Java™ Software Solutions

Foundations of Program Design

For our parents,
Leonard and Dorothy Lewis
John and Dolores Loftus

Java™ Software Solutions

Foundations of Program Design

John Lewis
Villanova University

William Loftus
WPL Laboratories, Inc.

▲ **ADDISON-WESLEY**

An imprint of Addison Wesley Longman, Inc.

Reading, Massachusetts • Harlow, England • Menlo Park, California
Berkeley, California • Don Mills, Ontario • Sydney • Bonn • Amsterdam
Tokyo • Mexico City

Editor-in-Chief	Lynne Doran Cote
Associate Editor	Deborah Lafferty
Production Manager	Karen Wernholm
Production Editor	Amy Willcutt
Marketing Manager	Tom Ziolkowski
Compositor	Michael and Sigrid Wile
Technical Artist	George Nichols
Copyeditor	Roberta Lewis
Text Design	Ron Kosciak
Indexer	Nancy Fulton
Proofreading	Phyllis Coyne et al.
Cover Designer	Diana Coe

Library of Congress Cataloging-in-Publication Data

Lewis, John, Ph.D.
    Java software solutions : foundations of program design / John
Lewis, William Loftus.
        p.   cm.
    Includes index.
    ISBN 0-201-57164-1
    1. Java (Computer program language)   2. Object-oriented
programming (Computer science)   I. Loftus, William.   II. Title.
    QA76.73.J38L49   1998
    005.13'3--dc21   97-19400
                                                                         CIP

Many of the designations used by manufacturers and sellers to distinguish their products are claimed as trademarks. Where those designations appear in this book, and Addison-Wesley was aware of a trademark claim, the designations have been printed in initial caps or all caps.

Cover image © Jerry Blank/SIS

Access the latest information about Addison-Wesley titles from our World Wide Web site: http://www.awl.com/cseng

3 4 5 6 7 8 9 10-MA-0100999897

Preface

We have designed this text for use in a first course in programming using the Java language. It serves as an introduction to computer science and forms a foundation for pursuing advanced computing topics. Our goal is to make students comfortable with object-oriented concepts so that they will be well-prepared to design and implement high-quality object-oriented software.

This text was formed out of our combined experiences with real-world programming and classroom teaching of Java. We have written this text from the ground up, with an object-oriented Java approach always in mind. When Java first emerged in mid-1995, most of the attention was focused on its applets and glitzy Web effects. Over time, people have come to realize its larger benefits as a powerful object-oriented language that is well-designed and pedagogically sound. We have discovered that students respond better, faster, and more enthusiastically to computing concepts when they are explained through Java.

In response to a strong initial interest, this text was first published in a preliminary version. Since then we have made several improvements to the text, rearranging topics to provide maximum versatility and adding more examples to help students better grasp important concepts. This edition has also been updated to fully embrace Java 1.1. This new version of Java provides many improvements over the earlier version, including a significant improvement to the GUI event model.

Object-Oriented Coverage

We introduce objects early in the text and consistently reinforce their use throughout. We have found that students find object-oriented concepts highly intuitive if they are presented in a clear, careful way. Introductory programmers can success-

v

fully master concepts like inheritance and polymorphism when these ideas are discussed in a straightforward and thorough manner.

The term object-oriented software development implies that the approach is oriented around objects, yet some people advocate postponing the introduction of objects until after many traditional procedural techniques are covered. Our view is that as soon as a design gets sophisticated enough to deserve multiple methods, it should use objects with methods in them. Methods should never be taught independent of their role in an object. We believe that educating students in object-oriented design will prepare them to be better programmers regardless of the language used.

GUI Coverage

We have experimented with a variety of approaches and have concluded that our students should not be asked to develop graphical user interfaces in Java too early. Introducing GUIs prior to a thorough coverage of classes, interfaces, and inheritance requires too many vague and misleading side discussions. We still cover applets, graphics, and animation early, but defer event-based interaction until suitable foundation material has been established.

The Four Cornerstones of the Text

This text is based upon four basic ideas that we believe make for a sound introductory text.

- *True object-orientation.* A true object-oriented text must do more than mention objects early. In this text, every situation and example reinforces the design principles of object-oriented programming. We establish as a fundamental guideline that the class that contains the main method should contain no additional methods; if other functionality is needed, it is provided through other classes and objects. This guideline is applied in all programs as soon as objects are introduced. (See the CD_Collection example in Chapter 4.)
- *Sound software engineering.* Students should be exposed to software engineering principles early in order to be prepared to develop high-quality software in the future. Software engineering concepts are integrated throughout the text and repeatedly reinforced so that students learn their importance from the start. For example, design and process issues are introduced in Chapter 3 and revisited in examples throughout the text. Furthermore, Chapters 11 and 15 are devoted to software engineering issues.
- *Integrated graphics.* Modern software systems are graphical. Introductory programming courses should cover graphics and graphical user interfaces. Various examples in this text, as early as the No_Parking applet in Chapter 2, use graphics to motivate and engage students. Furthermore, we

devote Chapter 7 to a complete investigation of basic Java graphics and Chapter 10 to GUIs and related topics. We introduce GUIs carefully, after students can appreciate the concepts of event-driven programming.

- *Balanced examples.* A text must contain a strong balance of smaller and larger examples. Smaller examples establish a foundation for students, whereas larger examples provide them with a more realistic context. We have intertwined small, readily understandable examples with larger, practical ones to give students and faculty a variety of examples to explore. We also balance the use of applications and applets throughout the text in order to give students a strong foundation in both approaches.

Paths Through the Text

This book is designed to be flexible, so that professors can tailor its presentation to the needs of their students. Professors can take a variety of different paths through the text; these paths include four major topics—object-oriented development, graphics and GUIs, software engineering, and Java language features. The initial chapters should be covered in the designated order, as they form the foundation on which to explore these topics.

Chapter 1 (Computer Systems) presents a broad overview of computing topics. It establishes some terminology concerning hardware, networks, and the World-Wide Web. Depending on the background of the student, this chapter can be covered quickly or left for outside reading. Chapter 2 (Software Concepts) begins the exploration of software development and introduces the concepts underlying the object-oriented approach. Students with previous software development exposure may only need to focus on portions of Chapter 2 as needed. Chapter 3 (Program Elements) provides just enough low-level detail, including basic control flow, in order to make the exploration of objects concrete.

Chapter 4 (Objects and Classes) is the springboard for the rest of the book. It describes how to define objects using classes and the methods and data that they contain. At this point the instructor has wide latitude in choosing the topics that will follow. Chapter 5 (More Programming Constructs) can be covered immediately to fill in additional low-level details, or it can be deferred to a later point. A more traditional course flow might also include Chapter 6 (Objects for Organizing Data) with its emphasis on arrays.

The remaining chapters can be organized in a variety of different ways based upon the needs of the instructor. Those instructors who want to emphasize object-oriented development can follow Chapter 4 with Chapter 8 (Inheritance) and Chapter 9 (Enhanced Class Design). The object-oriented issues should be covered prior to introducing the graphical user interface material in Chapter 10, although the basic graphics content of Chapter 7 can be covered any time after Chapter 4. A software engineering track can be followed by covering Chapters 11 and 15 (Software Development Process I and II) after the object-oriented material. To emphasize the Java language features, instructors can follow Chapters 4, 5, and 6 with Chapters 8, 9, and 14 (Advanced Flow of Control). We invite instructors to experiment with the ordering of chapters to best meet their own course needs.

Pedagogical features

This text contains numerous pedagogical features that help make the material more accessible to students. Some of the features we use are listed below:

- *Key Concepts.* The Key Concept designation is used throughout the book to draw special attention to fundamental ideas and important design guidelines.
- *In-Depth Focus boxes.* These boxes appear in several places throughout the text and provide a tiered coverage of material. They allow more advanced students to challenge their knowledge of the subject without overwhelming others. Instructors may choose to cover or skip this feature without any loss of continuity.
- *Code Callouts.* Blue type is used to call out and annotate important parts of the code. The second color allows students to better understand the code as they read through it.
- *Problem sets.* Each chapter of the book concludes with a set of problems, separated into three categories:
    - Self-Review Questions and Answers. These short-answer questions review the fundamental ideas and terms established in the chapter. They are designed to allow students to assess their own basic grasp of the material. The answers to these questions can be found at the end of the problem sets.
    - Exercises. These intermediate problems probe the underlying issues discussed in the chapter and integrate them with concepts covered in previous chapters. While they may deal with code, they do not involve any online activity.
    - Programming Projects. These consist of more involved problems that require design and implementation of Java programs. The projects vary widely in level of difficulty.
- *Java reference material.* The appendices contain a significant amount of language reference material. We have placed this material in appendices so that more of the text can focus on the important software concepts. Students can reference these appendices as needed throughout the course to learn more details of the Java language.
- *Java style guidelines.* Appendix G contains a proposed set of programming style guidelines. These guidelines are followed in the examples throughout the text.

- *Graphical design notation.* The object-oriented designs in the text are presented with a simple graphical notation. This allows students to read and use a design notation similar to professional development models.

Conventions

We use various conventions for indicating different types of material in the text. Important words and phrases are emphasized in *italics* on their first use. Code is presented in a monospaced font:

```
void cube (int num) {
   System.out.println ("The cube is " + (num*num*num));
} // method cube
```

and code elements, such as cube, maintain the code font in the text. Output is presented in a monospaced font surrounded by a colored box:

```
The cube is 9
```

Specific syntax of individual programming statements are shown in shaded boxes:

```
void cube (int num) {
   System.out.println ("The cube is " + (num*num*num));
} // method cube
```

In the sample run of a program, user input is shown in color:

```
> java Average
Enter a number (-1 to quit): 90
Enter a number (-1 to quit): 80
Enter a number (-1 to quit): 70
Enter a number (-1 to quit): -1
The average is 80
```

Pseudocode is presented in a script font:

```
prompt for and read the grade
    while (grade does not equal -1) {
    increment count
    sum = sum + grade;
    prompt for another grade
    read next grade
}
average = sum / count;
print average
```

Supplements

This book comes with a large variety of supplemental materials to assist in course preparation and execution. Links to all of the supplements can be found on the book's official Web site at `http://www.awl.com/cseng/author/lewis/java`. In addition to the supplements listed below, this site contains all examples from the book and additional Java examples not found in the book.

- *Instructor's Manual.* A manual has been created to assist professors in course preparation. It contains strategy suggestions for presenting material, answers to text exercises, solutions to selected programming projects, and a collection of potential test questions and answers. To obtain a copy of the Instructor's Manual, please contact your local Addison-Wesley sales representative.
- *Laboratory Manual.* A series of independent exercises support curricula that use a closed lab approach. Instructors can choose from a variety of labs, covering material found in each chapter of the text. The labs overlap to reflect the various ways that an instructor can approach the book. In addition to use in the laboratory environment, the lab exercises may also be assigned as outside work.
- *Integrated Web Presentation.* These Web pages allow an instructor to interactively present course notes, examples, and executable code entirely through a Web browser. At the instructor's discretion, the material can then be made available to students for further review at their own pace.
- *Transparency Masters.* Overhead slides are available for those who choose not to use the Integrated Web Presentation. Slides may be obtained in either Microsoft PowerPoint format or PostScript.

Acknowledgments

The creation of this text was an effort that extends well beyond the authors. If we have succeeded in our goals, it is largely due to the support we received from many sources.

First of all, we greatly appreciate the students who have participated in the courses in which preliminary versions of this text were used. Their feedback and suggestions have been quite helpful in the process of refining the book's content and presentation.

Lynne Doran Cote and Debbie Lafferty at Addison-Wesley have been outstanding in their editorial support and encouragement. Amy Willcutt was amazingly helpful and accommodating during the final production of the text, with the support of Karen Wernholm. Tom Ziokowski, Michael Hirsch, and Stacy Treco provided important insight and direction. Roberta (Bobbie) Lewis, of Lewis Editorial Services, was a pleasant and meticulous copyeditor. We appreciate their support of our vision for this book and their desire for quality above all else.

Many thanks go to our reviewers, listed below, who provided important, constructive comments and suggestions. They found numerous ways to improve the quality of the text and were never shy about expressing their opinion. Any errors that still exist in the book are solely the responsibility of the authors, as we can never seem to stop making changes.

Christopher Haynes	Indiana University
Lawrence Osborne	Lamar University
B. Ravikumar	University of Rhode Island
David Riley	University of Wisconsin, LaCrosse
Vijay Srinivasan	JavaSoft, Sun Microsystems Inc.
Shengru Tu	University of New Orleans
John J. Wegis	JavaSoft, Sun Microsystems Inc.
David Wittenberg	Brandeis University

Thanks also go to the many informal reviewers who have provided valuable feedback. Chief among them is Dan Joyce of Villanova University, who was instrumental in helping us revise our initial approach and who provided guidance through multiple revisions. Paul Gormley also provided significant and helpful comments on the content of the text.

Special thanks go to Pete DePasquale at Villanova University. He has been a tremendous help in many areas, including the development of Appendix O, the creation of exercises, and overall review. His assistance has been invaluable.

Many other people have helped in various ways. They include Ken Arnold, Bob Beck, Alan Dellinger, Tom DiSessa, Dan Hardt, John Loftus, Bob Pollack, Tim Ryan, Brent Schwartz, Ken Slonneger, Joe Tursi, and Mahesh Vanavada. Our apologies to anyone we may have forgotten.

The ACM Special Interest Group on Computer Science Education (SIGCSE) is a tremendous resource. Their conferences provide an opportunity for educators from all levels and all types of schools to share ideas and materials. If you are an educator in any area of computing and are not involved with SIGCSE, you're missing out.

The faculty in the Department of Computing Sciences at Villanova University and the staff at WPL Laboratories, Inc. have supported us both throughout this process. Their support is greatly appreciated.

Thanks also go to the following: Sun Microsystems (the network *is* the computer), FedEx (it often had to be there overnight), WaWa (open 24 hours, including holidays), Dominos (they deliver), Diet Coke (just for the taste of it), New Orleans (especially the House of Blues), sleep (we've read about this), coffee (the elixir of life), Altoids (curiously strong), a helpful student (for the goat), and the couch of science (the seat of inspiration).

Most importantly, thanks go to our wives. John thanks his wife Sharon for her love and understanding throughout this project, and for distracting him when he needed it. Bill thanks his wife Veena, for her undying love and support, his son Isaac, for his inspirational story "The Golden Mask," and his daughter Devi, for teaching him how to dress.

John Lewis
William Loftus

Contents

Chapter 5   More Programming Constructs   171

Chapter 6   Objects for Organizing Data   207

Computer Systems

This book is about writing well-designed software. To understand software, we must first have a fundamental understanding of its role in a computer system. Hardware and software cooperate in a computer system to accomplish complex tasks. The nature of that cooperation and the purpose of various hardware components are important prerequisites to the study of software development. Furthermore, computer networks have revolutionized the manner in which computers are used, and they now play a key role in even basic software development. This chapter explores a broad range of computing issues, laying the foundation for the study of software development.

Chapter Objectives

- Describe the relationship between hardware and software.
- Define various types of software and how they are used.
- Identify the core hardware components of a computer and explain their purpose.
- Explain how the hardware components interact to execute programs and manage data.
- Describe how computers are connected together into networks to share information.
- Explain the impact and significance of the Internet and the World-Wide Web.

1.1 Introduction

This section provides an overview of computers, defining some fundamental terminology and showing how the key pieces of a computer system interact.

Basic Computer Processing

A computer system is made up of hardware and software. The *hardware* components of a computer system are the physical, tangible pieces that support the computing effort. They include chips, boxes, wires, keyboards, speakers, disks, cables, plugs, printers, mice, monitors, and so on. If you can physically touch it and it can be considered part of a computer system, then it is computer hardware.

The hardware components of a computer are essentially useless without instructions to tell them what to do. A *program* is a series of instructions that the hardware executes, one after another. *Software* consists of programs and the data those programs use. Software is the intangible counterpart to the physical hardware components.

Key Concept Hardware components of a computer are useless without the instructions provided by a software program.

The key hardware components in a computer system are the following:

- central processing unit (CPU)
- main memory
- secondary memory devices
- input/output (I/O) devices

Each of these hardware components is described in detail in the next section. For now, let's simply examine their basic roles. The *central processing unit* (CPU) is the device which executes the individual commands of a program. *Input/output* (I/O) *devices,* such as the keyboard, mouse, and monitor, allow a human being to interact with the computer.

Software, both programs and data, are held in storage devices called memory, which fall into two categories: main memory and secondary memory. *Main memory* is the storage device in which the software is held when it is needed by the CPU. *Secondary memory* devices store programs and data in a relatively permanent manner. Two common secondary memory devices are floppy disks and hard disks. A

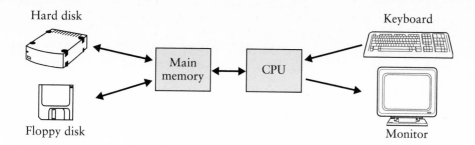

Figure 1.1   A simplified view of a computer system

floppy disk cannot store as much information as a hard disk, but it can be moved from computer to computer.

Figure 1.1 shows how information moves among the basic hardware components of a computer.

Suppose you have an executable program you wish to run. The program is stored on some secondary memory device, such as a hard disk.

When you instruct the computer to execute your program, a copy of the program is brought in from secondary memory and stored in main memory. The CPU reads the individual program instructions from main memory. Then the CPU executes the instructions one at a time until the program ends. The data that the instructions use, such as two numbers that will be added together, are also stored in main memory. They are either brought in from secondary memory or read from an input device such as the keyboard. During execution the program may display information to an output device, often a monitor.

> **Key Concept**   To execute a program, the computer copies the program from secondary memory to main memory. The CPU then reads the program instructions from main memory, executing them one at a time until the program ends.

The process of executing a program is fundamental to the operation of a computer. All computer systems basically work in the same way.

Software Categories

Software can be classified into many categories using various criteria. At this point we will simply differentiate between system programs and application programs.

The *operating system* is the core software of a computer. It performs two important functions. First, it provides a *user interface* so that the human user can interact with the machine. Second, the operating system manages computer resources such as the CPU and main memory. It determines when programs are allowed to run, where they are loaded into memory, and how hardware devices communicate. It is the job of the operating system to make the computer easy to use and ensure that it runs efficiently. Windows 95 and Unix are examples of popular operating systems.

 Key Concept   The operating system performs two important functions. It provides a user interface and manages computer resources.

An *application* is a generic term for just about any software other than the operating system. Word processors, missile control systems, database managers, and games can all be considered application programs. An application program usually has its own user interface that allows the user to interact with that particular program.

Key Concept   An application is a term for any software other than the operating system.

The user interface for most modern operating systems and applications are *graphical user interfaces* (GUI), which, as the name implies, make use of graphical screen elements. These elements include:

- *windows,* used to separate the screen into distinct work areas
- *pull-down menus,* which provide the user with a list of options
- *icons,* which are small images that represent computer resources, such as a file
- *buttons,* which can be "pushed" with a mouse click to indicate a user selection

In fact, the mouse is the primary input device used with graphical user interfaces, and GUIs are sometimes called *point-and-click interfaces.* The screen shot in Fig. 1.2 shows an example of a graphical user interface.

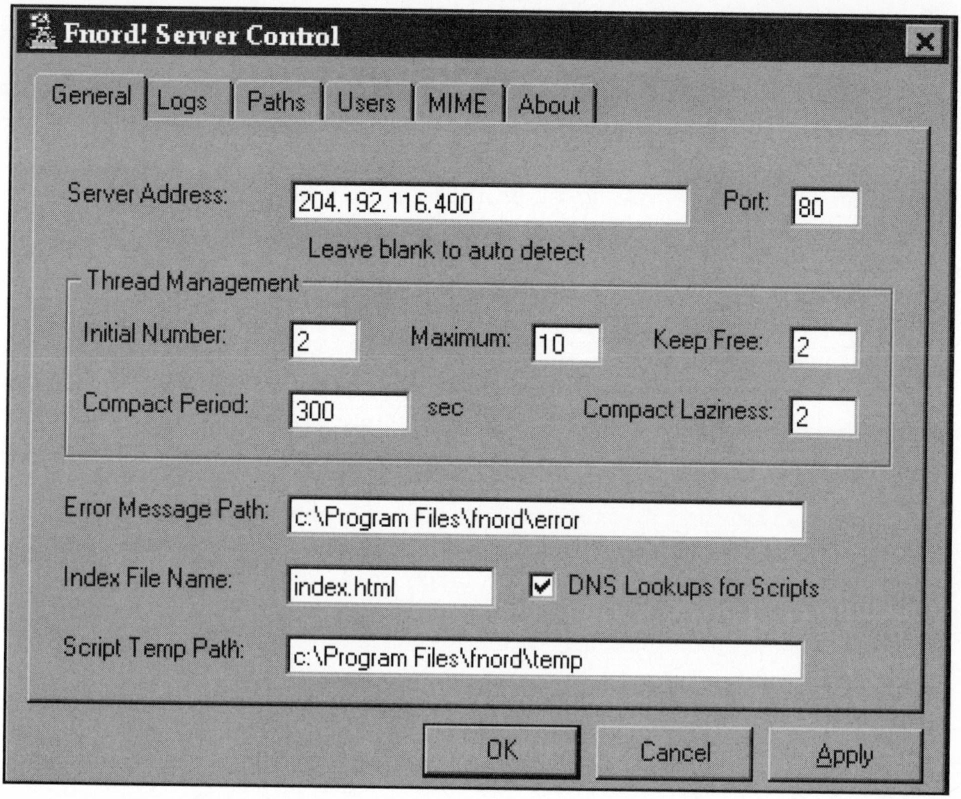

Figure 1.2   A graphical user interface (GUI)

▶ **Key Concept**   As far as the user is concerned, the interface *is* the program.

The interface to an application or operating system is an important part of the software because it is the only part of the program with which the user directly interacts. To the user, the interface *is* the program. Chapter 10 discusses graphical user interfaces in detail.

The focus of this book is the development of high-quality application programs. We explore how to design and write software that will perform calculations, make decisions, and control graphics. We use the Java programming language throughout the text to demonstrate various computing concepts.

Digital Computers

There are two fundamental techniques used to store and manage information: analog and digital. *Analog* information is continuous, in direct proportion to the source of the information. For example, a mercury thermometer is an analog device for measuring temperature. The mercury rises in a tube in direct proportion to the temperature outside the tube. Another example of analog information is an electronic signal used to represent the vibrations of a sound wave. The signal's voltage varies in direct proportion to the original sound wave. A stereo amplifier sends this kind of electronic signal to its speakers, which vibrate to reproduce the sound. We use the term analog because the signal is directly analogous to the information it represents. Figure 1.3 graphically depicts a sound wave captured by a microphone and represented as an electronic signal.

Digital technology breaks information down into discrete pieces and represents those pieces as numbers. The music on a compact disc is stored digitally, as a series of numbers. Each number represents the voltage level of one specific instance of the recording. Many of these measurements are taken in a short period of time, perhaps 40,000 measurements every second; the number of measurements per second is called the *sampling rate*. If samples are taken often enough, the discrete voltage measurements can be used to generate a continuous analog signal close enough to fool the human ear into thinking it is continuous sound.

Figure 1.4 shows the sampling of an analog signal. When analog information is converted to a digital format by breaking it into pieces, we say it has been *digitized*. Because the changes that occur in a signal between samples are lost, the sampling rate must be sufficiently fast.

Today's electronic computers are digital. Every kind of information, including text, pictures, numbers, audio, video, and even program instructions, is broken down into pieces. Each piece is represented as a number. The original information is maintained by storing those numbers.

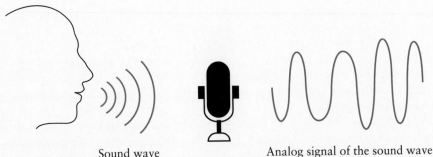

Sound wave   Analog signal of the sound wave

Figure 1.3   A sound wave and an electronic analog signal that represents it

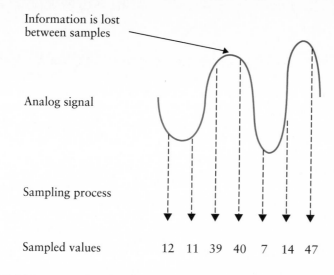

Information is lost between samples

Analog signal

Sampling process

Sampled values   12   11   39   40   7   14   47

Figure 1.4   Digitizing an analog signal

In-Depth Focus

Analog vs. Digital Signals

The distance that information can travel reliably across a wire depends on the type of signal used to carry it. An analog signal has continuously varying voltage, but a digital signal is discrete; that means the digital voltage changes dramatically between one extreme and the other. At any point, the voltage of a digital signal is considered to be either "high" or "low." Figure 1.5 compares these two types of signals.

As a signal moves down a wire, it gets weaker. That is, its voltage drops. To make sure a signal gets to its destination, amplifiers can be placed along the line to reinforce the strength of the signal. The trouble with an analog signal is that as it loses strength, it loses information. Since the information is directly analogous to the signal, any change in the signal changes the information. An amplifier can reinforce the signal but it cannot recover the changes in the signal up to that point. A digital signal also degrades, but can be reinforced so that no information is lost.

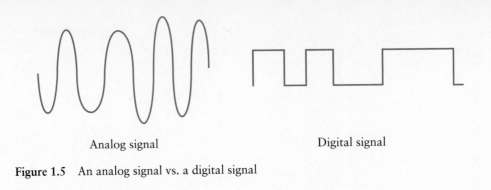

Analog signal   Digital signal

Figure 1.5   An analog signal vs. a digital signal

> **Key Concept**   Modern digital computers store information by breaking it down into pieces and representing each piece as a number.

Sampling is only one way to digitize information. For example, a sentence of text is stored on a computer as a series of numbers, where each number represents a single character in the sentence. Every letter, digit, and punctuation symbol has been assigned a number. Even the space character is assigned a number. Therefore the sentence

Hi, Heather.

is represented as a series of twelve numbers, as shown in Fig. 1.6. Note that the uppercase version of a letter is stored as a different number than the lowercase version, such as the 'H' and 'h' in the word Heather. They are considered to be separate and distinct characters.

Let's look at another example of digitization. A picture is stored digitally by breaking it up into small pieces called *pixels,* a term that stands for picture elements. Each pixel is stored as a separate number. A black and white picture can be

Hi, Heather.

72 105 44 32 72 101 97 116 104 101 114 46

Figure 1.6   Text is stored by mapping each character to a number.

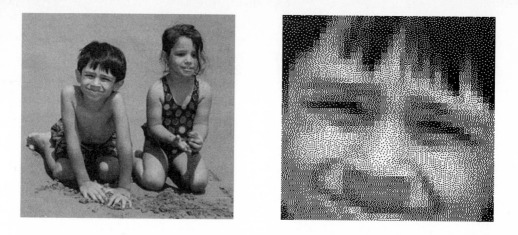

Figure 1.7 A digitized picture, with a small portion magnified

represented by storing each pixel as a zero (for white) or a one (for black). The picture can be reproduced when needed by reassembling the pixels that make it up. The more pixels used to represent a picture, the more realistic it looks when reproduced.

Figure 1.7 shows a black and white picture that has been stored digitally and an enlargement of a portion of that picture, which shows the individual pixels. Color pictures are more complicated, because each pixel cannot simply be represented as a 0 or 1. Since each pixel is one of several possible colors, several values are used to represent each pixel of a color picture.

Binary Numbers

A digital computer stores information as numbers, but those numbers are not stored as *decimal* values. All information in a computer is stored and managed as *binary* values. Unlike the decimal system, which has 10 digits (0 through 9), the binary number system has only two digits (0 and 1). A single binary digit is called a *bit*.

Key Concept Binary values are used to store all information in a computer. Binary is used because each digit is one of two possible values; therefore, the devices that store and move binary information are inexpensive and reliable.

All number systems work according to the same rules. The base value dictates how many digits we have to work with and indicates the place value of each digit in a number. The decimal number system is base 10, and the binary number system is base 2. Appendix B contains a detailed discussion of number systems.

Modern computers use binary numbers because the devices that store and move information are less expensive and more reliable if they only have to represent one of two possible values. Other than this characteristic, there is nothing special about the binary number system. Computers have been created that use other number systems to store information, but they aren't as convenient.

A single bit can represent two possible items or situations. The bit is either 1 or 0, similar to a light switch being either on or off. A pixel of a black and white picture can be represented as a single bit, by mapping the two possible values of the bit to the two possible colors of the pixel (white and black). If there are more than two items, such as in the pixels of a color picture, we must use more than one bit to represent each value.

Two bits, taken together, can represent four possible items because there are exactly four permutations of two bits (00, 01, 10, and 11). Similarly, three bits can represent eight unique items, because there are eight permutations of three bits. Figure 1.8 shows the relationship between the number of bits used and the number of items they can represent. In general, n bits can represent 2^n unique items. For every bit added, the number of items that can be represented doubles.

1 bit 2 items	2 bits 4 items	3 bits 8 items	4 bits 16 items
0 1	00 01 10 11	000 001 010 011 100 101 110 111	0000 0001 0010 0011 0100 0101 0110 0111 1000 1001 1010 1011 1100 1101 1110 1111

Figure 1.8 The number of bits used determines the number of items that can be represented.

Let's consider an example. Suppose you wanted to represent character strings in a language that contains 256 characters and symbols. You would need to use eight bits to store each character because there are 256 unique permutations of eight bits ($2^8 = 256$). Each permutation represents a specific character.

All of the hardware components of a computer system store and move bits of data. A digital signal is well suited for transmitting binary data. If the voltage is high on a digital signal, it is interpreted as a binary 1. If the voltage is low, it is interpreted as a binary 0.

1.2 Hardware Components

Let's examine the hardware components of a computer system in more detail. Consider the computer described in Fig. 1.9. What does it all mean? Is the system capable of running the software you want it to? How does it compare to other systems? These terms are explained throughout this section.

Computer Architecture

The architecture of a house defines its structure. Similarly, we use the term *computer architecture* to describe how the hardware components of a computer are put together. Figure 1.10 illustrates the basic architecture of a generic computer system. Information travels between components across a group of wires called a *bus*.

>> 200 MHz Pentium processor

>> 32 MB RAM (main memory)

>> 2.3 GB hard disk

>> 17" multimedia video display with 1280×1024 resolution

>> $12 \times$ speed CD ROM drive

>> 33,600 bps data/fax modem

Figure 1.9   The hardware specification of a particular computer

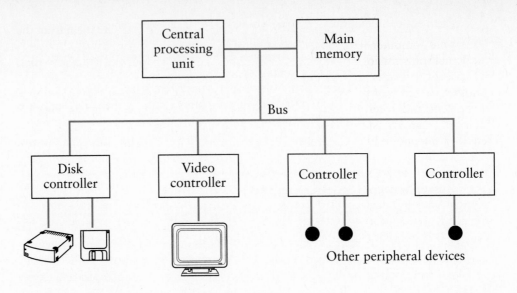

Figure 1.10   Basic computer architecture

> ◣ **Key Concept**   The core of a computer is made up of the CPU and the main memory.
> Main memory is used to store programs and data, and the CPU executes a program's
> instructions one at a time.

The CPU and the main memory make up the core of a computer. Main memory
stores programs and data that are actively in use and the CPU methodically executes
program instructions one at a time.

Suppose we have a program that computes the average of a list of numbers. The
program and the numbers must be stored in main memory while the program runs.
The CPU reads one program instruction from main memory and executes it. If an
instruction needs data to perform its task, such as a number in the list, the CPU
reads that information as well. This process repeats until the program ends. The
average, when computed, is stored in main memory to await further processing or
long-term storage in secondary memory.

Almost all devices in a computer system other than the CPU and main memory
are called *peripherals,* because they operate at the periphery, or outer edges, of the
system (although they may be in the same box). Human beings never directly interact with the CPU or main memory. Although they form the essence of the machine,
the CPU and main memory would not be useful without peripheral devices.

Controllers are devices that coordinate the activities of specific peripherals.
Every device has its own particular way of formatting and communicating data, and

part of the controller's role is to handle these idiosyncrasies and isolate them from the rest of the computer hardware. Furthermore, the controller often handles much of the actual transmission of information, allowing the CPU to focus on other activities.

All I/O devices and secondary memory devices are considered peripherals. Another category of peripherals are *data transfer devices*, which allow information to be sent and received between computers. The computer specified in Fig. 1.9 includes a data transfer device called a *modem*, which allows information to be sent across a telephone line. The modem in the example can transfer information at a rate of 33,600 *bits per second* (bps). It is called a data/fax modem because it can send and receive fax documents as well as basic data.

In some ways, secondary memory devices and data transfer devices can be thought of as I/O devices because they represent a source of information (input) and a place to send information (output). For our discussion, however, we define I/O devices as those that allow the human user to interact with the computer.

> ▶ **Key Concept**   I/O devices allow the human user to interact with the computer.

Input/Output Devices

Let's examine some I/O devices in more detail. The most common input devices are the keyboard and the mouse. Others include:

- *bar code readers,* such as the ones used at a grocery store checkout
- *light pens,* which can be touched to a monitor to indicate a user's action
- *microphones,* used by voice recognition systems that interpret simple voice commands
- *virtual reality devices,* such as gloves that interpret the movement of the user's hand
- *scanners,* which convert text, photographs, and graphics into machine-readable form

Monitors and printers are the most common output devices. Other examples are:

- *plotters,* which move pens across large sheets of paper
- *speakers,* for audio output
- *goggles,* for virtual reality display

Some devices can provide both input and output capabilities. A touch screen can detect the user touching the screen at a particular place, to indicate a choice between a set of options, for instance. Software that acknowledges the chosen option can then use the screen to display text and graphics in response. Touch screens are particularly useful in situations where the interface to the machine must be simple, such as at an information booth.

The computer described in Fig. 1.9 includes a monitor with a 17-inch diagonal display area. It has multimedia capabilities, which means it can display text, graphics, and video output. The monitor can display a grid of 1280 × 1024 pixels.

Main and Secondary Memory

Main memory is made up of a long series of small, consecutive *memory locations* as shown in Fig. 1.11. Associated with each memory location is a unique number called an *address*.

 Key Concept   An address is a unique number associated with each memory location. A memory address is used to both store and retrieve data from memory.

Key Concept   Data stored in a memory location overwrites and destroys any information that was previously held in that location. Data read from a memory location leaves the value in memory unaffected.

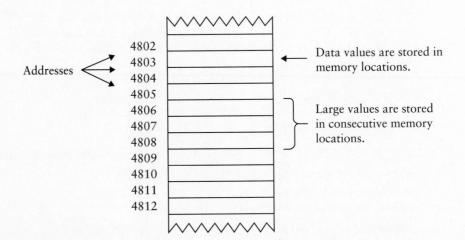

Figure 1.11   Memory locations

When data is stored in a memory location, it overwrites and destroys any information that was previously held in that location. However, data can be read from a memory location without affecting it.

On many computers, each memory location can hold one byte of information. A *byte* is made up of eight bits. If we need to store a value that cannot be represented in a single byte, such as a large number, then multiple, consecutive bytes are used to store the data.

The total *capacity* of a storage device such as main memory is the total number of bytes it can hold. Because these devices can store thousands or millions of bytes, it is necessary to become familiar with larger units of measure. Because computer memory is based on the binary number system, all units of storage are powers of two. A *kilobyte* (KB) is 1024, or 2^{10}, bytes. Some larger units of storage are a *megabyte* (MB), a *gigabyte* (GB), and a *terabyte,* as listed in Fig. 1.12. It's usually easier to think about these capacities by rounding them off. For example, most computer users think of a kilobyte as approximately one thousand bytes, a megabyte as approximately one million bytes, and so forth.

Many personal computers have 8, 16, or 32 megabytes of main memory. See, for example, the system described in Fig. 1.9. A large main memory allows large programs, and multiple programs, to run efficiently.

A special unit of storage is called a *word,* and the size of a word is different for different types of CPUs. Usually two, four, or eight bytes are combined to make up one word. The word size represents the amount of information that is moved through the machine at one time. The number of wires in the computer's bus correspond to the number of bits in a word for that computer. Each wire carries one bit, and an entire word is moved in one operation. The bigger the word size, the more information it can transfer in one operation. Thus we speak of 16-bit machines (with two-byte words), or 32-bit machines (with four-byte words), or 64-bit machines (with eight-byte words).

Main memory is usually *volatile,* meaning that the information stored in it will be lost if its electric power supply is turned off. When you are working on a computer, you should often save your work onto a secondary memory device such as a

Unit	Symbol	Number of Bytes
byte		$2^0 = 1$
kilobyte	KB	$2^{10} = 1024$
megabyte	MB	$2^{20} = 1,048,576$
gigabyte	GB	$2^{30} = 1,073,741,824$
terabyte	TB	$2^{40} = 1,099,511,627,776$

Figure 1.12   Units of binary storage

disk in case the power goes out or a plug is pulled. Secondary memory devices are usually *nonvolatile;* the information is retained even if the power supply is turned off.

> 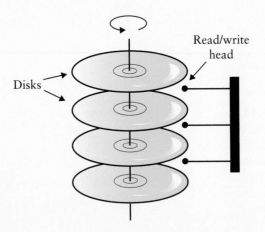 **Key Concept**   Main memory is usually volatile. Secondary memory devices are usually nonvolatile.

The most common secondary storage devices are hard disks and floppy disks. A high-density floppy disk can store 1.44 MB of information. The storage capacities of hard drives vary, but on personal computers capacities usually range between 0.5 and 9 GB, such as in the system described in Fig. 1.9.

A disk is a magnetic medium, on which bits are represented as magnetized particles. A read/write head passes over the spinning disk, reading or writing information as appropriate. A hard disk drive might actually contain several disks with several read/write heads, such as the one shown in Fig. 1.13.

To get an intuitive feel for how much information these devices can store, consider that all the information in this book, including pictures and formatting, requires about 6 MB of storage.

Magnetic tapes are also used as secondary storage, but are considerably slower than disks because of the way information is accessed. A disk is considered to be a *random-access device* since the read/write head can move directly to the information needed. But information on a tape can be accessed only by first getting past the intervening data. A tape must be rewound or fast forwarded to get to the appropriate position. A tape is therefore considered to be a *sequential-access device.* Tapes are usually only used to store information when it is no longer often used, or to provide a backup copy of the information on a disk.

Disks

Read/write head

Figure 1.13   A hard disk drive with multiple disks and read/write heads

Two other terms are used to describe memory devices: *random-access memory* (RAM) and *read-only memory* (ROM). It's important to understand these terms because they are often used and because their names can be misleading. The terms RAM and main memory are basically interchangeable. When contrasted with ROM, however, the term RAM seems to imply something it shouldn't. Both RAM and ROM are random-access devices because information that is stored on them can be obtained directly. RAM should probably be called read-write memory, since information can be both written to it and read from it. This feature distinguishes it from ROM. After information is created and stored on ROM, it cannot be altered (as the term read-only accurately implies). ROM is often embedded into the main circuit board of a computer and used to provide the preliminary instructions needed when the computer is initially turned on.

A *CD ROM* is a portable secondary memory device. CD stands for compact disk. It is accurately called ROM because information is stored permanently when the CD is created and cannot be changed. Like its musical CD counterpart, a CD ROM stores information in binary format. When the CD is initially created, a microscopic pit is burned into the disk to represent a binary 1, and the disk is left smooth to represent a binary 0. The bits are read by shining a low-intensity laser beam on the spinning disk. The laser beam reflects strongly from a smooth area on the disk, but weakly from a pitted area. A sensor looking for the reflection determines if each bit is a 1 or 0 accordingly.

The CD ROM drive described in Fig. 1.9 is characterized as having 12 $\times$ speed, distinguishing it from previous CD ROM technologies (6 $\times$ and 8 $\times$, for instance) relative to its data transfer rate. A typical CD ROM's storage capacity is approximately 630 MB.

The capacity of storage devices changes continually as technology improves. A general rule in the computer industry suggests that storage capacity doubles approximately every 18 months. However, this progress will eventually slow down as the capacities approach absolute physical limits.

The Central Processing Unit

The central processing unit (CPU) interacts closely with main memory to perform all fundamental processing in a computer. The CPU interprets and executes instructions, one after another, in a continuous cycle. It is made up of three important components as shown in Fig. 1.14. The *control unit* coordinates the processing steps, the *registers* provide a small amount of storage space in the CPU itself, and the *arithmetic/logic unit* performs calculations and makes decisions.

The control unit coordinates the transfer of data and instructions between main memory and the registers in the CPU. It also coordinates the execution of the circuitry in the arithmetic/logic unit to perform a particular operation on data stored in particular registers.

In many computers, some registers are set aside for special purposes. For example, the *instruction register* holds the current instruction being executed. The *program*

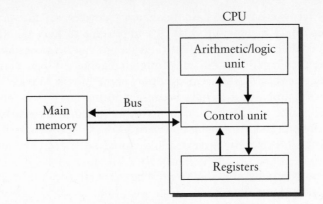

Figure 1.14 CPU components and main memory

counter is a register that holds the address of the next instruction to be executed. In addition to these and other special-purpose registers, the CPU also contains a set of general-purpose registers that are used for temporary storage of values as needed.

The concept of storing both program instructions and data in main memory together is the underlying principle of the *von Neumann architecture* of computer design, named after John von Neumann who first advanced this programming concept in 1945. These computers continually follow the *fetch-decode-execute cycle* depicted in Fig. 1.15. An instruction is fetched from main memory at the address stored in the program counter and put into the instruction register. The program counter is incremented at this point to prepare for the next cycle. Then the instruction is decoded electronically to determine which operation to carry out. Finally the control unit activates the correct circuitry to carry out the instruction, which may load a data value into a register or add two values together, for example.

The CPU is constructed on a chip called a *microprocessor,* a device that is part of the main circuit board of the computer. This board also contains ROM chips and communication sockets to which device controllers, such as the controller which manages the video display, can be connected.

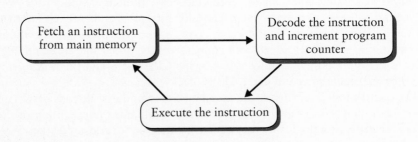

Figure 1.15 The continuous fetch-decode-execute cycle

Another crucial component of the main circuit board is the *system clock*. The clock generates an electronic pulse at regular intervals, which synchronizes the events of the CPU. The rate at which the pulses occur is called the *clock speed,* and varies depending on the processor. The computer described in Fig. 1.9 includes a Pentium processor that runs at a clock speed of 200 *megahertz* (MHz). The speed of the system clock provides a rough measure of how fast the CPU executes instructions. Similar to storage capacities, the speed of processors is constantly increasing with advances in technology, approximately doubling every 18 months.

Key Concept The speed of the system clock provides a measure of how fast the CPU executes instructions.

1.3 Networks

A single computer can accomplish a great deal, but connecting several computers together into networks can dramatically increase productivity and the ability to share information. A *network* is two or more computers connected together so they can exchange data. Using networks has become the normal mode of commercial computer operation. New technologies are emerging every day to capitalize on the connected environments of modern computer systems.

Key Concept A network consists of two or more computers connected together so they can exchange data. Connecting several computers together into networks can dramatically increase productivity and the ability to share information.

Figure 1.16 shows a simple computer network. One of the computers in the network has a printer connected to it. Because computers in a network can share information, any of these computers can print a document on that printer.

Another computer in Fig. 1.16, designated as a *file server,* is a computer in the network dedicated to storing programs and data that are needed by many network users. A file server usually has a large amount of secondary memory. When a network has a file server, each individual computer does not need its own copy of a program.

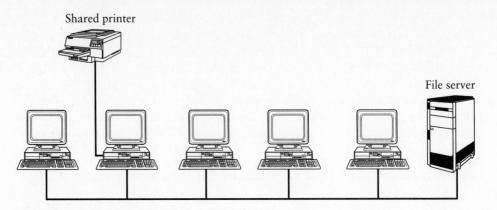

Figure 1.16   A simple network of computers

Network Connections

If two computers are directly connected, they can communicate in basically the same way that information moves across wires inside a single machine. When connecting only two geographically close computers, this solution works well, and is called a *point-to-point connection*. But consider the task of connecting many computers together. If point-to-point connections are used, then every computer is directly connected by a wire to every other computer in the network. A separate wire for each connection is not a workable solution because every time a new computer is added to the network, a new communication line will have to be installed for each computer already in the network. Furthermore, a single computer can handle only a small number of direct connections.

Figure 1.17 shows multiple point-to-point connections. Consider the number of communication lines that would be needed if only two or three additional computers were added to the network.

Contrast the diagrams in Fig. 1.16 and Fig. 1.17. All of the computers in the network shown in Fig. 1.16 share a single communication line. Each computer on the network has its own *network address*, which uniquely identifies it. These

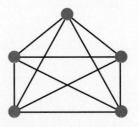

Figure 1.17   Point-to-point connections

addresses are similar in concept to the addresses in main memory, except that they identify individual computers instead of individual memory locations inside a single computer. A message is sent across the line from one computer to another by specifying the network address of the computer for which it is intended.

Key Concept Sharing a communication line is cost-effective and makes adding new computers to the network relatively easy. This sharing introduces delays because computers on the network cannot use the shared communication line at the same time.

Sharing a communication line is cost-effective and makes adding new computers to the network relatively easy. However, a shared line introduces delays. The computers on the network cannot use the communication line at the same time. They have to take turns sending information, which means they have to wait when the line is busy. Sometimes these delays are too restrictive.

One technique to improve network delays is to divide large messages into sections, called packets, then send the individual packets across the network intermixed with pieces of other messages sent by other users. The packets are collected at the destination and reassembled into the original message. This situation is similar to a group of people using a conveyor belt to move a set of boxes from one end to the other. If only one person were allowed to use the conveyor belt at a time, and that person had a large number of boxes to move, the others would be waiting a long time before they could use it. But by taking turns, each person can put one box on at a time, and they all can get their work done. It's not as fast as having a conveyor belt of your own, but it's not as slow as having to wait until everyone else is finished.

Local-Area and Wide-Area Networks

A *local-area network* (LAN) is a network designed to span short distances and a relatively small number of computers. Usually a LAN connects the machines in only one building, or in a single room. LANs are convenient to install and manage, and are highly reliable. As computers became increasingly small and versatile, LANs became an inexpensive way to share information throughout an organization. However, having a LAN is like having a telephone system that allows you to call only the people in your own town. We need to be able to share information across longer distances.

Key Concept LANs have become an inexpensive way to share information and resources throughout an organization.

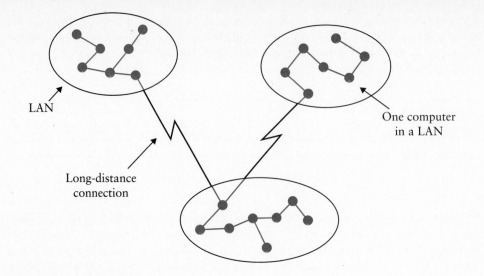

Figure 1.18   LANs connected into a wide-area network

A *wide-area network* (WAN) connects two or more LANs, often across long distances. Usually, one computer on each LAN is dedicated to handling the communication across a WAN. This technique relieves the other computers in a local-area network from having to perform the details of long-distance communication. Figure 1.18 shows several local-area networks connected into a wide-area network. The LANs connected by a WAN are often owned by different companies or organizations, and might even be located in different countries.

The impact of networks on computer systems has been dramatic. Computing resources can now be shared between many users, and communication using computers across the entire world is now possible. In fact, the use of networks is now so pervasive that some computers require network resources in order to operate.

Key Concept   The use of networks is so pervasive that some computers require network resources to operate.

The Internet

Throughout the 1970s, a United States government organization called the Advanced Research Projects Agency (ARPA) funded several projects to explore network technology. One result of these efforts was the ARPANET, a wide-area network that eventually was commercialized and became known as the Internet. The *Internet* is a network of networks. The term Internet comes from the WAN concept of *internetworking,* connecting many smaller heterogeneous networks together.

> ▶ **Key Concept**   The Internet is a network of networks.

In the mid and late 1980s, and throughout the 1990s, the Internet has grown incredibly. In 1983, there were fewer than 600 computers connected to the Internet. In 1997 that number has reached approximately 10 million. As more and more computers connect to the Internet, the ability to keep up with the larger number of users and heavier traffic has been difficult. New technologies have replaced the ARPANET several times since the initial development, each time providing more capacity and faster processing.

> ▶ **Key Concept**   TCP/IP is the software that controls the movement of messages across the Internet.

The software that controls the movement of messages across the Internet is called *TCP/IP* (pronounced by spelling out the letters, T-C-P-I-P). It is actually two separate entities, each containing many programs to control communication. TCP stands for *Transmission Control Protocol,* and IP stands for *Internet Protocol.* The IP software defines how information is formatted and transferred from the source to the destination. The TCP software handles problems such as pieces of information arriving out of their original order, or when information gets lost, which can happen if too much information converges at one location at the same time.

> ▶ **Key Concept**   Every computer connected to the Internet has an IP address that uniquely identifies it.

Every computer connected to the Internet has an *IP address* that uniquely identifies it among all other computers on the Internet. An example of an IP address is 204.192.116.2. Fortunately, the users of the Internet rarely have to deal with IP addresses. The Internet allows each computer to be given a name. Like IP addresses, the names must be unique. The Internet name of a computer is often referred to as its *Internet address*. Two examples of Internet addresses are `monet.vill.edu` and `kant.wpllabs.com`.

The first part of an Internet address is the local name of a specific computer. The rest of the address is the *domain name,* which indicates the organization to which the computer belongs. For example, `vill.edu` is the domain name for all computers at Villanova University, and `monet` is the name of a particular computer on that campus. Individual departments might add pieces to the name to uniquely distinguish their set of computers within the larger organization. A group called the *Internet Naming Authority* approves all domain names. Because the domain names are unique, many organizations can have a computer named `monet` without confusion.

The last part of each domain name usually indicates the type of organization to which the computer belongs. The suffix `edu` indicates an educational institution and the suffix `com` refers to a commercial business. For example, `wpllabs.com` refers to WPL Laboratories, Inc. Another common suffix is `org`, used by nonprofit organizations. Many computers, especially those outside of the United States, use a suffix that denotes the country of origin, such as `uk` for the United Kingdom.

When an Internet address is referenced, it gets translated to its corresponding IP address, which is used from that point on. The software that does this translation is called the *Domain Name System* (DNS). Each organization connected to the Internet operates a *domain server* that maintains a list of all computers at that organization and their IP address. It works somewhat like telephone directory assistance, in that you provide the name, and the domain server gives back a number. If the local domain server does not have the IP address for the name, it contacts another domain server that does.

> **Key Concept** The Internet has revolutionized computer processing by interconnecting computers across the world.

The Internet has revolutionized computer processing. Initially, the primary use of interconnected computers was to send electronic mail, but its capabilities continue to improve. One of the most significant uses of the Internet is the World-Wide Web.

The World-Wide Web

The Internet gives us the capability to exchange information. The *World-Wide Web* (WWW or simply the Web) makes the exchange of information easy. Web software provides a common user interface through which many different types of information can be accessed with the click of a mouse button.

The Web is based on the concepts of hypertext and hypermedia. The term *hypertext* was first used in 1965 to describe a way to organize information so that the flow of ideas was not constrained to a linear progression. In fact, that concept was entertained as a way to manage large amounts of information as early as the 1940s. Researchers on the Manhattan Project who were developing the first atomic bomb envisioned such an approach. The underlying idea is that documents can be linked at various points according to natural relationships so that the reader can jump from one document to another, following the appropriate path for that reader's needs. When other media components are incorporated, such as graphics, sound, and video, the resulting organization is called *hypermedia*.

Mosaic, the first graphical interface browser for the Web, was released in 1993. A *browser* is a software tool that loads and formats Web documents for viewing. Figure 1.19 shows a typical browser. The designer of a web document defines *links* to other web information that might be anywhere on the Internet. Some of the people who developed Mosaic went on to found the Netscape Communications Corporation and create the Netscape Navigator browser, which is shown in Fig. 1.19. It is currently one of the most popular systems for accessing information on the Web. Microsoft's Internet Explorer is another popular browser.

Browsers load and interpret documents that have been formatted using the *HyperText Markup Language* (HTML). An overview of Web publishing using HTML is given in Appendix K. The Java programming language has an intimate relationship with Web processing since links to Java programs can be embedded in HTML documents and executed through Web browsers. This relationship is explored in more detail in Chapter 2.

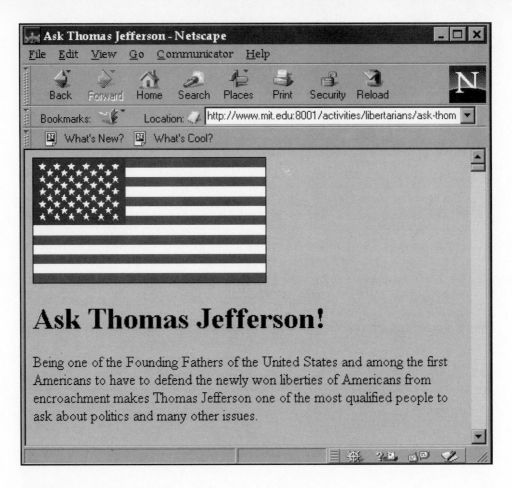

Figure 1.19   Netscape Navigator browsing an HTML document

Uniform Resource Locator

Information on the Web is found by identifying a *Uniform Resource Locator* (URL). A URL uniquely specifies documents and other information for a browser to obtain and display. An example URL is:

```
http://www.lycos.com
```

This particular URL will load a document that enables you to search the Web using particular words or phrases.

Key Concept A URL uniquely specifies documents and other information found on the Internet for a browser to obtain and display.

A URL contains several pieces of information. The first piece is a protocol, which determines the way the browser should communicate. The second piece is the Internet address of the machine on which the document is stored. The third piece of information is the file name of interest. If no file name is given, as is the case with the Lycos URL, browsers make a default selection (such as `index.html`). Let's look at another example URL:

```
http://www.wpllabs.com/vision.html
```

In this URL, the protocol is `http`, which stands for *HyperText Transfer Protocol*. The machine referenced is `www.wpllabs.com`, and `vision.html` is a file to be transferred to the browser for viewing. There are many other forms for URLs, but this form is the most common.

The terms Internet and World-Wide Web are sometimes used interchangeably, but there are important differences. The Web is essentially an information service including a set of software applications. It is not a network. Although it is used effectively with the Internet, it is not inherently bound to it. The Web can be used on a local-area network that is not connected to any other network, or even on a single machine to display HTML documents.

The Internet makes communication via computers all across the world possible. The Web makes accessing information across the Internet a straightforward and enjoyable activity. The Java programming language is another important evolutionary step that allows software to be easily exchanged and executed via the Web. The rest of this book explores the process of creating programs using Java.

Summary of Key Concepts

- Hardware components of a computer are useless without the instructions provided by a software program.
- To execute a program, the computer copies the program from secondary memory to main memory. The CPU then reads the program instructions from main memory, executing them one at a time until the program ends.
- The operating system performs two important functions. It provides a user interface and manages computer resources.

- An application is a term for any software other than the operating system.
- As far as the user is concerned, the interface *is* the program.
- Modern digital computers store information by breaking it down into pieces and representing each piece as a number.
- Binary values are used to store all information in a computer. Binary is used because each digit is one of two possible values; therefore, the devices that store and move binary information are inexpensive and reliable.
- The core of a computer is made up of the CPU and the main memory. Main memory is used to store programs and data, and the CPU executes a program's instructions one at a time.
- I/O devices allow the human user to interact with the computer.
- An address is a unique number associated with each memory location. A memory address is used to both store and retrieve data from memory.
- Data stored in a memory location overwrites and destroys any information that was previously held in that location. Data read from a memory location leaves the value in memory unaffected.
- Main memory is usually volatile. Secondary memory devices are usually nonvolatile.
- The speed of the system clock provides a measure of how fast the CPU executes instructions.
- A network consists of two or more computers connected together so they can exchange data. Connecting several computers together into networks can dramatically increase productivity and the ability to share information.
- Sharing a communication line is cost-effective and makes adding new computers to the network relatively easy. This sharing introduces delays because computers on the network cannot use the shared communication line at the same time.
- LANs have become an inexpensive way to share information and resources throughout an organization.
- The use of networks is so pervasive that some computers require network resources to operate.
- The Internet is a network of networks.
- TCP/IP is the software that controls the movement of messages across the Internet.
- Every computer connected to the Internet has an IP address that uniquely identifies it.
- The Internet has revolutionized computer processing by interconnecting computers across the world.
- The World-Wide Web is software that makes sharing information across a network easier.
- A browser is a software tool that loads and formats Web documents for viewing. These documents have been written using the HyperText Markup Language (HTML).

- A URL uniquely specifies documents and other information found on the Internet for a browser to obtain and display.

Self-Review Questions

1.1 What is hardware? What is software?

1.2 What are the two primary functions of an operating system?

1.3 What happens to information when it is stored digitally?

1.4 How many unique items can be represented with:
   a. 2 bits?
   b. 4 bits?
   c. 5 bits?

1.5 What are the two primary hardware components in a computer? How do they interact?

1.6 What is a memory address?

1.7 What does volatile mean? Which memory devices are volatile and which are nonvolatile?

1.8 What is a file server?

1.9 What is the origin of the term Internet?

Exercises

1.10 If a picture was made up of 64 possible colors, how many bits would be needed to store each pixel of the picture? Why?

1.11 Determine the storage capacity of main memory and secondary memory on your computer or on a computer in a lab to which you have access. Explain how you determined your answer.

1.12 How many bits are there in:
   a. 12 KB?
   b. 5 MB?
   c. 1 GB?

1.13 Explain the difference between random-access memory (RAM) and read-only memory (ROM).

1.14 A disk is a random-access device, but it is not RAM (random-access memory). Explain why and give an example of each.

1.15 Determine how your computer, or a computer in a lab to which you have access, is connected to others across a network. Is it linked to the Internet? Draw a diagram to show the basic connections in your environment.

1.16 Explain the differences between a local-area network (LAN) and a wide-area network (WAN). What is the relationship between them?

1.17 What is the total number of communication lines needed for a fully connected point-to-point network of eight computers? Nine computers? Ten computers? What is a general formula for determining this result?

1.18 Explain the difference between the Internet and the World-Wide Web.

1.19 List and explain the parts of the URL for:
   a. your school.
   b. the Computer Science department of your school.
   c. your professor's Web page.

1.20 Use a Web browser to access information through the World-Wide Web about the following topics. For each one, explain the process you used to find the information and record the specific URLs found.

   a. The Philadelphia Phillies baseball team
   b. Wine production in California
   c. The subway systems in four major cities throughout the world
   d. Vacation opportunities in the Caribbean

Answers to Self-Review Questions

1.1 The hardware of a computer system are its physical components such as a circuit board, monitor, or keyboard. Computer software are programs that are executed by the hardware, and the data that those programs use. Hardware is tangible but software is intangible. In order to be useful, hardware requires software and software requires hardware.

1.2 The operating system provides a user interface and efficiently coordinates the use of resources such as main memory and the CPU.

1.3 The information is broken down into pieces, and those pieces are represented as numbers.

1.4 a. 2 bits can represent four items because $2^2 = 4$.
    b. 4 bits can represent 16 items because $2^4 = 16$.
    c. 5 bits can represent 32 items because $2^5 = 32$.

1.5 The two primary hardware components are main memory and the CPU. Main memory holds the currently active programs and data. The CPU retrieves individual program instructions from main memory, one at a time, and executes them.

1.6 A memory address is a number that uniquely identifies a particular memory location in which a value is stored.

1.7 Main memory is volatile, which means the information that is stored in it will be lost if the power supply to the computer is turned off. Secondary memory devices are nonvolatile; therefore, the information that is stored on them is retained even if the power goes off.

1.8 A file server is a network computer that is dedicated to storing and providing programs and data that are needed by many network users.

1.9 The word Internet comes from the word internetworking, a concept related to wide-area networks (WANs). An internetwork connects one network to another. The Internet is a WAN.

Software Concepts

2

This chapter introduces the software concepts necessary to develop basic programs. It explores the relationships between various types of programming languages, and describes the software tools used in the development process. Furthermore, this chapter identifies some key elements of a Java program and introduces the underlying ideas of object-oriented programming in general. Finally, it demonstrates the relationship between the Java programming language and the World-Wide Web.

Chapter Objectives

- Dissect some Java programs, exploring the ideas of syntax and semantics.
- Explain the purpose and evolution of programming languages.
- Describe the various software tools used in program development.
- Define various categories of programming errors.
- Establish the fundamental principles of object-oriented programming.
- Explore the difference between a Java application and a Java applet.

2.1 A Java Program

A program is written in a particular *programming language* that determines the words and symbols that you can use to construct a program. A programming language also defines a set of rules that determine exactly how a programmer can combine the words and symbols of the language into programming statements. A *programming statement* is an instruction that is carried out when the program is executed.

Let's take a look at a simple, but complete, Java program. The following code prints a sentence, in this case a quote from Abraham Lincoln, to the screen:

A `class` definition contains methods.

The `main` method contains program statements.

```
// Prints a quote from Abraham Lincoln.
class Lincoln {

    public static void main (String[] args) {
        System.out.println ("Whatever you are, be a good one.");
    }  // method main

}  // class Lincoln
```

All Java applications have a similar basic structure. When executed, this program prints the following line of text:

```
Whatever you are, be a good one.
```

Despite its small size and simple purpose, this program contains several important features. Let's carefully dissect it and examine its pieces.

The first line of the program is a *comment,* which starts with the `//` symbol and continues to the end of the line. Comments don't affect what the program does, but are included to make the program easier to understand by humans. Programmers can and should include comments throughout a program to clearly identify the purpose of the program and describe any special processing. Any written comments or documents, including a user's guide and technical references, are called *documentation.* Comments included in a program are called *inline documentation.*

> **Key Concept** Comments do not affect a program's processing.

The second line in the program is the beginning of a `class` definition. A *class* is a collection of methods and data. This class is called `Lincoln`, though we could have named it just about anything we wished. The class definition runs from the first opening brace ({) to the final closing brace (}) on the last line of the program. All Java programs are defined using class definitions.

Inside the class definition is the `main` method. A *method* is a group of programming statements that are given a name. In this case, the name of the method is `main` and it contains only one programming statement. Like a class definition, a method is also delimited by braces.

The comments after the braces that terminate the method and the class are included to help the reader identify the end of the method or class. Like all comments, they are not required and do not affect how the program works. As a general rule, we include similar comments for all methods and classes in our programs.

All Java applications have a `main` method, which is where processing begins. Each programming statement in the `main` method is executed, one at a time in order, until the end of the method is reached. Then the program ends, or *terminates*. The `main` method definition in a Java program is always preceded by the words `public`, `static`, and `void`, which are defined later. The use of `String` and `args` do not come into play in this particular program and are also described later.

Key Concept   The `main` method must always be defined using the words `public`, `static`, and `void`.

The only line of code in the `main` method invokes another method called `println` (pronounced print line). We *invoke* a method when we want it to execute. Invoking a method is also referred to as *calling* the method. The `println` method prints specific characters to the screen. When the program is executed, it calls the `println` method to print the sentence, and because it is the only line in the program, the program then terminates.

The code for the `println` method is not defined in this program. The `println` method is part of the Java *Applications Programming Interface* (API). An API is a collection of preexisting software that we can use in our programs. The Java API is a standard set of classes that can be used in any Java program. The classes and methods in the Java API provide a variety of fundamental services that are not part of the language itself. The `println` method is one of thousands of API methods that we can use when we write programs. The full designation of the `println` method, `System.out.println`, indicates the class in the API that is being referenced.

Key Concept   There is a useful set of classes called the Java API that anyone can use when writing Java programs.

White Space

All Java programs use *white space* to separate words and symbols used in a program. White space consists of blanks, tabs, and newline characters. The phrase white space refers to the fact that, on a white sheet of paper with black printing, the space between the words and symbols is white. The way we use white space is important because it can emphasize parts of our code and can make programs easier to read.

Except when separating words, the computer ignores white space. It does not affect the execution of a program. This fact gives programmers a great deal of flexibility in how they format a program. The lines of a program should be divided in logical places and certain lines should be indented and aligned so that the program's underlying structure is clear.

Because white space is ignored, you could write a program in many different ways. For example, taking white space to one extreme, you could put as many words as possible on each line. The following program, Lincoln2, is formatted quite differently than Lincoln but prints the same message:

```
// A simple program that prints a message.
class Lincoln2 { public static void main (String[] args)
{ System.out.println ("Whatever you are, be a good one."); } }
```

Taking white space to the other extreme, you could write almost every word and symbol on a different line, such as in the following program, Lincoln3:

```
// A simple program that prints a message.
class
    Lincoln3
  {
                public
  static
      void
 main
          (
String
           []
    args
                )
  {
         System.out.println
            (
   "Whatever you are, be a good one."
      )
   ;
 }
     }
```

All three versions of Lincoln are technically valid and will execute in the same way, but they are radically different from a reader's point of view. Both of the latter examples show poor style and make the program difficult to understand. Appendix G contains guidelines for writing Java programs, including the appropriate use of white space. You may be asked to adhere to these or similar guidelines. In any case, you should adopt and consistently use a set of style guidelines in order to increase the readability of your code.

Comments

Let's examine comments in more detail. Comments are the only language feature that allows programmers to compose and communicate their thoughts independent of the code. Comments should provide insight to the author's intent when writing the program. A program is often used for many years, and it's likely that many modifications will be made to it over time. Often the original programmer will not remember the details of a particular program when, at some point in the future, modifications are required. Furthermore, it is often the case that the original programmer is not available to make the changes, and someone completely unfamiliar with the program needs to understand it. Therefore good documentation is essential.

However, as far as the Java programming language is concerned, comments are written without restriction to their content. Like white space, comments are ignored by the computer and they do not affect how the program executes. The comment in our Lincoln program represents one of two types of comments allowed in Java. It takes the following form:

```
// This is a comment.
```

This type of comment begins with a double slash (//) and continues to the end of the line. You cannot have any white space between the two slashes. The computer ignores any text between the double slash and the end of the line. A comment can follow code on the same line to document that particular line, as in the following example:

```
System.out.println ("Monthly Report");  // always use this title
```

The second form of a Java comment is:

```
/*  This is another comment.  */
```

This comment type does not use the end of a line to indicate the end of the comment. Anything between the initiating slash-asterisk (/*) and the terminating asterisk-slash (*/) is part of the comment, including the invisible *newline character* that represents the end of a line. Therefore, this type of comment can extend over multiple lines. There cannot be white space between the slash and the asterisk. If there is a second asterisk following the /* at the beginning of a comment, it can be used to automatically generate external documentation about your program. This process is described in Appendix L.

The two comment types can be used to create various documentation styles, such as:

```
// This is a comment on a single line.

// =================================================
// Some comments deserve to be blocked off to focus
// special attention.  Note that each of these lines
// is technically a separate comment.
// =================================================

/*
This is one comment
that spans several lines.
*/
```

Often programmers concentrate so much on writing code, they focus too little on documentation. You should develop good commenting practices, and follow them habitually. Comments should be well written, usually in complete sentences. They should not belabor ideas that are obvious, but provide greater insight into the intent of the code. The following examples are not good comments:

```
System.out.println ("hello");  // prints hello
System.out.println ("test");   // change this later
```

The first comment paraphrases the obvious purpose of the line and does not add any value to the statement. It is better to have no comment than a useless one. The second comment is ambiguous. What should be changed later? When is later? Why should it be changed?

Key Concept Inline documentation should provide insight into your code. It should not be ambiguous or belabor the obvious.

It is considered good programming style to use comments in a consistent way throughout an entire program. The guidelines in Appendix G suggest specific techniques for documenting your programs.

Identifiers, Reserved Words, and Literals

A programmer must make up words when writing a program, such as a class name or a method name. These words are called *identifiers*. Most identifiers have no predefined meaning in the language. The identifiers in the `Lincoln` program are `Lincoln`, `main`, `String`, `args`, and `System.out.println`. We simply chose to name the class `Lincoln`, but could have chosen many possible names. The identifiers `String` and `System.out.println` are not part of the Java language. They are defined in the Java API and are names that the authors of the Java API made up. The identifier `main` has a special significance, however, since it indicates where the execution of a Java application begins.

An identifier can be composed of any combination of letters, digits, the underscore character (`_`), and the dollar sign (`$`), but it cannot begin with a digit. Identifiers may be of any length. Therefore, `total`, `label7`, `next_stock_item`, and `$amount` are all valid identifiers, but `4th_word` and `coin#value` are not valid.

Both uppercase and lowercase letters can be used in an identifier, and the difference is important. Java is *case sensitive*, which means that two identifier names that only differ by the case of their letters are considered to be different identifiers. Therefore `total`, `Total`, `ToTaL`, and `TOTAL` are all different identifiers. However, you should not use multiple identifiers that differ only by their case because they can be easily confused.

The appropriate use of uppercase and lowercase letters in identifiers makes your code more readable. Although the Java language doesn't require it, using a consistent case format for each kind of identifier makes your identifiers easier to understand. For example, we use only lowercase letters for some identifiers, such as method names, but we use *title case* (uppercase for the first letter of each word) for class names. Throughout the text, we describe the preferred case style for each type of identifier as it is encountered, and guidelines for naming identifiers are given in Appendix G.

> **Key Concept**   Java is case sensitive. The uppercase and lowercase versions of a letter are distinct. You should use a consistent case convention for different types of identifiers.

An identifier can be of any length, but you should choose your names carefully. They should be descriptive but not overly verbose. You should avoid meaningless names such as a or x. An exception to this rule can be made if the short name is actually descriptive, such as using x and y to represent an *<x,y>* coordinate on a two-dimensional grid. Likewise, you should not use unnecessarily long names, such as the identifier `the_current_item_being_processed`. The name `current_item` would serve just as well. We use the underscore character to separate words in an identifier.

As you might imagine, the use of identifiers that are too verbose is a much less prevalent problem than the use of names that are not descriptive. Err to the side of readability, but a reasonable balance can almost always be found. Also, be careful when abbreviating words. You might think `cur_st_val` is a good name to represent the current stock value, but another person trying to understand your code is likely to have trouble figuring out what you meant. It might not even be clear to you two months after writing it.

> **Key Concept**   Variable names should be descriptive and readable, but not overly verbose.

Reserved words are identifiers that have a special meaning in a programming language and can only be used in predefined ways. The Java reserved words are listed in Fig. 2.1, in alphabetical order. Note that the words marked with an asterisk (*) are reserved for possible future use in later versions of the language, but currently have no meaning in Java. In the `Lincoln` program, the reserved words used are `class`, `public`, `static`, and `void`.

Literals are explicit data values that are used in a program. The only literal in the `Lincoln` program is the string of characters "`Whatever you are, be a good one.`" A *string* is a sequence of characters, such as a word or a sentence. The string

abstract	default	goto*	operator*	synchronized
boolean	do	if	outer*	this
break	double	implements	package	throw
byte	else	import	private	throws
byvalue*	extends	inner*	protected	transient
case	false	instanceof	public	true
cast*	final	int	rest*	try
catch	finally	interface	return	var*
char	float	long	short	void
class	for	native	static	volatile
const*	future*	new	super	while
continue	generic*	null	switch	

Figure 2.1   Java reserved words (* means reserved for possible future use).

literal is enclosed in double quotes so that it is treated as one entity. Otherwise, it would not be possible to determine where the string ended. Literals can also be numeric data values, such as 25, -14, 3.14159, and -0.4.

The `print` and `println` Methods

The `println` method prints the information sent to it, then moves to the next line. The `print` method is similar to `println`, but does not advance to the next line when completed. The `print` method is also part of the Java API. Let's look at another Java program, called `Countdown`, that invokes both of these methods.

```
// Demonstrates the difference between the print and
// println methods.
class Countdown {
   public static void main (String[] args) {
      System.out.print ("Three... ");
      System.out.print ("Two... ");
      System.out.print ("One... ");
      System.out.print ("Zero... ");
      System.out.println ("Liftoff!");
      System.out.println ("Houston, we have a problem.");
   } // method main

} // class Countdown
```

The `print` and `println` methods are part of the Java API.

When this program is executed, it produces the following output:

```
Three... Two... One... Zero... Liftoff!
Houston, we have a problem.
```

Note that the word `Liftoff` is printed on the same line as the first few words, even though it is printed using the `println` method. Remember that the `println` method moves to the next line *after* the information passed to it is printed. Let's look at another program that prints some information.

```
//  Demonstrates the string concatenation operator (+).
class Antarctica {

    public static void main (String[] args) {

        System.out.print ("The international " + "dialing code ");
        System.out.println ("for Antarctica is " + 672);

    }  // method main

}  // class Antarctica
```

672 is converted to a string then concatenated to the `string` literal.

The `Antarctica` program contains one call to `print` and another to `println`. The information passed to both methods contains the string concatenation operator (+). *String concatenation* means that two strings are combined into one, end to end. The call to `print` contains the expression

```
"The international " + "dialing code "
```

which takes the two strings and turns it into `"The international dialing code "`. This string could have been passed to `print` initially but was separated to demonstrate string concatenation. The strings are combined into one before it is sent to the `print` method. The call to `println` contains the expression

```
"for Antarctica is " + 672
```

which also uses the + operator. Note, however, that the + operator has a string and a number as operands. If either or both of the operands of the + operator are strings, then string concatenation is performed. The number 672 is automatically converted to the string "672"; then the strings are concatenated. As with the call to print, the concatenation occurs prior to calling println. The output of the Antarctica program is:

```
The international dialing code for Antarctica is 672
```

As you might imagine, the + operator is also used for arithmetic addition, as seen in the following program:

```
//  Adds two numbers together and prints the result.
class Sum {

    public static void main (String[] args) {

        System.out.println ("The sum of 6 and 9 is " + (6+9));

    }   // method main

}   // class Sum
```

The + operator represents both addition and string concatenation.

The Sum program uses the + operator twice. The first time it performs string concatenation and the second time it performs addition. Because of the extra parenthesis around 6+9, the addition is performed first, producing a result of 15. At that point we are left with a situation similar to the Antarctica program in which the + operator is used on a string and a number. The value 15 is converted to a string, the strings are concatenated together, and the string is sent to println, producing the following output:

```
The sum of 6 and 9 is 15
```

If the parentheses had not been used around the addition expression, the first + operator would have been executed first. The operation performed by the + operator depends on the types of the operands. Therefore the first + would have performed string concatenation on the string literal and the number 6. Then that string would be concatenated with the number 9, producing the string "The sum of 6 and 9 is 69", which is not the intended result. This issue is explored further in the next chapter.

Now that we have seen how to define some basic programs, let's explore programming languages in more detail.

2.2 Programming Languages

Suppose a particular person is giving travel directions to a friend. That person might express those thoughts in any one of several languages, such as English, French, or Italian. The directions are the same no matter which language is used to explain them, but the manner in which the directions are expressed is different. Furthermore, the friend must be able understand the language being used in order to follow the directions.

Similarly, a program can be written in many programming languages, such as Java, Ada, C, C++, Pascal, and Smalltalk. The task of the program is essentially the same, but the particular language statements used to express the instructions vary. Furthermore, a computer must be able to understand the instructions in order to carry them out.

This section explores the various categories of programming languages and describes the special programs used to execute them.

Programming Language Levels

Programming languages are often categorized into the following four groups. These groups basically reflect the historical development of computer languages:

- machine language
- assembly language
- high-level language
- fourth-generation language

In order for a program to run on a computer, it must be expressed in that computer's *machine language*. Each type of CPU has its own language. For that reason, you can't run a program specifically written for a Sun Workstation, with its Sparc processor, on an IBM PC, with its Intel processor.

Key Concept All programs must be translated to a particular computer's machine language in order to be executed.

Each machine language instruction can only accomplish a simple task. For example, a single instruction might only copy a value into a register or compare a value to zero. It might take four separate machine language instructions to add two numbers together and store the result. However, a computer can do millions of these instructions in a second, and therefore many simple commands can be quickly executed to accomplish complex tasks.

Machine language code is expressed as a series of binary digits and is extremely difficult for humans to read and write. Originally, programs were entered into the computer using switches or some similarly tedious method. Early programmers found these techniques to be time consuming and error prone.

These problems gave rise to the use of *assembly language*, which replaced binary digits with *mnemonics*, short English-like words that represent commands or data. It is much easier for programmers to deal with words than with binary digits. However, an assembly language program cannot be executed directly on a computer. It must first be translated into machine language.

Generally, each assembly language instruction corresponds to an equivalent machine language instruction. Therefore, similar to machine language, each assembly language instruction only accomplishes a simple operation. Although assembly language is an improvement over machine code from a programmer's perspective, it is still tedious to use. Both assembly language and machine language are considered to be *low-level languages*.

Today, most programmers use a *high-level language* to write software. A high-level language is expressed in English-like phrases, and thus is easier for programmers to read and write. A single high-level language programming statement can accomplish the equivalent of many, perhaps hundreds, of machine language instructions. The term high-level refers to the fact that the programming statements are expressed in a form that is removed from the machine language that is executed. Java is a high-level language, as are Ada, C, C++, Pascal, and Smalltalk.

Figure 2.2 shows equivalent expressions in a high-level language, assembly language, and machine language. The expressions add two numbers together. The assembly language and machine language in this example are specific to the Sparc processor.

The high-level language expression in Fig. 2.2 is readable and intuitive for programmers. It is similar to an algebraic expression. The equivalent assembly language code is somewhat readable but it is more verbose and less intuitive. The machine language is basically unreadable and much longer. In fact, only a small portion of the binary machine code to add two numbers together is shown in Fig. 2.2. The complete machine language code for this particular expression is over 400 bits long.

High-level language code must be translated into machine language in order to be executed. A high-level language insulates programmers from needing to know the underlying machine language for the processor on which they are working.

High-Level Language	Assembly Language	Machine Language

a + b	ld [%fp-20], %o0
	ld [%fp-24], %o1
	add %o0, %o1, %o0
		. . .
		1101 0000 0000 0111
		1011 1111 1110 1000
		1101 0010 0000 0111
		1011 1111 1110 1000
		1001 0000 0000 0000
		. . .

Figure 2.2   A high-level expression and its machine language equivalent

> **Key Concept**   Working with high-level languages allows the programmer to ignore the underlying details of machine language.

Some programming languages are considered to operate at an even higher level than high-level languages. They might include special facilities for automatic report generation or interaction with a database. These languages are called *fourth-generation languages,* or simply 4GLs, because they followed the first three generations of computer programming: machine, assembly, and high-level.

Compilers and Interpreters

Several special-purpose programs are needed to help with the process of developing new programs. They are sometimes called *software tools,* since they are used to build programs. Examples of basic software tools include an editor, a compiler, and an interpreter.

> **Key Concept**   Becoming proficient with software tools such as an editor can greatly enhance your efficiency.

Initially, an *editor* is used to type a program into a computer and store it in a file. There are many different editors with many different features. You should become familiar with the editor you will use regularly, since it can dramatically affect the speed at which you enter and modify your programs.

Once the source code is stored, it must be translated into machine language before it can be executed. This translation process can occur in a variety of ways. A *compiler* is a program that translates code in one language to equivalent code in another language. The original code is called *source code,* and the language into which it is translated is called the *target language.* For many traditional compilers, the source code is translated directly into a particular machine language. The translation process occurs once, and the resulting executable version of the program can be run whenever needed.

An *interpreter* is similar to a compiler but has an important difference. An interpreter interweaves the translation and execution activities. A small part of the source code, such as one statement, is translated and executed. Then another statement is translated and executed, and so on. One advantage of this technique is that it eliminates the need for a separate compilation phase, but the program generally runs more slowly because the translation process occurs during each execution.

The process often used to translate and execute Java programs combines the use of a compiler and an interpreter. This process is pictured in Fig. 2.3. The Java compiler translates Java source code into Java *bytecode,* which is a representation of the program in a low-level form similar to machine language code. The Java interpreter reads Java bytecode and executes it on a specific machine. Another compiler

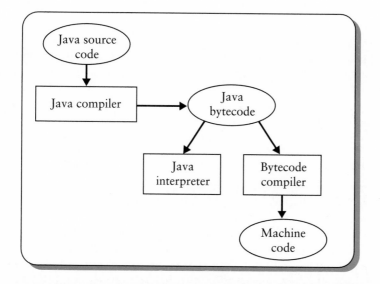

Figure 2.3   The Java translation and execution process

could translate the bytecode into a particular machine language for efficient execution on that machine.

 Key Concept   The Java compiler translates Java source code into Java bytecode. The Java interpreter translates and executes the bytecode.

The difference between Java bytecode and true machine language code is that Java bytecode is not tied to any particular processor type. This approach has the distinct advantage of making Java *architecture neutral,* and therefore easily *portable* from one machine type to another. There must be a Java interpreter or a bytecode compiler for each processor type on which you want to execute Java bytecode.

Key Concept   Java is architecture neutral because Java bytecode is not associated with any particular hardware platform. It can be executed on any machine with a Java interpreter.

Since the compilation process translates the high-level Java source code into a low-level representation, the interpretation process is more efficient than interpreting high-level code directly. Executing a program by interpreting its bytecode is still slower than executing machine code directly, but it is fast enough for most applications. Note that for efficiency, Java bytecode might be compiled into machine code.

The Java compiler and interpreter are part of the *Java Development Kit* (JDK), which also contains several other software tools that may be useful to a programmer. The tools in the JDK can be referenced directly by a user, or they might be part of an *Integrated Development Environment* (IDE), which combines an editor, compiler, and other Java support tools into a single application.

Syntax and Semantics

Each programming language has its own unique *syntax*. The syntax rules of a language dictate exactly how the vocabulary elements of the language can be put together to form statements. These rules must be followed in order to create a program. We've already discussed several Java syntax rules. For instance, the fact that an identifier cannot begin with a digit is a syntax rule. The fact that braces are used to delimit classes and methods is also a syntax rule. Appendix N formally defines the syntax rules for the Java programming language.

they avoid as many run-time errors as possible. For example, the program code could guard against the possibility of dividing by zero and handle the situation appropriately if it arises. In Java, many run-time errors are *exceptions* that can be caught and dealt with accordingly. Exceptions are covered in Chapter 14.

The third kind of software problem is a *logical error*. In this case, the software compiles and executes without complaint, but it produces incorrect results. For example, a logical error occurs when a value is calculated incorrectly or when a button does not appear in the correct place. A programmer must test the program thoroughly, comparing the expected results to those that actually occur. When defects are found, they must be traced back to the source of the problem in the code, and corrected. The process of finding and correcting defects in a program is called *debugging*. Logical errors can manifest themselves in many ways, and the actual root cause might be quite difficult to discover.

2.3   Compiling and Executing a Java Program

Once a program is saved into a file, the compiler is used to translate the Java source code into Java bytecode. The examples throughout this section use the basic software tools provided in the Java Development Kit. You may be using a different development environment, and the user interface may look different. However, you accomplish the same basic activities to get a program up and running in all development environments.

The name of the Java compiler is `javac`. To compile the `Lincoln` program, the source code must be stored in a file called `Lincoln.java`. The file name for a Java program must be the same name as the class which contains the `main` method, with an extension of `.java`. We use the > symbol to represent the command line prompt, and the input you enter is shown in color. You compile the program by submitting the file containing the source code to the compiler:

```
> javac Lincoln.java
>
```

If there are any compile-time errors in the program, the compiler detects them at this point and issues appropriate error messages. If there are no compile-time errors, the compiler creates a new file called `Lincoln.class`, which contains Java bytecode equivalent to the `Lincoln` source code program. Since a `.class` file is not a text file, you should not attempt to print or edit it.

Suppose that we had made a typing mistake when we entered our Lincoln program. For instance, a common mistake is to forget the semicolon that is necessary at the end of a statement. This is another example of a syntax rule. Suppose we have the following source code stored in the file Lincoln.java:

```
// This program contains a syntax error.  There should be
// a semi-colon after the println statement.
class Lincoln {
    public static void main (String[] args) {
        System.out.println ("Whatever you are, be a good one.")
    }  // method main
}  // class Lincoln
```

When we attempt to compile this file, we get a compile-time error message:

```
> javac Lincoln.java
Lincoln.java:5: ';' expected.
        System.out.println ("Whatever you are, be a good one.")
                                                              ^
1 error
>
```

Because an error was detected, the compiler does not produce bytecode. The error must be corrected and the program recompiled. This syntax error is very explicit. It indicates that on line 5 the character ' ; ' is expected. The offending line is written to the screen as part of the error message, and the carat character (^) points out the location on the line where the error was detected by the compiler. Depending on the type of error made, the error message may or may not direct you to the exact source of the problem. Each compiler produces slightly different error messages.

Once the program compiles without any compile-time errors (a *clean compile*), the resulting bytecode can be interpreted and executed. The name of the Java interpreter is java. A clean compile of Lincoln.java generates the bytecode file Lincoln.class. The interpreter can then be used to execute the program:

```
> java Lincoln
Whatever you are, be a good one.
>
```

The file being interpreted is Lincoln.class, not Lincoln.java. The .class portion of the file name is assumed by the interpreter. Do not include the .class extension when using the interpreter.

Using Command-Line Arguments

Let's examine another program that takes input from the command line when the bytecode is submitted to the interpreter. Any extra information on the command line when invoking the interpreter is called a *command-line argument*. It is one way to provide input to a program.

```
//  Prints a command line argument.
class Name_Tag {

   public static void main (String[] args) {
      System.out.println ("Hello.  My name is " + args[0]);
   }  // method main

}  // class Name_Tag
```

The `main` method always accepts possible command-line arguments.

The `main` method always accepts a potential list of command-line arguments. Any information typed after the file name when the program is submitted to the interpreter for execution is considered to be a command-line argument and can be referenced in the program. In this program, we call the list of arguments `args`. In the `Lincoln` program, command-line arguments could have been accepted but were never used.

The arguments are always treated as a list of character strings. The first argument in the argument list is designated as `args[0]`, the second as `args[1]`, then `args[2]`, and so on. The `Name_Tag` program only uses the first command-line argument. It invokes the `println` method to print a literal string concatenated with the value of `args[0]`.

If there are no compile-time errors in the program, submitting the `Name_Tag` source code to the compiler will produce the bytecode file called `Name_Tag.class`. The bytecode can now be submitted to the interpreter, this time with additional information on the command line.

```
> java Name_Tag John
Hello.  My name is John
>
```

The word John is read from the command line and stored as the first argument in the args list. So when the println method prints the value of args[0], the word John is printed. Note that without recompiling the program, we can execute the Name_Tag program again, giving it a different command-line argument, and produce a different result:

```
> java Name_Tag William
Hello.  My name is William
>
```

Programs that are GUI-based will usually not use command-line arguments for input because they are graphically oriented. Furthermore, if you use an integrated development environment, you will rarely use command-line arguments.

2.4 Object-Oriented Programming

Before examining more Java programs, we need to establish some of the fundamental principles on which Java programs are based. This section provides an introduction to the concepts of programming using objects.

Software Engineering

Programming languages were originally created to simplify the way programmers instruct the computer to perform certain actions. Since then they have evolved into tools that help us model the real world and solve problems. Early high-level languages, such as COBOL and FORTRAN, quickly became popular and are still used today. The move from low-level to high-level code allowed programmers to create software whose design reflected what the program did, rather than how it did it. These languages embody the *procedural* approach to developing software, in which programs are decomposed into manageable pieces called *procedures* or *functions* that are similar to methods. The procedural approach was a major achievement, but the focus was still on developing small, efficient programs. Programmers could better understand what they had written, but they did not have the techniques to proactively support the creation of high-quality software.

This situation did not change for many years. Throughout the 1960s and 1970s, the size and speed of a program were very important issues, because RAM and disk space were costly and processors were relatively slow.

Breakthroughs in digital electronics drove the cost of hardware down and made computers more powerful at the same time. Larger and more complicated programs were created to push the limits of hardware capabilities. Complex software systems are more difficult, and therefore more costly, to create. Figure 2.4 shows the nonlinear relationship between software complexity and the cost to develop it. Small increases in complexity can greatly increase costs. Habitually, large programming projects were delivered late and over budget. Furthermore, they were still error-ridden and hard to fix. This situation became known as the *software crisis*.

A primary cause of the software crisis was that programmers had no disciplined approach to the software development process. In the past several decades, many techniques have been proposed and used in an attempt to combat the software crisis. Certainly, some headway has been made. The term *software engineering* represents our efforts to engineer our software with some level of reliability. Even today, many software developers consider the term software engineering to be more aspiration than description.

Among the efforts to improve the process of large-scale software development was the introduction of *object-oriented programming* (OOP). As the name implies, a fundamental concept behind OOP is the use of objects. An object is a programming structure that groups related methods and the data those methods use. It is a mechanism that lets a programmer easily represent objects in the real world with objects in software. Furthermore, an object is designed to be a reusable entity that can be incorporated into multiple programs. *Object-oriented programming languages* were created to support the ideas behind object-oriented programming.

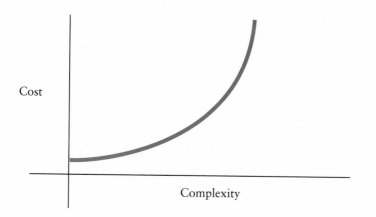

Figure 2.4 Software complexity vs. cost

Most modern high-level languages, including object-oriented languages, embody the ideas of *structured programming*. In this approach, the order in which program statements are executed follows a controlled path, without jumping around to various points in the program. In fact, object-oriented programming makes the most of many lessons learned in the past by adopting several techniques that have proven successful in the procedural approach and making them easier to use. Furthermore, an object-oriented approach provides additional techniques that have improved the development effort. For example, an object-oriented language provides mechanisms to create objects from existing ones, and so reuses past effort and saves development time.

Java is an object-oriented language. It represents an evolutionary step in software development, even among existing object-oriented languages, improving on previous techniques and contributing new, important characteristics, such as in its relationship with the Web.

Above all, an object-oriented approach promotes the development of programs by constructing them from software components. These components can often be reused in more than one situation. By having reusable code, the need to create new software for each new programming project is reduced; reusable code in turn reduces software development time and costs. New programs that reuse tested, reliable code are less error-prone, reducing costs further. The next section explores in more detail how software components are used to create programs.

Software Components

The basic purpose of software is to turn input into output. All programs can be thought of in this way. A simple example is a program that takes as input a list of numbers, then computes and prints their average. The program can be thought of as a process that transforms a list of numbers into the average.

A *software component* performs a specific task, transforming input into output, and can be combined with other components. A software component might be a piece of a larger program, or it might be a program that cooperates with other programs. Figure 2.5 depicts the concept of a software component transforming input into output.

Complicated programs use this same idea on a larger scale. A software system that controls the flight of an airplane takes input from the pilot using various con-

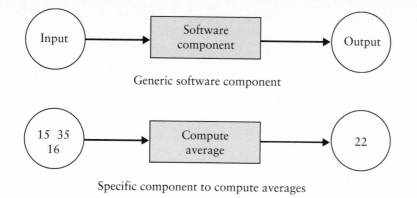

Generic software component

15 35
16 → Compute average → 22

Specific component to compute averages

Figure 2.5   Software as a transformation from input to output

trol levers and buttons, and transforms them into signals that control the plane's engines and wings.

Each internal part of a large, well-designed software system follows the same model of transforming input to output. Circles are used in Fig. 2.5 to represent both input and output because often the output of one component is used as the input to another. Most programs are designed and written today using software components that are linked together.

Figure 2.6 shows a system that is made up of two components. The first component uses three different inputs to generate an output. The second component uses two inputs, one of which is the output of the first component, to generate a single output. The way in which these components interact is as important as what

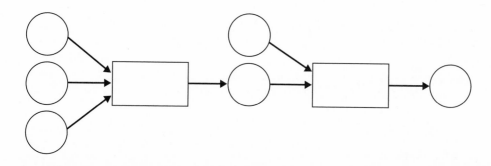

Figure 2.6   Two connected software components

is happening inside the components themselves. In an application program there may be hundreds of components linked together in a complicated structure. In a large software system there may be thousands of components.

> **Key Concept** Modern software systems are constructed from interacting and cooperating components. The output of one component may be used as the input to another.

These collections of linked components do not have to execute on a single computer. Using networks, the output of one component on one computer can be read as the input of another component on another computer. For example, consider one of the most popular uses of computers today: electronic mail (email). Suppose you wanted to send an email message from a computer in the United States to a friend in, say, Singapore. You can write a mail message using a software component that accepts what you type on the keyboard and stores it in a message. This component uses the email address of the computer to which your mail should be sent to create a new message in a particular format that contains the destination email address and the text of the message.

A similar component on another computer reads this message as input and decides if the message stays on the local machine or should be sent to another. If the message is not at its final destination, the component sends it over the network to another computer that is closer to the destination computer. This process is repeated until the destination computer receives the message, which is stored until the recipient reads the message using yet another software component. Figure 2.7 graphically depicts this process.

Note that across all of the computers in Fig. 2.7, there are only three different software components, one for composing email, one for sending email, and one for reading email. They are, essentially, replicated as needed to form a world-wide email system.

The object-oriented approach corresponds nicely with the ideas of component-based development. Let's take a look at some object-oriented concepts in more detail.

Objects and Classes

As discussed earlier in this chapter, an object in software groups related methods and data. A software object often represents a corresponding real-world object. Consider a computer game that races cars and uses a separate object to represent each car. The software car object reflects a real car to a certain extent. It is a soft-

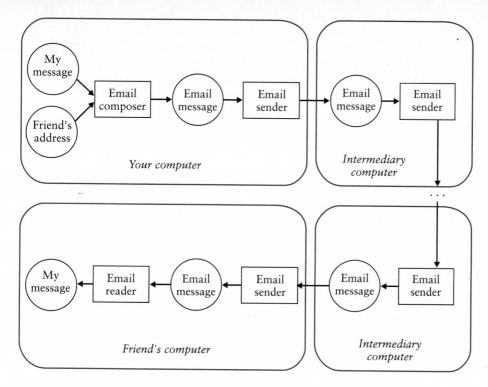

Figure 2.7   A software system for transferring email

ware component that transforms input to output. In this case, it may accept varia-tions in steering and pedal use, and produce as output a new position and speed. This is essentially what a real car does. It may also contain additional methods, such as one to draw the car on the screen. Figure 2.8 illustrates a real car represented as a software object.

An object is defined by a class. A *class* can be thought of as the blueprint of an object, or as a category of objects. For example, a particular car can be thought of as an object, while the concept of all cars can be thought of as a class. Figure 2.9 graphically depicts three specific objects: my first car, John's car, and Dad's car. The car class represents the idea of a car, and the three objects represent actual cars.

 Key Concept   A class is a description of a category. Objects are specific examples that fit within a category, and are described by classes.

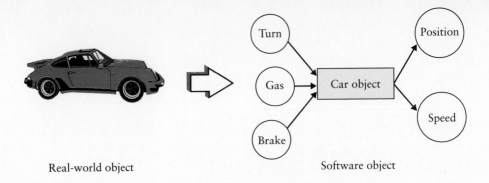

Real-world object   Software object

Figure 2.8   A real-world object represented as a software object

Classes can also be used to define other classes. For example, suppose we had a class that represents all vehicles, including cars, airplanes, and trains. It would contain the characteristics common to all vehicles, such as how fast they move. We can then use the vehicle class to create, or derive, our car class. It would contain all of the characteristics of a generic vehicle, and we could then add the specific details that make a car unique among other vehicle types. A class representing each specific vehicle type can be derived from the generic vehicle class.

The concept of deriving one class from another is called *inheritance*. By using one class to form the basis of another class definition, inheritance promotes reuse. Figure 2.10 shows an inheritance derivation in a *class diagram*. By convention, the arrows point from the new class to the class from which it was derived.

Key Concept   New classes can be derived from previously created classes. This derivation is called inheritance.

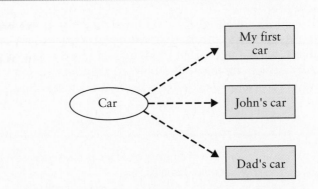

Figure 2.9   A car class and three car objects

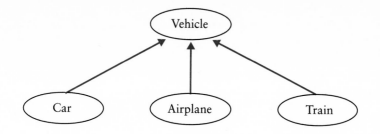

Figure 2.10   A class diagram, showing three new classes derived from an existing class

Objects, classes, and inheritance are three of the basic concepts used in object-oriented programming. They are explained in more detail in Chapters 4 and 8. The next section describes large collections of classes that are helpful in program development.

Key Concept   Objects, classes, and inheritance are three basic concepts used in object-oriented programming.

2.5   Class Libraries

A *class library* is a set of classes that support the development of programs. The classes in a class library are often related by inheritance. A compiler often comes with a class library, though class libraries can sometimes be obtained separately. The classes in a class library contain methods that are often invaluable to a programmer because of the special functionality they offer. In fact, programmers usually become dependent on the methods in a class library and begin to think of them as part of the language. But, technically, they are not in the language definition.

The Java Application Programming Interface (API) is a set of class libraries. Let's examine it in more detail.

The Java API

The classes of the Java API are grouped into packages. A *package* is a Java language element used to group related classes under a common name. Packages can be nested inside one another. All of the packages in the Java API, for instance, are collected into a

Package	Provides support to
java.applet	Create programs (applets) that are easily transported across the Web.
java.awt	Draw graphics and create graphical user interfaces; AWT stands for Abstract Windowing Toolkit.
java.beans	Define software components that can be easily combined into applications.
java.io	Perform a wide variety of input and output functions.
java.lang	General support; it is automatically imported into all Java programs.
java.math	Perform calculations with arbitrarily high precision.
java.net	Communicate across a network.
java.rmi	Create programs that can be distributed across multiple computers; RMI stands for Remote Method Invocation.
java.security	Enforce security restrictions.
java.sql	Interact with databases; SQL stands for Standard Query Language.
java.text	Format text for output.
java.util	General utilities.

Figure 2.11   The Java Platform API

single package that is simply called java. To refer to a package inside the java package, a period (pronounced dot) is used to separate the names, as in java.applet.

Key Concept   A package is a Java language element used to group related classes under a common name.

Figure 2.11 describes the packages that are part of the Java Platform API (version 1.1), which we refer to throughout the text as the Java API. These packages are available on any platform that supports Java software development.

Many of these packages support highly specific programming techniques and will not come into play in the development of basic programs. Let's discuss some of the packages you will initially find most useful.

The java.applet package contains classes that support the development of applets, which are Java programs that are intended to be linked to HTML documents and made accessible over the Web. Applets are discussed in more detail later in this chapter.

The `java.awt` package supports the use of graphics in a Java program. The abbreviation awt stands for *Abstract Windowing Toolkit*. It contains many classes that allow the user to draw shapes and text, as well as classes that support the development of complete graphical user interfaces (GUIs). The GUI classes allow the user to create buttons, menus, and many other graphical components through which a user can interact with a program.

The `java.io` package contains classes that assist the programmer in accomplishing various kinds of input and output. Network communication, however, is accomplished through the `java.net` package. The `java.util` package contains a set of general purpose utility classes that serve many purposes.

Finally, the `java.lang` package contains several classes that support primary language issues, such as mathematical functions. These classes are probably the most frequently used of all classes in the API. The `System` class, through which the `println` method is invoked, is part of this package.

Many classes of the Java API are discussed throughout this book. Appendix O serves as a general reference to the Java API.

The `import` Statement

When you want to use a class from the Java API in a program, you can use its fully qualified name, including the package name, every time it is referenced. For example, every time you want to refer to the `Graphics` class in the `java.awt` package, you can write `java.awt.Graphics`. However, completely specifying the package and class name each time it is needed quickly becomes monotonous. Java provides the `import` statement to simplify these references.

The `import` statement identifies the packages and classes of the Java API that will be used in a program, so that the full package name is not necessary on each reference. The `import` statement takes one of two forms:

```
import package.class;
```

or

```
import package.*;
```

The first form identifies a particular *class* that will be used in the program. For example, the following line imports the `Random` class of the `java.util` package:

```
import java.util.Random;
```

With this `import` statement at the top of the program, the `Random` class can be referenced inside the program without the package name. The second form of the `import` statement uses the asterisk (*) to indicate that any class inside the package might be used in the program. Therefore, the statement

```
import java.util.*;
```

allows all classes in the `java.util` package to be referenced in the program without the explicit package name. If only one class of a package is used in a program, import that class by name. Otherwise, use the * notation.

Because the `java.lang` package is so often used, it is automatically imported into all Java programs. Thus you do not need an explicit `import` statement to import the `java.lang` package or to use the classes contained in it. For example, the programs discussed earlier in this chapter refer to `System.out.println` even though they contain no `import` statement. The `System` class is defined in the `java.lang` package and is automatically available for use in any Java program.

With the basics of object-oriented programming established, and the use of packages in the Java API explained, we can now discuss a special and important type of Java program: the applet.

2.6 Java Applets

There are two kinds of Java programs: Java applets and Java applications. A *Java applet* is a Java program that is intended to be embedded into an HTML document, transported across a network, and executed using a Web browser. A *Java application* is a stand-alone program that can be executed using the Java interpreter. The programs seen earlier in this chapter, such as `Lincoln`, are Java applications.

 Key Concept   Applets are Java programs that are usually transported across a network and executed using a Web browser. Java applications are stand-alone programs that can be executed using the Java interpreter.

The Web enables users to send and receive various types of media, such as text, graphics, and sound, by using a point-and-click interface that is extremely convenient and easy to use. A Java applet was the first kind of executable program that could be retrieved using World-Wide Web software. Java applets are considered to be just another type of media that can be exchanged across the Web. However, Java applets do not have to be transported across a network. They can be viewed locally using a Web browser. For that matter, they don't even have to be executed through a Web browser at all. A tool in the Sun Java Development Kit called *appletviewer* can be used to interpret and execute an applet. We use appletviewer to display most of the applets in the book. However, usually the point of making a Java applet is to provide a link to it on a Web page and allow it to be retrieved and executed by World-Wide Web users anywhere in the world.

Java bytecode (not Java source code) is linked to an HTML document and sent across the Web. A version of the Java interpreter embedded in a Web browser is used to execute the applet once it reaches its destination. A Java applet must be compiled into bytecode format before it can be used with the Web.

There are some important differences between the structure of a Java applet and the structure of a Java application. Let's explore these differences by examining some applets.

Applet Examples

The overview of object-oriented programming concepts presented earlier in this chapter discusses the idea of inheritance, in which a class is created by deriving it from an existing class. Applets are a good example of this concept. The class that contains a Java applet must be derived from an existing class called Applet that is part of the Java API. The class you create for your applet need only focus on what you want your program to do. The details of how an applet works and interacts with the rest of the system is automatically provided by the Applet parent class through inheritance.

Because the Web browser that executes an applet is already running, applets can be thought of as a part of a larger program. As such they do not have a main method where execution starts. The paint method in an applet is automatically invoked by the applet. In the example below, the paint method is used to write a quotation by Confucius to the screen.

```
import java.applet.Applet;
import java.awt.*;

//  Prints a quote from Confucius.  Uses the drawString method
//  in an applet.
public class Confucius extends Applet {

   public void paint (Graphics page) {
      page.drawString ("Forget injuries, never forget kindness.",
                    50, 50);
      page.drawString ("-- Confucius", 70, 70);
   }  // method paint

}  // class Confucius
```

An applet is derived from the Applet class.

The paint method is automatically invoked by the applet.

The two import statements at the beginning of the program explicitly indicate the packages of the Java API that are used in the program. In this example, we need the

`Applet` class, which is in the `java.applet` package, and various graphics capabilities defined in the `java.awt` package.

Applets are usually graphically oriented, implying that the program will be drawing pictures in some sense. In fact, the quotation that is output in the `Confucius` applet is actually drawn on the screen rather than printed. In the example, the `paint` method uses a `Graphics` object called `page` to draw two character strings using the method `drawString`. The `drawString` method is defined in the `Graphics` class, and both are defined in the `java.awt` package of the Java API.

The Java reserved word `public`, used to define both the `Confucius` class and the `paint` method, is necessary. The same goes for the reserved word `void` used with the `paint` method. They specify particular characteristics of classes and methods and are explained later in the text.

The numeric values used in the call to `drawString` are the <*x,y*> coordinates where the string should be drawn. The origin (point <0,0>) for Java graphics is in the top left corner of the area defined for the applet. The *x* coordinate is along the horizontal axis, and the *y* coordinate is along the vertical axis. Figure 2.12 shows the results of executing the applet using the appletviewer tool. The coordinate system is discussed in more detail in Chapter 7.

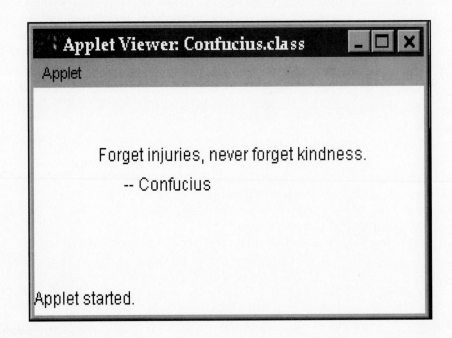

Figure 2.12 The `Confucius` applet

Even though it uses graphics to draw the character string, the Confucius applet is not very graphical. Let's look at another applet that uses two other graphics methods from the java.awt package of the Java API.

```
import java.applet.Applet;
import java.awt.*;

//  Draws a "No Parking" sign.
public class No_Parking extends Applet {

   public void paint (Graphics page) {
      page.drawString ("Parking", 50, 50);
      page.drawOval (45, 24, 43, 43);
      page.drawLine (82, 30, 51, 61);
   }  // method paint

}  // class No_Parking
```

The Graphics class contains several methods for drawing.

This applet draws the universal symbol for "no" (a circle with a diagonal line through it) superimposed over the word Parking to represent a "No Parking" sign. Figure 2.13 shows the execution of the No_Parking applet.

The first line of code inside the paint method calls drawString to output a string of characters, as it did in the Confucius applet. The call to drawOval

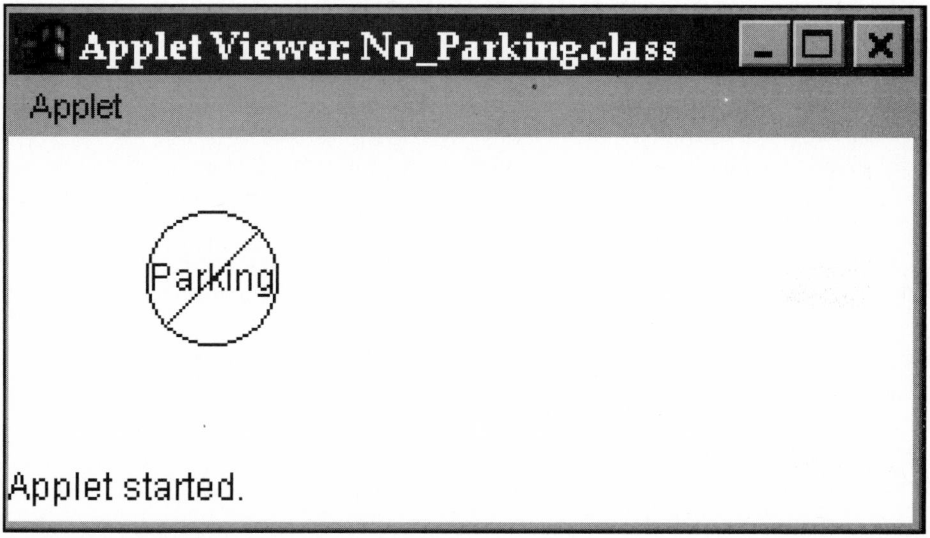

Figure 2.13   The No_Parking applet

draws an oval on the screen. The `drawOval` method uses four numeric values to determine how the oval is drawn. The first two values indicate the *<x,y>* coordinates of the top left "corner" of the oval (as if the oval were enclosed in a rectangle). The oval is positioned so that it will encircle the word `Parking`. The third value is the width of the oval and the fourth value is the height of the oval. Because the width and height of the oval are equal, the oval that is drawn is actually a circle. We compiled and ran the program several times, experimenting with the position and size of the oval until it was positioned around the word `Parking` correctly.

Finally, the `drawLine` method draws a line segment diagonally across the circle. The first two values used by the `drawLine` method indicate the *<x,y>* coordinate of one end of the line segment, and the last two values indicate the *<x,y>* coordinate of the end of the line segment. As with the drawing of the oval, the end points of the line segment were roughly determined initially, then refined by experimenting with the position. Careful planning with graph paper can minimize the amount of experimentation necessary to work with graphics. The `drawString`, `drawOval`, and `drawLine` methods represent only a small part of the drawing capabilities of the `Graphics` class.

HTML

In order for the applet to be transmitted over the Web and executed by a browser, it must be referenced in a HyperText Markup Language (HTML) document. An HTML document contains *tags* that specify formatting instructions and identify the special types of media that are to be included in a document. A Java program is considered to be a specific media type, just as text, graphics, and sound are.

An HTML tag is enclosed in angle brackets, as shown in the example below. The first tag is a comment and is ignored. The entire document is enclosed by an HTML tag which runs from `<HTML>` to `</HTML>`. Similar tags are used to define the head and body of the document. Words defined by the title tag usually appear in the title bar of the browser window. The `<H3>` tag requests that the enclosed text be highlighted as a heading (there are six levels of headings). The applet tag is used to embed a link to the `Confucius` applet in an HTML document. The applet tag also defines the width and height (in pixels) of the area in which the applet is displayed. Not all tags have a starting and ending tag, such as `<HR>`. That tag requests that a line, or horizontal rule, be drawn at that location in the document.

```
<! Confucius.html>
<HTML>
<HEAD>
<TITLE>The Confucius Applet</TITLE>
</HEAD>

<BODY>

<H3>The Confucius applet:</H3>
```

```
<APPLET CODE="Confucius.class" WIDTH=300 HEIGHT=150>
</APPLET>

<HR>
</BODY>
</HTML>
```

Note that the applet tag refers to the bytecode file of the `Confucius` applet, as opposed to the source code. Before an applet can be transported using the Web, it must be compiled into its bytecode format. Then, as shown in Fig. 2.14, the document can be loaded using a Web browser, which will automatically interpret and execute the applet. Appendix K contains a tutorial on HTML that can be used to create more sophisticated documents.

Summary of Key Concepts

- Comments do not affect a program's processing.
- The main method must always be defined using the words `public`, `static`, and `void`.
- There is a useful set of classes called the Java API that anyone can use when writing Java programs.

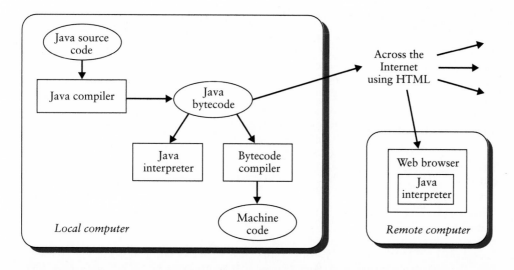

Figure 2.14   The Java translation and execution process (revised)

- You should always adhere to a set of guidelines that establish the way you format and document your programs.
- Appropriate use of white space makes your programs easier to read and understand.
- Inline documentation should provide insight into your code. It should not be ambiguous or belabor the obvious.
- Java is case sensitive. The uppercase and lowercase versions of a letter are distinct. You should use a consistent case convention for different types of identifiers.
- Variable names should be descriptive and readable, but not overly verbose.
- All programs must be translated to a particular computer's machine language in order to be executed.
- Working with high-level languages allows the programmer to ignore the underlying details of machine language.
- Becoming proficient with software tools such as an editor can greatly enhance your efficiency.
- The Java compiler translates Java source code into Java bytecode. The Java interpreter translates and executes the bytecode.
- Java is architecture neutral because Java bytecode is not associated with any particular hardware platform. It can be executed on any machine with a Java interpreter.
- The syntax rules of a programming language dictate the form of a program. The semantics dictates the meaning of the program statements.
- A computer follows our instructions exactly. The programmer is responsible for the accuracy and reliability of a program.
- A program must be syntactically correct or the compiler will not produce bytecode.
- Software development and maintenance is costly and prone to error. Object-oriented techniques and languages are designed to address these problems through reusable software and program designs that more closely model the real world.
- Modern software systems are constructed from interacting and cooperating components. The output of one component may be used as the input to another.
- A class is a description of a category. Objects are specific examples that fit within a category, and are described by classes.
- New classes can be derived from previously created classes. This derivation is called inheritance.
- Objects, classes, and inheritance are three basic concepts used in object-oriented programming.
- A package is a Java language element used to group related classes under a common name.
- Applets are Java programs that are usually transported across a network and executed using a Web browser. Java applications are stand-alone programs that can be executed using the Java interpreter.

Self-Review Questions

2.1 What is the relationship between a high-level language and machine language?

2.2 What is Java bytecode?

2.3 What is white space? How does it affect program execution? How does it affect program readability?

2.4 What do we mean by the syntax and semantics of a programming language?

2.5 What is object-oriented programming?

2.6 Categorize each of the following as either a class or an object:

    a. a coffee mug
    b. a coffee mug that has the words "Elvis Lives" on it
    c. Nancy's favorite coffee mug
    d. a speech
    e. the President's Inaugural Address
    f. the President's Inaugural Address that he gave Tuesday
    g. the United States
    h. the state of Pennsylvania
    i. Philadelphia

2.7 What is the difference between a Java application and a Java applet?

Exercises

2.8 Explain the process of translating and executing a Java program. How might the World-Wide Web be involved?

2.9 Give examples of the two types of Java comments. Explain the differences between them.

2.10 Which of the following are not valid Java identifiers? Why?

    a. `Factorial`
    b. `an_extremely_long_identifier_if_you_ask_me`
    c. `2nd_level`
    d. `level2`
    e. `highest$`
    f. `hook&ladder`

2.11 Why are the following valid Java identifiers not considered to be good identifiers?

    a. `i`
    b. `tot_val`
    c. `the_next_value_in_the_list`

2.12 Java is case sensitive. What does that mean?

2.13 Categorize each of the following situations as a compile-time error, run-time error, or logical error.

  a. multiplying two numbers when you meant to add them
  b. dividing by zero
  c. spelling a word wrong in the output
  d. producing inaccurate results
  e. typing a { when you should have typed (

2.14 Why is the English language ambiguous? Give two examples of English ambiguity (other than the example used in this chapter). Why is ambiguity a problem for programming languages?

2.15 What is the relationship between a class and an object?

2.16 Categorize each of the following as either a class or an object:

  a. a book
  b. the book Java Software Solutions
  c. my copy of Java Software Solutions with the dog-eared pages
  d. my dog
  e. the picture of my dog biting the mailman
  f. a car
  g. a Chrysler LeBaron

Programming Projects

2.17 Enter, compile, and run the following application:

```
class Test {
    public static void main (String [] args) {
        System.out.println ("Testing the Emergency Broadcast
                            Program");
    }
}
```

2.18 Introduce the following errors, one at a time, to the program in Problem 2.17. Record any error messages that the compiler produces. Fix the previous error each time before you introduce a new one. If no error messages are produced, explain why.

  a. Change Test to test.
  b. Change Emergency to emergency.
  c. Remove the first quotation mark in the string literal.
  d. Remove the last quotation mark in the string literal.
  e. Change main to man.

f. Change `println` to `bogus`.

g. Change `Broadcast` to `Brxoadxcaxst`.

h. Remove the semicolon at the end of the `println` statement.

i. Remove the last brace in the program.

2.19 Write an application that prints *Knowledge is Power*

a. on one line.

b. on three lines.

c. inside a box made up of the characters = and | .

2.20 Write an applet that prints *Knowledge is Power* inside an oval.

2.21 A mad-lib is a sentence with certain words left out. You ask people who don't know what the sentence is to give you words of particular parts of speech; these words are then inserted into the sentence to produce weird results. For example:

The _____ professor _____ my _____ , and I've never recovered.

This mad-lib needs an adjective, a verb (past tense), and a noun, in that order, in the three blanks. When the blanks are filled in, it might produce the following sentences:

The wise professor graded my paper, and I've never recovered.

The purple professor ate my computer, and I've never recovered.

Using this mad-lib, write a program that accepts three words as command-line arguments and prints the completed sentence. Run your program several times (without recompiling), providing different words.

2.22 Rewrite the program of Problem 2.21, creating a mad-lib that requires four blanks to be filled.

2.23 Create a personal web page using HTML (see Appendix K).

2.24 Write an applet that writes your name using the `drawString` method. Embed a link to your applet in an HTML document and view it using a Web browser.

2.25 Write an applet that draws a stick figure similar to the following:

Answers to Self-Review Questions

2.1 High-level languages allow a programmer to express a series of program instructions in English-like terms that are relatively easy to read and use. However, in order to execute, a program must be expressed in a particular computer's machine language, which consists of a series of bits basically unreadable by humans. A high-level language program must be translated into machine language before it can be run.

2.2 Java bytecode is a low-level representation of a Java source code program. The Java compiler translates the source code into bytecode, which can then be executed using the Java interpreter. The bytecode might be transported across the Web prior to being executed by a Java interpreter that is part of a Web browser.

2.3 White space is a term that includes the spaces, tabs, and newline characters that separate words and symbols in a program. The compiler ignores extra white space; therefore, it doesn't affect execution. However, it is crucial to use white space appropriately to make a program readable to humans.

2.4 Syntax rules define how the symbols and words of a programming language can be put together. The semantics of a programming language instruction determines what will happen when that instruction is executed.

2.5 Object-oriented programming is an approach to software development in which a program is defined by a set of objects that communicate and cooperate to accomplish tasks. The Java programming language supports the object-oriented approach.

2.6 The class or object categorization:
    a. Class; there are many coffee mugs.
    b. Class; the manufacturer probably made many such mugs.
    c. Object; the assumption is that Nancy has only one favorite.
    d. Class; there are many speeches, given by many people.
    e. Class; it's a specific kind of speech, but still a category.
    f. Object; it's a specific speech given once.
    g. Object; its class might be Country.
    h. Object; there is only one.
    i. Object; it's a specific city.

2.7 A Java applet is a Java program that is executed using a Web browser. Usually, the bytecode form of the Java applet is pulled across the Internet from another computer and executed locally. A Java application is a Java program that can stand alone. It does not require a Web browser in order to execute.

Program Elements

All programming languages have specific constructs that allow you to perform basic operations. These program elements are used to define the services an object contributes to a program. This chapter examines several of these programming elements. It also explores the basic activities that a programmer should go through when developing software. These activities form the cornerstone of high-quality software development and represent the first step toward a disciplined development process.

Chapter Objectives

- Declare and use variables.
- Identify and describe the Java primitive data types.
- Evaluate expressions according to a given precedence hierarchy.
- Perform basic decision-making and repetition.
- Perform basic input and output operations.

3.1 Primitive Data Types

Programs operate on data. Therefore, we must be able to refer to various kinds of data. Each data value has a specific *data type* that determines the kinds of operations that we can perform on it. Several common data types are built into the Java language and are called *primitive data types*. There are eight primitive types in Java: four variations of integers, two variations of floating point numbers, a boolean data type, and a character data type. Everything else is represented using objects. Let's examine the primitive data types in some detail.

> **Key Concept** Each value in memory is associated with a specific data type. This data type determines what operations we can perform on the data.

Integers and Floating Points

Java has two basic kinds of numeric values: integers (which have no fractional part) and floating points (which do). There are four integer data types (*byte, short, int, and long*) and two floating point data types (*float* and *double*). All of the numeric types differ by the amount of memory space used to store a value of that type, which determines the range of values that can be represented. The size of each data type is the same for all hardware platforms. All numeric types are *signed*, meaning that both positive and negative values can be stored in them. Figure 3.1 summarizes the numeric primitive types.

Type	Storage	Min Value	Max Value
byte	8 bits	−128	127
short	16 bits	−32,768	32,767
int	32 bits	−2,147,483,648	2,147,483,647
long	64 bits	−9,223,372,036,854,775,808	9,223,372,036,854,775,807
float	32 bits	Approximately −3.4E+38 with 7 significant digits	Approximately 3.4E+38 with 7 significant digits
double	64 bits	Approximately −1.7E+308 with 15 significant digits	Approximately 1.7E+308 with 15 significant digits

Figure 3.1 The Java numeric primitive types

Remember from our discussion in Chapter 1 that a bit can either be a 1 or a 0. Because each bit can represent two different states, a string of n bits can be used to represent 2^n different values. Appendix B describes number systems and these kinds of relationships in more detail.

When designing a program, you sometimes need to be careful about picking variables of appropriate size so that memory space is not wasted. For example, if a value will not vary outside of a range of 1 to 1000, then a two-byte integer (`short`) is large enough to accommodate it. On the other hand, when it's not clear what the range of a particular variable will be, you should provide a reasonable, even generous, amount of space. In fact, in most situations memory space is not a problem and you can usually afford generous assumptions.

Note that even though a regular floating point value supports very large (and very small) numbers, it only has seven significant digits. Therefore if it is important to accurately maintain a value such as 50341.2077, you need to use a `double`.

Java assumes all floating point literals are of type `double`. If you require that a floating point literal be treated as a `float`, then append an f or F to the end of the value, as in 2.718f or 123.45F. Numeric literals of type `double` can be followed by a d or D if desired.

Characters

Characters are another fundamental type of data used and managed on a computer. A *character set* is a list of characters in a particular order. Each programming language supports a particular character set that defines the valid values for a character variable in that language. Several character sets have been proposed, but only a few have been used over the years. The *ASCII character set* is a popular choice. ASCII stands for the American Standard Code for Information Interchange. The basic ASCII set uses seven bits per character, providing room to support 128 different characters, including:

- uppercase letters (A, B, C, etc.)
- lowercase letters (a, b, c, etc.)
- punctuation (period, semicolon, comma, etc.)
- digits (0 through 9)
- special symbols (such as ampersand, vertical bar, backslash)
- control characters (such as carriage return, null, end-of-text)

The *control characters* are sometimes called nonprintable or invisible characters because they do not have a specific symbol that represents them. Yet they are as valid as any other character and can be stored and used in the same ways. Many control characters have special meaning to certain software applications.

As computing became a world-wide endeavor, users demanded a more flexible character set to reflect other language alphabets. ASCII was extended to use eight bits per character and the number of characters in the set doubled to 256. The extended ASCII contains many accented and diacritical characters not used in English.

However, even with 256 characters, the ASCII character set cannot represent the world's languages, especially given the various Asian languages and their many thousands of ideograms. Therefore the developers of the Java programming language chose the *Unicode character set*, which uses 16 bits per character, supporting 65,536 unique characters. The characters and symbols from many languages are included in the Unicode definition. ASCII is essentially a subset of the Unicode character set. Portions of the Unicode character set are presented in Appendix C.

A character literal is expressed in a Java program with single quotes, such as `'b'` or `'J'` or `';'`. String literals are delineated using double quotes, as we've seen in several example programs. The `String` type is not a primitive data type in Java and is discussed in detail in later chapters.

Booleans

The *boolean* data type has only two valid values: true and false. A boolean variable is usually used to indicate if a particular condition is true or not. But it can also be used to represent any situation that has two states, such as a light bulb being on or off. Because a boolean value represents one of only two possible situations, only one bit is needed to store it. A boolean value cannot be converted to any other data type and any other data type cannot be converted to a boolean value. The words `true` and `false` are reserved in Java as boolean literals and cannot be used outside of this context.

Wrappers

For each primitive type there exists a *wrapper class*. A wrapper class contains the same type of data as its corresponding primitive type, but represents the information in a class. The wrapper classes are:

- Byte
- Short
- Integer
- Long
- Float
- Double
- Character
- Boolean
- Void

All wrapper classes are defined in the `java.lang` package of the Java API. Objects created from these classes can be used wherever objects are needed in a program instead of primitive types. They are also useful for converting a value of one type into another. For example, the `Integer` class contains a method to convert a string that contains a number into its corresponding integer value.

3.2 Variables and Assignment

Almost all programs manage data that are stored in variables. Let's explore how to declare and use them in a program.

Variables

A *variable* is a name for a location in memory used to hold a data value. When you declare a variable, you are instructing the compiler to reserve a portion of main memory space large enough to hold a particular type of value and indicating the name by which you will refer to that location. Consider the following program:

```
//  Shows the declaration and use of an integer variable.
class Piano_Keys {

   public static void main (String[] args) {
      int keys = 88;
      System.out.println ("The number of piano keys: " + keys);
   } // method main

} // class Piano_Keys
```

A variable declaration and initialization

The first line of the `main` method is the declaration of a variable named `keys` that holds an integer (`int`). The declaration also gives `keys` an initial value of `88`.

> **Key Concept**   A variable is a name for a memory location used to hold a value of a particular data type.

The general syntax used for a variable declaration is:

```
data-type variable-name;
```

or

```
data-type variable-name = initial-value;
```

The *variable-name* is an identifier that will hold values of type *data-type*. The *initial-value*, if provided, must conform to that type. If an initial value is not specified for a primitive variable, Java assigns a default value. In the case of integers, the default value is zero. However, you should not rely on these default initializations. In fact, most Java compilers give errors or warnings if you attempt to use a variable before you've explicitly given it a value.

In the program, two pieces of information are provided to the println method. The first is a string literal "The number of piano keys: ", and the second is the variable keys. When a variable is referenced, its current value is used. Therefore the Piano_Keys program prints the following line when executed:

```
The number of piano keys: 88
```

To be precise, when the call to println is executed, the value of keys is obtained and it is converted from an integer to a string. Then the two strings are concatenated together using the string concatenation operator, and then println prints one long string.

The Assignment Statement

Let's examine a program that changes the value of a variable:

```
//  Uses assignment to change a variable's value.
class United_States {

   public static void main (String[] args) {
      int states = 13;
      System.out.println ("States in 1776: " + states);
      states = 50;
      System.out.println ("States in 1959: " + states);
   } // method main

} // class United_States
```

An assignment statement overwrites the current value of a variable.

This program first declares an integer variable called states and initializes it to 13. It then prints out the current value of states. The next two lines in main change the value stored in the variable states and then print it out. The statement

```
states = 50;
```

is called an *assignment statement* because it assigns a value to a variable. The syntax of an assignment statement is:

```
variable-name = expression;
```

When executed, the `expression` on the right-hand side of the assignment operator (`=`) is evaluated, and the result is stored in the memory location indicated by the `variable-name`. In this example, the expression is simply a numeric literal, the number 50. More involved expressions are described later in this chapter.

A variable can only store one value of its declared type, and the new value overwrites the old one. In this case, when the value 50 is assigned to `states`, the original value 13 is overwritten and lost forever, as shown in Fig. 3.2. However, when a reference is made to a variable, such as when it is printed, the value of the variable is not changed.

 Key Concept   A variable can store only one value of its declared type.

The `United_States` program prints the following lines when executed:

```
States in 1776: 13
States in 1959: 50
```

The Java language is *strongly typed,* meaning you are not allowed to assign a value to a variable that is inconsistent with its declared type. For example, you cannot assign an integer value to a boolean variable, and vice versa. Trying to combine incompatible types will generate an error when you attempt to compile the program.

Before assignment | After assignment

states   states = 50;   states

13   50

Figure 3.2   A variable overwritten with a new value

Therefore, the expression on the right-hand side of an assignment statement must evaluate to a value compatible with the type of the variable on the left-hand side.

 Key Concept Java is a strongly typed language. Each variable is associated with a specific type for the duration of its existence, and you cannot assign a value of one type to a variable of an incompatible type. This feature helps prevent inadvertent errors.

Constants

Sometimes we use data that is constant throughout a program. For instance, you might write a program that deals with 23 students. It is often helpful to give a constant value a name, such as NUMBER_OF_STUDENTS, instead of using a literal value, such as 23, throughout the code.

Constants are identifiers and are similar to variables except that they hold a particular value for the duration of their existence. The compiler will produce an error message if you attempt to change the value of a constant using an assignment statement. In Java, if you precede a declaration with the reserved word final, the identifier is a constant. For example, the value of pi might be used throughout a program to compute the area of a circle. It can be declared as follows:

```
final double PI = 3.14159;
```

Key Concept Constants are similar to variables but they hold a particular value for the duration of their existence.

It is good practice to use constants instead of literal values in a program because they prevent inadvertent errors by not allowing their value to change. They also make code more readable by giving meaning to a possibly unclear value. Furthermore, if a value is used throughout a program and it needs to be modified, then the value only needs to be changed where the constant is declared. For example, if you decide that the value of PI needs to be carried to more decimal places, then you only have to change one declaration, and all uses of PI automatically reflect the change.

In this book we use uppercase letters when naming constants to distinguish them from regular variables. Constants cannot be declared inside a method, such as `main`. Furthermore, constants that are used by the `main` method must be declared using the Java reserved word `static`. We explain these restrictions in Chapter 4.

3.3   Input and Output

To be useful, programs need to be able to accept input and to display output. But the source of the input and the destination of the output can vary. Often programs read from and write to files on the disk drive. Sometimes input is accepted from the user through the keyboard or other input device and information is output to a monitor screen. In programs that communicate across a network, the source of input and the destination for output might be a network connection.

Streams

Java deals with all types of input and output (I/O) in basically the same way. Any source of input or destination for output is called a *stream*. Therefore we refer to various *input streams* and *output streams*. There are no input and output statements built into the Java language itself. All I/O is performed with the help of predefined class libraries that are provided with the Java programming environment. Most I/O operations are defined in the `java.io` package of the Java API. We've already seen the `println` and `print` methods, which make up only a small part of the I/O class library.

Key Concept   Java handles all input and output (I/O) in basically the same way. Any source of input or destination for output is called a stream.

There are three predefined standard streams:

- `System.in`, for reading input
- `System.out`, for writing output
- `System.err`, for writing error messages

Unless specified otherwise, `System.in` accepts information from the keyboard, and both `System.out` and `System.err` write to the screen. There are two output streams because sometimes it is helpful to direct the regular output of your programs to one destination and any error messages to another. Many other kinds of streams can be set up to read from and write to other places. The Java API environment has several predefined types of streams that can be used. However, at this point we focus on the standard streams.

The `print` and `println` methods send information to standard output because they are part of `System.out`. Reading from standard input is somewhat more involved than writing to standard output. Let's examine a program that reads a string of characters from the user and prints it back out.

```java
import java.io.*;

//  Reads a string from the user and prints it.
class Echo {

   public static void main (String[] args) throws IOException {

      BufferedReader stdin = new BufferedReader
         (new InputStreamReader(System.in));
      String message;

      System.out.println ("Enter a line of text:");
      message = stdin.readLine();
      System.out.println ("You entered: \"" + message + "\"");

   }  // method main

}  // class Echo
```

Sets up a text input stream from standard input

After being compiled, the program can be executed. A sample run of the program is presented below, with user input shown in colored type.

```
Enter a line of text:
Go Wildcats Go
You entered: "Go Wildcats Go"
```

In this program we make use of the `BufferedReader` class because it has the ability to read a string of characters. The `BufferedReader` class is defined in the `java.io` package, which is imported into the program. We redefine the standard input stream as a `BufferedReader` with the following declaration:

```java
BufferedReader stdin = new BufferedReader
   (new InputStreamReader(System.in));
```

At this point we will not go into detail about the new operator or other characteristics of this declaration except to say that we are creating an object to help with the

I/O activities. Object creation and use are covered in Chapter 4. The declaration creates a variable called `stdin`, which is a common abbreviation for standard input. The `stdin` variable can now use a method called `readLine`, which reads a string entered by the user at the keyboard.

In the `Echo` program, the first output message requests that the user enter a line of text. This kind of output statement is called a *prompt* because its purpose is to prompt the user to enter information. Prompts should be succinct and helpful. The `readLine` method reads the input string, which is then stored in a variable called `message` and printed.

The `readLine` method throws (issues) an exception if an error occurs while reading the input. Recall that an exception is a way that Java programs can handle certain situations or problems. Some exceptions are *checked* by the compiler; that is, the compiler insists that they either are dealt with or are thrown again when they occur. Other exceptions are *unchecked;* the compiler does not require that your program deal with them. The `readLine` method throws `IOException`, which is a checked exception. Therefore our `main` method must either catch and handle the exception or throw it again. By adding the phrase `throws IOException` after the header of the `main` method, we inform the compiler that if the exception is thrown by `readLine`, the exception will be thrown again. This decision implies that our program will abnormally terminate with a run-time error if there is a problem reading the input. Handling exceptions is covered in Chapter 14.

Escape Sequences

The input line read by the `Echo` program is printed inside quotation marks. Because quotations are used in the Java language to indicate the end of a string literal, we must use a special technique to print the quotation mark. The `\"` in a string literal is an example of an *escape sequence*. The backslash character (`\`) indicates the beginning of an escape sequence and the character or characters that follow are interpreted in a special way. In this program, the `\"` escape sequence means that the quotation mark should be printed and that it does not indicate the end of the string literal. Java recognizes several escape sequences, which are listed in Fig. 3.3.

Input and Output Buffers

When you are typing in your input in response to a prompt, you can use the Backspace key to delete some characters if you make a mistake. You have this option because the keystrokes you make are not being handled by the program immediately as they are typed. Your input characters are stored in a temporary location called an *input buffer*. Only after you press the Enter key does the program take the input and process it.

Similarly, all information sent to the standard output stream is written to a temporary area called an *output buffer*. Certain statements cause the information in the

Escape Sequence	Meaning
\b	backspace
\t	tab
\n	newline
\r	carriage return
\"	double quote
\'	single quote
\\	backslash

Figure 3.3 Java escape sequences

buffer to be displayed immediately on the output device; this process is often referred to as *flushing* the buffer. The println method automatically flushes the buffer, but the print method does not. The buffer can be explicitly flushed using the System.out.flush() method.

Key Concept Input information is stored in a temporary location called an input buffer. Similarly, all information sent to the standard output stream is written to a temporary area called an output buffer.

For the most part, you have to worry about explicitly flushing the buffer only when you want to ensure that your output is seen by the user immediately. This situation occurs when you want to prompt the user for information and want the user to be able to type a response on the same line as the prompt. To ensure that the prompt is displayed prior to waiting for the input, you explicitly flush the buffer. The following program demonstrates this process.

```
import java.io.*;

//  Reads strings, allowing the user to enter the input on
//  the same line as the prompt.
class Python {

    public static void main (String[] args) throws IOException {

        BufferedReader stdin = new BufferedReader
            (new InputStreamReader(System.in));
```

```
        String name, quest, color;

        System.out.print ("What is your name? ");
        System.out.flush();
        name = stdin.readLine();

        System.out.print ("What is your quest? ");
        System.out.flush();
        quest = stdin.readLine();

        System.out.print ("What is your favorite color? ");
        System.out.flush();
        color = stdin.readLine();
        System.out.println ("Name: " + name);
        System.out.println ("Quest: " + quest);
        System.out.println ("Color: " + color);

    }  // method main

}  // class Python
```

Flushing the buffer forces the prompt to appear.

This program prints questions and accepts answers (borrowed from a Monty Python scene). A sample run is shown below. Contrast this user interaction with that of the Echo program.

```
What is your name? Sir Galahad of Camelot
What is your quest? To Seek the Holy Grail
What is your favorite color? Blue, no...
Name: Sir Galahad of Camelot
Quest: To seek the Holy Grail
Color: Blue, no...
```

Numeric Input

One way to process numeric input is to read it as a string and then convert it to its corresponding numeric value. The following line of code converts a string to an integer value:

```
my_int = Integer.parseInt (my_string);
```

We can use similar techniques to convert a string to other primitive types. We introduced the `Integer` wrapper class in Chapter 2. The following program reads two strings, converts them to integers, adds them together and prints their sum.

```java
import java.io.*;

//  Reads two integers and prints their sum.
class Addition {

    public static void main (String[] args) throws IOException {
        BufferedReader stdin = new BufferedReader
            (new InputStreamReader(System.in));

        String string1, string2;
        int num1, num2, sum;

        System.out.println ("Enter a number:");
        string1 = stdin.readLine();
        num1 = Integer.parseInt (string1);

        System.out.println ("Enter another number:");
        string2 = stdin.readLine();
        num2 = Integer.parseInt (string2);

        sum = num1 + num2;
        System.out.println ("The sum is " + sum);

    }  // method main

}  // class Addition
```

Converts a string to an integer

A sample run of the `Addition` program might look like the following:

```
Enter a number:
33
Enter another number:
36
The sum is 69
```

Let's look at another version of the `Addition` program. It is shorter than the first one but accomplishes the same thing. In this version, the strings that are read as input are passed directly to the `parseInt` method without storing them in variables. Likewise, the sum is computed and printed without storing its value in a variable.

```
import java.io.*;

//  Reads two integers and prints their sum.
class Addition2 {

   public static void main (String[] args) throws IOException {
      BufferedReader stdin = new BufferedReader
         (new InputStreamReader(System.in));

      int num1, num2;

      System.out.println ("Enter a number: ");
      num1 = Integer.parseInt (stdin.readLine());

      System.out.println ("Enter another number:");
      num2 = Integer.parseInt (stdin.readLine());

      System.out.println ("The sum is " + (num1+num2));

   }  // method main

}  // class Addition2
```

Reads a string and
converts it in one line

3.4   Arithmetic Operators

Programming statements often involve *expressions*. These are combinations of operators and operands used to perform a calculation. The value calculated does not
have to be a number, but it often is. The operands used in the operations might be
literals, constants, variables, or other sources of data. The way we evaluate and use
expressions is fundamental to programming.

Key Concept   Many programming statements involve expressions. Expressions are
combinations of operators and operands used to perform a calculation.

   The usual arithmetic operations are defined for both integer and floating point
numeric types, including addition (+), subtraction (-), multiplication (*), and division (/). The remainder operator (%) returns the integer remainder after dividing its
second operand into its first.

The division operator performs different operations depending on the types of the operands. If both operands are integers, the / operator performs *integer division*, meaning that any fractional part of the result is truncated and discarded. If one or the other or both operands are floating point values, it performs *floating point division*, and the fractional part of the result is maintained. If either or both operands to +, -, and * are floating point values, the result is a floating point value. Both operands to % must be integers. Consider the following program:

```
//  Demonstrating the division operators.
class Division {

    public static void main (String[] args) {

        int oper1 = 9, oper2 = 4;
        double oper3 = 4.0;
        System.out.println ("Integer division: " + oper1/oper2);
        System.out.println ("Floating division: " + oper1/oper3);
        System.out.println ("Remainder division: " + oper1%oper2);

    }  // method main

}  // class Division
```

When executed, the output of the Division program is:

```
Integer division: 2
Floating division: 2.25
Remainder division: 1
```

Note that a variable declaration can have multiple variables of the same type declared on one line. Each variable on the line can be declared with or without an initializing value.

Operator Precedence

Operators can be combined into even more complicated expressions. For example, consider the following assignment statement:

```
result  =  14 + 8 / 2;
```

What is the result? It is 11 if the addition is performed first, or it is 18 if the division is performed first. The order of operator evaluation makes a big difference. In this case the division is performed before the addition, yielding a result of 18. You should note that in this and subsequent examples we have used literal values rather than variables to simplify the expression. The order of operator evaluation is the same even if the operands are variables.

All expressions are evaluated according to an *operator precedence hierarchy* that establishes the rules that govern the order in which operations are evaluated. In the case of arithmetic operators, multiplication, division, and the remainder operator all have equal precedence and are performed before addition and subtraction. Any arithmetic operators at the same level of precedence are performed left to right. Therefore, we say the arithmetic operators have a left-to-right *association*.

Precedence, however, can be forced in an expression by using parentheses. For instance, if we really wanted the addition to be performed first in the previous example, we could write the expression as follows:

```
result  =  (14 + 8) / 2;
```

Any expressions in parentheses are evaluated first. In complicated expressions, it is good practice to use parentheses even when it is not strictly necessary in order to make it clear how the expression is evaluated.

Key Concept   Java follows a well-defined set of rules that govern the order in which operators will be evaluated in an expression. These rules form an operator precedence hierarchy.

Parentheses can be nested, and the innermost nested expressions are evaluated first. Consider the expression:

```
result  =  3 * ((18 - 4) / 2);
```

In this example, the result is 21. First, the subtraction is evaluated, forced by the inner parentheses. Then, even though multiplication and division are at the same level of precedence and would be evaluated left to right, the division is evaluated first because of the outer parentheses. Finally, the multiplication is performed.

After the arithmetic operations are complete, then the computed result is stored in the variable on the left-hand side of the assignment operator (=). In other words, the assignment operator has a lower precedence than any of the arithmetic operators.

A precedence table, showing the relationships between the arithmetic operators, parentheses, and the assignment operator is shown in Fig. 3.4. We will expand this table as additional operators are discussed.

A *unary operator* has only one operand, while a *binary operator* has two. The + and – arithmetic operators can be both unary and binary. The binary versions accomplish addition and subtraction, and the unary versions represent positive and negative numbers. For example, –1 is an example of using the unary minus operator to make the value negative.

Precedence Level	Operator	Operation	Associates
1	+	unary plus	R to L
	−	unary minus	
2	*	multiplication	L to R
	/	division	
	%	remainder	
3	+	addition	L to R
	−	subtraction	
	+	string concatenation	
4	=	assignment	R to L

Figure 3.4   Java operator precedence

For an expression to be syntactically correct, the number of left parentheses must match the number of right parentheses and they must be properly nested. The following examples are not valid expressions:

```
result  =  ((19 + 8) % 3) - 4);   // not valid
result  =  (19 (+ 8 %) 3 - 4);    // not valid
```

3.5 Making Decisions

Unless otherwise specified, the execution of a program proceeds in a linear fashion. That is, it starts at the beginning and moves down one programming statement at a time until the program is complete. A Java program begins executing with the first line of the main method and proceeds step by step until it gets to the end of the main method. However, we can alter the flow of control through the code by using specific programming statements. This section describes a statement that provides basic decision-making capabilities. Other decision-making statements are discussed in in Chapter 5.

The if Statement

Most programming languages contain a set of statements that allow you to evaluate a condition and choose what will happen based on the result. These statements are called *selection statements* or *conditional statements*. The *if statement* is a selection statement found in many programming languages, including Java. Its syntax is:

```
if ( condition )
    statement;
```

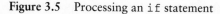 **Key Concept** An `if` statement allows a program to choose whether or not to execute a following statement.

The `condition` must be a boolean expression that evaluates to true or false. If the `condition` is true, then `statement` is executed. After `statement` is executed, processing continues with the next statement. If the `condition` is false, `statement` is skipped, and processing continues immediately with the next statement. This process is shown in Fig. 3.5.

The following example reads in an integer value representing the temperature and prints a message if it is below a particular threshold. The threshold value is declared as a constant.

```
import java.io.*;

//  Makes a decision about the temperature to determine if
//  a particular message should be printed.
class Temperature {
    final static int THRESHOLD = 65;
```

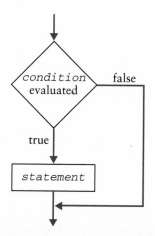

Figure 3.5   Processing an `if` statement

```
public static void main (String[] args) throws IOException {
    BufferedReader stdin = new BufferedReader
        (new InputStreamReader(System.in));

    System.out.println ("Enter the temperature:");
    int temperature = Integer.parseInt (stdin.readLine());

    System.out.println ("Current temperature: " + temperature);
    if (temperature < THRESHOLD)
        System.out.println ("It's cold in here!");
    System.out.println ("Wrapping up.");

}  // method main

}  // class Temperature
```

The condition determines if the `println` statement is executed.

The program prints the value of the temperature that it read as input. Then it uses an `if` statement to make a decision. The condition of the `if` statement uses the less than operator (<), which returns true if the left operand is less than the right operand. If the temperature is less than the value of THRESHOLD, then the `println` statement that prints `"It's cold in here."` is executed. If the condition is false, that `println` statement is skipped. Either way, the next line prints the `"Wrapping up."` message. The following is a sample run of the program:

```
Enter the temperature:
72
Current temperature: 72
Wrapping up.
```

Another sample run produces different results:

```
Enter the temperature:
50
Current temperature: 50
It's cold in here!
Wrapping up.
```

Boolean Expressions

A *boolean expression* evaluates to a true or false result. For example, the expression (total == sum) compares two integer variables to see if they contain the same value. The == symbol is the Java operator that tests for equality. Either `total` and `sum` contain the same value or they do not. The result is either true or false. Note that the equality operator (==) is different from the assignment operator (=).

The result of a boolean expression can be stored in a boolean variable, as in:

```
boolean answer = (total == sum);
```

More often, however, we use boolean expressions to determine if we want to perform one action or another. They give us the ability to make decisions.

In addition to checking for equality, Java provides an explicit operator to check for inequality and provides a whole series of relational operators. They are listed in Fig. 3.6. The less than operator (<) was used in the `Temperature` program in the previous section.

The equality and relational operators have precedence relationships similar to, and lower than, the arithmetic operators. Parentheses can be used with these operators as well. We update the precedence table in Fig. 3.7.

Block Statement

We may want to do more than one thing if the condition of an `if` statement is true. In Java, we can replace any single statement with a *block statement*. A block is a list of statements enclosed in braces. You've already seen these braces used to delimit the `main` method and a class definition. The following example revises the `Temperature` program to use a block in the selection statement.

```
import java.io.*;

//  Uses a statement block in a conditional.
class Temperature2 {
    final static int THRESHOLD = 65;
```

Operator	Meaning
==	equal to
!=	not equal to
<	less than
<=	less than or equal to
>	greater than
>=	greater than or equal to

Figure 3.6 Java equality and relational operators

Precedence Level	Operator	Operation	Associates
1	+	unary plus	R to L
	−	unary minus	
2	*	multiplication	L to R
	/	division	
	%	remainder	
3	+	addition	L to R
	−	subtraction	
	+	string concatenation	
4	<	less than	L to R
	<=	less than or equal	
	>	greater than	
	>=	greater than or equal	
5	==	equal	L to R
	!=	not equal	
6	=	assignment	R to L

Figure 3.7   Java operator precedence (expanded)

```
public static void main (String[] args) throws IOException {
   BufferedReader stdin = new BufferedReader
      (new InputStreamReader(System.in));

   System.out.println ("Enter the temperature:");
   int temperature = Integer.parseInt (stdin.readLine());

   System.out.println ("Current temperature: " + temperature);
   if (temperature < THRESHOLD) {
      System.out.print ("It's cold in here.");
      System.out.println ("But we'll survive.");
   }
   System.out.println ("Wrapping up.");

} // method main

} // class Temperature2
```

The body of the `if` statement is a block.

If the value entered for the temperature was 60, then the program's output would be:

```
Current temperature: 60
It's cold in here.  But we'll survive.
Wrapping up.
```

The `if-else` Statement

What if you want to do one thing if a condition is true and a different thing if the condition is false? You can add an `else` clause to an `if` statement, making it an *if-else statement,* to handle this kind of situation. The syntax of the `if-else` statement is:

```
if ( condition )
    statement1
else
    statement2
```

 Key Concept   An `If-else` statement allows a program to do one thing if a condition is true and a different thing if the condition is false.

If the *condition* is true, *statement1* is executed. If the *condition* is false, *statement2* is executed. They will not both be executed because the condition must always evaluate to either true or false. This processing is shown in Fig. 3.8.

Let's revise the `Temperature` program again so that it uses an `if-else` statement:

```
import java.io.*;

//   Uses an if-else statement to print one of two possible
//   messages.
class Temperature3 {
    final static int FREEZING_POINT = 32;

    public static void main (String[] args) throws IOException {
        BufferedReader stdin = new BufferedReader
            (new InputStreamReader(System.in));
```

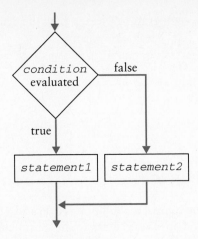

Figure 3.8   Processing an `if-else` statement

```
        System.out.println ("Enter the temperature:");
        int temperature = Integer.parseInt (stdin.readLine());

        System.out.println ("Current temperature: " + temperature);
        if (temperature <= FREEZING_POINT)
            System.out.print ("It's freezing in here. ");
        else
            System.out.println ("Above freezing.");
        System.out.println ("Wrapping up.");

    }  // method main

}  // class Temperature3
```

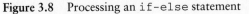

The statement in the `else` clause is executed if the condition is false.

If the user enters the value 85, the condition of the `if-else` statement is false, and thus the output of the program is:

```
Current temperature: 85
Above freezing.
Wrapping up.
```

Keep in mind that you can use a block statement anywhere a single statement is called for in the Java syntax to accomplish more than one thing. Therefore the `if` portion of an `if-else` statement might contain a block, or the `else` portion might contain a block, or both could. How you write them depends on what you want to accomplish.

Let's take a look at another example that uses a selection statement. The following program uses the Pythagorean theorem to determine if the three sides of a

Comparing Data

We all know what it means when we say that one number is less than another. But what does it mean to say one character is less than another? As we discussed in Section 3.1, characters in Java are based on the Unicode character set, which defines an ordering of all possible characters that can be used. Because the character `'a'` comes before the character `'b'` in the character set, we can say that `'a'` is less than `'b'`.

We can use the equality and relational operators on character data. For example, if two character variables `ch1` and `ch2` hold the values of two characters, we might determine their relative ordering in the Unicode character set with an `if` statement:

```
if (ch1 > ch2)
   System.out.println (ch1 + " is greater than " + ch2);
else
   System.out.println (ch1 + " is NOT greater than " + ch1);
```

The Unicode character set is structured so that all lowercase alphabetic characters (`'a'` through `'z'`) are continuous and in alphabetical order. The same is true of the uppercase alphabetic characters (`'A'` through `'Z'`) and the characters that represent digits (`'0'` through `'9'`). These relationships make it easy to sort characters and strings of characters. If you have a list of names, for instance, you can put them in alphabetical order based on the inherent relationships among characters in the character set. However, you cannot use the relational operators to compare entire strings to put them in alphabetical order. To compare strings you must use additional methods that are discussed in the next chapter.

Another interesting situation occurs when comparing floating point data. Specifically, you should rarely use the equality operator (==) when comparing floating point values. Two floating point values are equal, according to the == operator, only if every bit of their underlying representation is the same. If the values you are comparing are the results of computation, it may be unlikely that they are exactly equal even if they are close enough for your purposes. Therefore, a better way to check for floating point equality is to compute the absolute value of the difference between the two values and compare the result to some tolerance level. For example, you may choose a tolerance level of 0.00001. If the two floating point values are so close that their difference is less than the tolerance, then you are willing to consider them equal. Comparing two floating point values `f1` and `f2` could be accomplished as follows:

```
if (Math.abs(f1 - f2) < TOLERANCE)
    System.out.println ("Essentially equal.");
```

This code uses the absolute value method `abs` of the `Math` class, which is discussed further in Chapter 4. The value of the constant `TOLERANCE` should be appropriate for the situation.

triangle form a right triangle. Therefore, we need to determine if the square of the hypotenuse equals the sum of the squares of the other two sides.

```
import java.io.*;

// A program to determine if the length of three sides of a
// triangle represent a right triangle.
class Right_Triangle {

    public static void main (String[] args) throws IOException {
        BufferedReader stdin = new BufferedReader
            (new InputStreamReader(System.in));

        int hypotenuse_sq;   // calculated hypotenuse squared

        System.out.println ("Enter side 1:");
        int side1 = Integer.parseInt (stdin.readLine());
        System.out.println ("Enter side 2:");
        int side2 = Integer.parseInt (stdin.readLine());
        System.out.println ("Enter the hypotenuse:");
        int side3 = Integer.parseInt (stdin.readLine());

        hypotenuse_sq = (side1 * side1) + (side2 * side2);
        if ((side3*side3) == hypotenuse_sq)
            System.out.println ("It is a right triangle.");
        else
            System.out.println ("It is not a right triangle.");

    }  // method main

}  // class Right_Triangle
```

The program reads the values for two sides of a triangle, then reads the proposed hypotenuse. It calculates what the square of the hypotenuse would be and compares it to the square of the value given as the third side. The if-else statement prints the appropriate message.

If, for example, the user enters 3, 4, and 5 as the sides of the triangle, in that order, then the program's output would be:

```
It is a right triangle.
```

Note that the third side entered is assumed to be the triangle's hypotenuse. If the user enters 5, 4, and 3 in that order, the program would print that it is not a right triangle.

Nested `if` Statements

The body of an if statement could be another if statement. This situation is called a *nested if*. It allows you to make a decision given the results of a previous decision. The following program demonstrates a nested if statement.

```java
import java.io.*;

//  Uses a nested if to print one of three messages.
class Football_Choice {
   final static int HEADS = 1;
   final static int RECEIVE = 1;

   public static void main (String[] args) throws IOException {
      BufferedReader stdin = new BufferedReader
         (new InputStreamReader(System.in));

      System.out.println ("Enter 1 for heads or 2 for tails:");
      int coin = Integer.parseInt (stdin.readLine());
      System.out.println ("Enter 1 to receive and 2 to kickoff:");
      int choice = Integer.parseInt (stdin.readLine());

      if (coin == HEADS)
         if (choice == RECEIVE)
            System.out.println ("You won the toss and will receive.");
         else
            System.out.println ("You won the toss and will kickoff.");
```

An else is matched up with the most recent unmatched if.

```
        else
            System.out.println ("You lost the coin toss.");

    }  // method main

}  // class Football_Choice
```

An important situation arises due to nested `if` statements. It may seem that an `else` clause after a nested `if` could apply to either `if` statement. The semantics of the `if-else` statement is that an `else` clause is always matched to the closest unmatched `if` that came before it. However, if you're not careful you can easily mismatch it in your mind. This is another reason why appropriate, consistent indentation is crucial. Braces can be used to specify the `if` statement to which an `else` clause belongs.

Key Concept   A nested `if` allows the program to make a decision based on the results of a previous decision.

3.6   Repetition

Often when writing a program, it is necessary to repeat a statement or block many times. This task is accomplished with a *repetition statement*. Sometimes repetition statements are called *iteration statements* or *loops*. This section contains a discussion of one type of loop called a `while` statement. We discuss additional repetition statements in Chapter 5.

The `while` Statement

A `while` statement controls how many times another statement (or block) is executed. The syntax of a while statement is:

```
while ( condition )
    statement;
```

A `while` loop is similar to an `if` statement in that if the *condition* is true, the *statement* is executed. However, unlike the `if` statement, after the *statement* is executed, the *condition* is evaluated again. If it is still true, the *statement* is

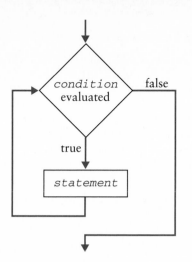

Figure 3.9   Processing a `while` statement

executed again. This repetition continues until the *condition* eventually becomes false; then processing continues with the statement after the body of the `while` loop. This process is shown in Fig. 3.9.

> **Key Concept**   A `while` statement allows a program to execute a statement many times.

Let's look at a program that uses a `while` loop. The `Counter` program simply prints the values from 1 to 5. Each iteration through the loop prints one value, then increments the counter. A constant called `LIMIT` is used to hold the maximum value that `count` is allowed to reach.

```
// Uses a while loop to count to 5.
class Counter {
   final static int LIMIT = 5;

   public static void main (String[] args) {
      int count = 1;
      while (count <= LIMIT) {
         System.out.println (count);
         count = count + 1;
      }
      System.out.println ("done");
```

The condition of a `while` loop is evaluated after each iteration.

```
    }  // method main

}  // class Counter
```

Note that the body of the while loop is a block containing two statements. Because the value of count is incremented each time, we are guaranteed that count will eventually reach the value of LIMIT. The output of this program is:

```
1
2
3
4
5
done
```

Let's look at another program that uses a while loop. The following program computes the factors of a number entered by the user. The loop checks each integer value from 1 to half of the input value (inclusive) to see if it evenly divides the input value and prints those that do.

```
import java.io.*;

//   Uses a while loop to print the factors of an input value.
class Factors {

    public static void main (String[] args) throws IOException {
        BufferedReader stdin = new BufferedReader
            (new InputStreamReader(System.in));

        int count = 1, number;

        System.out.println ("Enter a positive number:");
        number = Integer.parseInt (stdin.readLine());

        System.out.println ("The factors of " + number + " are:");
        while (count <= (number/2)) {
            if (number%count == 0)
                System.out.println (count);
            count = count + 1;
        }

    }  // method main

}  // class Factors
```

Note that the program will not list any factors if the user enters a negative number. A sample run of the Factors program is:

```
Enter a positive number:
20
The factors of 20 are:
1
2
4
5
10
```

Let's examine yet another program that uses a while loop. The Powers_of_Two program prints the first 10 powers of two.

```java
//   Uses the while statement to print the first ten powers
//   of two.
class Powers_of_Two {
   final static int LIMIT = 10;

   public static void main (String[] args) {
      int count = 1, power_of_two = 1;

      while (count <= LIMIT) {
         power_of_two = power_of_two * 2;
         System.out.print (power_of_two + "  ");
         count = count + 1;
      }

      System.out.println ();
      System.out.println ("All done.");

   }  // method main

}  // Powers_of_Two
```

The output of the Powers_of_Two program is shown below. The first println statement after the while loop moves the output to the next line; then another println statement prints the phrase "All done".

```
2  4  8  16  32  64  128  256  512  1024
All done.
```

Infinite Loops

What would have happened if we had forgotten to include the increment of count in the body of the while loop in the Powers_of_Two program? The variable count would never have been incremented and would have stayed below LIMIT. Thus the condition would never become false. This situation, called an *infinite loop*, is a common mistake inadvertently created by programmers. Be careful that the body of a loop is guaranteed to eventually make the condition of the loop false, so that the program can continue and eventually terminate. An infinite loop will continue processing until an error condition is encountered or until the user interrupts the processing.

The following program demonstrates an infinite loop.

```
//   This program contains an INFINITE LOOP!
class Forever {
   final static int LIMIT = 25;

   public static void main (String[] args) {
      int count = 1;
      while (count <= LIMIT) {
         System.out.println (count);
         count = count - 1;
      }
   }  // method main

}  // class Forever
```

The condition of an infinite loop is always true.

In this case, the initial value of count is 1 and it is decremented in the loop body. The while loop will continue as long as count is less than or equal to 25. Because count gets smaller with each iteration, the condition will always be true.

> **Key Concept**   Design your programs carefully to avoid infinite loops. The body of the loop must eventually make the loop condition false.

3.7   Developing Programs

Creating software involves much more than just writing code. This section introduces some of the basic programming activities necessary for developing software. There are four basic activities that are a part of any software development effort:

- establishing the requirements
- creating a design

- implementing the code
- testing the implementation

It would be nice if these activities, in this order, defined a step-by-step approach for developing software. However, although they may appear to be sequential, they almost never are. These activities overlap and interact. They are often integrated into a repetitive development strategy. Throughout this book, we continue to refine a software development process that incorporates these activities appropriately. For now, let's briefly discuss each one in turn.

Requirements

Software *requirements* specify what a program must accomplish. They indicate the tasks that a program should perform, but not how to perform them. Requirements often address user interface issues such as screen layouts, buttons, and menus. Essentially, requirements establish the characteristics that make the program useful for the end user. They also may apply constraints to your program, such as how fast tasks must be performed, and impose restrictions such as deadlines on the developer.

Key Concept Software requirements specify what a program must accomplish.

An initial set of requirements are often provided by the person or group who want the software developed. However, these initial requirements are often incomplete or ambiguous. The software developer must work to refine the requirements until all key decisions have been addressed.

Design

A software *design* specifies how a program will accomplish its requirements. The design lays out the classes and objects needed in a program and defines how they interact. A detailed design might even specify the individual steps that the code will follow.

Key Concept A software design specifies how a program will accomplish its requirements.

A civil engineer would never consider building a bridge without designing it first. The design of software is no less essential. Many problems in software are directly attributable to a lack of good design efforts. Alternatives need to be considered and explored. Often the first attempt at a design is not the best.

One of the most fundamental design issues is defining the algorithm to be used in the program. An *algorithm* is a step-by-step process for solving a problem. A recipe is an algorithm. Travel directions are an algorithm. Every program implements an algorithm; therefore you should spend time thinking about the algorithm before you write any code. An algorithm is often described using *pseudocode,* which is a mixture of code statements and English phrases. Pseudocode is sometimes called a *program design language* (PDL).

> **Key Concept** An algorithm is a step-by-step process for solving a problem.

When developing an algorithm, you should first analyze all of the requirements involved with that part of the problem. This step is necessary to ensure that the algorithm takes into account all aspects of the problem. Similar to writing an essay, the design of a program is often revised many times. After the design has been developed and refined, you can begin the implementation stage.

Implementation

Implementation is the process of writing source code. More precisely, implementation is the act of translating the design into a particular programming language. Too many programmers focus on implementation exclusively when it actually should be the least creative of all development activities. The important decisions should be made when establishing the requirements and creating the design. When implementing code, you should adhere to all established style guidelines.

> **Key Concept** Implementation is the process of writing source code, based on the design.

Testing

Testing a program involves running it multiple times with various input and observing the results. The goal of testing is to find errors. Running a program with specific input and producing the correct results only establishes that your program works for that particular input. It is important to repetitively test your program with various kinds of input.

By finding and fixing errors, you increase the reliability of your program. As more test cases execute without finding errors, your confidence in the program rises. Test cases should be created to ensure that a program accomplishes its intended purpose and fulfills its requirements.

3.8   Example: Test Average

Let's apply the basic program development activities to a particular problem. Suppose an instructor wants a program that will analyze test scores. The requirements are given initially as follows. The program will:

- accept a series of test scores
- compute the average test score
- determine the highest test score
- display the average and highest score

These requirements raise questions that need to be answered before we can design a suitable solution. Clarifying requirements often involves an extended dialog with the user. The instructor may very well have a clear vision about what the program should do, but this list of requirements does not specify enough detail.

For example, how many test scores should be processed? Is this program intended to handle a particular class size, or should it handle varying size classes? Is the input stored in a data file, or should it be read interactively? Should the average be computed to a specific degree of accuracy? Should the output be presented in any particular format? After conferring with the instructor, we establish that the program needs to handle a varying number of test scores each time it is run and that the input should be read interactively. Furthermore, the instructor wants the average computed to the nearest integer, and allows the developer to specify the output format.

Now that we have enough detail about the requirements, let's consider some design questions. Because there is no limit to the number of grades that can be entered, how should the user indicate that there are no more grades? We can address this situation in several possible ways. The program could prompt the instructor after each grade, asking if there are more grades to process. Or, the program could prompt the instructor initially for the total number of grades that will be entered, then allow exactly that many grades to be entered. Or, when prompted for a grade, the instructor could enter in a special value that indicates that there are no more grades to be entered.

The first option requires a lot more input from the instructor and therefore is too cumbersome a solution. The second option seems reasonable, but it forces the instructor to have an exact count of the number of grades to enter and therefore may not be convenient. The third option is reasonable, but before we can pick an appropriate value to end the input, we must ask additional questions. What is the range of valid grades? What would be an appropriate value to indicate the end of the grades? Values used in this way are called *sentinel values* and must be outside the range of normal input. After conferring with the instructor, we establish that a student cannot receive a negative grade, therefore the use of –1 as a sentinel value in this situation will work.

Let's sketch out the design of this program. The pseudocode for a program that reads in a list of grades and computes their average might be expressed as follows:

```
prompt for a grade.
input a grade.
while (grade does not equal –1) {
   increment count.
   sum = sum + grade;
   prompt for another grade.
   input the next grade.
}
average = sum / count;
print average
```

This algorithm only addresses the calculation of the average grade. Now we must augment the algorithm to compute the highest grade. As each grade is entered, we can keep track of the highest grade in a variable called max. The augmented pseudocode is now:

```
prompt for a grade.
input a grade.
max = grade;
while (grade does not equal –1) {
   increment count.
   sum = sum + grade;
   if (grade > max)
```

```
        max = grade;
    prompt for another grade.
    input the next grade.
}
average = sum / count;
print average and highest grade
```

Having planned out an initial algorithm for the program, the implementation can proceed. Consider the following solution to this problem:

```java
import java.io.*;

//   Determine the average and maximum grade of a set of test scores.
class Average {

    public static void main (String[] args) throws IOException {
        int grade, count = 0, sum = 0, max, average;

        BufferedReader stdin = new BufferedReader
            (new InputStreamReader (System.in));

        //  Get the first grade.  Give max that initial value.
        System.out.print ("Enter the first grade (-1 to quit): ");
        System.out.flush();
        grade = Integer.parseInt(stdn.readLine());

        max = grade;

        //  Read and process the rest of the grades.
        while (grade >= 0) {
            count = count + 1;
            sum = sum + grade;
            if (grade > max)
                max = grade;
            System.out.print ("Enter the next grade (-1 to quit): ");
            System.out.flush();
            grade = Integer.parseInt (stdn.readLine());
        }

        if (count == 0)
            System.out.println ("No valid grades were entered.");
        else {
            average = sum / count;
            System.out.println();
```

A running sum is calculated in order to compute the average.

A copy of the highest grade is held in `max`.

```
                  System.out.println ("Total number of students: " + count);
                  System.out.println ("Average grade: " + average);
                  System.out.println ("Highest grade: " + max);
              }
          } // method main

      } // class Average
```

Let's examine how this program accomplishes the stated requirements and critique the implementation. Then we can consider variations to this implementation.

After the variable declarations in the main method, we prompt the user to enter the value of the first grade. Prompts should provide information about any special input requirements. In this case, we inform the user that entering a value of –1 will indicate the end of the input.

The input is read as a string of characters using the readLine method, then converted to an integer value. The value of the variable max is set equal to the first grade entered. As the program reads and processes other grades, the value of max is modified as necessary to always hold the highest grade. After all the input is processed, the value left in max will be the highest grade of all students.

The while loop condition specifies that the loop body will be executed as long as the current grade being processed is greater than zero. Therefore, in this implementation any negative value will indicate the end of the input, even though the prompt suggests a specific value. This change is a slight variation on the original design and ensures that negative values of other than –1 will not be counted as grades.

After the user enters a positive grade initially, the body of the while loop is executed. The variable count is incremented. The variable count keeps track of the total number of grades entered. Note that the count variable was initialized to zero in its declaration. If it had not been initialized, the compiler would have complained that we were using a variable without first explicitly assigning an initial value to it. While not all variables in this program are initialized in their declarations, the code guarantees that they have all been assigned a value prior to being used.

The while loop uses sum to keep a running total of the grades, and the running total is used at the end the program to calculate the average. At the end of the loop body, the next grade is read. Then the loop condition is checked again and that grade is processed. Eventually, the user enters a negative value and the loop terminates.

If the user enters a negative value for the first grade, the body of the while loop will not execute at all and processing continues with the line after the body of the loop, which is an if statement. In this case, count was not changed from its original initialization value of zero, and the program prints a simple output message indicating that no valid grades were entered.

If at least one positive grade was entered, then count is not equal to zero after the loop, and the else portion of the if statement is executed. The average is computed by dividing the sum of the grades by the number of grades. Note that the if statement prevents us from attempting to divide by zero in situations where no valid grades are entered. We want to design robust programs that handle unexpected or erroneous input without a run-time error. This solution is robust up to a point because it processes any numeric input without a problem but would fail if a non-numeric, like a word, is entered at the grade prompt.

Because both `sum` and `count` are integer variables, the average calculation performs integer division, and therefore the fractional part of the result is discarded prior to assigning it to the variable `average`. Note that the result is truncated, not rounded. The truncation would happen even if `average` had been declared as a floating point number because the truncation occurs prior to the assignment. Finally, the appropriate output information is printed. A sample run of this program follows:

```
Enter the first grade (-1 to quit):  87
Enter the next grade (-1 to quit):  82
Enter the next grade (-1 to quit):  94
Enter the next grade (-1 to quit):  98
Enter the next grade (-1 to quit):  73
Enter the next grade (-1 to quit):  98
Enter the next grade (-1 to quit):  80
Enter the next grade (-1 to quit):  -1

Total number of students: 7
Average grade: 87
Highest grade: 98
```

Now let's consider another way to implement the program. One unflattering characteristic of the initial solution is that it repeats code. Note that the lines that prompt for, read, and convert a test score are essentially the same for the first grade and for all subsequent grades. This kind of redundancy is not good practice. If someone needed to modify this code later, they might change it in one place and not the other.

Eliminating the redundancy has some important implications. The original version uses the first grade to initialize the value of `max`. But because there is a lower bound on valid grades, we can initialize `max` to zero. Then as long as any grades are higher than zero, the value of `max` is replaced as before. Even if all grades in the list were zero, then `max` would still contain a correct value after the loop.

This change also implies that the only time we request a new grade is at the beginning of the body of the `while` loop. If we continue to use the check for a negative grade value as the condition of the `while` loop, we have to guarantee that we will enter the loop the first time. Therefore `grade` needs to be initialized to an arbitrary positive value. Also, we must be careful to avoid processing the sentinel value as part of the valid input.

Finally, let's output the average as a floating point number. Therefore `average` and at least one of the division operands, such as `sum`, need to be declared as floating point variables. Here is a second version of the program:

```java
import java.io.*;

//   Determine the average and maximum grade of a set of test scores.
//   A second version.

class Average2 {
    public static void main (String[] args) throws IOException {
        int grade = 9999, count = 0, max = 0;
        float sum = 0, average;
        BufferedReader stdin = new BufferedReader
            (new InputStreamReader (System.in));

        //   Read and process all grades.
        while (grade >= 0) {
            System.out.print ("Enter a grade (-1 to quit): ");
            System.out.flush();
            grade = Integer.parseInt (stdn.readLine());
            if (grade >= 0) {
                count = count + 1;
                sum = sum + grade;
                if (grade > max)
                    max = grade;
            }
        }

        if (count == 0)
            System.out.println ("No valid grades were entered.");
        else {
            average = sum / count;
            System.out.println();
            System.out.println ("Total number of students: " + count);
            System.out.println ("Average grade: " + average);
            System.out.println ("Highest grade: " + max);
        }
    } // method main

} // class Average2
```

To avoid processing the sentinel value, we had to insert another `if` statement whose condition basically duplicates the condition in the `while` loop. By avoiding one kind of redundancy, we have introduced another. Therefore, our second implementation is not necessarily better than the first, just different. The design and implementation of programs always involve these kinds of tradeoffs. Each situation must be critiqued for its particular characteristics and you should choose the most elegant, readable, and appropriate design for the situation.

Below is a sample run of the second version of the average program:

```
Enter a grade (-1 to quit):   87
Enter a grade (-1 to quit):   82
Enter a grade (-1 to quit):   94
Enter a grade (-1 to quit):   98
Enter a grade (-1 to quit):   73
Enter a grade (-1 to quit):   98
Enter a grade (-1 to quit):   80
Enter a grade (-1 to quit):   -1


Total number of students: 7
Average grade: 87.42857
Highest grade: 98
```

Many other requirements could have been specified for this problem. For instance, we might have been required to verify that the user types in valid grades. Suppose we knew the range of grades was strictly between 0 and 100, inclusive. We could add a check after the input is read to make sure it is in range and then produce an error message if it's not. We would also have to avoid processing the incorrect input as part of our list of grades. Note that while we can catch values that are out of the valid range, we can't catch incorrect values that happen to be in range. For example, we can't possibly tell that the user entered the value 87 when they meant to type 78.

Consider some other possible requirements: How would you change the program if you had to determine and produce the minimum grade? What if you knew there were exactly 17 students in the class? What if you wanted to keep the number of students general, but prompt the user for the specific number each time the program was executed? These variations are explored in the problem set at the end of the chapter.

Summary of Key Concepts

- Each value in memory is associated with a specific data type. This data type determines what operations we can perform on the data.
- Java has two kinds of numeric values—integers and floating point. There are four integer data types (byte, short, int, and long) and two floating point data types (float and double).

- A variable is a name for a memory location used to hold a value of a particular data type.
- A variable can store only one value of its declared type.
- Java is a strongly typed language. Each variable is associated with a specific type for the duration of its existence, and you cannot assign a value of one type to a variable of an incompatible type. This feature helps prevent inadvertent errors.
- Constants are similar to variables but they hold a particular value for the duration of their existence.
- Java handles all input and output (I/O) in basically the same way. Any source of input or destination for output is called a stream.
- Input information is stored in a temporary location called an input buffer. Similarly, all information sent to the standard output stream is written to a temporary area called an output buffer.
- Many programming statements involve expressions. Expressions are combinations of operators and operands used to perform a calculation.
- Java follows a well-defined set of rules that govern the order in which operators will be evaluated in an expression. These rules form an operator precedence hierarchy.
- An `if` statement allows a program to choose whether or not to execute a following statement.
- An `if-else` statement allows a program to do one thing if a condition is true and a different thing if the condition is false.
- A nested `if` allows the program to make a decision based on the results of a previous decision.
- A `while` statement allows a program to execute a statement many times.
- Design your programs carefully to avoid infinite loops. The body of the loop must eventually make the loop condition false.
- Software requirements specify what a program must accomplish.
- A software design specifies how a program will accomplish its requirements.
- An algorithm is a step-by-step process for solving a problem.
- Implementation is the process of writing source code based on the design.
- Testing a program involves running it multiple times with various input and observing the results.

Self-Review Questions

3.1 What is a variable?

3.2 Name the four kinds of Java integer data types? How are they different? Why is that difference important?

3.3 Name two specific purposes for the + operator.

3.4 What is a Java constant? How is it different from a Java variable?

3.5 Which character set does Java use? Why?

3.6 Explain the concept of operator precedence.

3.7 What is an infinite loop? Specifically, what causes it?

3.8 Name the four basic activities that are involved in a software development process.

Exercises

3.9 What is the result of the following expressions when `length` equals 8, `width` equals 3, and `height` equals 2.25? Assume `length` and `width` are integer variables, and `height` is a floating point variable.

a. `length / width`
b. `length / height`
c. `length % width`
d. `width % length`
e. `length * width + height`
f. `length + width * height`

3.10 Give an equivalent expression for the following:

a. `total < sum`
b. `MAX <= highest`
c. `intensity > threshold`

3.11 Explain three reasons to use constants in a program instead of literals.

3.12 Java is strongly typed. What does that mean?

3.13 What is wrong with the following code fragment? Using braces and correct indentation, rewrite it so that it produces correct output.

```
if (total == MAX)
    if (total < sum)
        System.out.println ("total equals MAX and total is
                            less than sum");
else
    System.out.println ("total is not equal to MAX");
```

3.14 What is wrong with the following code fragment? Will this code compile if it is part of a valid program? Explain completely.

```
if (length = MIN_LENGTH)
    System.out.println ("The length cannot be reduced
                        further.");
```

3.15 What is wrong with the following code fragment? What are three distinct ways it could be changed to remove the flaw?

```
count = 50;
while (count >= 0) {
    System.out.println (count);
    count = count + 1;
}
```

Programming Projects

3.16 Write a program that reads an integer value and prints the sum of all even integers between 2 and the input value, inclusive. Print an error message if the input value is less than 2. Prompt accordingly.

3.17 Write a program that reads an integer value between 0 and 100 (inclusive), representing the amount of a purchase in cents. Produce an error message if the input value is not in that range. If the input is valid, determine the amount of change that would be received from one dollar, and print the number of quarters, dimes, nickels, and pennies that should be returned. Maximize the coins with the highest value. Follow the format below. The user input is shown in color.

```
Enter the purchase amount [0-100]:  36
Your change of 64 cents is given as:
    2 Quarters
    1 Dimes
    0 Nickels
    4 Pennies
```

Hint: 64 / 25 equals 2, and 64 % 25 equals 14.

3.18 In Problem 3.17, the coins were always expressed as plural even if there was only one (1 Dimes). Modify your answer to print the singular form of the word for each coin when only one is used.

3.19 Modify the answer to Problem 3.17 to continue processing input values until a sentinel value of –1 is entered. Change the prompt accordingly and do not print an error message when the sentinel value is entered.

3.20 Modify the Football_Choice program so that it does not ask the receive / kickoff question unless the user wins the coin toss.

3.21 Modify the Average program to validate the grades entered to make sure they are in the range 0 to 100, inclusive. Print an error message if a grade is not valid; then continue to collect grades. Continue to use the sentinel value to indicate the end of the input, but do not print an error message when it is entered. Do not count an invalid grade or include it as part of the running sum.

3.22 Modify the `Average` program to determine and produce the minimum grade in addition to the maximum.

3.23 Modify the `Average` program to read and process exactly 17 grades.

3.24 Modify the `Average` program to prompt for and read the exact number of students in the class; then loop until exactly that many valid grades have been read.

Answers to Self-Review Questions

3.1 A variable is a place to store a value. It is the name we give to a memory location. When we refer to the variable name, we are referencing the value stored at the corresponding memory location.

3.2 The four Java integer types are `byte`, `short`, `int`, and `long`. They differ in the amount of room that is reserved in memory to store them, and therefore differ in the size of the integer value they can hold. A programmer should be careful to choose the appropriate size for the need.

3.3 The + operator can be used for arithmetic addition and for string concatenation.

3.4 A Java constant is declared like a variable, except the final modifier is used. The value of a constant cannot be changed, unlike a variable whose value can be changed as needed.

3.5 Java uses the Unicode character set because it provides 16 bits per character. Thus Java can store many more characters than ASCII and is attractive for an international environment.

3.6 Operator precedence determines how an expression gets evaluated. It is a set of rules that establishes which operators get evaluated first and how operators within the same precedence level associate.

3.7 An infinite loop is a repetition statement that never terminates. Specifically, the body of the loop never causes the condition to become false.

3.8 Software development consists of requirements analysis, design, implementation, and testing.

Objects and Classes

4

In Chapter 2 we briefly introduced the concept of object-oriented programming. You learned that objects are the primary building blocks of object-oriented software (as the name implies) and that a class is the blueprint from which an object is created. In Chapter 3 we examined some of the basic programming elements that make up an object and give it the ability to perform interesting tasks. In this chapter, we explore how to define classes, create objects from classes, and use objects to solve problems.

Chapter Objectives

- Create objects from classes and use them to perform their intended services.
- Use a class to define a set of objects, composed of variables and methods.
- Explain the concept of abstraction, on which all object-oriented concepts are based.
- Explain the advantages of encapsulation and the use of Java modifiers to accomplish it.
- Define a reference to an object and discuss how to use references appropriately.
- Explore the details of methods and parameter passing.
- Describe class variables and methods.
- Examine method overloading and discuss its proper uses.

4.1 Objects

What is an object? Think about objects in the world around you. How would you describe them? Let's use a ball as an example. A ball has particular characteristics such as its diameter, color, and elasticity. Formally, we say these characteristics contribute to the ball's *state* of being. We also describe a ball by what it does, such as the fact that it can be thrown, bounced, or rolled. These activities define the ball's *behavior*. All objects, including software objects, have a state and a set of behaviors. As we stated in Chapter 3, an object contains variables and methods. The values of the variables describe the object's state, and the methods define the object's behaviors.

> **Key Concept** An object contains variables and methods. The values of the variables define the state of the object and the methods define the behaviors of the object.

Consider a computer game that plays baseball. The baseball could be represented as an object. It would have variables to store its size and location, and methods that draw it on the screen and calculate how it moves when hit. The variables and methods defined in the ball object establish the state and behavior that are relevant to the ball's use in the computerized baseball game.

An object must also have a unique *identity* that distinguishes it from all other objects. Two objects can have the same types of variables with the same name, and those variables could contain the same values. Therefore two objects could have the same state. Thus state alone is not sufficient to distinguish two objects and provide a unique identity. In a program, an object's name is its identity.

Behaviors tend to apply to all objects of a particular type. For instance, in general, any ball can be thrown, bounced, or rolled. However, the state of an object and its behaviors work together. How high a ball bounces depends on its elasticity. The action is the same, but the specific result depends on its state. An object's behavior often modifies its state. For example, when a ball is rolled, its position changes.

Let's consider another situation. In software used to manage a university, a set of objects could represent the students on campus. Each object would contain the variables that store information about a particular student, such as name, address, major, courses taken, grades, and grade point average. It would also contain related code, such as a method that calculates the grade point average based on the student's grades.

Although software objects often represent tangible items, they don't have to. An error message can be an object, for instance. Don't limit the possibilities to tangible entities.

Classes

We briefly introduced classes in Chapter 2. Objects are defined by classes. A *class* is the model, or pattern, from which an object is created. Let's examine a particular analogy in order to explore the concept of a class.

Consider the blueprint created by an architect when designing a house. The blueprint defines the important characteristics of the house: walls, windows, doors, electrical outlets, and so forth. Once the blueprints are created, several houses can be built using the same blueprint, as depicted in Fig. 4.1. In one sense, the houses built from the blueprint are different. They are physically in different places, have different addresses, different furniture, and different people live in them. Yet, in many ways they are the "same" house. The layout of the rooms and other crucial characteristics are the same in each. To create a completely different house, we need a different blueprint.

A class is a blueprint of an object. It defines the types of data that will be held in an object, and defines the code for the methods. But a class is not an object any more than a blueprint is a house. After we have the class defined, we can create an object from it. The process of creating an object is called *instantiation*. Every object is an *instance* of a particular class. And, just as we can create several houses from the same blueprint, we can instantiate several objects from the same class. They are the same type of object, with the same methods, but each object is unique because each has its own data space with possibly different values.

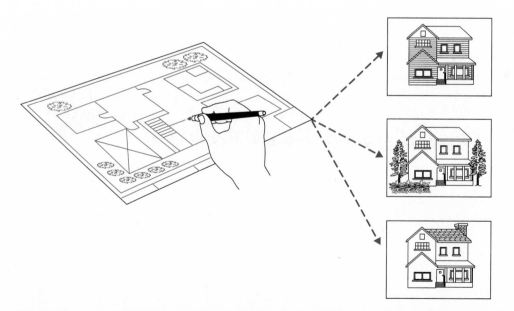

Figure 4.1   A house blueprint and three houses created from it

Instantiation and References

In many ways, a class can be thought of as the type of an object variable. Consider the following two declarations:

```
int total = 25;
Chess_Piece bishop = new Chess_Piece();
```

There are several similarities between these two lines. The first line declares that a variable called `total` holds a value of type integer. It is initialized to the value 25. The second line declares that a variable called `bishop` refers to an object created from class `Chess_Piece`. It is initialized to an object created using the `new` operator and a *constructor* of the `Chess_Piece` class. A constructor is similar to a method and is used to initialize the object. A constructor has the same name as the class.

The declaration and initialization of bishop could be separated onto two lines:

```
Chess_Piece bishop;
bishop = new Chess_Piece();
```

The first line declares the variable `bishop` to be a *reference to an object* of class `Chess_Piece`. At this point we still do not have an instantiated object. Variables in Java are either primitive types, like integers or characters, or they are references to objects. An object reference holds the address in memory where the object is stored. Until an actual object is assigned to the reference, it does not refer to anything. The second line creates an object of class `Chess_Piece` using the `new` operator and assigns it to the `bishop` reference variable.

After an object has been instantiated, you can use the *dot operator* to access its methods. We've used the dot operator many times, such as in calls to `System.out.println`. The dot operator is appended directly after the object reference name, then followed by the method being invoked. For example, the term `bishop.position()` in the following line of code invokes the `position` method in object `bishop`:

```
System.out.println ("The location is " + bishop.position());
```

Variables could be referenced using the dot operator in the same way if they were made available to the external environment. However, this type of access should not be allowed on variables; therefore you rarely use the dot operator to access a variable.

4.2   Using Predefined Classes

The Java Application Programming Interface (API) contains a large number of pre-defined classes for use in a program. This section describes a few of these classes and explores a few of their methods. A more detailed list of the contents of these and other classes can be found in Appendix O.

The `String` Class

Character strings in Java are not represented by a primitive type as are integers (`int`) or single characters (`char`). Strings are represented as objects of the `String` class, which is defined in the `java.lang` package. We've used character string literals, such as `"Enter a number"` in earlier examples. Now we can begin to explore the `String` class and the services it offers.

Once a `String` object contains a value, it cannot be lengthened, shortened, nor can any of its characters change. Thus we say that a string object is *immutable*. However, several methods in the `String` class return new strings that are often the result of modifying the original's value.

Though they are not primitive types, strings are so important and frequently used that Java provides an additional syntax for their declaration:

```
String name = "James Gosling";
```

Java creates a string object dynamically whenever a string literal is used. If that same literal is used again in the program, a reference is made to the original object that has that value. This prevents multiple, identical objects from being created. Because their values cannot change, this is a safe optimization.

There is also a constructor in the `String` class that accepts a `String` as a parameter and creates a unique `String` object with the same value. Therefore, the declaration

```
String name2 = new String (name);
```

creates a second `String` object called `name2` that has the value `"James Gosling"`.

A character in a string can be referred to by its position, or *index,* in the string. The index of the first character in a string is zero, the second character is one, and so on. Therefore, in the String "Hello", the index of the character 'H' is zero and the character at index 4 is 'o'.

Some useful methods of the String class are:

- charAt (int index)—returns the character at the specified index
- indexOf (char ch)—returns the index of the first occurrence of the specified character
- lastIndexOf (char ch)—returns the index of the last occurrence of the specified character
- endsWith (String suffix)—returns true if the string ends in the specified substring
- startsWith (String prefix)—returns true if the string begins with the specified substring
- equals (Object obj)—returns true if the string and the parameter contain the same characters
- equalsIgnoreCase (String str)—returns true if the string and the parameter differ only by case
- compareTo (String str)—returns a value that indicates if the string is lexically less than, equal to, or greater than the parameter
- toLowerCase ()—returns a string whose characters have been converted to lower case
- toUpperCase ()—returns a string whose characters have been converted to upper case
- length ()—returns the length of the string (number of characters)

The following program instantiates several String objects in a variety of ways, then exercises several String methods to demonstrate their use.

Multiple techniques for creating String objects

```
class Carpe_Diem {
    public static void main (String[] args) {
        String str1 = "Seize the day";
        String str2 = new String();
        String str3 = new String (str1);
        String str4 = "Day of the seize";
        String str5 = "Seize the day";
        System.out.println ("str1: " + str1);
        System.out.println ("str2: " + str2);
        System.out.println ("str3: " + str3);
        System.out.println ("str4: " + str4);
        System.out.println ("str5: " + str5);
        System.out.println();

        System.out.println ("Length of str1: " + str1.length());
        System.out.println ("Length of str2: " + str2.length());
```

```
         System.out.println();
         System.out.println ("Index of 'e' in str4: " +
             str4.indexOf('e'));
         System.out.println ("Last index of 'e' in str4: " +
             str4.lastIndexOf('e'));
         System.out.println ("The character at position 3 in str1: " +
             str1.charAt(3));
         System.out.println ("The substring of str1 from " +
             "position 6 to position 8: " + str1.substring(6, 9));
         System.out.println();
         if (str1 == str5)
             System.out.println ("str1 and str5 refer " +
                 "to the same object.");
         if (str1 != str3)
             System.out.println ("str1 and str3 do NOT refer " +
                 "to the same object.");
         if (str1.equals(str3))
             System.out.println ("str1 and str3 contain the same " +
                 "characters.");
         System.out.println();

         str2 = str1.toUpperCase();
         System.out.println ("str2 now refers to: " + str2);
         if (str1.equalsIgnoreCase(str2))
             System.out.println ("str1 and str2 contain the same " +
                 "characters (ignoring case).");
         str5 = str1.replace('e', 'X');
         System.out.println ("str5 now refers to: " + str5);
         System.out.println();

         System.out.println ("str1 starts with \"Seize\": " +
             str1.startsWith("Seize"));
         System.out.println ("Creating a string from a number: " +
             String.valueOf(22+33+44));
     } // method main
} // class Carpe_Diem
```

The phrase *Carpe diem* is Latin for "Seize the day." When executed, the Carpe_Diem program produces the following output:

```
str1: Seize the day
str2:
str3: Seize the day
str4: Day of the seize
str5: Seize the day
```

```
Length of str1: 13
Length of str2: 0


Index of 'e' in str4: 9
Last index of 'e' in str4: 15
The character at position 3 in str1: z
The substring of str1 from position 6 to position 8: the


str1 and str5 refer to the same object.
str1 and str3 do NOT refer to the same object.
str1 and str3 contain the same characters.


str2 now refers to: SEIZE THE DAY
str1 and str2 contain the same characters (ignoring case).
str5 now refers to: SXizX thX day
str1 starts with "Seize": true
Creating a string from a number: 99
```

The `StringTokenizer` Class

Often the characters in a string can be grouped into meaningful pieces. For example, the characters in a sentence can be grouped into individual words. The characters in the string `"75 69 81"` can be thought of as a series of integers separated by white space. To the Java compiler, a string is just a series of characters, but we can identify separate, possibly important, components within a string. Extracting and processing the data contained in a string is a common programming activity. The `java.util` package provides the `StringTokenizer` class to aid programmers in this task. The purpose of the `StringTokenizer` class is to break a string up into pieces, called *tokens,* based on a set of delimiters. The default delimiters used by the `StringTokenizer` class are the space, tab, carriage return, and newline characters.

Some useful methods of the `StringTokenizer` class are:

- `countTokens()`—returns the number of tokens a string was broken into
- `nextToken()`—returns the next token in the string

The following example creates a class called `Int_Reader` that sets up a `StringTokenizer` object to read multiple integer input values.

```
import java.io.*;
import java.util.StringTokenizer;
```

```
// Reads and prints ten integers separated by white space
// across any number of lines.
class Int_Reader {

   public static void main (String[] args) throws IOException {
      BufferedReader stdin = new BufferedReader
         (new InputStreamReader(System.in));
      StringTokenizer reader;
      reader = new StringTokenizer (stdin.readLine());
      int count = 1;
      while (count <= 10) {
         while (reader.countTokens() == 0)
            reader = new StringTokenizer(stdin.readLine());
         System.out.println ("Number is " +
            Integer.parseInt (reader.nextToken()));
         count = count + 1;
      }
   } // method main

} // class Int_Reader
```

Instantiating a new
`StringTokenizer`
object

Invoking the
`StringTokenizer`
method
`countTokens`

The input to this program could be spread out over multiple lines, with one or more white space characters between each number. Suppose the following input lines were used for the program:

```
746      27      498
   469      57
210   44
  102
69    540
```

Then the output of the `Int_Reader` program would be:

```
Number is 746
Number is 27
Number is 498
Number is 469
Number is 57
Number is 210
Number is 44
Number is 102
Number is 69
Number is 540
```

The Random Class

The need for random numbers occurs frequently when writing software. Games often use a random number to represent the roll of a die or to shuffle a deck of cards. A flight simulator may use random numbers to determine how often a simulated flight has engine trouble. A program designed to help a high school student prepare for the SATs may use random numbers to choose the next question to ask.

The Random class is defined in the java.util package and implements a pseudo–random number generator. A *random number generator* picks a number at random out of a range of values. A program that serves this role is technically pseudo-random, because a program has no means to actually pick a number randomly. A *pseudo–random number generator* performs a series of complicated calculations, starting with an initial *seed value,* and produces a number. Though they are technically not random (because they are calculated), the values produced by a pseudo–random number generator usually appear random, at least random enough for most situations.

Some useful methods of the Random class are:

- nextInt()—returns a random integer (across the entire int spectrum)
- nextFloat()—returns a random floating point value (between zero and one)

The following program simulates flipping a coin. It counts the number of heads and the number of tails produced. Flipping only a few coins, we can expect a large difference between the number of heads and the number of tails. As the number of flips grows we can expect the ratio of heads to tails to be approximately 50 percent.

```java
import java.io.*;
import java.util.*;

// This program simulates flipping a coin
class Flip {

    public static void main (String[] args) throws IOException {
        BufferedReader stdin = new BufferedReader
            (new InputStreamReader(System.in));
        Random coin = new Random();
        int count = 0, heads = 0, tails = 0;
        int number_flips, flip_result;

        System.out.print ("Enter the number of flips: ");
        System.out.flush();
        number_flips = Integer.parseInt (stdin.readLine());
        while (count <= number_flips) {
            flip_result = Math.abs (coin.nextInt()) % 2;
            if (flip_result == 0)
                heads = heads + 1;
```

Produces a random integer, either 0 or 1

```
        else
            tails = tails + 1;
        count = count + 1;
    }

    System.out.println ("The number of heads is " + heads);
    System.out.println ("The number of tails is " + tails);
  } // method main

} // class Flip
```

The following is a sample run of this program:

```
Enter the number of flips:   1000
The number of heads is 531
The number of tails is 469
```

The `nextInt` method of the `Random` class produces a random number from the entire domain of `int` values, including negatives. The program uses an absolute value function and the modulus division operator (`%`) to scale a random `int` value into the desired range (0 to 1). The absolute value function is part of the `Math` class, which is discussed in more detail later in this chapter.

The need to scale and shift a random number into an appropriate range is a common programming activity. If we had a `Random` object called `dice`, the following declaration could be used to simulate the roll of one die, producing values between 1 and 6:

```
int roll = Math.abs (dice.newInt()) %6 + 1;
```

The `Random` class can also produce random `bytes`, `floats`, and `doubles`.

4.3   Aliases

Because of Java's references to objects, the meaning of assignment for primitive types and for objects is different. Consider the following declarations of primitive data:

```
int num1 = 5;
int num2 = 12;
```

In the following assignment statement, a copy of the value that is stored in num1 is stored in num2:

```
num2 = num1;
```

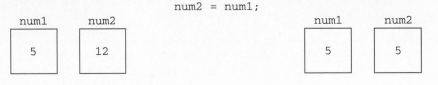

Before assignment   num2 = num1;   After assignment

Figure 4.2   Primitive data assignment

The original value of 12 in num2 is overwritten by the new value 5. The variables num1 and num2 still refer to different locations in memory, and both of those locations now contain the value 5. This situation is pictured in Fig. 4.2.

Now consider the following object declarations:

```
Chess_Piece bishop1 = new Chess_Piece();
Chess_Piece bishop2 = new Chess_Piece();
```

Initially, the references bishop1 and bishop2 refer to two different Chess_Piece objects. The following assignment statement, because it works on references instead of primitive data, has a different effect than the assignment of integer values:

```
bishop2 = bishop1;
```

The assignment copies the value of the reference from bishop1 to bishop2. The two references originally referred to different objects with unique data space for variables. After the assignment, both bishop1 and bishop2 refer to the same object, the one that bishop1 originally referred to, as shown in Fig. 4.3. These two references are now *aliases* of each other. All references to the object that was originally referenced by bishop2 are now gone and that object cannot be used again in the program.

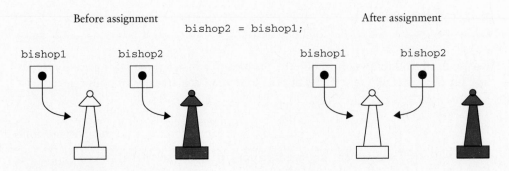

Figure 4.3   Reference assignment

One important implication of aliases is that when the state of one object changes, so does the other. If you change the state of `bishop1` for instance, you change the state of `bishop2` because they both refer to the same object. Aliases can be confusing unless they are managed carefully.

Defining your own classes, including constructors, is discussed in more detail later in this chapter. The next section describes several predefined classes from the Java API and demonstrates their use.

In-Depth Focus

Garbage Collection

When all references to an object are lost (perhaps by reassignment), that object can no longer contribute to the program. Because the use of an object is accomplished through a reference to the object, the program can no longer invoke its methods or use its variables. At this point the object is called *garbage* because it serves no useful purpose.

Java performs *automatic garbage collection*. When the last reference to an object is lost, the object becomes a candidate for garbage collection. Occasionally, the Java runtime executes a method that "collects" all of the objects marked for garbage collection and returns their allocated memory to the system for future use. The programmer does not have to worry about explicitly returning allocated memory.

However, if there is an activity that a programmer wants to accomplish in conjunction with the object being destroyed, the programmer can define a method called `finalize` in the object's class. The `finalize` method takes no parameters and uses a `void` return type. It will be executed by the Java runtime after the object is marked for garbage collection and before it is actually destroyed. The `finalize` method is not often used because the garbage collector performs most normal cleanup operations. However, it is useful for performing activities that the garbage collector does not address, such as closing files.

4.4 Defining Methods

We've already used many methods in various programs and we know that methods are part of a class. Let's now examine method definitions closely in preparation for defining our own classes.

A *method* is a group of programming language statements that are given a name. A method is associated with a particular class. Each method has a *method definition* that specifies the code that gets executed when the method is invoked. We've invoked the `println` method many times, but because we didn't write `println`, we have not been concerned about its definition. We call it assuming that it will do its job reliably.

When a method is called, the flow of control transfers to that method. One by one, the statements of that method are executed. When that method is done, control returns to the location where the call was made and execution continues. This process is pictured in Fig. 4.4.

We've defined the `main` method of a program many times. Its definition follows the same syntax as all methods:

```
return-type  method-name  ( parameter-list ) {
    statement-list
}
```

The header of a method includes the type of the return value, the method name, and a list of parameters that the method accepts. The list of statements that makes up the

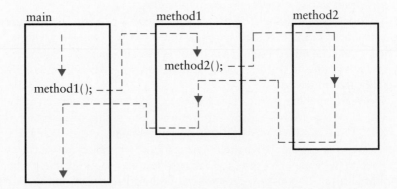

Figure 4.4 The flow of control following method invocations

body of the method are defined in a block. The following code is the definition of a method called `third_power`:

```
int third_power (int number) {
   int cube;
   cube = number * number * number;
   return cube;
}  // method third_power
```

A method may declare *local variables* in the body of the method for use only in that method. The variable `cube` in the `third_power` method is local to that method. Local variables cannot be accessed from outside of the method, even from other methods of the same class. In previous examples we've declared variables in the `main` method. These variables were local to the `main` method. Local variables do not exist except when the method is executing; therefore the value stored in a local variable is lost from one invocation of the method to the next. If you want a value to be maintained from one call to the next, you should define the variable at the class level. The declaration of a local variable can be mixed into the statement list, but it must be declared before it is used.

 Key Concept   A variable declared in a method is local to that method and cannot be used outside of it.

The `return` statement

Methods can return a value, whose type must correspond to the *return type* in the method header. The return type can be a primitive type or a reference to an object. When a method does not return any value, the reserved word `void` is used as the return type, as is always done with the `main` method. A return type must always be specified in the method header. The `return` statement in a method can take one of two forms:

```
return;
```

or

```
return expression;
```

The first form causes the processing flow to return to the calling location without returning a value. The second form returns to the calling method and specifies the value that is to be returned. If a return type other than `void` is specified in the method header, then the Java compiler insists that a `return` statement exist in the program and that a value of the proper type is returned.

▶▶ **Key Concept** A method must return a value consistent with the return type specified in the method header.

The following code is another way to define the `third_power` method, performing a calculation in the expression of the `return` statement. This modification eliminates the need for the local variable.

```
int third_power (int number) {
    return (number * number * number);
}   // method third_power
```

If there is no `return` statement in a method, processing continues until the end of the method is reached. If there is a `return` statement, then processing is stopped for that method when the `return` statement is executed, and control is returned to the statement that invoked the method.

It is usually not good practice to use more than one `return` statement in a method even though it is possible to do so. In general, a method should have one `return` statement as the last line of the method body unless it makes the method overly complex.

Parameters

A *parameter* is a value that is passed into a method when it is invoked. The *parameter* list in the header of a method specifies the types of the values that are passed and the names by which the called method will refer to the parameters in the method definition. In the method definition, the names of the parameters accepted are called *formal parameters*. In the invocations, the values passed into a method are called *actual parameters*. A method invocation and definition always specify the parameter list in parentheses after the method name. If there are no parameters, an empty set of parentheses are used.

The formal parameters are identifiers that essentially act as local variables for the method and whose initial value comes from the calling method. Actual parameters can be literals, variables, or full expressions that are evaluated and the result passed as the parameter. Let's look at an example:

```
public void acid_test (int substance1, float substance2) {
    String title = "Acid Test Order Form";
    generate_report (title, substance1, substance2);
}  // method acid_test
```

This example is a method called `acid_test`. The method generates a report by invoking another method called `generate_report`. The formal parameters for `acid_test` are `substance1` and `substance2`, as listed in the parameter list. Note that `substance1` and `substance2` also serve as actual parameters to the method invocation of `generate_report`. The variable `title` is a local variable in `acid_test`, and serves as an actual parameter for the call to `generate_report`.

When primitive data is passed, a copy of the value is assigned to the actual parameter. When objects are passed, a copy of the reference to the original object is assigned to the actual parameter. Therefore when an object is passed as a parameter, the formal parameter becomes an alias of the actual parameter. Another way to say this is that, in Java, primitive data is passed by value and objects are passed by reference.

 Key Concept An object is passed by reference when it is used as a parameter. Therefore the actual parameter and the formal parameter are aliases of each other.

Let's look at an example that tests the issue of parameter passing. Assume that we have a class `Num` that contains an `int` variable called `value`. The following program demonstrates passing the various data types:

```
// Demonstrates the effects possible using parameter passing.
class Parameter_Passing {

    public static void change_values
        (int formal1, int formal2, Num formal3,
         Num formal4, Num formal5) {

        System.out.println();
        System.out.println ("Before changing values");
        System.out.println ("Formal parameter 1: " + formal1);
        System.out.println ("Formal parameter 2: " + formal2);
```

```
                System.out.println ("Formal parameter 3: " + formal3);
                System.out.println ("Formal parameter 4: " + formal4);
                System.out.println ("Formal parameter 5: " + formal5);

```

Changes to primitive formal parameters are not reflected in `main`.

```
                formal2 = 5;
                formal4.value = 8;
                formal5 = new Num (20);

                System.out.println();
                System.out.println ("After changing values");
                System.out.println ("Formal parameter 1: " + formal1);
                System.out.println ("Formal parameter 2: " + formal2);
                System.out.println ("Formal parameter 3: " + formal3);
                System.out.println ("Formal parameter 4: " + formal4);
                System.out.println ("Formal parameter 5: " + formal5);
        } // method change_values

        public static void main (String[] args) {

                int actual1 = 6;
                int actual2 = 9;
                Num actual3 = new Num (7);
                Num actual4 = new Num (1);
                Num actual5 = new Num (10);

                System.out.println ("Before method call");
                System.out.println ("Actual parameter 1: " + actual1);
                System.out.println ("Actual parameter 2: " + actual2);
                System.out.println ("Actual parameter 3: " + actual3);
                System.out.println ("Actual parameter 4: " + actual4);
                System.out.println ("Actual parameter 5: " + actual5);

                change_values
                    (actual1, actual2, actual3, actual4, actual5);

                System.out.println();
                System.out.println ("After method call");
                System.out.println ("Actual parameter 1: " + actual1);
                System.out.println ("Actual parameter 2: " + actual2);
                System.out.println ("Actual parameter 3: " + actual3);
                System.out.println ("Actual parameter 4: " + actual4);
                System.out.println ("Actual parameter 5: " + actual5);

        } // method main
} // class Parameter_Passing
```

The output of this program is:

```
Before method call
Actual parameter 1: 6
Actual parameter 2: 9
Actual parameter 3: 7
Actual parameter 4: 1
Actual parameter 5: 10
Before changing values
Formal parameter 1: 6
Formal parameter 2: 9
Formal parameter 3: 7
Formal parameter 4: 1
Formal parameter 5: 10
After changing values
Formal parameter 1: 6
Formal parameter 2: 5
Formal parameter 3: 7
Formal parameter 4: 8
Formal parameter 5: 20
After method call
Actual parameter 1: 6
Actual parameter 2: 9
Actual parameter 3: 7
Actual parameter 4: 8
Actual parameter 5: 10
```

An actual parameter that is a primitive data type is unaffected by the method's effect on the associated formal parameter. If the formal parameter is assigned a new value, it affects the value of the formal parameter while the method is executing, but not the actual parameter. This case is demonstrated in the example by formal parameter `formal2`. An actual parameter that is an object type can be affected by what the method does to the associated formal parameter. If the method changes a value of the data in an object, then the data is also changed in the actual parameter. The variable `actual4` in the example demonstrates this case. However, if the formal parameter is assigned a completely new object, then the actual parameter is unaffected. The variable `actual5` in the example demonstrates this case.

Although these effects many seem arbitrary, they are related to the different rules for assignments between objects and primitive types. The different effects are a result of storing objects as references to the object's value rather than the actual object's value. Primitive-data-type actual parameters pass a copy of their value into the method, so changing the copy does not effect the original value stored in the actual parameter. The variables `actual1` and `actual2` are passed this way in the example. Object actual parameters pass a copy of their object's reference into the method. The actual parameter and the formal parameter have become aliases. Changing the value of data associated with the reference changes both what the formal parameter is referencing as well as what the actual parameter is referencing, because both parameters are referencing the same object's values. This type of change occurs to `actual4` in the example. Altering the copy of the reference to be a different reference, say, by assigning a new object to the formal parameter, will not change the original copy of the reference stored in the actual parameter. This type of change occurs to `actual5` in the example. Figure 4.5 traces the execution of the `Parameter_Passing` example showing how the values of the actual and formal parameters change.

4.5   Defining Classes

Now that we know how to define methods, let's explore how to define our own classes. Suppose we wanted to define a rectangle by its size and level of shading, where size is represented by its length and width, and shading is represented on a grey scale from 0 (white) to 100 (black). The rectangle object must also provide services to compute its area and change its shade.

Figure 4.6 shows a generic class specification, listing the variables and methods, and three objects instantiated from it. The variables `length`, `width`, and `shade` have different values in each object. The method that computes the area is the same for all of the rectangles, but the computed value is different value for each rectangle because it is based on the rectangle's unique `length` and `width`.

The basic syntax for defining a class in Java is:

```
class class-name {
    data-declarations
    constructors
    methods
}
```

> **Key Concept**   Classes define the variables for an object, but reserve no memory space for them. Each object, when instantiated, has unique storage space for variables, and therefore their values can be different. Methods, however, are shared among all objects of a class.

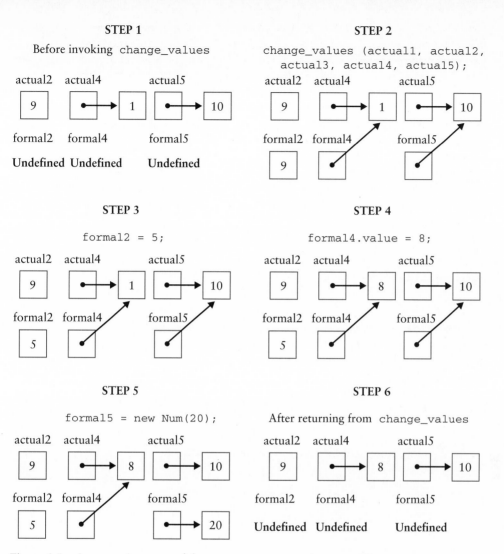

Figure 4.5 An execution trace of the `Parameter_Passing` example

A class can contain any number of variables and methods, which are collectively called the *members* of a class. The variables declared in a class are called *instance variables* because they don't exist until an instance of the class is created. When a method is invoked, it is done through a particular instance of the class. In the `Rectangle` example, the `area` method computes and returns the area of the specific rectangle through which the method was invoked, using the `length` and `width` values unique to that object. Furthermore, a variable in an object can be a reference to another object. An object that contains other objects is called an *aggregate object*.

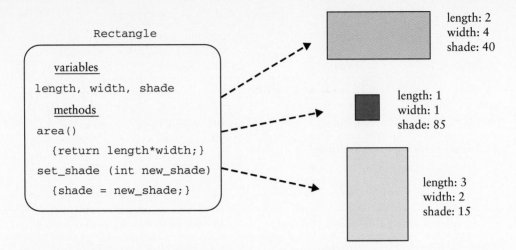

Figure 4.6 A class and three objects instantiated from it

The code below shows a Java definition of class `Rectangle`, with a more interesting version of the set_shade method than the one shown in Fig. 4.6:

```java
class Rectangle {
    final int MAX_LEVEL = 100;  // max shading level
    final int MIN_LEVEL = 0;    // min shading level
    int length, width, shade;

    Rectangle (int side1, int side2, int level) {
        length = side1;
        width = side2;
        shade = level;
    }  // constructor Rectangle

    int area () {
        return length * width;
    }  // method area

    void set_shade (int adjustment) {
        int new_level = shade + adjustment;

        if (new_level >= MIN_LEVEL)
            if (new_level <= MAX_LEVEL)
                shade = new_level;
            else
                System.out.println ("New shading level is too high.");
```

The constructor has the same name as the class.

A method defined in the class is invoked through an instance of the class.

```
        else
            System.out.println ("New shading level is too low.");
    } // method set_shade
} // class Rectangle
```

This definition contains the declarations of two integer constants (MAX_LEVEL and MIN_LEVEL) and three variables (length, width, and shade). It also contains two method definitions (area and set_shade) and one constructor (Rectangle).

You specify a constructor of the class using the class name. A constructor is similar to a method, but it has no return type and cannot return a value. A constructor can take parameters. The constructor code is executed when an object of this class is instantiated.

4.6 Encapsulation

You can think about an object in one of two ways. The view you take depends on what you are trying to accomplish at the moment. First, when you are designing and implementing an object, you need to think about the details of how an object works. You have to define the variables that will be held in the object and write the methods that make the object useful.

However, when you are designing a solution to a large problem, you have to think in terms of how the objects in your program interact. At that level, you only have to think about the services that an object provides, not on the details of how the services are accomplished.

For example, as long as a student object successfully calculates the grade point average when requested, we essentially don't need to worry about how the grades are represented or how the code that computes the grade point average is written. At the implementation stage, someone must concern themselves with those details, but establishing that a particular object will perform particular services is part of the design stage.

An object, from this second point of view, is a *black box*. The term black box refers to any part of a system whose inner workings and structure are currently hidden. The rest of the system only interacts with the object through a well-defined set of services that it provides.

The term *encapsulation* is used to describe the fact that objects are thought of as black boxes. An object encapsulates the methods and data that are contained inside it. Encapsulation is the main idea behind the *client-server model* of computing. An object is a server, providing services that other objects, the clients, can use.

Consider a program that plays chess. Each chess piece is represented as an object. Figure 4.7 shows a knight chess piece object as an encapsulated black box

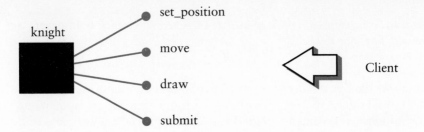

Figure 4.7   An encapsulated object with particular services

with services called `set_position`, `move`, `draw`, and `submit`. These services set the initial position of the piece on the chess board, move the piece during a game, draw the piece on the monitor screen, and submit the knight when another piece captures it. A client that uses the `knight` object requests these services by invoking the appropriate methods. The client does not need to know how these actions are accomplished.

An object is usually both a client and a server at the same time. To accomplish a particular service, an object may request a service of another object. For example, when the `knight` object moves to a position that contains a pawn, the knight's `move` method may invoke the pawn object's `submit` method, so that the pawn removes itself from play.

The methods that define the services that the object provides are called *service methods*. They can be invoked by a client. There may be additional methods in an object that do not define a service that is available to a client but instead help another method with its task. These types of methods are called *support methods*. For example, the `move` method of the `knight` object may invoke another method called `validate_move`, which makes sure that the requested move is valid before moving the knight. The `validate_move` method is part of the `knight` object but is not offered to the client as a service. Therefore the `validate_move` method is encapsulated inside the black box. The `move` method is a service method and the `validate_move` method is a support method.

> **Key Concept**   Objects are encapsulated. The rest of the system interacts with an object only through a well-defined set of services that it provides.

Encapsulation implies that an object should be self governing, which means that the variables contained in an object should only be modified within the object. Only the methods within an object should have access to the variables in that object.

If a client using an object needs to change the state of that object, then there should be service methods available that accomplish the change. A client should never be able to "reach in" and change the values of an object's variables directly.

Abstraction

It may appear that the distinction between the internal and external views of an object is unnecessary if the programmer using an object is also the one who defined it, but this is not true. A human being is capable of mentally managing around seven (plus or minus two) pieces of information in short-term memory. Beyond that, we start to lose track of some of the pieces. However, if we group pieces of information together, then those pieces can be managed as one "chunk" in our minds. We don't actively deal with all of the pieces in the chunk but can still manage it as a single entity. We therefore can deal with large quantities of information by organizing them into chunks. This concept is called *abstraction*. We can define it as hiding or ignoring the right details at the right time. All of the techniques in the object-oriented approach are rooted in the idea of using abstraction.

We use abstractions every day. Think about a car for a moment. You don't necessarily need to know how a four-cycle combustion engine works in order to drive a car. You just need to know some basic operations: how to turn it on with the key, how to put the car in gear, how to make it move with the pedals and steering wheel, and how to stop it. These operations define the way a person interacts with the car, just as the service methods define the way a client uses an object. These operations mask the details of what is happening inside the car that allow it to function. When you're driving a car, you're not usually thinking about the spark plugs igniting the gasoline that drives the piston that turns the crankshaft that turns the axel that turns the wheel. If we had to worry about all of these underlying details, we'd never be able to operate something as complicated as a car.

Initially, all cars had manual transmissions. The driver had to understand and deal with the details of changing gears with the stick shift. Eventually, automatic transmissions were developed, and the driver no longer had to worry about shifting gears. Those details were hidden by raising the level of abstraction.

Of course, someone has to deal with the details. The car manufacturer has to know the details in order to put the car together in the first place. A car mechanic relies on the fact that most people don't have the expertise or tools necessary to fix a car when it breaks. The level of abstraction must be appropriate for the situation. Some people prefer to drive a manual transmission car. A race car driver, for instance, needs to control the shifting manually for optimum performance. Knowing the appropriate level of abstraction is critical to defining the services for an object.

Encapsulation is an abstraction. A software object is an abstract entity in that we can view it from the outside without concerning ourselves with the details of how it works on the inside. We've been relying on the abstract nature of objects from our very first program in Chapter 2. The `println` method is a service provided by an object representing the standard output stream, called `out`. We use the `println` method without worrying about the details of how the string actually gets printed. Because it is abstracted, it is easy to start thinking of `println` as if it were a part of the Java language, when actually it is just a method that happens to have been written by someone else.

So whether or not you are the person implementing the object, the abstraction provided by encapsulation lets you deal with objects in a clear, consistent manner. The external view pushes the details out of the way so that we can deal with a large chunk of the system easily. At the appropriate time we can look inside the object and concern ourselves with the details, if we have to. The next section describes how we implement encapsulation in a Java program.

Visibility Modifiers

A *modifier* is a Java reserved word that is used to specify particular characteristics of a programming language construct. We've already seen one in use, `final`, which we used to declare a constant. Java has several modifiers that can be used in various ways. Some modifiers can be used together, whereas other combinations are invalid. All of the Java modifiers are discussed in Appendix F.

One use of modifiers is to specify the access characteristics of the members of a class. These modifiers are called *visibility modifiers* because they control to what extent a class member can be accessed and referenced. Thus they allow us to define the encapsulation characteristics of an object. The reserved words `public` and `private` are visibility modifiers that can be applied to the variables and methods of a class. If a variable or method is `public`, then it can be directly referenced from outside of the object. If a member is `private`, it cannot be referenced externally but can be used anywhere inside the class definition.

A client of an object must be able to reference service methods, which define the services an object provides, but it should not be able to directly invoke internal methods. Therefore, a `public` visibility modifier is appropriate for service methods, but any method that does not define a service for an object should be declared `private`. Note that the `main` method is always declared with `public` visibility, so that it can be executed by the interpreter. Remember that an object should be self governing, allowing variables to be changed only through a service provided by the object. Therefore, all variables should be declared with the `private` visibility modifier.

Let's revisit the definition of the `Rectangle` class, using appropriate visibility modifiers:

```
class Rectangle {
    private final int MAX_LEVEL = 100;   // max shading level
    private final int MIN_LEVEL = 0;     // min shading level
    private int length, width, shade;

    public Rectangle (int side1, int side2, int level) {
        length = side1;
        width = side2;
        shade = level;
    }  // constructor Rectangle

    public int area() {
        return length * width;
    }  // method area

    public void set_shade (int adjustment) {
        int new_level = shade + adjustment;

        if (new_level >= MIN_LEVEL)
            if (new_level <= MAX_LEVEL)
                shade = new_level;
            else
                System.out.println ("New shading level is too high.");
        else
            System.out.println ("New shading level is too low.");
    }  // method set_shade

}  // class Rectangle
```

Visibility modifiers determine the accessibility of a variable or method.

Note that all methods in the `Rectangle` class define external services and are therefore declared with `public` visibility. Constructors are used externally to instantiate objects of the class and cannot be declared `private`. Other uses for the modifiers `public` and `private`, and additional visibility designations, are discussed later in the text.

4.7   Example: CD Collection

The following example contains two classes. The Tunes class contains the main method of the program, which instantiates one object from class CD_Collection. A CD_Collection object contains two private data values and a set of methods. It is used to keep track of the number of compact discs in a collection and the value of that collection. The add_cds method adds a certain number of cds to the collection as well as their cost. The print method prints the current status of the collection, including the average cost of a CD. Note that the average cost is computed using a separate method.

The main method in class Tunes instantiates the CD collection, called music, with an initial set of CDs. It then adds some more CDs using the add_cds method and prints the status of the collection. Then it adds some more CDs and prints the status again.

```
// Instantiates an object to monitor the value of a
// collection of musical CDs
class Tunes {

    public static void main (String[] args) {

        CD_Collection music = new CD_Collection (5, 59, 69);

        music.add_cds (1, 10.99);
        music.add_cds (3, 39.34);
        music.add_cds (2, 24,73);

        music.print();

        music.add_cds (2, 20.82);
        music.acd_cds (4, 46.90);

        music.print();

    }   // method main

}   // class Tunes

// Represents a collection of CDs
class CD_Collection {
```

Instantiating a
CD_Collection
object

```
   private int num_cds;
   private double value_cds;

   public CD_Collection (int initial_num, double initial_val) {      The constructor ini-
      num_cds = initial_num;                                          tializes the data
      value_cds = initial_val;                                        values
   }  // constructor CD_Collection

   public void add_cds (int number, double value) {
      num_cds = num_cds + number;
      value_cds = value_cds + value;
   }  // method add_cds

   public void print() {
      System.out.println ("***************");
      System.out.println ("Number of CDs: " + num_cds);
      System.out.println ("Value of collection: $" + value_cds);
      System.out.println ("Average cost per CD: $" + average_cost());
   }  // method print
   private double average_cost() {                                   Support methods
      return value_cds / num_cds;                                    are not available to
   }  // method average_cost                                         the client

}  // class CD_Collection
```

Note that the average_cost method is declared private which means it supports the work of another method in the class (the print method) but cannot be called from the client of the object (main in class Tunes). Also note that the methods in class CD_Collection access the variables num_cds and value_cds without having to pass them in as parameters.

When executed, the CD_Collection program prints the following:

```
***************
Number of CDs: 11
Value of collection: $134.75
Average cost per CD: $12.25
***************
Number of CDs: 17
Value of collection: $202.47
Average cost per CD: $11.91
```

4.8   The `static` Modifier

We've seen how visibility modifiers allow us to specify the encapsulation characteristics of variables and methods in a class. Java has several other modifiers that determine other characteristics. For example, the `static` modifier associates a variable or method with its class, rather than with an object of the class, as described in the following sections.

Static Variables

So far, we've seen two categories of variables: those that are declared inside a method, called local variables, and those that are declared in a class but not inside a method, called instance variables. This second category of variables are called instance variables because they are accessed through a particular instance (an object) of a class. In general, each object has distinct memory space for each variable, so that each object can have a distinct value for that variable. Another kind of variable, called a *static variable* or *class variable,* can be shared among all instances of a class. There is only one copy of a static variable for all objects of a class. Therefore, changing the value of a static variable in one object changes it for all of the others. A local variable cannot be declared `static`.

To specify a static variable in Java, we use the reserved word `static`, as shown in the class definition below:

```
class Student {
    private static int count = 0;

    public Student() {
        count = count + 1;
    } // constructor Student

    public int number_of_students() {
        return count;
    } // method number_of_students

} // class Student
```

> The variable count is shared among all objects of the `Student` class.

Because `count` is declared with the modifier `static`, a new version of `count` is not created with each object of `Student` that is instantiated. There is one version of `count`, initialized to zero, that is shared among all objects created from the `Student` class. In this example, `count` is used to keep track of the total number of students. The constructor of `Student` increments `count` each time a new `Student` object is instantiated. At any point during its existence, any `Student` object can provide a client with the current value of `count` through the `number_of_students` method.

Constants, which are declared using the `final` modifier, are also often declared using the `static` modifier. Because the value of constants cannot be changed, there might as well be only one copy of the value across all objects of the class. Like static variables, constants cannot be declared inside a method.

Static Methods

Methods can also be declared using the `static` modifier. This kind of method is referred to as a *static method* or *class method*. A static method is not referenced through a particular instance of a class but through the class itself. You don't have to instantiate an object of the class to invoke a static method. Because static methods do not operate in the context of a particular object, they cannot reference instance variables, which only exist in an instance of a class. The compiler will issue an error if a static method attempts to use a nonstatic variable. They can, however, reference static variables, because static variables exist independent of specific objects.

The `main` method of a Java program must be declared `static` so that `main` can be executed by the interpreter without instantiating an object from the class containing `main`. Therefore the `main` method can only access static or local variables. Other examples of static methods are found in the Java API. For example, the `Math` class in the `java.lang` package contains several static mathematical operations on primitive types, including:

- `pow (double a, double b)`—raises a to the power b
- `cos (double a)`—returns the cosine of a
- `sqrt (double a)`—returns the square root of a
- `abs (int a)`—returns the absolute value of a

Because they operate on primitive types, there are no specific objects through which to invoke these methods. They are all declared as `static`, and no instantiated object is needed to use them.

Static methods are invoked using the class name, instead of the object name. The following declaration uses the `sqrt` method of the `Math` class to initialize a variable called `root`:

```
double root = Math.sqrt (33);
```

4.9 Method Overloading

When a program is compiled, a method invocation is *bound* to the appropriate definition. That is, code is inserted at the location of the method call to shift processing to the location of the method definition. After the method's code has been executed, control returns to the location of the call and processing continues.

The method name is often sufficient to indicate which method definition is being referenced by a given invocation. But in Java, as in other object-oriented languages, you can use the same method name for multiple methods. This technique is called *method overloading*. It is useful when you need to perform similar methods on different types of data.

The compiler must still be able to bind an invocation to a specific definition. If the method name for two or more definitions is the same, then additional information is used to uniquely identify the definition that is being referenced by a particular invocation. In Java, a method name can be used for multiple methods as long as some combination of the number of parameters, the types of those parameters, and the order of the types of parameters is distinct. A method's name along with the number, type, and order of its parameters is called the method *signature*. The compiler uses the complete method signature to bind a method invocation to the appropriate definition.

The compiler must be able to examine a method invocation, including the parameter list, and determine which specific definition is being referenced. If you attempt to specify two method names with the same signature, the compiler will issue an appropriate error message and will not create an executable system. There can be no ambiguity.

 Key Concept   An overloaded method is distinguished by its signature, which is the number, type, and order of the parameters.

The `println` method in the `PrintStream` class is an example of a method that is overloaded several times, each accepting a single type. A partial list of its various signatures is given below:

```
println (String s)
println (int i)
println (double d)
println (char c)
println (boolean b)
```

The following two lines of code actually invoke different methods that have the same name:

```
println ("The total number of students is: ");
println (count);
```

The first line invokes the `println` that accepts a string and the second, assuming `count` is an integer variable, invokes the `println` that accepts an integer. We often use a `println` statement that prints several distinct types, such as:

```
println ("The total number of students is: " + count);
```

But remember, the plus sign here is the string concatenation operator. First, the value in the variable `count` is converted to a string representation, then the two strings are concatenated into one longer string, and the definition of `println` that accepts a single string is invoked.

Overloading Constructors

Constructors are a primary candidate for overloading. By providing multiple versions of a constructor, you have a variety of ways to create and initialize an object. For instance, in addition to our original version of the `Rectangle` constructor, we could define two others:

```
public Rectangle() {
    length = 10;
    width = 20;
    shade = 50;
}

public Rectangle (int side1, int side2) {
    length = side1;
    width = side2;
    shade = 0;
}

public Rectangle (int side1, int side2, int level) {
    length = side1;
    width = side2;
    shade = level;
}
```

The first version takes no parameters and defines a default rectangle of a specific size and shade. The second allows the user to specify the size but provides a default shade. The third version is our original, which allows the user to explicitly define the initial value for all three variables.

Let's look at a simple, but complete, example. The following example demonstrates the use of overloaded constructors as well as overloaded methods. The Gambler class defines two overloaded constructors, and two overloaded double_it methods.

```java
// Example that demonstrates overloaded constructors and methods
public class Casino {
    public static void main (String[] args) {
        Gambler jim = new Gambler();
        Gambler joe = new Gambler (10, "Pizza");

        jim.double_it (20);
        joe.double_it ("Pizza");

        jim.claim();
        joe.claim();
    } // method main
} // class Casino


// Example with overloaded constructors and methods
class Gambler {

    private int winnings;
    private String consumed;

    public Gambler() {
        winnings = 0;
        consumed = "nothing";
    } // constructor Gambler

    public Gambler (int bet, String food) {
        winnings = bet;
        consumed = food;
    } // constructor Gambler

    public void double_it (int bet) {
        winnings = winnings + bet + bet;
    } // method double_it
```

Constructors and methods have distinguishing signatures.

```
public void double_it (String food) {
    consumed = consumed + " " + food;
} // method double_it

public void claim() {
    System.out.println
        ("I've eaten " + consumed + " and won " + winnings);
} // method claim
} // class Gambler
```

The Casino class main method declares two objects of Gambler, jim and joe. The instantiation of jim calls the default constructor. The instantiation of joe calls the constructor that accepts an int and String parameters. Both objects then call the double_it method. Because the call that jim makes contains an integer parameter, the first double_it method is invoked. The call that joe makes invokes the second double_it method, because the actual parameter is a String object. The output of this program is:

```
I've eaten nothing and won 40
I've eaten Pizza Pizza and won 10
```

4.10   Example: Purchase Power

Let's look at another program that makes use of the object-oriented concepts covered in this chapter. The following program is designed to provide insight into the way an object-oriented system is structured. It demonstrates the following:

- software objects used to represent real-world objects
- multiple classes in one program
- multiple objects instantiated from the same class
- objects cooperating via message passing to accomplish a task
- the use of constructors and visibility modifiers

Imagine a grocery store that has a program that keeps track of inventory and lets managers replenish out-of-stock items. Our example program simulates the sales and ordering of two products (beans and franks) by two managers (Jim and Bob).

Figure 4.8 shows the three classes used in the example. Each class is pictured with three sections: the first contains the class name, the second contains the variables in the class, and the third contains the signatures of the methods in the class.

The class Purchase_Power contains the main method of the program. It has an integer variable to store the number of sales, which is used to control how long

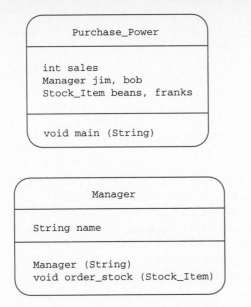

Figure 4.8 Three classes in the Purchase Power example

the simulation runs. It also instantiates two objects of class `Manager` and two objects of class `Stock_Item`. The `main` method drives the simulation by looping through several customer purchases of both items.

The class `Manager` represents a store manager. Each object instantiated from class `Manager` contains a string that holds the manager's name and a constructor that sets up the name. Each manager can order more stock of a particular item using the `order_stock` method. Because ordering stock is an operation performed by a manager, it is implemented by a method encapsulated in the `Manager` class.

Class `Stock_Item` represents a particular kind of store product. Each object instantiated from class `Stock_Item` contains an integer called `inventory`, which indicates the amount of the item the store currently has available. Each stock item has a name, stored as a string. Each stock item also has a reference to a `Manager` object, which indicates the manager responsible for stocking the item. The methods in class `Stock_Item` include a constructor that accepts a reference to the controlling `Manager` object and a string for the brand name. The method `brand` returns the name when needed. The `buy` method is invoked to simulate a customer attempting to buy some quantity of the item. If there is enough inventory to satisfy the purchase then the sale is made, otherwise the controlling manager reorders the stock. The act of reordering invokes the `replenish` method of a stock item, which increases its inventory.

The `Purchase_Power` program creates two `Manager` objects and two `Stock_Item` objects. All four objects are created in the `Purchase_Power` class. A reference to the appropriate `Manager` object is passed to a `Stock_Item` object

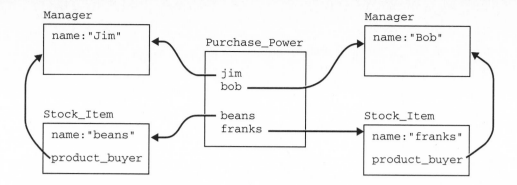

Figure 4.9 The objects in the Purchase_Power program

when it is created. Figure 4.9 shows the relationship between objects in the Purchase_Power program.

Here is the code for the Purchase_Power simulator:

```
class Purchase_Power {

   private final static int MAX_SALES = 100;
   private static int sales = 0;
   private static Manager jim = new Manager ("Jim");
   private static Manager bob = new Manager ("Bob");
   private static Stock_Item beans = new Stock_Item (jim, "beans");
   private static Stock_Item franks = new Stock_Item (bob, "franks");

   public static void main (String[] args) {
      while (sales < MAX_SALES) {
         if (beans.buy (2))
            sales = sales + 1;
         if (franks.buy (5))
            sales = sales + 1;
      }
   } // method main

} // class Purchase_Power

class Manager {
   private String name;
```

```
            public Manager (String id) {
                name = id;
            }   // constructor Manager

            public void order_stock (Stock_Item out_of_stock_item) {
                System.out.println ("Manager " + name + " is ordering more " +
                                    out_of_stock_item.brand());
                out_of_stock_item.replenish (10);
            }   // method order_stock

        }   // class Manager
        class Stock_Item {
            private int inventory = 0;
            private String name;
            private Manager product_buyer;

            public Stock_Item (Manager controller, String product_name) {
                name = product_name;
                product_buyer = controller;
            }   // constructor Stock_Item

            public String brand () {
                return name;
            }   // method brand

            public boolean buy (int amount) {
                boolean success = false;
                if ( amount <= inventory ) {
                    inventory = inventory - amount;
                    success = true;
                }
                else
                    product_buyer.order_stock (this);

                return success;
            }   // method buy

            public void replenish (int amount) {
                inventory = inventory + amount;
            }   // method replenish

        }   // class Stock_Item
```

The manager has the stock item replenish itself.

The stock item has the manager order more stock.

Note that objects of class `Stock_Item` contain a reference to a `Manager` object, but don't instantiate a `Manager` object themselves. This relationship is appropriate since a `Manager` is not a piece of a stock item, like a drawer is part of a desk. Good design practices dictate that you should only instantiate an object inside another object if it is truly part of the aggregate. In this program objects are passed to other objects that invoke their services. The output of this program demonstrates that different objects of the same class manage their own internal state. Because of the different amount being sold of beans and franks, managers reorder stock at different rates.

The output of this program is:

```
Manager Jim is ordering more beans
Manager Bob is ordering more franks
Manager Bob is ordering more franks
Manager Jim is ordering more beans
Manager Bob is ordering more franks
Manager Bob is ordering more franks
Manager Jim is ordering more beans
Manager Bob is ordering more franks
Manager Bob is ordering more franks
Manager Jim is ordering more beans
Manager Bob is ordering more franks
Manager Bob is ordering more franks
Manager Jim is ordering more beans
Manager Bob is ordering more franks
Manager Bob is ordering more franks
Manager Jim is ordering more beans
Manager Bob is ordering more franks
Manager Bob is ordering more franks
Manager Jim is ordering more beans
Manager Bob is ordering more franks
Manager Bob is ordering more franks
Manager Jim is ordering more beans
Manager Bob is ordering more franks
Manager Bob is ordering more franks
Manager Jim is ordering more beans
Manager Bob is ordering more franks
Manager Bob is ordering more franks
Manager Jim is ordering more beans
Manager Bob is ordering more franks
Manager Bob is ordering more franks
Manager Jim is ordering more beans
Manager Bob is ordering more franks
```

```
Manager Bob is ordering more franks
Manager Jim is ordering more beans
Manager Bob is ordering more franks
```

Finally, notice the use of the `this` reference when a manager orders stock (in the `buy` method). All methods in objects may use a special reference that is defined by the reserved word `this`. The `this` reference always refers to the current object that is executing the code. The `buy` method is a classic example of the need for an object to refer to itself. The `this` reference is generic in the class but refers to a particular object of class `Stock_Item` each time the `buy` method is invoked.

4.11   Example: `Storm` Applet

Let's look at an object-oriented Java applet. The following example is an applet called `Storm` that graphically simulates the effect of raindrops striking a puddle. The applet in this example demonstrates:

- using multiple classes and objects in the development of a Java applet
- using a static variable in the implementation of a class
- instantiating multiple objects from a single class
- passing objects as parameters
- passing primitive types as parameters

The following sections detail the various development activities involved in creating the applet.

Requirements

The `Storm` program should perform the following tasks.

- Simulate graphically the effects of raindrops on a puddle.
- Allow the program to be browsed over the Web.
- Create the effects of a raindrop by drawing a circle at a random location and then redrawing successively larger circles at the same location.
- Different raindrops should grow to different sizes.
- Many raindrops should be drawn at the same time.
- The applet should restart itself every time it is browsed.
- The simulation should stop after a short period of time.

Using this list as the initial set of requirements for the program, we can proceed to designing the program.

Design

What should we identify as classes? There are two physical objects represented in the requirements. The first is a raindrop and the second is a puddle. Raindrops have many requirements to fulfill, such as growing in size to simulate ripples and being represented many times simultaneously on the screen. Therefore we should be able to complete this program by using a class that represents the applet (already named `Storm`), and a class that represents a single raindrop, called `Raindrop`.

The `Raindrop` class should contain all the services related to raindrops. Raindrop objects need to grow in size. They need to support multiple copies simultaneously, and they need to be drawn at varying locations. So far, this leads us to assume that the `Raindrop` class will have a public constructor to enable us to instantiate multiple copies of the raindrop class, have a method called `set_position` that enables the position of the raindrop to be determined, and have a method called `ripple` that tells the raindrop object it should grow in size.

The `Storm` class needs to be derived from the `Applet` class. Because Storm is the controlling class, it creates multiple objects of the `Raindrop` class. Let's assume five objects of the `Raindrop` class are necessary. The pseudocode for the primary loop could be written as follows:

```
while (count is not greater than the maximum count) {
    call check_drop for 5 raindrop objects.
    increment count.
    call draw.
}
```

The `check_drop` method accepts a `Raindrop` object as a parameter. This method needs to determine if the drop has completed its rippling. If it has not, then the `ripple` method of the `Raindrop` class should be invoked. From this we can assume a need for a new method for the `Raindrop` class, called `visible`. This method should return a boolean that indicates whether or not the ripples of this particular raindrop are still visible or not. With this method, the `check_drop` pseudocode can be written as:

```
if (drop.visible( )) {
    drop.ripple( );
} else {
    calculate a new random x and y position for the drop.
    drop.set_position (x, y);
}
```

Before we can satisfy the requirement that the `Storm` applet restart the rain effect every time an HTML page containing the applet is viewed, we need to understand some rules associated with the methods of an applet. Applets have particular methods that have a special meaning. To accomplish our requirements, the special methods we need to understand are init and start methods. These methods are special because all applets are derived from the class Applet. Knowing this information, Web browsers assume all applets have these methods, and call them in a particular order. The init method is called once when the applet is first loaded into memory. The start method is called every time the applet is viewed by a browser. Therefore if we put all the code to implement the rain effect in the init method, the program would only run once. But, if we put the initialization code in init, and the algorithm that produces the rain effect in start, then the rain effect occurs every time the applet is viewed.

The pseudocode of the Storm class has imposed several more details on the Raindrop class. The visible method needs to be able to calculate when the circle has grown larger than the visible size of that particular raindrop. Also, the assigning of a position to the raindrop using set_position should reset the internal state of the object. This reset is necessary because once a raindrop is no longer visible, the check_drop pseudocode assumes that it can assign a new position. If the state of the object was not reset, then successive calls to the visible method would still return true.

Therefore, the set_position should reset the size of the raindrop to its initial value, and determine randomly how large the raindrop should grow. The visible method can be implemented by determining if the current size of the raindrop is smaller than its visible size. The drawing methods, as we saw in Chapter 2, are methods of a Graphics object. If we want a draw method in the Raindrop class, we need to pass into the draw method the applet's Graphics object. The implementation of the draw method then needs to call the drawOval method of the Graphics object.

Figure 4.10 shows the details of the classes just described.

<table>
<tr><td colspan="2">

Raindrop

```
Random new_size
int current_size
int visible_size
int x, y
```

```
boolean visible()
void set_position (int,int)
void ripple ()
void draw (Graphics)
```
</td><td>

Storm

```
Random position
Raindrop drop1, drop2, drop3, drop4, drop5
Graphics page
```

```
void init()
void start()
void draw (Graphics)
void check_drop (Raindrop)
```
</td></tr>
</table>

Figure 4.10   Class diagrams for the Storm program

Implementation

The following implementation of the `Storm` applet and the `Raindrop` class represent the above design. During implementation, some interesting characteristics of this program come to light. They are discussed after the program.

```java
import java.applet.Applet;
import java.awt.Graphics;
import java.util.Random;

//  Creates the effect of rain drops on a puddle
class Raindrop {

    private final int MAX_RIPPLE = 30;
    private final int RIPPLE_STEP = 2;

    private static Random new_size = new Random();

    private int current_size = 0;
    private int visible_size = 0;
    private int x = 1, y = 1;

    public boolean visible() {
        return current_size < visible_size;
    } // method visible

    public void set_position (int x_position, int y_position) {
        x = x_position;
        y = y_position;
        visible_size =
            Math.abs (new_size.nextInt() % MAX_RIPPLE) + 1;
        current_size = 1;
    } // method set_position

    public void ripple() {
        x = x - RIPPLE_STEP/2;
        y = y - RIPPLE_STEP/2;
        current_size = current_size + RIPPLE_STEP;
    } // method ripple

    public void draw (Graphics page) {
        page.drawOval (x, y, current_size, current_size);
    } // method draw
} // class Raindrop
```

```
//   The Storm class controls the raindrop loop in the start
//   method.
public class Storm extends Applet {

    private final int MAX_COUNT   = 500;
    private final int BUSY_WAIT    = 50000;
    private final int APPLET_SIZE = 200;

    private Random position = new Random();

    private Raindrop drop1;
    private Raindrop drop2;
    private Raindrop drop3;
    private Raindrop drop4;
    private Raindrop drop5;

    private Graphics page;
```

The init method is called once when the applet is loaded.

```
    public void init() {
        drop1 = new Raindrop();
        drop2 = new Raindrop();
        drop3 = new Raindrop();
        drop4 = new Raindrop();
        drop5 = new Raindrop();

        setSize (APPLET_SIZE, APPLET_SIZE);
        setVisible (true);

        page = getGraphics();
    } // method init
```

The start method is called each time the applet is displayed.

```
    public void start() {
        int count = 1;
        int wait;

        while (count < MAX_COUNT) {
            check_drop (drop1);
            check_drop (drop2);
            check_drop (drop3);
            check_drop (drop4);
            check_drop (drop5);
            count = count + 1;
            draw (page);
```

```
            wait = 0;
            while (wait < BUSY_WAIT) {
                wait = wait + 1;
            }
        }
    } // method start


    public void check_drop (Raindrop drop) {
        if (drop.visible()) {
            // if still visible ripple drop
            drop.ripple();
        } else {
            // if not visible assign a new random position for drop
            int x = Math.abs (position.nextInt() % APPLET_SIZE) + 1;
            int y = Math.abs (position.nextInt() % APPLET_SIZE) + 1;
            drop.set_position (x, y);
        }
    } // method check_drop


    public void draw (Graphics page) {
        // Clear the applet
        page.setColor(getBackground());
        page.fillRect (0, 0, APPLET_SIZE, APPLET_SIZE);
        page.setColor(getForeground());
        // Draw all the drops
        drop1.draw (page);
        drop2.draw (page);
        drop3.draw (page);
        drop4.draw (page);
        drop5.draw (page);
    } // method draw
} // class Storm
```

There are several interesting features of the implementation that should be noted. The main loop in the Storm class start method uses what is called a busy wait at the end of the loop. This is to cause the main loop to pause for a short period of time to create a realistic rain effect. The wait loop simply loops the number of times indicated by BUSY_WAIT, incrementing the wait variable.

Also note that the ripple method of the Raindrop class needs to adjust the x and y coordinates of the Raindrop object as it grows in size so that the circle grows out in all directions from a center point. If the coordinates were not adjusted, the circle would remain fixed in its upper left-hand corner and grow out on the bottom right.

Finally, the `Random` object `new_size` in the `Raindrop` class must be `static` to prevent each object of that class from having the same sequence of random visible sizes. On the other hand, the `Random` object called `position` in `Storm` does not need to be `static` because only one object (the applet) uses `position`.

System Test

The overriding requirement for the program is that it simulate the effects of raindrops on a puddle. A quick view of the running applet verifies that this requirement is met. Figure 4.11 show a snapshot of the running `Storm` applet.

The other important requirement to test is the ability of the applet to restart itself each time it is browsed. Displaying the applet in a browser is one way to test this requirement. Another way is to use the menu associated with the appletviewer program that allows us to restart the applet. Specifically, the menu item `Restart`

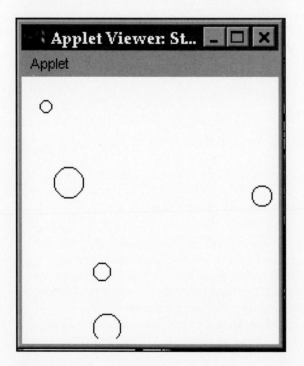

Figure 4.11   Snapshot of the `Storm` applet

will call the `start` method of the applet. Executing this several times provides the necessary feedback as to whether the applet is executing properly.

Summary of Key Concepts

- An object contains variables and methods. The values of the variables define the state of the object and the methods define the behaviors of the object.
- A class is a blueprint of an object; it reserves no memory space for data. Each object has its own data space; an object is an instance of a class.
- The `new` operator returns a reference to a newly created object.
- Multiple references can refer to the same object. These references are aliases of each other.
- A variable declared in a method is local to that method and cannot be used outside of it.
- A method must return a value consistent with the return type specified in the method header.
- An object is passed by reference when it is used as a parameter. Therefore the actual parameter and the formal parameter are aliases of each other.
- Classes define the variables for an object, but reserve no memory space for them. Each object, when instantiated, has unique storage space for variables, and therefore their values can be different. Methods, however, are shared among all objects of a class.
- Objects are encapsulated. The rest of the system interacts with an object only through a well-defined set of services that it provides.
- An abstraction hides details. A good abstraction hides the right details at the right time so that we can manage complexity and focus attention in the proper direction. All object-oriented concepts are based on abstraction.
- A static variable is shared among all instances of a class. A static method can be called through the class in which it is defined.
- An overloaded method is distinguished by its signature, which is the number, type, and order of the parameters.

Self-Review Questions

4.1 What is the difference between an object and a class?

4.2 How does the client-server model of computing relate to encapsulation?

4.3 What are constructors used for? How are they defined?

4.4 Explain the difference between an actual parameter and a formal parameter.

4.5 How is information passed back from a method?

4.6 What is a modifier?

4.7 Describe the following:

    a. public method
    b. private method
    c. public variable
    d. static variable
    e. static method

4.8 How are overloaded methods distinguished from each other?

Exercises

4.9 Explain why encapsulation is an abstraction and give a specific example other than the ones presented in this chapter.

4.10 Explain the difference between a method and a class.

4.11 Write an expression that uses the Random class to produce a random number between:

    a. 0 and 1.
    b. 1 and 100.
    c. 10 and 100.
    d. −5 and 55.
    e. 3 and 4.
    f. −10000 and 10000.

4.12 Write a method called uppercase that accepts a lowercase alphabetic character and returns its uppercase equivalent. If the parameter is not a lowercase letter, return it unchanged.

4.13 The value *N!* (pronounced *N*-factorial) is defined to be the product of the positive integers from 1 to *N*. Write a method to compute and return *N!*, where the value of *N* is passed in as a parameter.

4.14 Think about representing an alarm clock as a software object. Then:

    a. list some characteristics of the object that represent its state and behavior.
    b. define a class, as shown in Fig. 4.8, to represent the object.

4.15 Repeat the steps in Problem 4.14, representing a basketball stadium scoreboard.

4.16 Repeat the steps in Problem 4.14, representing a daily schedule planner.

4.17 Repeat Problem 4.14, using an object you come up with yourself. Describe a program that might make use of the class you define.

Programming Projects

4.18 Write a class called `Bank_Account` that stores the current balance of the account and contains two methods to debit and credit the account. Define a third method that returns the current balance. Pass a value into a constructor to set an initial balance. Write a `main` method that instantiates two bank accounts and exercises the methods of the class.

4.19 Write a class called `Triangle` that can be used to represent a triangle. It should include the following methods that return `boolean` values indicating if the particular property holds:

a. `is_right` (a right triangle)
b. `is_scalene` (no two sides are the same length)
c. `is_isosceles` (exactly two sides are the same length)
d. `is_equilateral` (all three sides are the same length)

4.20 Write a class called `String_Analyzer` that stores a string and provides several methods that determine and return the following characteristics. The string may contain several sentences. Each word in a sentence is separated by a single space character and each sentence is terminated with a period. One space separates each sentence. The characteristics that should be returned are:

a. the number of sentences in the string.
b. the number of words in the entire string.
c. the number of characters in the entire string.
d. the average number of words per sentence.
e. the average number of characters per word.
f. the length of the longest word (in characters).
g. the length of the longest sentence (in words).

Hint: Use the `charAt` and `lastIndexOf` methods from the `String` class in the Java API.

4.21 Write a class that uses the `StringTokenizer` class to identify the parts of a phone number. Assume that the format of the phone number is (nnn) nnn-nnnn. As an example, for the phone number of (610) 555-1212, 610 is the areacode, 555 is the exchange, and 1212 is the extension. The class should have at least three public methods: one that returns the area code, one that returns the exchange, and one that returns the extension.

Answers to Self-Review Questions

4.1 A class is the blueprint of an object. It defines the variables and methods that will be a part of every object that is instantiated from it. But a class reserves no memory space for variables. Each object has its own data space, and therefore its own state.

4.2 The client-server model views a software component in two ways: as a provider of services, and as a client that uses services. The focus is on what the services are, not on how they are accomplished; this focus is the basic premise of encapsulation.

4.3 Constructors are special methods in an object that are used to initialize the object when it is instantiated. A constructor has the same name as its class, and it does not return a value.

4.4 An actual parameter is the value or variable sent to a method when it is invoked. A formal parameter is the corresponding variable in the definition of the method; it takes on the value of the actual parameter so that it can be used inside the method.

4.5 An explicit `return` statement can be used to define the value that is returned from a method. The type of the return value must match the type specified in the method definition.

4.6 A modifier is a Java reserved word that can be used in the definition of a variable or method and that specifically defines certain characteristics of its use. For example, by declaring a variable with the private visibility, the variable cannot be directly accessed outside of the object in which it is defined.

4.7 The modifiers affect the methods and variables in the following ways:
   a. A public method is called a service method for an object because it can be invoked by the client of an object and defines a service that the object provides.
   b. A private method is called a support method. It cannot be invoked from outside the object and is used to support the activities of other methods in the class.
   c. A public variable is a variable that can be directly accessed and modified by a client. This explicitly violates the concept of encapsulation and therefore should be avoided.
   d. A static variable is also called a class variable because there is only one copy of it for all objects of the class, unlike instance variables for which there is a separate copy for each instantiated object.
   e. A static method is also called a class method because it can be invoked through the class name, without explicitly creating an object of that class.

4.8 Overloaded methods are distinguished by having their own signature, which includes the number, order, and type of the parameters. The return type is not part of the distinguishing signature.

More Programming Constructs

In addition to the constructs covered so far in the text, Java has several other operators, another selection statement, and two more loop variations. This chapter defines and explains these additional language constructs. Many of them provide alternative ways to accomplish the same functionality as techniques we've already discussed, and good programmers are careful to choose the appropriate construct for each situation. Some of the operators provide abilities that we haven't yet seen. The chapter begins with a discussion of the internal storage formats for primitive types.

Chapter Objectives:

- Describe the storage formats of primitive types.
- Explore the nuances of converting a value from one type to another.
- Define several additional Java operators.
- Explain the `switch` construct as an alternate selection statement.
- Explore the use of `do` and `for` loops as alternate repetition constructs.

5.1 Internal Data Representation

This section examines the underlying binary representation of primitive data types. Understanding the internal formats of data gives a programmer a better awareness of processing details and an increased confidence in certain activities, such as conversions from one data type to another.

Recall from Chapter 1 that the number of bits used to represent a value determines the range of values that can be represented. One bit can represent two things. Two bits can represent four things. In general, n bits can represent 2^n unique things.

What does the following string of binary digits represent?

```
0011101000101010
```

Who knows? It might represent a character, or an integer, or a floating point value, or a piece of a larger structure, or several smaller values run together. There is nothing inherent in the string itself that tells you what it is supposed to represent. Information in computer memory is just an organized collection of binary digits. Only when we take a specific string of bits and interpret them in a particular way do they have meaning. In the rest of this section we describe how certain primitive data types are represented in Java.

Representing Integers

As discussed in Chapter 3, the four types of Java integers all have a fixed size. Figure 5.1 reviews the Java integer data types. All Java numeric types are *signed*, which means a sign (positive or negative) is always associated with the value. The leftmost bit in the storage space for the number is called the *sign bit*. If the sign bit is one, then the number is negative. If it is zero, the number is positive.

All Java integer types are stored in *signed two's complement* format. The sign takes up one bit. The remaining bits store the value itself and dictate the range of

Type	Storage	Min Value	Max Value
byte	8 bits	–128	127
short	16 bits	–32,768	32,767
int	32 bits	–2,147,483,648	2,147,483,647
long	64 bits	–9,223,372,036,854,775,808	9,223,372,036,854,775,807

Figure 5.1 Java integer types

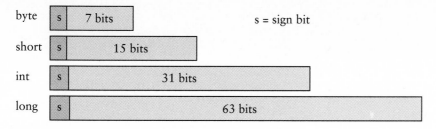

Figure 5.2 Java integer storage

values that can be stored for each type. For example, a `short` value uses one bit for the sign and 15 bits to store the value. Therefore it can represent values ranging from $-(2^{15})$ to $2^{15}-1$ or from -32768 to 32767. The storage sizes for Java integer types are pictured in Fig. 5.2.

In two's complement format, a positive value is represented as a straightforward binary number. A negative value is represented by inverting all of the bits in the corresponding positive binary number, then adding 1. For example, the `short` value 38 is represented as `0000000000100110` in binary. The value -38 is represented by first inverting all of the bits, yielding `1111111111011001`, then adding 1, yielding `1111111111011010`. Note that the sign bit is automatically converted when transforming a positive value into its two's complement negative representation. To decode a negative value, invert all of the bits, then add 1.

The use of two's complement format makes internal arithmetic processing easier. Furthermore, two's complement format prevents the case of "negative zero" from occurring. Let's try to make the value zero, represented as the 16-bit `short` value `0000000000000000`, into a negative number using two's complement format. First, we invert all of the bits to `1111111111111111`, then add 1, yielding `10000000000000000`. There are 17 bits in this new string. The leftmost bit "falls off" the left edge of the 16-bit storage space and is lost, leaving only the regular zero format.

Key Concept Two's complement format is a representation scheme for negative numbers that makes internal arithmetic processing easier.

Figure 5.3 shows several integer values and their internal binary format using signed two's complement representation.

Because we only have a fixed size in which to store a value, two related problems can occur. *Overflow* occurs when a value grows so large that it cannot be stored in the space allocated. Similarly, *underflow* occurs when a value grows so

Decimal Value	Type	Binary Representation
119	byte	01110111
−95	byte	10100001
7526	short	0001110101100110
−347	short	1111111010100100

Figure 5.3 Some integer values and their internal representation

small that it cannot be stored in the space allocated. The following program demonstrates overflow:

```
//  Demonstrates an overflow problem.
class Overflow {

    public static void main (String[] args) {

        byte num = 125;
        System.out.println ("num equals " + num);
        num = num + 1;
        System.out.println ("num equals " + num);
        num = num + 1;
        System.out.println ("num equals " + num);
        num= num + 1;
        System.out.println ("num equals " + num);
        num = num + 1;
        System.out.println ("num equals " + num);

    }  // method main

}  // class Overflow
```

The value of num overflows its storage space.

The output of this program is

```
num equals 125
num equals 126
num equals 127
num equals -128
num equals -127
```

Even though num was only incremented, it suddenly had a negative value. Why? The maximum value that can be stored in a byte is 127, represented as 01111111 in two's complement format. The sign bit indicates that it is a positive number, and the seven 1s equals 127 in binary. When you add 1 to that value, you get 10000000, which in two's complement is −128. When you add 1 to that number, you get 10000001, or −127. An overflow error occurred, producing the wrong results. Underflow causes similar problems. The solution to these problems is to always try to use types that provide enough storage space for the values you are using.

> **Key Concept**   Underflow and overflow can produce incorrect results. Always ensure that types with enough storage space for the possible range of values produced by calculations are used.

Representing Floating Point Values

Recall from Chapter 3 that there are two floating point data types in Java: float and double. Their ranges are summarized in Fig. 5.4.

A floating point number can be described with three values: the *sign*, which determines if it is a positive or negative value; the *mantissa*, which is a positive value that defines the significant digits of the number; and the *exponent*, which determines how the decimal point is shifted relative to the mantissa. A decimal number is therefore defined by the following formula:

$$sign * mantissa * 10^{exponent}$$

The sign is either 1 or −1. A positive exponent shifts the decimal point to the right, and a negative exponent shifts the decimal point to the left. For example, the number 148.69 is represented with a sign of 1, a mantissa of 14869, and an exponent of −2. The number −234000 is represented with a sign of −1, a mantissa of 234, and an exponent of 3.

Type	Storage	Min Value	Max Value
float	32 bits	approximately -3.4E + 38 with 7 significant digits	approximately 3.4E + 38 with 7 significant digits
double	64 bits	approximately -1.7E + 308 with 15 significant digits	approximately 1.7E + 308 with 15 significant digits

Figure 5.4   Java floating point types

Java follows a specific standard for representing floating point values. This standard was established by the International Electronic and Electrical Engineering (IEEE) organization and is commonly referred to as *IEEE 754*. It defines a floating point number with a sign, mantissa, and exponent, stored in binary. Because the base is different, a binary floating point number is defined by the following formula:

$$sign * mantissa * 2^{exponent}$$

In IEEE 754, a single sign bit is used to represent the sign (as it is with the integer types) for both a `float` and a `double`. In a `float`, 23 bits are reserved for the mantissa and 8 bits are reserved for the exponent. In a `double`, 52 bits are used to store the mantissa and 11 bits are used to store the exponent. Figure 5.5 shows the storage of the Java floating point types.

Three special values can be represented in the IEEE 754 floating point format: *positive infinity, negative infinity,* and *not a number*. The latter is displayed as `NaN` when printed. Unlike integer types, both positive and negative zero can be represented in a Java floating point value, but they are considered equal when compared using the equality operator `==`.

 Key Concept   Java uses the standard IEEE 754 floating point format to represent real numbers.

Representing Characters

Java characters are represented as members of the Unicode character set. A character set is simply an ordered list of specific characters. Each character corresponds to a numeric value that represents its location in the ordered list. By storing that number, we essentially store the character. Appendix C examines the Unicode character set in more detail.

A Unicode character is stored as an unsigned 16-bit integer. Because a character is unsigned, all 16 bits contribute to the value, giving characters a numeric range of

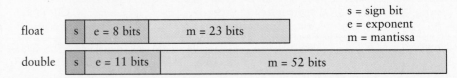

Figure 5.5   Java floating point storage

0 to $2^{16}-1$. Therefore 65,536 unique characters can be represented in the Unicode character set, although only a little over half of those are currently defined. Unicode contains many special symbols and is designed to be a truly international character set, representing languages from all over the world. A programmer will typically use only a small fraction of all possible characters.

The internal representation of a Java character is a 16-bit binary string. A straightforward conversion to the decimal number system gives the decimal numeric value associated with a particular Unicode character. Figure 5.6 shows a few characters from the Unicode character set and their decimal and binary values.

Because characters are stored as numbers, you can perform arithmetic operations on them. If the character variable ch currently holds the character 'A', its internal representation is the decimal value 65. When the following line of code is executed

```
ch = ch + 5;
```

the value of ch now stores the character 'F' because the decimal value of ch is 70. This characteristic can occasionally be helpful. For instance, if you take any uppercase letter and add 32 (the difference between 'A' and 'a'), you will get the letter's lowercase equivalent. If you subtract 48 (the value of '0') from any digit character ('0' through '9') and treat the result as an integer, you get the value of the digit.

Key Concept   Java uses the Unicode character set to represent characters. This representation enables programs to support many different languages.

Conversion Categories

Because Java is a strongly typed language, each data value is associated with a particular type. Sometimes it is helpful or necessary to convert a data value of one type to another type, but we must be careful that we don't lose important information in

Character	Decimal Value	Binary Representation
$	36	0000000000100100
j	74	0000000001001010
z	122	0000000001111010

Figure 5.6   Some Unicode characters

the process. For example, suppose a `short` variable that holds the number 1000 is converted to a `byte` value. Because a `byte` does not store enough bits to represent the value 1000, some bits would be lost in the conversion and the number represented in the byte would not keep its original value.

A conversion between one primitive type and another falls into one of two categories: widening conversions and narrowing conversions. *Widening conversions* are the safest because they usually do not lose information. They are called widening conversions because they go from one data type to another type that uses an equal or greater amount of space to store the value. Figure 5.7 lists the Java widening conversions.

For example, it is safe to convert from a `byte` to a `short` because a byte is stored in 8 bits and a `short` is stored in 16 bits. There is no loss of information. All widening conversions that go from an integer type to another integer type, or from a floating point type to another floating point type, preserve the numeric value exactly.

When converting from a signed integer to an integral type, the two's complement representation is extended, preserving the sign. A widening conversion from a character, which is unsigned, to an integral type fills the extra bits with zeros, making it a positive value.

Although widening conversions do not lose any information concerning the magnitude of a value, the widening conversions that result in a floating point value can lose precision. When converting from an `int` or a `long` to a `float`, or from a `long` to a `double`, some of the least significant digits may be lost. In this case, the resulting floating point value will be a rounded version of the integer value, following the rounding techniques defined in the IEEE 754 floating point standard.

Narrowing conversions are more likely to lose information than widening conversions. They often go from one type to a type that uses less space to store a value, and therefore some of the information may be compromised. Narrowing conversions can lose both numeric magnitude and precision. Therefore, in general, they should be avoided. Figure 5.8 lists the Java narrowing conversions.

From	To
byte	short, int, long, float, or double
short	int, long, float, or double
char	int, long, float, or double
int	long, float, or double
long	float or double
float	double

Figure 5.7   Widening conversions

From	To
byte	char
short	byte or char
char	byte or short
int	byte, short, or char
long	byte, short, char, or int
float	byte, short, char, int, or long
double	byte, short, char, int, long, or float

Figure 5.8   Narrowing conversions

An exception to the space-shrinking situation in narrowing conversions is when we convert a `byte` (8 bits) or `short` (16 bits) to a `char` (16 bits). These are still considered narrowing conversions because the sign bit is incorporated into the new character value. Since a character value is unsigned, a negative integer will be converted into a character that has no particular relationship to the numeric value of the original integer.

A narrowing conversion between a signed integer or a character and a particular integral type discards all but the N lowest-order bits, where N is the number of bits used to represent the new type. The new value may not have the same sign as the original.

Key Concept   Avoid narrowing conversions because they can lose information.

Note that boolean values are not mentioned in either widening or narrowing conversions. A boolean value cannot be converted to any other primitive type and vice versa.

A primitive type cannot be converted to a reference type and vice versa. Conversions between one reference type and another are explored in Chapter 8.

Performing Conversions

Now that we know which conversions are safe, let's explore the various ways in which a conversion can be accomplished. In Java, conversions can occur in three ways:

- assignment conversion
- arithmetic promotion
- casting

Assignment conversion occurs when a value of one type is assigned to a variable of another type, during which the value is converted to the new type. Only widening conversions can be accomplished through assignment. For example, if money is a `float` variable and dollars is an `int` variable, then the assignment statement

```
money = dollars;
```

would automatically convert the value in dollars to a `float`. Therefore, if dollars contained the value 25, after the assignment money would contain 25.0. However, if you attempted to assign money to dollars, the compiler would issue an error message alerting you to the fact that you are attempting a narrowing conversion that could lose information. If you really want to do this assignment, you would have to make the conversion explicit using a cast.

Assignment conversion also occurs when a parameter is passed to a method, because the act of passing a parameter essentially assigns one value to another. This change in data type is sometimes called a *method call conversion*.

Arithmetic promotion occurs automatically when certain arithmetic operators need to modify their operands in order to perform the operation. We've seen this type of conversion before. For example, when a floating point value called sum is divided by an integer value called count, the value of count is promoted to a floating point value automatically before the division takes place, producing a floating point result:

```
result = sum / count;
```

Casting is the most general form of conversion in Java. If a conversion can be accomplished at all in a Java program, it can be accomplished using a cast. A cast is a Java operator that is specified by a type name in parentheses. It is placed in front of the value to be converted:

```
(type)  value
```

For example, to convert money to an integer value, we could put a cast in front of it:

```
dollars = (int) money;
```

The cast returns the value in money, truncating any fractional part. If money contained the value 84.69, then after the assignment dollars would contain the value 84. Note, however, that the cast does not change the value in money.

Casts are helpful in many situations where we temporarily need to treat a value as another type. For example, if we want to divide the integer value `total` by the integer value `count` and get a floating point result, we could do it as follows:

```
result = (float) total / count;
```

First the cast operator returns a floating point version of the value in `total`. This operation does not change the value in `total`. Then, `count` is converted to a `float` via arithmetic promotion. Now the division operator will perform floating point division and produce the intended result. If the cast had not been included, the operation would have performed integer division and truncated the answer prior to assigning it to `result`. Also note that because the cast operator has a higher precedence than the division operator, the cast operates on the value of `total`, not on the result of the division.

5.2　More Operators

There are several operators in the Java language in addition to the ones discussed in Chapter 3. Some of them provide alternative ways to accomplish the same operations as other operators, whereas others provide new operations. They are grouped into the following categories:

- increment and decrement operators
- logical operators
- assignment operators
- the conditional operator

The following sections discuss each of these groups in turn. Then we reproduce the operator precedence hierarchy, incorporating all of the new operators. Yet another set of operators, called bitwise operators, are discussed in Appendix E.

Increment and Decrement Operators

The *increment operator* (++) adds 1 to any integer or floating point value. The two plus signs that make up the operator cannot be separated by white space. The *decrement operator* (--) is similar except that it subtracts 1 from the value. They are both unary operators because they operate on only one operand. The statement

```
count++;
```

causes the value of count to be incremented, and the result stored back into the variable count. Therefore, it is basically equivalent to the following statement:

```
count = count + 1;
```

The increment and decrement operators can be applied after the variable (such as count++), creating what is called the *postfix* form of the operator. The increment and decrement operators can also be applied before the variable (such as ++count), creating what is called the *prefix* form. When used alone in a statement, the prefix and postfix forms are basically equivalent. That is, it doesn't matter if you write

```
count++;
```

or

```
++count;
```

although when such a form is written as a statement by itself, it is usually written in its postfix form.

However, when the increment or decrement operator is used in a larger expression, it can yield different results depending on the form used. For example, if the variable count currently contains the value 15, then the statement

```
total = count++;
```

assigns the value 15 to total and the value 16 to count. Whereas the statement

```
total = ++count;
```

assigns the value 16 to both total and count. The value of count is incremented in both situations, but the value used in the larger expression depends on whether a prefix or postfix form of the increment operator is used, as described in Fig. 5.9.

Expression	Operation	Value of Expression
count++	add 1 to count	the original value of count
++count	add 1 to count	the new value of count
count--	subtract 1 from count	the original value of count
--count	subtract 1 from count	the new value of count

Figure 5.9 Prefix and postfix forms

Let's look at another example. Consider the following statement, assuming the current value of the integer variable sum is 25.

```
System.out.println (sum++ + "   " + ++sum + "   " + sum + "   " + sum--);
```

The first increment operator increases sum to 26 but sends the original value 25 to the println method. The second increment is a prefix form, which changes sum to 27 and sends 27 to the println method. Then the current value of sum, which is 27, is printed. Finally, sum is decremented back to 26, but the original value of 27 is sent to the println method. So the output of that statement is

```
25   27   27   27
```

and the value of sum is 26 after that line is complete.

Because of the subtle differences between the prefix and postfix forms of the increment and decrement operators, they should be used with care. As always, favor the side of readability.

The increment and decrement operators can also be applied to character values. When applied to a character variable, the increment operator changes the value of the variable to the next character in the Unicode character set. The decrement operator results in the previous Unicode character. The prefix and postfix versions work on characters and have the same subtleties as they do with arithmetic values.

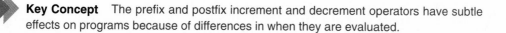

Key Concept   The prefix and postfix increment and decrement operators have subtle effects on programs because of differences in when they are evaluated.

Logical Operators

Java has three *logical operators* that take boolean operands and produce boolean results. They are listed and described in Fig. 5.10.

The ! operator is the *logical NOT* operation, also called the *logical complement*. The logical complement of a boolean value yields its opposite value. That is, if a boolean variable called found has the value false, then !found is true. Likewise, if found is true, then !found is false. The logical NOT does not change the value stored in found.

A logical operator can be defined by a *truth table* that lists all possible combinations of values for the variables involved in an expression. Because the logical

Operator	Description	Example	Result
!	logical NOT	! a	true if a is false and false if a is true
&&	logical AND	a && b	true if a and b are both true and false otherwise
||	logical OR	a || b	true if a or b or both are true and false otherwise

Figure 5.10 Java logical operators

NOT operator is unary, there are only two possible values for its one operand, true or false. The truth table for the ! operator is shown in Fig. 5.11.

The && operator performs a *logical AND*. The result is true if both operands are true, but false otherwise. Since it is a binary operator and each operand has two possible values, there are four combinations to consider. The truth table for && is shown in Fig. 5.12.

The result of the *logical OR* operator (\|\|) is true if one or the other or both operands are true, and false otherwise. It is also a binary operator, and its truth table is shown in Fig. 5.13.

The logical NOT has the highest precedence of the three logical operators, followed by logical AND, then logical OR. An expanded precedence table including the logical operators is presented later in this chapter.

 Key Concept Logical operators are a natural choice to implement a condition for a selection or repetition statement because they return a boolean value.

Logical operators are often used as part of a condition for a selection or repetition statement. For example, consider the following if statement:

```
if ( !done && (count > MAX) )
    System.out.println ("logical operators");
```

a	!a
false	true
true	false

Figure 5.11 Truth table for logical NOT (complement)

a	b	a && b
false	false	false
false	true	false
true	false	false
true	true	false

Figure 5.12   Truth table for logical AND

Under what conditions would the `println` statement be executed? The value of the boolean variable `done` is either true or false, and the NOT operator reverses that value. The value of `count` is either greater than MAX or it isn't. The truth table in Fig. 5.14 breaks down all of the possibilities.

An important chacteristic of the `&&` and `||` operators is that they are "short-circuited." That is, if their left operand is sufficient to decide the boolean result of the operation, then the right operand is not evaluated. This situation can occur with both operators but for different reasons. If the left operand of the `&&` operator is false, then the whole operation will be false, no matter what the value of the right operand. Likewise, if the left operand of the `||` is true, then the whole operation is true, no matter what the value of the right operand.

Sometimes you can capitalize on the fact that the operation is short-circuited. For example, the condition in the following `if` statement will not attempt to divide by zero if the left operand is false. If `count` has the value zero, then the left side of the `&&` operation is false, therefore the whole expression is false, and the right side is not evaluated.

```
if ( count != 0 && total / count > MAX )
   System.out.println ("testing");
```

Be careful when you count on these kinds of subtle programming language characteristics. Not all programming languages work the same way. As we have mentioned

a	b	a || b
false	false	false
false	true	true
true	false	true
true	true	true

Figure 5.13   Truth table for logical OR

done	count > MAX	!done	!done && (count > MAX)
false	false	true	false
false	true	true	true
true	false	false	false
true	true	false	false

Figure 5.14   A truth table for a specific condition

several times, you should always strive to make it extremely clear to the reader exactly how the logic of your program works.

Assignment Operators

As a convenience, several operators have been defined in Java that combine a basic operation with assignment. For example, the += operator can be used as follows

```
total += 5;
```

It has the same result as the statement

```
total = total + 5;
```

The right-hand side of the assignment operator can be a full expression. The expression on the right-hand side of the operator is evaluated, then that result is added to the current value of the variable on the left-hand side, and that value is stored in the variable. Therefore the statement

```
total += (sum - 12) / count;
```

is equivalent to

```
total = total + ((sum - 12) / count);
```

Many similar combination operators are defined in Java. They are listed in Fig. 5.15. The bitwise and boolean operators are described in Appendix E. There are no assignment operators that correspond to the logical operators !, &&, and || (though the boolean versions may suffice).

Operator	Description	Example	Equivalent Expression
=	assignment	x = y	x = y
+=	addition, then assignment	x += y	x = x + y
+=	string concatenation, then assignment	x += y	x = x + y
-=	subtraction, then assignment	x -= y	x = x - y
*=	multiplication, then assignment	x *= y	x = x * y
/=	division, then assignment	x /= y	x = x / y
%=	remainder, then assignment	x %= y	x = x % y
<<=	left shift, then assignment	x <<= y	x = x << y
>>=	right shift with sign, then assignment	x >>= y	x = x >> y
>>>=	right shift with zero, then assignment	x >>>= y	x = x >>> y
&=	bitwise AND, then assignment	x &= y	x = x & y
&=	boolean AND, then assignment	x &= y	x = x & y
^=	bitwise XOR, then assignment	x ^= y	x = x ^ y
^=	boolean XOR, then assignment	x ^= y	x = x ^ y
|=	bitwise OR, then assignment	x |= y	x = x | y
|=	boolean OR, then assignment	x |= y	x = x | y

Figure 5.15   Assignment operators

All of the assignment operators evaluate the entire expression on the right-hand side first, then use the result as the right operand of the other operation. Therefore, the statement

```
result *= count1 + count2
```

is equivalent to

```
result = result * (count1 + count2)
```

and the statement

```
result %= (highest - 40) / 2;
```

is equivalent to

```
result = result % ((highest - 40) / 2);
```

Some assignment operators perform particular functions depending on the types of the operands, just as their corresponding regular operators do. For example, if the operands to the += operator are strings, then it performs string concatenation.

The Conditional Operator

The Java *conditional operator* is a *ternary* operator because it requires three operands. The symbol for the conditional operator is usually written ?:, but it is not like other operators in that the two symbols that make it up are always separated. The general syntax for the conditional operator is:

```
condition ? expression1 : expression2
```

In many ways, the ?: operator is an abbreviated if-else statement. If the boolean *condition* is true, *expression1* is evaluated. If it is false, *expression2* is evaluated. Therefore the statement

```
total = (total > MAX) ? total + 1 : total * 2;
```

is basically equivalent to the following statement:

```
if (total > MAX)
   total = total + 1
else
   total = total * 2;
```

Because ?: is an operator, it returns a value. The two expressions must evaluate to the same type. The value that the conditional operator returns is the value of the expression that is evaluated, depending on the condition. Consider the following declaration:

```
int larger =  (num1 > num2) ? num1 : num2;
```

If num1 is greater than num2, then the value of num1 is returned and used to initialize the variable larger. If not, the value of num2 is returned and used. Similarly, the following statement prints the smaller of the two values:

```
System.out.println ("Smaller: " + (num1 < num2) ? num1 : num2);
```

The conditional operator is occasionally helpful to evaluate a short condition and return a result. It is not a replacement for an if-else statement, however, because the operands to the ?: operator are expressions, not necessarily full statements. Even when the conditional operator is a viable alternative, you should use it sparingly because it is not as readable as an if-else statement.

Precedence Revisited

Figure 5.16 shows the Java operator precedence for all operators discussed thus far in the text and includes the bitwise operators described in Appendix E. A complete precedence table with all Java operators is given in Appendix D. Operators with a lower precedence level number are evaluated before operators with higher precedence level numbers.

5.3 More Selection Statements

In Chapter 3 we introduced the `if` and the `if-else` selection statements. Now we will explore another selection statement called the `switch` statement, which directs the running program to follow one of many paths based on a single value. We also discuss the `break` statement in this section because it is often used with a `switch` statement.

The `switch` Statement

The *switch statement* is similar to the `if` statement except that it allows many values of an expression to be checked in a single statement. The syntax for the `switch` statement is:

```
switch (expression) {
    case value1:
        statement-list1
    case value2:
        statement-list2
    case ...
}
```

First, the `expression` is evaluated. Then execution transfers to the first statement identified by the `case` value that matches the result of the expression. The expression must be an integral type, such as an integer or a character. It cannot evaluate to a boolean or floating point value. Let's look at an example:

```
//   Counts the number of each vowel in a string.
class Vowels {

    public static void main (String[] args) {
```

Precedence Level	Operator	Operation	Associates
1	.	object member reference	L to R
	(*parameters*)	parameter evaluation and method invocation	
	++	postfix increment	
	--	postfix decrement	
2	++	prefix increment	R to L
	--	prefix decrement	
	+	unary plus	
	-	unary minus	
	~	bitwise NOT	
	!	logical NOT	
3	new	object instantiation	
	(*type*)	cast	
4	*	multiplication	L to R
	/	division	
	%	remainder	
5	+	addition	L to R
	+	string concatenation	
	-	subtraction	
6	<<	left shift	
	>>	right shift with sign	
	>>>	right shift with zero	
7	<	less than	L to R
	<=	less than or equal	
	>	greater than	
	>=	greater than or equal	
	instanceof	type comparison	
8	==	equal	L to R
	!=	not equal	
9	&	bitwise AND	L to R
	&	boolean AND	
10	^	bitwise XOR	L to R
	^	boolean XOR	
11	|	bitwise OR	L to R
	|	boolean OR	
12	&&	logical AND	L to R
13	||	logical OR	L to R

Figure 5.16 Java operator precedence (revised)

Precedence Level	Operator	Operation	Associates
14	? :	conditional operator	R to L
15	=	assignment	R to L
	+=	addition, then assignment	
	+=	string concatenation, then assignment	
	-=	subtraction, then assignment	
	*=	multiplication, then assignment	
	/=	division, then assignment	
	%=	remainder, then assignment	
	<<=	left shift, then assignment	
	>>=	right shift (sign), then assignment	
	>>>=	right shift (zero), then assignment	
	&=	bitwise AND, then assignment	
	&=	boolean AND, then assignment	
	^=	bitwise XOR, then assignment	
	^=	boolean XOR, then assignment	
	|=	bitwise OR, then assignment	
	|=	boolean OR, then assignment	

Figure 5.16   *(continued)*

```
int acount = 0, ecount = 0, icount = 0, ocount = 0;
int ucount = 0, other = 0, index = 0;
String quote = "We are the Borg.  Resistance is futile.";

while (index < quote.length()) {
    switch (quote.charAt (index)) {
        case 'a':
            acount++;
            break;
        case 'e':
            ecount++;
            break;
        case 'i':
            icount++;
            break;
        case 'o':
            ocount++;
            break;
```

The `switch` expression is matched to the appropriate case value.

```
                    case 'u':
                        ucount++;
                        break;
                    default:
                        other++;
                }
                index++;
            }

            System.out.println ("Quote: \"" + quote + "\"");
            System.out.println ("length = " + quote.length());
            System.out.println ("a: " + acount);
            System.out.println ("e: " + ecount);
            System.out.println ("i: " + icount);
            System.out.println ("o: " + ocount);
            System.out.println ("u: " + ucount);
            System.out.println ("other: " + other);

        } // method main

    } // class Vowels
```

The switch statement in the Vowels program is inside a loop that steps through each character in the string. The character at a particular position is used as the expression in the switch statement. Processing continues with the statement following the case value that matches the character. Each case in this example simply increments a counter to keep track of the number of each vowel that is encountered. The break statement causes the process flow to jump to the end of the switch statement body, and processing continues.

If no case value is found that matches the switch expression, control transfers to the default case. In Java, default is a reserved word. In the Vowels example, the default case counts all nonvowel characters that are encountered in the string. If no default section is provided in a switch statement and the expression does not match any given case value, then processing continues with the first statement after the switch body.

The output of the Vowels program is:

```
Quote: "We are the Borg.  Resistance is futile."
length = 39
a: 2
e: 6
i: 3
o: 1
u: 1
other: 26
```

Any `switch` statement can be implemented as a set of `if` statements. For example, the `switch` statement used in the `Vowels` program could be rewritten as a set of `if` statements:

```
if (quote.charAt (index) == 'a')
   acount++;
else if (quote.charAt (index) == 'e')
   ecount++;
else if (quote.charAt (index) == 'i')
   icount++;
else if (quote.charAt (index) == 'o')
   ocount++;
else if (quote.charAt (index) == 'u')
   ucount++;
else
   other++;
```

So why would we use a `switch` statement when we can always use `if` statements instead? There are several reasons. Perhaps most importantly, programs should be written so that they can be understood by a reader other than the author, and the `switch` is usually easier to read than a series of nested `if` statements. Second, the evaluated expression in the `switch` statement is repeated many times in an equivalent series of `if` statements that can become error prone when changes need to be made. Third, for a large `switch` statement, the compiler can generate slightly more efficient code than for the equivalent series of `if` statements. The choice to use a `switch` statement instead of a set of `if` statements depends on the nature of the problem being solved.

> **Key Concept** A `switch` statement can be implemented as a series of `if-then` statements.

The `break` statement is commonly used in `switch` statements to end the series of statements associated with a case value. In the `Vowels` program, it is used on every alternative except the `default` case. When the break statement is executed, the entire `switch` statement is terminated, and the statement following the `switch` statement is executed. Nevertheless, use of a `break` statement with every case value is not required. If the `break` statement is left out of one alternative, the execution will continue until it hits a break statement in another case alternative or the end of the `switch` statement is reached.

Key Concept   A break statement is necessary at the end of each case alternative in a switch statement to jump to the end of the switch.

The break statement also has another purpose, which we discuss in the next section as we explore additional repetition statements.

5.4   More Repetition Statements

We introduced the while statement in Chapter 3 as a fundamental repetition statement, or loop, which allows us to perform one or more statements repetitively. Java has two additional loops, the do statement and the for statement, which we will now explore. This section also discusses how the break statement can be used in a loop and how a similar construct, the continue statement, affects loop processing.

do Statement

The *do statement* is similar to the while statement, except that its termination condition is at the end of the body of the loop. The syntax of the do statement is:

```
do
    statement;
while (condition);
```

The do loop executes the *statement* in the loop body until the *condition* becomes false. The *condition* is evaluated at the end of the loop. Therefore the body of a do loop is always executed at least once. This process is shown in Fig. 5.17.

As always, we can use a block statement as the body of the loop if we need to do more than one thing repetitively. In fact, because the do loop uses the reserved word while, it is preferable to always use braces to indicate the beginning and the end of the loop body, even when it isn't necessary. This practice minimizes the con-

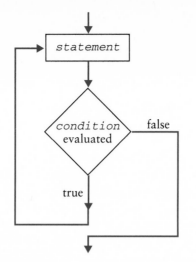

Figure 5.17 Processing a do statement

fusion that can result from reading the last line of the do statement and mistaking it for the first line of a while statement.

Let's look at an example that uses a do statement. The following program rolls a pair of dice and prints the result:

```
import java.io.*;
import java.util.Random;

//   Uses a do loop to roll two dice multiple times.
class Dice {

   public static void main (String[] args) throws IOException {

      BufferedReader stdin = new BufferedReader
         (new InputStreamReader (System.in));
      Random roll = new Random();
      int die1, die2;
      String again;

      do {
         System.out.println ("Rolling the dice...");
         die1 = Math.abs (roll.nextInt()) % 6 + 1;
         die2 = Math.abs (roll.nextInt()) % 6 + 1;
         System.out.println ("You rolled a " + (die1 + die2));
```

The body of the do loop executes at least once.

```
            System.out.print ("Roll again (y or n)? ");
            System.out.flush();
            again = stdin.readLine();

        } while (again.equals("y"));

    } // method main

} // class Dice
```

The do loop in the Dice program uses a Random object to simulate the die rolls, then prompts to see if the user wants to roll the dice again. This is an appropriate use for a do loop because the loop condition is determined by the user after the program has run at least once. If a while loop were used in this case, an initial value would have to be given to the variable again to ensure that the loop runs the first time. The do loop reflects the processing more realistically in this case.

If you know you want to perform the body of a loop at least once, then you probably want to use a do statement. Many of the while loops in previous examples could have, and probably should have, been written as do statements. A do loop has essentially the same properties as a while statement, so it must also be checked for termination conditions to avoid infinite loops and other problems.

> **Key Concept**   A do statement executes its loop body at least once.

for Statement

The while and the do statements are good to use when you don't initially know how many times you want to execute the loop body. The *for statement* is another repetition statement that is particularly well suited for executing the body of a loop a specific number of times. The syntax of the for statement is:

```
for (initialization; condition; increment)
    statement;
```

The header of a for loop contains three parts separated by semicolons. Executing the for statement starts by executing the *initialization* statement. Then the *condition* is evaluated. If it is false, processing continues with the first statement after the for loop. If the *condition* is true, the *statement* that makes up the

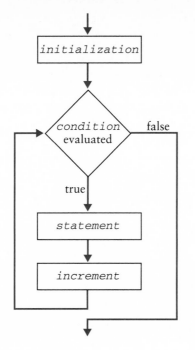

Figure 5.18   Processing a `for` statement

body of the `for` loop is executed. After the body of the loop is executed, the *increment* statement is executed. Then the *condition* is evaluated again, and the loop body is repeated if the *condition* is still true. After each execution of the loop body, the *increment* statement is executed. This process continues until the *condition* becomes false, as shown in Fig. 5.18.

Note that the *initialization* portion is only performed once, but the *increment* portion is executed after each iteration of the loop. The execution of a `for` loop is equivalent to the following code that uses a `while` statement:

```
initialization;
while (condition) {
    statement;
    increment;
}
```

Let's examine a program that uses a `for` loop. The following example modifies the `Dice` program we used earlier to roll the dice a specific number of times.

```
import java.util.Random;

//   Uses a for loop to roll two dice 1000 times.  It counts
//   the number of snake eyes (2) that occur.
class Dice2 {

   private final static int MAX_ROLLS = 1000;

   public static void main (String[] args) {

      Random roll = new Random();
      int die1, die2, snake_eyes = 0;

      for (int count=1; count <= MAX_ROLLS; count++) {
         die1 = Math.abs (roll.nextInt()) % 6 + 1;
         die2 = Math.abs (roll.nextInt()) % 6 + 1;

         if (die1 + die2 == 2)
            snake_eyes++;
      }

      System.out.print ("Out of " + MAX_ROLLS + " rolls, ");
      System.out.println ("you rolled snake eyes " + snake_eyes +
         " times.");

   } // method main

} // class Dice2
```

The `for` loop iterates a predetermined number of times.

The `Dice2` program uses a `for` loop that increments a variable called `count` from 1 to the value of `MAX_ROLLS`. Each iteration of the loop rolls the dice and counts the number of times that snake eyes (the value 2) comes up. The variable `count` is called a *loop control variable*.

Note that the initialization portion of the loop header actually declares the variable `count`, as well as initializing it. This practice is commonly used when the loop control variable is not needed outside of the loop body. Because `count` is declared in the `for` loop header, its scope is limited to the loop body and cannot be referenced elsewhere.

The loop control variable is set up, checked, and modified by the actions in the loop header. It can be referenced inside the loop body, but should not be modified.

The increment portion of the `for` loop does not have to perform a simple increment. For example, the following `for` loop prints the value of the loop control variable as its value changes in steps of 2:

```
for (num=1; num <= 100; num += 2)
   System.out.println (num);
```

Let's look at another example. The following `for` loop prints several powers of 5:

```
for (num=5; num <= 78125; num *= 5)
   System.out.println (num);
```

 Key Concept   A `for` statement is usually used when a loop will be executed a set number of times.

Using the `break` Statement in Loops

We've seen how the `break` statement can be used in a `switch` statement. The `break` statement can also be used in the body of any loop. Its effect on a loop is similar to its effect on a `switch` statement. The execution of the loop is stopped, and the statement following the loop is executed. Consider the following `for` loop:

```
for (int num=1; num <= 20; num++) {
   if (num == 12)
      break;
   System.out.println ("num is " + num);
}
```

The loop is set up to execute the body of the loop 20 times, but the `break` statement is executed when num becomes 12. Once a `break` has been executed, the condition of the loop is not evaluated again. Processing continues with the statement after the loop.

It is never necessary to use a `break` statement in a loop. An equivalent loop can always be written without it. Because the `break` statement causes program flow to jump from one place to another, using a `break` in a loop is not good practice. Its use is tolerated in a `switch` statement because an equivalent `switch` statement cannot be written without it. But you can and should avoid it in a loop.

The `continue` Statement

When a *continue statement* is executed in a loop, the remainder of the loop body is skipped and another iteration of the loop begins. The `continue` statement is similar to a *break*, but the loop condition is evaluated again, and the loop body is executed

Expressions and the `for` statement

The `for` statement is unique, since it combines three expressions to control a loop. Intermixing various types of expressions with the `for` loop can produce interesting and sometimes unexpected results. Consider the following `for` statement header:

```
for (int count=1; count <= MAX_ROLLS; count++)
```

Because the increment expression uses a postfix increment operator we can rewrite the loop, producing the same number of iterations, but not the same exact results:

```
for (int count=1; count++ <= MAX_ROLLS;)
```

This change causes the loop to iterate between 2 and `MAX_ROLLS + 1`. Note that the increment expression is left empty because the increment occurs after the conditional expression is evaluated. Using the prefix increment operator instead of the postfix increment operator:

```
for (int count=1; ++count <= MAX_ROLLS;)
```

the result is changed again. In this case, `count` would be incremented before the evaluation of the condition. Even though theses changes were subtle, the impact on the execution of the `for` statement is dramatic. For this reason, using a complicated condition is not considered good programming practice.

In the header of a `for` loop each of the expressions is optional. Consider the `for` statement:

```
for (;;)
```

When the initialization part is left out, no initialization is performed. When the condition is left out, the condition is always considered to be true (therefore it is an infinite loop). When the increment part is left out, no increment operation is performed.

In general, the simple forms of the `for` statement, with each portion in the header clearly specified, are preferred and lead to fewer errors in programs.

if it is still true. Consider the following `for` statement. It is identical to the earlier example, except that a `continue` statement is executed when num becomes 12.

```
for (int num=1, num <= 20, num++) {
   if (num == 12)
      continue;
   System.out.println ("num is " + num);
}
```

When num is 12, the `continue` statement causes the `println` statement to be skipped for that iteration. But the `for` loop still increments the value of num to 13 and reevaluates the condition. Because the condition is still true (13 is less than 20), processing precedes. The `continue` statement will not be executed again because num will never again be 12. Therefore the `for` loop prints the value of num from 1 to 11, skips 12, then prints its value from 13 to 20.

Like the `break` statement, the `continue` statement can always be avoided in a loop, and for the same reasons, it should be.

Labels

In Java, it is possible to put a *label* on a line and refer to the label in a `break` or `continue` statement. The syntax of a `break` statement is either

```
break;
```

or

```
break label;
```

and the syntax of a `continue` statement is either

```
continue;
```

or

```
continue label;
```

A label is usually used only if a `break` or `continue` is used inside nested loops. For a `break` statement, the flow of control is transferred to the statement after the labeled statement. For a `continue` statement, control is transferred to the beginning of the loop identified by the label.

As we discussed earlier, the `break` and `continue` statements should not be used in a loop. Therefore, there is no need to use labels either, and they should be avoided.

Summary of Key Concepts

- Two's complement format is a representation scheme for negative numbers that makes internal arithmetic processing easier.
- Underflow and overflow can produce incorrect results. Always ensure that types with enough storage space for the possible range of values produced by calculations are used.
- Java uses the standard IEEE 754 floating point format to represent real numbers.
- Java uses the Unicode character set to represent characters. This representation enables programs to support many different languages.
- Avoid narrowing conversions because they can lose information.
- The prefix and postfix increment and decrement operators have subtle effects on programs, because of differences in when they are evaluated.
- Logical operators are a natural choice to implement a condition for a selection or repetition statement because they return a boolean value.
- A `switch` statement can be implemented as a series of `if-then` statements.
- A `break` statement is necessary at the end of each case alternative in a `switch` statement to jump to the end of the `switch`.
- A `do` statement executes its loop body at least once.
- A `for` statement is usually used when a loop will be executed a set number of times.

Self-Review Questions

5.1 What is a character set?

5.2 Which character set is used by Java? Why was this character set chosen?

5.3 Convert the decimal number −44 into two's complement binary representation.

5.4 Consider the following two's complement binary number: `10111011`. What value does it represent in decimal?

5.5 Explain why every operator must have a precedence.

5.6 What is the primary reason for using the following iteration statements: `while`, `do`, and `for`?

5.7 How can the `switch` statement be replaced with a series of `if-else` statements?

5.8 What is the difference between the `break` and `continue` statements? When should they be used?

Exercises

5.9 Represent the following integer values in two's complement using eight bits:
   a. −100
   b. 32
   c. −32
   d. −40
   e. −128
   f. 127
   g. −127

5.10 The following binary numbers are stored in two's complement format. What are their decimal equivalents?
   a. 01010101
   b. 10101010
   c. 00001000
   d. 10001111
   e. 01110000
   f. 10111011
   g. 00111111
   h. 11111111

5.11 Compare and contrast the Java representations of integer and floating point numbers.

5.12 What is the value of the integer variables `total` and `num` after each of the following statements? Assume the variables `total` and `num` contain the values 2 and 3, respectively, at the beginning of each statement.
   a. `total = ++ num;`
   b. `num = total ++;`
   c. `total = ++ num + num ++;`

5.13 What is the value of the integer variable `total` after each of the following statements? Assume the variables `total`, `num1`, and `num2` contain the values 2, 3, and 4, respectively, at the beginning of each statement.
   a. `total *= 5;`
   b. `total %= 4;`
   c. `total += num1 - num2 * 4;`
   d. `total = (num1 == 7) ? num1 : num2;`

5.14 Write a `switch` statement that counts the letters `'a'`, `'e'`, `'m'`, and `'t'` in a string called `str`.

5.15 Write a `switch` statement that evaluates an integer between the numbers 1 through 12 inclusive and prints a string that represents the corresponding month name. Print an error message if the integer value is not valid.

5.16 Rewrite the following `switch` statement using `if-else` statements:

```
switch (number) {
   case 1:
       System.out.println ("digits");
       break;
   case 10:
       System.out.println ("tens");
       break;
   case 100:
       System.out.println ("hundreds");
       break;
   case 1000:
       System.out.println ("thousands");
       break;
   case 10000:
       System.out.println ("ten thousands");
       break;
   default:
       System.out.println ("error");
}
```

5.17 What is the output of the following code:

```
index = 1;
do {
   System.out.println (index);
   index++;
} while (index < 10);
```

5.18 What is the output of the following code:

```
index = 1;
do {
   System.out.println (index);
} while (index < 10);
```

5.19 Write the following code using a do loop:

```
index = 1;
while (index < 10) {
   System.out.println (index);
   index++;
}
```

5.20 Repeat Problem 5.19 using a `for` loop.

5.21 Write the following code using a `for` loop:

```
index = 1;
while (index < 10) {
    index++;
    System.out.println (index);
}
```

Programming Projects

5.22 Write a program that prints in two columns the values 1, 2, etc., up to 25, and a running sum of those values. For example, the following is a table for the values 1 through 5:

```
Value   Sum
  1      1
  2      3
  3      6
  4      10
  5      15
```

5.23 Implement a class that may be used by a bank that uses a `for` loop to compute compound interest. Its constuctor should accept a starting balance, interest rate, and the number of times to compute the interest. The class should have appropriate methods that allow a larger program to compute and use compound interest. Write a main program to exercise the class.

5.24 Implement a class named `Grade_Histogram` that provides a method to read a series of letter grades (A, B, C, D, E, F) from a user and counts the number of each grade. Also, provide a method that prints a histogram of the letter-grades distribution. The class implementation should make use of the `switch` statement and the `for` statement. Test the class implementation using an appropriate `main` program and input.

5.25 Rewrite the class in Problem 5.24 to be an applet, where the histogram is graphically represented.

5.26 Write a program that presents several numbered menu choices to a user. The choices should represent information about your home state. The menu choices should be state name, state capitol, state bird, state flower, state population, and quit. The program should print out a menu and solicit input from the user. When the user indicates a choice, the appropriate information is printed. After each selection is made, the menu choices are reprinted and the user is prompted for another selection. The user can continue to select menu choices until the quit option is chosen. If an invalid menu choice is made, an error message should be printed. Implement the program using a `switch` statement and a `do` loop.

Answers to Self-Review Questions

5.1 A character set equates a unique number to each character. A programming language uses a particular character set. A character, when stored in memory, is converted to its numeric equivalent. This conversion is necessary because memory devices store only numeric values.

5.2 Java uses the Unicode character set. Since each Unicode character is stored as a 16-bit binary string, Unicode is capable of storing many thousands of characters and symbols, and is used to represent characters from many languages across the world.

5.3 The decimal value 44 is represented in binary as `00101100`. To negate it, invert all of the bits to `11010011`, then add 1, yielding `11010100`. Therefore, -44 is represented in two's complement format as `11010100`.

5.4 The value `10111011` has a 1 in the sign bit (far left); therefore this two's complement value represents a negative number. To convert it, invert all of the bits to `01000100`, then add 1, yielding `01000101`, which is 67 in decimal. Therefore, `10111011` in two's complement format represents -67.

5.5 Evaluation of expressions involving operators should not be ambiguous. If every operator did not have a precedence there would be multiple ways to evaluate expressions.

5.6 Use a `while` statement when you want to use a statement as long as a particular condition is true. Use a `do` statement for the same reason as a `while`, except that you want the loop body to be executed at least once. Use a `for` statement to repeat a statement a set number of times. Any of these loops can be rewritten in either of the other two forms.

5.7 A `switch` statement can always be rewritten as a series of `if-else` statements by creating an if condition for each case value in the `switch`. The statements associated with each case value are executed in the appropriate `if` statement. It is very difficult to rewrite a `switch` statement that does not use a `break` statement at the end of each case.

5.8 A `break` statement will terminate the execution of the body of the switch or loop. A `continue` statement begins the next iteration of the loop in which it is contained.

Objects for
Organizing Data

6

There are many language features that help you manage and organize data. We often want to gather objects or primitive data in a form that is easy to access and modify. This chapter introduces arrays, which are programming constructs that group data into ordered lists. They are a fundamental component of most high-level languages. We then explore the Vector class in the Java API, which provides capabilities similar to arrays. Finally, this chapter revisits the support Java provides for string management, extending our discussion of the StringTokenizer class and introducing the StringBuffer class.

Chapter Objectives

- Define and use arrays for basic data organization.
- Describe how arrays and array elements are passed as parameters.
- Explore how arrays and other objects can be combined to manage complex information.
- Examine the Vector class and the costs of its versatility.
- Revisit the StringTokenizer class to process string information.
- Compare and contrast the String and StringBuffer classes.

6.1 Arrays

An array is a simple but powerful programming language construct used to group and organize data. When writing a program that manages a large amount of information, such as a list of 100 names, it is not feasible to declare separate variables for each piece of data. Arrays solve this problem by letting us declare one variable that can hold multiple values.

Basic Arrays

An *array* is an ordered list of values. Each value is stored at a specific, numbered position in the array. The number corresponding to each position is called an *index* or a *subscript*. Figure 6.1 shows an array of integers and the indexes that correspond to each position. The array is called `height` and it contains integers that represent several people's heights in inches.

In Java, array indexes always begin at zero. Therefore, the value stored at index 5 is actually the sixth value in the array. The array in Fig. 6.1 has 11 values, indexed from zero to 10.

To access a value in an array, you use the name of the array followed by the index in square brackets. For example, the following expression refers to the ninth value in the array `height`:

```
height[8]
```

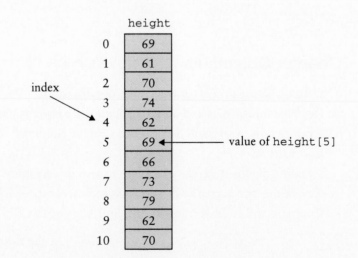

Figure 6.1   An array called `height` containing integer values

According to Fig. 6.1, `height[8]` (pronounced height-sub-eight) contains the value 79. Don't confuse the value of the index, in this case 8, with the value stored in the array at that index, in this case 79.

▶ **Key Concept**   A Java array of size *N* is indexed from 0 to *N*−1.

The expression `height[8]` refers to a single integer stored at a particular memory location. It can be used wherever an integer variable can be used. Therefore, you can assign a value to it, use it in calculations, print its value, and so on. Furthermore, because array indexes are integers, you can use integer expressions to determine the index into an array. These concepts are demonstrated in the following lines of code:

```
height[2] = 72;

height[count] = feet * 12;

average = (height[0] + height[1] + height[2]) / 3;

System.out.println ("The middle value is " + height[MAX/2]);

pick = height[rand.nextInt()%11];
```

In Java, arrays are objects. To create an array, the reference to the array must be declared. The array can then be instantiated using the `new` operator, which allocates memory space to store values. The following code represents the declaration for the array shown in Fig. 6.1:

```
int[] height = new int[11];
```

The variable `height` is declared to be an array of integers (`int[]`). An array contains multiple values all having the same type. For example, we can create an array that can hold integers or an array that can hold strings, but not an array that can hold both integers and strings. Note that the type of the variable (`int[]`) does not include the size of the array. The instantiation of height, using the `new` operator, reserves the memory space to store 11 integers indexed from 0 to 10. Once an array is declared to be a certain size, the number of values it can hold cannot be changed.

The following program creates an array called `list` that can hold 15 integers, and loads it with successive increments of 10. It then changes the value of the sixth element in the array (at index 5). Finally, it prints all values stored in the array. It is often convenient to use `for` loops when handling arrays because the number of positions in the array is constant. Figure 6.2 shows the array as it changes during program execution.

```
//  Shows basic array declaration and use.
class Basic_Array {
    final static int LIMIT = 15;
    final static int INCREMENT = 10;

    public static void main (String[] args) {
        int[] list = new int[LIMIT];
```

An array is an object that must be instantiated.

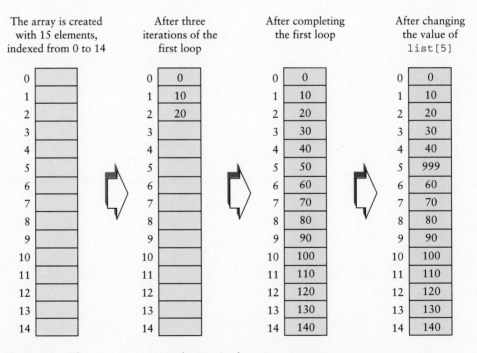

| The array is created with 15 elements, indexed from 0 to 14 | After three iterations of the first loop | After completing the first loop | After changing the value of `list[5]` |

Figure 6.2 The array `list` as it changes in the `Basic_Array` program

```
    // Initialize array values
    for (int index = 0; index < LIMIT; index++)
        list[index] = index * INCREMENT;

    list[5] = 999;  // Change one array value

    for (int index = 0; index < LIMIT; index++)
        System.out.print (list[index] + "  ");

    System.out.println ();
  }  // method main

}  // class Basic_Array
```

Note that a constant called LIMIT is used in several places in the Basic_Array program: to declare the size of the array, to control the for loop that initializes the array values, and to control the for loop that prints the values. The use of constants in this way is a good practice. It makes your program more readable and easier to modify. For instance, if the size of the array needed to change, only one line of code (the constant declaration) would need to be modified.

When executed, the Basic_Array program prints the following:

```
0  10  20  30  40  999  60  70  80  90  100  110  120  130  140
```

The square brackets used to indicate the index of an array are treated as an operator in Java. Therefore, just like the + operator or the <= operator, the *index operator* ([]) has a precedence relative to the other Java operators that determines when it is executed. It has the highest precedence of all Java operators.

The index operator performs automatic *bounds checking,* which requires that the index is in range for the array being referenced. Whenever a reference to an array element is made, the index must be greater than or equal to zero and less than the size of the array. For example, suppose an array called prices is created with 25 elements. The valid indexes for the array are from 0 to 24. Whenever a reference is made to a particular element in the array (such as prices[count]), the value of the index is checked. If it is in the valid range of indexes for the array (0 to 24), the reference is carried out. If the index is not valid, an exception called ArrayIndexOutOfBoundsException is thrown.

Key Concept Bounds checking ensures that an index used to refer to an array element is in range. The Java index operator performs automatic bounds checking.

Because array indexes begin at zero and go up to one less than the size of the array, it is easy to inadvertently create *off-by-one errors* in a program. When referencing array elements, be careful to ensure that the index stays within the array bounds. This problem is specifically noted in the review checklist in Appendix H.

Another important characteristic of Java arrays is that their size is held in a constant called `length` in the array object. It is a `public` constant, and therefore can be referenced directly. For example, after the array `prices` is created with 25 elements, the constant `prices.length` contains the value 25. Its value is set once when the array is first created and cannot be changed. The `length` constant, which is an integral part of each array, can be used when the array size is needed instead of using a separate constant (as we did in the `Basic_Array` program).

Let's look at another example. The following program reads 10 integers into an array called `numbers`, and then prints them in reverse order.

```java
import java.io.*;

// Reads a set of integers from the user, storing them in an
// array, then prints them in the opposite order.
class Reverse_Numbers {

    public static void main (String[] args) throws IOException {
        int[] numbers = new int[10];
        BufferedReader stdin = new BufferedReader
            (new InputStreamReader (System.in));

        System.out.println ("The size of the array is: " +
                                numbers.length);

        for (int index = 0; index < numbers.length; index++) {
            System.out.print ("Number " + index + ": ");
            System.out.flush();
            numbers[index] = Integer.parseInt (stdin.readLine());
        }

        System.out.println ("Numbers in reverse:");
        for (int index = numbers.length-1; index >= 0; index-)
            System.out.print (numbers[index] + "  ");

        System.out.println ();

    } // method main

} // class Reverse_Numbers
```

A sample run of the `Reverse_Numbers` program might be:

```
The size of the array is: 10
Number 0: 1
Number 1: 2
Number 2: 3
Number 3: 4
Number 4: 5
Number 5: 6
Number 6: 7
Number 7: 8
Number 8: 9
Number 9: 10
Numbers in reverse:
10  9  8  7  6  5  4  3  2  1
```

Note that in the `Reverse_Numbers` program the array `numbers` is declared to have 10 elements and therefore is indexed from 0 to 9. The index range is controlled in the `for` loops using the `length` field of the array object. You should carefully control the initial value of loop control variables and the conditions that terminate loops, to guarantee that only valid indexes are used to reference an array element.

The next example uses two arrays: one to hold the test scores of a group of students and another to hold modified scores after they are adjusted (if necessary) so that the average grade is approximately equal to 75. The program reads the original list of test scores from the user.

```java
import java.io.*;

//  Read and adjust a set of test scores.
class Adjust_Test_Scores {
   private final static int DESIRED = 75;
   private final static int STUDENTS = 10;

   public static void main (String[] args) throws IOException {
      BufferedReader stdin = new BufferedReader
         (new InputStreamReader (System.in));
      int[] test = new int[STUDENTS], shifted = new int[STUDENTS];
      int sum = 0, bonus;
      float average;
```

```
System.out.println ("Enter " + test.length + " grades:");
for (int grade = 0; grade < STUDENTS; grade++) {
    test[grade] = Integer.parseInt (stdin.readLine());
    sum += test[grade];
}

average = (float) sum / STUDENTS;
System.out.println ("Average = " + average);
bonus = DESIRED - (int) average;
if (bonus <= 0)
    System.out.println ("No adjustment required");
else {
    System.out.println ("Original  Adjusted");
    for (int grade = 0; grade < STUDENTS; grade++) {
        shifted[grade] = test[grade] + bonus;
        System.out.print ("   " + test[grade]);
        System.out.println ("          " + shifted[grade]);
    }
}
} // method main

} // class Adjust_Test_Scores
```

Two arrays processed in parallel

If the following values were entered as input to the `Adjust_Test_Scores` program (one per line): 91, 67, 69, 54, 94, 60, 69, 82, 67, and 81, then the program would produce the following output:

```
Average = 73.4
Original  Adjusted
   91        93
   67        69
   69        71
   54        56
   94        96
   60        62
   69        71
   82        84
   67        69
   81        83
```

Note that a constant called `STUDENTS` is used throughout the program in various ways. The constants `test.length` or `shifted.length` could have been used in the same situations, but probably wouldn't have conveyed as much information to the user. A programmer must assess each situation and decide the best course of action when it comes to the use of constants, especially when dealing with arrays. There is no one best answer that will work in all situations.

Alternate Array Syntax

Syntactically, there are two ways to declare an array reference in Java. The first, which is used in the previous examples and throughout this book, is by associating the brackets with the type of the values stored in the array. The second technique is to associate the brackets with the name of the array. Therefore, the following two declarations are equivalent:

```
int[] grades;
```

```
int grades[];
```

Although there is no difference between these declaration techniques as far as the compiler is concerned, the first is consistent with other types of declarations. Consider the following declarations:

```
int total, sum, result;
```

```
int[] grade1, grade2, grade3;
```

In the first declaration, the type of the three variables, `int`, is given at the beginning of the line. Similarly, in the second declaration, the type of the three variables, `int[]`, is also given at the beginning. In both cases, the type applies to all variables in that particular declaration.

When the alternative form of array declaration is used, it can lead to confusing situations, such as the following:

```
int grade1[], grade2, grade3[];
```

The variables `grade1` and `grade3` are declared to be arrays of integers, but `grade2` is a single integer. Although most declarations declare variables of the same type, this example declares variables of two different types. Why did the programmer write a declaration this way? Is it a mistake? Should `grade2` be an array? This confusion is eliminated if the array brackets are associated with the element's type.

Therefore we associate the brackets with the element's type throughout this book. The coding guidelines in Appendix G reinforce this style decision.

Initializer Lists

An important alternative technique for instantiating arrays is the use of an *initializer list* that lists the initial values for the elements of the array. It is essentially the same idea as initializing a variable of a primitive data type in its declaration, except that an array requires several values. The items in an initializer list are separated by commas and delimited by braces ({ }). When an initializer list is used, the new operator is not used. The size of the array is determined by the number of items in the initializer list. For example:

```
int[] scores = {87, 98, 69, 54, 65, 76, 87, 99};
```

The array scores is instantiated as an array of eight integers, indexed from 0 to 7. An initializer list can only be used when an array is first declared.

Key Concept   An initializer list can be used to instantiate the array object, instead of using the new operator. The size of the array and its initial values are determined by the initializer list.

The type of each value in an initializer list must match the type of the array elements. Let's look at another example:

```
char[] letter_grades = {'A', 'B', 'C', 'D', 'F'};
```

In this case, the variable letter_grades is declared to be an array of five characters, and the initializer list contains character literals. The following program demonstrates the use of an initializer list to instantiate an array:

```
//  Uses an initilizer list to set up an array containing
//  prime numbers.
class Primes {

    public static void main (String[] args) {
        int[] primes = {2, 3, 5, 7, 11, 13, 17, 19};
```

An array created using an initializer list

```
      System.out.println ("The first few prime numbers:");
      for (int prime = 0; prime < primes.length; prime++)
         System.out.print (primes[prime] + "   ");
      System.out.println ();

   }  // method main

}  // class Primes
```

When executed, the `Primes` program prints the following:

```
The first few prime numbers:
2   3   5   7   11   13   17   19
```

Example: Monthly Sales

Let's look at a more involved example using arrays. The following program uses a class called `Monthly_Sales` that provides services to:

- compute the total sales for the year
- compute the average sales per month
- determine the month of the highest sales
- return the sales value for a particular month
- print a table showing the month number and corresponding sales

The program provides an end-of-the-year analysis for a fictitious company. The `main` method in the `Sales_Analysis` class instantiates one `Monthly_Sales` object and exercises it.

An array called `revenue` is maintained by the `Monthly_Sales` class and is used by most of its methods. The `revenue` array contains the total sales for each month of one year and is created using an initializer list. The array is declared with 13 elements so that it can be indexed from 0 to 12. The first element at index zero is ignored in the program. This way, the index for each sales value corresponds to the month number, 1 through 12, in which those sales were made.

```
//  Performs a year-end analysis on some sales data.
class Sales_Analysis {

   public static void main (String[] args) {
      Monthly_Sales sales = new Monthly_Sales ();
      int best;
```

```java
        System.out.println ("End of the Year Report");
        System.out.println ();
        sales.print_table();
        System.out.println ("Total sales: " + sales.total ());
        System.out.println ("Average sales: " + sales.average ());
        best = sales.highest_month();
        System.out.print ("Best month was " + best + " with revenue ");
        System.out.println (sales.months_revenue (best));
    }  // method main


}  // class Sales_Analysis


//  Contains the sales data and methods to perform the analysis.
class Monthly_Sales {
    private final int JANUARY = 1;
    private final int DECEMBER = 12;
    private int [] revenue = {0, 1692, 2504, 2469,
                                 1826, 2369, 3699,
                                 2383, 2697, 2569,
                                 1986, 2692, 2536};


    public int total () {
        int sum = 0;
        for (int month = JANUARY; month <= DECEMBER; month++)
            sum += revenue[month];
        return sum;
    }  // method total


    public int average () {
        return  total() / DECEMBER;
    }  // method average


    public int highest_month () {
        int highest = JANUARY;
        for (int month = JANUARY+1; month <= DECEMBER; month++)
            if (revenue[highest] < revenue[month])
                highest = month;
        return highest;
    }  // method highest_month
```

```java
    public int months_revenue (int month) {
        return revenue[month];
    }  // method months_revenue

    public void print_table () {
        System.out.println ("Month\tSales");
        for (int month = JANUARY; month <= DECEMBER; month++)
            System.out.println ("  " + month + "\t" + revenue[month]);
        System.out.println ();
    }  // method print_table

}  // class Monthly_Sales
```

When executed, the `Sales_Analysis` program produces the following output:

```
End of the Year Report
Month    Sales
  1      1692
  2      2504
  3      2469
  4      1826
  5      2369
  6      3699
  7      2383
  8      2697
  9      2569
 10      1986
 11      2692
 12      2536
Total sales: 29422
Average sales: 2451
Best month was 6 with revenue 3699
```

As with all objects, an array reference is initialized to `null` if it is not explicitly made to refer to an array object when the variable is declared. Furthermore, when an array object is instantiated, each element in the array is initialized to its appropriate default value unless explicitly initialized in the declaration. For example, each integer in an array of integers is initialized to zero when that array is first instantiated. However, as with all other variables, for clarity you should not rely on default initializations.

Arrays of Objects

Arrays can have references to objects as elements. For example, consider the following declaration:

```
String[] words = new String[25];
```

The variable words is an array of references to String objects. The new operator in the declaration instantiates the array, and reserves space for 25 String references, but it does not create any String objects. Each String that is assigned to the array must be instantiated separately.

 Key Concept Instantiating an array of objects only reserves room to store references. The objects that are stored in each element must be instantiated separately.

Let's look at a program that uses an array of objects. The following program creates an array of String objects and prints them out:

An array can hold references to objects.

```
//  Sets up and prints an array of String objects.
class Children {

    public static void main (String[] args) {
        String[] name_list = {"Joshua", "Bethany", "Megan", "Eric"};

        for (int name = 0; name < name_list.length; name++)
            System.out.println (name_list[name]);
    }  // method main

}  // class Children
```

The initializer list in the declaration instantiates the array of String references. Then, because a String literal automatically instantiates a String object, each

String literal in the initializer list creates an actual object to which the elements of the array refer. When executed, the Children program prints the following:

```
Joshua
Bethany
Megan
Eric
```

The formal parameter to the main method is always an array of String objects. This array is used to store command-line arguments, as discussed in Chapter 2.

The following program is similar to the previous example, except that the strings stored in the array are read in from the user. The declaration of the variable names instantiates an array of seven String references. The String objects that are assigned to the array elements are instantiated by the readLine method. After reading the list of strings, the program prints them out in reverse order.

```java
import java.io.*;

//  Reads several strings into an array and prints them
//  in reverse order.
class Presidents {

   public static void main (String[] args) throws IOException {
      BufferedReader stdin = new BufferedReader
         (new InputStreamReader (System.in));
      String[] names = new String[5];

      System.out.println ("Enter " + names.length + " Presidents:");
      for (int name = 0; name < names.length; name++)
         names[name] = stdin.readLine();

      System.out.println ("The names you entered, in reverse:");
      for (int name = names.length-1; name >= 0; name-)
         System.out.println (names[name]);
   }  // method main

}  // class Presidents
```

Let's look at a sample run of the program:

```
Enter 5 presidents:
Clinton
Bush
Reagan
Carter
Ford
The names you entered, in reverse:
Ford
Carter
Reagan
Bush
Clinton
```

Fairly complex information management structures can be created using only arrays and other objects. For example, an array could contain objects, and each of those objects could contain several variables and the methods that use them. Those variables could themselves be arrays, and so on. The design of a program should capitalize on the ability to combine these constructs to create the most appropriate representation for all information.

Let's look at another program, called Roll_Call. It uses a class called Membership to manage a list of members of an organization. The Membership class uses an array of objects instantiated from another class called Member. The Member class contains information about each member, including their name and membership number. Figure 6.3 graphically depicts how the objects and arrays are arranged to represent the roster of members. The main method instantiates a Membership roster, which in turn instantiates several Member objects. It then uses the method find_member to search the membership list for a particular membership number. The find_member method implements a simple *linear search,* which steps

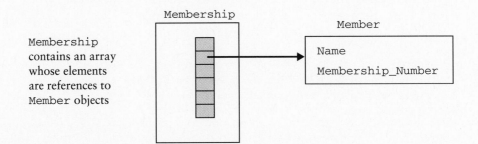

Figure 6.3 Using arrays and objects to represent information

through the entire array one element at a time until it finds the desired object or until it reaches the end of the array. Other types of search techniques are explored in Chapter 13. Before terminating, the `main` method prints the entire roster of members.

```
//  Creates and searches a membership list.
class Roll_Call {

    public static void main (String[] args) {
        Membership roster = new Membership();
        Member person;
        System.out.println();
        person = roster.find_member(26911);
        if (person == null)
           System.out.println ("No match found");
        else {
           System.out.println ("The search found the following member:");
           person.print();
        }
        System.out.println();
        roster.print();
    }  // method main

}  // class Roll_Call

//  Stores the membership list and methods to search it.
class Membership {

    private Member[] member_list;
    private int num_members;

    public Membership() {
        num_members = 4;
        member_list = new Member[4];
        member_list[0] = new Member ("Johnny Storm", 70469);
        member_list[1] = new Member ("Sue Richards", 69048);
        member_list[2] = new Member ("Reed Richards", 26911);
        member_list[3] = new Member ("Ben Grimm", 89696);
    }  // constructor Membership

    public Member find_member (int target) {
        int index = 0;
        while (index < num_members) {
            if (member_list[index].get_membership_number() == target)
                return member_list[index];
```

```
                    index++;
            }
            return null;
    }   // method find_member

    public void print() {
        System.out.println ("\nMember\t\tId #");
        for (int person=0; person < num_members; person++)
            member_list[person].print();
    }   // method print

}   // class Membership

//  Represents an individual club member.
class Member {

    private String name;
    private int membership_number;

    Member (String member_name, int id_number) {
        name = member_name;
        membership_number = id_number;
    }   // constructor Member

    public int get_membership_number() {
        return membership_number;
    }   // method get_membership_number

    public void print() {
        System.out.println (name + "\t" + membership_number);
    }   // method print

} // class Member
```

When executed, the Roll_Call program produces the following output:

```
The search found the following member:
Reed Richards    26911
Member           Id #
Johnny Storm     70469
Sue Richards     69048
Reed Richards    26911
Ben Grimm        89696
```

Arrays as Parameters

An entire array can be passed as a parameter to a method. Because an array is an object, when an entire array is passed as a parameter, a copy of the reference to the original array is passed. The method can change an element of the array permanently, because it is referring to the original element value. The method cannot change the reference itself, because a copy of the original reference is sent to the method. These rules are consistent with the rules that govern any object type.

Key Concept An entire array can be passed as a parameter, making the formal parameter an alias to the original.

An element of an array can be passed to a method as well. If the type of the element is a primitive type, a copy of the value is passed. If that element is a reference to an object, a copy of the object reference is passed. The impact of changes made to a parameter inside the method depends on the type of the parameter, as described in Chapter 4.

The following program instantiates two arrays, then attempts to modify them in various ways using methods. The Array_Test class contains the main method that creates the arrays. The Array_Parameters class contains several methods that accept arrays or array elements as parameters and performs simple modifications to them.

```
//  Exercises parameter passing with arrays.
class Array_Test {

   public static void main (String[] args) {
      Array_Parameters tester = new Array_Parameters ();
      int[] list = {11, 22, 33, 44, 55};
      int[] list2 = {99, 99, 99, 99, 99};

      tester.print ("Original array:", list);
      tester.pass_element (list[0]);
      tester.print ("After passing one element:", list);
      tester.change_elements (list);
      tester.print ("After changing individual elements:", list);
      tester.change_reference (list, list2);
      tester.print ("After attempting to change a reference:", list);
      tester.copy_array (list, list2);
```

```
            tester.print ("After copying each array element:", list);
            list = tester.return_reference (list2);
            tester.print ("After returning a reference:", list);
        }   // method main

    }   // class Array_Test

    //   Contains methods that modify parameters.
    class Array_Parameters {
        public void pass_element (int num) {
            System.out.println ("The value of num is " + num);
            num = 1234;
            System.out.println ("The value of num is now " + num);
        }   // method pass_element

        public void change_elements (int[] mylist) {
            mylist[2] = 77;
            mylist[4] = 88;
        }   // method change_elements

        public void change_reference (int[] mylist, int[] mylist2) {
            mylist = mylist2;
        }   // method change_reference

        public void copy_array (int[] mylist, int[] mylist2) {
            for (int index=0; index < mylist.length; index++)
                mylist[index] = mylist2[index];
        }   // method copy_array

        public int[] return_reference (int[] mylist2) {
            mylist2[1] = 9876;
            return mylist2;
        }   // method return_reference

        public void print (String message, int[] mylist) {
            System.out.println (message);
            for (int index=0; index < mylist.length; index++)
                System.out.print (mylist[index] + "   ");
            System.out.println ();
        }   // method print

    }   // class Array_Parameters
```

When executed, the `Array_Test` program prints the following:

```
Original array:
11  22  33  44  55
The value of num is 11
The value of num is now 1234
After passing one element:
11  22  33  44  55
After changing individual elements:
11  22  77  44  88
After attempting to change a reference:
11  22  77  44  88
After copying each array element:
99  99  99  99  99
After returning a reference:
99  9876  99  99  99
```

The call to the `pass_element` method passes a copy of one integer to the method as a parameter called `num`. The value of `num` is changed within the method, but it has no effect on the original array.

The call to `change_elements` passes a reference to the original array to the method. The parameter is called `mylist`, and is actually a copy of the original reference. But it refers to the same array object (the same memory space) as the original. Essentially, the `mylist` parameter is an alias of the original `list` variable. Therefore, when changes are made to individual elements, those changes are made to the original elements.

The call to `change_reference` passes references of two arrays as parameters. Both of these references are copies of the originals. One parameter is assigned the value of the other, essentially making them aliases of the same array for the duration of the method. But when that method returns, the original references are unchanged. Note that the array corresponding to the first parameter is not made a candidate for garbage collection when the reference `mylist` is overwritten because there is still a reference to it, namely `list` in the main method.

The call to `copy_array` passes references of two arrays as parameters. Both of the parameters are copies of the original references, but refer to the original array elements. Therefore, when the values of each element are copied from one array to the other, the original elements are modified, and those changes are reflected after the method returns. At this point, the variables `list` and `list2` refer to two separate array objects that contain the same element values.

The call to `return_reference` passes a copy of a reference to an array as a parameter. It changes one element of the array, which changes the original. It then uses a `return` statement to return that reference (which is actually a copy of the reference). In the main method, the returned reference is assigned to the variable `list`, overwriting its current reference. Now `list` and `list2` are aliases to the same array, and the array object previously referred to by `list` is a candidate for garbage collection.

Multidimensional Arrays

The arrays we've examined so far have all been *one-dimensional* arrays because they represent a simple list of values. As the name implies, a *two-dimensional* (2D) array has values in two dimensions, often referred to as rows and columns. It therefore uses two indexes to refer to a value. Figure 6.4 compares a one-dimensional array with a two-dimensional array. An array can have two, three, or even more dimensions. Any array with more than one dimension is called a *multidimensional array*.

Technically, Java does not support multidimensional arrays. However, it supports them in effect because a one-dimensional array can have an array as an element. An array whose element type is `array-of-integer` is essentially a two-dimensional array of integers.

Brackets are used to represent each dimension in the array. An initializer list can be used to instantiate the array, where each element is itself an array initializer list. Because each array is a separate object, the lengths of each row could be different, as shown in the following program. Each dimension has a beginning index of zero. As with one-dimensional arrays, a programmer must be careful to stay within the bounds of each dimension of a multidimensional array. The `length` constant contains the size of each individual array. For example, the variable `table[2].length` contains the size of the third row in the array.

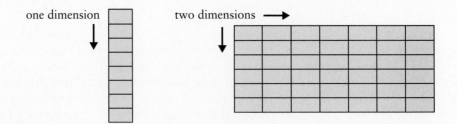

Figure 6.4   A one-dimensional array and a two-dimensional array

```
//  Creates and prints a multi-dimensional array.
class Multi_Array_Test {

   public static void main (String[] args) {
      Multi_Array chart = new Multi_Array();
      chart.print();
      System.out.println();
      for (int column=0; column < 4; column++)
         System.out.println ("Sum of column " + column +
                             ": " + chart.sum_column (column));
   }  // method main

}  // class Multi_Array_Test

//  Stores a 2D array of integers.
class Multi_Array {
   int[][] table = { {28, 84, 47, 72}, {69, 26}, {91, 40, 28},
                     {42, 34, 37}, {13, 26, 57, 35} };

   public void print() {
      for (int row=0; row < table.length; row++) {
         for (int column=0; column < table[row].length; column++)
            System.out.print (table[row][column] + "   ");
         System.out.println();
      }
   }  // method print

   public int sum_column (int column) {
      int sum = 0;
      for (int row=0; row < table.length; row++)
         if (column < table[row].length)  // ignore rows without column
            sum += table[row][column];
      return sum;
   }  // method sum_column

}  // class Multi_Array
```

An initializer list can be used with multidimensional arrays.

A 2D array requires two separate indexes.

The `main` method in the `Multi_Array_Test` program instantiates an object of class `Multi_Array`, which in turn instantiates a two-dimensional array of integers. The rows of the 2D array contain a different number of values. The method `print` in the `Multi_Array` class prints the entire 2D array of values. The `sum_column` method computes the sum of all values in a particular column, ignoring the rows that do not have a value in that column. The output of the `Multi_Array_Test` program is:

```
28   84   47   72
69   26
91   40   28
42   34   37
13   26   57   35
Sum of column 0: 243
Sum of column 1: 210
Sum of column 2: 169
Sum of column 3: 107
```

Key Concept   A multidimensional array is implemented in Java as an array of arrays. Therefore each element could have a different length.

Let's look at another example. Suppose a soda manufacturer held a taste test for four new flavors to see if each one was worthy of the investment of more time and money to make it a new part of their product line. The company got 10 people to try each new flavor and give it a score from 1 to 5, where 1 means poor and 5 means excellent. The following program stores the results of that survey in a two-dimensional array called `results`. The row corresponds to the soda and the column corresponds to the person who tasted it. That is, each row holds the responses that all testers gave for one particular soda flavor, and each column holds the responses of one person for all sodas. Because each tester tried all four sodas, there is the same number of columns in each row.

```
//  Produces the results of a soda taste test.
class Soda_Survey {

   public static void main (String[] args) {
      Soda_Scores test = new Soda_Scores();

      for (int soda=0; soda < test.num_sodas(); soda++)
         System.out.println ("Soda " + (soda+1) + " is " +
            (test.worthy(soda, 3) ? "worthy." : "not worthy."));
   }  // method main

}  // class Soda_Survey
```

```
//  Stores the taste test scores with methods to analyze the
//  results.
class Soda_Scores {
   private final int RESPONDENTS = 10;
   private final int SODAS = 4;
   private int[][] results = { {3, 4, 5, 2, 1, 4, 3, 2, 4, 4},
                               {2, 4, 3, 4, 3, 3, 2, 1, 2, 2},
                               {3, 5, 4, 5, 5, 3, 2, 5, 5, 5},
                               {1, 1, 1, 3, 1, 2, 1, 3, 2, 4} };

   public int num_sodas() {
      return SODAS;
   }  // method num_sodas

   public boolean worthy (int soda, int level) {
      int count = 0;
      for (int person=0; person < results[soda].length; person++)
         if (results[soda][person] >= level)
            count++;
      return (count > RESPONDENTS/2);
   }  // method worthy

}  // class Soda_Scores
```

The `boolean` method called `worthy` returns true if more than half of the respondents gave a particular soda a certain score level, and false otherwise. In the `Soda_Survey` program, the call to `worthy` uses a score level of 3 to make the determination, producing the following output:

```
Soda 1 is worthy.
Soda 2 is not worthy.
Soda 3 is worthy.
Soda 4 is not worthy.
```

Its fairly easy to picture a two-dimensional array as a table. A three-dimensional array could be drawn as a cube. But once you are past three dimensions, multidimensional arrays might seem to be hard to visualize. However, each dimension is simply a subdivision of the previous one, and it is often best to think of a multidimensional array in this way.

For example, suppose we wanted to store the number of students attending universities across the country, broken down in a meaningful way. We might represent it as a four-dimensional array of integers. The first dimension is an array of states.

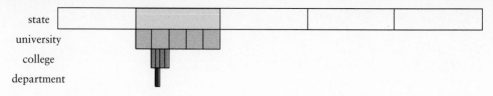

state
university
college
department

Figure 6.5 A four-dimensional array

Each state contains an array of the universities in that state. Each university contains an array of the colleges in that university. Each college contains an array of departments, which stores the number of students in that department. These subdivisions can be pictured as shown in Fig. 6.5.

Two-dimensional arrays are fairly common. However, care should be taken when deciding to create multidimensional arrays in a program. When dealing with large amounts of data that are managed at multiple levels, other information and the methods to manage that information will probably be required. In the previous example, for instance, it is far more likely that each state would be represented by an object, which may contain an array to store information about each university, and so on.

 Key Concept   Using an array with more than two dimensions is rare in an object-oriented system because intermediate levels are usually represented as separate objects.

6.2   The Vector Class

The Vector class is part of the `java.util` package of the Java API. It provides a service similar to an array in that it can store a list of values and reference them by an index. But whereas an array remains a fixed size throughout its existence, a Vector object can dynamically grow and shrink as needed. A data element can be inserted into or removed from any location of a vector with a single method invocation.

Key Concept   A Vector object is similar to an array, but it can dynamically change size as needed.

Dynamic Arrays

Unlike an array, a vector is not declared to store a particular type. A `Vector` object manages a list of references to the `Object` class. A reference to any type of object can be added to a vector. Because vectors store references, a primitive type must be stored in an appropriate wrapper class in order to be stored in a vector. Appendix O contains a complete description of `Vector`.

The `Vector` class provides several methods to manage the list, including:

- `addElement (Object element)`
- `removeElement (Object element)`
- `contains (Object element)`
- `elementAt (int index)`
- `firstElement ()`
- `lastElement ()`
- `size ()`

The `addElement` method adds an object to the end of the vector. The `removeElement` method removes the specified object from the vector. Note that the parameter to `removeElement` is an alias to an object in the vector that is to be removed. The act of removing an element reduces the length of the vector by one. The `contains` method returns true if the specified object is present anywhere in the vector. The `elementAt` method returns the object at the specified index. The `firstElement` method returns a reference to the first element in the vector (but doesn't remove it from the vector). Similarly, the `lastElement` method returns a reference to the last element in the vector (but doesn't remove it). The `size` method returns the number of objects in the vector.

Consider the following example, which instantiates a `Vector` called `band`. The method `addElement` is used to add several `String` objects to the vector, in a particular order. After printing the vector using `println`, the method `removeElement` deletes the second name in the list, and adds another name. Then the vector is printed again.

```
import java.util.Vector;

//  Uses a Vector object to store a list of strings.
class Beatles {

   public static void main (String[] args) {
      Vector band = new Vector();

      band.addElement ("Paul");
      band.addElement ("Pete");
      band.addElement ("John");
      band.addElement ("George");
```

Any object can be added to a `Vector`.

```
      System.out.println (band);

      band.removeElement ("Pete");
      band.addElement ("Ringo");

      System.out.println (band);
   }  // method main

}  // class Beatles
```

The `println` method is overloaded so that it accepts any object, including a `Vector`, and presents it in a form suitable for printing. This process is discussed in more detail later in the text. The output of the program is:

```
[Paul, Pete, John, George]
[Paul, John, George, Ringo]
```

The next example demonstrates several `Vector` methods. The `Vector` object called `song` stores several objects of different types. Note that the primitive types are stored using an object of their wrapper class, and that one of the items in the song vector is another vector called `authors`.

```
import java.util.Vector;

//  Fills a Vector object with various object types.
class ZZ_Top {

   public static void main (String[] args) {
      Vector song = new Vector();

      String name = new String ("ZZ Top's Greatest Hits");
      Integer track = new Integer (6);
      String title = "Cheap Sunglasses";
      Double price = new Double (15.95);
      Vector authors = new Vector (2);

      authors.addElement ("Gibbons");
      authors.addElement ("Hill");

      song.addElement (track);
      song.addElement (title);
      song.addElement (authors);
```

```
        song.addElement (price);
        song.insertElementAt (name, 0);

        System.out.println (song);

        authors.addElement ("George");

        System.out.println (song);

        System.out.println ("song size: " + song.size());
        System.out.println ("authors size: " + authors.size());
        System.out.println ("song begins: " + song.firstElement());
        System.out.println ("authors begins: " + authors.firstElement());
        System.out.println ("song ends: " + song.lastElement());
        System.out.println ("authors ends: " + authors.lastElement());

        authors.setElementAt ("Frank", authors.indexOf ("George"));

        System.out.println (song);

        song.removeAllElements();

        System.out.println (song);
    }  // method main

}  // class ZZ_Top
```

The output of the ZZ_Top program is:

```
[ZZ Top's Greatest Hits, 6, Cheap Sunglasses, [Gibbons, Hill],
15.95]
[ZZ Top's Greatest Hits, 6, Cheap Sunglasses, [Gibbons, Hill,
George], 15.95]
song size: 5
authors size: 3
song begins: ZZ Top's Greatest Hits
authors begins: Gibbons
song ends: 15.95
authors ends: George
[ZZ Top's Greatest Hits, 6, Cheap Sunglasses, [Gibbons, Hill,
Frank], 15.95]
[]
```

As we've seen, the objects stored and used in a Vector object can be of different reference types. The methods of the Vector class are designed to accept references to the Object class as parameters, thus allowing a reference to any kind of object to be passed to it. Note that an implication of this implementation is that the elementAt method's return type is an Object reference. In order to retrieve a specific object from the Vector class, the returned object must be cast to its original class. The Object class and its relationship to other classes is explained further in Chapter 8.

> **Key Concept** The abstraction provided by Vector objects mask some fairly inefficient processing.

The processing of an array is significantly slowed down when capacity is enlarged and when insertions are made that cause a great deal of element copying. A Vector, with its dynamic characteristics, is a useful abstraction of an array but the abstraction masks some underlying activity that can be fairly inefficient. Chapter 16 discusses some alternative forms of data organization that do not have this unattractive overhead.

In-Depth Focus

Vector Efficiency

The Vector class is implemented using arrays. When a Vector object is instantiated, it is created with an initial *capacity* that defines the number of references it can currently handle. Elements can be added to the vector without needing to allocate more memory until it reaches this capacity. When required, the capacity is expanded to accommodate the new need.

When an element is inserted into the middle of a vector, all of the elements at higher indexes are copied into their new locations in the vector. This process is illustrated in Fig. 6.6. If several elements are inserted, this copying is repeated many times over.

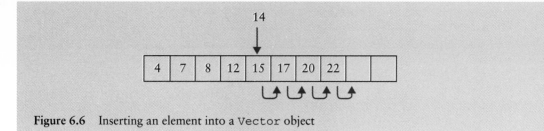

Figure 6.6   Inserting an element into a `Vector` object

6.3   Strings Revisited

We've been using strings throughout the text, and in Chapter 4 we introduced some of the methods of the `String` class. In Chapter 4 we also introduced the `StringTokenizer` class, which can be used to process string information. In this section we continue our discussion of string processing, exploring the `StringTokenizer` class in more detail and introducing the `StringBuffer` class.

Using `StringTokenizer`

When using the `StringTokenizer` class, you can specify which characters act as token delimiters. When processing a sentence, for example, you might specify spaces and punctuation characters to separate tokens. For a Unix directory name, such as `"/home/lewis/work"`, the user could specify the slash character as the delimiter. The delimiters determine how tokens are found in a `StringTokenizer` object.

The `StringTokenizer` class has three constructors:

- `StringTokenizer (String str);`
- `StringTokenizer (String str, String delimiters);`
- `StringTokenizer (String str, String delimiters`
  `                   boolean returndel);`

All of the constructors require a `String` parameter that contains the string to be tokenized. Two of the constructors use another `String` parameter that defines the set of delimiters to be used when tokenizing the string. If left unspecified, the tokens are delimited with white space, as defined by the string `" \n\r\t"`. In addition, one constructor accepts a boolean parameter that determines if the delimiters themselves should be returned as tokens. If left unspecified, the delimiters are not returned as tokens. Appendix O contains a complete specification of the StringTokenizer class.

The methods of the StringTokenizer class include:

- hasMoreTokens()
- nextToken()
- nextToken (String delimiters)
- countTokens()

The hasMoreTokens method returns true if there are more tokens in the string that have not yet been processed. The nextToken method returns a String object that represents the next token in the string. An overloaded version of the nextToken method allows you to specify the delimiters to use to process the next token. This new delimiter set remains in effect for subsequent calls to nextToken until you explicitly change it again. The countTokens method returns the number of tokens left to process in the string.

 Key Concept   The default delimiters for a *StringTokenizer* object are white space characters. The delimiters can also be explicitly set.

Let's look at an example that uses a StringTokenizer object. The following program separates a quote from Voltaire into tokens using the default white space delimiters.

```
import java.util.StringTokenizer;

//  Breaks a sentence into individual words using a
//  StringTokenizer.
public class Voltaire {

    public static void main (String[] args) {
        String quote = "Use, do not abuse; neither abstinence " +
                        "nor excess renders a man happy.";
        StringTokenizer words = new StringTokenizer (quote);

        System.out.println ("Characters: " + quote.length());
        System.out.println ("Tokens: " + words.countTokens());

        while (words.hasMoreTokens()) {
            System.out.println (words.nextToken());
```

```
      }
   }  // method main

}  // class Voltaire
```

This program creates a `StringTokenizer` object called `words` that is used to tok-enize the `String` object `quote`. The initial call to `countTokens` returns the number of tokens in the entire string. The `while` loop uses the `hasMoreTokens` method as its termination condition. The body of the loop prints each token on a separate line. The `StringTokenizer` object maintains the current position in the string being tokenized. Each call to the `nextToken` method returns the next token in the string and updates its current position. Note that the `countTokens` method returns the number of tokens still left to be processed based on its current position. The output of the `Voltaire` program is:

```
Characters: 69
Tokens: 12
Use,
do
not
abuse;
neither
abstinence
nor
excess
renders
a
man
happy.
```

Note that, unlike our natural tendency to group punctuation with white space, the comma and semicolon are part of the tokens that were returned from the `nextToken` method. Because the comma and semicolon are not part of the default delimiter set, they are considered part of a token. Suppose we had used the follow-ing constructor:

```
StringTokenizer Tokenizer = new StringTokenizer (Voltaire, ";,");
```

Now the delimiters for tokens are defined to be the semicolon and the comma, and the output of the program would be:

```
Characters: 69
Tokens: 3
Use
 do not abuse
 neither abstinence nor excess renders a man happy.
```

Note that the comma and semicolon are no longer part of any token, because they were defined to be token delimiters. Also note that the space character is now considered part of a token, including the space after punctuation characters. Therefore, the last two lines of the output begin with a space character.

Let's look at another example. A URL used with the Web consists of three basic pieces: a protocol, an Internet address, and a resource (such as a file). The string "http://www.wpllabs.com/vision.html" contains a URL that references a file called vision.html on the machine at the Internet address www.wpllabs.com using the http protocol. Reading the URL as a single string is convenient, but not very useful when you need detailed information. The following program uses StringTokenizer to implement a class called URL_Tokenizer that decomposes a URL into its essential parts.

```java
import java.util.StringTokenizer;

//  Prints the pieces of a URL.
public class URL_Tokens {

   public static void main (String[] args) {
      URL_Tokenizer url = new URL_Tokenizer
         ("http://www.wpllabs.com/vision.html");

      System.out.println ("Protocol: " + url.get_protocol());
      System.out.println ("Address : " + url.get_address());
      System.out.println ("Resource: " + url.get_resource());
   }  // method main

}  // class URL_Tokens

//  Uses a StringTokenizer to separate the basic pieces of a URL.
class URL_Tokenizer {

   private String protocol;
   private String address;
   private String resource;
```

```
public URL_Tokenizer (String URL_Text) {
    StringTokenizer URL = new StringTokenizer (URL_Text, ":");
    protocol = URL.nextToken();
    address  = URL.nextToken (":/");
    resource = URL.nextToken ("");
}  // constructor URL_Tokenizer

public String get_protocol() {
    return protocol;
}  // method get_protocol

public String get_address() {
    return address;
}  // method get_address

public String get_resource() {
    return resource;
}  // method get_resource

}  // class URL_Tokenizer
```

Token delimiters can be changed dynamically.

The output from this program is:

```
Protocol: http
Address : www.wpllabs.com
Resource: /vision.html
```

The class `URL_Tokenizer` has a single constructor that performs most of the work of the class. The constructor accepts a single `String` parameter containing a URL. The constructor uses `StringTokenizer` to break up the url into meaningful parts.

The first token, delimited by a colon, is the protocol. The delimiter of a colon is specified in the `StringTokenizer` constructor. The first call to `nextToken` returns a string representing the name of the protocol, in this case `"http"`.

The next token of interest is the address, which follows the two slashes. The second call to `nextToken` retokenizes the string, from its current position, using the characters of a colon and a slash as the new delimiters. Using the colon and the slash makes sure that the `nextToken` method will not return the colon.

The last piece of information in the URL string is the resource. The final call to `nextToken` uses the null string to define the delimiter set. Therefore it returns the rest of the string.

The `StringBuffer` Class

The `String` class manages the use of immutable strings, which cannot change in size or content once they are created. However, there is sometimes a need to have a *dynamic string* that can be modified during program execution. The Java API offers the `StringBuffer` class as partial support of this type of string.

The major benefit of dynamic strings is their ability to modify their content after they are instantiated. For instance, you might insert characters into the middle of a string, or append characters to the end of a string, or delete characters, or replace characters. The `StringBuffer` class supports most of these activities. It does not, however, allow you to delete specific characters. This limitation exists because the `StringBuffer` class was originally created to implement the string concatenation operator (+), and was not intended as a general-purpose class. Most of the capabilities of the `StringBuffer` class can be accomplished by working with regular `String` objects, using substrings and string concatenation.

> **Key Concept**   A `StringBuffer` object provides a string whose value can change, but most of the functionality of the `StringBuffer` can be accomplished with strings and string concatenation.

The methods of the `StringBuffer` class include:

- `append (char c)`
- `insert (int index, char c)`
- `charAt (int index)`
- `setCharAt (int index, char c)`
- `setLength (int newlength)`
- `reverse()`
- `length()`

The `append` method adds a character to the end of the `StringBuffer`. The `insert` method inserts a character into the `StringBuffer` at the specified index. The process of appending or inserting a character increases the size of the `StringBuffer` by 1. Actually, both the `append` and `insert` methods are over-loaded many times so that you can append and insert various types of data, including numeric types and strings. The `charAt` method returns the character stored at the specified index (but does not remove it). The `setCharAt` method changes the character at the specified index. The `setLength` method sets the length of the `StringBuffer`, which may truncate and eliminate some existing characters. The `reverse` method inverts the characters stored in the `StringBuffer`. The `length` method returns the current length of the `StringBuffer`.

Let's look at an example that uses `StringBuffer`. The following program creates three StringBuffer objects and modifies them in various ways.

```java
//  Uses StringBuffer to store and modify string data.
public class Money {

    public static void main (String[] args) {
        StringBuffer text1 = new StringBuffer();
        StringBuffer text2 = new StringBuffer(" m");
        StringBuffer text3 = new StringBuffer ("1 dollar");

        text1.append (1);
        text1.append (" p");
        text1.append ('e');
        text1.append ('n');
        text1.append ("ny");

        text2.insert (0, 1);
        text2.insert (2, "di");
        text2.insert (5, 'e');

        System.out.println (text1);
        System.out.println (text2);
        System.out.println (text3);
        text3.reverse ();
        System.out.println (text3);
    }  // method main

}  // class Money
```

Characters can be inserted into a `StringBuffer`.

The output of this program is:

```
1 penny
1 dime
1 dollar
rallod 1
```

Summary of Key Concepts

- A Java array of size N is indexed from 0 to $N-1$.
- A Java array is an object. Memory space for the array elements are reserved by instantiating the array using the new operator.

- Bounds checking ensures that an index used to refer to an array element is in range. The Java index operator performs automatic bounds checking.
- An initializer list can be used to instantiate the array object, instead of using the new operator. The size of the array and its initial values are determined by the initializer list.
- Instantiating an array of objects only reserves room to store references. The objects that are stored in each element must be instantiated separately.
- An entire array can be passed as a parameter, making the formal parameter an alias to the original.
- A multidimensional array is implemented in Java as an array of arrays. Therefore each element could have a different length.
- Using an array with more than two dimensions is rare in an object-oriented system because intermediate levels are usually represented as separate objects.
- A Vector object is similar to an array, but it can dynamically change size as needed.
- The abstraction provided by Vector objects mask some fairly inefficient processing.
- The default delimiters for a StringTokenizer object are white space characters. The delimiters can also be explicitly set.
- A StringBuffer object provides a string whose value can change, but most of the functionality of the StringBuffer can be accomplished with strings and string concatenation.

Self-Review Questions

6.1 Explain the concept of array bounds checking. What happens when a Java array reference has an index value that is not valid?

6.2 Describe the process of creating an array. When is memory allocated for the array?

6.3 What is an off-by-one error? How does it relate to arrays?

6.4 What does an array initializer list accomplish?

6.5 How is an array of objects created?

6.6 Can an entire array be passed as a parameter? How is this accomplished?

6.7 How are multidimensional arrays implemented in Java?

6.8 What are the advantages of using a Vector as opposed to an array? What are the disadvantages?

6.9 What are the default delimiters for the StringTokenizer class?

6.10　What is the difference between a `String` object and a `StringBuffer` object?

Exercises

6.11　Which of the following are valid declarations? Which instantiate an array object? Explain your answers.

a. `int primes = {2, 3, 4, 5, 7, 11};`
b. `float elapsed_times[] = {11.47, 12.04, 11.72, 13.88};`
c. `int[] scores = int[30];`
d. `int[] primes = new {2,3,5,7,11};`
e. `int[] scores = new int[30];`
f. `char grades[] = {'a', 'b', 'c', 'd', 'f'};`
g. `char [] grades = new char[];`

6.12　Describe five programs that are difficult to implement without using arrays.

6.13　Describe what occurs in the following code:

```
int[] numbers = {3, 2, 3, 6, 9, 10, 12, 32, 3, 12, 6};
for (int count = 1; count <= numbers.length; count++) {
    System.out.println (numbers[count]);
}
```

How can any problems identified be corrected?

6.14　Write an array declaration with any necessary supporting classes to represent the following statements:

a. Students' names for a class of 25 students
b. Students' grades for a class of 10 students
c. Credit-card transaction lines that contain a transaction number, a merchant name, and a charge
d. Students' names for a class and homework grades for each student
e. For each employee of the LL International Corporation, the employee number, hire date, and the amount of the last five raises

6.15　Write a method that accepts an array of integers and sums the values stored in the array.

6.16　Write a method that accepts an array of integers and prints out various statistics, such as highest number, lowest number, and number of items in the array.

6.17　Write a method that accepts two array parameters and switches the contents of the arrays. What happens when the arrays are different sizes? What happens when one of the arrays is null?

6.18 Describe a program for which you would use the Vector class instead of arrays to implement choices. Describe a program for which you would use an array instead of the Vector class. Explain your choices.

6.19 When using the StringTokenizer class, what are the tokens for the following strings if the delimiters are defined to be " , . : * # "?

a. "This is a test, which may or may not work."
b. "What are the tokens in this statement?"
c. "All work and no play makes Jack a dull boy. All work and no play makes Jack a dull boy."
d. "jad:John Doe:/usr/jad:/bin/csh"
e. "#%^&$%**(&^@#%$#@#"

6.20 What are some improvements that could be made to the StringTokenizer class to help break down strings?

6.21 The StringBuffer class can be used to simulate what occurs when using the + operator on strings. Write the calls to the methods of a StringBuffer object to implement the following use of the + operator:

```
line = "The " + "cat " + "in " + "the " + "hat "
```

Programming Projects

6.22 Modify the Storm applet from Chapter 4 so that the set of raindrops are stored in an array.

6.23 Design and implement an application that reads an arbitrary number of integers that are in the range 0 to 50 inclusive and counts how many occurrences of each is entered. After all input has been processed, print all of the values (with the number of occurrences) that were entered one or more times.

6.24 Modify the program in Problem 6.23 so that it works for numbers in the range between −25 and 25.

6.25 Modify the program in Problem 6.23 so that it works for any integer values. *Hint:* Use two arrays—one to store the value entered and one to store the number of occurrences.

6.26 Design and implement an application that creates a histogram, which allows you to visually inspect the frequency distribution of a set of values. The program should read in an arbitrary number of integers that are in the range 1 to 100 inclusive; then produce a chart similar to the one below that indicates how many input values fell in the range 1–10, 11–20, and so on. Print one asterisk for each value entered.

```
1 - 10   | *****
11 - 20  | **
21 - 30  | ********************
31 - 40  |
41 - 50  | ***
51 - 60  | ********
61 - 70  | **
71 - 80  | *****
81 - 90  | *******
91 - 100 | ********
```

6.27 The lines in the histogram of Problem 6.26 will be too long if a large number of values are entered. Modify the program so that it prints an asterisk for every five values in each category. Ignore leftovers. For example, if a category had 17 values, print three asterisks in that row. If a category had 4 values, do not print any asterisks in that row.

6.28 Design and implement an application that computes and prints the mean and standard deviation of a list of integers. Assume that there will be no more than 50 input values. Compute both the mean and standard deviation as floating point values.

6.29 Design and implement a class called `Big_Number` that stores a number up to 25 digits long. Store the individual digits of the number in an array. Create another class called `Big_Calculations` that contains the static methods `add`, `subtract`, `multiply`, and `divide` to perform arithmetic operations on "big" numbers. Each method should accept two `Big_Number` objects as parameters to be used as operands and should return a `Big_Number` object as a result. Create another class that contains a `main` method that instantiates several `Big_Number` objects and performs various calculations.

6.30 The L&L Bank can handle up to 30 customers that have savings accounts. Design and implement a program that manages the accounts. Each customer has a name, phone number, and an account balance. Allow each customer to make deposits and withdrawals. Produce appropriate error messages for invalid transactions. Also provide a method to add 3 percent interest to all accounts whenever it is invoked.

6.31 Design and implement an applet that draws a checkerboard with five red and eight black checkers on it in various locations. Store the checkerboard as a two-dimensional array.

6.32 Modify the applet in Problem 6.31 so that the program determines if any black checkers can jump any red checkers. Under the checkerboard, print the position (row, column) of all black checkers that have possible jumps.

Answers to Self-Review Questions

6.1 Whenever a reference is made to a particular array element, the index operator ensures that the value of the index is greater than or equal to zero and less than the size of the array. If it is not within the valid range, an ArrayIndexOutOfBounds exception is thrown.

6.2 Arrays are objects. Therefore, like all objects, to create an array you first create a reference to the array (its name). Then you instantiate the array itself, which reserves memory space to store the array elements. The only difference between a regular object instantiation and an array instantiation is the bracket syntax. The bracket syntax of int[] count = new int[25]; is an example.

6.3 An off-by-one error occurs when program processing misses the boundary of an array or similar structure by one. These errors include forgetting to process a boundary element and attempting to process a nonexistent element. Array processing is susceptible to off-by-one errors because their indexes begin at zero and run to one less than the size of the array.

6.4 An array initializer list is used in the declaration of an array to set up the initial values of its elements. An initializer list instantiates the array object, so no new operator is needed.

6.5 An array of objects holds references to the object type specified as the array element. The array of object references and the element objects are instantiated separately.

6.6 An entire array can be passed as a parameter that passes a reference to the array into the method. Any changes made to the array elements will be reflected outside of the method.

6.7 A multidimensional array is implemented in Java as an array of array objects. The arrays that are elements of the outer array could also contain arrays as elements. This nesting process could continue for several levels, but usually does not.

6.8 One advantage of using a Vector is that it stores references to the Object class, which allows any object to be stored in it. In addition, a Vector object can dynamically grow and shrink as needed. A disadvantage of the Vector class is that it copies a significant amount of data in order to insert and delete elements, and this process is inefficient.

6.9 The default delimiters of the `StringTokenizer` class are standard white space characters (space, newline, carriage return, and tab). You can explicitly set the delimiters to other characters in the `StringTokenizer` constructor or in the `nextToken` method.

6.10 You cannot change the contents of a `String` object once it is created, whereas you can change the contents of a `StringBuffer` object by using a variety of methods.

Graphics

7

Graphics play a primary role in modern computing systems. As the saying goes, "A picture is worth a thousand words." Graphics can be used to communicate information faster and easier than using text or numbers. In previous chapters, we have used graphic methods to draw lines and rectangles, and to draw character strings. However, we have only scratched the surface of Java's graphics capabilities. The `java.awt` package provides a large variety of graphical classes and methods. In this chapter, we focus on using color, drawing shapes, and managing fonts. Chapter 10 describes the creation of graphical user interfaces (GUIs).

Chapter Objectives

- Describe the `Graphics` class and its underlying role.
- Explore the use of predefined and programmer-defined colors.
- Draw shapes, including ovals, rectangles, arcs, and polygons.
- Explain how to change fonts and modify their appearance.
- Perform simple animations using graphics.

7.1 The Graphics Class

The `Graphics` class is the cornerstone of all drawing and graphical user interface (GUI) facilities in Java. It is defined in the `java.awt` package of the Java API, as are almost all classes related to graphics. The abbreviation `awt` stands for *abstract windowing toolkit*.

The `Graphics` class contains all methods for creating line drawings, including shapes such as rectangles, ovals, arcs, and polygons. It also has facilities to control colors and manage fonts. In previous chapters, we've seen the basic use of the methods `drawString`, `drawLine`, `drawOval`, and `drawRect`. These methods are part of the `Graphics` class. This chapter contains a more complete discussion of these and other graphic methods.

Each `Graphics` object represents a particular drawing surface. Each applet, for instance, has a `Graphics` object associated with it. Any methods called through that `Graphics` object will affect the applet. The `Graphics` object defines a *graphics context* through which we manage all graphic activities on that surface.

 Key Concept   An object of the `Graphics` class represents a particular drawing surface and contains methods for drawing shapes on that surface.

The `Graphics` class is somewhat special in that the programmer does not instantiate it. Because the details of drawing graphics are unique for each type of computer system, the `Graphics` class is *device dependent*. The `Graphics` object corresponding to a particular surface is obtained either by using the `getGraphics` method of the surface, or by accepting it as a parameter to a method that is invoked automatically, such as `paint`.

The Graphics Coordinate System

Each drawing surface associated with a `Graphics` object is referenced relative to a simple coordinate system, shown in Fig. 7.1. Each point in the coordinate system corresponds to a *pixel*, a term that stands for picture element. Each pixel is identified by an <x, y> coordinate. The top left corner of the area is coordinate <0, 0>. The x-axis coordinates get larger as you move to the right and the y-axis coordinates get larger as you move down. A drawing surface, such as an applet, has a particular width and height. Therefore the bottom-right corner of the area is coordinate <*width* −1, *height* −1>. Anything drawn outside of that defined area will not be visible.

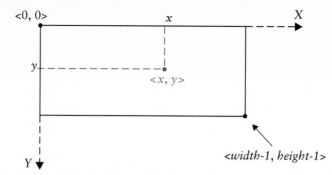

Figure 7.1 The Java coordinate system

Key Concept Each <x, y> coordinate represents a single pixel. The top-left corner is coordinate <0, 0>. All coordinate values are positive.

The following applet demonstrates the use of the `Graphics` class and the coordinate system. The `paint` method first calls the applet's `setSize` method to set its drawing area. The parameters to the `setSize` method specify the applet's width and height in pixels. The size of an applet can also be set in HTML code that refers to it.

```
import java.applet.Applet;
import java.awt.*;

// Shows two points on the coordinate system.
public class Coordinates extends Applet {

   public void paint (Graphics page) {
      setSize (300, 200);
      page.drawRect (0, 0, 299, 199);
      page.drawLine (50, 50, 250, 100);
      page.drawString ("<50, 50>", 25, 45);
      page.drawString ("<250, 100>", 225, 115);
   } // method paint

} // class Coordinates
```

The size of a drawing surface can be changed dynamically.

The call to the `drawRect` method draws a rectangle around the outer edge of the applet's drawing area. Recall from our previous use of the `drawRect` method

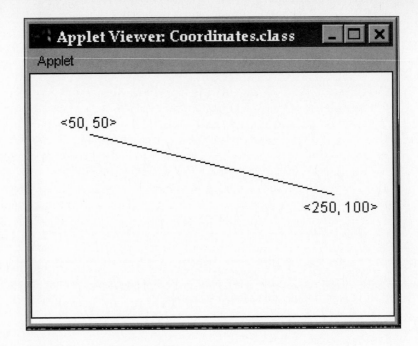

Figure 7.2 The Coordinates applet

that the first two parameters specify the <x, y> coordinate of the upper-left corner of the rectangle, and the last two parameters specify the rectangle's width and height in pixels. The call to drawLine draws a line segment from one coordinate, represented by the first two parameters, to a second coordinate, represented by the last two parameters. The two calls to the drawString method label the end points of the line segment. The output of the applet is shown in Fig. 7.2.

Note that the applet's paint method accepts a Graphics object as a parameter. The object, which is called page in this example, is associated with the applet. Therefore methods such as drawRect and drawLine, when invoked through that object, draw on the applet surface.

If a call to a drawing method specifies that a shape should be drawn outside of the boundaries of the drawing surface, then it simply will not be seen. Similarly, if only part of a shape is within the drawing surface coordinates, then only that part will be seen. Specifying a shape with a negative or zero width or height will cause no shape to be drawn.

 Key Concept Any portion of a shape drawn outside of the drawing surface area will not be displayed.

7.2 Color

Color can be used effectively to enhance the appearance of graphics by highlighting and contrasting various elements of a picture. In Java, a programmer uses the `Color` class, which is part of the `java.awt` package, to define and manage colors. Each instance of the `Color` class represents a single color, though the class also contains several `static` instances of itself to provide a basic set of predefined colors. It also contains methods to define and manage many other colors.

All colors can be specified as a mix of three primary colors: red, green, and blue. In Java, as in many other computer languages and applications, colors are specified by three numbers that are collectively referred to as an *RGB value*. RGB stands for Red-Green-Blue. Each of the three numbers range from 0 to 255, and represent the contribution of a particular primary color. The precise level of each primary color determines the overall color. For example, high values for red and green combined with a low level of blue results in a shade of yellow.

Key Concept A color is defined by an RGB value that specifies the relative weight given to the primary colors red, green, and blue.

For each drawing surface there is a *foreground color* that specifies the color in which shapes or text are drawn. The programmer can change the foreground color for a surface over the course of a program's execution. The foreground color defaults to black. The `setColor` method in the `Graphics` class specifies a new foreground color for the associated surface. The `getColor` method returns the foreground color.

Predefined Colors

The `Color` class contains several `final static Color` objects that define some basic colors. Because they are `static`, they can be referenced using the class name and without instantiating a separate `Color` object. Because they are `final`, their definitions cannot be changed. The predefined colors are listed in Fig. 7.3.

Notice the RGB values for the predefined colors. They range from (0, 0, 0) for black to (255, 255, 255) for white. The colors red, green, and blue maximize their particular color and minimize the other two, such as (0, 0, 255) for blue. Various other RGB combinations are used to define a set of common colors in this list.

Color	Object	RGB Value
black	Color.black	0, 0, 0
blue	Color.blue	0, 0, 255
cyan	Color.cyan	0, 255, 255
gray	Color.gray	128, 128, 128
dark gray	Color.darkGray	64, 64, 64
light gray	Color.lightGray	192, 192, 192
green	Color.green	0, 255, 0
magenta	Color.magenta	255, 0, 255
orange	Color.orange	255, 200, 0
pink	Color.pink	255, 175, 175
red	Color.red	255, 0, 0
white	Color.white	255, 255, 255
yellow	Color.yellow	255, 255, 0

Figure 7.3   Predefined colors in the Color class

> **Key Concept**   The Color class has several common colors predefined.

The following applet, called Nature, uses the setColor method to change the foreground color at various points in the program. It also demonstrates the use of the applet's setBackground method, which sets the color of the background for the entire applet area. The output of Nature is shown in Fig. 7.4, but is best appreciated when displayed on a color monitor.

```
import java.applet.Applet;
import java.awt.*;

// Writes two strings in different colors.
public class Nature extends Applet {

    public void paint (Graphics page) {
        setBackground (Color.white);
        page.setColor (Color.red);
        page.drawRect (10, 15, 125, 85);
        page.setColor (Color.green);
```

The foreground color can be changed with setColor.

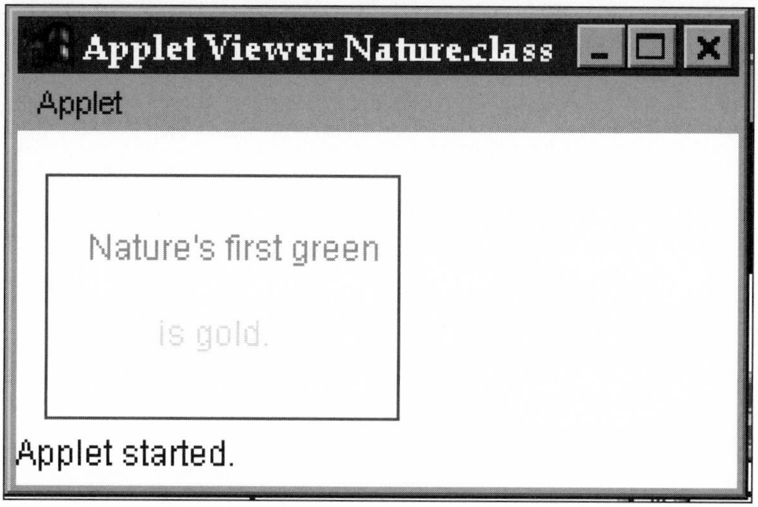

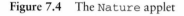

Figure 7.4   The Nature applet

```
        page.drawString ("Nature's first green", 25, 45);
        page.setColor (Color.yellow);
        page.drawString ("is gold.", 50, 75);
    } // method paint

} // class Nature
```

Defining Colors

In addition to the predefined colors, we can create many other specific colors in a Java program. The constructors of the Color class are:

- Color (int red, int green, int blue)
- Color (float red, float green, float blue)
- Color (int rgb)

The first constructor of the Color class accepts three integer parameters, representing the RGB value for the new color. For example:

```
Color brown = new Color (107, 69, 38);
```

Another constructor of the Color class accepts three floating point values to define the color. Like the previous constructor, the parameters represent the RGB value for the color, except this time they are expressed on a scale from 0.0 to 1.0. The third

`Color` constructor takes one integer parameter, in which bits 0 through 7 represent the blue contribution, bits 8 through 15 represent green, and bits 16 through 23 represent red.

Because the value of each primary color contribution can range from 0 to 255, we can define over 16 million different colors (256^3). The differences between some of these are so subtle that it is difficult, if not impossible, to distinguish between them. For example, the RGB values (255, 200, 0) and (255, 200, 1) are technically different colors (shades of orange), but the human eye could not tell them apart. Furthermore, some monitors are not able to display all of the possible colors that can be defined in Java, and they will use the closest color possible in each situation.

> **Key Concept** Over 16 million colors can be defined in a Java program, but nearly identical colors cannot be differentiated by the human eye. Most systems can only display a small subset of all possible colors.

The `Color` methods `getRed`, `getGreen`, and `getBlue` return an integer between 0 and 255 that represents the contribution of a particular primary color. Therefore, given the shade of brown defined earlier, the method invocation `brown.getGreen()` would return 69.

The `brighter` method returns a `Color` object that is a bit brighter than the one through which the method is invoked. Similarly, the `darker` method returns a `Color` object that is a bit darker. These methods are often helpful to create a palette of slightly different shades of a particular color. For example:

```
Color brighter_brown = brown.brighter();
```

XOR Mode

When two, overlapping, filled shapes are drawn, the last shape drawn overwrites the overlapped portion of the shape underneath. When those shapes are drawn in the same color, the shapes merge because their edges become indistinguishable. Drawing can occur in either normal mode or *XOR mode*. The XOR mode allows overlapping shapes to remain distinct. The XOR mode is turned on by using the `setXORMode` method of the `Graphics` class. This method accepts a `Color` parameter, that specifies the *XOR mode color*.

When a pixel is drawn in normal mode, the pixel is assigned the foreground color. But if the XOR mode has been set, the color assigned to the pixel is calculated using the pixel's current color and the XOR mode color. Therefore any shape drawn will always contrast with the color it is being drawn upon.

The XOR effect is reversible. If you draw the same pixel twice while the XOR mode is set, the pixel's color is returned to its original color. Therefore, if a shape is drawn twice in the same position, the effect is that the first shape is erased by the second.

▶ **Key Concept**　　The XOR mode can be used to erase a shape after it is drawn.

The following applet demonstrates the use of XOR mode. Its output is shown in Fig. 7.5. First, two nonintersecting rectangles are drawn. Then, two rectangles are drawn with a slight overlap, showing the effect of the XOR mode. Finally, one rectangle is drawn exactly on top of the first, essentially erasing the first so that nothing is displayed.

```java
import java.awt.*;
import java.applet.*;

// Demonstrates the use of XOR Mode
public class XOR_Demo extends Applet {

    public void paint (Graphics page) {

        page.setXORMode (Color.gray);

        page.fillRect (10,10,20,20);
        page.fillRect (40,10,20,20);

        page.fillRect (100,10,20,20);
        page.fillRect (110,20,20,20);
```

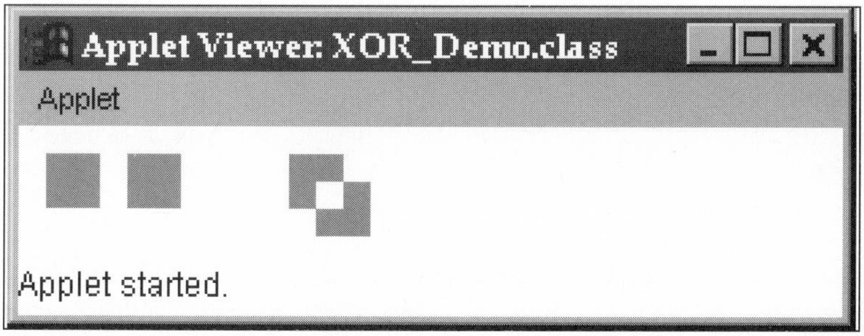

Figure 7.5　The XOR_Demo applet

XOR mode causes the second rectangle to "erase" the first.

```
        page.fillRect (140,10,20,20);
        page.fillRect (140,10,20,20);

    }   // method paint

}   // class XOR_Demo
```

7.3   Drawing Shapes

The Java API, through the `Graphics` class, directly supports the drawing of lines, ovals, rectangles, arcs, polygons, and polylines. A circle is simply a specific kind of oval, just as a square is a specific kind of rectangle. Polygons include many specific kinds of shapes such as triangles and hexagons because polygons can have any number of sides of any length. A polyline is a series of line segments connected end to end.

The `Graphics` class also allows you to specify whether you want a shape filled or not. An unfilled shape shows only the outline of the shape, and is otherwise transparent (you can see any underlying graphics). A filled shape is solid between its edges, and it overwrites any underlying graphics. The foreground color is used to draw the outline of the shape (as well as its interior if the shape is filled).

> **Key Concept**   Most shapes can be drawn filled (opaque) or unfilled (as an outline).

We've been drawing lines throughout previous chapters using the `drawLine` method, and there is little more to add. Lines cannot be filled, and you cannot specify their thickness (they are always one pixel wide). You can simulate the drawing of a thicker line by drawing multiple lines side by side, or by a series of filled circles, or by a rectangular filled polygon. Thick lines that are drawn vertically or horizontally can also be simulated using filled rectangles or ovals.

The following sections describe the details of drawing ovals, rectangles, arcs, polygons, and polylines.

Ovals

An oval can be defined by a rectangle that surrounds it. Figure 7.6 shows an oval and its *bounding rectangle*. In the `Graphics` methods used to draw ovals, the parameters specify the top-left corner of the bounding rectangle and its width and height in pixels.

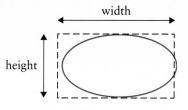

width

height

Figure 7.6 An oval and its bounding rectangle

The `Graphics` class contains two methods to draw ovals:

- `drawOval (int x, int y, int width, int height)`
- `fillOval (int x, int y, int width, int height)`

Both methods accept the same parameters. The first two specify the <*x*, *y*> coordinate of the top-left corner of the bounding rectangle. The third and fourth parameters specify the width and height of the bounding rectangle. An oval cannot be drawn at an angle. Its width and height are always perpendicular to the *x* and *y* axes. The `drawOval` method draws an unfilled oval, and the `fillOval` method draws a filled oval.

The following applet exercises the `drawOval` and `fillOval` methods. Its output is shown in Fig. 7.7.

```
import java.applet.Applet;
import java.awt.*;

// Draws ovals of various sizes.
public class Ovals extends Applet {

   public void paint (Graphics page) {
      page.drawOval (20, 20, 30, 50);
      page.drawOval (70, 40, 60, 10);
      page.drawOval (150, 30, 30, 30);  // a circle

      page.fillOval (30, 100, 50, 30);
      page.drawRect (100, 100, 50, 30);  // bounding rectangle
```

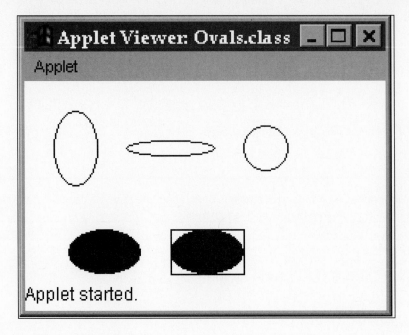

Figure 7.7   The `Ovals` applet

```
    page.fillOval (100, 100, 50, 30);
  } // method paint

} // class Oval
```

The next example, called `Rotating_Disk`, produces a simple animation. It repetitively draws filled ovals of varying sizes in order to simulate a disk rotating around a central vertical axis. Each oval is slightly less or more wide than the previous one, so that it appears as if the disk is being viewed at an angle as it rotates.

```
import java.applet.Applet;
import java.awt.*;

// Uses ovals to simulate a rotating disk.
public class Rotating_Disk extends Applet {

   public void paint (Graphics page) {
      int width = 0, height = 40;
      int x = 100, y = 100, warp = 1;

      page.setXORMode (getBackground());
      for (int change=1; change < 200; change++) {
```

```
      width += warp * 2;
      x -= warp;
      if (width == 0 || width == 40)
        warp *= -1;   //switch between growing and shrinking

      page.fillOval (x, y, width, height);
      for (int pause=1; pause <= 100000; pause++);
      page.fillOval (x, y, width, height); // erase oval
    }
  } // method paint

} // class Rotating_Disk
```

The width of each oval is changed to simulate rotation.

The height of all of the ovals is kept at 40 pixels. The width of each oval is increased or decreased by two pixels from the previous one. Whether the ovals are growing or shrinking in width depends on the variable warp, which has either the value 1 or −1. If warp is positive, the ovals are growing in size, and if negative, they are shrinking. The value of warp is changed when the oval reaches a width of 0 (when shrinking) or 40 (when growing). The x coordinate of each oval changes as the oval's size changes to keep all ovals centered around a common point. The top-left corner of the bounding rectangle of the initial oval is <100, 100>.

In the example, the XOR mode is set to the color of the background of the applet; this setting allows an oval to be erased by drawing it again in the same position. Unlike rectangles, the Graphics class does not have a specific method for erasing a drawn oval. A for loop with no body is used to create a short pause between drawing an oval and erasing it.

Figure 7.8 shows how the shape of the ovals change over time. You should execute the program to see how the dynamic changes create the illusion of a rotating disk.

Rectangles

Using the methods in the Graphics class, a rectangle can be drawn filled or unfilled, and it can have rounded corners or a slight three-dimensional effect. The methods for drawing rectangles are:

- drawRect (int x, int y, int width, int height)
- fillRect (int x, int y, int width, int height)
- clearRect (int x, int y, int width, int height)
- drawRoundRect (int x, int y, int width, int height, int arc_width, int arc_height)
- fillRoundRect (int x, int y, int width, int height, int arc_width, int arc_height)

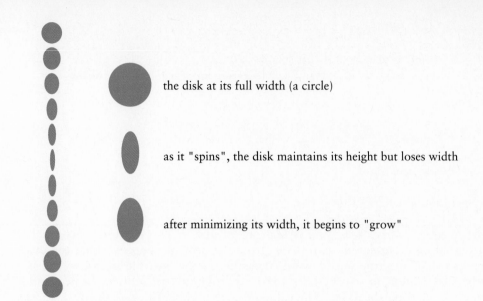

the disk at its full width (a circle)

as it "spins", the disk maintains its height but loses width

after minimizing its width, it begins to "grow"

Figure 7.8   The changing shape of the ovals in the `Rotating_Disk` applet

- `draw3DRect (int x, int y, int width, int height, boolean raised)`
- `fill3DRect (int x, int y, int width, int height, boolean raised)`

The first two parameters for all of these functions indicate the <*x, y*> coordinate of the upper-left corner of the rectangle. In the case of a rounded rectangle, the <*x, y*> coordinate indicates the upper-left corner of the bounding rectangle, as it does with ovals. The third and fourth parameters represent the width and height of the rectangle in pixels.

There is a class called `Rectangle` defined in the `java.awt` package, but it is not used to draw rectangles. All methods to draw rectangles are in the `Graphics` class. The `Rectangle` class is used to specify rectangular regions in various situations throughout the `java.awt` package.

The `drawRect` and `fillRect` methods draw unfilled and filled rectangles, respectively, in the foreground color. The `clearRect` method draws a rectangle in the current background color and can be used to erase an existing rectangle. The following program exercises the `drawRect` and `fillRect` methods. Its output is shown in Fig. 7.9.

```
import java.applet.Applet;
import java.awt.*;
```

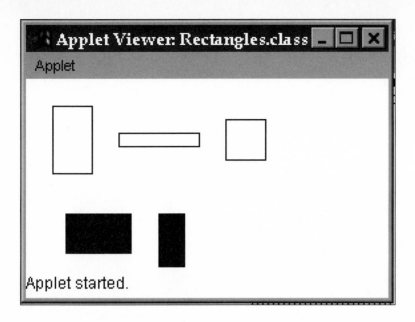

Figure 7.9 The `Rectangles` applet

```
// Draws various types of rectangles.
public class Rectangles extends Applet {

   public void paint (Graphics page) {
      page.drawRect (20, 20, 30, 50);
      page.drawRect (70, 40, 60, 10);
      page.drawRect (150, 30, 30, 30);   // a square

      page.fillRect (30, 100, 50, 30);
      page.fillRect (100, 100, 20, 40);
   } // method paint

} // class Rectangles
```

The `drawRoundRect` and `fillRoundRect` methods draw rectangles with rounded corners. The corners are rounded as specified by the last two parameters of the methods, which indicate the arc width and the arc height. These values are actually the width and height of an oval that, when superimposed over the corner of the rectangle, dictate the shape of the rounded edge. Figure 7.10 shows two rectangles with rounded corners of different sizes. The arc width and height need not be equal. If the arc width and arc height are the same, the rounded corners will be a quarter circle. All four corners of a rectangle are rounded in the same way.

Figure 7.10   Two rounded rectangles with different arc specifications

> **Key Concept**   An oval is used to define the shape of the corners of a rounded rectangle.

The following program exercises the `drawRoundRect` and `fillRoundRect` methods, and the output is shown in Fig. 7.11.

```
import java.applet.Applet;
import java.awt.*;

// Draws various types of rounded rectangles.
public class Rounded_Rectangles extends Applet {

   public void paint (Graphics page) {
      page.drawRoundRect (20, 20, 50, 50, 25, 25);
      page.drawOval (20, 20, 25, 25);  // oval defines the rounded
                                       // corner
```

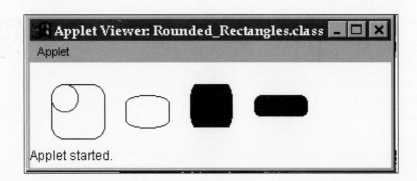

Figure 7.11   The `Rounded_Rectangles` applet

```
        page.drawRoundRect (90, 30, 40, 30, 40, 15);

        page.fillRoundRect (150, 20, 40, 40, 10, 30);
        page.fillRoundRect (210, 30, 50, 20, 15, 15);
    } // method paint

} // class Rounded_Rectangles
```

The arc width and height shape the rectangle's corner.

The `draw3DRect` and `fill3DRect` methods draw a rectangle with a slight three-dimensional effect. That effect is created by a highlight that appears on two adjacent sides of the rectangle. The last parameter of both methods is a boolean value that indicates whether the rectangle should be raised (if true) or lowered (if false). A raised rectangle has the highlight on the bottom and right sides of the rectangle. A lowered rectangle has the highlight on the top and left sides. The following program exercises these two methods. Its output is shown in Fig. 7.12.

```
import java.applet.Applet;
import java.awt.*;

// Draws various 3D rectangles.
public class Three_D_Rectangles extends Applet {

    public void paint (Graphics page) {
        setBackground (Color.white);
        setForeground (Color.gray);
        page.draw3DRect (20, 20, 50, 50, true);
        page.fill3DRect (90, 20, 50, 50, true);
        page.draw3DRect (160, 20, 50, 50, false);
```

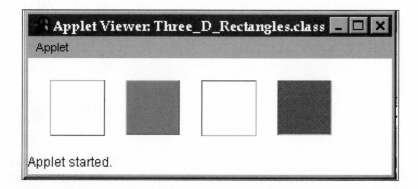

Figure 7.12   The `Three_D_Rectangles` applet

```
        page.fill3DRect (230, 20, 50, 50, false);
    } // method paint

} // class Three_D_Rectangles
```

Arcs

An arc is a segment of an oval. The Graphics class supports the following two
methods for drawing arcs:

- `drawArc (int x, int y, int width, int height, int start_angle, int arc_angle)`
- `fillArc (int x, int y, int width, int height, int start_angle, int arc_angle)`

A filled arc includes lines drawn from each end point of the arc to the center of
the oval used to define the arc, with the area between the lines and the arc filled with
the foreground color. Both methods contain the same parameters. The first two
specify the <x, y> coordinate of the top-left corner of the bounding rectangle of the
oval of which the arc is a part. The next two parameters specify the width and
height of the bounding rectangle. The last two parameters are the start angle and the
arc angle that define the portion of the oval that makes up the arc.

The *start angle* indicates where the arc begins and the *arc angle* determines the
sweep of the arc. Note that the arc angle does not indicate where the arc ends, but
rather its range. The start angle and the arc angle are measured in degrees. The
origin for the start angle is an imaginary horizontal line passing through the center
of the oval and can be referred to as 0°.

Key Concept An arc is a segment of an oval; the segment begins at a specific start
angle and extends for a distance specified by the arc angle.

Figure 7.13 shows the oval and arc indicated in the following call:

```
drawArc (10, 10, 60, 30, 20, 90);
```

The arc defined by the call to drawArc in Fig. 7.13 is the portion of the oval that
extends from 20° to 110°. The sweep of the arc covers 90°. The following program
draws this arc. Its output is shown in Fig. 7.14.

drawArc (10, 10, 60, 30, 20, 90)

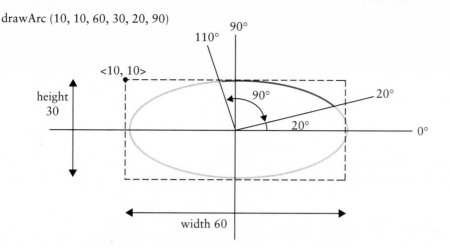

Figure 7.13   An arc defined by an oval, a start angle, and an arc angle

```
import java.applet.Applet;
import java.awt.*;

// Draws an arc.
public class Arc extends Applet {
   public void paint (Graphics page) {

      page.drawLine (140, 5, 140, 55);
      page.drawLine (105, 30, 175, 30);
```

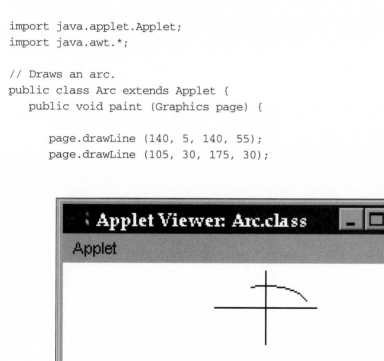

Figure 7.14   The Arc applet

The start angle
and arc angle
define an arc of an
oval.

```
        page.drawArc (110, 15, 60, 30, 20, 90);
    } // method paint

} // class Arc
```

There are actually two ways to specify any start angle. A positive start angle indicates the angle from the origin line in a counterclockwise direction. A negative start angle indicates the angle from the origin line in a clockwise direction. The origin line can be referred to as 0°, 360°, or −360°. Therefore, relative to the origin line, a starting angle of 45° and a starting angle of −315° are the same starting point. An arc angle can also be positive or negative. A positive arc angle sweeps counter-clockwise, and a negative arc angle sweeps clockwise.

> **Key Concept**   Because angles can be specified with negative values, each arc can be defined by four unique combinations of start and arc angles.

Therefore, the same arc can be specified using any of four different combinations of start and arc angles. For example, the following four calls to `drawArc` will all draw the top quarter of a circle, as shown in Fig. 7.15:

- `drawArc (10, 10, 50, 50, 45, 90);`
- `drawArc (10, 10, 50, 50, -315, 90);`
- `drawArc (10, 10, 50, 50, 135, -90);`
- `drawArc (10, 10, 50, 50, -225, -90);`

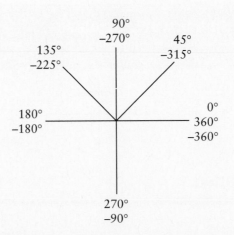

Figure 7.15   Positive and negative starting angles to specify an arc

Figure 7.16 The Arcs applet

The following program exercises the drawArc and fillArc methods by using both positive and negative start and arc angles. The output of the program is shown in Fig. 7.16.

```
import java.applet.Applet;
import java.awt.*;

// Draws various arcs.
public class Arcs extends Applet {

   public void paint (Graphics page) {
      page.drawArc (10, 10, 50, 50, 45, 225);
      page.drawArc (70, 10, 30, 70, -180, 180);
      page.fillArc (130, 10, 60, 60, -180, -90);
      page.fillArc (190, 10, 50, 50, 45, 270);
      page.fillArc (250, 10, 80, 40, -225, 180);
   } // method paint

} // class Arcs
```

Polygons

A polygon is a multisided figure. In Java, it is defined using a series of <x, y> points that indicate the end points of the line segments of the polygon sides. The java.awt package contains a Polygon class, which can be used to specify a polygon to be drawn. The methods that accomplish the drawing, however, are in the Graphics class. The polygon-drawing methods are:

- drawPolygon (int[] xpoints, int[] ypoints, int numpoints)
- drawPolygon (Polygon poly)

- `fillPolygon (int[] xpoints, int[] ypoints, int numpoints)`
- `fillPolygon (Polygon poly)`

Both `drawPolygon` and `fillPolygon` are overloaded. In one form, they take three parameters. The first two parameters are both arrays of integers. Taken together, the first two parameters represent the <x, y> coordinates of the end points of the line segments of the polygon sides. The third parameter is the number of points in the coordinate list. The second version of these methods take a single parameter that is a `Polygon` object, which already encapsulates the coordinates of the polygon sides. The `addpoint` method of the Polygon class is used to add points to the polygon. A filled polygon is drawn with all interior areas filled with the foreground color.

A polygon is always closed. If the last <x, y> coordinate pair in the coordinate list is not the same as the first coordinate pair in the list, the drawn figure is automatically closed by connecting the last point to the first point.

Key Concept A polygon is always a closed shape. The last point is automatically connected back to the first one.

The following program exercises the `drawPolygon` and `fillPolygon` methods. Its output is shown in Fig. 7.17.

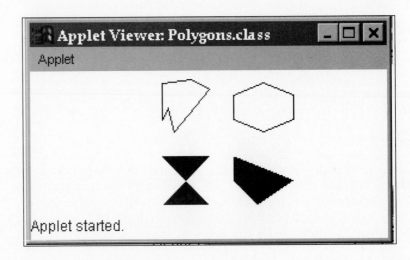

Figure 7.17 The `Polygons` applet

```
      page.drawString (quote, 10,40);
      page.setFont (new Font ("Helvetica", Font.ITALIC, 16));
      page.drawString (quote, 10,60);
      page.setFont (new Font ("Helvetica", Font.PLAIN, 18));
      page.drawString (quote, 10,80);
   } // method paint

} // class Entropy
```

7.5   Example: Bouncing Ball

Let's look at an example that uses some graphic methods to perform another simple animation. The following program implements a class that represents a ball attached to a rubber band. The program simulates what happens when the ball is pulled down and released.

The ball is represented by a circle, and the rubber band as a line. The bouncing effect is produced by erasing the previously drawn circle and line by using the XOR mode technique, and redrawing the circle attached to a shorter line or a longer line. When redrawn many times in sequence the effect of a bouncing ball is produced.

Note that various constants are used to slow the execution of the applet. The slow-down is necessary so that the simulation can produce a bouncing effect that looks realistic. A snapshot of the running applet is shown in Fig. 7.20.

```
import java.applet.Applet;
import java.awt.*;

// Simulates a ball on a rubber band.
public class Bouncing_Ball extends Applet {

   private final int PAUSE = 100000;
   private final int SIZE = 300;

   private Ball ball = new Ball(150, 10, 250, 200);
   private Graphics page;

   public void init() {
      setVisible(true);
      setSize (SIZE, SIZE);
      page = getGraphics();
```

Scaling Fonts

A continuing problem with fonts is choosing the correct sized font for an application. What happens when a user resizes a window of an applet? Unless specifically coded to respond to the change, the applet will write using font sizes that are inappropriate for the new size of the applet. This problem can be avoided by resizing the font to an appropriate smaller or larger point size. The Java API provides methods in the `Font` class and the `FontMetrics` class to implement this feature. The following method sets the font of a particular `Graphics` object to an appropriate size.

```
void set_font_size (String str, int width, Graphics page) {
    Font font = page.getFont();
    FontMetrics sizer = page.getFontMetrics();
    while (width <= sizer.stringWidth (str)) {
        font = new Font (font.getName(), font.getStyle(),
            font.getSize() - 1);
        page.setFont (font);
        sizer = page.getFontMetrics();
    }
} // method set_font_size
```

The method accepts three parameters: a `String` that contains the characters to be represented, the `width` into which the string must fit, and a `Graphics` object on which the string is drawn. Using the `stringWidth` method of the `FontMetrics` class, we can determine the amount of space that `str` will use when written in the current font. If this space is greater than the acceptable `width`, then the font size must be reduced. This method repetitively calculates a new font that is one point size smaller than the current font. The `while` loop iterates until the string will fit in the width allotted. The methods `getName`, `getStyle`, and `getSize` of the `Font` class are used to return the current font's name, style, and size, respectively.

You can call this method prior to calling `drawString` to ensure that your string will fit in a particular location, no matter what font or font size you are using.

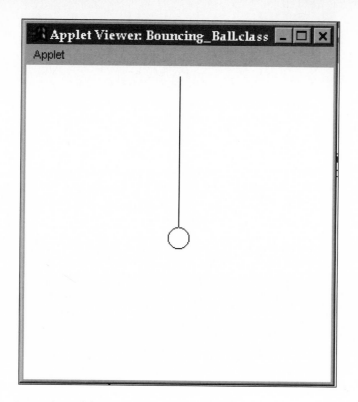

Figure 7.20 A snapshot of the `Bouncing_Ball` applet

```
      page.setXORMode (getBackground());
   } // method init

   public void start() {
      for (int pause = 1; pause < PAUSE; pause++);
      while (ball.moving())
         ball.bounce (page);
   } // method start

} // class Bouncing_Ball

// Draws the ball and simulates its movement.
class Ball {

   private final int MOVE = 2;
   private final float DISTANCE = 0.97f;
```

```
private final int SIZE = 20;
private final int PAUSE = 1000000;

private int x;
private int start_y;
private int end_y;
private int length;

private boolean moving_up = true;

Ball (int new_x, int new_start_y,
      int new_end_y, int new_length) {
   x = new_x;
   start_y = new_start_y;
   end_y = new_end_y;
   length = new_length;
} // constructor Ball

void move() {
   if (moving_up) {
      end_y = end_y - MOVE;
   } else {
      end_y = end_y + MOVE;
   }
} // method move

void draw_ball (Graphics page) {
   page.drawOval (x-(SIZE/2), end_y, SIZE, SIZE);
   page.drawLine (x, start_y, x, end_y);
} // draw_ball

public boolean moving () {
   return length != 0;
} // method moving

public void bounce (Graphics page) {
   for (int count = 1; count < length; count += MOVE) {
      draw_ball(page);
      for (int pause = 1; pause < PAUSE/length; pause++);
      draw_ball(page);
      move();
   }
```

```
      moving_up = !moving_up;
      length = (int) (DISTANCE * length);
   } // method bounce

} // class Ball
```

Summary of Key Concepts

- An object of the `Graphics` class represents a particular drawing surface and contains methods for drawing shapes on that surface.
- Each <x, y> coordinate represents a single pixel. The top left corner is coordinate <0, 0>. All coordinate values are positive.
- Any portion of a shape drawn outside of the drawing surface area will not be displayed.
- A color is defined by an RGB value that specifies the relative weight given to the primary colors red, green, and blue.
- The `Color` class has several common colors predefined.
- Over 16 million colors can be defined in a Java program, but nearly identical colors cannot be differentiated by the human eye. Most systems can only display a small subset of all possible colors.
- The XOR mode can be used to erase a shape after it is drawn.
- Most shapes can be drawn filled (opaque) or unfilled (as an outline).
- A bounding rectangle is often used to define the position of the "upper-right corner" of curved shapes such as an oval.
- An oval is used to define the shape of the corners of a rounded rectangle.
- An arc is a segment of an oval; the segment begins at a specific start angle and extends for a distance specified by the arc angle.
- Because angles can be specified with negative values, each arc can be defined by four unique combinations of start and arc angles.
- A polygon is always a closed shape. The last point is automatically connected back to the first one.
- A polyline is similar to a polygon except that a polyline is not a closed shape.
- Each computer system supports a specific set of fonts.

Self-Review Questions

7.1 Describe the Java coordinate system.

7.2 How many predefined colors are there in the Java API?

7.3 What is the difference between a filled shape and an unfilled shape?

7.4 What is a bounding rectangle?

7.5 What is the start angle and arc angle of an arc?

7.6 What is the difference between a polygon and a polyline?

7.7 Explain three ways that you could draw a triangle in a Java applet.

7.8 How are three-dimensional rectangles created in Java?

Exercises

7.9 Exactly how many colors can you define in a Java program? Why might you not be able to make use of all of them?

7.10 Write a Java declaration that creates a new `Color` object that represents a shade of purple. Explain how this is accomplished.

7.11 Define the color you created in Problem 7.10 using the `Color` constructor that accepts floating point values.

7.12 Explain what the XOR mode is and how it can be used to erase shapes once they are drawn.

7.13 Write four different `drawArc` method invocations that will draw the bottom half of a circle that has a radius of 10 pixels. Make sure each call draws the same arc in the same position.

7.14 Describe the relationship between an arc and an oval as they are drawn in Java. Explain the relationship of these shapes to a rounded rectangle. Give specific examples other than those found in this chapter.

Programming Projects

7.15 Design and implement an applet that draws a red stop sign with black letters.

7.16 Design and implement an applet that draws a bullseye by drawing five concentric circles centered around two lines forming a crosshair. Fill every other circle with a different color.

7.17 Design and implement an applet that draws a square using the `drawRoundRect` method.

7.18 Design and implement an applet that draws a rounded rectangle using only lines and arcs.

7.19 Design and implement an applet that appears to draw a circle divided into eight equal "pie-wedge" sections. Color each section with a different color. *Hint:* Use the `fillArc` method.

7.20 Design and implement an applet that defines a class called `My_Graphics`. This class contains a method called `my_drawRoundRect` that implements a functionality equivalent to that of the `drawRoundRect` method. Instantiate and test your class.

7.21 Design and implement an applet that simulates the actions of a traffic light. Use the `drawRect` method to create the background of the traffic light and the `drawOval` method to create the three lamps. Apply a dark initial color to each lamp; then, in a sequence that simulates the normal operation of a traffic light, change the color of the lamps. Repeat the sequence several times.

7.22 Design and implement an applet that simulates a yo-yo moving up and down its string. Allow the yo-yo to come to rest eventually at the string's full length. Use the `Bouncing_Ball` applet as a guide.

7.23 Design and implement an applet that simulates the swinging movement of a pendulum.

7.24 A clacker is a desktop toy that has five metal balls suspended on wires and lined up in a row. When one ball on one end is raised and released, it strikes the other balls. The action sends the ball on the other end bouncing away. When that ball returns, the original ball rebounds in the same way. This process continues, with the bouncing balls moving a lesser distance each time, until they eventually come to rest. Design and implement an applet that simulates the movement of a clacker.

7.25 Modify the program in Problem 7.24 so that the clacker movement is simulated as two balls are raised and released. (This action causes the two balls on the other end to respond accordingly.)

7.26 Design and implement an applet in which a rubber ball appears to bounce along a floor from left to right. Use the `setXORMode` method to erase the ball as it moves. Store the coordinates of the ball's path in an array.

7.27 Design and implement an applet that simulates an aerial view of a ball rolling around a rectangular box and rebounding off of the walls. Allow the simulation to run until the ball has rebounded 25 times.

Answers to Self-Review Questions

7.1 The Java coordinate system is used to reference any drawing surface. The top-left corner represents coordinate <0, 0>. The *x* axis increases to the right and the *y* axis increases down.

7.2 There are 13 colors defined in the `Color` class of the Java API, although a programmer can define many more if desired. The defined colors are: black, blue, red, yellow, green, white, orange, pink, gray, cyan, magenta, light gray, and dark gray. They are represented as static constants in the `Color` class. The constants are referenced through the class name, such as `Color.red`.

7.3 An unfilled shape draws only the outline of the shape, in the foreground color, with the background color (or whatever was drawn beneath it) showing through. A filled shape draws the shape in the foreground color and fills in the shape with that color.

7.4 A bounding rectangle is a rectangle that encompasses a curved shape such as an oval in order to specify its position, width, and height.

7.5 An arc is part of an oval. The start angle specifies one end point of the arc on the oval. The arc angle specifies how much of the oval is used for the arc.

7.6 A polygon is a multisided, closed shape defined by a set of points. A polyline is a set of line segments, connected end to end, but is not closed.

7.7 To draw a triangle, you could draw each side separately using the `drawLine` method, so that the end points of the line segments corresponded appropriately. Another way to draw a triangle would be to use the `drawPolygon` method, specifying two of the three corner coordinates. A third way would be to use the `drawPolyline` method, specifying all three corner coordinates.

7.8 A 3D rectangle is created using the `draw3DRect` or `fill3DRect` methods. They draw a rectangle with two adjacent edges highlighted, giving the illusion of depth. The rectangle can be raised or lowered based on the value of a parameter.

Inheritance

8

This chapter explains inheritance, a fundamental technique for organizing and creating classes. It is a simple but powerful idea that influences the way we design an object-oriented software system. Furthermore, inheritance enhances our ability to reuse classes in multiple situations and programs. Polymorphism, which is also described in this chapter, is an object-oriented concept related to inheritance that provides a versatile way to use objects consistently and elegantly. Inheritance is a cornerstone of object-oriented design and therefore influences much of the material covered in the remainder of this text.

Chapter Objectives

- Derive new classes from existing ones.
- Explain how inheritance supports software reuse.
- Add and modify methods and variables in child classes.
- Extend simple class derivations into well-designed class hierarchies.
- Define polymorphism and demonstrate its usefulness.

8.1 Creating Subclasses

Inheritance was introduced briefly in Chapter 2. It allows a software designer to derive a new class from an existing one. Inheritance is a powerful software development technique and a defining characteristic of object-oriented programming.

Derived Classes

We discussed in Chapter 4 the idea that a class is to an object as a blueprint is to a house. A class establishes the structure and purpose of an object, but reserves no memory space for variables. Classes are the plan, and objects are the embodiment of that plan.

Many houses can be created from the same blueprint, and they are essentially the same house in different locations with different people living in them. But suppose you wanted a house that was similar to another, but had some fundamentally different characteristics. You want to start with the same basic blueprint but need to modify it to suit your needs. Many housing developments are created this way. The houses in the development have the same core layout, but they can have unique features. For instance, they might all be split-level homes with the same bedroom, kitchen, and living-room configuration, but some have attached garages, or fireplaces, or full basements, while others do not.

It's likely that the housing developer commissioned a master architect to create a single blueprint establishing the basic design of all houses in the development. Then a series of new blueprints were created, starting with the original layout, but including variations designed to please different buyers. The act of creating the series of blueprints was simplified since they all begin with the same underlying structure, yet the variations give them unique characteristics that may be very important to the owners.

> **Key Concept**   Inheritance is the act of deriving a new class from an existing one. It is analogous to creating a new house blueprint from an existing blueprint that has similar characteristics.

This process is similar to the object-oriented concept of *inheritance,* in which a new class is *derived* from an existing one. The new class automatically contains some or all of the variables and methods in the original class. The software designer can then add new variables and methods to the newly derived class, or modify the inherited ones, to define the class appropriately.

New classes can be created via inheritance faster, easier, and cheaper than by writing them from scratch. At the heart of inheritance is the idea of *software reuse*. By using existing software components to create new ones, we capitalize on all of the effort that went into the design, implementation, and testing of the existing software.

Key Concept   A primary purpose of inheritance is to reuse existing software.

Keep in mind that the word class comes from the idea of classifying groups of objects with similar characteristics. Classification schemes often use levels of classes that relate to each other. For example, all mammals share certain characteristics: they are warm-blooded, have hair, and bear live offspring. Now consider a subset of mammals, such as horses. All horses are mammals, and have all of the characteristics of mammals. But they also have unique features that make them different from other mammals.

If we map this idea into software terms, an existing `Mammal` class would have certain variables and methods that describe the state and behavior of mammals. A `Horse` class could be derived from the existing `Mammal` class, automatically inheriting the variables and methods contained in `Mammal`. New variables and methods can then be added to the derived class, to distinctly define a horse. Inheritance nicely models many situations found in the natural world.

The derivation process should establish a specific kind of relationship between two classes; this relationship is called an *is-a relationship*. In this relationship the derived class should be a more specific version of the original. For example, a horse *is-a* mammal. Not all mammals are horses, but all horses are mammals.

The original class that is used to derive a new one is called the *parent class,* or *superclass,* or *base class*. The derived class is called a *child class,* or *subclass*. Java uses the reserved word `extends` to indicate that a new class is being derived from another. The basic syntax for specifying an inherited class is:

```
class child-class extends parent-class {
    // class contents
}
```

This syntax represents the definition of the class `child-class`. The child class automatically inherits an initial set of methods and variables from the `parent-class`. The inherited variables and methods can be used by the child class as if they had been declared locally in the child class.

Recall that to create an applet we define a class that extends the `Applet` class defined in the `java.applet` package of the Java API. The `Applet` class already contains the details of getting an applet running, so that the derived class is free to focus on the purpose of that particular applet.

Let's look at an example of inheritance in Java. In the following application, the class `Words` contains the `main` method, which instantiates one object of class `Dictionary`. The `Book` class is the parent of `Dictionary`, but it is never instantiated.

```
//  Instantiates a derived class and invokes its inherited
//  and local methods.
class Words {

    public static void main (String[] args) {
        Dictionary webster = new Dictionary ();
        webster.page_message ();
        webster.definition_message ();
    }  // method main

}  // class Words

//  Serves as a parent class.
class Book {

    protected int pages = 1500;

    public void page_message () {
        System.out.println ("Number of pages: " + pages);
    }  // method page_message
}  // class Book

//  Dictionary contains two data values (one inherited) and two
//  methods (one inherited).
class Dictionary extends Book {

    private int definitions = 52500;

    public void definition_message () {
        System.out.println ("Number of definitions: " + definitions);
```

Calling an inherited method

Dictionary is derived from Book

```
    System.out.println ("Definitions per page: " +
                            definitions/pages);
 }  // method definition_message

}  // class Dictionary
```

The class `Dictionary` is derived from `Book` using the `extends` keyword in the definition of `Dictionary`. Inheritance relationships are often depicted graphically, as shown in Fig. 8.1. By convention, the arrow points to the parent class.

The `Dictionary` class automatically inherits the definition of the `page_message` method and the `pages` variable. Therefore, it is as if the `page_message` method and the `pages` variable were declared inside the `Dictionary` class. Note that the `definition_message` method uses the `pages` variable and that both the `page_message` and `definition_message` methods are invoked through the `Book` object called `webster`. When executed, the program produces the following output:

```
Number of pages: 1500
Number of definitions: 52500
Definitions per page: 35
```

The `protected` Modifier

Not all variables and methods are inherited in a derivation. The visibility modifiers used to declare them determine which variables and methods get inherited and which do not. Specifically, variables and methods that are declared `public` are inherited by the child class, and those declared `private` are not. The `page_mes-sage` method was inherited by `Dictionary` in the `Words` program because it is declared `public`.

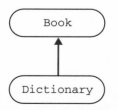

Figure 8.1   Graphical notation for showing a derived class

Key Concept   Visibility modifiers determine which variables and methods are inherited. Protected visibility provides the best encapsulation while still permitting inheritance.

However, by declaring a variable `public` so that it is inherited by a derived class, we violate the principle of encapsulation (established in Chapter 4). Therefore, Java provides a third visibility modifier: `protected`. Note that the variable `pages` is declared with `protected` visibility in the `Words` program. When a variable or method is declared with `protected` visibility, it retains some of its encapsulation properties and it is inherited by a derived class. The encapsulation with `protected` visibility is not as tight as it would be if the variable or method were declared `private`, but it is better than if it were declared `public`. The nuances of these visibility modifiers are discussed further in Chapter 9 and are explained in a summary of all Java modifiers in Appendix F.

Inheritance is a one-way street. No new variables or methods declared in the `Dictionary` class can be used by the `Book` class. For instance, the `Book` class cannot invoke the `definition_message` method.

Inherited variables and methods retain the affect of their original visibility modifier. For example, the `page_message` method is still considered `public` in its inherited form. Therefore it can be invoked through an object of the `Dictionary` class, as it is in the `main` method.

Key Concept   Inherited variables and methods keep their original visibility characteristics in the subclass.

The `super` Reference

Constructors are an exception to the inheritance process. They are not inherited by a derived class, even though they have `public` visibility. Let's look at a variation of the `Words` program that addresses this issue:

```
//  Instantiates a derived class using multiple
//  constructors and the super reference.
class Words2 {

   public static void main (String[] args) {
      Dictionary webster = new Dictionary (1500, 52500);
      webster.page_message();
```

```
         webster.definition_message();
     }   // method main

}   // class Words2

//  Book's constructor sets up Book's data.
class Book {

    protected int pages;

    public Book (int num_pages) {
        pages = num_pages;
    }   // constructor Book

    public void page_message () {
        System.out.println ("Number of pages: " + pages);
    }   // method page_message

}   // class Book

//  Dictionary's constructor calls Book's constructor
//  using the super references.
class Dictionary extends Book {

    private int definitions;

    public Dictionary (int num_pages, int num_definitions) {
        super (num_pages);
        definitions = num_definitions;
    }   // constructor Dictionary

    public void definition_message () {
        System.out.println ("Number of definitions: " + definitions);
        System.out.println ("Definitions per page: " +
                            definitions/pages);
    }   // method definition_message

}   // class Dictionary
```

Invoking the parent's constructor using super

The output of the Words2 program is the same as it is for the original Words program. However, this time constructors are used to set up Book and Dictionary objects. Because Dictionary inherits the variable pages from Book, a Dictionary object needs to initialize it in its constructor. But the Book class already has a constructor that initializes pages. Because constructors are not inherited, the

Book constructor cannot be invoked directly in `Dictionary`. However, we can use the *super reference* to invoke a constructor of the superclass. The super reference is used in the `Dictionary` constructor to invoke the constructor of the `Book` class, passing in the initial value of the `pages` variable to be initialized. The `Dictionary` constructor then proceeds to initialize its own variable, `definitions`.

▶ **Key Concept** The `super` reference can be used to invoke the parent's constructor.

A child's constructor is responsible for calling the parent's constructor. The first line of a constructor should use the `super` reference call to a constructor of the parent class. If no such call exists, Java will automatically make a call to `super()` at the beginning of the constructor. This rule ensures that all data of a parent class are initialized before the child class constructor begins to execute. The `super` reference for invoking a parent's constructor can only be used in the child's constructor, and if included it must be the first line of the constructor.

The `super` reference can also be used to reference other variables and methods in the parent's class, as we discuss later in this chapter.

Defined versus Inherited

We need to carefully examine a subtle feature of inheritance at this point. The visibility modifiers determine if a variable or method is inherited into a subclass. If a variable or method is inherited, then it can be referenced directly in the subclass by name, as if it were declared locally in the subclass. However, all variables and methods are *defined* for a derived class, so that they can be referenced indirectly if needed. Consider the following example:

```
//   Instantiates a derived class which indirectly uses
//   variables and methods that are not inherited.
class Eating {

   public static void main (String[] args) {
      Pizza special = new Pizza (275);
      System.out.println ("Calories per serving: " +
         special.calories_per_serving());
   }  // method main

}  // class Eating
```

```
//  Represents a food item with methods to compute
//  total calories and calories per serving.
class Food {

    final private int CALORIES_PER_GRAM = 9;
    private int fat;
    protected int servings;

    public Food (int num_fat_grams, int num_servings) {
        fat = num_fat_grams;
        servings = num_servings;
    }  // constructor Food

    private int calories() {
        return fat * CALORIES_PER_GRAM;
    }  // method calories

    public int calories_per_serving() {
        return (calories() / servings);
    }  // method calories_per_serving

}  // class Food

//  Represents a pizza as a food item with eight servings.
class Pizza extends Food {

    public Pizza (int amount_fat) {
        super (amount_fat, 8);
    }  // constructor Pizza

}  // class Pizza
```

Private data is
defined but not
inherited

Private methods
can be invoked
implicitly

The output of this program is:

```
Calories per serving: 309
```

This example defines a class Food that stores the amount of fat and the number
of servings for a particular food item. From Food we derive a subclass called
Pizza, which assumes that there are eight servings. The Pizza constructor uses the
super reference to invoke the constructor of Food.

Note that the Pizza object called special is used to invoke the method
calories_per_serving, which is defined as a public method and is therefore
inherited by Pizza. However, calories_per_serving calls calories, which

references `fat` and `CALORIES_PER_GRAM`. Note that the method `calories` and the values `fat` and `CALORIES_PER_GRAM` are all `private`. The `Pizza` constructor passes in a value for the fat content, which is used in the calculations. Even though no object of class `Food` has been instantiated, these `private` variables and methods are available, indirectly, to the child class `Pizza`. The `Pizza` class cannot refer to them directly by name, because they are not inherited, but they are defined.

> **Key Concept** All variables and methods are defined for a subclass, but they are not necessarily inherited. Only inherited variables and methods can be referenced by name in a derived class.

Figure 8.2 lists each variable and method declared in the `Food` class, and indicates whether it is defined and/or inherited in the `Pizza` class.

Note that all items are defined in the `Pizza` class. No matter how an item is declared, it is defined in the `Pizza` class. In this example, each of the items that are not inherited can be accessed through a method that is inherited.

Student Example

Let's look at another example of inheritance. The following program derives the class `Grad_Student` from `Student`. This derivation follows the *is-a* relationship because a graduate student is a student. In this case, the `Grad_Student` class inherits the variables `name` and `num_courses`, and the method `info`. It then augments its definition with variables and methods concerning financial support.

Items declared in `Food` class	Defined in `Pizza` class	Inherited in `Pizza` class
`CALORIES_PER_GRAM`	yes	no, because the constant is private
`fat`	yes	no, because the variable is private
`servings`	yes	yes, because the variable is protected
`Food`	yes	no, because constructors are not inherited
`calories`	yes	no, because the method is private
`calories_per_serving`	yes	yes, because the method is public

Figure 8.2   Items from `Food` class defined in `Pizza`

```
//  Instantiates student and grad student objects and
//  invokes their methods.
class School {

    public static void main (String[] args) {
        Student sammy = new Student ("Sammy", 5);
        Grad_Student pete = new Grad_Student ("Pete", 3,
            "Teaching Assistant", 8.75);

        sammy.info();

        System.out.println();

        pete.info();
        pete.support();
    }  // method main

}  // class School

//  Represents one student that is currently taking a certain
//  number of courses.
class Student {

    protected String name;
    protected int num_courses;

    public Student (String student_name, int classes) {
        name = student_name;
        num_courses = classes;
    }  // constructor Student

    public void info () {
        System.out.println ("Student name: " + name);
        System.out.println ("Number of courses: " + num_courses);
    }  // method info

}  // class Student

//  Represents a grad student, who may receive financial
//  support.
class Grad_Student extends Student {

    private String source;
    private double rate;
```

```
public Grad_Student (String student_name, int classes,
        String support_source, double hourly_rate) {
    super (student_name, classes);
    source = support_source;
    rate = hourly_rate;
}   // constructor Grad_Student

public void support () {
    System.out.println ("Support source: " + source);
    System.out.println ("Hourly pay rate: " + rate);
}   // method support

}   // class Grad_Student
```

The output of the program is:

```
Student name: Sammy
Number of courses: 5
Student name: Pete
Number of courses: 3
Support source: Teaching Assistant
Hourly pay rate: 8.75
```

The Grad_Student constructor uses the super reference to invoke the constructor of Student, then initializes its own variables. The main method instantiates one Student object and one Grad_Student object. The Grad_Student object is used to invoke the local method support and the inherited method info.

8.2 Overriding Methods

When a child class defines a method with the same name and signature as the parent, we say that the child's version *overrides* the parent's version in favor of its own. The need for overriding occurs often in the inheritance derivation process.

> **Key Concept** A child class can override (redefine) a parent's definition of an inherited method.

Let's look at a simple example that demonstrates method overriding in Java. The following program defines a parent class called Thought and a child class called Advice. Both have a method called message. The message method is inherited by the Advice class, but Advice overrides it with a new definition.

```java
//  Instantiates two objects and prints a message from each.
//  The second message is overridden.
class Messages {

   public static void main (String[] args) {
      Thought parked = new Thought();
      Advice dates = new Advice();

      parked.message();
      dates.message();

   }  // method main

}  // class Messages


//  Defines a message method.
class Thought {

   public void message() {
      System.out.println ("I feel like I'm diagonally parked " +
                          "in a parallel universe.");
      System.out.println();

   }  // method message

}  // class Thought


//  Overrides the message method.
class Advice extends Thought {

   public void message() {
      System.out.println ("Warning: Dates in calendar are " +
                          "closer than they appear.");
      System.out.println();
   }  // method message

}  // class Advice
```

Advice overrides the message method

When executed, the program produces the following output:

```
I feel like I'm diagonally parked in a parallel universe.

Warning: Dates in calendar are closer than they appear.
```

The type of the object that is used to invoke a method determines which version of the method is actually executed. When `message` is invoked using the `parked` object, the `Thought` version of `message` is executed. When `message` is invoked using the `dates` object, the `Advice` version of `message` is executed. This flexibility allows two objects that are related by inheritance to use the same naming conventions for methods that accomplish the same task in different ways.

 Key Concept The class of the object determines which version of an overridden method is invoked.

Employee Example

Let's look at another example that uses overriding. A class representing an `Employee` for a company is used to derive an `Executive` employee class, as shown in Fig. 8.3.

The derived class uses the `super` reference to invoke the parent's constructor. The `pay` method defined for `Employee` is overridden in the `Executive` class in order to incorporate a possible bonus. The `Executive` class also defines new variables and methods as needed. Two employees and one executive are instantiated in the main method, then each one's `pay` method is invoked.

```
//  Creates several employees, including an executive, and
//  pays them.
class Firm {

    public static void main (String[] args) {
        Executive sam = new Executive ("Sam", "123 Main Line",
            "555-0469", "123-45-6789", 1923.07);
        Employee carla = new Employee ("Carla", "456 Off Line",
            "555-0101", "987-65-4321", 846.15);
        Employee woody = new Employee ("Woody", "789 Off Rocker",
            "555-0000", "010-20-3040", 769.23);

        woody.print();
        System.out.println ("Paid: " + woody.pay());
        System.out.println();
```

Shadowing Variables

It is possible for a child class to redefine variables that were inherited from the parent. This technique is called *shadowing* variables. It is similar to the process of overriding methods, but creates some confusing subtleties. Consider the following code:

```
//  Demonstrates variable shadowing.
class Shadow {

   public static void main (String[] args) {
      Child darkness = new Child();
      darkness.print_num();
   }  // method main

}  // class Shadow

class Parent {
   int number = 34;
}  // class Parent

//  Redefines the variable number.
class Child extends Parent {

   int number = 35;

   public void print_num() {
      System.out.println ("The number is: " + number);
   }  // method message

}  // class Child
```

When executed, this program produces the following output:

```
The number is: 35
```

Note that number is actually redeclared, not just reassigned a new value. When print_num is invoked, the newly defined version of the variable number is used. Shadowing variables often leads to confusing code and is usually not necessary. In this case, the child class could have changed the value of the variable without creating a new version of it. In general, shadowing variables should be avoided.

Figure 8.3   Parent and child classes representing specific kinds of employees

```
        carla.print();
        System.out.println ("Paid: " + carla.pay());
        System.out.println();
```

The pay method is
overridden

```
        sam.print();
        sam.award_bonus (2000);
        System.out.println ("Paid: " + sam.pay());
        System.out.println();

    }  // method main

}  // class Firm

//  Represents one employee
class Employee {

    protected String name;
    protected String address;
    protected String phone_number;
    protected String social_security_number;
    protected double pay_rate;

    public Employee (String emp_name, String emp_address,
            String emp_phone, String emp_ssnumber, double emp_rate) {
        name = emp_name;
        address = emp_address;
        phone_number = emp_phone;
        social_security_number = emp_ssnumber;
        pay_rate = emp_rate;
    }  // constructor Employee

    public double pay () {
        return pay_rate;
    }  // method pay
```

```
        public void print () {
            System.out.println (name + "   " + social_security_number);
            System.out.println (address);
            System.out.println (phone_number);
        }  // method print

}  // class Employee


//   Represents one executive, which is an employee that can
//   earn a bonus.
class Executive extends Employee {

    private double bonus;

    public Executive (String exec_name, String exec_address,
            String exec_phone, String exec_ssnumber, double exec_rate) {
        super (exec_name, exec_address, exec_phone, exec_ssnumber,
            exec_rate);
        bonus = 0;  // bonus yet to be awarded
    }  // constructor Executive

    public void award_bonus (double exec_bonus) {
        bonus = exec_bonus;
    }  // method award_bonus

    // Executive pay is the regular salary plus a one-time bonus
    public double pay () {
        double paycheck = super.pay() + bonus;
        bonus = 0;
        return paycheck;
    }  // method pay

}  // class Executive
```

Explicitly invoking a parent's method using super

Note that Sam's pay method is an overridden version that uses the super reference to invoke the pay method of the Employee class. This process demonstrates the use of super to explicitly refer to a parent's method. This technique is often used when dealing with overridden methods. Though the new version of pay could simply refer to the pay_rate, which it inherited, the use of the super reference guarantees consistency with the parent class. If the process of paying a regular employee changes, the Executive class automatically takes it into account.

> **Key Concept** The `super` reference can be used to explicitly invoke any method from a parent class. This technique is often used in overridden methods to call the parent's version of the method.

The output of the program is:

```
Woody    010-20-3040
789 Off Rocker
555-0000
Paid: 769.23

Carla    987-65-4321
456 Off Line
555-0101
Paid: 846.15

Sam    123-45-6789
123 Main Line
555-0469
Paid: 3923.07
```

Savings Accounts Example

This example defines classes that represent a bank `Savings_Account` and a special type of savings account, called a `Bonus_Saver_Account`. Both types of accounts are savings accounts through which you can make deposits and withdrawals. However, the `Bonus_Saver_Account` is designed with incentives to encourage faster savings accumulation. Both types of accounts earn interest, but the `Bonus_Saver_Account` earns more. Furthermore, there is a financial penalty every time a withdrawal is made from a bonus account.

```
//  Manages savings accounts.
class Accounts {

    public static void main (String[] args) {
        Savings_Account savings =
            new Savings_Account (4321, 8921.39, 0.02);
        Bonus_Saver_Account big_savings =
            new Bonus_Saver_Account (6543, 1225.00, 0.02);
```

```
      savings.add_interest();
      big_savings.add_interest();

      savings.deposit (390.23);
      big_savings.deposit (250.45);

      savings.withdrawal (432.34);
      big_savings.withdrawal (875.95);

   }  // method main

}  // class Accounts

//  Represents a single savings account with the ability to
//  make deposits and withdrawals.  The account earns interest.
class Savings_Account {

   protected int account;
   protected double balance;
   protected double rate;

   public Savings_Account (int account_num, double initial_balance,
                           double interest_rate) {
      account = account_num;
      balance = initial_balance;
      rate = interest_rate;
   }  // constructor Savings_Account

   public void deposit (double amount) {
      balance += amount;
      System.out.println ("Deposit into account " + account);
      System.out.println ("Amount: " + amount);
      System.out.println ("New balance: " + balance);
      System.out.println ();
   }  // method deposit

   public boolean withdrawal (double amount) {

      boolean result = false;

      System.out.println ("Withdrawal from account " + account);
      System.out.println ("Amount: " + amount);
```

```
         if (amount > balance)
            System.out.println ("Insufficient funds.");
         else {
            balance -= amount;
            System.out.println ("New balance: " + balance);
            result = true;
         }
         System.out.println();

         return result;

      }  // method withdrawal

      public void add_interest () {
         balance += balance * rate;
         System.out.println ("Interest added to account: " + account);
         System.out.println ("New balance: " + balance);
         System.out.println();
      }  // method add_interest

}  // class Savings_Account

//  A bonus savings account earns extra interest, but there
//  is a penalty for withdrawals.
class Bonus_Saver_Account extends Savings_Account {

      private final int PENALTY = 25;
      private final double BONUS_RATE = 0.03;

      public Bonus_Saver_Account (int account_num,
               double initial_balance, double interest_rate) {
         super (account_num, initial_balance, interest_rate);
      }  // constructor Super_Saver_Account

      public boolean withdrawal (double amount) {
         System.out.println ("Penalty incurred: " + PENALTY);
         return super.withdrawal (amount+PENALTY);
      }  // method withdrawal

      public void add_interest () {
         balance += balance * (rate + BONUS_RATE);
         System.out.println ("Interest added to account: " + account);
         System.out.println ("New balance: " + balance);
         System.out.println();
```

```
}   // method add_interest

}   // class Bonus_Saver_Account
```

The inherited method `deposit` is shared by both `Savings_Account` and `Bonus_Saver_Account`. However, the derived class overrides the definition of `withdrawal` and `add_interest`. Note that the new version of `withdrawal` uses the `super` reference to invoke the `withdrawal` method of the parent. The output of the program is:

```
Interest added to account: 4321
New balance: 9099.82

Interest added to account: 6543
New balance: 1286.25

Deposit into account 4321
Amount: 390.23
New balance: 9490.05

Deposit into account 6543
Amount: 250.45
New balance: 1536.7

Withdrawal from account 4321
Amount: 432.34
New balance: 9057.71
Penalty incurred: 25

Withdrawal from account 6543
Amount: 900.95
New balance: 635.75
```

In this and earlier examples, we've seen only simple derivation. That is, we've only used one class to derive one new one. But inheritance can be used to form rich hierarchies, as discussed in the next section.

8.3   Class Hierarchies

A child class of one parent can itself be the parent of another derived class. Furthermore, multiple classes can be derived from a single parent. Therefore, inheritance relationships often develop into *class hierarchies*. Figure 8.4 shows a class

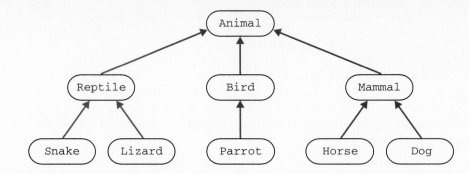

Figure 8.4   A class hierarchy of animals

hierarchy that incorporates the inheritance relationship between classes `Mammal` and `Horse`.

> ▶ **Key Concept**   The child of one class can be the parent of one or more other classes, creating a class hierarchy.

There is no limit to the number of children a class can have, or on the number of levels to which a class hierarchy can extend. Two children of the same parent are called *siblings*. Large programs are often made up of hundreds or even thousands of classes, with many objects instantiated from a number of classes. A small program might be made up of a single class. Classes that make up a program do not all have to be related by inheritance, though programs are often constructed using several hierarchy clusters.

A characteristic of good class hierarchies is that common features are kept as high in the hierarchy as reasonably possible. That way, only specific differences are established in a child class, which explicitly identifies the characteristics that make the class unique. Furthermore, this approach maximizes the ability to reuse. Common traits are established high in the hierarchy for the child classes to use.

> ▶ **Key Concept**   Common features should be located near the top of a class hierarchy, maximizing reuse potential.

The inheritance mechanism is transitive. That is, a parent passes along a trait to a child class, and that child class passes it along to its children, and so on. An inherited feature might have originated in the immediate parent, or possibly from several levels higher from a more distant ancestor class.

Remember to maintain the *is-a* relationship when building class hierarchies. As hierarchies grow, it is easier to forget this fundamental and important guideline.

> **Key Concept** You should maintain the *is-a* relationship between all derived classes in a class hierarchy.

Revising and Extending Hierarchies

Although it would be nice to avoid modifications to existing classes, such revisions to class hierarchies are common and necessary in order to maintain a clean design. Remember that it is good practice to store characteristics as high in a class hierarchy as is reasonable.

Figure 8.5 shows a class hierarchy that extends the basic savings account relationship we examined in the previous section. A higher-level, generic `Bank_Account` class can be used to collect all features common to all bank accounts. The `Checking_Account` and `Savings_Account` classes are derived from it, and `Bonus_Saver_Account` is derived from `Savings_Account`, as it was earlier.

Consider the following code that implements and exercises the modified class hierarchy design:

```
//  Creates and uses various bank accounts.
class Accounts2 {
```

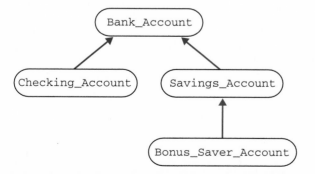

Figure 8.5 A class hierarchy for bank accounts

```java
        public static void main (String[] args) {
            Savings_Account savings =
                new Savings_Account (4321, 5028.45, 0.02);
            Bonus_Saver_Account big_savings =
                new Bonus_Saver_Account (6543, 1475.85, 0.02);
            Checking_Account checking =
                new Checking_Account (9876, 269.93, savings);


            savings.deposit (148.04);
            big_savings.deposit (41.52);
            savings.withdrawal (725.55);
            big_savings.withdrawal (120.38);
            checking.withdrawal (320.18);


        }  // method main


    }  // class Accounts2


    //  Represents a generic bank account with deposits and
    //  withdrawals.
    class Bank_Account {
```

Common features
are kept in high-
level classes

```java
        protected int account;
        protected double balance;


        public Bank_Account (int account_num, double initial_balance) {
            account = account_num;
            balance = initial_balance;
        }  // constructor Bank_Account


        public void deposit (double amount) {


            balance += amount;
            System.out.println ("Deposit into account " + account);
            System.out.println ("Amount: " + amount);
            System.out.println ("New balance: " + balance);
            System.out.println ();


        }  // method deposit
```

```java
    public boolean withdrawal (double amount) {

        boolean result = false;

        System.out.println ("Withdrawal from account " + account);
        System.out.println ("Amount: " + amount);
        if (amount > balance)
            System.out.println ("Insufficient funds.");
        else {
            balance -= amount;
            System.out.println ("New balance: " + balance);
            result = true;
        }
        System.out.println();

        return result;

    }  // method withdrawal


}  // class Bank_Account


//  A checking account has an overridden withdrawal method
//  that makes use of overdraft protection.
class Checking_Account extends Bank_Account {

    private Savings_Account overdraft;

    public Checking_Account (int account_num, double initial_balance,
                             Savings_Account protection) {
        super (account_num, initial_balance);
        overdraft = protection;
    }  // constructor Checking_Account

    public boolean withdrawal (double amount) {

        boolean result = false;

        if ( ! super.withdrawal (amount) ) {
            System.out.println ("Using overdraft...");
            if ( ! overdraft.withdrawal (amount-balance) )
```

A reference to another account object

```
                    System.out.println ("Overdraft source insufficient.");
                else {
                    balance = 0;
                    System.out.println ("New balance on account " +
                                            account + ": " + balance);
                    result = true;
                }
            }
            System.out.println();


            return result;


        }   // method withdrawal


    }   // class Checking_Account


// A savings account earns interest.
class Savings_Account extends Bank_Account {

    protected double rate;


    public Savings_Account (int account_num, double initial_balance,
                            double interest_rate) {
        super (account_num, initial_balance);
        rate = interest_rate;

    }   // constructor Savings_Account


    public void add_interest () {
        balance += balance * rate;
        System.out.println ("Interest added to account: " + account);
        System.out.println ("New balance: " + balance);
        System.out.println();
    }   // method add_interest


}   // class Savings_Account


// A bonus savings account earns extra interest, but there
// is a penalty for withdrawals.
```

```
class Bonus_Saver_Account extends Savings_Account {


   private final int PENALTY = 25;
   private final double BONUS_RATE = 0.03;


   public Bonus_Saver_Account (int account_num,
              double initial_balance, double interest_rate) {
      super (account_num, initial_balance, interest_rate);
   }  // constructor Super_Saver_Account


   public boolean withdrawal (double amount) {


      System.out.println ("Penalty incurred: " + PENALTY);
      return super.withdrawal (amount+PENALTY);


   }  // method withdrawal


   public void add_interest() {
      balance += balance * (rate + BONUS_RATE);
      System.out.println ("Interest added to account: " + account);
      System.out.println ("New balance: " + balance);
      System.out.println();
   }  // method add_interest


}  // class Bonus_Saver_Account
```

The basic deposit and withdrawal methods are now defined in the Bank_Account class, as are variables to define the account number and current balance. Only savings accounts earn interest, therefore the interest rate and add_interest method are defined in Savings_Account. Bonus_Saver_Account overrides add_interest and withdrawal, as it did in the earlier Accounts program.

The Checking Account class stores a reference to a Savings_Account object that can be used in case a withdrawal is attempted against insufficient funds. This feature is called overdraft protection. If an overdraft is attempted, the extra funds needed to cover the withdrawal are taken from the Savings_Account. This leaves the Checking_Account with a zero balance. This process makes for a fairly interesting withdrawal method in the Checking_Account class, which overrides the definition in the Bank_Account class.

When executed, the program prints the following:

```
Deposit into account 4321
Amount: 148.04
New balance: 5176.49

Deposit into account 6543
Amount: 41.52
New balance: 1517.37

Withdrawal from account 4321
Amount: 725.55
New balance: 4450.94

Penalty incurred: 25
Withdrawal from account 6543
Amount: 145.38
New balance: 1371.99

Withdrawal from account 9876
Amount: 320.18
Insufficient funds.

Using overdraft...
Withdrawal from account 4321
Amount: 50.25
New balance: 4400.69
New balance on account 9876: 0
```

Alternative Hierarchies

There is not a single best hierarchy organization for all situations. The decisions made when designing a class hierarchy restrict and guide more detailed design decisions and implementation options, and must be made carefully.

▶ **Key Concept**   There is no single class hierarchy that is appropriate for all situations.

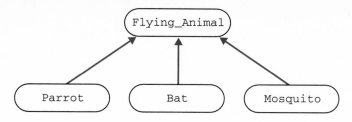

Figure 8.6   An alternate hierarchy that includes birds

In earlier examples we discussed grouping animals by their major biological classifications, such as `Mammal`, `Bird`, and `Reptile`. However, in a different situation, the same animals might logically be organized in a different way. For example, as shown in Fig. 8.6, the class hierarchy may be organized around a function of the animals, such as their ability to fly. In this case, a `Parrot` class and a `Bat` class would be siblings derived from a general `Flying_Animal` class.

This class hierarchy is as valid and reasonable as the original one. It depends on the need of the programs that use the hierarchies.

The `Object` class

In Java, all classes are derived ultimately from the `Object` class. If a class definition doesn't use the `extend` clause, then that class is derived from the `Object` class by default. The following two class definitions are equivalent:

```
class Bank_Account {
}
```

and

```
class Bank_Account extends Object {
}
```

Key Concept   All Java classes are derived, directly or indirectly, from the `Object` class.

Because all classes are derived from `Object`, any `public` method of `Object` can be invoked on any object created in any Java program. Some interesting methods of the `Object` class are:

- `toString()`   Returns a `String` that represents the object
- `equals (Object obj)`   Returns true if this object and `obj` are the same (i.e., aliases)
- `hashCode()`   Returns a unique number for an object

The `toString` method is particularly useful because it allows any object to be converted to a `String`. Any newly defined class can override the `toString` method to provide a `String` representation for that particular class. Most of the classes in the Java API have overridden `toString` to provide a text representation appropriate for the class. If `toString` is invoked on a class that has not overridden it, the `Object` version is used; this version prints the name of the class followed by a hexadecimal hash code for the class.

> **Key Concept**   The `toString` method is defined in the `Object` class and therefore is inherited by every class in every Java program.

Consider the following example:

```
import java.awt.Point;

//  Instantiates several objects and calls their toString
//  method.
class Test_toString {

    public static void main (String[] args) {
        Integer num = new Integer (25);
        Point origin = new Point (0, 0);
        Any_Class my_class = new Any_Class();

        String num_string = num.toString();
        String point_string = origin.toString();
        String class_string = my_class.toString();

        System.out.println (num_string);
        System.out.println (point_string);
        System.out.println (class_string);

    }  // method main
```

All objects have a `toString` method

```
}  // class Test_toString

//  This class does nothing important, but it overrides the
//  toString method of the Object class.
class Any_Class {

   public String toString() {
      return "I am Any_Class";
   }  // method toString

}  // class Any_Class
```

Both the `Integer` wrapper class and the `Point` class have implemented their own `toString` method. The `Any_Class` class, which is implicitly derived from `Object`, overrides `toString` as well. The output of the program is:

```
25
java.awt.Point[x=0,y=0]
I am Any_Class
```

8.4 Polymorphism

The word polymorphism means "having many forms." It is a rather awkward word that describes an elegant and relatively simple concept in object-oriented programming. *Polymorphism* is the technique by which a reference that is used to invoke a method can actually invoke different methods at different times, depending on the nature of the method invocation.

References and Class Hierarchies

In Java, a reference that is declared to refer to an object of a particular class can be used to refer to an object of any class to which it is related by inheritance. For example, if the class `Mammal` is used to derive a class `Horse`, then a reference to `Mammal` can be used to refer to an object of class `Horse`. This ability is shown in the code segment below:

```
Mammal m = new Mammal();
Horse h = new Horse();
m = h;  // a valid assignment
```

The reverse operation, assigning the `Mammal` object to a `Horse` reference, is also valid, but requires an explicit cast. Usually, because Java is strongly typed, when a value of one type is assigned to a variable of a different type, it creates a compile-time error. But if the two classes are related by inheritance, the assignment can be made. Therefore, after the assignment above, both references refer to the horse object. But one reference is of type `Mammal` and the other reference is of type `Horse`.

Key Concept An object reference can be used to refer to any object created from a class that is related to the reference type by inheritance.

This variation of type compatibility makes sense when you remember that an inheritance relationship is also an *is-a* relationship. Since a `Horse` is a `Mammal`, it is reasonable for a reference to a mammal be allowed to refer to a horse.

The ability for references of one class to refer to an object of another class is the key to polymorphism. When a reference is used to invoke a method, the class of the object being referred to determines which method is invoked, not the type of the reference.

For instance, let's assume that both `Mammal` and `Horse` have a method called move. The `Horse` class has overridden the definition of move that it inherited from `Mammal`. When the method invocation m.move() is invoked, it is not necessarily the `Mammal`'s version of move that is executed. It depends on the type of object that the reference m refers to at the moment the invocation is made. If it refers to a `Mammal` object, then the `Mammal` version of move is executed. If it refers to a `Horse` object, then the `Horse` version of the move method is executed. In this situation, the expression m.move() is polymorphic. The same reference has many forms, or definitions, that it can use.

Key Concept A polymorphic reference uses the type of the object, not the type of the reference, to determine which version of an overridden method to invoke.

Let's look at a simple example that uses polymorphism. It is similar to the `Messages` program presented earlier in this chapter.

```
//  Prints a message from two objects, then uses a
//  polymorphic reference to print one of them again.
class Messages2 {
```

```
    public static void main (String[] args) {
        Thought territory = new Thought();
        Advice cliche = new Advice();

        territory.message();
        cliche.message();

        territory = cliche;
        territory.message();

    } // method main

} // class Messages

// Defines a message method.
class Thought {

    public void message() {
        System.out.println ("Some people get lost in thought " +
                            "because it's unfamiliar territory.");
        System.out.println();
    } // method message

} // class Thought

// Overrides the message method.
class Advice extends Thought {

    public void message() {
        System.out.println ("Avoid cliches like the plague.");
        System.out.println();
    } // method message

} // class Advice
```

Compatible references support polymorphism

Two objects are instantiated in the main program: one from class Thought and one from class Advice. The references that are used to access the objects are called territory and cliche. Initially, both are used to print their respective messages. Then territory is assigned the value of cliche. This assignment is possible because territory and cliche are related by inheritance. The Thought object to which territory originally referred is now a candidate for garbage collection, and territory and cliche are now aliases of each other, both referring to the original Advice object. When message is invoked through the territory reference, the Advice version of message is invoked. The type of the object being referred to (`Advice`), not the type of the reference (`Thought`), is used to determine which polymorphic method is invoked. The output of the program is:

```
Some people get lost in thought because it's unfamiliar territory.
Avoid cliches like the plague.
Avoid cliches like the plague.
```

Let's look at another example. We saw in Chapter 4 that the `Vector` class can store any type of object reference. It is polymorphism that provides this ability. A `Vector` is defined to store `Object` references. Because all objects are derived ultimately from the `Object` class, all objects can be assigned to an `Object` reference.

The following program creates four objects, two from the `Integer` wrapper class and two from the `Point` class. These objects are stored in a `Vector` object. A loop is used to scan through the `Vector` and retrieve the stored objects one at a time. The objects are referenced by an `Object` reference called `something`.

```java
import java.awt.Point;
import java.util.Vector;

//   Demonstrates the polymorphic nature of a Vector.
class Variety {

    public static void main (String[] args) {

        Vector collector = new Vector();

        Integer num1 = new Integer (10);
        collector.addElement (num1);

        Point origin = new Point (0, 0);
        collector.addElement (origin);

        Integer num2 = new Integer (37);
        collector.addElement (num2);

        Point corner = new Point (12, 45);
        collector.addElement (corner);

        int temp;
        Object something;
        for (int count=0; count < 4; count++) {
            something = collector.elementAt (count);
```

```
        if (something instanceof Integer) {
            temp = ((Integer)something).intValue() + 20;
            System.out.println (something + " + 20 = " + temp);
        } else
            System.out.println ("Point: " +  something);
    }

  } // method main

} // class Variety
```

The instanceof operator identifies the object's true class

The instanceof operator is a reserved word in Java and is used to determine if a reference currently refers to an object of a particular class. It returns a boolean result. If the reference currently refers to an Integer, the value is obtained using the intValue method. Note that something must be cast to an Integer before the reference to intValue is allowed. In both cases, the toString method of the object converts the object to a String to be printed. The output of the program is:

```
10 + 20 = 30
Point: java.awt.Point[x=0,y=0]
37 + 20 = 57
Point: java.awt.Point[x=12,y=45]
```

Paying Employees Example

The single derivation shown earlier in Fig. 8.3, in which the Executive class is extended from the Employee class, is now revised and extended into the hierarchy shown in Fig. 8.7. A generic Staff_Member class serves as the root of the class hierarchy, and both Volunteer and Employee are derived from it. An Hourly class was also added, derived from Employee.

Because volunteers do not get paid, they are not considered to be employees. However, they share many common characteristics of employees, such as name and address. Therefore the Staff_Member class holds the information common to all workers at the company. This process caused several of the values that were originally stored in the Employee class to be moved into the Staff_Member class.

The following example uses polymorphism with the employee classes. The purpose of the program is to pay all employees. Note how polymorphism simplifies this process. Because each class of employee has its own version of the pay method, the payment process is potentially complicated. But with polymorphism, the same reference can be used for all employees to invoke the correct method.

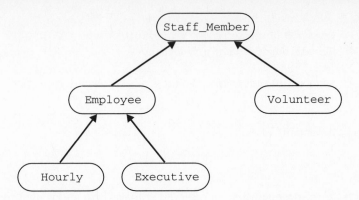

Figure 8.7   A class hierarchy for an office staff

```
//  Creates a list of personnel for a firm and pays them.  The
//  pay method is polymorphic and defined in multiple places.
class Firm2 {

   public static void main (String[] args) {

      Staff personnel = new Staff();

      personnel.payday();

   }  // method main

}  // class Firm2

//  Represents the entire staff of the firm.  Contains a method
//  to pay all staff members.
class Staff {

   Staff_Member[] staff_list = new Staff_Member[6];

   public Staff() {
      staff_list[0] = new Executive ("Sam", "123 Main Line",
         "555-0469", "123-45-6789", 1923.07);
      staff_list[1] = new Employee ("Carla", "456 Off Line",
         "555-0101", "987-65-4321", 846.15);
      staff_list[2] = new Employee ("Woody", "789 Off Rocker",
         "555-0000", "010-20-3040", 769.23);
```

An array of staff members holds many reference types

```
        staff_list[3] = new Hourly ("Diane", "678 Fifth Ave.",
           "555-0690", "958-47-3625", 8.55);
        staff_list[4] = new Volunteer ("Norm", "987 Suds Blvd.",
           "555-8374");
        staff_list[5] = new Volunteer ("Cliff", "321 Duds Lane",
           "555-7282");

        ((Executive)staff_list[0]).award_bonus (5000);
        ((Hourly)staff_list[3]).add_hours (40);

    }  // constructor Staff


    public void payday() {

        double amount;

        for (int count=0; count < staff_list.length; count++) {
           staff_list[count].print();
           amount = staff_list[count].pay();
           if (amount == 0.0)
               System.out.println ("Thanks!");
           else
               System.out.println ("Paid: " + amount);
           System.out.println ("**********************");
        }

    }  // method payday

}  // class Staff


//  Represents a generic staff member.
class Staff_Member {

    protected String name;
    protected String address;
    protected String phone_number;

    public Staff_Member (String emp_name, String emp_address,
            String emp_phone) {
        name = emp_name;
```

A polymorphic call to pay

```
         address = emp_address;
         phone_number = emp_phone;
      }  // constructor Staff_Member


      public double pay() {
         return 0.0;
      }  // method pay


      public void print() {
         System.out.println ("Name: " + name);
         System.out.println ("Address: " + address);
         System.out.println ("Phone: " + phone_number);
      }  // method print


}  // class Staff_Member


//  Represents an unpaid volunteer.
class Volunteer extends Staff_Member {

      public Volunteer (String emp_name, String emp_address,
            String emp_phone) {
         super (emp_name, emp_address, emp_phone);
      }  // constructor Volunteer


      public double pay() {
         return 0.0;
      }  // method pay


}  // class Volunteer


//  Represents one paid employee.
class Employee extends Staff_Member {

      protected String social_security_number;
      protected double pay_rate;

      public Employee (String emp_name, String emp_address,
            String emp_phone, String emp_ssnumber, double emp_rate) {

         super (emp_name, emp_address, emp_phone);
         social_security_number = emp_ssnumber;
```

```
        pay_rate = emp_rate;

    }  // constructor Employee


    public double pay() {
        return pay_rate;
    }  // method pay


    public void print() {
        super.print();
        System.out.println ("SS number: " + social_security_number);
        System.out.println ("Pay rate: " + pay_rate);
    }  // method print


}  // class Employee


//  Represents one executive, which is an employee that can
//  earn a bonus.
class Executive extends Employee {

    private double bonus;

    public Executive (String exec_name, String exec_address,
            String exec_phone, String exec_ssnumber, double exec_rate) {


        super (exec_name, exec_address, exec_phone, exec_ssnumber,
            exec_rate);
        bonus = 0;   // bonus yet to be awarded


    }  // constructor Executive


    public void award_bonus (double exec_bonus) {
        bonus = exec_bonus;
    }  // method award_bonus


    // Executive pay is the regular salary plus a one-time bonus
    public double pay() {
        double paycheck = super.pay() + bonus;
        bonus = 0;
```

```
            return paycheck;
    }   // method pay


    public void print() {
        super.print();
        System.out.println ("Current bonus: " + bonus);
    }   // method print


}   // class Executive


//  Represents an hourly employee, which tracks the number of
//  hours worked during the current pay period.
class Hourly extends Employee {

    private int hours_worked;

    public Hourly (String hr_name, String hr_address,
           String hr_phone, String hr_ssnumber, double hr_rate) {

        super (hr_name, hr_address, hr_phone, hr_ssnumber, hr_rate);
        hours_worked = 0;

    }   // constructor Hourly


    public void add_hours (int more_hours) {
        hours_worked += more_hours;
    }   // method add_hours


    public double pay() {
        return pay_rate * hours_worked;
    }   // method pay


    public void print() {
        super.print();
        System.out.println ("Current hours: " + hours_worked);
    }   // method print


}   // class Hourly
```

When executed, the `Firm2` program produces the following output:

```
Name: Sam
Address: 123 Main Line
Phone: 555-0469
SS number: 123-45-6789
Pay rate: 1923.07
Current bonus: 5000
Paid: 6923.07
**********************
Name: Carla
Address: 456 Off Line
Phone: 555-0101
SS number: 987-65-4321
Pay rate: 846.15
Paid: 846.15
**********************
Name: Woody
Address: 789 Off Rocker
Phone: 555-0000
SS number: 010-20-3040
Pay rate: 769.23
Paid: 769.23
**********************
Name: Diane
Address: 678 Fifth Ave.
Phone: 555-0690
SS number: 958-47-3625
Pay rate: 8.55
Current hours: 40
Paid: 342
**********************
Name: Norm
Address: 987 Suds Blvd.
Phone: 555-8374
Thanks!
**********************
Name: Cliff
Address: 321 Duds Lane
Phone: 555-7282
Thanks!
**********************
```

Summary of Key Concepts

- Inheritance is the act of deriving a new class from an existing one. It is analogous to creating a new house blueprint from an existing blueprint that has similar characteristics.
- A primary purpose of inheritance is to reuse existing software.
- Inherited variables and methods can be used in the derived class as if they had been declared locally.
- Visibility modifiers determine which variables and methods are inherited. Protected visibility provides the best encapsulation while still permitting inheritance.
- Inherited variables and methods keep their original visibility characteristics in the subclass.
- The `super` reference can be used to invoke the parent's constructor.
- All variables and methods are defined for a subclass, but they are not necessarily inherited. Only inherited variables and methods can be referenced by name in a derived class.
- A child class can override (redefine) a parent's definition of an inherited method.
- The class of the object determines which version of an overridden method is invoked.
- The `super` reference can be used to explicitly invoke any method from a parent class. This technique is often used in overridden methods to call the parent's version of the method.
- The child of one class can be the parent of one or more other classes, creating a class hierarchy.
- Common features should be located near the top of a class hierarchy, maximizing reuse potential.
- You should maintain the *is-a* relationship between all derived classes in a class hierarchy.
- There is no single class hierarchy that is appropriate for all situations.
- All Java classes are derived, directly or indirectly, from the `Object` class.
- The `toString` method is defined in the `Object` class and therefore is inherited by every class in every Java program.
- An object reference can be used to refer to any object created from a class that is related to the reference type by inheritance.
- A polymorphic reference uses the type of the object, not the type of the reference, to determine which version of an overridden method to invoke.

Self-Review Questions

8.1 Describe the relationship between a parent class and a child class.

8.2 How does inheritance support software reuse?

8.3 Why would a child class override one or more of the methods of its parent class?

8.4 Why is the `super` reference important to a child class?

8.5 What is the defining characteristic of a class hierarchy?

8.6 What is polymorphism?

8.7 How is overriding related to polymorphism?

Exercises

8.8 Draw a class hierarchy containing classes that represent different types of clocks.

8.9 Show the details (variables and method names) of two different classes described in Problem 8.8.

8.10 Show an alternative hierarchy for the hierarchy in Problem 8.8. Explain why it may be a better or worse approach than the original.

8.11 Draw and annotate a class hierarchy representing students in a university.

8.12 Present pseudocode for a method that can invoke the methods of every object that can be created from the classes in Problem 8.11. Is polymorphism important to this process? Why or why not?

Programming Projects

8.13 Experiment with a simple derivation. Write a constructor for a child class that does not explicitly refer to the constructor of the parent. What happened? Why?

8.14 Design and implement a set of classes that define the employees of a hospital: doctor, nurse, administrator, surgeon, receptionist, janitor, and so on. Include methods in each class that are named according to the services provided by that person and that print an appropriate message. Create a main method to instantiate and exercise several of the classes.

8.15 Design and implement a set of classes that define various types of reading material: books, novels, magazines, textbooks, and so on. Include data values that describe various attributes of the material such as the number of pages and the names of the primary characters. Include methods that are named appropriately for each class that print a message. Create a `main` method to instantiate and exercise several of the classes.

8.16 Design and implement a class that simulates a VCR remote control. The class should have various methods for interacting with the TV as well as recording and playing tapes. Extend the VCR remote-control class to create a different type of remote control. Add a method to the subclass that provides additional or less functionality for the remote control. Create a `main` method which instantiates several different remote controls and exercises the various class methods.

8.17 Design and implement a set of classes that keeps track of various sports statistics. Have each low-level class represent a certain sport. Tailor the services of the classes to the sport in question, and move common attributes to the higher-level classes as appropriate. Create a `main` method to instantiate and exercise several of the classes.

8.18 Design and implement a set of classes that keeps track of various demographic information about a set of people. Let each class focus on a particular aspect of data collection. Create a `main` method to instantiate and exercise several of the classes.

Answers to Self-Review Questions

8.1 A child class is derived from a parent class using inheritance. The methods and variables of the parent class automatically become a part of the child class, subject to the rules of the visibility modifiers used to declare them.

8.2 Because a new class can be derived from an existing one, the characteristics of the parent class can be reused without the error-prone process of copying and modifying code.

8.3 A child class may prefer its own definition of a method in favor of the definition provided for it by its parent. In this case, the child overrides the parent's definition with its own.

8.4 The `super` reference can be used to call the parent's constructor, which cannot be invoked directly by name.

8.5 Any derivation in a class hierarchy should represent an *is-a* relationship. That is, the child is a more specific version of the parent. If this relationship does not hold, then inheritance is being used improperly.

8.6 Polymorphism is the ability for a reference of one class to refer to an object of another. In Java, a reference to a parent class can be used to refer to an object of the child class.

8.7 When a child class overrides the definition of a parent's method, two versions of that method exist. If a polymorphic reference is used to invoke the method, the specific version of the method that gets invoked is determined by the type of the object being referred to, not by the type of the reference variable.

Enhanced
Class Design

9

An appropriate organization of class relationships is the cornerstone of good object-oriented design. It provides flexibility so that the design can change over time without significant rewriting of existing software. An elegant organization communicates the intent of the design, and leads to appropriate implementation decisions, as opposed to arbitrary choices that often cause errors. This chapter explains abstract classes, interfaces, and packages. These techniques allow greater flexibility and potential reuse for the software that we write.

Chapter Objectives:

* Define abstract classes and their relationship to subclasses.
* Explain interfaces for use in tagging classes.
* Explore the polymorphic support provided by abstract classes and interfaces.
* Show how to group a collection of related and interdependent classes into a package.

9.1 Abstract Classes and Methods

An abstract class allows a generic concept to be represented in a class hierarchy. Because it is not concrete, an *abstract class* is a class that cannot be instantiated. Typically, abstract classes contain abstract methods. An *abstract method* is a method that does not contain an implementation. In practice abstract classes are used in a class hierarchy in which a class defines only part of its implementation and expects its children classes to fill in the gaps. Let's look at some examples in which abstract classes and methods can be applied.

> **Key Concept**   An abstract class represents a generic concept in a class hierarchy. An abstract method is a method that does not contain an implementation.

Example: Food

Consider Fig. 9.1, which shows a class that represents the generic concept of a food and three classes derived from it:

Assume for an application using this hierarchy that we want to add a method to the Food class called slogan, which would return a String that represents a marketing quote. Each subclass of Food should override slogan to provide a quote specific to the food in question. Choosing the slogan is straightforward for the classes Beans, Franks, and Pepperoni, but what slogan should we choose for the base Food class? The slogan would have to be general enough to cover all possible subclasses that might be derived from Food. Nothing specific seems appropriate, because we really want the slogan to be specific to each food type, not just food. One solution is to provide a slogan method in Food that returns a meaningless

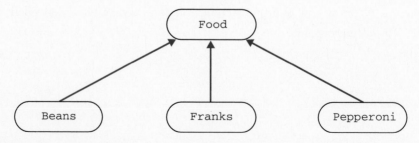

Figure 9.1   Food class hierarchy

value, such as an empty `String`. Fortunately, abstract methods offer a cleaner alternative. An abstract method provides a means for the `Food` class to define that a `slogan` method should exist in all its subclasses, without providing a meaningless implementation in `Food` class itself. The following is an example of an abstract method that the `Food` class might use:

```
abstract public String slogan();
```

Note that instead of a body of statements following the method header that would be its implementation, the header is terminated with a semicolon. The lack of an implementation identifies this method as abstract. Also, note that the modifier `abstract` is used to further identify the method as abstract. An abstract method does not specify how a method is implemented, but what it accepts as parameters and what it returns. In this case, the `slogan` method does not accept any parameters and returns a `String`.

Much like an abstract method, a class is abstract if it is marked using the `abstract` modifier. Let's look at an example.

```
// Demonstrates using a class derived from an abstract class
public class Dinner {

    public static void main (String[] args) {
        Pepperoni slice = new Pepperoni();
        System.out.println (slice.slogan());
    } // method main

} // class Dinner

// Shows an example definition of a class with a
// single abstract method
abstract class Food {

    // returns a marketing slogan for the food
    abstract public String slogan();

} // class Food

// Derives a class from an abstract class implementing
// the Food's abstract method
class Pepperoni extends Food {

    public String slogan() {
        return "Great for pizza!";
    } // method slogan

} // class Pepperoni
```

An abstract class is defined using the `abstract` modifier

An abstract method has no statements following the method header

The `Food` class is abstract because it is marked using the `abstract` modifier. In addition, the class contains one abstract method called `slogan`. The `Pepperoni` class is derived from the abstract `Food` class and overrides the `slogan` method.

The output of this application is:

```
Great for pizza!
```

 Key Concept A nonabstract class derived from an abstract parent must override all of its parent's abstract methods.

Example: File Structure

Choosing which methods should be abstract is a design decision that affects the entire application. Such choices should only be made after much reflection and experimentation. By carefully using the abstract class, we can ensure that future maintainers of the application understand where the software was designed to remain flexible.

Let's look at a more involved example. Consider the class hierarchy in Fig. 9.2. This hierarchy describes different types of files that are processed by a program. The program can handle three different types of files: text, binary, and image. For

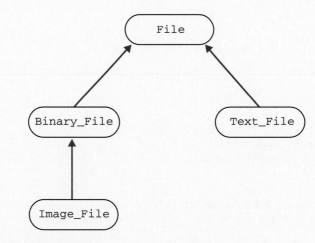

Figure 9.2 `File` class hierarchy

all file types the program will keep track of its name and size. The following code implements these file types using a base class, called `File`, to group common functionality.

```
// Demonstrates the use of an abstract class
public class Printer {

   public static void main (String[] args) {
      byte[] logo_data  = {41, 42, 49, 44};
      Text_File report = new Text_File
         ("Sand Reconner", 66, "One two three");
      Image_File logo = new Image_File
         ("Number 1", 45, logo_data);

      Print_Logger daily = new Print_Logger();

      daily.log(report);
      daily.log(logo);
   } // method main

} // class Printer

// Represents a single file
abstract class File {

   protected String id;
   protected int size;

   public File (String file_id, int file_size) {
      id = file_id;
      size = file_size;
   } // constructor File

   public String name() {
      return id;
   } // method name

   // returns the contents of the file
   abstract public String print();

} // class File

// Represents a single file containing text
class Text_File extends File {

   protected String text;
```

A nonabstract method in an abstract class

```
        public Text_File (String id, int size, String file_contents) {
            super(id, size);
            text = file_contents;
        } // constructor Text_File

        public String print() {
            return text;
        } // method print

    } // class Text_File


    // Represents a single file contain binary data
    class Binary_File extends File {

        protected byte[] data;

        public Binary_File (String id, int size, byte[] file_data) {
            super(id, size);
            data = file_data;
        } // constructor Binary_File

        public String print() {
            return "";
        } // method print

    } // class Binary_File

    // Represents a single file containing an image
    class Image_File extends Binary_File {

        public Image_File (String id, int size, byte[] file_data) {
            super(id, size, file_data);
        } // constructor Image_File

        public String print() {
            return new String (data);
        } // method print

    } // class Image_File


    // Prints to sdtin objects that are being printed
    class Print_Logger {
```

```
public void log (File file) {
    System.out.println (file.name() + " : " + file.print());
} // method log

} // class Print_Logger
```

An abstract class can be used as a data type

The `File` class is defined to be abstract because it contains an abstract method called `print`. Notice that the `File` class, even though it is an abstract class, contains data and completely implemented methods. Abstract and nonabstract methods can be freely intermixed in the definition of an abstract class. In this case, each subclass of `File` will inherit and be able to use the data and methods.

Key Concept An abstract class can intermix abstract and nonabstract method definitions.

Because we want to be able to create objects of `Binary_File`, `Image_File`, and `Text_File`, these classes cannot be abstract; therefore they must override the abstract `print` method defined in the `File` class. The print method of the `Binary_File` class does not return the internal representation of the file, but an empty string instead. The `print` method of the `Image_File` class converts its internal data into a string. The `print` method of the `Text_File` class returns the internal string representing the file.

Coding the `File` class using the abstract method `print` explicitly forces all children derived from `File` to choose how to implement the `print` method. Without using abstract methods, children classes would not be forced to make such a choice. They can use the inherited `print` method of their parent class.

Deriving Subclasses

The previous examples show subclasses being derived from abstract classes. Let's look at the details associated with this relationship. It would be a contradiction for an abstract method to be modified as `final` or `static`. Because a final method cannot be overridden in subclasses, an abstract final method would have no way of being made nonabstract in subclasses. A static method can be invoked by using the class name without declaring an object of the class. This method of invocation implies that an implementation must exist for the method. Because abstract methods have no implementation, an abstract static method would make no sense.

Any class containing one or more abstract methods must be declared as an abstract class. However, an abstract class doesn't have to contain abstract methods, it merely needs to be declared as `abstract` using the `abstract` modifier. There are no restrictions as to where in a class hierarchy an abstract class needs to be defined. For example, an abstract class can be derived from a nonabstract parent, but usually abstract classes are more useful located higher in the class hierarchy and closer to the base class. Classes derived from an abstract parent class do not have to override all the abstract methods of their parents. However, if they do not override all abstract methods then the child class must also be declared as an abstract class. In essence, through inheritance the child class contains abstract methods.

An abstract class can be used as a placeholder for its subclasses. Consider the following method:

```
public void print_list (File[] file_list) {
    for (int index = 0; index < file_list.length; index++) {
        System.out.println (file_list[index].print());
    }
}
```

This method will accept an array of objects that are derived from the `File` class. Because abstract classes cannot be instantiated, we can assume that only subclasses that have overridden the abstract `print` method are referenced by the array `file_list`. This use of an abstract class is a common technique for writing classes that are reusable. We can replace the class hierarchy rooted at the `File` class with a completely different hierarchy, without ever affecting the `print_list` method.

Key Concept An abstract class can be used in every way that a class can be used, except that it cannot be instantiated.

9.2 Interfaces

An interface is a collection of constants and abstract methods. These are not classes, but they can be used in the definition of a class. The following is the general syntax of an interface specification:

```
interface interface-name {
    constants-declarations
    abstract-method-declarations
}
```

A class implements an interface by providing method implementations for each of the methods defined in the interface declaration. Classes that implement an interface use the implements keyword and the interface's name.

```
class class-name implements interface-name {
    implementation-of-methods-named-in-interface
}
```

Methods in an Interface

Let's look at a small example that demonstrates an interface and its use:

```
// Demonstrates using a class that implements an interface
public class Soap_Box {

    public static void main (String[] args) {
        Kant immanual = new Kant();
        System.out.println (immanual.pontificate());
    } // method main

} // class Soap_Box

// Shows an example definition of an interface with a
// single method
interface Philosopher {

    // return a statement made by a philosopher
    String pontificate();

} // class Philosopher

// Defines a class that implements an interface by implementing
// the Philosopher's abstract method
class Kant implements Philosopher {

    public String pontificate() {
        return "Follow the Categorical Imperative!";
    } // method pontificate

} // class Kant
```

An interface uses abstract methods similar to abstract classes

A class implementing an interface

Kant is a class that implements the interface Philosopher. The Philosopher class contains a single method called pontificate. To properly implement `Philosopher`, `Kant` must provide an implementation of the `pontif-icate` method.

Looking closer at the interface `Philosopher`, one might notice that no modifiers are used on the `pontificate` method. The only modifiers allowed are `public` and `abstract`. However, these are not needed, because by default all methods in an interface are public and abstract. This default is very similar to the way in which abstract methods in an abstract class cannot be declared `final` or `static`.

Key Concept All methods in an interface are by default declared to be `public` and `abstract`.

Constants in an Interface

Let's look at another example that involves constants defined in an interface. The following example shows an interface that defines a series of constants related to file protections:

```
// Defines several constants used to determine file protections
interface File_Protection {

    // file can be executed
    int EXECUTE = 2;
    // file can be read from
    int READ = 4;
    // file can be written to
    int WRITE = 6;
} // interface File_Protection
```

Declarations in an `interface` are always `public` and `final`

```
// provides some utility routines to determine
// protections
class Protections implements File_Protection {

    public boolean is_readable (int protection) {
        return (protection == READ);
    } // method is_readable
```

Constants from an interface can be used as if they were declared locally

```
    public boolean is_writable (int protection) {
        return (protection == WRITE);
    } // method is_writable
```

```
    public boolean is_executable (int protection) {
        return (protection == EXECUTE);
    } // method is_executable

} // class Protections
```

The constant EXECUTE in the `File_Protection` interface looks like a variable declaration; however, it is not. The modifiers `public` and `final` are implicitly added to all such declarations in an interface. Therefore, the declaration

```
int EXECUTE = 2;
```

can be rewritten as:

```
public final int EXECUTE = 2;
```

Although abstract methods in an interface must have implementations provided for them by an implementer's class, `constant` declarations do not. Constants from an interface can be used as if they were declared locally in the class itself.

> ► **Key Concept** Constants declared in interface can be used as if they were declared locally in a class that implements the interface.

Using Interfaces

The previous sections have shown how an interface can be used in the implementation of a class. However, interfaces can be used in other ways. Interfaces can extend other interfaces to add constants or more abstract classes. For example, the following interface extends the `File_Protection` interface by adding three more constants.

```
// Demonstrates extending an interface with another interface
interface Extended_File_Protection extends File_Protection {

    // file has an access control list
    int ACL = 4;
    // file can be deleted
    int DELETE = 5;
    // file can be copied
    int COPY = 6;

} // interface Extended_File_Protection
```

Interfaces can be linked in a hierarchy with other interfaces

A class that implements this interface will be able to use the constants READ, WRITE, EXECUTE, ACL, DELETE, and COPY, as if they were defined locally.

Interfaces are not part of a class's inheritance hierarchy. Let's look at the File hierarchy shown in Fig. 9.2, that we first implemented using abstract classes, and let's see how it might be implemented using interfaces instead.

```
// Demonstrates the use of interfaces
public class Printer2 {

    public static void main (String[] args) {
        byte[] logo_data  = {41, 42, 49, 44};
        Text_File report = new Text_File
            ("Sand Reconner", 66, "One two three");
        Image_File logo = new Image_File
            ("Number 1", 45, logo_data);

        Print_Logger daily = new Print_Logger();

        daily.log(report);
        daily.log(logo);
    } // method main

} // class Printer2


// Represents a single file
class File {
```

The File class does not have a print method any longer

```
    protected String id;
    protected int size;

    public File (String file_id, int file_size) {
        id = file_id;
        size = file_size;
    } // constructor File

    public String name() {
        return id;
    } // method name

} // class File
```

```java
// Represents a single file containing text
class Text_File extends File implements Printable {

    protected String text;

    public Text_File (String id, int size, String file_contents) {
        super(id, size);
        text = file_contents;
    } // constructor Text_File

    public String print() {
        return text;
    } // method print

} // class Text_File


// Represents a single file contain binary data
class Binary_File extends File {

    protected byte[] data;

    public Binary_File (String id, int size, byte[] file_data) {
        super(id, size);
        data = file_data;
    } // constructor Binary_File
} // class Binary_File


// Represents a single file containing an image
class Image_File extends Binary_File implements Printable {

    public Image_File (String id, int size, byte[] file_data) {
        super(id, size, file_data);
    } // constructor Image_File

    public String print() {
        return new String (data);
    } // method print

} // class Image_File
```

Subclass of `File` that needs to print now implements `Printable`

```
// Identifies classes that are able to be printed
interface Printable {

    String name();
    // returns the name of the objects being printed

    String print();
    // returns data to be printed


} // interface Printable

// Prints to sdtin objects that are being printed
class Print_Logger {

    public void log (Printable file) {
        System.out.println (file.name() + " : " + file.print());
    } // method log

} // class Print_Logger
```

Interfaces can be
used as data types

Note that the method `print` is not required on all classes derived from the
`File` class, just those classes that implement the `Printable` interface. Therefore, a
list of `File` classes or subclasses cannot be guaranteed to have print methods.
Fortunately, we can use the name of the interface as a class type, so that the log
method of the `Print_Logger` class can accept as a parameter a `Printable` class.
A formal parameter data type that is an interface can accept as an actual parameter
any class that implements the interface. In the example, the `log` method of the
`Print_Logger` class can accept as a parameter an object that is of the `Text_File`
or `Image_File` class.

 Key Concept A formal parameter data type that is an interface can accept as an
actual parameter any class or subclass that implements the interface.

More than one interface can be implemented by a class. Suppose we had a class
that needed to print its result based on the protection scheme of a file. The following
class will accept a list of files and protections and print out a list of the files that are
readable:

```
// Implements a class that will store and list a set of
// filenames and protections
class Readable_Files implements File_Protection, Printable {
    File[] files;
    int[] permissions;


    Readable_Files (File[] file_list, int[] permissions_list) {
        files = file_list;
        permissions = permissions_list;
    } // constructor Readable_Files


    public String name() {
        return "Readable files";
    } // method name


    public String print() {
        String printable_list = "";
        for (int index = 0; index < files.length; index++) {
            if (permissions[index] == READ) {
                printable_list = printable_list + " " +
                    files[index].name();
            }
        }
        return printable_list;
    } // method print


} // class Readable_Files
```

A class can imple-
ment more than
one interface

The Readable_Files class implements both the File_Protection and
the Printable interfaces. The File_Protection interface only has constant
declarations, so no methods are required in Readable_Files. The constant READ
from this interface is used in the implementation of the print method. The
Printable interface requires two methods to be implemented in this class. The
first is name, which accepts no parameters and returns a String, and the second is
print, which also accepts no parameters and returns a String.

If we have class hierarchies and abstract classes, why do we need interfaces?
Class hierarchies allow the designer to group classes by parent-child relationships.
Unfortunately, it is often very difficult to implement a single class hierarchy for an
application. Usually, multiple class hierarchies are used. The AWT is an example of
using multiple hierarchies. While abstract classes work well for a single hierarchy,
they are limited because they can only affect methods to be implemented in child
classes of themselves. What happens when we have two abstract classes and we

want to use them both on the same object? Since a class can have only one immediate parent, this dual usage is impossible using abstract classes. Interfaces classes contained in two different class hierarchies can be substituted for each other, as if they were subclasses of the same class.

Key Concept   Interfaces allow multiple hierarchies to be used in an application.

Encapsulation and Information Hiding

The use of abstract classes and interfaces plays an important role in the encapsulation and hiding of information in a software application. Most software projects are written by many people. The larger a software project becomes, the more important

In-Depth Focus

Multiple Inheritance

Java's approach to inheritance in object-oriented programming is called single inheritance. This is because a derived class can only have one parent. Many object-oriented languages will allow a child class to have multiple parents. This approach is called multiple inheritance. Multiple inheritance is useful for describing objects that are in between two categories or classes. For example, a pickup truck is part car and part truck. If we had a class for trucks, we'd like to derive a pickup truck from that class, but since a pickup truck is smaller than a standard truck and more like a car, we'd like to derive it from the car class, as shown in Fig. 9.3. With single inheritance, we cannot support both decisions. With multiple inheritance, we can.

Multiple inheritance is very powerful, but it comes with a price. What if both truck and car have methods with the same name? Which method would pickup truck inherit? The answer to this question is complex, and it depends on the highly system-dependent rules of the system supporting multiple inheritance.

Java uses interfaces to provide some of the functionality that multiple inheritance supports. While a class can be derived from only one parent, it can implement many different interfaces. To complete our example, a pickup truck could be derived from a truck and implement a car interface. Because interfaces can be derived from other interfaces, an entire alternative to a class hierarchy can be defined for an application, i.e., an interface hierarchy.

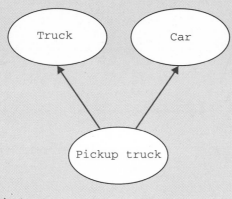

Figure 9.3 Multiple inheritance

encapsulation and information hiding become. Imagine if every programmer on a project was forced to understand the details of the work being done by other programmers. Encapsulation and information hiding reduce the number of details a programmer needs to understand about a software system in order to work effectively.

> **Key Concept** Interfaces and abstract classes can be used to encapsulate and hide details of a software system.

By using abstract classes and interfaces, a programmer can identify the bounds between the different parts of a software system without having to provide details about their implementation. Because abstract classes and interfaces do not specify how something is to be done, but rather that something must be done, they are a good mechanism for defining parts early in a project. After defining a good set of interface and abstract classes, various programmers can work in parallel.

9.3 Packages

Having class hierarchies allows us to group similar classes together. However, we cannot use class hierarchies to group different hierarchies together. It is often useful, however, to be able to group different class hierarchies together. For example, suppose we have a collection of classes that allows us to simulate a car. We have a class hierarchy for body types, a class hierarchy for wheels, a class hierarchy for engines, and so on. It is convenient to group these different class hierarchies together under a single name to show that they are conceptually related. Packages provide this function in Java.

> ▶ **Key Concept**   A package is used to group similar and interdependent classes together under a single name.

Defining Packages

Packages in Java allow a collection of classes to be grouped together under a single name. Other classes can make use of the package by referencing the package name. To create a package, the programmer must do two things. The first is to identify the files and classes that belong to the package. The second is to collect all the compiled version of the classes into a subdirectory associated with the package name.

The syntax for packages is:

```
package package-name;

class class-name {
    ...
}
```

The class `class-name` is marked as part of the package `package-name`. The package clause must be located at the top of a file. All classes in the file are added to the package. Classes that are public are available to every other class. Classes with no modifier are available to any other class in the same package. The package phrase can be repeated on as many files as is necessary to group a series of classes into one package. Every class must be contained in a package. If there is no package declaration in a file, then the classes in that file belong to a default, unnamed package.

Let's look at a simple example. The following code exists in the file `Reader.java`. The class simplifies the interface to reading an integer or string from standard input:

Classes in the same file with a `package` statement are included in that package

```
package Simple_IO;
// Place the reader class into the Simple_IO package

import java.io.*;

// Defines some simple input routines
public class Reader {
```

```
   public static int read() throws IOException {
      BufferedReader stdin = new BufferedReader
         (new InputStreamReader (System.in));
      String value = stdin.readLine();
      return Integer.parseInt (value);
   } // method read

   public static String read_line() throws IOException {
      BufferedReader stdin = new BufferedReader
         (new InputStreamReader (System.in));
      return stdin.readLine();
   } // method read_line

} // class Reader
```

By placing the package statement at the beginning of this file, the class `Reader` has been tagged as part of the `Simple_IO` package. After compiling this class, we should have a file `Reader.class` created by the compiler. In order for the package to be fully implemented, the compiled class files need to be copied into a directory with the same name as the package. In our example, we would copy the `Reader.class` file to `.../Simple_IO/Reader.class`. Note that this is a Unix file-naming convention. On Windows95, the filename would be `...\Simple_IO\Reader.class`. The placement of this directory is usually identified by an environment variable called `CLASSPATH`. Refer to the documentation of the Java compiler you are using for more specifics on these directories.

Usually, a package contains more than just one or two classes. Other classes can be added to this package by performing a similar process. For example, let's add another class to the `Simple_IO` package similar to the `Reader` class, but this class is for writing to standard output.

```
package Simple_IO;

// a class to define simple output
public class Writer {

   public static void write (int value) {
      System.out.println (value);
   } // method write

   public static void write_line (String line) {
      System.out.println (line);
   } // method write_line

} // class Writer
```

Multiple files can have the same `package` statement

Package names can contain a dot (.). This is often used to indicate a relationship between parts of two or more packages. For example, `java.lang` and `java.io` are two different packages, but they are related. The commonality of their name implies this, but it is not enforced in the Java language. However, many Java compilation systems allow the commonality of the packages to be represented in how they are stored. For example, the `.java` and `.class` files for `Simple_IO` package are stored in a directory called `Simple_IO`. The `.java` and `.class` files for the `java.io` package are stored in a directory called `java` in a subdirectory called `io`. The files for the `java.lang` package are also stored in a directory called `java`, in a subdirectory called `lang`.

Using Packages

Recall that we introduced the import statement in Chapter 2. Let's review them in more detail. The syntax for the `import` statement is:

```
import package.class;
```

or

```
import package.*;
```

Any number of `import` statements can appear in a Java program. The `import` statements must immediately follow the package declaration, or if no package declaration exists, be at the top of the file.

A package name has the form of one or more identifiers separated by dots. The first version of an `import` statement shortens a class name in the current file to be just the class name. The second version of an `import` statement allows all classes defined in the package to be visible to the classes in the current file. By default, the `java.lang` package is implicitly imported into every class.

Let us look at an example of how to define and use packages. In the `Simple_IO` package we defined earlier, we have two classes. The following code imports the `Simple_IO` package and exercises methods of the `Reader` and `Writer` classes:

```
import java.io.IOException;
import Simple_IO.*;

// Exercises some methods of classes in the Simple_IO package
class Simple_IO_Test {

    public static void main (String[] args) throws IOException {
        int value = Reader.read();
```

Classes in `Simple_IO` can be referenced directly

```
      String line = Reader.read_line();
      Writer.write (value);
      Writer.write_line (line);
   } // method main

} // class Simple_IO_Test
```

The importation of `Simple_IO` allows the `Simple_IO_Test` class to refer to the `Reader` and `Writer` class directly. Since the methods of these classes are static, we can refer to them without declaring an object. Notice how much easier it is to read a number from standard input by using the `Simple_IO` package.

If two or more imported packages have the same name, that name cannot be referenced except as an explicit package reference. For example, in `Simple_IO_Test` if we had imported `java.io.*` instead of `java.io.IOException`, the class `Reader` would not be directly referenced in the class. The name `Reader` was made ambiguous by the two import statements because a `Reader` class existed in both `Simple_IO` and `java.io`.

Key Concept   A class name that exists in both of the packages being imported into a class cannot be referenced without a qualifier.

The following example shows how to create objects using a fully qualified class name by prefacing each class with its package name.

```
// Using the Simple_IO package without any import statements
class Simple_IO_Test2 {

   public static void main (String[] args)
      throws java.io.IOException {
      int value = Simple_IO.Reader.read();
      String line = Simple_IO.Reader.read_line();
      Simple_IO.Writer.write (value);
      Simple_IO.Writer.write_line (line);
   } // method main

} // class Simple_IO_Test2
```

A class in a package can always be referenced by its fully qualified name

Notice that when a program uses fully qualified class names, no `import` statements are necessary.

The next example imports the `Write` class from the `Simple_IO` package, but no other classes.

A single class can
be named in an
import statement

```
import Simple_IO.Writer;

// Using the Simple_IO package with an explicit class imported
class Simple_IO_Test3 {

    public static void main (String[] args)
        throws java.io.IOException {
        int value = Simple_IO.Reader.read();
        String line = Simple_IO.Reader.read_line();
        Writer.write (value);
        Writer.write_line (line);
    } // method main

} // class Simple_IO_Test3
```

Note that `Simple_IO.Reader`, because it was not imported, is referenced using its fully qualified name.

Summary of Key Concepts

- An abstract class represents a generic concept in a class hierarchy. An abstract method is a method that does not contain an implementation.
- A nonabstract class derived from an abstract parent must override all of its parent's abstract methods.
- An abstract class can intermix abstract and nonabstract method definitions.
- An abstract class can be used in every way that a class can be used, except that it cannot be instantiated.
- All methods in an interface are by default declared to be `public` and `abstract`.
- Constants declared in interface can be used as if they were declared locally in a class that implements the interface.
- A formal parameter data type that is an interface, can accept as an actual parameter any class or subclass that implements the interface.
- Interfaces allow multiple hierarchies to be used in an application.
- Interfaces and abstract classes can be used to encapsulate and hide details of a software system.
- A package is used to group similar and interdependent classes together under a single name.
- A class name that exists in both of the packages being imported into a class cannot be referenced without a qualifier.

Self-Review Questions

9.1 What is the difference between a class and an abstract class?

9.2 What is the difference between a class and an interface?

9.3 What is the difference between an abstract class and an interface?

9.4 What is the purpose of an interface?

9.5 What is a package?

9.6 What happens when two packages that contain the same class name are imported into the same class?

Exercises

9.7 How can a class be designed so that it can only be instantiated by other classes in its package, but is visible to classes outside of its package. *Hint:* Focus on the constructor.

9.8 Design an abstract class for printing objects. The class should include methods for producing various forms suited for printing. The class should include postscript, rich-text format, and ASCII text.

9.9 Design an interface for printing objects. The class should include methods for producing postscript, rich-text format, and ASCII text.

9.10 Explain, using the Java API, the following method invocations. Define what packages, interfaces, classes, objects, and methods are involved.

```
a. int number = Math.abs (-12);
b. System.out.println ("Hello");
c. BufferedReader stdin = new BufferedReader(new
                            InputStreamReader (System.in));
d. applet.getAudioClip (this.getCodeBase(), "bark.au");
```

Assume that applet is an object of `java.applet.Applet`, and that the following packages were imported: `java.lang`, `java.io`, `java.applet`, and `java.util`.

9.11 Review the `Enumeration` interface of the Java API and describe how it can be used in a program that contains lists of `Student` objects. Assume that `Student` objects contain information on a particular student, such as name, id number, and GPA.

9.12 Identify three interfaces in the Java API and why they are used.

9.13 Explain the process of creating a package on the particular development environment you are using.

Programming Projects

9.14 Modify the pay method of the `Staff_Member` class in Chapter 8 to make use of abstract classes or interfaces.

9.15 Design and implement a program that uses an interface to define a set of methods called `print_verbose`, `print_normal`, and `print_brief`. Create two classes, `Phone_List` and `Address_List` that implement the interface, printing the information in the appropriate manner.

9.16 Design and implement a program that uses two abstract classes, one derived from the other. From the child, derive a concrete class that gives definitions to all abstract methods inherited from both classes.

9.17 Design and implement a class hierarchy that represents different shapes, such as lines, circles, and squares. Design and implement an interface that enables objects to be drawn in an applet. Modify the shape hierarchy to make use of the interface where appropriate. The modification should allow applets to be written that can draw different shapes in an applet by using classes in the hierarchy. Write an applet that exercises the methods of the modified shape hierarchy.

9.18 Modify the end program in Problem 9.17 to use an abstract class instead of an interface.

9.19 Modify the end program in Problem 9.17 to not use abstract classes or interfaces.

9.20 Incorporate the shape hierarchy developed in Problem 9.17 into a `Shape` package. Write a program to import and use the package.

9.21 Further develop the `Simple_IO` package shown as an example in this chapter to support a large number of simplified IO methods.

Answers to Self-Review Questions

9.1 A class can be instantiated; an abstract class cannot. Abstract classes often contain abstract methods that do not have implementations.

9.2 A class can be instantiated; an interface cannot. A class implements an interface by giving a definition for each method defined in the interface.

9.3 An abstract class may have some methods defined. An interface contains no defined methods. Neither can be instantiated. A class can implement many interfaces, but can only be derived from a single abstract class.

9.4 An interface is used to define a common set of methods and constants for classes that are often contained in different class hierarchies.

9.5 A package is language construct used for grouping classes with interdependent or similar characteristics. A package can be imported into a program as a unit.

9.6 The class names that are in both classes must be referred to using a qualified name, because an unqualified name in this situation is ambiguous.

Graphical User Interfaces

10

M ost modern software includes a graphical user interface (GUI) through which the user interacts with the program. This chapter describes the techniques for creating a GUI using the Java API. An important part of the chapter is its description of event-driven programming; this concept is crucial to the implementation of graphical interfaces. The chapter also examines various GUI components and the layout managers that govern their positions on the screen. It concludes with an example that demonstrates several of the concepts discussed in the chapter.

Chapter Objectives

- Explain how components are used to define GUIs.
- Explain a model for GUI-based programs.
- Define events and event-driven programming.
- Use the `Canvas` class to define custom GUI components.
- Explore the properties of the GUI components defined in the Java API.
- Describe how layout managers specify the positioning of components inside containers.

10.1 GUI Elements

A graphical user interface is composed of many pieces. Java provides a set of classes derived from a `Component` class to construct GUIs. This class hierarchy is often referred to as the *GUI Components*. Figure 10.1 describes some of the popular GUI components.

Components can be grouped together by the use of special GUI components known as containers. Arranging the components within a container class is the job of a layout manager. The layout manager decides based on a set criteria where each component should be placed. By nesting component containers and choosing appropriate layout managers, an entire component hierarchy can be created that is used for the visual presentation of a program's GUI.

The graphical user interface often allows a user to perform many possible actions. Depending on the options provided by a particular program, the user might press a graphic button, or type characters into a text field, or move a scrollbar. The program must be able to recognize that a certain action has occurred and respond to it appropriately. The GUI components generate *events* that indicate that specific

GUI Component	Description
Label	Displays a line of text.
TextField	Displays a line of text. It may allow the user to edit its contents, one way to accept typed user input.
TextArea	Displays several lines of text. Like a text field, it may allow editing.
List	Displays a list of selectable items.
PushButton	A single button designed to initiate some action when pushed.
Choicebuttons	A single button that displays a list of choices when pushed. The current choice is shown next to the button.
CheckBoxButtons	A button that can be toggled on or off. Often a group of checkbox buttons are used to define a set of options. Multiple options can be chosen at the same time.
RadioButtons	A group of buttons that defines a set of options from which a user can choose. Only one option can be selected at any given time.
Scroll bar	A sliding bar used to indicate a position or a relative value.
Scroll panel	A region that has an associated scroll bar with predefined event handlers.
PullDownMenu	A set of options from which a user can choose, located at the top of a window.
PopUpMenu	A set of options from which a user can choose, located at a defined location.
Canvas	A general surface used for creating customized GUI components.

Figure 10.1 Some GUI components

Event	Description
Label	Generated by a combination of user actions and indicates that a command should be performed.
Adjustment	Generated by movement of a scrollbar, etc, and indicates that a value has been adjusted or changed.
Component	Generated by a change such as resize or movement to a component.
Focus	Generated by a change in focus, such as a component losing or gaining focus.
Item	Generated by selecting an item from a list or a group. Indicates that the state of an item has changed, for example, a checkbox being checked.
Key	Generated by a keyboard action, such as a key press or release.
Mouse	Generated by various mouse buttons and movement.
Text	Generated by text objects and indicates that the text represented by the object has changed.
Window	Generated by actions on a window, such as closing or iconifying it.

Figure 10.2   GUI Events

actions have occurred. *Event-driven programming* is a technique for constructing software that operates in response to events as they occur. Figure 10.2 describes some of the common events used in Java event-driven programs. The events must be detected by a program and handled appropriately.

> **Key Concept**   Event-driven programming is a technique used in software that operates a program in response to events as they occur.

10.2   Event-Driven Programming

Let's look at an example of a simple graphical interface. The following applet contains a `TextField` object and a `Label` object. When characters are typed into the `TextField` followed by a newline (return or enter), the phrase is repeated in the label. Figure 10.3 shows the running applet.

The following code implements the `Mimic` applet. The applet's `init` method initializes the applet's graphical user interface. The `update_label` method implements

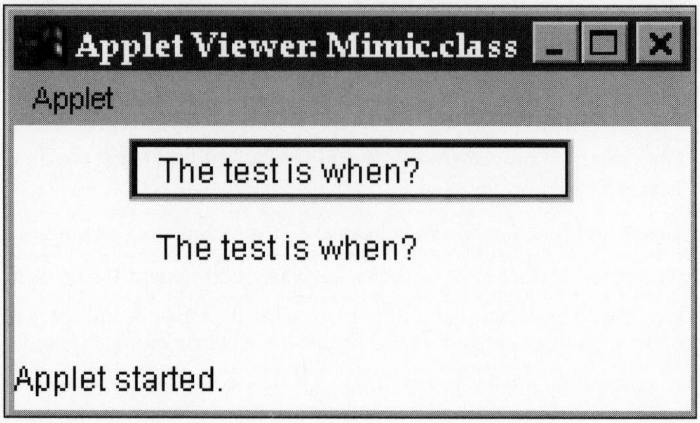

Figure 10.3 The `Mimic` applet

the main purpose of the applet, which is to update a label based on what a user types into a text field. Note that there is no explicit call to the `update_label` method inside of the applet itself. This method is invoked when an action event occurs. In this case the `ActionEvent` is generated by the text field when the user enters a newline character.

```
import java.applet.Applet;
import java.awt.*;
import java.awt.event.*;

// Demonstrates a simple component and an action event
public class Mimic extends Applet {

   Mimic_GUI gui = new Mimic_GUI (this);

   public void init() {
      gui.init();
   } // method init

   public void update_label() {
      System.out.println("Action");
      gui.update_label (gui.get_quote());
   } // method set_uppercase
} // class Mimic
```

The applet uses two additional classes to accomplish its goals: `Mimic_GUI` and `Mimic_Action_Listener`. The `Mimic_GUI` class declares various parts of the graphical user interface and arranges them appropriately. This applet is composed of two GUI components: a TextField and a Label. Both of these components are hooked to the applet using the applets add method.

Mimic_GUI also associates the listener object of the Mimic_Action_Listener class with the quote TextField object. This association is done using the addActionListener method of the TextField class. When the quote object detects an ActionEvent (such as a newline being typed into the text field) all of the listeners that have been registered using the addActionListener method of the text field will be called. In this case, only one object has been added as a listener.

```
// Constructs the graphical user interface
class Mimic_GUI {

    private Label label = new Label ("No news is good news.");
    private TextField quote = new TextField(20);

    private Mimic applet;
    private Mimic_Action_Listener listener;

    public Mimic_GUI (Mimic mimic_applet) {
        applet = mimic_applet;
        listener = new Mimic_Action_Listener (applet);
    } // Constructor Mimic_GUI

    public void init() {
        applet.add (quote);
        applet.add (label);

        applet.resize (250,100);

        // Add all associated listeners
        quote.addActionListener (listener);
    } // method init

    public void update_label (String message) {
        label.setText (message);
    } // method update_label

    public String get_quote() {
        return quote.getText();
```

The GUI is segregated from the rest of the program

```
        } // method get_quote


} // class Mimic_GUI
```

The listener classes must provide very specific methods. These methods are enforced on the listeners by requiring listeners to implement particular interfaces. In this case, the `ActionListener` interface is implemented by the `Mimic_Action_Listener`. This particular interface requires a listener for action events to provide the method `actionPerformed`. When the object associated with the listener detects an action event, the `actionPerformed` method of the listener is invoked. The Mimic listener proceeds to invoke the `update_label` method of the applet.

Listener classes implement appropriate listener interfaces

```
// Handles the action events for Mimic
class Mimic_Action_Listener implements ActionListener {

    private Mimic applet;

    public Mimic_Action_Listener (Mimic listening_applet) {
        applet = listening_applet;
    } // constructor Mimic_Action_Listener

    public void actionPerformed (ActionEvent event) {
        applet.update_label();
    } // method actionPerformed

} // class Mimic_Action_Listener
```

Let's identify the parts of the `Mimic` example that can be extended for most GUI programs. The basic model for a GUI program is to separate the entire program into three different parts:

- the GUI that is responsible for constructing the user interface and for connecting events to listeners
- the listener part that implements the appropriate interface for the type of event of interest
- the code that performs the program's action associated with the event

---

Key Concept The basic model for GUI programs contains three parts: GUI, listeners, and program-specific code.

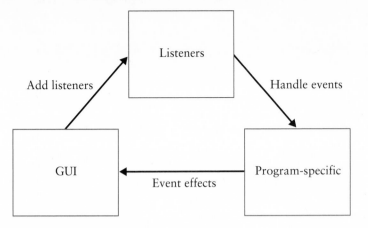

Figure 10.4 GUI program model

```
} // constructor Mimic_Action_Listener

public void actionPerformed (ActionEvent event) {
    applet.update_label();
} // method actionPerformed

} // class Mimic_Action_Listener
```

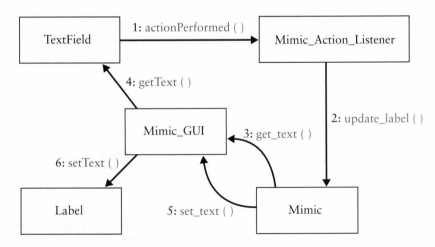

Figure 10.5 Mimic scenario diagram

Event Interfaces

Each type of event has its own particular listener interface. Figure 10.6 shows a complete table of events, their listener interfaces, their association methods, and the classes that support them. These classes operate similarly to the `Listener` defined in the `Mimic` example.

Let's look at an applet that lets a user explore how events are generated by user actions. The applet uses a listener class that implements many of the listener interfaces. The program acknowledges a series of mouse and keyboard events by printing a message that describes each event as it occurs. It also keeps a running total of the number of events processed and displays that information as it changes. Figure 10.7 shows a snapshot of the applet.

The program uses two classes. The first class is the `Events` class which `extends Applet`. This class serves as both the program-specific code and the GUI code for the program. The class creates the GUI components, arranges them, and associates them with listeners. The second class, called `Universal_Listener`, is a single class that implements many different listener interfaces. The result of the events being listened for is a log entry. The log is implemented in the GUI as a `TextArea`.

```java
import java.awt.*;
import java.awt.event.*;
import java.applet.*;

// Interactively shows when and how events are generated
public class Events extends Applet {

    private TextArea log = new TextArea (10, 65);
    private int count = 0;
    private Label count_label = new Label("", Label.CENTER);

    private Universal_Listener listener = new
        Universal_Listener (log, count_label);

    public void init() {
        add ("North", new Label ("Event Logging", Label.CENTER));
        add ("Center", log);
        add ("South", count_label);

        addComponentListener(listener);
        log.addFocusListener(listener);
        log.addKeyListener(listener);
        log.addMouseListener(listener);
        log.addMouseMotionListener(listener);
```

Event Class	Listener Interface Methods	Association Method	Generated by Class
ActionEvent	interface ActionListener actionPerformed(ActionEvent)	addActionListener removeActionListener	Button List TextField MenuItem
WindowEvent	interface WindowListener windowClosing(WindowEvent) windowOpened(WindowEvent) windowIconified(WindowEvent) windowDeiconified(WindowEvent) windowClosed(WindowEvent) windowActivated(WindowEvent) windowDeactivated(WindowEvent)	addWindowListener removeWindowListener	Window
ComponentEvent	interface ComponentListener componentMoved(ComponentEvent) componentHidden(ComponentEvent) componentResized(ComponentEvent) componentShown(ComponentEvent)	addComponentListener removeComponentListener	Component
AdjustmentEvent	interface AdjustmentListener adjustmentValueChanged(AdjustedEvent)	addAdjustmentListener removeAdjustmentListener	Scrollbar
ItemEvent	interface ItemListener itemStateChanged(ItemEvent)	addItemListener removeItemListener	Checkbox Checkbox- MenuItem Choice List
MouseEvent	interface MouseListener mouseDragged(MouseEvent) mouseMoved(MouseEvent) interface MouseMotionListener mousePressed(MouseEvent) mouseReleased(MouseEvent) mouseEntered(MouseEvent) mouseExited(MouseEvent) mouseClicked(MouseEvent)	addMouseListener removeMouseListener addMouseMotionListener removeMouseMotionListener	Component
KeyEvent	interface KeyListener keyPressed(KeyEvent) keyReleased(KeyEvent) keyTyped(KeyEvent)	addKeyListener removeKeyListener	Component
FocusEvent	interface FocusListener focusGained(FocusEvent) focusLost(FocusEvent)	addFocusListener removeFocusListener	Component
TextEvent	interface TextListener textValueChanged(TextEvent)	addTextListener removeTextListener	TextComponent

Figure 10.6 `Listener` interfaces and related classes

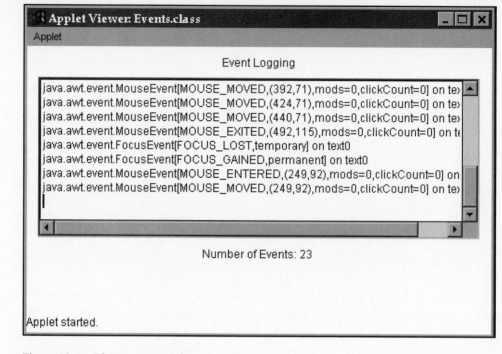

Figure 10.7 The Events applet

```
      setSize (500, 300);
   } // method init
} // class Events


class Universal_Listener implements ComponentListener,
      MouseMotionListener, MouseListener, KeyListener,
      FocusListener {

   private TextArea log;
   private Label    count_label;
   private String count_text = "Number of Events: ";
   private int count = 0;

   public Universal_Listener (TextArea log, Label count_label) {
      this.log = log;
      this.count_label = count_label;
   } // constructor Universal_Listener
```

One class as a listener for multiple event types

```java
private void log_event (AWTEvent event) {
    count++;
    count_label.setText (count_text + count);
    log.append (event.toString() + "\n");
} // method log_event


public void componentMoved (ComponentEvent event) {
    log_event (event);
} // method componentMoved
public void componentHidden (ComponentEvent event) {
    log_event (event);
} // method componentHidden
public void componentResized (ComponentEvent event) {
    log_event (event);
} // method componentResized
public void componentShown (ComponentEvent event) {
    log_event (event);
} // method componentShown
public void mouseDragged (MouseEvent event) {
    log_event (event);
} // method mouseDragged
public void mouseMoved (MouseEvent event) {
    log_event (event);
} // method mouseMoved
public void mousePressed (MouseEvent event) {
    log_event (event);
} // method mousePressed
public void mouseReleased (MouseEvent event) {
    log_event (event);
} // method mouseReleased
public void mouseEntered (MouseEvent event) {
    log_event (event);
} // method mouseEntered
public void mouseExited (MouseEvent event) {
    log_event (event);
} // method mouseExited
public void mouseClicked (MouseEvent event) {
    log_event (event);
} // method mouseClicked
public void keyPressed (KeyEvent event) {
    log_event (event);
} // method keyPressed
public void keyReleased (KeyEvent event) {
    log_event (event);
```

```
      } // method keyReleased
   public void keyTyped (KeyEvent event) {
      log_event (event);
   } // method keyTyped
   public void focusGained (FocusEvent event) {
      log_event (event);
   } // method focusGained
   public void focusLost (FocusEvent event) {
      log_event (event);
   } // method focusLost
} // class Universal_Listener
```

Executing and experimenting with this applet will give you a better understanding of when and how events are generated by user actions.

10.3   Components and Containers

As we saw in the Mimic applet, GUIs are made up of components that allow the user to interact with a program in particular ways. For example, the Mimic applet combined a TextField and Label component. Figure 10.1 gives a succinct description of some GUI components that are defined in the java.awt package.

Each of these GUI components is defined by a class or set of classes in the java.awt package. Most of those classes are derived from Component, which defines several methods that are shared by all components. The Component class provides basic drawing support, event handling, image handling, and control of color and fonts. The particular methods defined in the Component class are discussed at the appropriate points in this chapter, and the complete contents of the class are given in Appendix O.

Before exploring particular GUI components in detail, we must first discuss how containers are used to organize and present to the user. We must also examine the way in which a program determines that a user event, such as a mouse-button click, has occurred.

Key Concept   Each of the GUI components is defined by a class or set of classes in the java.awt package.

Containers

A special set of components are called *containers;* these are used to group components into manageable units and help with their presentation on the screen. An
applet is a container. The examples in this chapter are written as applets, and other
GUI components such as buttons are added to them to be displayed. Several other
types of containers are also defined in the Java API, each with their own specific
purpose. They are all derived from a common `Container` class, which is a child of
`Component`, as shown in Fig. 10.8. A brief description of these classes is given in
Fig. 10.9.

Key Concept   Containers are a special set of components that are used to group components into manageable units and help with their presentation on the screen. An applet
is a container.

`Containers` are subdivided into those that must be attached to another
graphical surface (`Panel` and `Applet`) and those that can be moved independently
(`Window` and its children). A panel or applet can only be displayed on another
graphical surface. An applet is attached to a Web browser or applet viewer, and a
panel must be added to another container in order to be displayed. A `Window`,
`Frame`, or `Dialog` object is created as its own "floating" surface, whose edge can
be grabbed with the mouse pointer and moved to a different location on the screen.

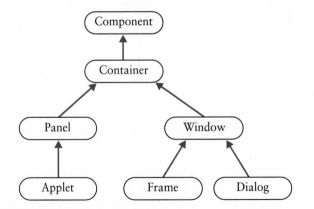

Figure 10.8   The class hierarchy for containers

Containers	Description
Container	The parent of all classes that can contain other components. It cannot be instantiated.
Panel	A container used to organize and group components. It is added to another container.
Applet	A panel that is meant to be displayed in a Web browser.
Window	A container that can be repositioned by the program user. It has no borders, no title bar, and no menu bar.
Frame	A window that has a border and a title bar. It supports the use of menus. It can be reduced to an icon by the application user.
Dialog	A window created to deal with a specific situation. It is *modal*; that is, it can block all application user input until the dialog object is dismissed.

Figure 10.9   Java container classes

A component is added to a container using the add method of the Container class. A component can only be a part of one container at a time. If you add a component to a container, it is automatically removed from any other container it was in.

Component Hierarchies

Since containers are components, a container can be added to another container. The look of a graphical interface is controlled in part by the way containers and other components are put together. These relationships form a *component hierarchy*.

Let's look at another example that derives a class called Rings from Canvas, and uses the paint method of Rings to draw a small graphic. Figure 10.10 shows a snapshot of the applet.

Three unique objects of that class are created. Two are added to a panel called group. One Ring object, and the panel containing two other Ring objects, are added to the applet.

```
import java.applet.Applet;
import java.awt.*;

public class Rings_Display extends Applet {

   private Panel group = new Panel();
   private Rings rings1 = new Rings();
   private Rings rings2 = new Rings();
   private Rings rings3 = new Rings();

   public void init() {
      add (rings1);
```

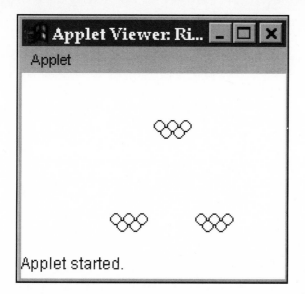

Figure 10.10 The `Rings_Display` applet

Two canvases on one panel

```
        group.add (rings2);
        group.add (rings3);
        add (group);
        resize (200, 150);
    } // method init
} // class Rings_Display


class Rings extends Canvas {
    private Dimension size = new Dimension (60, 60);

    public void paint (Graphics page) {
        page.drawOval (30,30,8,8);
        page.drawOval (40,30,8,8);
        page.drawOval (50,30,8,8);
        page.drawOval (35,35,8,8);
        page.drawOval (45,35,8,8);
    } // method paint

    public Dimension minimumSize() {
        return size;
    } // method minimumSize
```

```
      public Dimension preferredSize() {
         return minimumSize();
      } // method preferredSize
} // class Rings
```

Because a `Canvas` has a width and height of zero by default, it would not be visible unless the methods `minimumSize` and `preferredSize` are defined. The `Canvas` class is described in greater detail later in this chapter and in Appendix O. The output of the program is shown in Fig. 10.10. Although it is not visible, the second and third graphics are joined on a single panel. When the window is resized, and the graphics are repositioned, the graphics on the panel will always move as a single unit.

 Key Concept   Because a `Canvas` has a width and height of zero by default, it is not visible unless the methods `minimumSize` and `preferredSize` are overridden.

The component hierarchy of the `Rings_Display` applet can be described by the diagram in Fig. 10.11. The component hierarchy of a program is particularly important when handling user events such as a button push. This issue is discussed later in this chapter.

The way the components are arranged inside the container is also important. The method for deciding the arrangement is done by a layout manager. Layout managers use different strategies for deciding how components in a container are presented.

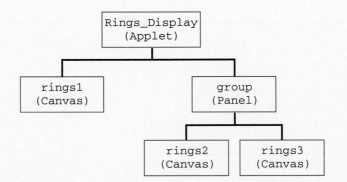

Figure 10.11   The component hierarchy of the `Rings_Display` applet

10.4 GUI Components

GUI components defined in the Java API cover an assortment of mechanisms used to interact with the user. They are all derived from the `Component` class and are used for drawing, event handling, image handling, and control of font and color. All components are defined by classes in the `java.awt` package.

Labels

Labels are components that specify a line of text to be included in the GUI. They are defined by the `Label` class. Labels are not selectable and cannot be modified by the user.

Key Concept   Labels specify a line of text in the GUI.

When a label is added to a container that is governed by a layout with a specific width, such as a grid cell, the label can be aligned to the left, right, or center of that area. The alignment is left by default. Three `static` integer constants in the `Label` class, called `LEFT`, `RIGHT`, and `CENTER`, can be used to specify the alignment.

The `Label` class has three constructors:

- `Label()`
- `Label (String label)`
- `Label (String label, int alignment)`

One constructor takes no parameters and has no initial text. Another accepts a parameter that specifies the label's initial text. The third sets up its initial text and alignment. Some of the methods of the `Label` class are listed below.

- `void setText (String label)`
- `void setAlignment (int Alignment)`
- `String getText()`
- `int getAlignment()`

The text of a label and its alignment can be set explicitly using the methods `setText` and `setAlignment`. The current text and the alignment can be retrieved using the `getText` and `getAlignment` methods. The `Mimic` applet is an example that uses a `Label`.

Text Fields and Text Areas

A text field is a GUI component that displays a single line of text. Under program control you can specify whether or not the user is allowed to edit the contents of the field. Because they may be edited, they can be used to get input from the user.

▶ **Key Concept**   A text field displays a single line of text. The programmer specifies if the user can edit the contents of the field.

A text area is similar to a text field, except that it lets you view and edit multiple lines of text. You can specify its size when it is instantiated. Scroll bars are attached along the bottom and right side of the text area, no matter how much text is actually contained in it. If the text requires more room than is provided by the visible portion of the text area, the scrollbars can be used to bring the desired portion of the text into the visible area.

A text field is defined by the `TextField` class, and a text area is defined by the `TextArea` class. Both of these classes are subclasses of the `TextComponent` class, which contains several important methods used by both. All three classes are part of the `java.awt` package and are described in Appendix O. `TextComponent` has no `public` constructor and therefore cannot be instantiated.

The constructors of `TextField` are:

- `TextField()`
- `TextField (int columns)`
- `TextField (String text)`
- `TextField (String text, int columns)`

The first two constructors do not specify an initial text string, while the others do. Two of them accept an integer that specifies the width of the text field in columns (characters). The constructors of `TextArea` are similar to those of `TextField`, except that the size of a text area is specified using rows and columns:

- `TextArea()`
- `TextArea (int rows, int columns)`
- `TextArea (String text)`
- `TextArea (String text, int rows, int columns)`

The following methods are defined in the `TextComponent` class and are used by both text fields and text areas:

- `void setText (String text)`
- `String getText()`

- `String getSelectedText()`
- `void setEditable (boolean b)`

The `setText` method explicitly specifies the text to be displayed, and `getText` returns the current text. The method called `getSelectedText` returns a string corresponding to the portion of the text that is currently selected. The `setEditable` method accepts a boolean that specifies if the text field or text area can be edited.

The following applet uses a text field to accept user input representing a Fahrenheit temperature. When the user presses the Enter key, the temperature is converted to Celsius. The result is printed in a label and in a text area that serves as an ongoing log of all conversions. The user can continue to perform temperature conversions until terminating the applet.

A screen shot of the `Fahrenheit` converter applet is shown in Fig. 10.12.

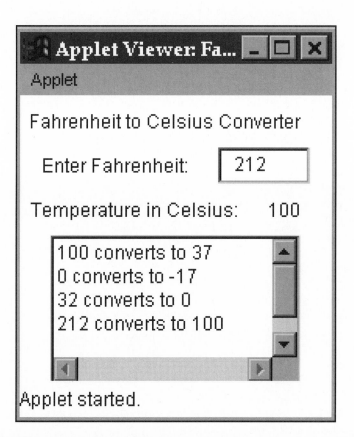

Figure 10.12   The `Fahrenheit` applet

The following program implements the `Fahrenheit` applet. The implementation uses the `ActionEvent` associated with the `TextField` component to determine when to respond.

```java
import java.applet.Applet;
import java.awt.*;
import java.awt.event.*;

//  Converts temperatures from fahrenheit to celsius.
public class Fahrenheit extends Applet {

    private Label title = new Label ("Fahrenheit to Celsius Converter");
    private Label question = new Label ("Enter Fahrenheit:");
    private Label answer = new Label ("Temperature in Celsius:");

    private TextField fahrenheit = new TextField (5);
    private Label celsius = new Label ("N/A");
    private TextArea log = new TextArea (5, 20);

    private Fahrenheit_Listener listener = new
        Fahrenheit_Listener (this);

    public void init() {
        fahrenheit.addActionListener (listener);
        log.setEditable (false);
        add (title);
        add (question);
        add (fahrenheit);
        add (answer);
        add (celsius);
        add (log);
        resize (200,200);
    } // method init

    public void convert() {
        int fahrenheit_temperature, celsius_temperature;
        String text = fahrenheit.getText();

        fahrenheit_temperature = Integer.parseInt (text);
        celsius_temperature = (fahrenheit_temperature-32)*5/9;

        celsius.setText (Integer.toString (celsius_temperature));
        log.append (text + " converts to " +
                    celsius.getText() + "\n");
```

```
      } // method convert
} // class Fahrenheit

//  The listener class for the textfield.
class Fahrenheit_Listener implements ActionListener {
   private Fahrenheit applet;

   public Fahrenheit_Listener (Fahrenheit listening_applet) {
      applet = listening_applet;
   } // constructor Fahrenheit_Listener

   public void actionPerformed(ActionEvent action) {
      applet.convert();
   } // method actionPerformed
} // class Fahrenheit_Listener
```

Lists

The GUI component defined by the List class can be used to display a list of selectable strings. The size of the list box is specified by the number of visible rows in it. However, the list can contain any number of strings and, when necessary, a scroll bar appears on the right edge of the list box.

Key Concept   The List class can be used to display a list of selectable strings.

An item in a list can be selected with a single mouse click. You can allow multiple items in the list to be selected at the same time. Methods in the List class can be used to retrieve the selected text for processing. Furthermore, each item in the list can be specified by an index corresponding to its position. The first item in the list is at index 0.

The constructors for the List class are:

- List()
- List (int rows, boolean multipleSelections)

The first constructor creates a list of no visible size and limits the user to selecting only one item at a time. The second constructor accepts an integer parameter that specifies the size of the list box, and a boolean parameter that specifies whether multiple items in the list can be selected at the same time.

Some of the key methods defined in the `List` class are:

- `void addItem (String item)`
- `void addItem (String item, int index)`
- `boolean isMultipleMode()`
- `void setMultipleMode (boolean b)`
- `int countItems()`
- `void clear()`
- `void delItem (int index)`
- `String getitem (int index)`
- `String getSelectedItem()`
- `String[] getSelectedItems()`

The overloaded `addItem` methods either add a new item to the end of the list or add it at a particular index in the list. The `isMultipleMode` method returns a boolean indicating whether the list currently allows multiple selections to occur. That characteristic can be set explicitly using `setMultipleMode`.

The `countItems` method returns the number of items in the list. To remove items from the list, you could use `clear`, which removes all items from the list, or `delItem`, which removes the item at the specified index. Finally, the method `getSelectedItem` returns the currently selected string. If multiple selections are allowed, `getSelectedItems` returns an array containing the group of selected strings.

Buttons

The `java.awt` package supports four distinct types of buttons. Each button type serves a different purpose and is used in specific situations, as described in Fig. 10.13.

Key Concept The Java API package supports four distinct types of buttons. Each button type serves a different purpose and is used in specific situations.

A push button is defined by the `Button` class. It can either be created with a label or without, using the following constructors:

- `Button()`
- `Button (String label)`

A choice button is defined by the `Choice` class. It only has one constructor, which accepts no parameters. Options are added to the choice list and acknowledged by the following methods:

- `void addItem (String item)`
- `int getItemCount()`

Button Type	Description
Push button	A single button set up to initiate some action when pushed.
Choice button	A single button that displays a list of choices when pushed. The current choice is shown next to the button at all times.
Checkbox button	A button that can be toggled on or off. Often a group of checkbox buttons are used to define a set of options. Multiple options can be chosen at the same time.
Radio buttons	A single button that displays a list of choices when pushed. The current choice is shown next to the button at all times.

Figure 10.13   Button types defined in the `java.awt` package

- `String getItem (int item)`
- `int getSelectedItem()`
- `String getSelectedItem()`
- `void select (int index)`
- `void select (String string)`

Items in the choice list can be recognized by their index in the list or by the name of the item itself. A particular item can be selected using either of the overloaded `select` methods, and its value obtained by using the `getSelectedItem` methods. The `addItem` method allows new items to be inserted at currently selected index.

Checkbox buttons and radio buttons are defined using the `Checkbox` class. A checkbox button does not need to be grouped, since multiple options are allowed. However, radio buttons are defined by using the `CheckboxGroup` class in addition to the `Checkbox` class. The constructors of `Checkbox` are:

- `Checkbox()`
- `Checkbox (String label)`
- `Checkbox (String label, CheckboxGroup group, boolean state)`

A checkbox can be created with a string that explains the option, a checkbox group to which it belongs, and a boolean indicating the checkboxes' initial state. Section 10.6 shows an extended example using various types of buttons.

Scrollbars

A text area automatically has a scrollbar attached to its bottom and right sides, so that text that cannot be seen in the visible area can be scrolled into view. Similarly, a list box will attach a scrollbar to its right side if the number of items in the list becomes larger than the visible area. However, a scrollbar is also a GUI component and can be created and used by itself for any situation if a value needs to be set from a given range. Scrollbars are also helpful to specify the relative position of objects on the screen.

Key Concept   Scrollbars are helpful to specify the relative position of objects on the screen and to set a value from a given range.

A scrollbar is created by instantiating the `Scrollbar` class. The constructors of `Scrollbar` are:

- `Scrollbar()`
- `Scrollbar (int orientation)`
- `Scrollbar (int orientation, int value, int visible, int minimum, int maximum)`

The last constructor can be used to specify the scrollbar's orientation by using the constants `HORIZONTAL` or `VERTICAL`, the scrollbar's initial value, the scrollbar's visible size, and the minimum and maximum values for the scrollbar at its end points. If the orientation is not set, it defaults to vertical. If the `value`, `visible`, `minimum`, and `maximum` are not specified, they default to zero.

A scrollbar can be clicked in various areas to indicate how far the scrollbar should move. The arrows at each end indicate a unit increment. The areas between the scroll box and the arrows indicate a block increment. How far these increments move the scrollbar can be set using some of the following methods:

- `void setUnitIncrement (int increment)`
- `void setBlockIncrement (int increment)`
- `void setValue (int value)`
- `void setValues (int value, int visible, int minimum, int maximum)`
- `int getUnitIncrement ()`
- `int getBlockIncrement ()`
- `int getValue ()`
- `int getMaximum ()`
- `int getMinimum ()`
- `int getOrientation ()`
- `int getVisibleAmount ()`

Several other methods in the list return the current state of various scrollbar characteristics.

The following applet uses a scrollbar to zoom a picture in and out. The picture begins as a small rectangle above the horizontal scrollbar. As the scrollbar is moved, the picture looms larger. A snapshot of the applet is shown in Fig. 10.14.

The program uses the `AdjustmentListener` interface to create a class that can respond to the changes in the scrollbar's position. Setting the scrollbar's maximum size to the same size as the largest possible picture, directly associates the value of the scrollbar's position to the dimensions of the picture. As an `AdjustmentEvent` is detected, the `adjustmentValueChanged` method of the

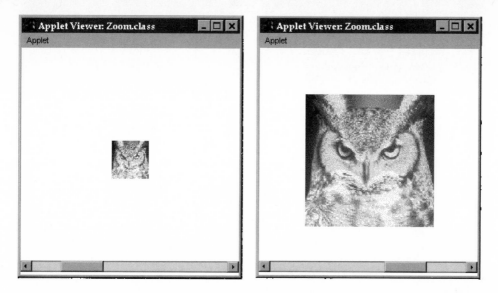

Figure 10.14 The Zoom applet

Zoom_Adjustment_Listener object is invoked. This method in turn calls the Zoom applet's zoom_image method for setting the dimensions of the image and repainting of the applet.

```
import java.applet.*;
import java.awt.*;
import java.awt.event.*;

// Zooms in and out on an Image controlled by a scrollbar
public class Zoom extends Applet {

    private final int SIZE = 300;

    private Scrollbar bar =
        new Scrollbar(Scrollbar.HORIZONTAL, 10, 64, 10, SIZE);
    private Zoom_Listener listener = new Zoom_Listener (this);

    private int current_size = 10;
    private Image picture;

    public void init() {
        setLayout (new BorderLayout());
        setBackground (Color.white);
        bar.addAdjustmentListener (listener);
```

```
            picture = getImage (getDocumentBase(), "owl.gif");
            add (bar, "South");
            setSize (SIZE, SIZE);
            setVisible (true);
        } // method init

        public void zoom_image (int size) {
            current_size = size;
            repaint();
        } // method zoom_image

        public void paint (Graphics page) {
            page.drawImage (picture, SIZE/2-current_size/2,
                SIZE/2-current_size/2, current_size, current_size, this);
        } // method draw

} // class Zoom

// The AdjustmentEvent Listener for Zoom
class Zoom_Listener implements AdjustmentListener {
    private Zoom applet;

    public Zoom_Listener (Zoom zoom_applet) {
        applet = zoom_applet;
    } // constructor Zoom_Listener

    public void adjustmentValueChanged (AdjustmentEvent event) {
        applet.zoom_image (event.getValue());
    } // method adjustmentValueChanged

} // class Zoom_Listener
```

A scrollbar generates `Adjustment` events

10.5   Layout Managers

Every container uses a *layout manager* to arrange its components. There are several predefined layout managers in the java.awt package. This section describes how each layout manager affects the manner in which components are presented. They are described in Fig. 10.15. Each layout manager is defined by its own class in the java.awt package.

Layout Manager	Description
Flow Layout	Lays out components from left to right, moving to new rows as necessary. It is the default layout manager for Panel and Applet.
Border Layout	Defines five areas to which components can be added: north, south, east, west, and center. It is the default layout manager for Window and its children.
Card Layout	Displays only one component at a time, which is resized to fill the container.
Grid Layout	Lays out components in the specified number of rows and columns. It makes all components equal in size.
Grid Bag Layout	Lays out components in grid, but allows a component to span multiple rows and columns.

Figure 10.15   Predefined layout managers

Key Concept   Every container uses a layout manager to arrange its components.

The layout manager used by a particular container can be explicitly set by using the setLayout method of the Container class. The getLayout method returns the current layout manager used for a particular container.

Flow Layout

All panels and applets use flow layout by default. As components are added to a container that is governed by the flow layout manager, they are placed in a row from left to right. If a component cannot be added to a row in the remaining space, a new row is started. All components on a row are centered vertically, so the midpoints of components of different heights are aligned.

Figure 10.16 shows two snapshots of an applet using the flow layout. The applet displays five buttons. The position of each button relative to its order is determined by the order of the calls to the container's add method. The distinctive feature of the flow layout can be seen when the applet is resized to be small. The flow layout rearranges the buttons to fit as many on a row as possible, starting new rows as necessary. In the first snapshot we see one row of two buttons followed by another row of three buttons. When the applet is resized, the buttons are rearranged to take advantage of the new size. In the second snapshot all the buttons fit in a single row. Notice that the buttons are only as large as needed to display their label. The following is the implementation of the Flow applet.

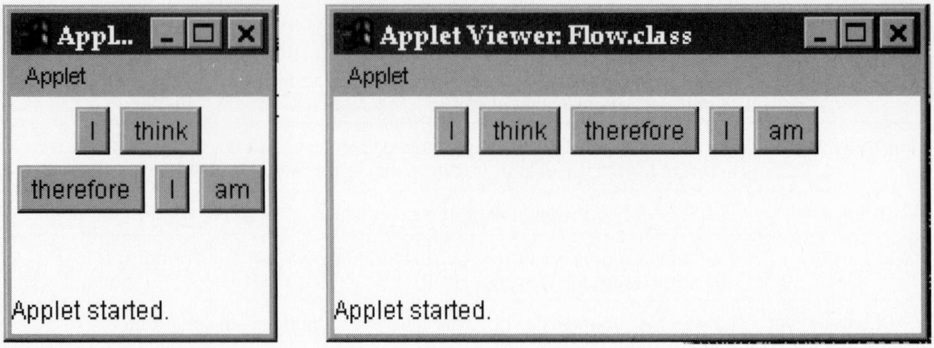

Figure 10.16 The Flow applet

```java
import java.applet.Applet;
import java.awt.*;

// Show how the flow layout manager works
public class Flow extends Applet {

    Button button1 = new Button ("I");
    Button button2 = new Button ("think");
    Button button3 = new Button ("therefore");
    Button button4 = new Button ("I");
    Button button5 = new Button ("am");

    public void init() {
        setLayout (new FlowLayout());
        add (button1);
        add (button2);
        add (button3);
        add (button4);
        add (button5);
        setVisible(true);
    } // method init
} // class Flow
```

Explicitly setting
the layout manager

By default, the components used are centered on each row. That is, all empty space on the row is divided in half and placed on either end, with the components grouped together in the middle. The alignment can be explicitly specified using the constants LEFT, CENTER, or RIGHT.

A flow layout manager lets the programmer specify the size of the gaps between components. The horizontal gap specifies the space between components on a row, and the vertical gap specifies the space between rows. The gaps are measured in pixels.

A flow layout manager is defined by the `FlowLayout` class, which has the following constructors:

- `FlowLayout()`
- `FlowLayout (int align)`
- `FlowLayout (int align, int hgap, int vgap)`

The last constructor accepts parameters specifying the alignment, horizontal gap, and vertical gap to be used by that particular flow layout manager. If the gaps are not specified, they default to five pixels. If the alignment is not specified, it defaults to `CENTER`.

Grid Layout

A grid layout manager places components in a grid with a specific number of rows and columns. Each component occupies exactly one cell in the grid, which is filled left to right and top to bottom. All cells in a grid are the same size.

Figure 10.17 shows two snapshots of an applet using the grid layout. This particular example uses a 2 × 3 grid, filling it with only five button components. When this applet is resized, all of the buttons grow in proportion to the new size.

The following is the implementation of the `Grid` applet.

```
import java.applet.Applet;
import java.awt.*;
```

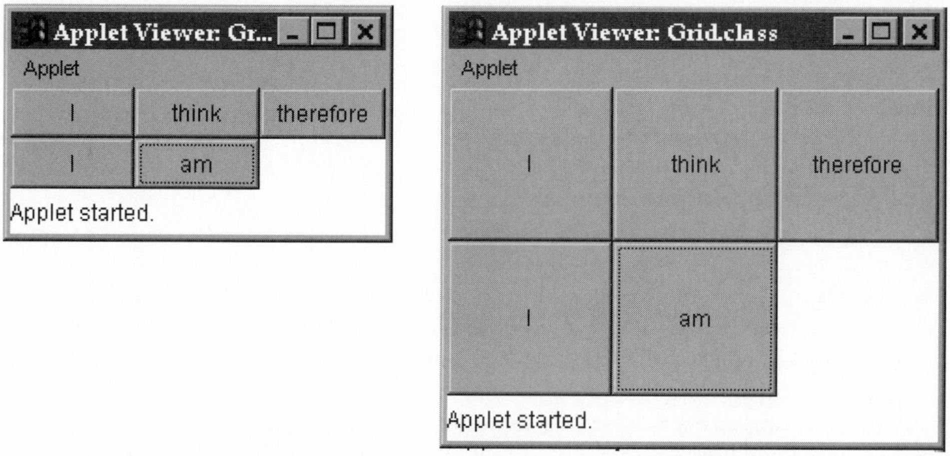

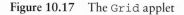

Figure 10.17   The `Grid` applet

```
// Show how the grid layout manager works
public class Grid extends Applet {

    Button button1 = new Button ("I");
    Button button2 = new Button ("think");
    Button button3 = new Button ("therefore");
    Button button4 = new Button ("I");
    Button button5 = new Button ("am");

    public void init() {
        setLayout (new GridLayout(2,3));
        add (button1);
        add (button2);
        add (button3);
        add (button4);
        add (button5);
        setVisible(true);
    } // method init
} // class Grid
```

produces a grid of 2 rows by 3 columns

The GridLayout class has the following constructors:

- GridLayout (int rows, int columns)
- GridLayout (int rows, int columns, int hgap, int vgap)

Both constructors specify the number of rows and columns in the grid. The second constructor also has parameters to specify the horizontal gap and the vertical gap between rows and columns of the grid. The gaps are measured in pixels and default to zero if not specified. Specifying a zero for the number of rows or columns results in the number being determined by the other value. For example, if the number of rows is specified as zero, and the number of columns is four, then the number of rows will be the total number of components divided by four. The number of rows and columns cannot both be set to zero.

Border Layout

A border layout defines five locations in which to place components: North, South, East, West, and Center. The locations are positioned relative to each other, as shown in Fig. 10.18, but can have widely varying sizes and may not be used at all. The total space is distributed among the locations of the border layout that are used.

When a component is added to a container governed by a border layout, one of the five locations must be specified. Only one component should be placed in each location. If you wish to have multiple components in a location, group them using a

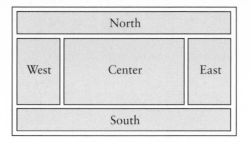

Figure 10.18 The border layout locations

panel and add the panel to the container with the border layout. An example of this type of grouping can be seen in the program explored in Section 10.6.

The size of each location depends on the size of the component that is added to it. The North and South locations are as wide as the container and as tall as the component's preferred height. The West and East locations are as wide as the component's preferred width and as tall as the space between the North and South components. The Center location is as wide as the space between the West and East components and as high as the space between the North and South components.

Figure 10.19 shows two snapshots of an applet using the border layout. As this applet is resized, the center component grows in both the horizontal and vertical directions. The North and South components grow in the horizontal direction, and the East and West components grow in the vertical direction. The following code is the implementation of the Border applet.

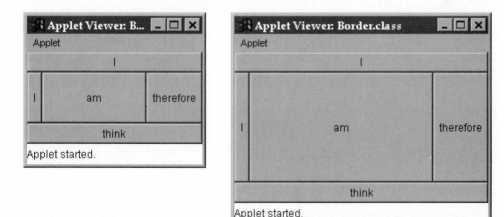

Figure 10.19 The Border applet

```
import java.applet.Applet;
import java.awt.*;

// Show how the border layout manager works
public class Border extends Applet {

    Button button1 = new Button ("I");
    Button button2 = new Button ("think");
    Button button3 = new Button ("therefore");
    Button button4 = new Button ("I");
    Button button5 = new Button ("am");

    public void init() {
        setLayout (new BorderLayout ());
        add (button1, "North");
        add (button2, "South");
        add (button3, "East");
        add (button4, "West");
        add (button5, "Center");
        setVisible(true);
    } // method init
} // class Border
```

BorderLayout
works in five
distinct areas

Notice that the position of the components in the border layout is not determined by the sequence of calls to the container's add method. A second parameter is used to identify a component's location, e.g., "North", "South", "East", "West", and "Center".

The BorderLayout class has the following constructors:

- BorderLayout ()
- BorderLayout (int hgap, int vgap)

The second constructor accepts parameters that specify the horizontal and vertical gaps between the locations in the border layout. The horizontal gap specifies the space between the West, Center, and East locations. The vertical gap specifies the space between the North location and the middle locations, and between the South location and the middle locations. If the constructor with no parameters is used, then a horizontal and vertical gap of zero is used.

Card Layout

Although many components may be added to a container using a card layout manager, only one component is displayed at a time. The components are ordered according to the order in which they were added to the container. The currently visible component is resized to take up the entire visible area of the container.

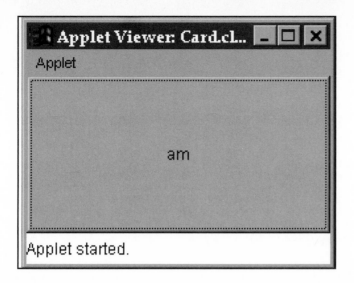

Figure 10.20   The `Card` applet

Figure 10.20 shows an applet using the card layout manager. Five buttons have been added to the applet, but only the last one is currently visible. The following code implements the `Card` applet.

```
import java.applet.Applet;
import java.awt.*;

// Show how the card layout manager works
public class Card extends Applet {

    Button button1 = new Button ("I");
    Button button2 = new Button ("think");
    Button button3 = new Button ("therefore");
    Button button4 = new Button ("I");
    Button button5 = new Button ("am");
    CardLayout layout = new CardLayout();

    public void init() {
        setLayout (layout);
        add (button1, "One");
        add (button2, "Two");
        add (button3, "Three");
        add (button4, "Four");
        add (button5, "Five");
```

```
            setVisible(true);
    } // method init

    public void start() {
        for (int cards = 1; cards < 50; cards++) {
            layout.next(this);
            for (int pause = 1; pause < 400000; pause++);
        }
    } // method start
} // class Card
```

CardLayout
components are
stacked

The CardLayout class has the following constructors:

- CardLayout()
- CardLayout (int hgap, int vgap)

The second constructor accepts parameters that specify the horizontal and vertical gaps around the edges of the currently visible card. If not specified, the gaps default to zero pixels.

The following methods are defined in the CardLayout class:

- void first (Container cont)
- void last (Container cont)
- void next (Container cont)
- void previous (Container cont)
- void show (Container cont, String name)

Each of these methods control which component is currently visible in the container specified by the cont parameter. The first and last methods make visible the first or last component in the ordered list, respectively. The next method shows the next component in the list, relative to the currently visible component. The example cycles through all the components added to the applet using this method. The previous method is similar, except that it shows the previous component in the list. The show method explicitly indicates which component to display using component's name. The show method can only be used after the addLayoutComponent method is used to associate a String with a particular component.

Grid Bag Layout

Like a grid layout, a grid bag layout is designed as a two-dimensional grid of rows and columns, but not all of the cells in the grid are the same size. A component may span multiple cells.

A grid bag layout manager is defined by the GridBagLayout class, which has only one constructor that accepts no parameters. A grid bag has no cells initially.

They are automatically created as components are added. Not all cells need to be occupied.

Every component in a grid bag layout is associated with a series of constraints, as defined by the class called `GridBagConstraints`. The constraints determine the size and position of a component in the grid bag. Figure 10.21 shows the vast number of options available to constrain components.

With the options in Fig. 10.21 a wide variety of layouts can be created. Figure 10.22 shows two snapshots of an applet using the `GridBag` layout manager.

This applet demonstrates how to define rows for the gridbag and how to control the effects on components when the entire applet is resized. The first "I" and the "am" buttons do not resize at all. The second "I" button expands in both directions, and the "think" and "therefore" buttons grow in different directions. The following code implements this applet.

```
import java.applet.Applet;
import java.awt.*;


// Show how the flow layout manager works
public class Grid_Bag extends Applet {

   private Button button1 = new Button ("I");
   private Button button2 = new Button ("think");
   private Button button3 = new Button ("therefore");
   private Button button4 = new Button ("I");
   private Button button5 = new Button ("am");


   private GridBagLayout gridbag = new GridBagLayout ();


   private void first_row (Button button) {
      GridBagConstraints constraints = new GridBagConstraints ();


      constraints.gridwidth = GridBagConstraints.REMAINDER;
      constraints.anchor    = GridBagConstraints.WEST;


      gridbag.setConstraints (button, constraints);
      add (button);
   } // method first_row


   private void second_row (Button button1, Button button2) {
      GridBagConstraints constraints = new GridBagConstraints ();
```

GridBagLayout
works with a
GridBagConstraints
specification

Constraint Field	Description	Assignment Values	Default
anchor	When the component is smaller than its grid location, this field specifies where to locate it.	CENTER EAST NORTH NORTHEAST NORTHWEST SOUTH SOUTHEAST SOURTHWEST WEST	CENTER
fill	Direction the component is allowed to grow when there is extra space that can be filled.	BOTH HORIZONTAL NONE VERTICAL	NONE
gridx	Represents the x location of the component in the grid coordinates.	RELATIVE x integer value of a grid location	RELATIVE
gridy	Represents the y location of the component in the grid coordinates.	RELATIVE y integer value of a grid location	RELATIVE
gridwidth	Width of the component in cells.	RELATIVE REMAINDER Size integer value in cells	1
gridheight	Height of the component in cells.	RELATIVE REMAINDER Size integer value in cells	1
ipadx	Padding in pixels to be added to a component in the x direction.	Size integer value of pixels for padding	0
ipady	Padding in pixels to be added to a component in the y direction.	Size integer value of pixels for padding	0
insets	Padding to be used for internal edge of cells containing the component.	insets class representing appropriate internal padding	0,0,0,0
weightx	The x direction growth factor for the component.	Integer value to be used to create a growth ratio with other components in the grid	0
weighty	The y direction growth factor for the component.	Integer value to be used to create a growth ratio with other components in the grid	0

Figure 10.21 Fields of the `GridBagConstraints` class

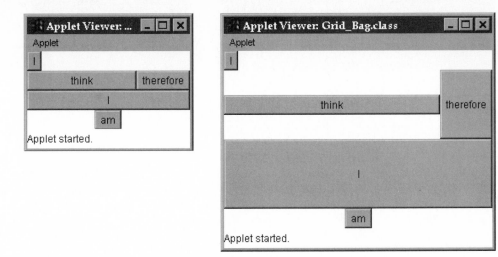

Figure 10.22   The Grid_Bag applet

```
    constraints.gridwidth = 8;
    constraints.fill      = GridBagConstraints.HORIZONTAL;
    constraints.weightx   = 1.0;


    gridbag.setConstraints (button1, constraints);
    add (button1);
    constraints = new GridBagConstraints();


    constraints.gridwidth = GridBagConstraints.REMAINDER;
    constraints.fill      = GridBagConstraints.VERTICAL;
    constraints.weighty   = 1.0;


    gridbag.setConstraints (button2, constraints);
    add (button2);
} // method second_row

private void third_row (Button button) {
    GridBagConstraints constraints = new GridBagConstraints();

    constraints.gridwidth = GridBagConstraints.REMAINDER;
    constraints.fill      = GridBagConstraints.BOTH;
    constraints.weighty   = 1.0;
```

```
            gridbag.setConstraints (button, constraints);
            add (button);
    } // method third_row


    private void fourth_row (Button button) {
        GridBagConstraints constraints = new GridBagConstraints();


        constraints.gridwidth = GridBagConstraints.REMAINDER;


        gridbag.setConstraints (button, constraints);
        add (button);
    } // method fourth_row


    public void init() {
        setLayout(gridbag);


        first_row (button1);
        second_row (button2, button3);
        third_row (button4);
        fourth_row (button5);


        setVisible(true);
    } // method init
} // class Grid_Bag
```

The applet is written to show how each row is constructed. The first_row method declares a constraint for the "I" button. The gridwidth variable of the constraint is set to REMAINDER, which indicates that the "I" button will be the last component on this row. The anchor variable of the constraint is set to WEST, which indicates that the component should remain as far left as possible. Assuming the default of NONE for fill, the "I" button remains the same size no matter how large the applet is resized. The second_row method allows the "think" button to grow horizontally by setting the fill to HORIZONTAL and the weightx to 1. Also, the cell size for the "think" button is set to eight times what the previous row used by setting the gridwidth to 8. The "therefore" button is allowed to grow vertically by setting the fill to VERTICAL and the weighty to 1. This button is the last component on the second row, because the gridwidth is set to REMAINDER. The third_row method allows the second "I" button to grow in both the vertical and the horizontal directions by setting the fill to BOTH. The last row, defined by the fourth_row method, sets gridwidth to REMAINDER, so there is only one button in the row. The button remains centered since the default value of anchor is CENTER. The button remains the same size as the applet is resized because the default for `fill` is `NONE`. Overall the `GridBag` applet provides a very flexible applet for creating nonuniform applet layouts.

10.6   Example: Quotes

The following applet demonstrates the use of various kinds of buttons. Its output is pictured in Fig. 10.23. A quote is printed using a label. As various buttons are used, the quote itself changes, or the way the quote is presented changes. The category of the quote (comedy, philosophy, or carpentry) is determined by the series of radio buttons in the middle. Two push buttons control whether the text appears in all uppercase letters or all lowercase letters. A choice button on the bottom-left corner allows the user to choose the font in which the quote appears. Two checkbox buttons on the right side determine the style in which the quote appears. Because multiple checkboxes can be selected at one time, the quote can be in plain text, italics, bold, or italics and bold. The applet uses a grid layout and a flow layout.

The program is an extended example of the model for GUI-based programs. The program is separated into four classes. The first class is the applet, which contains the commands supported by this program and methods associated with each command. A simple command is `BOLD`, which will invoke the appropriate code to put the quote at the top of the applet in boldface type. The second class is `Quote_GUI`, which creates objects for the GUI components and constructs the component hierarchy. The third and fourth class implement various types of `event listeners` that are used by the `Quote_GUI` class. The listener classes use a `private` variable to record a command that should be performed. This example is different from the previous one in that the `Quote_GUI` class creates a separate object for every type of listener, and associates each object with a particular GUI component.

```java
import java.applet.Applet;
import java.awt.*;
import java.awt.event.*;

// Demonstrates several types of events that interact to
// change and highlight several quotes.
public class Quotes extends  Applet {

    String[] text = {"Take my wife, please.",
                     "We move our legs ourselves.",
                     "Measure twice, cut once."};

    Label quote = new Label (text[0], Label.CENTER);
```

Defining Custom LayoutManager

If none of the predefined layout managers will support the type of application being developed, a customized layout manager can be created. The LayoutManager interface defines the methods that are necessary for a class to be used as a layout manager. The methods are:

- void addLayoutComponent (String name, Component comp)
- void layoutContainer (Container cont)
- void removeLayoutComponent (Component comp)
- Dimension minimumLayoutSize (Container cont)
- Dimension preferredLayoutSize (Container cont)

The methods addLayoutComponent and removeLayoutComponent are called by a container when a component is added to the container. A customized layout manager needs to keep track of the components associated with the layout for any particular container. A common method for doing this tracking is to use the Hashtable class. When calling addLayoutComponent, the component passed in is put into the hash table. The removeLayoutManager needs to be able to remove the component from the hash table. The method layoutContainer needs to be able to arrange all the components stored according to their constraints. What the constraints mean is determined by the implementation of the LayoutManager object. Similar to the way BorderLayout works, specific instructions can be provided to the container when the object is added. To implement a stable and pleasing layout, particular attention needs to be paid to the size of the current container (including its insets, which define the amount of space to be left blank around the inner edge of the container). Also, the LayoutContainer needs to calculate the placement of components based on their size, the size of the current applet, and any constraints. The method miminumLayoutSize specifies how small the layout size can be without affecting the components laid out inside of it. The preferredLayoutSize provides the appropriate size for the layout manager to look visually appealing.

After all of these methods are implemented and tested, they can be used in the same manner as the predefined layout managers.

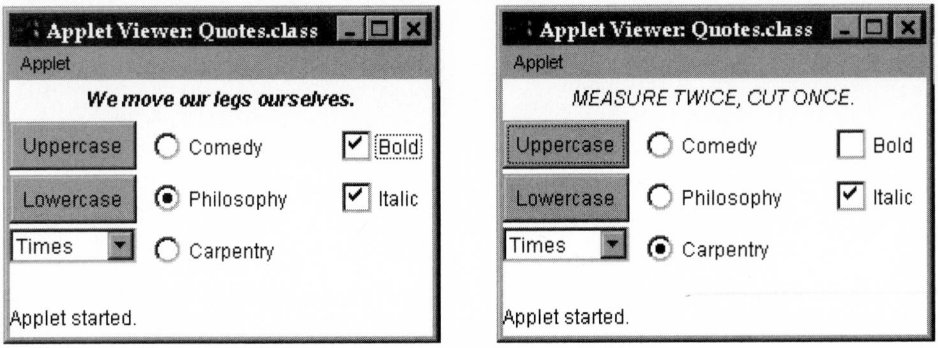

Figure 10.23 The Quotes applet

```java
final public static int UPPERCASE  = 1;
final public static int LOWERCASE  = 2;
final public static int FONT       = 3;
final public static int COMEDY     = 4;
final public static int PHILOSOPHY = 5;
final public static int CARPENTRY  = 6;
final public static int BOLD       = 7;
final public static int ITALIC     = 8;

Quote_GUI gui = new Quote_GUI (this);

public void init() {
   quote.setFont (new Font ("Times", Font.PLAIN, 12));
   gui.init (quote);
} // method init

public void set_uppercase() {
   quote.setText (quote.getText().toUpperCase());
} // method set_uppercase

public void set_lowercase() {
   quote.setText (quote.getText().toLowerCase());
} // method set_lowercase

public void set_comedy() {
   quote.setText (text[0]);
} // method set_comedy
```

```
public void set_philosophy() {
   quote.setText (text[1]);
} // method set_philosophy

public void set_carpentry() {
   quote.setText (text[2]);
} // method set_carpentry

public void set_font (String font) {
   quote.setFont (new Font (font,
      quote.getFont().getStyle(), 12));
} // method set_font

public void set_italics (boolean on) {
   Font font = quote.getFont();
   int style = font.getStyle();

   // Turn italic on or off if not already set.
   if (on) {
      if (! font.isItalic())
         style += Font.ITALIC;
   } else {
      if (font.isItalic())
         style -= Font.ITALIC;
   }
   quote.setFont (new Font (font.getName(), style, 12));
} // method set_italics

public void set_bold (boolean on) {
   Font font = quote.getFont();
   int style = font.getStyle();

   // Turn bold on or off if not already set.
   if (on) {
      if (! font.isBold())
         style += Font.BOLD;
   } else {
      if (font.isBold())
         style -= Font.BOLD;
   }
   quote.setFont (new Font (font.getName(), style, 12));
} // method actionPerformed
} // class Quotes
```

```
// Constructs the graphical user interface and associates
// event listeners
class Quote_GUI {

    private Quotes applet;

    private Panel letters = new Panel();
    private Panel domain = new Panel();
    private Panel style = new Panel();

    private Button uppercase = new Button ("Uppercase");
    private Button lowercase = new Button ("Lowercase");
    private Choice font_choice = new Choice();

    private CheckboxGroup topic = new CheckboxGroup();
    private Checkbox comedy =
        new Checkbox ("Comedy", topic, true);
    private Checkbox philosophy =
        new Checkbox ("Philosophy", topic, false);
    private Checkbox carpentry =
        new Checkbox ("Carpentry", topic, false);

    private Checkbox bold = new Checkbox ("Bold");
    private Checkbox italic = new Checkbox ("Italic");

    private Quote_Action_Listener uppercase_listener;
    private Quote_Action_Listener lowercase_listener;
    private Quote_Item_Listener bold_listener;
    private Quote_Item_Listener italic_listener;
    private Quote_Item_Listener font_listener;
    private Quote_Item_Listener comedy_listener;
    private Quote_Item_Listener philosophy_listener;
    private Quote_Item_Listener carpentry_listener;

    public Quote_GUI (Quotes quote_applet) {
        applet = quote_applet;
        uppercase_listener =
            new Quote_Action_Listener (applet, Quotes.UPPERCASE);
        lowercase_listener =
            new Quote_Action_Listener (applet, Quotes.LOWERCASE);

        bold_listener =
            new Quote_Item_Listener (applet, Quotes.BOLD);
        italic_listener =
```

A listener for each button

```
                new Quote_Item_Listener (applet, Quotes.ITALIC);
         font_listener =
                new Quote_Item_Listener (applet, Quotes.FONT);
         comedy_listener =
                new Quote_Item_Listener (applet, Quotes.COMEDY);
         philosophy_listener =
                new Quote_Item_Listener (applet, Quotes.PHILOSOPHY);
         carpentry_listener =
                new Quote_Item_Listener (applet, Quotes.CARPENTRY);
    } // Constructor Quote_GUI

    public void init (Label quote) {

         // setup the component hierarchy
         font_choice.addItem ("Courier");
         font_choice.addItem ("Times");
         font_choice.addItem ("Helvetica");

         letters.setLayout (new GridLayout (4,1,3,3));
         letters.add (uppercase);
         letters.add (lowercase);
         letters.add (font_choice);

         domain.setLayout (new GridLayout (4,1));
         domain.add (comedy);
         domain.add (philosophy);
         domain.add (carpentry);

         style.setLayout (new GridLayout (4,1));
         style.add (bold);
         style.add (italic);

         applet.setLayout (new BorderLayout(10,2));
         applet.add ("North", quote);
         applet.add ("West", letters);
         applet.add ("Center", domain);
         applet.add ("East", style);

         applet.resize (260,150);

         // Add all associated listeners
         uppercase.addActionListener (uppercase_listener);
         lowercase.addActionListener (lowercase_listener);
```

```
      font_choice.addItemListener (font_listener);
      comedy.addItemListener (comedy_listener);
      philosophy.addItemListener (philosophy_listener);
      carpentry.addItemListener (carpentry_listener);
      bold.addItemListener (bold_listener);
      italic.addItemListener (italic_listener);
   }
}


// Handles the item events for the domain of the quote,
// style, and font.
class Quote_Item_Listener implements ItemListener {

   private Quotes applet;
   private int command;

   public Quote_Item_Listener (Quotes listening_applet,
                               int listening_command) {
      applet  = listening_applet;
      command = listening_command;
   } // constructor Quote_Item_Listener

   public void itemStateChanged (ItemEvent event) {
      switch (command) {
         case Quotes.FONT:
            applet.set_font ((String)(event.getItem()));
            break;
         case Quotes.COMEDY:
            applet.set_comedy();
            break;
         case Quotes.PHILOSOPHY:
            applet.set_philosophy();
            break;
         case Quotes.CARPENTRY:
            applet.set_carpentry();
            break;
         case Quotes.BOLD:
            applet.set_bold
               (event.getStateChange() == ItemEvent.SELECTED);
            break;
         case Quotes.ITALIC:
            applet.set_italic
               (event.getStateChange() == ItemEvent.SELECTED);
            break;
```

```
                     default:
                         System.out.println ("Illegal Item " +
                             event.toString());
                 }
         } // method actionPerformed
} // class Quote_Item_Listener


// Handles the action events for the Uppercase and Lowercase
// buttons
class Quote_Action_Listener implements ActionListener {

    private Quotes applet;
    private int     command;
    public Quote_Action_Listener (Quotes listening_applet,
                                  int listening_command) {
        applet  = listening_applet;
        command = listening_command;
    } // constructor Quote_Action_Listener

    public void actionPerformed (ActionEvent event) {
        switch (command) {
            case Quotes.UPPERCASE:
                applet.set_uppercase();
                break;
            case Quotes.LOWERCASE:
                applet.set_lowercase();
                break;
            default:
                System.out.println ("Illegal Action " +
                    event.toString());
        }
    } // method actionPerformed
} // class Quote_Action_Listener
```

Summary of Key Concepts

- Event-driven programming is a technique used in software that operates a
  program in response to events as they occur.
- The basic model for GUI programs contains three parts: GUI, listeners, and
  program-specific code.

- Each of the GUI components is defined by a class or set of classes in the `java.awt` package.
- Containers are a special set of components that are used to group components into manageable units and help with their presentation on the screen. An applet is a container.
- Because a `Canvas` has a width and height of zero by default, it is not visible unless the methods `minimumSize` and `preferredSize` are overridden.
- Labels specify a line of text in the GUI.
- A text field displays a single line of text. The programmer specifies if the user can edit the contents of the field.
- The `List` class can be used to display a list of selectable strings.
- The Java API supports four distinct types of buttons. Each button type serves a different purpose and is used in specific situations.
- Scrollbars are helpful to specify the relative position of objects on the screen and to set a value from a given range.
- Every container uses a layout manager to arrange its components.
- Event-driven programming is a technique used in software that operates a program in response to events as they occur.

Self-Review Questions

10.1 What is the primary difference between a window and a panel?

10.2 What is an event?

10.3 What is a container?

10.4 What is a layout manager?

10.5 What is the component hierarchy?

10.6 Why would one use a `Label` instead of a `TextField`?

10.7 What is the basic model for GUI programs?

10.8 Why are there many different GUI components?

Exercises

10.9   Explain the relationship between a container and a layout manager.

10.10 Compare and contrast a grid layout manager and a flow layout manager.

10.11 Name three different ways that scrollbars are used in GUI components defined by the Java API.

10.12 Draw the component hierarchy for the `Quotes` applet.

10.13 Draw the component hierarchy for the `Fahrenheit` applet.

10.14 Write a class that will create a panel that contains a `Label` and a `TextField`. A constructor of the class should accept a parameter that determines what the `Label` of the panel should contain and the size of the `TextField`.

10.15 Choose one of the examples from Section 10.5 and change the layout manager it uses. Document the effect and explain why it occurs. What were the deciding factors in choosing a new layout manager?

10.16 Draw a scenario diagram for receiving the `ItemEvent` in the `Quotes` program.

10.17 Explain how the separation of the GUI portion of an application leads to flexible programs.

10.18 Explain the difference between an `ActionEvent` and an `ItemEvent`. When would you use one over the other?

10.19 Explain how the component hierarchy is different from the inheritance hierarchy.

10.20 Describe the benefits of event-driven programming. Why are most GUI programs event driven?

10.21 How would you rewrite the `Quotes` program using the `GridBagLayoutManager` instead of the three panels and the use of `GridLayoutManager`.

10.22 Repeat problem 10.21 using the `Grid LayoutManager` instead of the `GridBag LayoutManager`.

Programming Projects

10.23 Write a program that simulates a traffic light with a short delay between states.

10.24 Write a program that uses the mouse pointer to be able to scribble on an applets `Graphics` context. Assume that you can use the `drawLine` method of the `Graphics` class and a `MouseMotionListener`.

10.25 Write a program that draws a circle around the place at which the mouse is currently located on an applet. The program should track the motion of the mouse, erase an old circle, and draw a new circle at the last known position of the mouse.

10.26 Write a program that displays the current time and date, updated regularly.

10.27 Add a choice button to the program described in Problem 10.26 to choose the time zone for which the clock should display information.

10.28 Write a program that implements a mouse odometer. As the mouse moves across the screen, the odometer is updated to indicate the distance the mouse has traveled in pixels. Add a button to reset the odometer.

10.29 Write a program that accepts and checks a person's password. To prevent misuse, asterisks should be printed as the user types the password. (See the setEchoChar method of the TextField class.) Print an appropriate message depending on whether the user types a correct or incorrect password.

10.30 Write a program that will act as a countdown clock. Allow the user to enter the number of ticks (not necessarily seconds). On a button click, count backwards from the starting point to zero. When zero is reached, print an appropriate message.

10.31 Extend the program described in Problem 10.30 to add a pause/resume button that allows the user to stop and restart the countdown. Add only one button, whose label is "pause" when the countdown is running and "resume" when it is not.

10.32 Modify the Quotes program by adding another button that allows the user to change the size of the quote.

Answers to Self-Review Questions

10.1 A window is not attached to another container, while a panel must be. The user can move a window from one point to another on the screen.

10.2 An event is a situation that arises in software, often in response to a user action such as a mouse button click. A program can be written to process and respond to particular events.

10.3 A container is a Java component that can contain other components. It is used to organize and display a graphical user interface.

10.4 A layout manager controls the format and relative positions of the components in a GUI. Each Java container is governed by a layout manager.

10.5 The order in which you put components in containers defines a component hierarchy. Careful planning of the component hierarchy can facilitate high-quality GUI development.

10.6 A Label cannot be modified by the user by typing over it, whereas the contents of a TextField can be modified if it is made editable. If you don't want a user to change a value, you don't even want to hint that there may be the possibility. Using a `TextField` could give the user the wrong idea.

10.7 There are three elements: the GUI with its components presented in a particular manner, the listeners that are ready to respond to events, and the other program code that handles all other processing.

10.8 There are many GUI components because there are many ways to interact with a system. Some components are particularly well suited to certain types of interactions. It is the challenge of the interface developer to design the user interface for maximum ease and functionality.

The Software Development Process I

11

The quality of software is only as good as the process used to create it. In Chapter 3, we introduced four basic activities that are a part of any software development effort: requirements, design, implementation, and testing. For successful software development, it is crucial to refine these activities into a well-defined process that can be applied repeatedly and consistently. This chapter integrates these activities into a basic iterative development process. This process is illustrated using an extended example that synthesizes many of the programming concepts explored thus far in the book.

Chapter Objectives

* Explore several different approaches to developing software.
* Explain the life cycle of a software system and its implications for software development.
* Explain an iterative design process that uses prototypes and multiple evaluations.
* Explore the ways in which prototyping is applied during software design.
* Show how to use graphical images in a Java program.
* Demonstrate a software process by using a nontrivial example.
* Show various graphical approaches, such as scenario diagrams, used when designing software.

11.1 Software Development Models

A program goes through many phases from its initial conception to its ultimate demise. This sequence is often called the *life cycle* of the program. Too often, a programmer focuses on the particular issues of getting a program to run, to the point of ignoring other important characteristics. The development stage is only a small part of a program's overall life. Developing high-quality programs requires an appreciation for what happens to a program after its initial development. This section discusses the life cycle of a program and defines a development process model.

Software Life Cycle

The life cycle of a program is shown in Fig. 11.1. All programs go through three fundamental stages: development, use, and maintenance. Initially, the idea for a program is conceived by a software developer or by a user who has a particular need. The new program is created in the *development* stage. At some point the new program is considered to be complete and is turned over to the users. The version of the program that is made available to the users is often called a *release* of the program.

Almost certainly, users will discover problems with the program. They also often have suggestions for new features that they would like to see added to the program in order to make it more useful. The defects and ideas for new features are conveyed back to the developer, and the program undergoes maintenance.

Software *maintenance* is the process of modifying a program in order to enhance it or fix problems. The changes are made to a copy of the program, so the user can still use the original release while the program is being maintained. When the changes are serious enough or numerous enough, a new version of the program

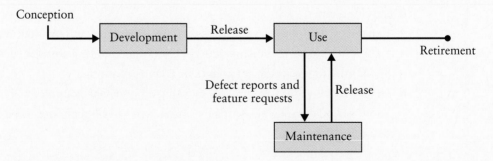

Figure 11.1 The life cycle of a program

is released for use. A program might be maintained many times over, resulting in several releases.

Key Concept Maintaining software is the process of modifying a program in order to enhance it or fix problems.

For a variety of reasons, a developer may decide that it is no longer worth the effort to maintain an existing program and therefore releases no further versions of it. Eventually, a program will outlive its usefulness, and users will abandon it or seek another solution. This eventual demise is sometimes referred to as the program's *retirement* from active use.

The duration of a program's life cycle varies greatly depending on the purpose of the program, how useful it is, and how well it is constructed. The development portion of a program can vary from a few weeks to many years. Likewise, a program may be used and maintained for many years. Figure 11.2 shows a typical ratio of comparing the time spent in development versus the time spent using and maintaining a program.

Since a significant amount of time can go by between the initial development and the maintenance tasks, the original developers are rarely the same people who maintain it. Therefore, the success of a maintenance task, such as fixing a defect, depends on the ability of a new developer to understand the program, determine what the problem is, and correct it.

Key Concept The maintainers of a program are often not the program's original developers.

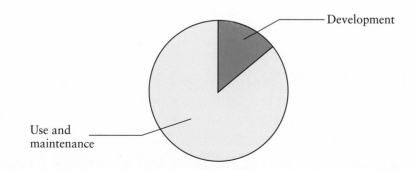

Figure 11.2 Comparing phases of a program's life cycle

The ability to read and understand a program depends on how well it is designed, implemented, and documented. It depends on how classes are derived and how objects are used. It depends on how elegantly methods accomplish their goals and on how closely coding guidelines are followed. In short, the ability to read and understand a program depends on the effort put into the development process.

When requirements are not clearly established, and when designs are not thought out carefully, the software created can be unnecessarily complex and difficult to understand. The more complex a program is, the easier it is to introduce errors during development, and the more difficult it is to remove these errors when they are found. The earlier the problems are discovered, the easier and less costly they are to correct.

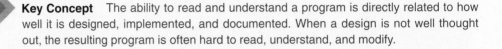

Key Concept   The ability to read and understand a program is directly related to how well it is designed, implemented, and documented. When a design is not well thought out, the resulting program is often hard to read, understand, and modify.

Writing a program without careful planning is as absurd as building a house without pouring a foundation or working from a blueprint. The builder may actually create some kind of structure, even one that looks good on a superficial examination. However, it is likely that the structure will fail to meet the safety requirements of the local building code, and it will not stand up to severe weather nearly as well as a house that has been carefully designed. Likewise, a program that is created in an ad hoc fashion, with little or no attention to requirements or design, is likely to contain many defects and will not perform well when used.

Key Concept   Rushing through the development stage often leads to significant increases in the effort expended during maintenance.

Even small changes in the development effort can radically reduce the effort necessary during maintenance. For example, including meaningful documentation in your program can significantly help anyone who must add a feature or correct a defect. Following coding guidelines can help in similar ways.

The bars in Fig. 11.3 show two possible relationships between the development effort and the effort required for maintenance tasks. The bottom bar shows that even with small increases in the effort expended during development, significant savings in maintenance effort can be gained. The effort put into the development stage is an investment that will reduce the overall effort required throughout the life

Development	Maintenance

Development	Maintenance

Figure 11.3   Development effort relative to maintenance effort

cycle of the program. A good programmer has the long-term effects in mind while performing short-term activities.

In some ways, putting a little extra effort into program development is like brushing your teeth. To many children, brushing teeth is often a chore that they try to avoid. To an adult, brushing is simply part of a daily routine, necessary for a lifetime of healthy teeth. It only takes a few minutes, and its not a big deal, unless you go for a long time without doing it. Similarly, the mature software developer realizes that even small, unobtrusive activities can have a dramatic effect over the life of the program, even if the results are not immediately apparent.

Therefore, the goal of writing software is not to minimize the amount of time it takes to develop a program, but to minimize the overall amount of effort required to create and maintain a useful program. With this goal in mind, the development process should be well defined and rigorously followed.

Development Process Models

Too often, programmers follow the *build-and-fix* approach depicted in Fig. 11.4. In it, a programmer creates an initial version of a program, then continually modifies it until it has reached some level of acceptance. The testing activities to discover errors are not systematic or carefully planned, and therefore problems often go undiscovered. The programmer is simply reacting to problems, as opposed to creating something worthy in the first place. Therefore, the so-called build-and-fix model is not really a development model at all.

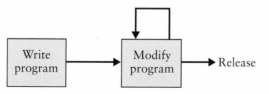

Figure 11.4   The build-and-fix approach

A program produced using the build-and-fix approach is a product of ad hoc, reckless activities. Although some problems might have been eliminated during the development, the overall quality of the product has never been addressed. Defects that still exist will be difficult to isolate and correct. Enhancements to the program will also be challenging because the system was never designed well in the first place.

> **Key Concept**   A program produced using the build-and-fix approach is a product of ad hoc, reckless activities.

As discussed in Chapter 3, the following activities need to be specifically addressed during development: establishing requirements, creating a design, implementing the design, and testing the implementation. How do we best incorporate these activities into a precise development strategy?

One of the first development process models was offered in the early 1970s. It is called the *waterfall model*, and is depicted in Fig. 11.5.

The waterfall model is linear, with one stage followed directly by the next. In fact, the name of the waterfall model comes from the implication that information is flowing in one direction from stage to stage until the final release is created. It does not allow for an earlier stage to be revisited after a new stage is begun.

It would be nice if all of the requirements of a program were completely specified and analyzed before the design activities are started. Likewise, it would be nice to have all of the design decisions made before the implementation begins. Unfortunately, it almost never works out that cleanly. No matter how carefully the requirements are established, or how thoroughly the design is analyzed, it is impos-

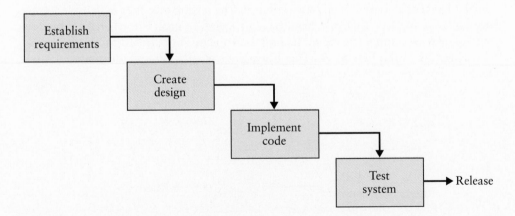

Figure 11.5   An unrealistic approach: The waterfall model

sible to predict the future, and there will always come a time when the developer realizes an earlier decision was in error.

Furthermore, since stages are not revisited in the waterfall model, a tremendous effort needs to go into each stage to ensure its completeness. However, sometimes proceeding to later stages is an efficient way to discover the issues that have not been addressed in the earlier stages. But the next stage should not be entered unless it can be honestly estimated that a large percentage of the tasks in the previous stage have been accomplished.

Therefore, a realistic model must take into account that the development activities are somewhat overlapping. However, we must be careful not to degenerate into a build-and-fix approach. We need a flexible development model with interacting activities, while still maintaining rigorous attention to each stage, ensuring the quality of the overall product.

An Iterative Process

An *iterative process* is one that allows a software developer to cycle through the different development activities. Earlier stages can be revisited, formally, allowing proper changes to be made when needed. Figure 11.6 shows an initial version of an iterative process.

The process in Fig. 11.6 is essentially the waterfall model with backtracking. That is, when new information is uncovered that changes the requirements or design, we have a way to formally go back and modify the affected stages.

The danger of backtracking is that the developer might rely on it too much. This model is not intended to reduce the amount of effort that goes into developing the initial requirements prior to starting on the design. Likewise, the design of a program should still be well established before beginning implementation. The backtracking activity should be used primarily to correct problems uncovered in later stages.

Another technique that can greatly enhance this process model is called prototyping. A *prototype* is a program that is created to explore a particular concept. Sometimes a programmer simply doesn't know how to accomplish a particular task, or whether a certain requirement is feasible, or if the user interface is acceptable to

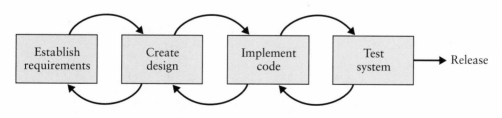

Figure 11.6   An iterative process

the client. Prototypes can be used to explore all of these issues, instead of proceeding on an assumption that may later prove unwise.

> **Key Concept** Prototypes can be used to explore design issues in a program, instead of proceeding on an assumption that may later prove unwise.

For example, a programmer might have had little experience dealing with a particular API class. Before committing to its use, the programmer may produce a small program that exercises the class in order to establish that it is a viable choice to use in the design. Another prototype might be created to test the feasibility of a requirement that states that the program should solve a quadratic equation and print the result within 100 milliseconds. A third prototype might be created that shows a simplified version of the user interface. The developer and the client can then discuss the "look and feel" of the program to see if it is acceptable.

A prototype can often pinpoint problems that lists of requirements might obscure or miss altogether. It can be used to reject certain design or implementation decisions before they become a problem. And it can clarify the user's intentions. It is not uncommon, after a project is complete, for a user to make a statement such as: "I know that's what I said I wanted, but that's not what I meant."

Figure 11.7 shows a revised iterative process model that incorporates the ability to create prototypes during any development stage in order to explore unknown issues.

Figure 11.7 also shows another necessary step at each stage in the process. Before moving on to the next stage, the results of the current stage must be evalu-

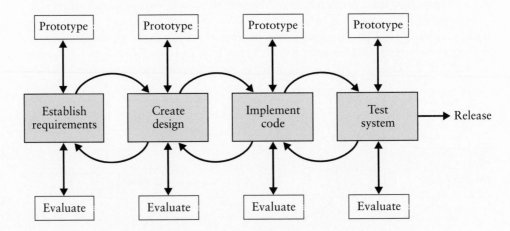

Figure 11.7   An iterative model with prototyping and evaluation

ated. That is, prior to moving on to creating a design, the requirements should be carefully evaluated to ensure that they are complete, consistent, and unambiguous. Prior to implementation, the design should be evaluated to make sure that each requirement is adequately addressed.

The evaluation of the implementation should determine how faithfully the implementation represents the design. This is often done through a *code walkthrough,* which is a meeting in which several people read the code and discuss its merit. A walkthrough might also evaluate how well the code conforms to a coding standard. Evaluating the testing stage includes determining if the tests that are planned will adequately show that the program satisfies the requirements.

Key Concept A design or code walkthrough is a meeting in which several people read and critique a software design or implementation. The purpose of the walkthrough is to improve the quality of the design and software produced by a group.

In addition to iterating between the different phases of developing a program, the entire model can be used to develop a program iteratively. One iteration of the entire model might be to build a program that represents a subset of the overall requirements or to build a specific part of a program (such as the graphical user interface). Figure 11.8 shows several iterations of the entire model shown in Fig. 11.7. Usually, a useful part of the program is developed on each iteration, and that is used as part of the requirements and design stages of the next increment.

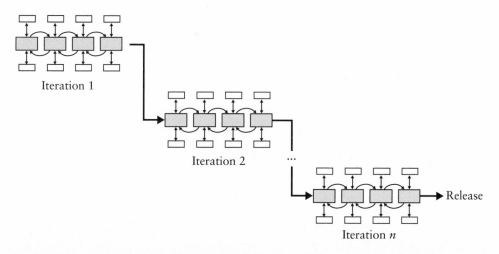

Figure 11.8 An iterative development approach

Testing Techniques

Testing a program involves running it multiple times with various input and observing the results. The goal of most testing is to find errors; therefore, a good test should be defined as a test that uncovers a problem in a program. This kind of testing is known as *defect testing*. The focus of defect testing is to increase the reliability of a program by finding and fixing errors. Over time, the number of errors that are being found should decrease, and general confidence in the program increase.

> **Key Concept** The goal of most testing is to find errors; therefore, a good test should be defined as a test that uncovers a problem in a program.

A *test case,* to be effective, is a set of inputs, user actions, or other initial conditions and expected output. By having the conditions that can cause a possible error appropriately documented, each test can be repeated. When a defect can be repeatedly shown, programmers can execute the failed testing step multiple times during debugging and thereby identify the cause of the problem.

Because programs operate on a large number of possible inputs, it is not feasible to create test cases for all possible input or user actions. For example, to exhaustively test a single integer parameter would require billions of test cases, one case for every possible value the parameter might hold. Many of these test cases end up being so similar that they are not actually testing anything different about the program, and are therefore a wasted effort. Let's take a closer look at two techniques for testing: black box and white box.

> **Key Concept** Because programs operate on a large number of possible inputs, it is not feasible to create test cases for all possible input or user actions.

Black-box testing exercises a class only through its `public` methods and variables. Essentially this technique tests the programs and classes as if they are black boxes; that is, the technique assumes no knowledge of how a class or method is implemented. This testing method is closely associated with the requirements for the program and how it will ultimately be used. Often test cases are derived directly from the requirements. A set of specific inputs to a program should produce an expected set of outputs. Every `public` method or variable should be called or set with the appropriate input values.

The input data for a test case should be selected by defining equivalence categories. An *equivalence category* is a collection of inputs that are expected to produce similar outputs. For example, a square root method has two equivalence categories: positive integers and negative integers. For this method, positive integers will produce valid output, and negative integers will not produce valid output.

For each possible input, the equivalence categories have defined boundaries. Because all values of an equivalence category essentially test the same features of a program, there is only a need for one or two test cases inside the equivalence boundary. However, the boundary itself should be tested exhaustively. For an integer boundary, an exhaustive test would use the exact value of the boundary, the boundary −1, and the boundary +1. Test cases should be defined that use these cases, plus one or two cases within the boundary.

Let's look at an example. Consider a program that is using an integer to represent a number between 0 and 99 that stands for the years 1900 to 1999. There are two boundaries for this variable, 0 and 99. These boundaries define three different regions to test. The areas are the maximum negative integer to 0, 0 to 99, and 99 to the maximum positive integer. Therefore, we should devise test cases that use −1000, −1, 0, 1, 50, 98, 99, 100, and 1000 as values for this variable. Of course, for a complete test case, we should also define the expected output of these values.

White-box testing, also known as glass-box testing, exercises the internal structure and implementation of a class or method. The goal of white-box testing is to ensure that every part of a program is executed at least once by using knowledge of how a program is implemented. This testing is done by mapping out the different possible paths through the code, and ensuring that the input associated with the test cases causes every path to be executed. This type of testing is often called a *statement coverage*. Usually, paths through the code are controlled by various control flow statements that use conditional expressions, such as an `if` statement. In order to get every path through the program executed at least once, the input data values for the test cases need to control the values for the conditional expressions so that every possible path is executed at least once. For example, the input data of one or more test cases should cause an `if` statement condition to evaluate to true in at least one case and then to false in at least one case. Covering both true and false values in the `if` statement will guarantee that both the paths through the `if` statement will be executed. Similarly for `while` statements, the termination condition needs to be evaluated at least once so that the body of the `while` statement is executed. Controlling via input data the value of conditional expressions in a program so that all paths of a program are executed is known as *conditional coverage*.

11.2   Requirements: Robot Search Simulator

Having reviewed the development life cycle, let's use the iterative process model to develop a program for the research and development (R&D) group of a robotics firm. This company develops robots for working in various environments into which humans cannot easily go, such as the inside of a nuclear power plant, outer space, the bottom of the ocean, toxic dumps, and so on. This company is currently developing a new series of robots.

Robot Search Problem

Our job is to develop a program to test the search strategies for a new series of robots. In particular, a robot must be able to traverse an area while avoiding obstacles. Quite often a robot's purpose is to search for some goal, such as radioactive material inside a nuclear power plant. Our program will simulate and graphically demonstrate several different search patterns for robots. By doing simulated searches, the various search strategies can be compared, and the robotic engineers can decide how they want their robots to behave before they actually manufacture them.

The robotic engineers provided an initial set of requirements:

- The program will be able to test multiple search algorithms.
- The program must be available to multiple sites around the world.
- Robot movement in the program should avoid danger as indicated by an obstacle sensor.
- A robot will stop when its search goal is encountered.
- Robot movement in the program will take into account walls and barriers as the robot would do in a room.
- Initially, two robots will be simulated, one performing a random search and one performing a diagonal search (though the program should be able to support all four search patterns shown in Fig. 11.9).

Revising Requirements

Notice that the requirements as provided by the user are often sparse, ambiguous, and leave many questions unanswered. For example, how many search algorithms must be supported? One requirement simply says multiple search algorithms, and another implies that there will be four (although only two initially). What does initially mean? What does danger mean? Is that the same thing as a barrier? Is a barrier different from an obstacle? Is a wall a barrier? Are there multiple barriers or goals? Are there different types of barriers and goals? What does "take into account" mean when a robot encounters a wall or barrier? What happens when one robot runs into another?

> **Key Concept**   The requirements as provided by the user are often sparse, ambiguous, and leave many questions unanswered. They need to be made as complete and consistent as possible before a programmer begins a design.

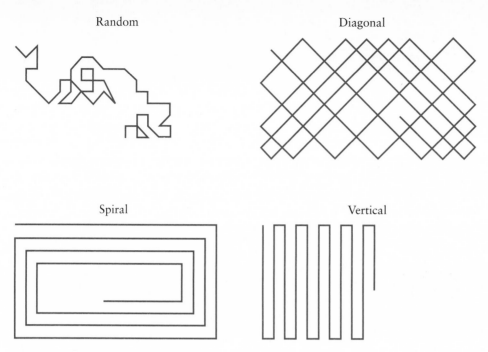

Figure 11.9   Robot search patterns

Establishing requirements often involves talking to the user to clear up any misunderstandings. This process could be long and tedious. After multiple discussions with the robotic engineers, the following revised set of requirements was created:

- The simulator shall graphically depict the top view of a rectangular room.
- Two distinct robot images shall graphically traverse the room in two distinct patterns: random and diagonal.
- The random search pattern shall pick a random direction each time the robot moves.
- All robots shall move at the same rate of speed.
- The diagonal search pattern shall move in a diagonal line relative to the room.
- There shall be one goal for both robots, graphically represented as an X at a fixed point in the room.
- There shall be one obstacle in the room, graphically represented as a rectangle.
- Robots shall start their search in the northwest (upper-left) corner of the room.
- When a wall or obstacle is encountered, the robot shall rebound (reverse direction) and continue moving.
- Robots shall ignore each other, as if they are not in the same room at the same time.

- Each robot shall continue moving until the goal is encountered.
- The program shall terminate when all robots have encountered the goal.
- The program can use images to represent robots.

Even this list does not completely answer all questions, but it does provide a good representative set, enabling the design to begin. A real requirements document would attempt to enumerate as many requirements as possible, and to provide a description of each one.

These derived requirements are usually very specific. They deal with how results will be presented, how the program should start up, and when the program should terminate. Quite often, customers request more than is actually reasonable. Explicitly stating the requirements helps everyone clearly understand and agree upon the goals of the program.

Notice that most of the requirements were written using the auxiliary verb *shall*. Using a particular and somewhat unusual verb for stating requirements, removes some (but not all) of the ambiguity inherent in English. This practice is common when stating requirements, so that programmers know which requests must be accomplished versus those that are suggestions. For example, the last statement in the above list would not be an explicit requirement, since it uses the auxiliary verb *can*.

 Key Concept   Requirements are often stated using the verb *shall,* so that they are easy to identify in a document.

Now that we have a relatively complete set of requirements we can begin the design of the program. Remember, however, that in most cases it is impossible to get all the requirements established before design work or implementation is accomplished. Often during the development of a program the requirements need to be revisited to make sure new requirements are explicitly stated.

11.3   Design

The design of a software system is an iterative process. An initial set of objects is chosen based on the requirements and general problem description of the software to be written. As behaviors and scenarios are developed for these objects, the need for other objects becomes apparent. By defining these new objects and including them into new scenarios, the design is fleshed out.

> **Key Concept**   The design of a software system is an iterative process.

As the design matures, the objects are abstracted into classes. As classes are defined, common functionality is grouped into parent classes, and unique functions specified in child classes. As part of class definitions, public behaviors of the classes are also defined.

The initial design effort focuses on the overall structure of the program. The individual algorithms for methods are usually specified using pseudocode. Implementation of the program can begin after most of the design structure and most of its algorithm are completed.

Objects and Classes

In the problem description and requirements of the robot search simulation, there are several physical objects that can be represented in software. These are:

- robot
- goal
- obstacle

Robots are the main object of the simulation. The requirements specify several behaviors that the software object must implement. These include moving around a simulated room while searching for a goal, and drawing themselves graphically. If we equate these behaviors with `public` methods for robots, then robots will have a `move` method and a `draw` method. Reviewing the requirements for the goal and obstacle, they also must be able to draw themselves. Figure 11.10 shows an initial definition of the classes for the robot simulator.

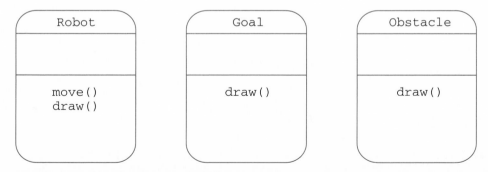

Figure 11.10   Initial classes in the robot simulator

The need to control the robots introduces another class, Robot_Sim. According to the requirements, the program should terminate when all robots have reached the goal. Using the methods defined for robots, we can write pseudocode for the main loop of the program as follows:

```
draw the goal.
draw the obstacle.
while (any robots are still searching for the goal) {
  Move all robots.
  Draw all robots in their new position.
}
```

Reviewing this pseudocode, we can see that there is a need for the Robot class to have a method that determines if the robot has reached its goal. For the robot to determine if it has reached the goal, it must be able to query the goal object. Based on this observation, we can add a detect_goal method to the Robot class, and a collide method to the Goal class.

For the Robot move method, the requirements state that different robots should be able to move in different patterns while searching for the goal. This requirement could be satisfied by implementing a complicated move method, or it could be satisfied by defining new classes derived from the Robot class that would implement the various search patterns. The latter choice is more object-oriented. It allows the child classes to share everything of the parent through inheritance while defining a unique search pattern in each child's overridden move method. It also allows many different types of robots to be implemented without complicating the Robot class itself. Figure 11.11 shows a possible class hierarchy for the robots' search patterns called for in the requirements.

As we further develop the move method, the Obstacle class needs to have a collide method that the robot's move method can invoke. Consider the following scenario for a Random_Robot move method in Fig. 11.12.

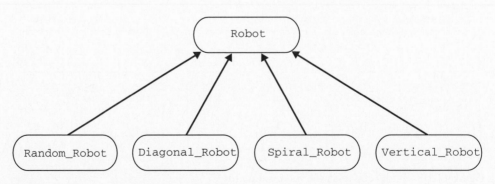

Figure 11.11 A class hierarchy for robots

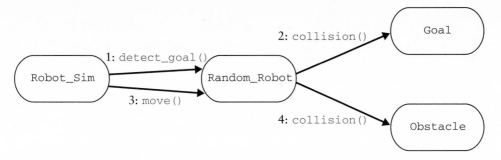

Figure 11.12 A scenario diagram that shows the movement of a robot

The scenario diagram shows the classes of each object, with arrows indicating method invocation. The numeral on the method invocation indicates the sequence of the invocation.

In this scenario, the `Robot_Sim` class calls the `detect_goal` method of the `Random_Robot` class in order to determine if the `Random_Robot`'s `move` method should be called. To determine if the `Random_Robot` has detected the goal, it must invoke the `collision` method of the `Goal` class. If the `Random_Robot` has not detected the goal, then its `move` method is invoked by the `Robot_Sim` class. In determining a proper move, the robot must consider if its movement collides with the `Obstacle`.

Now that we've fleshed out more of the details of the class design, Fig. 11.13 shows a more complete description of the classes for the robot simulation program.

Algorithms

Looking closer at the `move` method of the random robot, we can see from Fig. 11.14 that two random numbers are necessary to generate a random movement in one of eight directions. The `move` method first determines the next potential position for

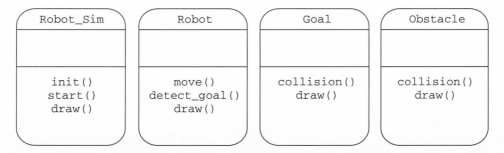

Figure 11.13 The `primary` classes in the robot simulator

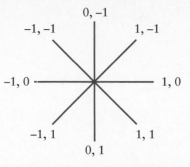

Figure 11.14 Determining a direction for the robot using two random numbers

the robot using two random numbers. Each random number is scaled to produce the value −1, 0, or 1. Each random number corresponds to one of the two axes along which the robot can move. If the x direction random number is −1, the robot moves west and if it is 1, it moves east. An x direction of 0 means the robot does not move along the x (east–west) axis at all. The y direction variable adjusts the robots position in a similar way along the y (north–south) axis. After the next position for the robot is determined, a collision with an obstacle or a wall should be considered.

The following pseudocode shows the basic algorithm for the move method of the Random_Robot class.

```
x_try = x + (pixels to move * random number from -1 to 1);
y_try = y + (pixels to move * random number from -1 to 1);

// Determine if the chosen direction is blocked
if (position at (x_try, y_try) is not blocked by obstacle) {
  x = x_try;
  y = y_try;
}

// Determine if the chosen direction is blocked by a wall
// West or East wall
if (x < 0)
  x = 1;
else if (x > largest possible x position)
  x = largest possible x position - 1;

// North or South wall
if (y < 0)
  y = 1;
else if (y > largest possible y position)
  y = largest possible y position - 1;
```

The `move` method for the other types of child classes for robots would be similar.

Prototype

As the design of the software classes has evolved, we've made an assumption. This assumption is that robots, as derived from the `Robot` class, should be able to draw themselves without any knowledge about other classes in the program. This seems like a reasonable assumption since we have used the `Graphics` class in previous programs to draw a line, draw a circle, or draw a string. Each of these tasks was done by calling various methods of an object of the `Graphics` class. By examining the `Graphics` class, a method called `drawImage` to draw predefined images can be found that is similar to ones we've used before. However, there are several parameters to `drawImage` with which we are not familiar, `Image` and `ImageObserver`. A prototype program could be used to experiment with unfamiliar methods or techniques to determine a solution's feasibility.

The following program demonstrates a proof-of-concept of a moving image in an applet. There are several features of the program to note. The first is that two images are used: one that represents the robot image to be drawn on the screen, and another that represents an empty position (i.e., no robot). To make the image move, the code draws an empty position image where the robot was, and then the robot image at the new location. The second feature to notice is the use of `this`, which refers to the `Applet` object, in the `getImage` and `drawImage` method invocations.

```java
import java.applet.*;
import java.awt.*;
import java.awt.image.*;


// Demonstrates the moving images across an applet
public class Image_Prototype extends Applet {

    Image robot_image;
    Image background_image;

    public void init() {
        robot_image = getImage
            (getDocumentBase(), "diagonal.gif");
        background_image = getImage
            (getDocumentBase(), "background.gif");
        setSize (300,300);
```

Loads image stored in diagonal.gif

```
            setVisible (true);
      } // method init

      public void start() {
         Graphics page = getGraphics();
         int x = 1, y = 1;
         // walk the images across the screen
         while (x < 300) {
            x++;
            y++;
            page.drawImage (background_image, x, y, this);
            page.drawImage (robot_image, x, y, this);
         }
      } // method start

} // class Image_Prototype
```

11.4   Implementation

With the most important issues of requirements and design established, we can now move on to discuss the implementation. The following sections contain a complete program that implements the robot simulator. Each class is discussed in detail.

The program is broken into six files in which each file represents a public class. The six files are:

- Robot_Sim.java
- Robot.java
- Diagonal_Robot.java
- Random_Robot.java
- Goal.java
- Obstacle.java

The following sections detail the implementation of these public classes.

Classes Obstacle and Goal

The Obstacle and Goal classes describe two elements in the simulated room. The obstacle is drawn as a simple rectangle, and the goal is drawn as the character X.

The Obstacle class stores the <*x,y*> coordinate of the upper-left corner and the length and width in pixels of the obstacle. The constructor sets the initial value for these variables. The parameters for the constructor represent the coordinates for

Throw-away and Evolutionary Prototypes

There are essentially two kinds of prototyping techniques. One type of prototype is a "quick and dirty" test of an idea or concept. These prototypes are often done very quickly and with little regard to software engineering principles. Their purpose is to validate an idea or approach, not to be used in the final system. These types of prototypes are known as *throw-away* prototypes because once they are written and proved their point, they are discarded.

Although creating throw-away prototypes is a great way to solidify requirements and design, it can be costly. Another kind of prototyping that is more cost effective is known as evolutionary prototyping. An *evolutionary prototype* starts as a small part of a software system to be developed and is added to in an incremental fashion until the software is complete. Usually, each prototype stage implements a particular requirement, and is a useful piece in and of itself.

The Internet is a good example of an evolutionary prototype that evolved into a usable and productive software system. Before the development of the Internet, it was unknown how to connect many computers together, so that they could communicate. The original contract from DARPA that created the Internet was a contract to prototype a network. As the fledgling Internet grew in functionality, it was used by more and more government researchers, and DARPA funded more evolutionary prototyping. After the use of the Internet grew to a significant size, DARPA stopped the funding of prototyping efforts, and commercial and academic prototyping increased. In fact, the Web is the outgrowth of prototyping efforts by researchers in different geographical locations to share documents easily.

the upper-left and lower-right corners. The constructor calculates the length and width of the obstacle from these coordinates.

The `boolean` method `collision` returns true if the next possible position of the robot is blocked by the obstacle. The method determines if the edge of the robot image has crossed over the boundary of the obstacle. The parameters of the method represent the <*x,y*> coordinates of the upper-left corner of the robot image. Since the robot can approach the obstacle from many different directions, the code must detect if any edge of the robot image has intersected the area of the obstacle. First the `collision` method calculates the center point of the robot image, then determines if that point falls within an appropriate border area surrounding the obstacle, as shown in Fig. 11.15. Since the center point of the robot image is used to detect a collision, the border area around the obstacle is half of the width of the robot image.

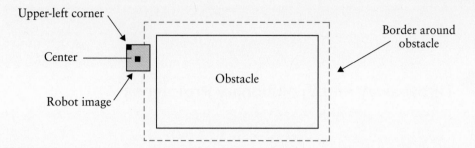

Figure 11.15 Detecting a robot colliding with an obstacle

The draw method in the Obstacle class simply calls the AWT method drawRect to draw a rectangle.

The following code implements the Obstacle class.

```
import java.awt.*;

// Obstacle objects represent things that would block a robot.
public class Obstacle {
    private int x, y; // corner point
    private int length, width;

    public Obstacle (int x1, int y1, int x2, int y2) {
        x = x1;
        y = y1;
        length = x2 - x;
        width = y2 - y;
    } // constructor Obstacle

    public boolean collision (int scan_x, int scan_y) {
        // Calculate the center point of a robot image
        // where scan_x and scan_y represent the upper left
        // corner.
        int center_x = scan_x + (Robot.BORDER_SIZE);
        int center_y = scan_y + (Robot.BORDER_SIZE);

        boolean collided = false; // Assume no collision
        // If the center of the robot is within the area
        // of the obstacle, the obstacle is blocking the
        // robots movement.
```

```
        if (center_x >= x - Robot.BORDER_SIZE)
            if (center_x <= x + length + Robot.BORDER_SIZE)
                if (center_y >= y - Robot.IMAGE_SIZE)
                    if (center_y <= y + width + Robot.IMAGE_SIZE)
                        collided = true;
        return collided;
    } // method collision

    public void draw (Graphics page) {
        page.drawRect (x, y, length, width);
    } // method draw

} // class Obstacle
```

Determine if a collision has occurred

The `Goal` class represents the item that the robots are trying to find during the simulation. It is similar to the `Obstacle` class in that it has a particular position and representation in the simulated room and must be detected by a moving robot.

Initially, the `Goal` class defines a constant `CHARACTER_SIZE`, which is used to determine how big the goal is in the simulated room. The class also stores the *<x,y>* coordinates of the `X` that represents the goal. These coordinates are set by the constructor.

The `collision` method of the `Goal` class is similar to the detect method of the `Obstacle` class. The difference between the two is that the goal is represented as a point with a border around it, and the obstacle is represented as a rectangle with a border around it. Therefore, the `collision` method of `Goal` does not need to consider the length or width of the goal itself.

The `draw` method of the `Goal` class uses the `AWT` method `drawString` to draw the goal. The `drawString` method draws the string at the specified coordinate, extending it up and to the right as the font requires. Therefore, unlike the `Obstacle` class, which stores the coordinate of the upper-left corner of the obstacle, the `Goal` class stores the coordinate of the bottom-left corner of the character `X` that represents the goal. The `collision` method takes this orientation into account.

The following code implements the `Goal` class.

```
import java.awt.*;

// The Goal class represents the object that the robots are
// searching for.
public class Goal {
    private final int CHARACTER_SIZE = 10;
    private int x, y;   // Coordinate of the goal

    public Goal (int x1, int y1) {
        x = x1;
        y = y1;
```

```
    } // constructor Goal

    public boolean collision (int scan_x, int scan_y) {
        // Calculate the center point of a robot image
        // where scan_x, scan_y represent the upper left corner.
        int center_x = scan_x + Robot.BORDER_SIZE;
        int center_y = scan_y + Robot.BORDER_SIZE;
        boolean collided = false; // Assuming goal is not found
        // If the center of the robot is within the border
        // of the goal, the robot has found the goal.
        if (center_x >= x)
            if (center_x <= x + CHARACTER_SIZE)
                if (center_y >= y - CHARACTER_SIZE)
                    if (center_y <= y)
                        collided = true;
        return collided;
    } // method collision

    public void draw (Graphics page) {
        page.drawString ("X", x, y);
    } // method draw
} // class Goal
```

Notice that there are many similarities between the `Obstacle` and `Goal` classes. A valid alternative design might define a base class for these similarities and derive these classes from it. This alternative is explored as a programming exercise at the end of the chapter.

Classes `Robot`, `Random_Robot`, and `Diagonal_Robot`

All specific robot classes are derived from the general `Robot` class. Methods and variables common to all robots should be implemented in this class. In this implementation the `Robot` class contains all methods necessary for specific robots except for the move method, which defines how a specific robot searches the simulated room.

The `Robot` class declares three constants: `IMAGE_SIZE`, which defines the size of the robot GIF image in pixels; `BORDER_SIZE`, which defines the detection border surrounding the obstacle and goal; and `MOVE_PIXELS`, which defines how many pixels each robot moves in a single turn. `MOVE_PIXELS` is defined as `protected` since only the move method of a specific robot class should reference it.

The `Robot` class stores the <x,y> coordinates of its location, and the <x,y> coordinates of its previous location. The previous location is used to erase a robot image after the robot moves to its next position. The class also stores the robot image and a background image using the `Image` class from the `java.awt.image` package. The background image is nothing more than a solid rectangular image with the same color as the applet's background, and is used to erase a robot's image after the robot moves to a new location.

In addition, the `Robot` class stores references to an `Obstacle` and a `Goal`, and a reference to the applet itself. The applet is needed as a vehicle through which additional information is obtained, such as loading GIF images.

The `Robot` constructor initializes all the variables of the class. Notice that the `image_name` parameter represents the file name that stores the GIF image for a particular robot. The method `getImage` is used to load the GIF into memory. Notice also that the file name of the background image is hard-coded into the constructor, since it is the same for all robots.

The `move` method in the `Robot` class is intentionally left empty, because moving is the one behavior that is specific to each particular robot type. Thus each child class must override it in order to be useful. In fact, the `move` method could have been declared as `abstract`, as discussed in Chapter 9.

The `detect_goal` method is used to determine if the goal has been reached by calling the `collision` method of the `Goal` class. The `collision` method determines if the current location of the robot is close enough to the goal to consider it found.

The `draw` method of the `Robot` class is called after a robot has moved to a new location. It first draws the background image at its previous location to erase the robot's image at that location. It then draws the robot image at the new location, and then saves that location in anticipation of the robot's next move.

The following code implements the `Robot` class.

```
import java.applet.*;
import java.awt.*;
import java.awt.image.*;

// Robot is the parent class for all robots
public abstract class Robot {

    public static final int IMAGE_SIZE = 10;
    public static final int BORDER_SIZE = IMAGE_SIZE/2;

    protected final int MOVE_PIXELS = 1;
    protected int x, y;  // Robot's current location
    private int previous_x, previous_y;
    private Image robot_image;
    private Image background_image; // Used to erase robot images
    protected Goal prize;
    protected Obstacle block;
    protected Applet applet;  // Applet containing robots
```

```
        public Robot (Applet applet1, Obstacle block1, Goal prize1,
                      int x1, int y1, String image_name) {
            // Save object references
            applet = applet1;
            prize = prize1;
            block = block1;

            // Save starting position
            x = x1;
            y = y1;
            previous_x = x1;
            previous_y = y1;

            // Load images of robot and the background from the
            // applet's location.
            robot_image = applet.getImage
                (applet.getDocumentBase(), image_name);
            background_image = applet.getImage
                (applet.getDocumentBase(), "background.gif");
        } // constructor Robot

        // Since this is the parent class for robots, no particular
        // movement is defined.
        abstract public void move();

        // detect_goal returns true if the Robot's location
        // is over the Goal's location.
        public boolean detect_goal() {
            return prize.collision (x, y);
        } // method detect_goal

        public void draw (Graphics page) {
            page.drawImage
                (background_image, previous_x, previous_y, applet);
            page.drawImage (robot_image, x, y, applet);
            previous_x = x; // save x,y for next undraw
            previous_y = y;
        } // method draw
    } // class Robot
```

Load a picture of a robot

Method that must be implemented by children classes

The Diagonal_Robot class and the Random_Robot class define two specific types of robots. They differ in the image used to represent them in the simulated room and in the pattern used to search for the goal. They both are derived from the general Robot class and therefore inherit its methods and variables.

The diagonal robot follows a diagonal path to search for the goal. To accomplish moving in this manner, the class defines two variables: `x_direction` and `y_direction`. These variables toggle between the values 1 and −1. When `x_direction` is 1, the robot will attempt to move toward increasing values on the x axis, and when `x_direction` is −1, the robot will attempt to move in the opposite direction. Similarly, the `y_direction` variable controls the robot's movement along the y axis. Initially, the robot is moving down and towards the right (southwest in the simulated room) as indicated by initial values for `x_direction` and `y_direction`.

The `Diagonal_Robot` class contains a constructor that uses the `super` reference to pass all of its parameters to the constructor of the Robot class and a string containing the file name of the GIF image for this robot.

The `move` method attempts to move the robot in its current direction, but takes into account that it could be blocked by an obstacle or a wall. The `x_try` and `y_try` variables are set to the coordinates of the next potential position of the robot. The `move` method then calls the obstacle's `collision` method to determine if a robot in that position would collide with the obstacle. If the robot is not blocked by the obstacle, its position is updated. If it is blocked, the robot is moved to another position as if it had rebounded off the obstacle. After checking for a collision with an obstacle, the method ensures that the robot is not moving into a wall of the simulated room.

The following code implements the `Diagonal_Robot` class.

```
import java.applet.*;

// This robot moves in diagonal lines, rebounding
// off walls and the obstacle in search of the goal.
public class Diagonal_Robot extends Robot {
   private int x_direction = 1;
   private int y_direction = 1;

   public Diagonal_Robot (Applet applet, Obstacle block, Goal prize,
                          int x, int y) {
      super (applet, block, prize, x, y, "diagonal.gif");
   } // constructor Diagonal_Robot

   // Move in diagonal lines
   public void move() {
      // Calculate where the robot is going to move
      int x_try = MOVE_PIXELS * x_direction + x;
      int y_try = MOVE_PIXELS * y_direction + y;

      // Determine if robot's movement would be blocked
      // by an obstacle.
      if (! block.collision (x_try, y_try)) {
```

Assume the robot's next move

Check for a collision

```
                        // Movement is unobstructed
                        x = x_try;
                        y = y_try;
                    } else {
                        // The robot is blocked by an obstacle.  Try to move
                        // in only the X or Y direction.
```

Check to see if the robot is only partially blocked

```
                        if (block.collision (x, y_try)) {
                            // blocked along y axis
                            y_direction = - y_direction;
                            x = x_try;
                        } else {
                            // blocked along x axis
                            x_direction = - x_direction;
                            y = y_try;
                        }
                    }


                    //  Check for collisions with walls

                    // West or East wall
                    if (x <= 0) {
                        x = 1;
                        x_direction = - x_direction;
                    } else if (x >= Robot_Sim.LENGTH - Robot.IMAGE_SIZE) {
                        x = Robot_Sim.LENGTH - Robot.IMAGE_SIZE - 1;
                        x_direction = - x_direction;
                    }

                    // North or South wall
                    if (y <= 0) {
                        y = 1;
                        y_direction = - y_direction;
                    } else if (y >= Robot_Sim.WIDTH - Robot.IMAGE_SIZE) {
                        y = Robot_Sim.WIDTH - Robot.IMAGE_SIZE - 1;
                        y_direction = - y_direction;
                    }
                } // method move

            } // class Diagonal_Robot
```

The Random_Robot class is similar to the Diagonal_Robot class in that it represents a specific type of robot that searches for the goal in a specific manner. In this case, on each move the robot randomly picks one of nine possible positions in which to move (eight primary directions or no movement at all).

The `Random_Robot` class instantiates an object called `random_movement` from the `Random` class (defined in the `java.util` package) for use in the `move` method. The constructor for this class is exactly the same as the constructor for the `Diagonal_Robot` class except for the file name of the robot image.

The `move` method first determines the next potential position for the robot by using two random numbers. After the next position for the robot is determined, a collision with an obstacle or a wall is considered, similar to the processing in the `Diagonal_Robot` class.

The following code implements the `Random_Robot` class.

```
import java.applet.*;

// Random_Robot move around randomly until the goal is found.
public class Random_Robot extends Robot {

   // Create an object to product random numbers
   private java.util.Random random_movement =
      new java.util.Random();

   public Random_Robot (Applet applet, Obstacle block, Goal prize,
                        int x, int y) {
      super (applet, block, prize, x, y, "random.gif");
   } // constructor Random_Robot

   public void move() {

      int x_try, y_try;

      // Randomly choose which direction the movement
      // should be in.
      int x_direction =
         (Math.abs (random_movement.nextInt()) % 3) - 1;
      int y_direction =
         (Math.abs (random_movement.nextInt()) % 3) - 1;

      x_try = x_direction * MOVE_PIXELS + x;
      y_try = y_direction * MOVE_PIXELS + y;

      // Determine if the chosen direction is blocked or will hit
      // a wall.
      if (! block.collision (x_try, y_try)) {
         x = x_try;
         y = y_try;
      }
```

Randomly choose a new position

```
      // West or East wall
      if (x < 0)
         x = 1;
      else if (x > Robot_Sim.LENGTH - Robot.IMAGE_SIZE)
         x = Robot_Sim.LENGTH - Robot.IMAGE_SIZE - 1;

      // North or South wall
      if (y < 0)
         y = 1;
      else if (y > Robot_Sim.WIDTH - Robot.IMAGE_SIZE)
         y = Robot_Sim.WIDTH - Robot.IMAGE_SIZE - 1;
   } // method move

} // class Random_Robot
```

Class `Robot_Sim`

The `Robot_Sim` class is the driver of the robot simulation program. It is derived from `Applet` and uses the `init` and `start` methods to control the execution of the simulation. The class defines the constants `LENGTH` and `WIDTH` that represent the size of the applet in pixels. This size also defines the size of the simulated room in which the robots move. The class then instantiates objects representing an obstacle, a goal, and an array of two robots. The object `page` is instantiated from the `Graphics` class to enable the program to draw on the applet.

The `init` and `start` methods are automatically called when the applet is loaded. The `init` method instantiates the array of robots, sets up the `page` object, and calls the `show` method of the applet to display the graphics. The `start` method uses a `boolean` flag called `moving` that indicates if any of the robots are still searching for the goal. Each pass through the `while` loop allows each robot to move. Processing continues until all robots find the goal.

The `draw` method in the `Robot_Sim` class uses the `drawRect` method to draw the walls of the simulated room and then calls the `draw` method of all other objects in the room.

The following code implements the `Robot_Sim` class.

```
import java.applet.*;
import java.awt.*;
import java.awt.image.*;

// Robot_Sim provides a framework to test various algorithms
// for robot search patterns.
public class Robot_Sim extends Applet {
   public static final int LENGTH = 300;
```

```java
public static final int WIDTH = 200;
private Obstacle block = new Obstacle (100, 100, 130, 120);
private Goal prize = new Goal (180, 131);


// Robots
Robot[] robots = new Robot[2];


private Graphics page;  // Area for drawing simulated room

public void init() {
   // Instantiate the robots
   robots[0] = new Random_Robot (this, block, prize, 1, 1);
   robots[1] = new Diagonal_Robot (this, block, prize, 1, 1);
   // Obtain the Graphics object for drawing from the applet
   setVisible (true);
   page = getGraphics();
} // method init


public void start() {
   boolean moving = true;


   // Loop to control simulation
   while (moving) {
      moving = false;
      // Robot movement
      for (int index = 0; index < robots.length; index++)
         if (! robots[index].detect_goal()) {
            robots[index].move();
            moving = true;
         }
      draw (page);
   }
} // method start


public void draw (Graphics page) {
   // Border around robots representing a room
   page.drawRect (0, 0, LENGTH, WIDTH);
   // Call draw for all robots
   for (int index = 0; index < robots.length; index++)
      robots[index].draw (page);
   // Call draw for remaining objects
```

Move robots until
they find the goal

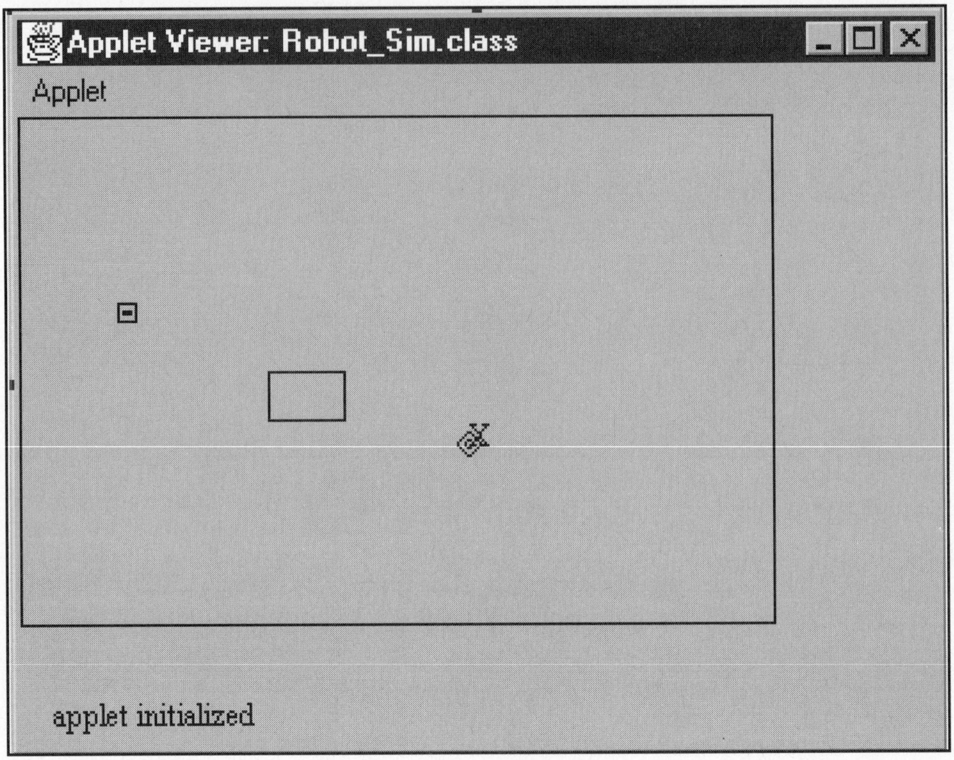

Figure 11.16 The robot search applet

```
      block.draw (page);
      prize.draw (page);
   } // method draw
} // class Robot_Sim
```

Figure 11.16 shows a screen shot of the executing robot search applet.

Summary of Key Concepts

- Maintaining software is the process of modifying a program in order to enhance it or fix problems.

- The maintainers of a program are often not the program's original developers.
- The ability to read and understand a program is directly related to how well it is designed, implemented, and documented. When a design is not well thought out, the resulting program is often hard to read, understand, and modify.
- Rushing through the development stage often leads to significant increases in the effort expended during maintenance.
- A program produced using the build-and-fix approach is a product of ad hoc, reckless activities.
- Prototypes can be used to explore design issues in a program, instead of proceeding on an assumption that may later prove unwise.
- A design or code walkthrough is a meeting in which several people read and critique a software design or implementation. The purpose of the walkthrough is to improve the quality of the design and software produced by a group.
- The goal of most testing is to find errors; therefore, a good test should be defined as a test that uncovers a problem in a program.
- Because programs operate on a large number of possible inputs, it is not feasible to create test cases for all possible input or user actions.
- The requirements as provided by the user are often sparse, ambiguous, and leave many questions unanswered. They need to be made as complete and consistent as possible before a programmer begins a design.
- Requirements are often stated using the verb *shall,* so that they are easy to identify in a document.
- The design of a software system is an iterative process.

Self-Review Questions

11.1 What are the three major stages in the life cycle of a program?

11.2 How is the effort expended during development related to the effort expended on maintenance tasks?

11.3 Describe the build-and-fix approach to software development.

11.4 What is the main problem with the waterfall model?

11.5 What is a prototype?

11.6 What is a code walkthrough?

11.7 Why are requirements sometimes expressed using the verb *shall?*

11.8 What are two important elements of a test case?

11.9 How is white-box testing different from black-box testing?

Exercises

11.10 Create a scenario diagram for drawing the simulated room and its contents.

11.11 Write the pseudocode for the move method of the spiral robot.

11.12 Write the pseudocode for the move method of the vertical robot.

11.13 Suppose we wanted to use robots defined by different inheritance hierarchies. What language features would you use to implement the program?

11.14 Assume you are using a black-box technique for testing the Robot class. Write a plan showing how you would test this class. What are the necessary equivalent categories for this class?

11.15 Assume you are using a black-box technique for testing the Obstacle class. Write a plan showing how you would test this class. What are the necessary equivalent categories for this class?

11.16 Assume you are using a white-box technique for testing the Robot class. Write a plan showing how you would test this class.

11.17 Assume you are using a white-box technique for testing the Obstacle class. Write a plan showing how you would test this class.

11.18 Assume you are using a white-box technique for testing the Robot_Sim class. Write a plan showing how you would test this class.

11.19 Develop a complete set of test cases for the Robot class.

11.20 Design a component hierarchy for a graphical user interface for the Robot_Sim class.

Programming Projects

11.21 When the robot search simulator is running, the speed of the robots depends on the type of system on which you execute the program and how many other programs are running at the time. Modify the program to change the speed of the robots.

11.22 The move method in the Random_Robot class allows the random robot to decide not to change positions at all during a particular move (a decision that doesn't get it any closer to the goal). Modify the robot search simulator so that the random robot makes a move to a new position on each turn.

11.23 Modify the robot search simulator so that the `random` robot does not revisit the same location that it occupied during its last turn.

11.24 Design and write a class called `Spiral_Robot` that implements the spiral search pattern seen in Fig. 11.9. Incorporate this new class into the `Robot_Sim` program.

11.25 Design and write a class called `Vertical_Robot` that implements the spiral search pattern seen in Fig. 11.9. Incorporate this new class into the `Robot_Sim` program.

11.26 Notice that the `Goal` class and the `Obstacle` class have many similarities. Modify the design and implementation of the program so that these two classes are derived from a new class called `Room_Item`.

11.27 Modify the robot search simulator to include multiple obstacles and multiple goals.

11.28 An easy way to trace the paths that robots travel is to change the background color of the applet. This can be done by setting a parameter in the HTML applet tag. Make this modification to the robot search simulator.

11.29 In the `Robot_Sim` class, the main control loop uses a flag called `moving`. Modifying this flag in the body of the `while` can become awkward as the number of robots in the program grows. Create a new class called `Controller` that encapsulates the purpose of this flag.

11.30 Design and implement a graphical user interface for the `Robot_Sim` program.

Answers to Self-Review Questions

11.1 The three major stages in the life cycle of a program are its initial development, its active use by the users, and subsequent maintenance tasks to fix defects and make enhancements.

11.2 The effort put into the development of a program can have a significant effect on maintenance. The earlier problems are discovered, the easier and less expensive it is to correct them. Small and often unobtrusive tasks during development that are designed to enhance the quality of the product can lead to a significant reduction in maintenance efforts. Any maintenance tasks that still need to be done are easier to accomplish in a carefully designed and implemented system.

11.3 The build-and-fix development approach simply involves writing a program, then modifying it until it is considered to be acceptable by some ill-defined criteria. No specific attention to the quality of the program is given either when it is initially created or through the reckless modifications that follow. The build-and-fix approach is not a development process at all.

11.4 The primary limitation to the waterfall model is that it does not allow back-tracking. That is, its focus is on completely finishing each stage prior to starting the next—not a realistic or feasible expectation. Development activities naturally overlap to some degree.

11.5 A prototype is a quickly constructed program created to demonstrate an idea or prove the feasibility of a requirement. It is often used to illustrate the user interface in order to clarify the user's needs. Prototypes can be used at any development stage.

11.6 A code walkthrough is a special meeting at which the programmer and several other developers sit down to discuss a program, often line by line. The intention is to find problems with the design or logic of the program, and to verify that coding standards are followed. It is an effective tool for enhancing the quality of a program.

11.7 Requirements, especially those that are created after a thorough evaluation of the user's specifications, are often written using the verb *shall* in order to specifically distinguish between statements that are considered mandatory versus those that are suggestions or otherwise optional.

11.8 A test case should always include a set of input data, which can be comprised of data values, user actions, and so on, and the expected output for the input.

11.9 Black-box testing deals only with the public parts of a class, testing only the inputs and outputs associated with public methods and variables. White-box testing deals with the internal structure of a class, testing the various paths of execution.

Recursion

12

Recursion is a powerful programming technique that provides elegant solutions to certain problems. This chapter serves as an introduction to recursive processing. It contains an explanation of the basic concept underlying recursion, then explores the use of recursion in programming. Several specific problems are solved using recursion, demonstrating its versatility, simplicity, and elegance.

Chapter Objectives

- Explain the underlying concepts of recursion.
- Examine recursive methods and unravel their processing steps.
- Define infinite recursion and discuss the ways to avoid it.
- Explain when recursion should be used and when it should not.
- Demonstrate the use of recursion to solve problems.

12.1 Recursive Thinking

As we've seen many times, a method can call another method to accomplish a goal. What we haven't seen yet, however, is that a method can call itself. *Recursion* is a programming technique in which a method calls itself in order to fulfill its purpose. But before we get into the details of how we use recursion in a program, we need to explore the general concept of recursion first. The ability to think recursively is essential to being able to use it as a programming technique.

> **Key Concept**　Recursion is a programming technique, but the key is to be able to think recursively.

In general, recursion is the process of defining something in terms of itself. For example, consider the following definition of the word `decoration`:

```
decoration  -  any ornament or adornment used to decorate something
```

The word `decorate` is used to define the word `decoration`. You may recall your grade school teacher telling you to avoid such *recursive definitions* when explaining the meaning of the word. However, in many situations, recursion is a simple and appropriate way to express an idea or definition. For example, suppose we wanted to formally define a list of one or more numbers, separated by commas. Such a list can be defined recursively as either a number or as a number followed by a comma followed by a list. Another way to express that definition is:

A LIST is a:　number
　　or a:　number　comma　LIST

This recursive definition of LIST defines each of the following lists of numbers:

```
24, 88, 40, 37
96, 43
14, 64, 21, 69, 32, 93, 47, 81, 28, 45, 81, 52, 69
70
```

No matter how long a list is, the recursive definition describes it. A list of one element, such as in the last example, never follows the recursive part of the definition (the part which refers to itself). For any list longer than one element, the recursive

```
LIST:   number comma LIST

          24     ,     88, 40, 37

                      number comma LIST

                        88      ,    40, 37

                              number comma LIST

                                40     ,    37

                                            number

                                              37
```

Figure 12.1   A recursive definition of a list

part is followed as many times as necessary, until the last element is reached. Figure 12.1 shows how one particular list of numbers corresponds to the recursive definition of LIST.

Infinite Recursion

Note that the definition of LIST contains one option that is recursive, and one option that is not. The part of the definition that is not recursive is called the *base case*. If all options had a recursive element, then the recursion would never end. For example, if the definition of a list was "a number followed by a comma followed by a list," then no list could ever end. This problem is called *infinite recursion*. It is similar to an infinite loop, except that the "loop" occurs in the definition itself.

▶ **Key Concept**   Any recursive definition must have a nonrecursive part, called the base case, that permits the recursion to eventually end. The algorithm must ensure that the base case is eventually reached.

Like the infinite-loop problem, a programmer must be careful to design algorithms so that they avoid infinite recursion. Any recursive definition must have a base case that does not result in following a recursive option. Furthermore, the structure of the recursive definition must ensure that the base case is eventually reached. The base case of the LIST definition is a single number that is not followed by a comma. In other words, when the last number in the list is reached, the base case option terminates the recursive path.

Recursion in Math

Mathematical formulas are often expressed recursively. For example, the definition of *N!* (pronounced *N* factorial) is defined for any positive integer *N* as the product of all integers between 1 and *N* inclusive. Therefore:

```
3!  =  3*2*1  =  6
```

and

```
5!  =  5*4*3*2*1  =  120.
```

The definition of *N!* can be expressed recursively as:

$$1! = \quad 1$$
$$N! = \quad N\,(N-1)!$$

The base case of this definition is 1!, which is defined to be 1. All other values of *N!* are defined recursively as *N* times the value (*N* − 1)!. Therefore 50! is equal to 50 * 49!. And 49! is equal to 49 * 48!. And 48! is equal to 48 * 47!. This process continues until you get to the base case of 1. Because *N!* is defined for only positive integers, this definition is complete and will always conclude with the base case.

> **Key Concept**   Mathematical problems and formulas are often expressed recursively.

The next section describes how recursion is accomplished in programs.

12.2   Recursive Programming

Let's use a simple mathematical operation to demonstrate the concepts of recursive programming. Consider the process of summing the values between 1 and *N* inclusive, where *N* is any positive integer. The sum of the values from 1 to *N* can be expressed as *N* plus the sum of the other *N* − 1 values. That sum can be expressed similarly, and so on, as shown in Fig. 12.2.

For example, the sum of the values between 1 and 20 is equal to 20 plus the sum of the values between 1 and 19. Continuing this idea, the sum of the values between 1 and 19 is equal to 19 plus the sum of the values between 1 and 18. This may sound like a funny way to think about this problem, but it is a simple example that can be used to demonstrate how recursion is programmed.

$$\sum_{i=1}^{N} i \;=\; N \;+\; \sum_{i=1}^{N-1} i \;=\; N \;+\; N-1 \;+\; \sum_{i=1}^{N-2} i$$

$$=\; N \;+\; N-1 \;+\; N-2 \;+\; \sum_{i=1}^{N-3} i$$

$$\vdots$$

$$=\; N \;+\; N-1 \;+\; N-2 \;+\; \cdots \;+\; 2 \;+\; 1$$

Figure 12.2 The sum of the numbers 1 through N, defined recursively

In Java, as in many other programming languages, a method can call itself. Each call to the method creates a new environment in which to work. All local variables and parameters are newly defined with their own unique data space every time the method is called. Each parameter is given an initial value based on the new call. Each time a method terminates, processing returns to the method that called it (which may be an earlier invocation of the same method). These rules are essentially no different than those governing any regular method invocation.

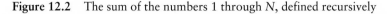

Key Concept Each recursive call to a method creates new local variables and parameters.

A recursive solution to the summation problem is defined by the following recursive method called sum:

```
//  This method returns the sum of 1 to N
public int sum (int N) {
   int result;
   if (N == 1)
      result = 1;
   else
      result = N + sum (N-1);
   return result;
}
```

A recursive call to the sum method

Note that this method essentially embodies our recursive definition that the sum of the numbers between 1 and N is equal to N plus the sum of the numbers between 1 and $N-1$. The call to sum is recursive because it is calling itself. The parameter passed to sum is decremented each time sum is called, until it reaches the base case of 1.

Suppose the `main` method calls `sum`, passing it an initial value of 1, which is stored in the parameter N. Since N is equal to 1, the result of 1 is returned to `main` and no recursion occurs.

Now let's trace the execution of the method when it is passed an initial value of 2. Since N does not equal 1, the method `sum` is called again with an argument of N–1, or 1. This is a new call to the method `sum`, with a new parameter N and a new local variable `result`. Since this N is now equal to 1, the result of 1 is returned without further recursive calls. Control returns to the first version of `sum`. The return value of 1 is added to the initial value of N in that call to `sum`, which is 2. Therefore `result` is assigned the value 3, which is returned to the `main` method. The method called from `main` correctly calculates the sum of the integers from 1 to 2, and returns the result of 3.

> **Key Concept**   A careful trace of recursive processing can provide insight into the way it is used to solve a problem.

The base case in this example is when N equals 1, at which point no further recursive calls are made. The recursion begins to fold back into the earlier versions of the `sum` method, returning the appropriate value each time. Each return value contributes to the computation of the sum at the higher level. Without the base case, infinite recursion would result. Each call to a method usually requires additional memory space, therefore infinite recursion often results in a run-time error indicating that memory has been exhausted.

Trace the `sum` function with different initial values of N until this processing becomes familiar. Figure 12.3 traces the recursive calls when `main` invokes `sum` to determine the sum of the integers from 1 to 4. Each box represents a copy of the method as it is invoked. Invocations are shown as solid lines, and returns as dotted lines. The return value `result` is shown at each step. The recursive path is followed completely until the base case is reached; then the calls begin to return their result up through the chain.

Recursion vs. Iteration

Of course, there is a nonrecursive solution to the summation problem we just explored. One way to compute the sum of the numbers between 1 and N inclusive in an iterative manner is:

```
sum = 0;
for (int number = 1; number <= N; number++)
    sum += number;
```

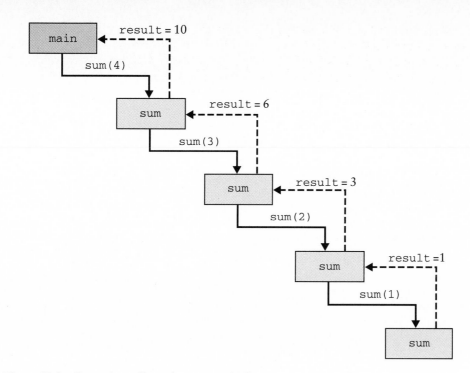

Figure 12.3   Recursive calls to the sum method

This solution is certainly more straightforward than the recursive version. We used the summation problem to demonstrate recursion because it is simple, not because you would use recursion to solve it under normal conditions. Recursion has the overhead of multiple method invocations, and in this case presents a more complicated solution than its iterative counterpart.

Key Concept   Recursion is the best way to solve some problems, but for other problems it is more complicated than the iterative solution. A programmer must evaluate each situation to determine the appropriate approach.

A programmer must decide when to use recursion and when not to use it. The best approach depends on the problem being solved. All problems can be solved in an iterative manner, but in some cases the iterative version is much more complicated. Recursion, for some problems, allows us to create relatively short, elegant solutions.

Direct vs. Indirect Recursion

Direct recursion occurs when a method invokes itself, such as when sum calls sum. *Indirect recursion* occurs when a method invokes another method, eventually resulting in the original method being invoked again. For example, if method m1 calls method m2, which invokes method m1, we can say that m1 is indirectly recursive. The amount of indirection could be several levels deep, as when m1 invokes m2, which invokes m3, which invokes m4, which invokes m1. Figure 12.4 depicts a situation with indirect recursion. Method invocations are shown with solid lines, and returns are shown with dotted lines. The entire invocation path is followed, then the recursion unravels following the return path.

Indirect recursion requires all of the same attention to base cases that direct recursion does. Furthermore, it can be more difficult to trace because of the intervening method calls. Therefore, extra care is warranted when designing or evaluating indirectly recursive methods. Ensure that the indirection is truly necessary and clearly explained in documentation.

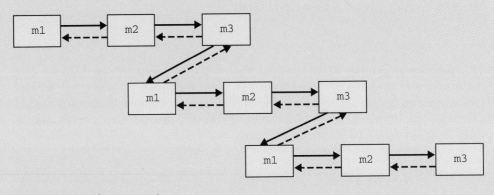

Figure 12.4   Indirect recursion

The next section explores several problems and their recursive solutions.

12.3 Using Recursion

Each of the following sections describe a particular recursive problem. For each one, let's examine exactly how recursion plays a role in the solution and how the base case is used to terminate the recursion. Also, think about how complicated a nonrecursive solution for each problem would be.

Repeating Pictures

Carefully examine Fig. 12.5. It shows an applet that displays several pictures. There are actually three unique pictures among all of the ones shown. The entire area is divided into four equal quadrants, separated by lines. A picture of the world (with a circle indicating the Himalayan mountain region) is shown in the top-right quadrant. The bottom-left quadrant contains a picture of Mt. Everest. In the bottom-right quadrant is a picture of a mountain goat.

The interesting part of the picture is the top-left quadrant. It contains a copy of the entire collage, including itself. In this smaller version you can see the three simple pictures in their three quadrants. And again, in the upper-left corner, the picture is repeated (including itself). This repetition continues for several levels. It is similar to the effect you can create when looking at a mirror in the reflection of another mirror.

This visual effect is created quite easily using recursion. The following applet contains a `paint` method that invokes another method called `draw_pictures`. The `draw_pictures` method accepts a parameter that defines the size of the area in which pictures are displayed. It draws the three standard images using `drawImage`. Then the `draw_pictures` method draws the upper left quadrant recursively. On each invocation, if the drawing area is large enough, the `draw_pictures` method is invoked again, using a smaller drawing area. Eventually, the drawing area becomes so small that the recursive call is not performed.

```
import java.applet.Applet;
import java.awt.*;

// Demonstrates a recursive drawing routine
public class Repeating_Pictures extends Applet {

    private final int SIZE = 300; // Size of applet
    private final int STOP = 20;  // Smallest picture size
    private final int OFFSET = 2; // Picture offset from lines
```

Figure 12.5 The Repeating_Pictures applet

```
private Image world;
private Image everest;
private Image goat;

public void init() {
    world = getImage (getDocumentBase(), "world.gif");
    everest = getImage (getDocumentBase(), "everest.gif");
    goat = getImage (getDocumentBase(), "goat.gif");
    setSize (SIZE, SIZE);
}  // method init
```

```
public void draw_pictures (int size, Graphics page) {
    // Draw lines to create four quadrants
    page.drawLine (size/2, 0, size/2, size); // vertical
    page.drawLine (0, size/2, size, size/2); // horizontal

    // Draw three images in different quadrants
    page.drawImage (world, 0+OFFSET, size/2+OFFSET,
                    size/2-(OFFSET*2), size/2-(OFFSET*2), this);
    page.drawImage (everest, size/2+OFFSET, 0+OFFSET,
                    size/2-(OFFSET*2), size/2-(OFFSET*2), this);
    page.drawImage (goat, size/2+OFFSET, size/2+OFFSET,
                    size/2-(OFFSET*2), size/2-(OFFSET*2), this);

    // Draw the entire picture again in the first quadrant
    if (size > STOP)
        draw_pictures (size/2, page);

} // method draw_pictures

public void paint (Graphics page) {
    draw_pictures (getSize().width, page);
} // method paint

} // class Repeating_Pictures
```

A recursive call decreases the size of the drawing area each time

Each time the `draw_pictures` method is invoked, the size passed as a parameter is used to determine the area in which the pictures are presented, relative to the coordinates <0,0>. The two lines defining the four quadrants are drawn relative to the size of the current drawing area. The `drawImage` method automatically scales the pictures to fit in the area indicated.

The base case of the recursion in this problem specifies a minimum size for the drawing area. Because the size is decreased each time, eventually the base case is reached and the recursion stops. This is the reason that the upper-right corner is empty in the smallest version of the collage.

Palindrome

A palindrome is a string that reads the same forward and backward. Examples of palindromes are "radar" and "able was I ere I saw elba." In the following example, the class `Palindrome_Tester` uses a recursive method called `ptest` to determine if a string is a palindrome:

```
//  Determines if several strings are palindromes.
class Palindromes {
```

```
public static void main (String[] args) {
    Palindrome_Tester tester = new Palindrome_Tester();


    System.out.println ("radar is a palindrome? "
        + tester.ptest ("radar"));
    System.out.println ("abcddcba is a palindrome? "
        + tester.ptest ("abcddcba"));
    System.out.println ("able was I ere I saw elba is a palindrome? "
        + tester.ptest ("able was I ere I saw elba"));
    System.out.println ("hello is a palindrome? "
        + tester.ptest ("hello"));
    System.out.println ("abcxycba is a palindrome? "
        + tester.ptest ("abcxycba"));
}   // method main


}   // class Palindromes


//  Uses recursion to determine if a string is a palindrome.
class Palindrome_Tester {


    public boolean ptest (String str) {
        boolean result = false;
        if (str.length() <= 1)
            result = true;
        else
            if (str.charAt (0) == str.charAt (str.length()-1))
                result = ptest (str.substring (1, str.length()-1));
        return result;
    }   // method ptest


}   // class Palindrome_Tester
```

Each call to ptest shrinks the string by 2 characters

We can state the definition underlying the ptest method recursively: A string is a palindrome if its first and last characters are the same, and if the substring in the middle is a palindrome. A string of length 1 or 0 is a palindrome, and defines the base case for this problem. The recursive call to palindrome is made only if the first and last characters of the string match.

The output of the `Palindromes` program is:

```
radar is a palindrome? true
abcddcba is a palindrome? true
able was I ere I saw elba is a palindrome?
true
hello is a palindrome? false
abcxycba is a palindrome? false
```

Trace the execution of each of these palindrome tests. Note that a palindrome can have either an odd or even number of characters. The string "radar", for instance, contains five characters with a single 'd' in the center, whereas the string "abcdd-cba" contains eight characters, with two 'd' characters in the center. Both an odd and even number of characters are handled by the recursive method since the base case is defined as a string of length 0 or 1.

Also note that the string "hello" is immediately determined to be a non-palindrome, since the 'h' and the 'o' do not match. However, several levels of recursive calls are made before the string "abcxycba" is ruled out.

The palindrome problem is a good example of a case where the choice between recursion and iteration must be carefully considered. The recursive solution is fairly elegant and straightforward. However, there is a relatively simple iterative solution as well. Comparing the two versions is left as an exercise.

Maze

Solving a maze involves a great deal of trial and error: following a path, backtracking when you cannot go further, and trying other options. Such activities often are handled nicely using recursion. The following program sets up a maze using a two-dimensional array of integers. Initially, a 1 indicates a clear path, and a 0 indicates a blocked path. As the maze is solved, these array elements are changed to other values to indicate attempted and successful paths through the maze.

The only valid moves through the maze are in the four primary directions: up, down, right, and left. No diagonal moves are allowed. The goal is to start in the upper-left corner of the maze (0, 0) and find a path that reaches the bottom-right corner. In this example, the maze is 8 rows by 13 columns, although the code is designed to handle a maze of any size.

The `Maze_Search` class contains the `main` method, which instantiates the maze, prints out its initial configuration, solves the maze if possible, and prints out the solved version of the maze.

```java
class Maze_Search {

    public static void main (String[] args) {
        Maze labyrinth = new Maze();

        labyrinth.print_maze();
        if (labyrinth.solve(0, 0))
            System.out.println ("Maze solved!");
        else
            System.out.println ("No solution.");
        labyrinth.print_maze();
    }  // method main

}  // class Maze_Search

class Maze {
    int[][] grid = {{1,1,1,0,1,1,0,0,0,1,1,1,1},
                    {1,0,1,1,1,0,1,1,1,1,0,0,1},
                    {0,0,0,0,1,0,1,0,1,0,1,0,0},
                    {1,1,1,0,1,1,1,0,1,0,1,1,1},
                    {1,0,1,0,0,0,0,1,1,1,0,0,1},
                    {1,0,1,1,1,1,1,1,0,1,1,1,1},
                    {1,0,0,0,0,0,0,0,0,0,0,0,0},
                    {1,1,1,1,1,1,1,1,1,1,1,1,1}};

    public void print_maze () {

        System.out.println();
        for (int row=0; row < grid.length; row++) {
            for (int column=0; column < grid[row].length; column++)
                System.out.print (grid[row][column]);
            System.out.println();
        }
        System.out.println();

    }  // method print_maze

    public boolean solve (int row, int column) {
        boolean done = false;
```

```
        if (valid (row, column)) {
            grid[row][column] = 3;   // cell has been tried
            if (row == grid.length-1 && column == grid[0].length-1)
                done = true;   // maze is solved
            else {
                done = solve (row+1, column);   // down
                if (!done)
                    done = solve (row, column+1);   // right
                if (!done)
                    done = solve (row-1, column);   // up
                if (!done)
                    done = solve (row, column-1);   // left
            }
            if (done)   // part of the final path
                grid[row][column] = 7;
        }

        return done;
    }   // method solve

    private boolean valid (int row, int column) {
        boolean result = false;

        // check if cell is in the bounds of the matrix
        if (row >= 0 && row < grid.length &&
            column >= 0 && column < grid[0].length)

            //  check if cell is not blocked and not
            //  previously tried
            if (grid[row][column] == 1)
                result = true;

        return result;
    }   // method valid

}   // class Maze
```

Multiple recursive calls to the solve method

The recursive method is called solve. It returns a boolean value that indicates whether a solution was found. First the method determines if a move to that row and column is valid. A move is considered valid if it stays within the grid boundary and if the grid contains a 1 in that location, indicating that a move in that direction is not blocked. The initial call to solve passes in the upper-left location (0, 0).

If the move is valid, the grid entry is changed from a 1 to a 3, marking this location as visited so that later we don't retrace our steps. Then the solve method determines if the maze has been completed by having reached the bottom-right location. Therefore, there are actually three possibilities of the base case for this problem that will terminate a recursive path:

- an invalid move because it is out of bounds
- an invalid move because it has been tried before
- a move that arrives at the final location

If the current location is not the bottom-right corner, we search for a solution in each of the primary directions, if necessary. First, we look down by recursively calling the `solve` method and passing in the new location. The logic of the `solve` method starts all over again using this new position. A solution is either ultimately found by starting down from the current location, or it's not found. If it's not found, we try moving right. If that fails, we try up. Finally, if no other direction has yielded a correct path, we try left. If no direction from the current location yields a correct solution, then there is no path from this location, and `solve` returns false.

If a solution was found from the current location, then the grid entry is changed to a 7. Therefore, when the final maze is printed, the zeros still indicate a blocked path, a 1 indicates an open path that was never tried, a 3 indicates a path that was tried but failed to yield a correct solution, and a 7 indicates a part of the final solution of the maze. The output of the program is:

```
1110110001111
1011101111001
0000101010100
1110111010111
1010000111001
1011111101111
1000000000000
1111111111111
Maze solved!
7770110001111
3077707771001
0000707070300
7770777070333
7070000773003
7077777703333
7000000000000
7777777777777
```

Note that there are several opportunities for recursion in each call to the `solve` method. Any or all of them might be followed, depending on the maze configuration. Carefully trace the execution of this code while following the maze array to see how the recursion solves the problem.

Summary of Key Concepts

- Recursion is a programming technique, but the key is to be able to think recursively.
- Any recursive definition must have a nonrecursive part, called the base case, that permits the recursion to eventually end. The algorithm must ensure that the base case is eventually reached.
- Mathematical problems and formulas are often expressed recursively.
- Each recursive call to a method creates new local variables and parameters.
- A careful trace of recursive processing can provide insight into the way it is used to solve a problem.
- Recursion is the best way to solve some problems, but for other problems it is more complicated than the iterative solution. A programmer must evaluate each situation to determine the appropriate approach.

Self-Review Questions

12.1 What is recursion? What is recursive programming?

12.2 What is infinite recursion?

12.3 When is a base case needed for recursive processing?

12.4 Is recursion necessary?

12.5 When should recursion be avoided?

Exercises

12.6 Write a recursive definition of a valid Java identifier (see Chapter 2).

12.7 Write a recursive definition of x^y (x to the power y), where x and y are integers and $y > 0$.

12.8 Write a recursive definition of $i * j$ (integer multiplication), where $i > 0$. Define the multiplication process in terms of integer addition.

12.9 Write a recursive definition of the Fibonacci numbers. The Fibonacci numbers are a sequence of integers, each of which is the sum of the previous two numbers. The first two numbers in the sequence are 0 and 1. Explain why you would not normally use recursion to solve this problem.

12.10 Trace the execution of the `Palindromes` program when it is run against the string "wxyzzyxw." Produce a diagram similar to the one shown in Fig. 12.3. Explain the processing of each step.

12.11 Repeat Problem 12.10 using the string "abcba." What is the primary difference between the string used in Problem 12.10 and this one? Explain how the program handles that difference.

12.12 Repeat Problem 12.10 using the string "abcxycba."

12.13 Write an iterative version of the `Palindromes` program. Compare and contrast it with the recursive version presented in this chapter.

12.14 Write a recursive method to determine and print the value of $N!$ (N factorial) using the definition given in this chapter. Explain why you would not normally use recursion to solve this problem.

12.15 Write a recursive method to reverse a `String`. Explain why you would not normally use recursion to solve this problem.

Programming Projects

12.16 Redesign and implement the recursive program that calculates the sum of the integers between 1 and N to match the recursive definition below. Trace your solution using an N of 5.

$$\sum_{i=1}^{N} i = \sum_{i=1}^{\frac{N}{2}} i + \sum_{i=\frac{N}{2}+1}^{N} i$$

12.17 Design and implement a program that implements Euclid's algorithm for finding the greatest common divisor of two positive integers. The greatest common divisor is the largest integer that divides both values without producing a remainder. In a class called `Divisor_Calc`, define a method called gcd that accepts two integers, num1 and num2. The algorithm is defined as follows:

- gcd (num1, num2) is num2 if num2 <= num1 and num2 divides num1
- gcd (num1, num2) is gcd (num2, num1) if num1 < num2
- gcd (num1, num2) is gcd (num2, num1%num2) otherwise

12.18 Modify the maze problem so that it prints out the path of the final solution without storing it.

12.19 Design and implement a recursive program that solves the Non-Attacking Queens problem. Determine how eight queens can be positioned on an eight-by-eight chessboard so that none of them are in the same row, column, or diagonal as any other queen. There are no other chess pieces on the board.

12.20 In the language of an alien race, all words take the form of Blurbs. A Blurb is a Whoozit followed by one or more Whatzits. A Whoozit is the character x followed by zero or more ys. A Whatzit is a q followed by either a z or a d, followed by a Whoozit. Design and implement a recursive program that generates random Blurbs in this alien language.

12.21 Design and implement a recursive program to determine if a string is a valid Blurb as defined in Problem 12.20.

Answers to Self-Review Questions

12.1 Recursion is the act of defining something in terms of itself. Recursive programming allows a method to call itself, solving a smaller version of the problem each time, until the terminating condition is reached.

12.2 Infinite recursion has no terminating condition or one that is improperly specified. The recursive path is followed forever. In a recursive program, infinite recursion will often result in an error that indicates that available memory has been exhausted.

12.3 A base case is always required to terminate recursion and begin the process of returning through the calling hierarchy. Without the base case, infinite recursion would result.

12.4 Recursion is not necessary. Every recursive algorithm can be written in an iterative manner. However, some problem solutions are much more elegant and straightforward when written recursively.

12.5 Avoid recursion when the iterative solution is simpler and more easily understood. Recursion has the overhead of multiple method calls and is not always intuitive.

Sorting and Searching

13

Two important and recurring programming tasks are the process of arranging a list in a particular order and the process of locating an item within a group. These activities are referred to as sorting and searching. Many algorithms have been designed to perform these tasks and each has its own unique characteristics. This chapter serves as an introduction to some basic sorting and searching techniques.

Chapter Objectives

- Explore the implementation and application of selection sort and insertion sort algorithms.
- Define a generic sort for objects.
- Explore the implementation and application of linear search and binary search.
- Examine a recursive implementation of binary search.
- Explore the implementation and application of hashing.

13.1 Sorting

Sorting is the process of arranging a list of items into a well-defined order. For example, you may want to alphabetize a list of names, or put a list of grades into descending numeric order. Many sorting algorithms have been developed and critiqued over the years. In fact, sorting is considered to be a classic area of study in computer science.

This section examines two relatively simple sorting algorithms: selection sort and insertion sort. Complete coverage of various sorting techniques is beyond the scope of this book. Instead we want to introduce the topic, establish some fundamental ideas, and motivate the need for further investigation. Furthermore, we do not delve into a detailed analysis of the algorithms, but focus on the strategies involved and general characteristics. After investigating the selection sort and insertion sort algorithms, we develop a general sorting interface that can be used to define a sort for any list of objects.

> **Key Concept**　Selection sort and insertion sort are two sorting algorithms that define the processing steps for putting a list of values into a well-defined order.

Selection Sort

The *selection sort* algorithm sorts a list of values by repetitively putting a particular value into its final, sorted, position. In other words, for each position in the list, the algorithm selects the value that should go in that position, and puts it there.

> **Key Concept**　Selection sort works by putting each value into its final position, one at a time.

Suppose we wanted to put a list of numeric values into ascending order. The general strategy of selection sort is: Scan the entire list to find the smallest value. Exchange that value with the value in the first position of the list. Scan the rest of the list (all but the first value) to find the smallest value, and exchange it with the value in the second position of the list. Scan the rest of the list (all but the first two values) to find the smallest value, and exchange it with the value in the third position of the list. Continue this process for each position in the list. When complete, the list is sorted. Figure 13.1 demonstrates the use of the selection sort algorithm.

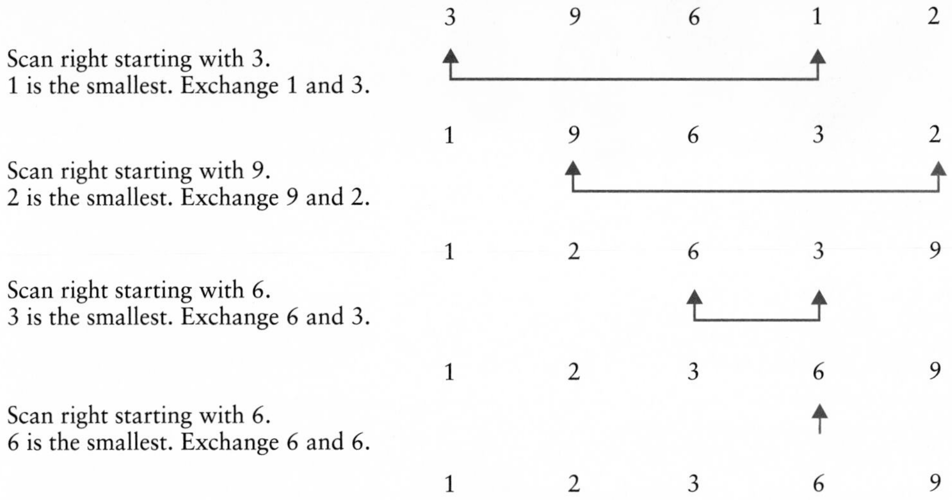

3	9	6	1	2

Scan right starting with 3.
1 is the smallest. Exchange 1 and 3.

1	9	6	3	2

Scan right starting with 9.
2 is the smallest. Exchange 9 and 2.

1	2	6	3	9

Scan right starting with 6.
3 is the smallest. Exchange 6 and 3.

1	2	3	6	9

Scan right starting with 6.
6 is the smallest. Exchange 6 and 6.

1	2	3	6	9

Figure 13.1   Selection sort example

The following example uses a selection sort to arrange a list of values into ascending order:

```
//  Demonstrates the use of selection sort.
public class Selection_Sort_Test {

   public static void main (String[] args) {
      int[] numbers = {3, 9, 6, 1, 2};

      Selection_Sort.sort (numbers);

      for (int index = 0; index < numbers.length; index++)
         System.out.println (numbers[index]);

   }  // method main

}  // class Selection_Sort_Test

//  Contains a method that implements a selection sort
//  on an array of integers.
class Selection_Sort {

   public static void sort (int[] numbers) {
      int min, temp;
```

The outer loop
checks each posi-
tion.
The inner loop
finds the smallest
value.

```
    for (int index = 0; index < numbers.length-1; index++) {
        min = index;
        for (int scan = index+1; scan < numbers.length; scan++)
            if (numbers[scan] < numbers[min])
                min = scan;

        // swap the values
        temp = numbers[min];
        numbers[min] = numbers[index];
        numbers[index] = temp;
    }
    }  // method sort

}  // class Selection_Sort
```

The output of this program is:

```
1
2
3
6
9
```

The selection sort implementation uses two loops to sort an array of integers. The outer loop controls the position in the array where the next smallest value will be stored. The inner loop finds the smallest value in the rest of the list by scanning all positions greater than or equal to the index specified by the outer loop. When the smallest value is found, it is exchanged with the value stored at index. This exchange is done in three assignment statements by using an extra variable called temp. This type of exchange is often called *swapping*.

> **Key Concept**   Swapping is the process of exchanging two values. Swapping requires three assignment statements.

Note that because this algorithm finds the smallest value during each iteration, the result is an array sorted in ascending order (i.e., smallest to largest). It can easily be changed to put values in descending order by finding the largest value each time.

Insertion Sort

The *insertion sort* algorithm sorts a list of values by repetitively inserting a particular value into a subset of the list that has already been sorted. One at a time, each unsorted element is inserted at the appropriate position in that sorted subset until the entire list is in order.

> **Key Concept**   Insertion sort works by inserting each value into a previously sorted subset of the list.

Let's again consider the process of sorting a list of numeric values into ascending order. The general strategy of insertion sort is: Sort the first two values in the list relative to each other by exchanging them if necessary. Insert the list's third value into the appropriate position relative to the first two (sorted) values. Then insert the fourth value into its proper position relative to the first three values in the list. Each time an insertion is made, the number of values in the sorted subset increases by one. Continue this process until all values in the list are completely sorted.

When sorting an array of values, the insertion process requires that the other values in the list shift to make room for the inserted element. Figure 13.2 demonstrates the use of insertion sort algorithm.

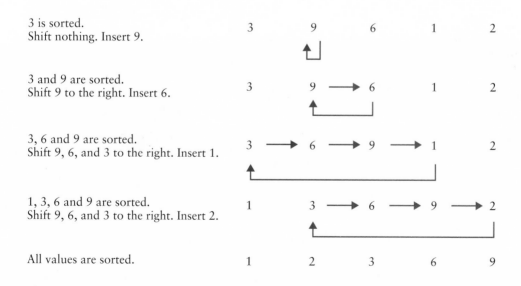

3 is sorted.
Shift nothing. Insert 9.

3 and 9 are sorted.
Shift 9 to the right. Insert 6.

3, 6 and 9 are sorted.
Shift 9, 6, and 3 to the right. Insert 1.

1, 3, 6 and 9 are sorted.
Shift 9, 6, and 3 to the right. Insert 2.

All values are sorted.

Figure 13.2   Insertion sort example

The following example uses an insertion sort.

```java
//   Demonstrates the use of insertion sort.
public class Insertion_Sort_Test {

   public static void main (String[] args) {
      int[] numbers = {3, 9, 6, 1, 2};


      Insertion_Sort.sort (numbers);


      for (int index = 0; index < numbers.length; index++)
         System.out.println (numbers[index]);


   }  // method main


}  // class Insertion_Sort_Test


//   Contains a method that implements an insertion sort
//   on an array of integers.
class Insertion_Sort {

   public static void sort (int[] numbers) {

      for (int index = 1; index < numbers.length; index++) {
         int key = numbers[index];
         int position = index;


         // shift larger values to the right
         while (position > 0 && numbers[position-1] > key) {
            numbers[position] = numbers[position-1];
            position--;
         }


         numbers[position] = key;
      }
   }  // method sort
}  // class Insertion_Sort
```

The condition determines where the current value should be inserted.

The output of the `Insertion_Sort_Test` program is identical to that of the `Selection_Sort_Test` program:

```
1
2
3
6
9
```

Similar to the selection sort program, this sort uses two loops to sort an array of integers. In the insertion sort, however, the outer loop controls the `index` in the array of the next value to be inserted. The inner loop compares the current insert value with values to its left (which make up a sorted subset of the entire list). If the current insert value is less than value at `position`, then that value is shifted to the right. Shifting continues until the proper position is opened to accept the insert value. Each iteration of the outer loop adds one more value to the sorted subset of the list, until the entire list is sorted.

Comparing Sorts

There are a variety of reasons for choosing one sorting algorithm over another: an algorithm's simplicity, its level of efficiency, the amount of memory it uses, and the type of data being sorted. An algorithm that is easier to understand is also easier to implement and debug. However, often the simplest sorts are the most inefficient ones. *Efficiency* is usually considered to be the primary criteria when comparing sorting algorithms. In general, a sorting algorithm is less efficient than another if it performs more comparisons than the other. There are several algorithms that are more efficient than the two we examined, but they are also more complex.

Key Concept   Sorts are often compared by their efficiency, which is often defined as the number of comparisons required to perform the sort.

Both selection sort and insertion sort have essentially the same level of efficiency. Both have an outer loop and an inner loop with similar properties, if not purposes. The outer loop is executed once for each value in the list, and the inner loop compares the value in the outer loop with most if not all of the values in the rest of the list. Therefore, both algorithms perform approximately n^2 number of comparisons, where n is the number of values in the list. We say that both selection sort and insertion sort are algorithms of *order n^2*. More efficient sorts perform fewer comparisons and are of a smaller order, such as $n \log_2 n$. These sorts, and their analysis, are beyond the scope of this book.

Key Concept   Both selection sort and insertion sort algorithms are of order n^2. Other sorts are more efficient.

Because both selection sort and insertion sort have the same general efficiency, the one you choose is a fairly arbitrary choice. Selection sort is usually easy to understand and will often suffice in many situations. Some people find insertion sort to be a good choice when they are continually adding values to a list while keeping the list in sorted order, because that process is essentially the strategy that the insertion sort technique uses anyway.

Sorting Objects

Each of the previous sort examples is designed to sort an array of integers. Often it is necessary to sort other kinds of data, including objects. In fact, it is helpful to have a generic sorting method that can sort any list of objects. The following example defines an `interface` called `Sortable` that lists the methods necessary to create a generic sort. The class `Object_Sort` contains a `sort` method that operates on any object that implements the `Sortable` interface.

Key Concept   A generic sort for any list of objects can be created by using an interface that requires sort-specific methods.

An object that implements `Sortable` contains a collection of other objects. The objects in this collection can be sorted, no matter what those objects are. The interface guarantees that the collection defines the necessary methods to determine an ordering among the objects. Because operations such as "less than" are not defined for all objects, we need a comparison operation to determine the relative ordering of any two objects in a list. The interface ensures that we define one, called `compare`. Other methods, such as one to set the value of a list item at a particular position, are also included in the interface. Note that the interface does not assume that the list is stored in an array.

Compare the sort method defined in the Object_Sort class with the sort method in the Insertion_Sort class from the previous example. Note the similarities and differences. This sort implements an insertion sort, but it is defined for generic objects and invokes methods of the Sortable interface to accomplish its task.

```java
import java.net.*;

// Creates a sortable object (a URL list) and sorts it.
public class Object_Sort_Test {

    public static void main (String[] args)
                      throws MalformedURLException {
        Search_Engines engines = new Search_Engines();

        Object_Sort.sort (engines);

        for (int index = 0; index < engines.length(); index++)
            System.out.println (engines.value_at(index));
    }  // method main

}  // class Object_Sort_Test

//  Contains the abstract methods to sort any list of Objects.
interface Sortable {
    // returns true if left > right
    boolean compare (Object left, Object right);
    // returns the object at the specified position
    Object value_at (int position);
    // sets the value of the specified position
    void set_value (Object value, int position);
    // returns the number of items in the list
    int length();
}  // interface Sortable

//  Contains a sort method for any collection of Sortable
//  objects.  The sort is an insertion sort.
class Object_Sort {

    public static void sort (Sortable items) {

        for (int index = 1; index < items.length(); index++) {
            Object key = items.value_at (index);
```

An interface for any list of sortable objects.

```
                      int position = index;

                      while (position > 0 &&
                              items.compare (items.value_at (position-1), key)) {
                          items.set_value (items.value_at (position-1), position);
                          position--;
                      }
                      items.set_value (key, position);
                  }
              }  // method sort

          }  // class Object_Sort

          //  Contains a list of urls that are search engines and
          //  the methods that allow them to be sorted by host name.
          class Search_Engines implements Sortable {

              private URL[] sites = new URL[5];

              public Search_Engines() throws MalformedURLException {
                  sites[0] = new URL ("http://www.lycos.com");
                  sites[1] = new URL ("http://www.yahoo.com");
                  sites[2] = new URL ("http://www.webcrawler.com");
                  sites[3] = new URL ("http://www.excite.com");
                  sites[4] = new URL ("http://www.infoseek.com");
              } // constructor Search_Engines

              public boolean compare (Object left, Object right) {
                  URL site1 = (URL) left;
                  URL site2 = (URL) right;
                  String host1 = site1.getHost();
                  String host2 = site2.getHost();
                  if (host1.compareTo(host2) > 0)
                      return true;
                  else
                      return false;
              }  // method compare

              public Object value_at (int index) {
                  return (sites[index]);
              }  // method value_at

              public void set_value (Object value, int index) {
                  sites[index] = (URL)value;
              }  // method set_value
```

The class must
define methods to
assist the sorting
process.

```
    public int length() {
        return (sites.length);
    }  // method length


}  // class Search_Engines
```

This example sorts a list of URL objects. The Search_Engines class creates an array of five URL objects and implements all of the methods required by the Sortable interface. Only the methods in the Search_Engines class deal with URL objects. The Object_Sort class can be used to sort objects of other types, as long as they implement Sortable.

The output of the Object_Sort_Test program is:

```
http://www.excite.com/
http://www.infoseek.com/
http://www.lycos.com/
http://www.webcrawler.com/
http://www.yahoo.com/
```

13.2   Searching

Searching is the process of determining if a particular item, often called the *target value*, is included in a list of items, and if so, where. As with sorting, many search techniques have been devised, and one may be more appropriate in a particular situation than another. Some searching algorithms require that the list is already in sorted order. The three search techniques described in this section are linear search, binary search, and hashing.

Linear Search

The algorithm to perform a *linear search* was examined briefly in Chapter 6. It is the simplest search but not the most efficient. It is a brute-force approach that does not require the values in a list to be sorted or in any other particular format prior to being searched.

Suppose we have a list of numeric values, and we want to determine the position of a particular value in the list, if it is there at all. The general strategy of the linear search is: Starting with the first item in the list, examine each successive item, terminating when the target value is found or the end of the list is reached.

The following example implements a linear search, returning the index of the target element if it is found, and the value −1 (which is outside the range of valid indexes) if it is not in the list at all. Note that there may be duplicate values in the list and that this approach returns the index of the first item that matches the target value.

```java
//  Demonstrates the use of a linear search.
public class Linear_Search_Test {

   public static void main (String[] args) {
      int numbers[] = {7, -3, 7, 2, 8, -1, 3, 2, 5, 6, 7};

      System.out.println ("The index of 6 is " +
         Linear_Search.search (numbers, 6));
   }  // method main
}  // class Linear_Search_Test

//  Contains a method that implements a linear search
//  on an array of integers.

class Linear_Search {

   public static int search (int[] numbers, int target) {
      int index = 0;

      while (index < numbers.length) {
         if (target == numbers[index])
            return index;  // target found
         index++;
      }

      return -1;  // target not found
   }  // method search

}  // class Linear_Search
```

The output of this program is:

```
The index of 6 is 9
```

Since the list is not sorted or organized in any other particular way, the target value may be in any position in the list. Therefore every item in the list must be examined to determine that the target value is not in the list.

Binary Search

The *binary search* algorithm is significantly more efficient than a linear search, but requires that the list being searched has already been sorted. This assumption allows quick elimination of large portions of the list.

> **Key Concept** The binary search algorithm requires that the list is sorted, but provides significant improvements in efficiency over a linear search.

Let's again consider the task of finding a particular numeric value in a list of integers, except that this time the values are sorted (we'll assume ascending order). The general strategy of binary search is: Examine the value in the middle of the list. If it is the target value, the search is over. If not, we capitalize on the fact that the middle value that we just examined divides the list into two halves. The first half contains values that are less than or equal to the middle value, and the second half contains values that are greater than or equal to the middle value. Immediately, we can eliminate half of the data from further consideration because we know that the target value will be found in one half or the other (if at all). If the target value is less than the middle value, then the search continues with the first half of the list, and if not, the search continues with the second half. The appropriate half can be searched with the same binary search technique. That is, the middle value of the appropriate half is examined and either finds the target or eliminates half of the remaining values. Note that with only two comparisons, three-quarters of the data have been taken out of consideration. This process continues until the target value is found, or all possible locations in the list have been eliminated.

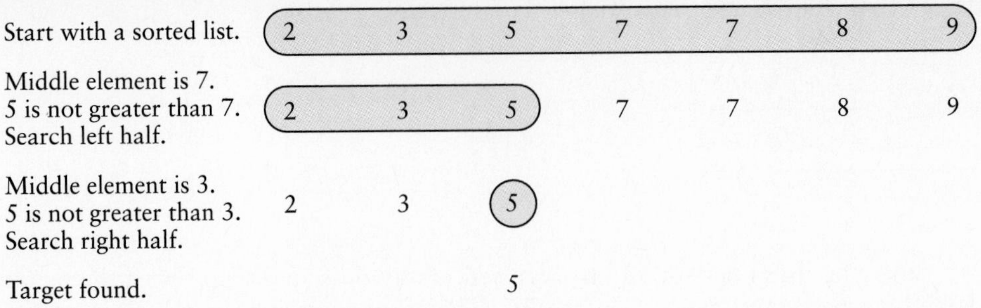

| Start with a sorted list. | 2 | 3 | 5 | 7 | 7 | 8 | 9 |

Middle element is 7.
5 is not greater than 7.
Search left half.

| | 2 | 3 | 5 | 7 | 7 | 8 | 9 |

Middle element is 3.
5 is not greater than 3.
Search right half.

2   3   ⑤

Target found.

5

Figure 13.3   Binary search example, searching for 5

▶▶ **Key Concept**   Each comparison in a binary search eliminates half of the remaining values under consideration.

Figure 13.3 depicts the process of a binary search on a list of sorted integers. At each iteration, the circled values in the figure represent the subset of the original list that is still under consideration.

Binary search takes its name from the fact that each comparison eliminates half of the data being considered. This characteristic makes it an extremely efficient search, but the algorithm will not work unless the data is already sorted.

The following example demonstrates one way to implement a binary search algorithm:

```
//  Finds a value using a binary search.
public class Binary_Search_Test {

   public static void main (String[] args) {
      int[] numbers = {2, 3, 5, 7, 7, 8, 9};

      System.out.println ("The index of 5 is " +
         Binary_Search.search (numbers, 5));
   }  // method main

}  // class Binary_Search_Test

//  Contains a method that implements a binary search
//  on an array of integers.
class Binary_Search {
```

```
    public static int search (int[] numbers, int target) {

        int index;
        int left = 0, right = numbers.length - 1;

        while (left <= right) {
            index = (left + right) / 2;

            if (target == numbers[index])
                return index;   // target found

            if (target > numbers[index])
                left = index + 1;
            else
                right = index - 1;
        }

        return -1;  // target not found

    }  // method search

}  // class Binary_Search
```

The binary search examines the "middle" value.

The output of this program is:

```
The index of 5 is 2
```

This implementation of binary search uses the integers `left` and `right` to mark the boundaries of the region in the array still under consideration. Initially, `left` is set to the first position in the array (zero), and `right` is set to the last position in the array. At each iteration, half of the data is eliminated from consideration by updating either the `left` or `right` boundary.

The middle element is picked by dividing the sum of `left` and `right` by 2. When the number of elements under consideration is even, there are two possible choices for the middle element. This implementation selects the left choice, since the division operator truncates any remainder. This decision is basically arbitrary. Note that the search terminates as soon as any occurrence of the target value is found, which may not be the first occurrence of it in the list.

The loop terminates when either the target value is found, or when the `left` and `right` boundaries "cross" each other (i.e., `right` is less than `left`). The crossing boundaries indicate that no more values are under consideration and that

Search Analysis

We compared sorting algorithms by evaluating the number of comparisons that were made to accomplish the sort. We can compare search techniques in a similar way.

First let's consider the linear search. A value we are searching for can be anywhere in the list, and possibly not present at all. Because there is no special ordering of the values, it will take, on average, $n/2$ number of comparisons to find an item that is in the list containing n elements. Searching for an item that is not in the list requires n comparisons, until we exhaust all possibilities. In general, you need to make one pass through the list for each linear search, which means the algorithm is of *order n*. Remember that the selection search and insertion search algorithms are both of order n^2. This number seems reasonable because we certainly do more comparisons to sort a list (with those techniques) than we do to find a value using a linear search.

Now consider the binary search algorithm. For each comparison, we are able to eliminate half of the existing data under consideration. Therefore, the first comparison eliminates half of the data. The second comparison eliminates another one-quarter of the total data. The third comparison eliminates another one-eighth of the total data. When searching a large amount of data, this quick elimination is quite beneficial. We certainly examine only a fraction of the total number of values stored in the list. Therefore the binary search algorithm is much more efficient than linear search. In fact, because we eliminate half of the data under consideration each time, the binary search technique is of *order* $\log_2 n$. However, keep in mind that this increased search efficiency can only be accomplished if the list is sorted first.

the target value is not present in the list. The value -1 is returned from the search method in this case.

A Recursive Binary Search

Let's examine a recursive version of the binary search algorithm. The general strategy is basically the same, but the implementation is different.

> **Key Concept** A recursive version of a binary search has the same general strategy for finding the target value as the iterative version.

First, note that the `main` method is essentially the same as it was in our previous example, calling the `search` method with only two parameters: the list of numbers and the target value. This time, however, the class that contains the binary search contains two methods. The `search` method simply makes the first call to the `recursive_binary_search` method, which actually conducts the search. Because the calls to `search` are identical in both examples, it doesn't matter if the search is conducted recursively or not (from the perspective of any method that calls `search`). That implementation detail is hidden in the class.

```java
//  Finds a value using a binary search.
public class Binary_Search_Test2 {

   public static void main (String[] args) {
      int[] numbers = {2, 3, 5, 7, 7, 8, 9};

      System.out.println ("The index of 5 is " +
         Binary_Search2.search (numbers, 5));
   }  // method main

}  // class Binary_Search_Test2

//  Contains methods that implement a recursive binary
//  search on an array of integers.
class Binary_Search2 {

   public static int search (int[] numbers, int target) {

      int left = 0, right = numbers.length - 1;

      return recursive_search (numbers, target, left, right);

   }  // method search

   private static int recursive_search (int[] numbers, int target,
               int left, int right) {

      int index = (left + right) / 2;

      if (left > right) // target not found
         return -1;
      else if (target == numbers[index])  // target found
         return index;
      else if (target > numbers[index])
         return recursive_search (numbers, target, index+1, right);
      else
```

The parameters narrow the recursive search on the appropriate "half."

```
        return recursive_search (numbers, target, left, index-1);
    }   // method recursive_search

}   // class Binary_Search2
```

The recursive binary search method has a base case with two possibilities. The recursion will stop if the left and right boundaries "cross," which means the possible locations for the target value have been exhausted and the target value is not in the list. The recursion will also stop if the target value is found. These criteria for stopping the search are essentially the same as they were for the iterative binary search example.

If the base-case situations do not apply, the method will execute one of two possible recursive invocations, depending on which half of the list should be searched. The target value is compared to the middle value, and the search boundaries are modified by the parameters that are passed to the recursive_search method. Specifically, index+1 is used as the new left boundary if the target value is greater that the middle value, or index-1 is used as the new right boundary otherwise.

This recursive version of the binary search produces the same output as the iterative version does:

```
The index of 5 is 2
```

Hashing

Hashing is a technique for storing items so that they can be found efficiently. Items are stored in a *hash table*. Hashing involves a series of specific calculations to determine where in the hash table a certain value should be stored. Later, the same calculations can be used to find a value quickly. Hashing is often thought of as an advanced data-organization technique, but we present it here because Java provides strong API support for hashing, making it a simple technique to use if you understand the basic strategy.

> **Key Concept**   In hashing, a value is computed that determines where in the hash table a value will be stored.

Suppose we have a series of strings that we want to store in a hash table, so that we can easily look them up later. The general strategy of hashing is: A number, called a *hash code* (or *hash value*), is calculated from the target value using a *hash method* (or *hash function*). The hash code is then scaled to the size of the hash table, often using the remainder operator (%). The result, called a *hash index*, designates the position of the target value in the hash table. A *collision* occurs when two or more data values produce the same hash code and, consequently, the same hash table index. One way to resolve a collision is to create a list of values at each possible hash index in the table. There are other techniques for resolving collisions that we will not explore in this text. Figure 13.4 depicts the hashing technique.

Suppose we wanted to count the number of occurrences of each word in Edgar Allan Poe's poem "The Raven." Figure 13.4 shows the list at hash index 12, which contains four words from the first two lines of the poem:

```
Once upon a midnight dreary, while I pondered, weak and weary,
Over many a quaint and curious volume of forgotten lore
```

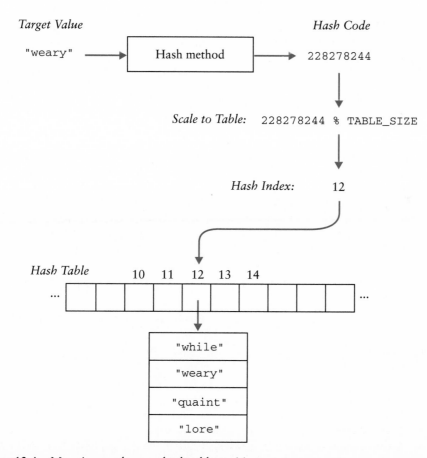

Figure 13.4   Mapping a value to a hash table position

This problem can be solved by associating a counter with each word stored in the hash table. As each word in the poem is encountered, we search the hash table for it. If it is present, its counter is incremented. If it is not present, the word is added to the end of the list at its hash index.

This problem is an appropriate one to solve with hashing, because we don't know what words we will encounter, and therefore can't list them all initially. Furthermore, there are many words in the poem, and we need an efficient way to search for them as they are encountered. Hashing addresses both of these concerns effectively.

The Java language and the API directly support hashing. Specifically, the `Object` class contains a hash method called `hashCode`, which uses the object's value to calculate its hash code. This method is inherited by all objects and can be overridden. In addition, the `java.util` package contains a class called `Hashtable`, which implements a general hashing scheme. Programs that need to use hashing techniques can instantiate an object of `Hashtable`, which encapsulates most of the hashing process. The details of the `Hashtable` class are discussed in Appendix O.

Summary of Key Concepts

- Selection sort and insertion sort are two sorting algorithms that define the processing steps for putting a list of values into a well-defined order.
- Selection sort works by putting each value into its final position, one at a time.
- Swapping is the process of exchanging two values. Swapping requires three assignment statements.
- Insertion sort works by inserting each value into a previously sorted subset of the list.
- Sorts are often compared by their efficiency, which is often defined as the number of comparisons required to perform the sort.
- Both selection sort and insertion sort algorithms are of order n^2. Other sorts are more efficient.
- A generic sort for any list of objects can be created by using an interface that requires sort-specific methods.
- A linear search examines each value in turn until the target is found or the end of the list is reached.
- The binary search algorithm requires that the list is sorted, but provides significant improvements in efficiency over a linear search.
- Each comparison in a binary search eliminates half of the remaining values under consideration.
- A recursive version of a binary search has the same general strategy for finding the target value as the iterative version.

- In hashing, a value is computed that determines where in the hash table a value will be stored.

Self-Review Questions

13.1 Sort the following list of numbers using selection sort showing the list at intermediate stages:

9 5 4 2 1 6

13.2 Repeat Problem 13.1 using the insertion sort.

13.3 Explain why a binary search algorithm is efficient. What assumption is being made?

13.4 Explain why hashing is an efficient searching method.

13.5 Why is a linear search part of hashing?

Exercises

13.6 Explain what happens when multiple values occur in the list to be sorted using:

a. selection sort.
b. insertion sort.

13.7 Trace the steps when sorting the following list: 23, 48, 49, 69, 12, 85, 20, 37, 51, 69, 23 using:

a. selection sort.
b. insertion sort.

13.8 Trace the steps when sorting the following list: 70, 60, 50, 40, 30, 20, 10 using:

a. selection sort.
b. insertion sort.

13.9 Trace the steps when sorting the following list: 11, 22, 33, 44, 55, 66, 77, 88, 99 using:

a. selection sort.
b. insertion sort.

13.10 Compare the different executions of each sort with the lists in Problem 13.8 and Problem 13.9. How many comparisons are made in each?

13.11 What optimization can be performed during a linear search if the data is sorted?

13.12 What would happen if the list used in a binary search was not sorted?

13.13 Why are three assignment statements necessary to exchange two values, as seen in the selection sort? What is the role of the `temp` variable in the selection sort example?

Programming Projects

13.14 Modify the linear search method to optimize the search if you assume the list is sorted. In other words, don't examine any more values than you need to in order to assert that the target value is not present.

13.15 Each of the sorting algorithms presented in this chapter arranges lists of numbers in ascending order. Rewrite the sort algorithms to arrange a list in descending order.

13.16 Design and implement a program that reads every word of a paragraph of text and counts the occurrences of each word. Use hashing as part of the solution.

13.17 Design and implement a program that sorts a list of `People` objects, each of which contains a name, age, and salary. Allow the list to be sorted by any of these values, depending on the sort method invoked.

13.18 Design and implement a generic binary search algorithm. Exercise the class by storing a list of employees, and searching for individuals by name.

13.19 Modify the algorithms for the selection sort and the insertion sort to count the:
- number of comparisons.
- number of exchanges.
- number of times each loop is executed.

Answers to Self-Review Questions

13.1 The incremental steps are:

```
9 5 4 2 1 6
1 5 4 2 9 6
1 2 5 4 9 6
1 2 4 5 9 6
1 2 4 5 9 6
1 2 4 5 6 9
```

13.2 The incremental steps are:

```
9 5 4 2 1 6
5 9 4 2 1 6
4 5 9 2 1 6
2 4 5 9 1 6
1 2 4 5 9 6
1 2 4 5 6 9
```

13.3 The binary search algorithm is efficient because each comparison eliminates half of the remaining data. This algorithm will work only if the list being searched is previously sorted.

13.4 Hashing is efficient since it uses a calculation to determine the position of a value in the hash table instead of performing many comparisons.

13.5 A linear search is required in hashing to find an item among all items stored at the same hash index.

Advanced Flow
of Control

14

J ava has two additional techniques for controlling the flow of execution in a program: exceptions and threads. Exceptions allow us to define a distinct execution flow to handle erroneous or unusual situations. Threads allow us to define multiple execution flows through a program that operate concurrently. This chapter explores both techniques, explaining when they should be used and how to apply them.

Chapter Objectives

- Explain the concept of exception flows.
- Explain how to catch and process exceptions.
- Define new exceptions and throw them.
- Examine the process of exception propagation.
- Explain the use of the `finally` clause in an exception handler.
- Explain the concept of multiple threads.
- Create separate threads and show how they interact.
- Demonstrate the problems associated with shared data.
- Explain how threads can be synchronized.
- Explore additional thread controls.

14.1 Exceptions

As we've discussed briefly in other parts of the text, problems that arise in a Java program generate exceptions and errors. An *exception* is an object that defines an unusual or erroneous situation. An exception is *thrown* by a program or the runtime environment, and can be caught and handled appropriately. An *error* is similar to an exception, except that an error generally represents an unrecoverable situation, and should not be caught.

> **Key Concept** Both errors and exceptions represent unusual or invalid processing, but whereas an exception can be caught and handled, an error should not.

Java has a predefined set of exceptions and errors that may occur during the execution of a program. The general concept of exceptions and errors are defined by the classes `Exception` and `Error`, which are derived from the `Throwable` class. Specific exceptions and errors are derived from them. Appendix M contains a list of many of the errors and exceptions defined in the Java API. Appendix O contains class diagrams that show how exceptions and errors are derived.

Exception handling is important to software design because it allows a programmer to divide a program into a normal execution flow and an *exception execution flow*. This separation is useful for several reasons:

- Debugging code is easier because exceptions help pinpoint errors quickly.
- Predefined classes in the Java API often throw exceptions, allowing the programmer to decide how to handle a particular situation.
- Most programs spend approximately 80 percent of their execution time in 20 percent of the code (the normal flow). An elegant design isolates the normal flow into a clear and efficient section of code.
- Some programs have a requirement that they should never abnormally terminate (crash).

> **Key Concept** Handling exceptions creates a separate execution flow that is appropriately distinct from the normal execution flow.

We can now discuss the various techniques for dealing with exceptions. A program can be designed to process an exception in one of three ways. It can:

- not handle the exception at all.
- handle the exception where it occurs.
- handle the exception at another point in the program.

We explore each of these approaches in the following sections.

Exception Messages

If an exception is not handled at all by the program, the program will terminate (abnormally) and produce a message that describes what exception occurred and where in the program it was produced. You should read the exception output carefully because it is often helpful in tracking down the cause of a problem.

Let's look at the output of an exception. An `ArithmeticException` is thrown when an invalid arithmetic operation is attempted, such as dividing by zero. The following code produces this exception:

```
// Produces an exception.
public class Zero {

    public static void main (String[] args) {
        int numerator = 10;
        int denominator = 0;
        System.out.println (numerator / denominator);
    }  // method main

}  // class Zero
```

> Throws an
> `ArithmeticException`

Because there is no code in this program to explicitly handle the exception, the program will terminate when the exception occurs, producing the following output:

```
java.lang.ArithmeticException: / by zero
    at Zero.main(Zero.java:7)
```

The first line indicates which exception was thrown and provides some information about why it was thrown. In this example, the exception is `ArithmeticException`, which is defined in the `java.lang` package of the Java API. The message "`/ by zero`" is given as the reason the exception was thrown. The remaining lines are the *call stack trace,* which tell us where the exception occurred. In this case, there is only one line in the call stack trace, but there may be several depending on where the exception originated in the program. The first line of the trace indicates the method, file, and line number where the exception occurred. The other lines in the trace, if present, indicate the methods that were called to get to the method that produced the exception. In this program, there is only one method, and it produced the exception; therefore there is only one line in the trace.

▶ **Key Concept** The messages printed by a thrown exception indicate the nature of the problem and a stack trace that shows the methods that were invoked.

The stack trace information is also available by calling several methods of the exception class that is being thrown. The method `getMessage()` returns a string explaining the reason the exception was thrown. The method `printStackTrace()` prints the call stack trace to the `System.err` stream.

The `try` Statement

Let's now examine how we catch and handle an exception when it is thrown. The *try statement* identifies a block of statements that may throw an exception. A *catch clause*, which follows a `try` block, defines how a particular kind of exception is handled. A `try` block can have several `catch` clauses associated with it. Each `catch` clause is called an *exception handler*. The syntax of the `try` statement is:

```
try {

    statement-list1

} catch (exception-class1 variable1) {

    statement-list2

} catch (exception-class2 variable2) {

    statement-list3;

} catch ...
```

When a `try` statement is executed, the statements in the `try` block (`statement-list1`) are executed. If no exception is thrown during the execution of `statement-list1`, processing continues with the statement following the `try` statement (after all of the `catch` clauses). This situation is the normal execution flow and would occur most of the time.

If an exception is thrown at any point during the execution of *statement-list1,* control is immediately transferred to the appropriate `catch` handler. That is, control transfers to the first `catch` clause whose *exception class* corresponds to the class of the exception that was thrown. For instance, if the class of the thrown exception matches the class specified by *exception-class2* (and didn't match *exception-class1*), then control transfers to the second `catch` clause and *statement-list3* is executed. After executing the statements in the `catch` clause, control transfers to the statement after the entire `try` statement.

Key Concept Each `catch` clause on a `try` statement handles a particular kind of exception that may get thrown from the `try` block.

The following program demonstrates the use of the `try` statement. The `User_Reader` class contains a method called `get_integer` that prompts the user for a numeric value, reads the input as string, and converts it to an integer. The conversion operation, which is accomplished by calling `parseInt`, is put in a `try` block. The `parseInt` method produces an exception if the string to be converted does not represent a valid integer. The `catch` clause that matches `NumberFormatException` prints an error message. Input is read from the user until a valid number is entered.

```
import java.io.*;

//  Adds two numbers that are read from the user.
public class Adding {
   public static void main (String[] args) {

      int num1 = User_Reader.get_integer ("Enter a number: ");
      int num2 = User_Reader.get_integer ("Enter another number: ");

      System.out.println ("The sum is " + (num1+num2));

   } // method main
} // class Adding

// Processes input from the user.
class User_Reader {
```

```
public static int get_integer (String prompt) {

    BufferedReader stdin = new BufferedReader
        (new InputStreamReader(System.in));
    int number = 0;
    boolean valid = false;

    // repeat until a valid number is typed by the user
    while (! valid) {
        System.out.print (prompt);
        System.out.flush ();
        try {
            number = Integer.parseInt (stdin.readLine());
            valid = true;
        } catch (NumberFormatException exception) {
            System.out.println ("Invalid input. Try again.");
        } catch (IOException exception) {
            System.out.println ("Input problem. Terminating.");
            System.exit(0);
        }
    }

    return number;

} // method get_integer

} // class User_Reader
```

The `try` block defines a scope for exceptions.

The `catch` clauses handle particular exception types.

The following is a sample run of this program:

```
Enter in a number:  a
Invalid input. Try again.
Enter in a number:  12
Enter in another number: play it again sam
Invalid input. Try again.
Enter in another number:  twelve
Invalid input. Try again.
Enter in another number:
Invalid input. Try again.
Enter in another number:  43
The sum is 36
```

The next section explores the ability to catch and handle an exception at various points in a program.

Exception Propagation

If an exception is thrown and no catch clause applies, control is immediately returned to the method that invoked the method that produced the exception to see if it is caught and handled at that outer level. This process is called *propagating* the exception. If the exception is not caught in the calling method, control is passed to the method that called it. The propagation continues until the exception is caught and handled, or until it is passed out of the main method, which terminates the program and produces an exception message.

Key Concept   If an exception is not caught and handled where it occurs, it is propagated to the calling method.

To catch an exception at an outer level, the method that produces the exception must be invoked inside a try block that has catch clauses to handle it. The following program succinctly demonstrates the process of exception propagation. The main method invokes method level1, which invokes level2, which invokes level3, which produces an exception. Method level3 does not catch the exception, so control is transferred back to level2. But level2 does not catch it either, so control is transferred back to level1. Because the invocation of level2 is made inside a try block (in method level1), the exception is caught and handled at that point.

```
class Propagation_Demo {
    static public void main (String[] args) {

        Exception_Scope demo = new Exception_Scope();

        System.out.println ("program beginning");
        demo.level_1();
        System.out.println ("program ending");

    }  // method main
}  // class Propagation_Demo

class Exception_Scope {
```

```
                    public void level3 (int adjustment) {
                        int current = 1;
                        System.out.println ("level3 beginning");
Throws an excep-        current = current / adjustment;
tion in a nested        System.out.println ("level3 ending");
method invocation   }   // method level3


                    public void level2() {
                        System.out.println ("level2 beginning");
                        level3 (0);
                        System.out.println ("level2 ending");
                    }   // method level2


                    public void level1() {
                        System.out.println ("level1 beginning");
                        try {
                            level2();
Catches the         } catch (ArithmeticException problem) {
exception at a          System.out.println (problem.getMessage());
calling method         error.printStackTrace();
                        }
                        System.out.println ("level1 ending");
                    }   // method level1


                }   // class Exception_Scope
```

The output of the `Propagation_Demo` program has several interesting parts:

```
program beginning
level1 beginning
level2 beginning
level3 beginning
/ by zero
java.lang.ArithmeticException: / by zero
        at Exception_Scope.level3(Exception_Demo.java:18)
        at Exception_Scope.level2(Exception_Demo.java:24)
        at Exception_Scope.level1(Exception_Demo.java:31)
        at Exception_Demo.main(Exception_Demo.java:7)
level1 ending
program ending
```

The first four lines of the output are printed as various methods are invoked. The next line is generated by printing the string returned from the method `getMessage`, which is defined in the `Throwable` class from which all exception objects are derived. In this example, the `getMessage` method is explicitly called in the `catch` clause that handles the exception. The message generally explains why the exception was thrown (in this case a division by zero was attempted).

> **Key Concept**   Methods defined in each exception object can be invoked to get the message indicating the reason the exception was thrown and to print the call stack trace.

The next line and all the indented lines are part of a stack trace that was produced by calling the exception's `printStackTrace` method. The stack trace indicates that line 18 of the program, in method `level3`, contains the statement that caused the exception to be thrown (the division operation). The rest of the stack trace defines the methods that were called to get to that point: `level3` was called from `level2` at line 24 of the program, `level2` was called from `level1` at line 31 of the program, and `level1` was called from `main` at line 7 of the program.

A programmer must pick the most appropriate level at which to catch and handle an exception. There is no single best answer. It depends on the situation and the design of the system. Sometimes the right approach will be not to catch an exception at all, and let the program terminate.

> **Key Concept**   A programmer must carefully consider how exceptions should be handled, if at all, and at what level of the method calling hierarchy.

Let's consider one more important detail concerning error propagation. Recall from Chapter 3 that some exceptions are checked, and others are unchecked. A checked exception must be explicitly acknowledged in the code, even if it isn't caught and handled. If a method could produce a checked exception (that isn't caught), a `throws` clause must be added to the method's header to explicitly indicate that the method could throw that exception. By adding the `throws` clause, we are acknowledging that the method will propagate the exception if it occurs. Throughout the text, we've added a `throws` clause to the `main` method header to indicate that an `IOException` might be thrown (which would cause the program to terminate). We had to add the `throws` clause because `IOException` is a checked exception, and methods that could throw it were being invoked from `main`. If a method catches and handles a checked exception, no `throws` clause is needed.

The `throw` Statement

Until this point, all exceptions we have seen have been generated by the runtime environment or by a method in the Java API. A programmer can also create an exception and throw it as needed. Exceptions are created by deriving a new exception class from an existing one, and instantiating it. The *throw statement* causes an exception to begin propagating. The syntax for the `throw` statement is:

```
throw exception-variable;
```

A `throw` statement causes the execution of the program to transfer to the first applicable `catch` clause, if it is thrown within a `try` block, or to propagate to the calling method. The transfer is immediate, and any statements following the `throw` statement are not executed. The following example demonstrates the act of throwing a programmer-defined exception:

```java
import java.io.IOException;

// Demonstrates creating and throwing your own exception.
public class Throw_Demo {

    public static void main (String[] args) throws Ooops {
        Ooops problem = new Ooops ("Alert!");
        throw problem;
        System.out.println ("Never gets here.");
    } // method main

} // class Throw_Demo

// Represents a special exception in our program.
class Ooops extends IOException {
```

The `throw` statement explicitly throws an exception.

Defines a new exception

```
    Ooops (String message) {
        super (message);
    } // constructor Ooops

} // class Ooops
```

The exception thrown in this program is not caught, so the program terminates abnormally and produces the following output:

```
Ooops: Alert!
        at Throw_Demo.main(Throw_Demo.java:8)
```

Note that the invocation of the `println` method in `main` is never executed. The `throw` statement preceding it immediately transfers control in order to handle the exception. Usually, a `throw` statement is nested inside a selection statement that evaluates a condition to determine if the exception should be thrown. If it isn't thrown, processing continues normally.

The `finally` Clause

A `try` statement can have an optional *finally clause*. The `finally` clause defines a section of code that is executed no matter how the `try` block is exited. Most often a `finally` block is used to manage resources or to guarantee that particular parts of an algorithm are executed. The syntax for a `try` statement that includes a `finally` clause is:

```
try {
    statement-list1
} catch (exception-class1 variable1) {
    statement-list2
} catch ...

} finally {

    statement-list3

}
```

If no exception is generated in the `try` block, the statements in the finally block are executed after *statement-list1* is complete. If an exception is generated in the try block, control first transfers to the appropriate catch clause. After executing the exception-handling code, control transfers to the finally block and its statements are executed. A finally block, if present, should be listed after all catch clauses.

> **Key Concept** The finally clause of a try block is executed whether or not the try block is exited normally or because of a thrown exception.

Note that a try block does not have to have a catch clause at all. If there are no catch clauses, a finally block can be used by itself, if that is appropriate for the situation.

14.2 Threads

The normal flow of control through a program is sequential. One statement is executed and when it is done the next statement is executed, and so on. A *thread* is a programming mechanism that allows us to have more than one task happening at the same time in a program. By "at the same time," we mean one of two things: *parallel processing,* in which there are two or more CPUs available on which multiple tasks are literally being executed at the same instant, or *concurrent processing,* in which multiple tasks are sharing one CPU but their processing steps are intertwined. As far as our discussion of threads go, it really doesn't matter which way you think about it. We will use the term concurrent from here on to refer to threads that run "at the same time." Figure 14.1 visually contrasts a sequential flow with a concurrent flow.

Let's be more precise in our definition of a thread. A thread is a sequential flow of execution through a program that occurs at the same time another sequential flow of execution is processing the same program. Such a program is called *multithreaded.* The concurrent threads are not necessarily processing the same program statements at the same time. The order in which the threads execute statements can become quite important.

> **Key Concept** One thread can be executing the statements of a program at the same time another thread is executing the statements of the same program. They are not necessarily executing the same statements at the same time, however.

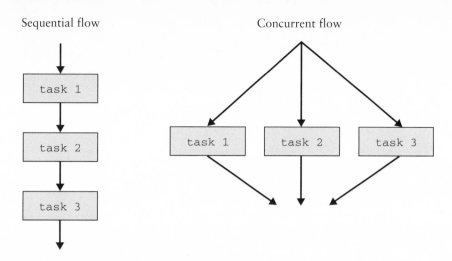

Sequential flow

Concurrent flow

Figure 14.1   Sequential vs. Concurrent Processing

Although programming multiple threads is more complicated than a single sequential flow of control, the power of concurrent processing is significant. Threads enable programs to mimic real-life activities of many people or things working in a common frame of reference at the same time. The rest of this section describes how threads are created and used safely.

Creating Threads

You can create a thread in a Java program in one of two ways. The first way is to extend the `Thread` class and override its `run` method. The second way is to create a class that implements the `Runnable` interface (which requires that a `run` method be created), then pass that object to the constructor of a newly created `Thread` object. The second technique has the advantage of allowing the threaded class to be derived from a class other than `Thread`, if desired.

Key Concept   Java threads can be created in two ways: by deriving a new thread from the `Thread` class or by implementing the `Runnable` interface.

Using the first of these two techniques, the following example creates and executes three threads. Each thread prints a string one hundred times.

```
//  Creates three threads that run concurrently.
public class Simultaneous {

    public static void main (String[] args) {
        Soda one = new Soda ("Coke");
        Soda two = new Soda ("Pepsi");
        Soda three = new Soda ("Diet Coke");

        one.start();
        two.start();
        three.start();
    } // method main

} // class Simultaneous

//  A thread that prints a message 100 times.
class Soda extends Thread {

    private String name;

    Soda (String str) {
        name = str;
    } // constructor Soda

    public void run() {
        for (int count = 0; count < 100; count++)
            System.out.println (name);
    } // method run

} // class Soda
```

The start method begins thread processing.

The run method defines the concurrent code.

Each thread is an instantiation of Soda, which is a subclass of Thread. A thread begins executing when its start method is invoked. The start method creates the separate thread of execution and invokes the run method, which has been overridden in the Soda class. Note the interesting discontinuity: you define a run method that contains the statements that will execute in the thread, but you invoke the start method to begin the thread's processing.

Key Concept   Each thread has a run method that defines the concurrent activity, but you invoke the thread's start method to begin its processing.

Initially, there is only one flow of control through this program—the flow that is executing the main method. When that flow executes the start method of object `one`, a separate thread begins executing. Because it is a separate thread, the main flow immediately returns from the `start` method of object `one` and invokes the `start` method of object `two`, which starts another thread executing. The main flow then invokes the `start` method of object `three`, starting a third thread.

At this point, all three threads are executing the `run` method of class `Soda` concurrently. So instead of printing 100 of the first message, then 100 of the second message, then 100 of the third message, the messages get intermixed. Each thread prints a few of its messages, then another thread takes over. Each thread eventually gets a chance to print its message 100 times, but they are interspersed among the other messages. A possible and partial output of this program is:

```
Coke
Coke
Pepsi
Pepsi
Pepsi
Diet Coke
Diet Coke
Coke
Pepsi
Pepsi
...
```

Knowing how to create and execute a thread is just the beginning. Threads open the door to various complications in a program, and these are discussed in the next section.

A Problem with Threads

While the ability to split a program into small, separately executing parts is important for many problems, it also complicates their implementation. The `Simultaneous` program in the previous section creates three separate threads, but all three threads have their own data. When multiple threads share data, we must be careful to ensure that the shared data is accessed properly.

> **Key Concept** When two or more threads share data, unintended processing sequences can occur that produce incorrect results.

Consider the following situation: A husband and wife have a joint savings account at a bank. Both have the ability to make withdrawals from the account through an automatic teller machine (ATM). One day, the husband happens to use the ATM at the east branch of the bank, while at the same time the wife is using the ATM at the west branch of the bank. If the software controlling the account's withdrawals is threaded in an unsafe manner, sharing the same balance, the inaccurate processing sequence pictured in Fig. 14.2 could occur.

Suppose both people want to withdraw 300 dollars from an account with a current balance of 531 dollars. The withdrawal software first checks to see if the balance can cover the withdrawal amount. If the check occurs at essentially the same time, both threads can conclude that there is enough money to make the withdrawal. Then one thread reduces the balance to 231 dollars, and the second thread reduces the balance to a negative amount. The account is now overdrawn even though the software is theoretically designed to prevent it.

This situation demonstrates a general problem: Multiple threads accessing shared data can cause inappropriate processing to occur solely because of the timing of the thread executions. You may think that the chances of this kind of unfortunate timing would be rare, but it turns out that this problem comes up quite a bit in certain types of processing. The next section discusses a solution to the multithreaded, shared-data problem.

Synchronization

The trouble with shared data would be eliminated if we could guarantee that no two threads were accessing it at the same time. Java allows us to *synchronize* the execution of a particular method. If the synchronized modifier is applied to the definition of a method, only one thread can be executing that method at any one time. Note that this does not specifically dictate which thread will use it first. It simply prevents another thread from entering the method until the thread that is currently using it exits.

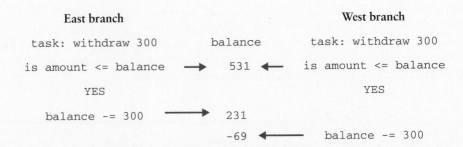

Figure 14.2   Unsafe concurrent transactions among threads sharing data

The following program simulates the bank account situation discussed in the last section. It uses the `synchronized` modifier on the `withdrawal` method to ensure the processing will be safe.

```
//  Manages savings accounts using ATMs.
class ATM_Accounts {

   public static void main (String[] args) {
      Savings_Account savings =
         new Savings_Account (4321, 531);

      ATM west_branch = new ATM (savings);
      ATM east_branch = new ATM (savings);

      west_branch.start();
      east_branch.start();
   }  // method main

}  // class ATM_Accounts

//  Represents a single savings account with the ability
//  to make withdrawals.
class Savings_Account {
   protected int account;
   protected int balance;

   public Savings_Account (int account_num, int initial) {
      account = account_num;
      balance = initial;
   }  // constructor Savings_Account

   public synchronized boolean withdrawal (int amount) {

      boolean result = false;
      System.out.println ("Withdrawal from account " + account);
      System.out.println ("Amount: " + amount);

      if (amount <= balance) {
         balance -= amount;
```

Only one thread at a time can execute a `synchronized` method.

```
            System.out.println ("New balance: " + balance);
            result = true;
        } else
            System.out.println ("Insufficient funds.");

        System.out.println();

        return result;

    }   // method withdrawal

}   // class Savings_Account

// A thread that makes a withdrawal.
class ATM extends Thread {

    Savings_Account account;

    ATM (Savings_Account savings) {
        account = savings;
    } // constructor ATM

    public void run () {
        account.withdrawal (300);
    } // method run

} // class ATM
```

The output of the `ATM_Accounts` program is shown below. Note that it is not clear which thread (`east_branch` or `west_branch`) is making the successful withdrawal first, because the threads are not forced to occur in any particular order. However, the `synchronized` modifier guarantees that the messages will not get intermixed because one thread executes the `withdrawal` method to completion before the other is allowed to start executing it.

```
Withdrawal from account 4321
Amount: 300
New balance: 231
Withdrawal from account 4321
Amount: 300
Insufficient funds.
```

Let's be more precise about the synchronized modifier. As soon as one thread begins executing a synchronized method, the entire object of which that method is a part becomes *locked,* and no other thread can execute any synchronized method in that object. This allows you to create multiple methods that access shared data. For example, our ATM account could also have a deposit method that accesses the balance. Then one thread could be in withdrawal and another thread would be prevented from making a deposit until the withdrawal was complete.

> **Key Concept**   When a thread executes a synchronized method, it locks the object so that no other thread can execute any synchronized method in that object.

Controlling Threads

Threads have several methods that can be used to control thread processing. Two of them are:

- suspend()—temporarily halts a thread's execution
- resume()—resumes a suspended thread's execution at the point it left off

In-Depth Focus

The synchronized Statement

There is also a statement associated with the synchronized reserved word. It follows the following syntax:

```
synchronized (expression)
    statement
```

The *expression* must result in an object. The synchronized statement locks that object while it executes the *statement*. This allows you to execute synchronized code without having to invoke a synchronized method in the object on which the lock is based. The *statement* is executed as if it were a synchronized method of the locked object. Usually, the *statement* is a block.

These two methods work in concert to control when a thread is active. Another method can be used to temporarily halt a thread's processing for a specific amount of time:

- `sleep (long milliseconds)`—suspends the thread for the specified number of milliseconds

The thread will resume processing after the specified time has elapsed. Actually, the thread will sleep for at least the specified amount of time. Thread scheduling and the accuracy of the system clock can interfere with the exact timing.

> **Key Concept**   The `Thread` class defines several methods that enable us to control its processing.

Let's revisit the `Bouncing_Ball` problem, first seen in Chapter 7, and make it threaded. By putting the animation in a thread, we can then control it with the various methods at our disposal. For instance, a pause was implemented in our first version of the program using a `for` loop that had no body. We had to adjust the number of iterations of the loop to make the animation look smooth. The trouble with that approach is that the speed of the processor on which the program runs affects how the applet looks. We can replace the pause loop with a call to the `sleep` method of the thread. This call will suspend the thread for a consistent amount of time (which is our real goal). Then the pause will be independent of the processor speed.

> **Key Concept**   The `sleep` method is a good technique for pausing a program because it is not tied to the speed of the processor.

We can also add a frame with two buttons, labeled suspend and resume, which invokes the appropriate thread-control methods. As the ball bounces up and down, the user can click the suspend button to freeze the animation, and a click of the resume button allows the animation to continue from the point it was suspended.

The following program implements these changes:

```java
import java.awt.event.*;
import java.applet.Applet;
import java.awt.*;

// Simulates a ball on a rubber band.
public class Bouncing_Ball2 extends Applet {
```

```
        private final int SIZE = 300;

        private Ball ball = new Ball(150, 10, 250, 200);
        private Graphics page;

        private Control_Panel controls;

        public void init() {
           setVisible (true);
           setSize (SIZE, SIZE);
           page = getGraphics();
           page.setXORMode (getBackground());
        } // method init

        public void start() {
           controls = new Control_Panel (Thread.currentThread());
           controls.start();
           ball.pause();
           while (ball.moving()) {
              ball.bounce (page);
           }
        } // method start

} // class Bouncing_Ball2

// Various buttons that suspend and resume execution of the
// applet thread.
class Control_Panel extends Thread {

        private Button suspend = new Button ("suspend");
        private Button resume = new Button ("resume");
        private Frame frame = new Frame ("Bouncing Ball Control Panel");
        private Thread applet_thread;

        Control_Panel (Thread applet_thread) {
           this.applet_thread = applet_thread;
        } // constructor Control_Panel

        public void run() {
           Resume_Action resume_action =
              new Resume_Action (applet_thread);
           Suspend_Action suspend_action =
              new Suspend_Action (applet_thread);
```

```
                    suspend.addActionListener (suspend_action);
                    resume.addActionListener (resume_action);
                    frame.setLayout (new FlowLayout());
                    frame.add (suspend);
                    frame.add (resume);
                    frame.pack();
                    frame.setLocation (250, 200);
                    frame.setVisible (true);
                } // method run
            } // class Control_Panel


            // Action for the suspend button
            class Suspend_Action implements ActionListener {

                Thread applet_thread;

                Suspend_Action (Thread applet_thread) {
                    this.applet_thread = applet_thread;
                } // Constructor Suspend_Action

                public void actionPerformed(ActionEvent action) {
                    applet_thread.suspend();
                } // method actionPerformed
            } // class Suspend_Action


            // Action for the suspend button
            class Resume_Action implements ActionListener {

                Thread applet_thread;

                Resume_Action (Thread applet_thread) {
                    this.applet_thread = applet_thread;
                } // constructor Resume_Action

                public void actionPerformed(ActionEvent action) {
                    applet_thread.resume();
                } // method actionPerformed
            } // class Resume_Action


            // Draws the ball and simulates its movement.
            class Ball {

                private final int MOVE = 2;
                private final float DISTANCE = 0.97f;
```

Suspends the
animation

Resumes the
animation

```
private final int SIZE = 20;
private final int PAUSE = 5;

private int x;
private int start_y;
private int end_y;
private int length;

private boolean moving_up = true;

Ball (int new_x, int new_start_y,
      int new_end_y, int new_length) {
   x = new_x;
   start_y = new_start_y;
   end_y = new_end_y;
   length = new_length;
} // constructor Ball

public void pause() {
   try {
      Thread.currentThread().sleep (PAUSE);
   } catch (InterruptedException exception) {
     System.out.println ("have an exception");
     // ignore the exception and continue
   }
} // method pause

void move() {
   if (moving_up) {
      end_y = end_y - MOVE;
   } else {
      end_y = end_y + MOVE;
   }
} // method move

void draw_ball (Graphics page) {
   page.drawOval (x-(SIZE/2), end_y, SIZE, SIZE);
   page.drawLine (x, start_y, x, end_y);
} // draw_ball

public boolean moving () {
   return length != 0;
} // method moving
```

Pauses the animation for a short time

```
   public void bounce (Graphics page) {
      for (int count = 1; count < length; count += MOVE) {
         draw_ball(page);
         pause();
         draw_ball(page);
         move();
      }
      moving_up = !moving_up;
      length = (int) (DISTANCE * length);
   } // method bounce
} // class Ball
```

A snapshot of the running applet, with its separate control panel frame, is shown in Fig. 14.3.

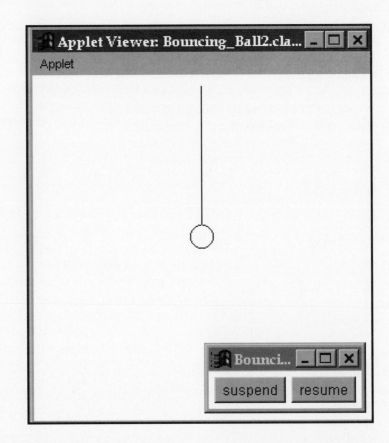

Figure 14.3 The Bouncing_Ball2 applet

Summary of Key Concepts

- Both errors and exceptions represent unusual or invalid processing, but whereas an exception can be caught and handled, an error should not.
- Handling exceptions creates a separate execution flow that is appropriately distinct from the normal execution flow.
- The messages printed by a thrown exception indicate the nature of the problem and a stack trace that shows the methods that were invoked.
- Each `catch` clause on a `try` statement handles a particular kind of exception that may get thrown from the `try` block.
- If an exception is not caught and handled where it occurs, it is propagated to the calling method.
- Methods defined in each exception object can be invoked to get the message indicating the reason the exception was thrown and to print the call stack trace.
- A programmer must carefully consider how exceptions should be handled, if at all, and at what level of the method calling hierarchy.
- The `throws` clause on a method header must be included for checked exceptions that are not caught and handled in the method.
- An exception can be defined by a programmer and thrown, when the appropriate conditions arise, by using the throw statement.
- The `finally` clause of a `try` block is executed whether or not the `try` block is exited normally or because of a thrown exception.
- One thread can be executing the statements of a program at the same time another thread is executing the statements of the same program. They are not necessarily executing the same statements at the same time, however.
- Java threads can be created in two ways: by deriving a new thread from the `Thread` class or by implementing the `Runnable` interface.
- Each thread has a `run` method that defines the concurrent activity, but you invoke the thread's `start` method to begin its processing.
- When two or more threads share data, unintended processing sequences can occur that produce incorrect results.
- Synchronization is the process of protecting a portion of a program so that two threads do not access shared data at the same time.
- When a thread executes a `synchronized` method, it locks the object so that no other thread can execute any `synchronized` method in that object.
- The `Thread` class defines several methods that enable us to control its processing.
- The `sleep` method is a good technique for pausing a program because it is not tied to the speed of the processor.

Self-Review Questions

14.1 What is an exception?

14.2 What are the three approaches to handling exceptions?

14.3 What information is contained in a thrown exception message?

14.4 What is the semantics of a `try` statement?

14.5 When does a `finally` block in a `try` statement get executed?

14.6 What is a threaded program?

14.7 What is the danger of accessing data from multiple threads?

14.8 What does the `synchronized` modifier do?

14.9 What does the `sleep` method do?

Exercises

14.10 Explain how an exception propagates through a method call stack.

14.11 Design a `main` method using pseudocode that will prevent any thrown exception from terminating the program.

14.12 Compare and contrast the `throws` clause with the `throw` statement.

14.13 Explain how threads can be implemented when there is only a single CPU on which a program may execute.

14.14 Test the `Simultaneous` program presented in this chapter. Several messages from each thread are printed before another thread takes over. Explain.

Programming Projects

14.15 Modify a program from the previous chapters so that it uses exceptions to prevent reading incorrectly formatted data.

14.16 Design and implement a program that creates two new exceptions with messages "Too High!" and "Too Low!". Read integer input from the user and throw the appropriate exception if the value is out of the range 25 to 75, inclusive. Catch the exceptions and print their message using the getMessage method. Process exactly five valid (in range) values.

14.17   Modify the program in Problem 14.16 so that the two exceptions are caught at different levels in a method-calling hierarchy.

14.18   Modify the Simultaneous program presented in this chapter to produce five threads from five sodas. Add a single counter shared by all five threads that counts the total number of messages printed. Protect the counter using a synchronized method.

14.19   Modify the ATM_Accounts program presented in this chapter to include a synchronized deposit method.

14.20   Modify the Storm applet presented in Chapter 4, so that it is threaded and has buttons to suspend, resume, and terminate the applet.

Answers to Self-Review Questions

14.1   An exception is an object that represents an unusual or erroneous situation. It can be thrown to indicate that the situation has occurred. Exception handlers can be designed to catch and process the exception when it is thrown.

14.2   An exception can be ignored, which will cause a program to terminate; handled at the point it occurs; or handled at another level in the method call stack.

14.3   A thrown exception message contains an indication of the reason the exception was thrown, and a call stack trace that shows the method, including line numbers, that were called to get to the point where the problem occurred.

14.4   A try statement defines a context for exception handling. If an exception is thrown within the scope of the try block, the exception is matched to the first catch handler that corresponds to the exception that was thrown. If there is no appropriate catch clause, the exception propagates to the calling method, where it may be caught and handled at that level.

14.5   If the try block exits normally, the finally block is executed immediately. If the try block produces an exception, the appropriate exception handler is processed, and then the finally block is executed.

14.6   A threaded program is a program that may be executing multiple versions of itself at the same time. Each thread in the program represents a separate sequential flow that can occur concurrently with other threads.

14.7   Data shared among threads can be corrupted by inappropriate processing that occurs because of the unfortunate timing between thread statements.

14.8   The `synchronized` modifier specifies a method that can be accessed by only one thread at a time. In fact, when a thread enters a `synchronized` method, it locks the entire object so that no thread can enter any `synchronized` method in the object.

14.9   The `sleep` method suspends a thread for a specified number of milliseconds. It is useful for creating a timed pause in a program.

The Software Development Process II

15

I n Chapter 11 we introduced a basic software development life cycle that focused on the following activities: requirements analysis, system design, program implementation, and system testing. This chapter revises that development model into an evolutionary approach and applies it specifically to object-oriented software. The revised process is used to create a graphical applet that allows the user to solve a sliding tile puzzle.

Chapter Objectives

- Explore an evolutionary approach to object-oriented design and implementation.
- Define an object-oriented software development process.
- Demonstrate the development process.
- Explore graphical techniques to capture and represent design decisions.

15.1　An Object-Oriented Development Process

Recall the development model described in Chapter 11. The core parts of this model are shown again in Fig. 15.1. This model steps through the four key activities of software development and stresses the need to be able to iteratively revisit various activities in order to refine the decisions made in those stages. However, this model is fairly simplistic and doesn't specifically refer to object-oriented development.

This section explores the iterative relationship between the initial design of a program and its implementation as highlighted in Fig. 15.1. In particular it expands these phases into an evolutionary development technique as described in the next section.

Evolutionary Development

Our revised, object-oriented development process is shown in Fig. 15.2. One important difference between the two processes is that the design activity in the revised version is divided into two stages: architectural design (also called high-level design), and detailed design. The *architectural design* establishes the general high-level guidelines to be used when constructing any part of the software program, and is done at the beginning of the software development process. The *detailed design* documents the specific methods and algorithms used by specific parts of the system, and is now done as part of an iterative activity called a *refinement*.

> **Key Concept**　The architectural design establishes the general high-level guidelines to be used when constructing any part of the software program.

Each refinement focuses on fleshing out one aspect of the overall software program. The refinement cycle is done many times, until all parts of a program are com-

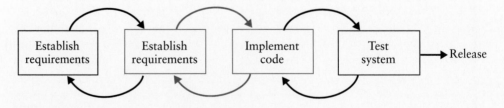

Figure 15.1　The design and implement cycle

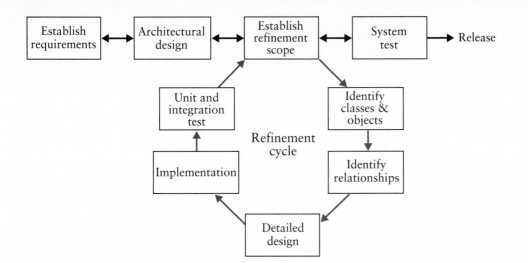

Figure 15.2   An object-oriented software development process

pleted and tested. At this point the entire system needs to be tested and the software released to the user. Usually, the cycle continues until the program is considered "good enough" to be released. What "good enough" means is different for every program, and depends heavily on what the user expectations are.

Key Concept   A refinement focuses on a single aspect of a program, such as the user interface or a particular algorithm.

Because the design stages are broken up, the interactions between design and implementation are better controlled and focused. Each refinement concentrates on one aspect of a program, such as designing the user interface, and the design steps in the refinement are focused on only that aspect. This reduces the overall level of complexity the design needs to address during each refinement.

By following these smaller design cycles with their implementation, the consequences of design decisions are known at a more appropriate time, soon after the design of that refinement is completed, but before the entire design is completed. In this way, the information uncovered during implementation can affect changes in the design of the current refinement and all future refinements. Also, by arranging refinements in a way that the various refinement cycles are independent, i.e., they are not dependent on one another, many refinements can be done at the same time by different implementation teams.

Object-oriented programming is particularly well suited for this type of process, since it supports many types of abstraction. These abstraction techniques make it possible for the design and implementation to work hand-in-hand. By using techniques such as modularity and encapsulation to isolate what has not yet been specified by a refinement, an implementation for a refinement can be completed and tested. For example, a complicated algorithm for a program might be written as a method that accepts all the correct parameters necessary to implement the algorithm, but it might contain no statements, or just a simple `System.out.println`. This type of method is known as a *stub*. A future refinement is necessary to fully implement the algorithm. However, the current refinement can call the existing stub implementation.

Key Concept   Object-oriented programming is particularly well suited for the refinement process because it supports many types of abstraction, such as modularity and encapsulation.

The following sections describe the details of each step of the process shown in the refinement cycle of Fig. 15.2.

Establish Refinement Scope

Establishing the refinement scope determines what will be worked on during the current refinement. The scope can be very broad, addressing a large portion of a program, or it might be focused on a particular detail of the program. Typical refinements might include the following:

- Create the user-interface for a program.
- Flesh out the algorithm for a portion of a program.
- Create the output results of a program.
- Develop a class library to be used in writing other parts of the program.
- Flesh out a requirement or feature of a program.

The size of a refinement is a tradeoff between the resources we have to write the program and the complexity of the program. If there are many programmers that will be writing and designing a particular program, the scope of one refinement can be larger than if there is only one part-time programmer working on the program. In addition, if the area of the refinement is particularly complex, then a refinement might focus on only one small aspect of that complexity, allowing for many refinement cycles to complete that part of the program.

Also, a refinement can focus on unknown parts of a program. Similar to prototypes described in Chapter 11, a refinement can be used to elicit information about a particularly undefined part of the program. This could be an area where the requirements are vague, so the purpose of the refinement is to solidify the requirements. Another reason could be that a specific programmer has never implemented a similar feature in another program and is unsure of the right approach or implication of various design choices.

After the scope of the refinement has been established and documented, the design process can begin.

Identifying Classes and Objects

As part of the architectural design and before we are able to identify classes and objects, the program is usually broken down into parts. For example, consider designing the software to control a printer. Some part of the software must deal with arranging the print on paper, some part needs to control the various options of the printer switches, such as off-line, test, and form-feed buttons, and another part needs to control the data port used to transmit documents to the printer.

At this stage, our goal is to identify all the known requirements related to the current refinement and associate them with some part of the software. These parts are not necessarily classes. In fact, one part may eventually be broken down into a set of related classes, much like one of the Java API packages. In essence, we are making a first cut at the roles and responsibilities of this refinement cycle.

Once the various roles of the refinement have been identified, we can now make some guesses about what the objects in this system are. Having a first cut on the objects, we should be able to arrange them into groups that represent the various objects' classes. This is a critical step in the process, since the definition of classes will determine how easy or how hard modifications to the software will be in the future. However, it is also an impossible task to identify the perfect set of classes the first time through a refinement cycle. Therefore, rather than focusing on creating the best possible class structure, we should concentrate on creating a satisfactory class structure, that is, a set of classes that will enable us to successfully implement the current refinement. If during the later stages of the refinement cycle the choice of classes causes difficulties during detailed design, this stage can be revisited to identify more appropriate class structures.

One rule of thumb for choosing objects and classes, as described in Chapter 4, is the association of software with physical entities or hardware components that they control. Objects that map to physical entities are easier to understand since an analogy can be made with the software. However, as software becomes more complex, there is a greater need for objects that represent intangible ideas, such as an object that controls access and use of several other objects.

> **Key Concept**   One rule of thumb for choosing objects and classes is the association of software with physical entities or hardware components that they control.

When the objects and classes are being enumerated, some of their details become obvious. Often a general understanding of the types of methods each class should support is known at the time the class is identified. For example, a class related to controlling a robot should have a method associated with the robot's movement. These class assumptions should be documented and tested using scenario diagrams. Note that not all details of the class will be known at this point in the refinement cycle.

Another consideration is reuse of existing classes. A programmer should not want to write all parts of a program from scratch, but instead augment the program with software written by others. Class libraries that exist should be incorporated into this process where appropriate and as much as possible. Incorporating these classes should also help guide the programmer's choices of other objects and classes needed for the refinement. For example, one could program a graphical user interface without ever using the AWT class library. You could use the `Graphics` class and implement their own buttons and other GUI features. However, much time and effort would be spent on parts of the program that could have been served better by using the AWT.

> **Key Concept**   A programmer should strive to reuse existing software components.

Identifying Relationships

Once a basic set of classes and objects is identified, the way in which each class relates to the others should be described. These classes should exhibit various relationships with each other, such as common state and behavior relationships, or perhaps one class simply needs to use another class.

An initial step is to group classes that have similar roles and common behavior. The *"is-a"* relationship, related to inheritance, should be a common relationship among these classes. A parent class might be introduced that contains the common elements of each class, and then each class can be derived from the parent.

Identifying this relationship and creating common parent classes can greatly reduce the amount of code that needs to be written during the implementation stage of the refinement.

Another type of relationship between classes can be expressed using Java's interfaces. An interface, as described in Chapter 9, is used to identify a role the class may play in an alternate hierarchy. Often interfaces represent patterns in the software that cannot be represented using the inheritance hierarchy.

Classes that are related, but not part of an inheritance hierarchy, can often be grouped into packages. This type of grouping accomplishes two goals. The first is to provide insight to a user of these classes that there are many classes necessary to support a particular program feature or requirement. The AWT packages are an example of this type of class. The second is for implementation purposes. Packages allow certain implementation techniques that are difficult or impossible to accomplish otherwise. For example, package scope allows a method of a class to be available to the implementation of other classes in the same package, but not to classes outside of the package.

A different type of association is the use relationship. The *use relationship* is an association based on how a class will be implemented. It is not related to inheritance, interfaces, or packages. If a class A requires an object of class B for its implementation, then we say that A uses B. A use relationship is often drawn using a single line with a circle on the end. Often the line is labeled with the exact nature of the use relationship. The class attached to the circle is being used by the other class. Figure 15.3 shows a simple use relationship between two classes, where Class1 uses Class2 in its implementation. The labels n and m represent the cardinality of the relationship. If Class1 used five objects of Class2, then n would be 1 and m would be 5. If these labels are left off of a use relationship it can be assumed that both ends are of cardinality 1.

Key Concept   The use relationship is an association based on how a class will be implemented. It is not related to inheritance, interfaces, or packages.

Since the set of classes and objects represent a refinement of part of a program, each of the classes should be associated with another in some way, either

Figure 15.3   A use relationship

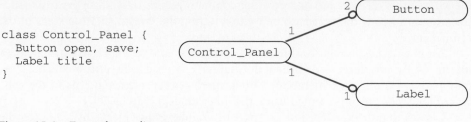

```
class Control_Panel {
  Button open, save;
  Label title
}
```

Figure 15.4   Example use diagram

through inheritance, interfaces, packages, or via a use relationship. Therefore, by the end of this phase the purpose of each class and the reason for the refinement should be clear. The relationship between classes should be documented using a class diagram. This diagram should show all the inheritance hierarchies and use relationships identified in this step. An example of the use diagram is shown in Fig. 15.4.

Detailed Design

Once we have an understanding of how the program will work with respect to classes and objects, we need to flesh out the smaller details. All of the public methods need to be identified. These include all the methods that a class needs to work according to the assumptions documented in previous refinement phases. Public methods of a class are often used in concert with methods of other classes. This information is expressed and verified using scenario diagrams.

 Key Concept   Scenario diagrams are used to express and verify the methods and classes identified during the detailed design.

Next we must identify the exact use of other objects and classes. The use of other classes can be done in many ways. An object of the class can be declared locally, or it can be passed as a parameter, or it can be a public object declared in another class. These decisions should be made and verified using pseudocode and scenario diagrams. Lastly, the details of any complex algorithmic portion of a method should be described in pseudocode. The pseudocode should convey how a method will process various input data provided by parameters into output. This step should tie together all of the previous steps of the refinement, so that the design can be walked through and checked against the requirements related to this refinement.

Implementation

At this stage of the refinement, we have enough information to start the implementation of the classes described in the previous stages. The implementation should be carried out using an efficient and clean coding style following guidelines such as those described in Appendix G. The code written should match the pseudocode and the design as enumerated by the various design documents produced so far. Of course, reusing existing class implementations and methods should be considered before implementing a class from scratch.

The implementation is a concrete representation of the design. At this point, it should be clear whether or not the class structure and the design are appropriate to the refinement at hand. If there are difficulties implementing a particular design feature cleanly, the design should be reevaluated using this new perspective, and design changes made. The stages of a refinement should be considered iterative among themselves.

> **Key Concept** The implementation of a program should be a concrete representation of the design.

This stage includes compiling all the code written. If there is a portion of the program that is being ignored during this refinement, a class or interface needs to be written that represents how this refinement might interact with the yet-to-be designed portion of the software.

Unit and Integration Testing

Once the software is written, it must be tested to ensure that it performs as expected. This is called a *unit test;* it tests a particular class instantiation to ensure its proper execution. Unit testing often involves simulating the input to a particular method and checking the output for correctness. Eventually, these refinements will have to be integrated with previously written pieces of the program (usually produced by an earlier refinement). The integrated pieces need to be tested to see if they interact together properly. This is called an integration test. Often integration testing involves executing program code from multiple classes and testing the results for correctness. The relationship between unit and integration testing is the same as the relationship between a class and a program.

Stub Methods

Often during a refinement a program will need to use a class, method, or object that is not part of the current refinement. Because we want to address all parts of the code associated with the current refinement, we'd like to leave a placeholder for the reference and then continue on with development. The placeholder would be replaced with a fully implemented version of the class, method, or object during a future refinement. This type of placeholder is often called a *stub*. The following is a stub for a simple input routine:

```
// Gets input from the user
class User {

    // A stub method for testing purposes
    int prompt_for_number() {
        return 42; // Need to replace with a dialog box         Simulating actual
    } // method prompt_for_number                                user input

} // class User
```

By defining the class and the method (including its signature), the rest of a program can be written and tested. After the other parts are completed, we can replace the `prompt_for_number` method with an appropriate implementation that actually prompts the user for an input value.

Stubs are also a useful technique for debugging a complex program. Because complex programs are difficult to trace, bugs are often difficult to find. Stubs can be used to simplify a program and isolate a problem. For example, if a program is producing an incorrect result, but we are not sure what part of the algorithm is causing the problem, we can stub out portions of the algorithm with known values (such as in the example above). When the problem disappears, we know that the last portion stubbed out was at least partly the cause of the problem. This technique can be repeated until the real problem is identified.

Key Concept Once the software is written, it must be tested to ensure that it performs as expected.

15.2   Example: Slide Puzzle

This section demonstrates the use of the object-oriented development process described in the previous section. The program to be developed presents the user with a slide puzzle to solve. A slide puzzle consists of a square board of tiles that can be shifted around until they are in a final configuration. The goal is to solve the puzzle as quickly as possible.

Requirements

The requirements for the program can be stated as follows:

- The program shall be accessible on the World-Wide Web.
- The program shall present a 3×3 playing board, forming nine positions. At any time eight of the positions will contain a tile, and one of the positions will be "empty."
- Each tile is a portion of a picture. When assembled in the final configuration, the tiles form the complete picture. The goal of the puzzle is to move tiles around the board until they are in the final configuration.
- A tile adjacent to the empty position can be moved into the empty position, leaving its original position empty.
- The user indicates the tile to move with a mouse click. Only one tile can be moved at a time.
- When the program is initially loaded, a default picture is chosen for display, with its tiles distributed randomly in the board positions.
- The user interface shall include controls that allow the user to:
  - choose the picture that the puzzle presents.
  - reshuffle the current puzzle.
  - see the puzzle in its final, solved configuration, effectively abandoning the challenge of solving the puzzle.
- At least four different pictures will be presented as choices for the puzzle.

- When the user chooses a picture, the current puzzle is replaced by the new picture with its tiles randomly distributed.
- When the user solves the puzzle by moving the tiles into their correct position, the program will display a message to that effect.

Since the puzzle must be accessible over the Web, it will be written as an applet. The requirements provide some freedom in the controls used, so careful decisions must be made concerning the interface. Once any questions about the requirements are resolved, the developer's attention can turn to the architectural design.

Architectural Design

The high-level design of the puzzle is rather simple. The main data of the puzzle is the state of the board. The main properties of the puzzle are its presentation via a user interface, and the movement of tiles. A major decision relates to how we store the board. If we assume that there is only one representation of the board in the program, then all the other parts of the program must be related to it. Figure 15.5 shows the overall architecture of the program.

Another architectural decision is to create a movement control portion of the software that is the only part of the program that changes the state of the board. This implies that any software that needs to move board pieces must interact with movement control. Movement control can take input from either the user interface, or a class that the board object acts on on behalf of the user, such as the reshuffler or the solver part of the program.

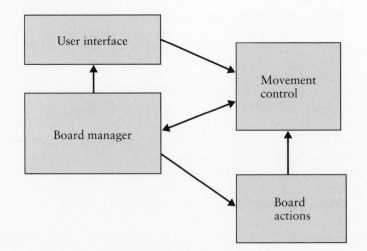

Figure 15.5   Graphical view of the high-level design

Refinements

After careful consideration, the developer could define several refinements for the slide puzzle program:

- Develop the basic user interface, showing the tile positions and button controls.
- Allow tile movement and mouse events.
- Load an image, dividing it into tiles, and randomly distributing them on the board.
- Provide the functionality to start a new puzzle and reshuffle the existing puzzle.
- Determine when the user correctly solves the puzzle and acknowledge it.
- Produce the final solution when the user requests it.

Since the number and content of the refinements is dependent on the experience of the developer, the refinements for this project could have been broken down in other ways, separated into smaller pieces, or grouped into larger ones. For example, starting a new puzzle and reshuffling the existing puzzle could be treated as separate refinements if that makes the developer more comfortable.

The following section steps through the refinement loop for the first refinement listed above, the development of the basic user interface. The complete program for the slide puzzle can be downloaded from the text's Web site (see the Preface for details). Several additional refinements are left as programming projects at the end of this chapter.

Refinement: The User Interface

Since the user interface is a significant part of this project, it is spread over three different refinements. The first refinement is concerned with building the basic structure and layout of the user interface. The first activity of a refinement is to identify the classes and objects appropriate for that refinement. The requirements associated with this refinement are:

- The program shall be accessible on the World-Wide Web.
- The program shall present a 3 × 3 playing board, forming nine positions. At any time eight of the positions will contain a tile, and one of the positions will be "empty."
- The user interface shall include controls that allow the user to:
  - reshuffle the current puzzle.
  - see the puzzle in its final, solved configuration, effectively abandoning the challenge of solving the puzzle.

This list was chosen since it represents the requirements that affect the structural layout of the user interface. The first requirement can be satisfied by implementing the program as an applet. In this case, we need a class derived from `Applet` that will

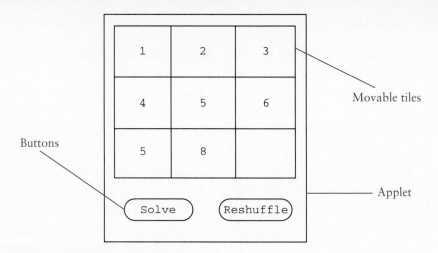

Figure 15.6 Sample user interface drawing

serve as the primary class for the program. This class will be called the Slider class. A drawing of the parts of the user interface are shown in Fig. 15.6.

The board users play on is another class that is needed. This class will be called Board class. The board needs to hold at least eight different positions and one empty position. We can propose another class, called Tile, which represents what is located at these positions.

A common user interface component that provides controls to the user is the Button class. We can provide a button for reshuffling and for solving the puzzle. Since we will need to arrange these user interface components so that the Layout manager interacts with them properly, several Panel class objects may be needed. From this short discussion we can see the need for the following classes:

- Slider (derived from Applet)
- Board
- Tile
- Button
- Panel

The next stage of a refinement is to identify the relationships between classes. We've already identified that the Slider class will be derived from Applet since we want the puzzle to be playable over the Web. We can assume that the Board class should be derived from the Panel class since it will be used to display collections of Tile objects. Since the Tile objects must eventually be capable of displaying images, a logical conclusion is to derive the Tile class from the

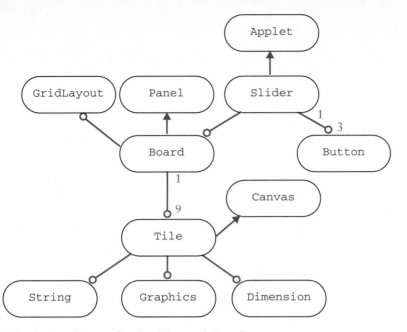

Figure 15.7 A class diagram for the slide puzzle interface

`java.awt.Canvas` class. The `Canvas` class is a generic user interface component that allows the drawing of images upon it. Figure 15.7 shows a class diagram of these relationships.

Since this refinement creates the overall structure of the user interface, with little functionality behind it, it does not require much detailed design. There are no significant algorithms to implement at this time. During this refinement, we are primarily concerned with the paint methods and layout managers, to ensure that all pieces are displayed in their appropriate positions. The scenario diagram in Fig. 15.8 shows the invocations of the `paint` and `repaint` methods from various objects.

The following code represents the implementation of this first refinement. The `Slider` class is the applet that controls the interface, which is made up of a `Board` class derived from `panel` and several `Button` objects. The `Board` consists of nine `Tile` objects, formatted using the `GridLayout` manager. The `init` method of the Slider class uses the applet's `add` method to link the various user interface objects together and call the `setup` method for the board. The call to the `board` object's `setup` method uses the `Canvas`'s `add` method to link eight of the `Tile` objects to the board. The various paint methods are linked together as shown in Fig. 15.8. The `Tile`'s paint method draws a rectangle and writes the number associated with the object in the middle. This code will eventually be replaced by code that manages graphical images by later refinements of the program.

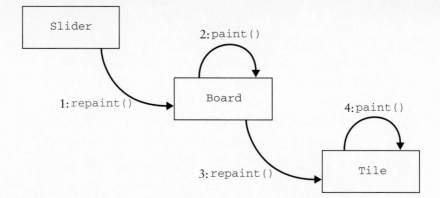

Figure 15.8 A scenario diagram showing the display methods

```
import java.io.*;
import java.awt.*;
import java.applet.*;

// Presents a slide puzzle with control buttons.
public class Slider extends Applet {

    final static int SIZE = 150;

    Board tiles = new Board();
    Panel buttons = new Panel();

    Button solve = new Button ("Solve");
    Button reshuffle = new Button ("Reshuffle");

    public void init() {

        // Put buttons on a panel so that they use
        // the flow manager to be shown side-by-side
        buttons.add (solve);
        buttons.add (reshuffle);

        // Add the tiles contained formatted by GridBag and
        // the buttons formatted using flow to this applet
        // using flow. This provides the required user interface
        // layout
        add (tiles);
        add (buttons);

        tiles.setup();
```

The buttons are
on their own panel.

```
         setSize (SIZE+100,SIZE+100);
    } // method init


    public void paint (Graphics page) {
        tiles.repaint();
    } // method paint


} // class Slider


// Represents a single tile in the game
class Tile extends Canvas {

    final private int SIZE = Slider.SIZE/3;


    private String title;


    Tile (String title1) {
        title = title1;
    } // Constructor Tile


    public void paint (Graphics page) {
        page.drawRect (0,0,SIZE-2,SIZE-2);
        page.drawString (title, SIZE/2, SIZE/2);
    } // method paint


    public Dimension getMinimumSize() {
        return new Dimension (SIZE, SIZE);
    } // method getMinimumSize


    public Dimension getPreferredSize() {
        return getMinimumSize();
    } // method getPreferredSize


} // class Tile


// Panel that holds nine tiles.
class Board extends Panel {

    private Tile[] tiles = {
        new Tile ("1"), new Tile ("2"), new Tile ("3"),
        new Tile ("4"), new Tile ("5"), new Tile ("6"),
        new Tile ("7"), new Tile ("8"), new Tile ("") };
```

The board stores nine `Tile` objects in an array.

```
        public void setup() {
            setLayout (new GridLayout (3,3)); // Create the 3x3 matrix
            for (int number_of_tiles = 0;
                 number_of_tiles < tiles.length;
                 number_of_tiles++) {
               add (tiles[number_of_tiles]);
            }
        } // method setup

} // class Board
```

The implementation must go through a thorough unit test. Because this refinement only presents the interface, with essentially no functionality behind it, the testing may be nothing more than a visual inspection of the graphical layout of the interface components. Furthermore, since this is our first refinement of the project, there is no earlier portion with which to integrate the code, and no specific integration testing is required. As additional refinements are accomplished, they are integrated into this framework. Figure 15.9 shows a snapshot of the running applet.

Summary of Key Concepts

- The architectural design establishes the general high-level guidelines to be used when constructing any part of the software program, and is done at the beginning of the software development process.
- A refinement focuses on a single aspect of a program, such as the user interface or a particular algorithm.
- Object-oriented programming is particularly well suited for the refinement process because it supports many types of abstraction, such as modularity and encapsulation.
- The size of a refinement is a tradeoff between the resources available to write the program and the complexity of the program.
- One rule of thumb for choosing objects and classes is the association of software with physical entities or hardware components that they control.
- A programmer should strive to use existing software components.
- The use relationship is an association based on how a class will be implemented. It is not related to inheritance, interfaces, or packages.
- Scenario diagrams are used to express and verify the methods and classes identified during the detailed design.
- The implementation of a program should be a concrete representation of the design.

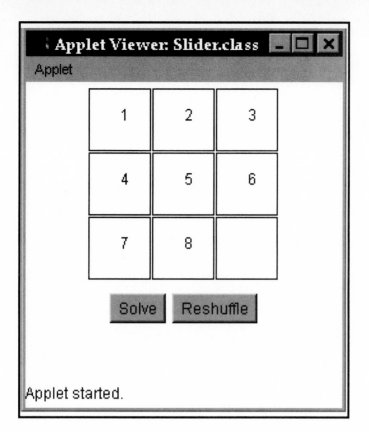

Figure 15.9 Snapshot of Slider applet

- Once the software is written, it must be tested to ensure that it performs as expected.

Self-Review Questions

15.1 What is evolutionary software development?

15.2 What is a program refinement?

15.3 When is a program good enough to release?

15.4 Why is the development model in this chapter considered to be object-oriented?

15.5 How is integration testing different from unit testing?

15.6 What does a scenario diagram show?

15.7 What is a use relationship?

Exercises

15.8   Compare and contrast the development model shown in Chapter 11 and the model in this chapter.

15.9   Consider the development of a software program to perform library book management. The system should be able to catalog all books, record books being borrowed and returned, and associated fines related to books returned late.

a. Identify several possible refinements, such as book borrowing, for the system.
b. Identify several objects and classes for the book borrowing refinement.
c. Identify possible relationships between classes and objects in the book borrowing refinement.
d. Draw a class diagram showing a class hierarchy and use relationships.

15.10 Consider the development of a software program to implement a graphical sketch pad. The system should be able to draw and delete different shapes, such as a circle and square, define different colors to use when drawing shapes, and render text.

a. Identify several possible refinements, such as the user interface, for the system.
b. Identify several objects and classes for the user interface refinement.
c. Identify possible relationships between classes and objects in the user interface refinement.
d. Draw a class diagram showing a class hierarchy and use relationships.

15.11 Consider the development of a software program to simulate an airport. The system should be able to simulate takeoffs and landings of planes on different runways, simulate an air traffic controller's screen, and allow an operator to control the takeoff, landing, and flying attributes of planes (such as course and speed).

a. Identify several possible refinements, such as plane simulation, for the system.
b. Identify several objects and classes for the plane simulation refinement.
c. Identify possible relationships between classes and objects in the plane simulation refinement.
d. Draw a class diagram showing a class hierarchy and use relationships.

Programming Projects

15.12 Add a counter to the slide puzzle that keeps track of the number of moves the user makes. Reset the counter to zero whenever a new puzzle is started.

15.13 Add a control to the slide puzzle to allow the user to select the number of cells that make up the puzzle (3×3, 4×4, or 5×5).

15.14 Add a timer to the slide puzzle that indicates the passing of time so that the user can strive to complete the puzzle in a minimum amount of time. Provide controls so that the user can pause and restart the timer. Reset the timer whenever a new puzzle is started.

15.15 Extend Problem 15.14 so that the program keeps track of a list of the top 10 "high scores"—the low values on the timer. Provide controls that allow the user to display the high score table and to clear its entries.

Answers to Self-Review Questions

15.1 Evolutionary software development is a controlled iterative process that creates a program as a series of well-defined refinements. Evolutionary development acknowledges our limited ability to plan all details of the program design and implementation initially.

15.2 Each refinement in an iterative development process focuses on one particular aspect of a software system. For example, the purpose of one refinement may be to develop the user interface. Another refinement may focus on the necessary database access that has to occur in the system. A refinement allows the programmer to target a particular task while keeping the overall architectural design in mind.

15.3 In most situations, it is not feasible to exhaustively prove that a program produces correct results. Therefore the concept of a program being "good enough" is a function of many factors, including test results and user needs. Each development project has its own characteristics that drive the schedule. Unfortunately, the quality of the software is only one factor.

15.4 Although the development model discussed in this chapter contains activities similar to those in the earlier model, these phases specifically address issues related to the object-oriented approach, such as identifying the relationships between classes.

15.5 Unit testing is the process of testing individual software components; it may often require the creation of stub modules to simulate the other portions of the system. Integration testing is the process of testing a collection of components, focusing on the way the components interact.

15.6 A scenario diagram depicts the messages that are passed between objects (the methods that are invoked) to get a particular task accomplished.

15.7 A use relationship between two classes implies that some method in one class uses the services of the other. A user relationship could also mean that one object is an aggregate that contains one or more objects of the other class.

Data Structures

A dvanced problem solving often requires advanced techniques for organizing and managing information. The term *data structures* refers to the various ways information can be organized and used. Many data structures have been developed over the years, and some of them have become classics. A data structure can often be implemented in a variety of ways. This chapter explains how data structures can be implemented using references to link one object to another. It also serves as an introduction to some specific data structures.

Chapter Objectives

- Examine the difference between static and dynamic implementations.
- Explore the concept of an Abstract Data Type (ADT).
- Define and use dynamically linked lists.
- Define queue and stack ADTs.
- Use dynamic structures to implement queues and stacks.

16.1   Dynamic Structures

Arrays are considered to be *static* structures because they have a fixed size through-out their existence. (Note that this use of static does not have the same meaning as it has when used as the Java reserved word.) Vectors are more dynamic than arrays in that they can grow and shrink in size as necessary. However, the Vector class is implemented by creating and destroying arrays, a process that is not efficient. Furthermore, arrays and vectors are good at representing linear relationships, such as lists, but are not as suited to other types of organizations. We need a better approach.

> **Key Concept**   A static data structure has a fixed size for the duration of its existence, whereas a dynamic data structure grows a d shrinks as needed.

Using references, we can create whatever types of structures are most appropri-ate for the situation. If implemented carefully, they can be quite efficient to search and modify. Structures created this way are considered to be *dynamic*, since their size is determined dynamically, as they are used, and not by their declaration.

Using References to Link Objects

Remember from Chapter 4 that all objects are created dynamically using the new operator. A variable used to keep track of an object is actually a reference to the object. Recall that a declaration such as:

```
Book my_book = new Book ("The Cuckoo's Egg");
```

actually accomplishes two things: it declares my_book to be a reference to a Book, and it instantiates an object of class Book. An object and its reference can be depicted as shown in Fig. 16.1.

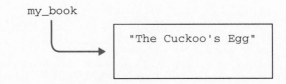

Figure 16.1   A reference to an object

Consider an object that contains a reference to another object of the same type. For example:

```
class Node {
    int info;
    Node next;
}
```

Two objects of this class can be instantiated and chained together by having the next reference of one Node object refer to the other. The second object's next reference can refer to a third Node object, and so on, creating a *linked list*. The first node in the list could be referenced using a separate variable. The last node in the list would have a next reference that is null, indicating the end of the list. This situation is pictured in Fig. 16.2. For this example, the information stored in each Node class is a simple integer, but keep in mind that we could define a class to contain any amount of information of any type.

 Key Concept   A dynamically linked list is managed by storing and updating references to objects.

Let's look at an example. The following program demonstrates the use of references to chain a set of objects together into a list. Note that the next data value in the class Book is declared public, but this practice is not good programming style. Later in the chapter we will see the proper way to handle this issue. The Library program creates a linked list of Book objects, then scans through the list, printing the book titles.

```
//   Sets up a dynamically linked list.  Scans through the
//   list, printing the items one at a time.
public class Library {
```

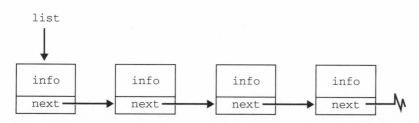

Figure 16.2   A linked list

```
public static void main (String[] args) {

    Book current, books;

    // Set up first entry in list
    books = new Book ("The Hitchhiker's Guide to the Galaxy");

    // Create and add additional books
    books.next = new Book ("Jonathan Livingston Seagull");
    books.next.next = new Book ("A Tale of Two Cities");
    books.next.next.next = new Book ("Java Software Solutions");

    // Print the list
    current = books;
    while (current != null) {
        System.out.println (current.get_title());
        current = current.next;
    }

} // method main

} // class Library

// The Book class holds the book title and a reference to another
//  book.  The reference is public, which is not good style.
class Book {

    private String title;
    public Book next;  // refers to the next book in the list

    Book (String new_title) {
        title = new_title;
        next = null;
    } // constructor Book

    public String get_title() {
        return title;
    } // method get_title

} // class Book
```

Referencing the second, third, and fourth book in the list.

Each new Book object that is created is assigned to the previous book's next reference. Since the constructor initializes the next reference to null, the last node in the list always has a null value for next. The loop that prints the book titles terminates when that `null` reference is encountered, indicating that the end of the list has been reached. The variable `current` is a reference to a `Book`, and is used to refer to each book in the list one at a time.

When executed, the `Library` program produces the following output:

```
The Hitchhiker's Guide to the Galaxy
Jonathan Livingston Seagull
A Tale of Two Cities
Java Software Solutions
```

One of the main problems with the `Library` program is that the `main` method manipulates the `next` references directly. The objects instantiated from class `Book` do not manage themselves, and thus break a fundamental tenet of object-oriented programming. This issue is explored further in the next section.

Abstract Data Types

An *abstract data type* (ADT) is a collection of data and the particular operations that are allowed on that data. A list ADT, for example, would define the operations that can be used with the list, such as add, delete, and print. The data is often managed using a data structure. An ADT is considered abstract because the operations you perform on it are separated from the underlying implementation. For instance, a list could be implemented as an array or as a linked list. The interface provided by the list ADT could be the same for either implementation.

Objects are perfectly suited for defining ADTs since an object, by definition, has a well-defined interface whose implementation is hidden in the class. The data that is represented, and the operations that manage the data, are encapsulated together inside the object. An encapsulated ADT is more reusable and reliable, since its interaction with the rest of the system is controlled.

 Key Concept   An abstract data type hides the implementation of a data structure behind a well-defined interface. This characteristic makes objects a perfect way to define ADTs.

The `Library` program defines a `Book` class that contains a public data value called `next`. The management of the list of books is not hidden behind a set of well-defined operations. The linked list of books is directly accessed and changed by commands such as:

```
books.next = new Book ("Jonathan Livingston Seagull");
```

Therefore the `Library` program violates the principles behind good object design and the techniques of abstract data types, two concepts that are highly related. The next section investigates a better list solution.

In-Depth Focus

Coupling and Cohesion

An abstract data type reduces the connection between the ADT and the code that uses the ADT to a small, well-defined set of operations. This supports the software engineering concepts of coupling and cohesion. *Coupling* is the strength of the relationship between two software components. *Cohesion* is the strength of the relationship among the parts of a single software component. That is, coupling is the glue that holds two separate components together, and cohesion is the glue inside a single component that allows it to be thought of as a single piece. A bond is created between two items when they both use a common piece of information, or when one item interacts with another, or when they both support a common purpose.

We want to minimize the amount of coupling between any two pieces of our system. By minimizing coupling, we localize the processing. Any change we make will more likely be confined to a small portion of the program. When errors occur, their effect will have less chance of propagating to other parts of the system, and the errors will be easier to track down and correct.

On the other hand, we want to maximize the amount of cohesion in any given piece of the software. The more tightly related the parts of an item are, the cleaner the design is and the more logical its operations are. This concept is consistent with our goal that a method should only accomplish one logical function, and that an object should represent a single concept or entity. Figure 16.3 depicts the relationship between two items in a software system, and the relationship among the parts of a given item.

An abstract data type confines the implementation of the data structure and presents a specific set of operations by which another part of the system can interact with it. All details of the implementation are hidden behind the interface. The client of the ADT need only know what the interface operations are, not how they are implemented. Therefore, by definition, an ADT minimizes the coupling between the ADT and its client, and maximizes the cohesion within the ADT implementation.

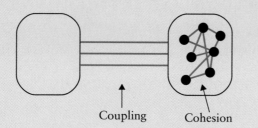

Coupling   Cohesion

Figure 16.3   Coupling and cohesion bonds

16.2   Lists

A list is a general data structure that can be used in a variety of circumstances. Therefore a list abstract data type could include many types of operations. For now we only consider the actions of adding new nodes to the end of the list, and printing the list.

A Dynamically Linked List

The following program accomplishes the same goal as the original `Library` program: to set up a linked list of `Book` objects, then scan through the list and print their titles. However, in this version of the program, the list of books is encapsulated inside the `Book_List` class. The `main` method only sends messages to the `books` object to add new books and to print the entire book list.

```
//   Sets up a list of books, then prints them.  The details of
//   the list implementation is encapsulated in an object.
public class Library2 {

   public static void main (String[] args) {

      Book_List books = new Book_List ();

      books.add ("The Hitchhiker's Guide to the Galaxy");
      books.add ("Jonathan Livingston Seagull");
      books.add ("A Tale of Two Cities");
      books.add ("Java Software Solutions");

      books.print ();
```

```
        } // method main

} // class Library2

//  The Book_List class encapsulates all list operations.
class Book_List {

    private Book list;

    Book_List() {
       list = null;
    } // constructor Book_List

    public void add (String new_title) {
       Book new_book = new Book (new_title);
       Book current;

        if (list == null)
           list = new_book;
        else {
           current = list;
           while (current.get_next() != null)
              current = current.get_next();
           current.set_next (new_book);
        }
    } // method add

    public void print () {
       Book current = list;
       while (current != null) {
          current.print();
          current = current.get_next();
       }
    } // method print

} // class Book_List

//  The Book class stores a title and a reference to another book.
class Book {
    private String title;
    private Book next;  // refers to the next book in the list

    Book (String new_title) {
       title = new_title;
```

Creating a new book node to be added.

Adding it to the end of the list.

Each Book object controls its own next pointer.

```
      next = null;
   } // constructor Book


   public Book get_next () {
      return next;
   } // method get_next


   public void set_next (Book next_book) {
      next = next_book;
   } // method set_next


   public void print() {
      System.out.println (title);
   } // method print


} // class Book
```

The book list is embodied inside the Book_List class. From outside of the class, it is not known how the list is implemented, nor is it really important. The Book_List class provides a set of methods that allow the user to maintain the list of books. That set of methods, specifically add and print, define the operations to the Book_List ADT. Furthermore, the Book class itself is well encapsulated, with all data declared as private and methods provided to accomplish any updates necessary.

Other methods could be included in the Book_List ADT. The add method provided always adds a new book to the end of the list. Another method called insert could be defined to add a node anywhere in the list (to keep it sorted, for instance). A parameter to insert could indicate the value of the node after which the new node should be inserted. The picture in Fig. 16.4 shows how the references would be updated to insert a new node.

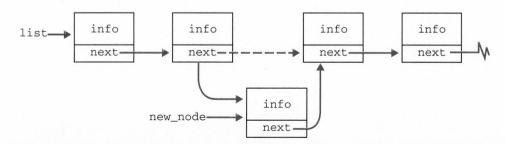

Figure 16.4   Inserting a node into the middle of a list

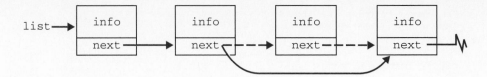

Figure 16.5 Deleting a node from a list

> ▶ **Key Concept**   A versatile list ADT contains insert and delete operations, which can be implemented by carefully manipulating object references.

Another operation that would be helpful in the list ADT would be a `delete` method, to remove a particular node. Recall that by removing all references to an object, it becomes a candidate for garbage collection. Figure 16.5 shows the way references would be updated to delete a node from a list. Care must be taken to accomplish the modifications to the references in the proper order to ensure that other nodes are not lost and that references continue to refer to valid, appropriate nodes in the list.

Other Dynamic List Implementations

Many variations on list implementations can be used, depending on the specific needs of the program being designed. For example, in some situations it may make your processing easier to implement a *doubly linked list* in which each node has not only a reference to the next node in the list, but also another reference to the previous node in the list. The `Node` class might be declared as follows:

```
class Node {
    int info;
    Node next, prev;
}
```

A doubly linked list is pictured in Fig. 16.6. Note that, like a single linked list, the next reference of the last node is null. Similarly, the previous node of the first

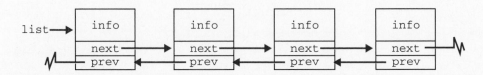

Figure 16.6 A doubly linked list

node is null, since there is no node that comes before the first one. This type of structure makes it easy to move back and forth between nodes in the list, but it is somewhat more trouble to set up and modify.

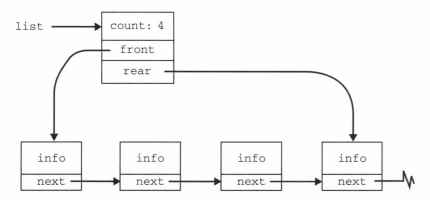

Key Concept   There are many variations on the implementation of dynamic linked lists.

Another implementation of a linked list could include a header node for the list that has a reference to the front of the list and another to the rear. A rear reference makes it easier to add new nodes to the end of the list. The header node could contain other information, such as a count of the number of nodes currently in the list. The declaration of the header node would be similar to the following:

```
class List_Header {
    int count;
    Node front, rear;
}
```

Note that the header node is not of the same class as the Node class to which it refers. A linked list that is implemented using a header node is pictured in Fig. 16.7.

Other linked list implementations could be created. For instance, the use of a header can be combined with a doubly linked list, or the list could be maintained in sorted order. The implementation should cater to the type of processing that is necessary. Some extra effort to maintain a more complex data structure may be worthwhile if it makes common operations on the structure more efficient.

Figure 16.7   A list with front and rear references

16.3 Queues

A *queue* is similar to a list, except that it has restrictions on the way you put items on and take items off. Specifically, a queue uses *first-in, first-out* (FIFO) processing. That is, the first item put on the list is the first item that comes off the list. Think about a line of people waiting at a bank. You enter the queue at the back, and work your way to the front. Eventually you come off of the front of the line to be processed (served by the teller). Figure 16.8 depicts the FIFO processing of a queue.

 Key Concept   A queue is a linear data structure that manages data in a first-in, first-out manner.

A Queue ADT

A queue data structure typically has the following operations:

- `enqueue`—adds an item to the rear of the queue
- `dequeue`—removes an item from the front of the queue
- `empty`—returns true if the queue is empty

The following program implements a queue and exercises it with some simple strings. The queue ADT is written to manage the `Object` class; therefore any object can be added to the queue.

```
class QTrek {

   public static void main (String[] args) {
      Queue ship = new Queue();

      if (ship.empty())
         System.out.println ("Ship deserted.");
```

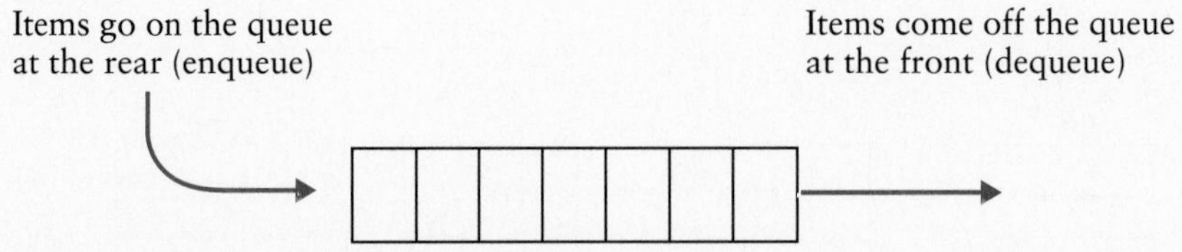

Items go on the queue at the rear (enqueue)

Items come off the queue at the front (dequeue)

Figure 16.8   A queue, with FIFO processing

```
        ship.enqueue ("Pickard");
        ship.enqueue ("Data");
        ship.enqueue ("Troi");

        if (ship.empty())
           System.out.println ("The ship is empty.");

        System.out.println (ship.dequeue());
        System.out.println (ship.dequeue());
        System.out.println (ship.dequeue());

        if (ship.empty())
           System.out.println ("Abandon ship!");
    }   // method main

}   // class QTrek

class Queue {
    Queue_Item first, last;

    boolean empty() {
        return first == null;
    }   // method empty

    void enqueue (Object item) {
        Queue_Item new_item = new Queue_Item (item);
        if (first != null) {
           last.set_next (new_item);
           last = new_item;
        } else {
           last = new_item;
           first = last;
        }
    }   // method enqueue

    Object dequeue () {
        if (first != null) {
           Object result = first.get_item();
           first = first.get_next();
           return result;
        } else {
           return null;
        }
    }   // method dequeue
```

Adding an item to the back of the queue

Removing an item from the front of the queue

```
}   class Queue

class Queue_Item {
    private Object item;
    private Queue_Item next;

    Queue_Item (Object qitem) {
        item = qitem;
        next = null;
    }   // constructor Queue_Item

    Object get_item() {
        return item;
    }   // method get_item

    Queue_Item get_next() {
        return next;
    }   // method get_next

    void set_next (Queue_Item qitem) {
        next = qitem;
    }   // method set_next
}   // class Queue_Item
```

When executed, the QTrek program produces the following output:

```
Ship deserted.
Pickard
Data
Troi
Abandon ship!
```

16.4   Stacks

Like the list and queue data structures, a *stack* is a linear construct, meaning that it maintains its information in a straight line. However, unlike the queue, whose items go in on one side and come out on the other, interaction with a stack occurs only at one end. The last item to go on a stack is the first item to come off, like a stack of trays in a cafeteria. A stack processes information in a *last-in, first-out* (LIFO) manner, as shown in Fig. 16.9.

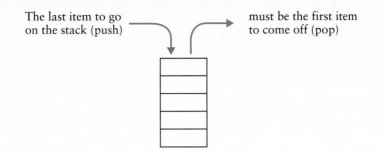

The last item to go on the stack (push) · · · must be the first item to come off (pop)

Figure 16.9 A stack, with LIFO processing

▶ **Key Concept** A stack is a linear data structure that manages data in a last-in, first-out manner.

The Stack Class

A typical stack ADT contains the following operations:

- push—pushes an item onto the top of the stack
- pop—removes an item from the top of the stack
- peek—retrieves the top item of the stack without removing it
- empty—returns true if the stack is empty

The `java.util` package of the API contains a class called `Stack` that implements a stack data structure. It contains methods that correspond to the standard stack operations, plus a method that searches for a particular object in the stack. The signatures for these methods are:

```
public Object push (Object obj)
public Object pop ()
public Object peek ()
public boolean empty ()
public int search (Object obj)
```

The `Stack` class is derived from `Vector`. The `search` method returns an integer corresponding to the position in the stack of the particular object. This type of searching is not usually considered to be part of the classic stack ADT.

Note that the `Stack` operations operate on the `Object` class. Since all objects are derived from the `Object` class, any object can be pushed onto a stack. If primitive types are to be stored, they must be converted to objects using the corresponding wrapper class. Unlike the `Stack` class, there is no `Queue` class defined in the Java API. The `Vector` class, however, can be thought of as a list implementation.

Example: Message Decoding

The following program accepts a string of characters that it interprets as a secret message. The program decodes the message and prints it. A coded message has each individual word in the message reversed. Words in the message are separated by a single space. The program uses the `Stack` class to push the characters of each word on the stack. When an entire word has been read, it is popped off the stack in reverse order and printed.

```java
import java.io.*;
import java.util.Stack;


//    Decodes a message by reversing each word in a string.
public class Decode {

    public static void main (String[] args) throws IOException {
        BufferedReader stdin = new BufferedReader
            (new InputStreamReader(System.in));
        Stack word = new Stack();
        String message;
        int index = 0;


        System.out.println ("Enter the coded message:");
        message = stdin.readLine();
        System.out.println ("The decoded message is:");

        while (index < message.length()) {

            // push word onto stack
            while (index < message.length() && message.charAt(index)
                    != ' ') {
                word.push (new Character(message.charAt(index)));
                index++;
            }
```

Using the pre-defined `Stack` class

```
        // print word in reverse
        while (!word.empty())
            System.out.print (((Character)word.pop()).charValue());
        System.out.print (" ");
        index++;
    }

    System.out.println();

} // method main

} // class Decode
```

Popping an Object and casting it as a Character

The following is a sample run of the Decode program.

```
Enter the coded message:
ehT neerg yeknom sah tfel sih hcrep
The decode message is:
The green monkey has left his perch
```

Summary of Key Concepts

- A static data structure has a fixed size for the duration of its existence, whereas a dynamic data structure grows and shrinks as needed.
- A dynamically linked list is managed by storing and updating references to objects.
- An abstract data type hides the implementation of a data structure behind a well-defined interface. This characteristic makes objects a perfect way to define ADTs.
- A versatile list ADT contains insert and delete operations, which can be implemented by carefully manipulating object references.
- There are many variations on the implementation of dynamic linked lists.
- A queue is a linear data structure that manages data in a first-in, first-out manner.
- A stack is a linear data structure that manages data in a last-in, first-out manner.

Self-Review Questions

16.1 What is a dynamic structure?

16.2 Why are objects a good choice for implementing an abstract data type?

16.3 What is a doubly linked list?

16.4 What is a header node for a linked list?

16.5 How is a queue different from a list?

16.6 What is a stack?

16.7 What is the Stack class?

Exercises

16.8 Suppose current is a reference to a Node object and that it currently refers to a specific node in a linked list. List, in pseudocode, the steps that would delete the node following current from the list. Carefully consider the cases in which current is referring to the first and last nodes in the list.

16.9 Modify your answer to Problem 16.8 assuming that the list was set up as a doubly linked list, with next and prev references.

16.10 Suppose current and new_node are references to Node objects. Assume current currently refers to a specific node in a linked list and new_node refers to an unattached Node object. List, in pseudocode, the steps that would insert new_node behind current in the list. Carefully consider the cases in which current is referring to the first and last nodes in the list.

16.11 Modify your answer to Problem 16.10 assuming that the list was set up as a doubly linked list, with next and prev references.

16.12 Show the contents of a queue after the following operations are performed. Assume the queue is initially empty. Does it matter how the dequeue operations are intermixed with the enqueue operations? Does it matter how the enqueue operations are intermixed among themselves? Explain.

```
enqueue (45);
enqueue (12);
enqueue (28);
dequeue();
dequeue();
enqueue (69);
```

```
enqueue (27);
enqueue (99);
dequeue();
enqueue (24);
enqueue (85);
enqueue (16);
dequeue();
```

16.13   Show the contents of a stack after the following operations are performed. Assume the stack is initially empty. Does it matter how the pop operations are intermixed with the push operations? Does it matter how the push operations are intermixed among themselves? Explain.

```
push (45);
push (12);
push (28);
pop();
pop();
push (69);
push (27);
push (99);
pop();
push (24);
push (85);
push (16);
pop();
```

Programming Projects

16.14   Design and implement an application that maintains a linked list of objects instantiated from a class called CD, where each node represents a compact disk in an audio collection. In each node, keep track of the title of the CD, the artist's name, and the number of tracks on the CD. In a class called Tunes, define a main method that adds various CDs to the collection. Print the list when complete.

16.15   Modify the Library2 program presented in this chapter by adding delete and insert operations into the Book_List class. The insert method should be based on a compare method in the Book class that determines if one book title comes before another alphabetically. In the main method, exercise various insertion and deletion operations. Print the book list when complete.

16.16 Design and implement a version of selection sort (from Chapter 13) that operates on a linked list of nodes that each contain an integer.

16.17 Design and implement a version of insertion sort (from Chapter 13) that operates on a linked list of nodes that each contain an integer.

16.18 Design and implement an application that simulates the customers waiting in line at a bank. Use a queue data structure to represent the line. As customers arrive at the bank, customer objects are put on the end of the line with an enqueue operation. When the teller is ready to service another customer, the customer object is taken off the queue with a dequeue operation. Print a message each time an operation occurs during the simulation.

16.19 We are familiar with *infix expressions,* in which an operator is positioned between its two operands. A *postfix expression* puts the operators after its operands. Keep in mind that an operand could be the result of another operation. This eliminates the need for parentheses to force precedence. For example, the infix expression

```
(5 + 2) * (8 - 5)
```

is equivalent to the following postfix expression

```
5 2 + 8 5 - *
```

The evaluation of a postfix expression is fairly easy when you use a stack. As you progress through a postfix expression from left to right, you encounter operands and operators. If you encounter an operand, push it on the stack. If you encounter an operator, pop two operands off the stack, perform the operation, and push the result back on the stack. When you have processed the entire expression, there will be one value on the stack, which is the result of the entire expression.

Design and implement an application that evaluates a postfix expression that operates on integer operands using the arithmetic operators +, -, *, /, and %. You may want to use a `StringTokenizer` object to assist in the parsing of the expression.

Answers to Self-Review Questions

16.1 A dynamic data structure is one constructed using references to link various objects together into a particular organization to facilitate its use. It is dynamic because it can grow and shrink dynamically as needed. New objects can be created and added to the structure, or obsolete objects can be removed from the structure, by adjusting references between objects in the structure.

16.2 An abstract data type is a collection of data and the operations that can be performed on that data. An object is essentially the same thing, in that we encapsulate related variables and methods in an object. Therefore an object is an appropriate way to represent an ADT.

16.3 Each node in a doubly linked list has references to both the node that comes before it in the list and the node that comes after it in the list. This organization allows for easy movement forward and backward in the list.

16.4 A header node for a linked list is a special node that holds information about the list, such as references to the front and rear of the list and an integer to keep track of how many nodes are currently in the list.

16.5 A queue is a linear data structure, like a list, but it has more constraints concerning its use. A general list can be modified by inserting or deleting nodes anywhere in the list, but a queue only adds nodes to one end (enqueue) and takes them off of the other (dequeue). The difference is largely conceptual, determined by the purpose of the structure for a given situation.

16.6 A stack is a linear data structure that adds (pushes) and removes (pops) nodes from one end. It manages information using a last-in, first-out (LIFO) approach.

16.7 The `Stack` class is defined in the `java.util` package of the Java API. It implements a generic stack ADT. The `Stack` class stores `Object` references, so the stack can be used to store any kind of object.

Glossary

abstract—A Java reserved word that serves as a modifier for classes, interfaces, and methods. An abstract class cannot be instantiated, and is used to specify bodiless abstract methods that are given definitions by derived classes. Interfaces are inherently abstract.

abstract class—See abstract.

abstract data type—A collection of data and the operations that are defined on that data. An abstract data type might be implemented in a variety of ways, but the interface operations are consistent. Abbreviated ADT.

abstract method—See abstract.

abstraction—The concept of hiding details. If the right details are hidden at the right times, abstraction can significantly help control complexity and focus attention on appropriate issues.

Abstract Windowing Toolkit—The package in the Java API (java.awt) that contains classes related to graphics and graphical user interfaces. Abbreviated AWT.

access—The ability to reference a variable or invoke a method from outside the class in which it is declared. Controlled by the visibility modifier used to declare the variable or method. Also called scope or level of encapsulation. See also: visibility modifier.

access modifier—See visibility modifier.

actual parameter—The value passed to a method as a parameter. See also: formal parameter.

address—(1) A numeric value that uniquely identifies a particular memory location in a computer's main memory. (2) A designation that uniquely identifies a computer among all others on a network.

aggregate object—An object that contains variables that are references to other objects.

algorithm—A step-by-step process for solving a problem. A program is based on one or more algorithms.

alias—A reference to an object that is currently also referred to by another reference. Each reference is an alias of the other.

analog—A representation that is in direct proportion to the source of the information. See also: digital.

applet—A Java program that is linked into an HTML document, then retrieved and executed using a Web browser, as opposed to a stand-alone Java application.

appletviewer—A software tool that interprets and displays Java applets through links in HTML documents. Part of the Java Development Kit (JDK).

API—See Application Programming Interface.

application—(1) A generic term for any program. (2) A Java program that can be run without the use of a Web browser, as opposed to a Java applet.

Application Programming Interface—A set of classes that define services for a programmer. Not part of the language itself, but often relied upon to perform even basic tasks. Abbreviated API. See also: class library.

arc angle—When defining an arc, the radial distance that defines the arc's length. See also: start angle.

architectural design—A high-level design that identifies the large portions of a software system and key data structures. See also: detailed design.

architecture—See computer architecture.

architecture neutral—Not specific to any particular hardware platform. Java code is considered to be architecture neutral since it is compiled into bytecode, then interpreted on any machine with a Java interpreter.

arithmetic operator—An operator that performs a basic arithmetic computation, such as addition or multiplication.

arithmetic promotion—The act of promoting the type of a numeric operand to be consistent with the other operand.

array—A programming language construct used to store an ordered list of primitive values or objects. Each element in the array is referenced using a numerical index from 0 to $N - 1$, where N is the size of the array.

ASCII—A popular character set used by many programming languages. ASCII stands for American Standard Code for Information Interchange. It is a subset of the Unicode character set, which is used by Java.

assembly language—A low-level language that uses mnemonics to represent program commands.

assignment conversion—Some data types can be converted to another in an assignment statement. See widening conversion.

assignment operator—An operator that results in an assignment to a variable. The = operator performs basic assignment. Many additional assignment operators perform additional operations prior to the assignment, such as the *= operator.

association—See operator association.

AWT—See Abstract Windowing Toolkit.

background color—The color of the background on an applet or HTML page. See also: foreground color.

Backus-Naur Form—A notation for representing language syntax using a formal grammar. Abbreviated BNF.

base—The numerical value on which a particular number system is based. It determines the number of digits available in that number system and the place value of each digit in a number. See also: binary, octal, decimal, hexadecimal, place value.

base 2—See binary.

base 8—See octal.

base 10—See decimal.

base 16—See hexadecimal.

base case—The situation that terminates recursive processing, allowing the active recursive methods to begin returning to their point of invocation.

base class—See superclass.

behavior—The functional characteristics of an object, defined by its methods. See also: state, identity.

binary—The base-2 number system. Modern computer systems store information as strings of binary digits.

binary operator—An operator that uses two operands.

binary search—A searching algorithm that requires that the list be sorted. It repetitively compares the "middle" element of the list to the target value, narrowing the scope of the search each time. See also: linear search.

binary string—A series of binary digits (bits).

binding—The process of associating an identifier with the construct that it represents. For example, the process of binding a method name to the specific definition that it invokes.

bit—A binary digit, either 0 or 1.

bit shifting—The act of shifting the bits of a data value to the left or right, losing bits on one end and inserting new bits on the other.

bits per second—A measurement rate for data transfer devices. Abbreviated bps.

bitwise operator—An operator that manipulates individual bits of a value, either by calculation or shifting.

black-box testing—Producing and evaluating test cases based on the input and expected output of a software component. The test cases focus on covering the equivalence categories and boundary values of the input. See also: white-box testing.

block—A group of programming statements and declarations delimited by braces ({ }).

BNF—See Backus-Naur Form.

boolean—A Java reserved word representing a logical primitive data type that can only take the values `true` or `false`.

boolean expression—An expression that evaluates to a true or false result, primarily used as conditions in selection and repetition statements.

boolean operator—Any of the bitwise operators AND (&), OR (|), or XOR (^) when applied to `boolean` operands. The results are equivalent to their logical counterparts, except that boolean operators are not short-circuited.

bounding rectangle—A rectangle that delineates a region in which an oval or arc is defined.

boundary values—The input values corresponding to the edges of equivalence categories. Used in black-box testing.

bounds checking—The process of determining if an array index is in bounds, given the size of the array. Java performs automatic bounds checking.

break—A Java reserved word used to interrupt the flow of control by breaking out of the current loop or `switch` statement.

browser—Software that retrieves HTML documents across network connections and formats them for viewing. A browser is the primary vehicle for accessing the

World-Wide Web. See also: Netscape Navigator.

bug—A slang term for a defect or error in a computer program.

build-and-fix approach—An approach to software development in which a program is created without any significant planning or design, then modified until it reaches some level of acceptance. It is a prevalent, but unwise, approach.

bus—A group of wires in the computer that carry data between components such as the CPU and main memory.

byte—A unit of binary storage equal to eight bits. (2) A Java reserved word that represents a primitive integer type, stored using eight bits in two's complement format.

bytecode—The low-level format into which the Java compiler translates Java source code. The bytecodes are interpreted and executed by the Java interpreter, perhaps after transportation over the Internet.

byvalue—A Java reserved word that is not currently used. It may be used in the future to specify parameters that are passed by value into methods.

capacity—See storage capacity.

case—(1) A Java reserved word that is used to identify each unique option in a `switch` statement. (2) The orientation of an alphabetic character (uppercase or lowercase).

case sensitive—Differentiating between the uppercase and lowercase versions of an alphabetic letter. Java is case sensitive; therefore the identifier `total` and the identifier `Total` are considered to be different identifiers.

cast—(1) A Java reserved word that is not currently used. (2) A Java operation expressed using a type or class name in parentheses to explicitly convert and return a value of one data type into another.

catch—A Java reserved word that is used to specify an exception handler, defined after a try block.

CD ROM—An optical secondary memory medium that stores binary information in a manner similar to a musical compact disc.

central processing unit—The hardware component that controls the main activity of a computer, including the flow of information and the execution of commands.

char—A Java reserved word that represents the primitive character type. All Java characters are members of the Unicode character set and are stored using 16 bits.

character set—A ordered list of characters, such as the ASCII or Unicode character sets. Each character corresponds to a specific, unique numeric value within a given character set. A programming language adopts a particular character set to use for character representation and management.

character string—A series of ordered characters. Represented in Java using the `String` class and string literals such as `"hello"`.

checked exception—A Java exception that must be either caught or explicitly thrown to the calling method. See also: unchecked exception.

child class—See subclass.

class—(1) A Java reserved word used to define a class. (2) The blueprint of an object. The model that defines the variables and methods an object will contain when instantiated.

class diagram—A diagram that shows the relationships between classes, including inheritance and use relationships.

class hierarchy—The treelike structure created when classes are derived from other classes through inheritance.

class library—A set of classes that define useful services for a programmer. See also: Application Programmer Interface.

class method—A method that can be invoked using only the class name. An instantiated object is not required, as it is with instance methods. Defined in a Java program by using the `static` reserved word.

CLASSPATH—An operating system setting that determines where the Java interpreter searches for class files.

class variable—A variable that is shared among all objects of a class. It can also be referenced through the class name, without instantiating any object of that class. Defined in a Java program by using the `static` reserved word.

client-server model—A manner in which to construct a software design based on objects (clients) making use of the services provided by other objects (servers).

coding guidelines—A series of conventions that describe how programs should be constructed. They make programs easier to read, exchange and integrate. Sometimes referred to as coding standards, especially when they are enforced.

coding standard—See coding guidelines.

cohesion—The strength of the relationship among the parts within a software component. See also: coupling.

collision—The process of two hash values producing the same hash code. See also: hashing, hash code.

command-line arguments—The values that follow the program name on the command line. Accessed within a Java program through the `String` array parameter to the `main` method.

comment—A programming language construct that allows a programmer to embed human-readable annotations into the source code. See also: documentation.

compiler—A program that translates code from one language to equivalent code in another language. The Java compiler translates Java source code into Java bytecode. See also: interpreter.

compile-time error—Any error that occurs during the compilation process, often indicating that a program does not conform to the language syntax or that an operation was attempted on an inappropriate data type. See also: syntax error, logical error, run-time error.

component—Any portion of a software system that performs a specific task, transforming input to output. See also: GUI component.

component hierarchy—The relationships among graphical components of a user interface. See also: container.

computer architecture—The structure and interaction of the hardware components of a computer.

concatenation—See string concatenation.

condition—A `boolean` expression used to determine if the body of a selection or repetition statement should be executed.

conditional coverage—A strategy used in white box testing in which all conditions in a program are executed, producing both `true` and `false` results. See also: statement coverage.

conditional operator—A Java ternary operator that evaluates one of two expressions based on a condition.

conditional statement—See selection statement.

const—A Java reserved word that is not currently used.

constant—An identifier that contains a value that cannot be modified. Used to make code more readable and to facilitate changes. Defined in Java using the `final` modifier.

constructor—A special method in a class that is invoked when an object is instantiated from the class. Used to initialize the object.

container—A Java GUI component that can contain other components. See also: component hierarchy.

control characters—See nonprintable characters.

controller—Hardware devices that control the interaction between a computer system and a particular kind of peripheral.

coupling—The strength of the relationship between two software components. See also: cohesion.

CPU—See central processing unit.

data structure—Any programming construct, either defined in the language or by a programmer, used to organize data into a format to facilitate access and processing. Arrays, linked lists, and stacks can all be considered data structures.

data type—The designation that specifies the set of values (which may be infinite). For example, each variable has a data type that specifies the kinds of values that can be stored in it.

data transfer device—A hardware component that allows information to be sent between computers, such as a modem.

debugger—A software tool that allows a programmer to step through an executing program and examine the value of variables at any point. See also: jdb.

decimal—The base-10 number system, which humans use in everyday life. See also: binary.

default—A Java reserved word that is used to indicate the default case of a `switch` statement, used if no other cases match.

default visibility—The level of access designated when no explicit visibility modifier is used to declare a class, interface, method, or variable. Sometimes referred to as package visibility. Classes and interfaces declared with default visibility can be used within their package. A method or variable declared with default visibility is inherited and accessible by all subclasses in the same package.

defect testing—Testing designed to uncover errors in a program.

defined—Existing for use in a derived class, even if it can only be accessed indirectly. See also: inheritance.

delimiter—Any symbol or word used to set the boundaries of a programming language construct, such as the braces ({}) used to define a Java block.

derived class—See subclass.

design—(1) The plan for implementing a program, which includes a specification of the classes and objects used and an expression of the important program algorithms. (2) The process of creating a program design.

desk check—A type of review in which a developer carefully examines a design or program to find errors.

detailed design—(1) The low-level algorithmic steps of a method. (2) The development stage at which low-level algorithmic steps are determined.

development stage—The software life-cycle stage in which a software system is first created, preceding use, maintenance, and eventual retirement.

digital—A representation that breaks information down into pieces, which are in turn represented as numbers. All modern computer systems are digital.

digitize—The act of converting an analog representation into a digital one by breaking it down into pieces.

dimension—The number of index levels of a particular array.

direct recursion—The process of a method invoking itself. See also: indirect recursion.

do—A Java reserved word that represents a repetition construct. A do statement is executed one or more times. See also: while, for.

documentation—Supplemental information about a program, including comments in a program's source code and printed reports such as a user's guide.

domain name—The portion of an Internet address that specifies the organization to which the computer belongs.

Domain Name System—Software that translates an Internet address into an IP address using a domain server. Abbreviated DNS.

domain server—A file server that maintains a list of Internet Addresses and their corresponding IP addresses.

double—A Java reserved word that represents a primitive floating point numeric type, stored using 64 bits in IEEE 754 format.

doubly linked list—A linked list with two references in each node: one that refers to the next node in the list and one that refers to the previous node in the list.

dynamic binding—The process of associating an identifier with its definition during run time. See also: binding.

dynamic data structure—A set of objects that are linked using references, which can be modified as needed during program execution.

editor—A software tool that allows the user to enter and store a file of characters on a computer. Often used by programmers to enter the source code of a program.

efficiency—The characteristic of an algorithm that specifies the required number of a particular operation in order to complete its task. For example, the efficiency of a sort can be measured by the number of comparisons required to sort a list. See also: order.

else—A Java reserved word that designates the portion of code in an if statement that will be executed if the condition is false.

encapsulation—The characteristic of an object that limits access to the variables and methods contained in it. All interaction with an object occurs through a well-defined interface that supports a modular design.

equality operator—One of two Java operators that returns a boolean result based on whether two values are equal (==) or not equal (!=).

equivalence category—A range of functionally equivalent input values as specified by the requirements of the software component. Used when developing black-box test cases.

error—(1) Any defect in a design or program. (2) An object that can be thrown and processed by special catch blocks, though usually errors should not be caught. See also: compile-time error, syntax error, logical error, run-time error, exception.

escape sequence—In Java, a sequence of characters beginning with the backslash character (\), used to indicate a special situation when printing values. For example, the escape sequence \t specifies that a horizontal tab should be printed.

exception—(1) A situation that arises during program execution that is erroneous or out of the ordinary. (2) An object that can be thrown and processed by special catch blocks. See also: error.

exponent—The portion of a floating point value's internal representation that specifies how far the decimal point is shifted. See also: mantissa.

expression—A combination of operators and operands that produce a result.

extends—A Java reserved word used to specify the parent class in the definition of a child class.

event—(1) A user action, such as a mouse click or key press. (2) An object that represents a user action, to which the program can respond. See also: event-driven programming.

event-driven programming—An approach to software development in which the program is designed to acknowledge that an event has occurred and act accordingly. See also: event.

false—A Java reserved word that serves as one of the two boolean literals (true and false).

fetch-decode-execute—The cycle through which the CPU continually obtains instructions from main memory and executes them.

FIFO—See first-in, first-out.

file server—A computer in a network, usually with a large secondary storage capacity, which is dedicated to storing software that are needed by many network users.

final—A Java reserved word that serves as a modifier for classes, methods, and variables. A final class cannot be used to derive a new class. A final method cannot be overridden. A final variable is a constant.

finalize—A Java method defined in the Object class that can be overridden in any other class. It is called after the object becomes a candidate for garbage collection and before it is destroyed. It can be used to perform "clean-up" activity that is not performed automatically by the garbage collector.

finalizer method—A Java method, called finalize, that is called before an object is destroyed. See also: finalize.

finally—A Java reserved word that designates a block of code to be executed when an exception is thrown, after any appropriate catch handler is processed.

first-in, first-out—A data management technique in which the first value that is stored in a data structure is the first value that comes out. Abbreviated FIFO. See also: queue, LIFO.

float—A Java reserved word that represents a primitive floating point numeric type, stored using 32 bits in IEEE 754 format.

flushing—The process of forcing the contents of the output buffer to be displayed on the output device.

font—A specification that defines the distinct look of a character when it is printed or drawn.

for—A Java reserved word that represents a repetition construct. A for statement is executed zero or more times, and is usually used when a precise number of iterations are known.

foreground color—The color in which any current drawing will be rendered. See also: background color.

formal parameter—An identifier that serves as a parameter name in a method. It receives its initial value from the actual parameter passed to it. See also: actual parameter.

fourth-generation language—A high-level language that provides built-in functionality beyond that of traditional high-level languages, such as automatic report generation or database management.

function—A named group of declarations and programming statements that can be invoked (executed) when needed. A function that is part of a class is called a method. Java has no functions because all code is part of a class.

future—A Java reserved word that is not currently used.

garbage—(1) An unspecified or uninitialized value in a memory location. (2) An object that cannot be accessed anymore because all references to it have been lost.

garbage collection—The process of reclaiming unneeded dynamically allocated memory. Java performs automatic garbage collection of objects that no longer have any valid references to them.

generic—A Java reserved word that is not currently used.

gigabyte—A unit of binary storage, equal to 2^{30} (approximately 1 billion) bytes. Abbreviated GB.

goto—(1) A Java reserved word that is not currently used. (2) An unconditional branch.

grammar—A representation of language syntax that specifies how reserved words, symbols, and identifiers can be combined into valid programs.

graphical user interface—Software that provides the means to interact with a program or operating system by making use of graphical images and point-and-click mechanisms such as buttons and scroll bars. Abbreviated GUI.

graphics context—The drawing surface and related coordinate system on which a drawing is rendered or GUI components placed.

GUI component—A visual element, such as a button or slide bar, that are used to make up a graphical user interface (GUI).

hardware—The tangible components of a computer system, such as the keyboard, monitor, and circuit boards.

hashing—A technique for storing items so that they can be found efficiently. Items are stored in a hash table at a position specified by a calculated hash code. See also: hash method.

hash code—An integer value calculated from any given data value or object, used to determine where a value should be stored in a hash table. Also called a hash value. See also: hashing.

hash method—A method that calculates a hash code from a data value or object. The same data value or object will always produce the same hash code. Also called a hash function. See also: hashing.

hash table—A data structure in which values are stored for efficient retrieval. See also: hashing.

hexadecimal—The base-16 number system, often used as an abbreviated representation of binary strings.

hierarchy—An organizational technique in which items are layered or grouped to reduce complexity.

high-level language—A programming language in which each statement represents many machine-level instructions.

HTML—See HyperText Markup Language.

hybrid object-oriented language—A programming language that can be used to implement a program in a procedural manner or an object-oriented manner, at the programmer's discretion. See also: pure object-oriented language.

hypermedia—The concept of hypertext extended to include other media types such as graphics, audio, video, and programs.

hypertext—A document representation that allows a user to easily navigate through it in other than a linear fashion. Links to other parts of the document are embedded at the appropriate places to allow the user to jump from one part of the document to another. See also: hypermedia.

HyperText Markup Language—The notation used to define Web pages. Abbreviated HTML. See also: World-Wide Web, browser.

identifier—Any name that a programmer makes up to use in a program, such as a class name or variable name.

identity—The designation of an object, which, in Java, is an object's reference name. See also: state, behavior.

IEEE 754—A standard for representing floating point values. Used by Java to represent `float` and `double` data types.

if—A Java reserved word that specifies a simple conditional construct. See also: else.

immutable—The characteristic of something that does not change. For example, the contents of a Java character string are immutable once it has been defined.

implementation—(1) The process of translating a design into source code. (2) The source code that defines a method, class, abstract data type, or other programming entity.

implements—A Java reserved word that is used in a class declaration to specify that the class implements the methods specified in a particular interface.

import—A Java reserved word that is used to specify the packages and classes that are used in a particular Java source code file.

index—The integer value used to specify a particular element in an array.

index operator—The brackets ([]) in which an array index is specified.

indirect recursion—The process of a method invoking another method, which eventually results in the original method being invoked again. See also: direct recursion.

infinite loop—A loop that does not terminate because the condition controlling the loop never becomes false.

infinite recursion—A recursive series of invocations that does not terminate because the base case is never reached.

infix expression—An expression in which the operators are positioned between the operands on which they work. See also: postfix expression.

inheritance—The ability to derive a new class from an existing one. Inherited variables and methods of the original (parent) class are available in the new (child) class as if they were declared locally.

initialize—To give an initial value to a variable.

initializer list—A comma separated list of values, delimited by braces ({ }), used to initialize and specify the size of an array.

inline documentation—Comments that are included in the source code of a program.

inner—A Java reserved word that is not currently used.

input / output devices—Hardware components that allow the human user to interact with the computer, such as a keyboard, mouse, and monitor.

input / output buffer—A storage location for data on its way from the user to the computer (input buffer) or from the computer to the user (output buffer).

insertion sort—A sorting algorithm in which each value, one at a time, is inserted into a sorted subset of the entire list. See also: selection sort.

inspection—See walkthrough.

instance—An object, created from a class. Multiple objects can be instantiated from a single class.

instanceof—A Java reserved word that is also an operator, used to determine the class or type of a variable.

instance method—A method that must be invoked through a particular instance of a class, as opposed to a class method.

instance variable—A variable that must be referenced through a particular instance of a class, as opposed to a class variable.

instantiation—The act of creating an object from a class.

int—A Java reserved word that represents a primitive integer type, stored using 32 bits in two's complement format.

integration test—The process of testing software components that are made up of other interacting components. Stresses the communication between components rather than the functionality of individual components.

interface—(1) A Java reserved word that is used to define a set of bodiless methods that will be implemented by particular classes. (2) The set of messages to which an object responds, defined by the methods that can be invoked from outside of the object. (3) The techniques through which a human user interacts with a program, often graphically. See also: graphical user interface.

interpreter—A program that translates and executes code on a particular machine. The Java interpreter translates and executes Java bytecode. See also: compiler.

Internet—The most pervasive wide-area network in the world; it has become the primary vehicle for computer-to-computer communication.

Internet address—A designation that uniquely identifies a particular computer or device on the Internet.

Internet Naming Authority—The governing body that approves all Internet addresses.

invocation—See method invocation.

IP address—A series of several integer values, separated by periods (.), that uniquely identifies a particular computer or device on the Internet. Each Internet address has a corresponding IP address.

I/O devices—See input / output devices.

is-a relationship—The relationship created through properly derived classes via inheritance. The subclass *is-a* more specific version of the superclass.

ISO-Latin-1—A 128 character extension to the ASCII character set defined by the

International Standards Organization. The characters correspond to the numeric values 128 through 255 in both ASCII and Unicode.

iteration—(1) One execution of the body of a repetition statement. (2) One pass through a cyclic process, such as an iterative development process.

iteration statement—See repetition statement.

iterative development process—A step-by-step approach for creating software, which contains a series of stages that are performed repetitively.

Java—The programming language used throughout this text to demonstrate software development concepts. Described by its developers as object-oriented, robust, secure, architecture neutral, portable, high-performance, interpreted, threaded, and dynamic.

Java API—See Application Programmer Interface.

Java Development Kit—A collection of software tools available free from Sun Microsystems, the creators of the Java programming language. Abbreviated JDK.

java—The Java command-line interpreter, which translates and executes Java bytecode. Part of the Java Development Kit (JDK).

javac—The Java command-line compiler, which translates Java source code into Java bytecode. Part of the Java Development Kit (JDK).

javadoc—A software tool that creates external documentation in HTML format about the contents and structure of a Java software system. Part of the Java Development Kit (JDK).

javah—A software tool that generates C header and source files, used for imple-menting `native` methods. Part of the Java Development Kit (JDK).

javap—A software tool that disassembles a Java class file, containing unreadable bytecode, into a human-readable version. Part of the Java Development Kit (JDK).

Java Virtual Machine—The underlying software system through which Java bytecode is executed.

jdb—The Java command-line debugger. Part of the Java Development Kit (JDK).

JDK—See Java Development Kit.

JVM—See Java Virtual Machine.

kilobyte—A unit of binary storage, equal to 2^{10}, or 1024 bytes. Abbreviated K or KB.

label—An identifier in Java used to specify a particular line of code. The `break` and `continue` statements can jump to a specific, labeled line in the program.

LAN—See local-area network.

last-in, first-out—A data management technique in which the last value that is stored in a data structure is the first value that comes out. Abbreviated LIFO. See also: stack, FIFO.

layout manager—An object that specifies the presentation of GUI components.

life cycle—The stages through which a software product is developed and used.

LIFO—See last-in, first-out.

linear search—A search algorithm in which each item in the list is compared to the target value until the target is found or the list is exhausted. See also: binary search.

link—(1) A designation in a hypertext document that "jumps" to a new docu-ment (or to a new part of the same docu-ment) when followed. (2) A connection between two items in a dynamically linked structure, represented as an object reference.

linked list—A dynamic data structure in which objects are linked using references.

literal—A primitive value used explicitly in a program, such as the numeric literal 147 or the string literal `"hello"`.

local-area network—A computer network designed to span short distances and connect a relatively small number of computers. Abbreviated LAN. See also: wide-area network.

local variable—A variable defined within a method, which does not exist except during the execution of the method.

logical error—A problem stemming from inappropriate processing in the code. It does not cause an abnormal termination of the program, but produces incorrect results. See also: compile-time error, syntax error, run-time error.

logical line of code—A logical programming statement in a source code program, which may extend over multiple physical lines. See also: physical line of code.

logical operator—One of the operators that perform a logical NOT (!), AND (&&), or OR (|), returning a boolean result. The logical operators are short-circuited, meaning that if their left operand is sufficient to determine the result, the right operand is not evaluated.

long—A Java reserved word that represents a primitive integer type, stored using 64 bits in two's complement format.

loop—See repetition statement.

loop control variable—A variable whose value specifically determines how many times a loop body is executed.

low-level language—Either machine language or assembly language, which are not as convenient to construct software in as high-level languages are.

machine language—The native language of a particular CPU. Any software that runs on a particular CPU must be translated into its machine language.

main memory—The volatile hardware storage device where programs and data are held when they are actively needed by the CPU. See also: secondary memory.

maintenance—(1) The process of fixing errors in or making enhancements to a released software product. (2) The software life cycle phase in which the software is in use and changes are made to it as needed.

mantissa—The portion of a floating point value's internal representation that specifies the magnitude of the number. See also: exponent.

megabyte—A unit of binary storage, equal to 2^{20} (approximately 1 million) bytes. Abbreviated MB.

member—A variable or method in an object or class.

memory—Hardware devices that store programs and data. See also: main memory, secondary memory.

memory location—An individual, addressable cell inside main memory into which data can be stored.

memory management—The process of controlling dynamically allocated portions of main memory, especially the act of returning allocated memory when it is no longer required. See also: garbage collection.

method—A named group of declarations and programming statements that can be invoked (executed) when needed. A method is part of a class.

method definition—The specification of the code that gets executed when the method is invoked. The definition includes declarations of local variables and formal parameters.

method invocation—A line of code that causes a method to be executed. It specifies any values that are passed to the method as parameters.

method call conversion—The automatic widening conversion that can occur when a value of one type is passed to a formal parameter of another type.

method overloading—See overloading.

mnemonic—A word or identifier that specifies a command or data value in an assembly language.

modal—Having multiple modes (such as a dialog box).

modem—A data transfer device that allows information to be sent along a telephone line.

modifier—A designation used in a Java declaration that specifies particular characteristics to the construct being declared.

monitor—The screen in the computer system that serves as an output device.

multidimensional array—An array that uses more than one index to specify a value stored in it.

multiple inheritance—Deriving a class from more than one parent, inheriting methods and variables from each. Not supported in Java.

NaN—An abbreviation that stands for "not a number," which is the designation for an inappropriate or undefined numeric value.

narrowing conversion—A conversion between two values of different but compatible data types. Narrowing conversions could lose information because the converted type usually has an internal representation smaller than the original storage space. See also: widening conversion.

native—A Java reserved word that serves as a modifier for methods. A native method is implemented in another programming language.

natural language—A language that humans use to communicate, such as English or French.

negative infinity—A special floating point value that represents the "lowest possible" value. See also: positive infinity.

nested if statement—An if statement that has as its body another if statement.

Netscape Navigator—A popular World-Wide Web browser.

network—Two or more computers connected together so that they can exchange data and share resources.

network address—See address.

new—A Java reserved word that is also an operator, used to instantiate an object from a class.

newline character—A nonprintable character that indicates the end of a line.

nonprintable characters—Any character, such as escape or newline, that does not have a symbolic representation that can be displayed on a monitor or printed by a printer. See also: printable characters.

nonvolatile—The characteristic of a memory device that retains its stored information even after the power supply is turned off. Secondary memory devices are nonvolatile. See also: volatile.

null—A Java reserved word that is a reference literal, used to indicate that a reference does not currently refer to any object.

number system—A set of values and operations defined by a particular base value that determines the number of digits available and the place value of each digit.

object—(1) The primary software construct in the object-oriented paradigm. (2) An encapsulated collection of data variables and methods. (3) An instance of a class.

object-oriented programming—An approach to software design and implementation that is centered around objects and classes. See also: procedural programming.

octal—The base-8 number system, sometimes used to abbreviate binary strings. See also: hexadecimal.

off-by-one error—An error caused by a calculation or condition being off by one, such as when a loop is set up to access one too many array elements.

operand—A value on which an operator performs its function. For example, in the expression 5 + 2, the values 5 and 2 are operands.

operating system—The collection of programs that provide the primary user interface to a computer and manage its resources, such as memory and the CPU.

operator—(1) A Java reserved word that is not currently used. (2) A symbol that represents a particular operation in a programming language, such as the addition operator (+).

operator association—The order in which operators within the same precedence level are evaluated, either right to left or left to right. See also: operator precedence.

operator overloading—Assigning additional meaning to an operator. Operator overloading is not supported in Java, though method overloading is.

operator precedence—The order in which operators are evaluated in an expression as specified by a well-defined hierarchy.

order—The dominant term in an equation that specifies the efficiency of an algorithm. For example: selection sort is of order n^2.

outer—A Java reserved word that is not currently used.

overflow—A problem that occurs when a data value grows too large for its storage size, which can result in inaccurate arithmetic processing. See also: underflow.

overloading—Assigning additional meaning to a programming language construct, such as a method or operator. Method overloading is supported by Java, but operator overloading is not.

overriding—The process of modifying the definition of an inherited method to suit the purposes of the subclass. See also: shadowing variables.

package—A Java reserved word that is used to specify a group of related classes.

package visibility—See default visibility.

parameter—(1) A value passed from a method invocation to its definition. (2) The identifier in a method definition that accepts the value passed to it when the method is invoked. See also: actual parameter, formal parameter.

parameter list—The list of actual or formal parameters to a method.

parent class—See superclass.

pass by reference—The process of passing a reference to a value into a method as the parameter. In Java, all objects are managed using references, so an object's formal parameter is an alias to the original. See also: pass by value.

pass by value—The process of making a copy of a value and passing the copy into a method. Therefore, any change made to the value inside the method is not reflected in the original value. All Java primitive types are passed by value.

peripheral—Any hardware device other than the CPU or main memory.

persistence—The ability of an object to stay in existence after the executing program that creates it terminates. Java currently has no built-in mechanisms to support object persistence.

physical line of code—A line in a source code file, terminated by a newline or similar character. See also: logical line of code.

pixel—A picture element. A digitized picture is made up of many pixels.

place value—The value of each digit position in a number, which determines the overall contribution of that digit to the value. See also: number system.

pointer—A variable that can hold a memory address. Instead of pointers, Java uses references, which provide essentially the same functionality as pointers but without the complications.

point-to-point connection—The link between two networked devices that are connected directly by a wire.

polymorphism—An object-oriented technique by which a reference that is used to invoke a method can result in different methods being invoked at different times. A Java reference can point to any type of object in its inheritance ancestry, and all Java method invocations are polymorphic in that they invoke the method of the object type, not the reference type.

portability—The ability of a program to be moved from one hardware platform to another without having to change it. Because Java bytecode is not related to any particular hardware environment, Java programs are considered portable. See also: architecture neutral.

positive infinity—A special floating point value that represents the "highest possible" value. See also: negative infinity.

postfix expression—An expression in which an operator is positioned after the operands on which it works. See also: infix expression.

postfix operator—In Java, an operator that is positioned behind its single operand, whose evaluation yields the value prior to the operation being performed. Both the increment (++) and decrement (--) operators can be applied postfix. See also: prefix operator.

precedence—See operator precedence.

prefix operator—In Java, an operator that is positioned in front of its single operand, whose evaluation yields the value after the operation has been performed. Both the increment (++) and decrement (--) operators can be applied prefix. See also: postfix operator.

primitive data type—A data type that is predefined in a programming language.

printable characters—Any character that has a symbolic representation that can be displayed on a monitor or printed by a printer. See also: nonprintable characters.

private—A Java reserved word that serves as a visibility modifier for methods and variables. Private methods and variables are not inherited by subclasses, and can only be accessed in the class in which they are declared.

procedural programming—An approach to software design and implementation that is centered around procedures (or functions) and their interaction. See also: object-oriented programming.

program—A series of instructions executed by hardware, one after another.

Program Design Language—A language in which a program's design and algorithms are expressed. Abbreviated PDL. See also: pseudocode.

programming language—A specification of the syntax and semantics of the statements used to create a program.

programming language statement—An individual instruction in a given programming language.

prompt—A message or symbol used to request information from the user.

protected—A Java reserved word that serves as a visibility modifier for methods and variables. Protected methods and variables are inherited by all subclasses and are accessible from all classes in the same package.

prototype—A program used to explore an idea or prove the feasibility of a particular approach.

pseudocode—Structured and abbreviated natural language used to express the algorithmic steps of a program. See also: Program Design Language.

pseudo–random number—A value generated by software that performs extensive calculations based on an initial seed value. The result is not truly random, because it is based on a calculation, but it is usually random enough for most purposes.

public—A Java reserved word that serves as a visibility modifier for classes, interfaces, methods, and variables. A public class or interface can be used anywhere. A public method or variable is inherited by all subclasses, and is accessible anywhere.

pure object-oriented language—A programming language that enforces, to some degree, software development using an object-oriented approach. See also: hybrid object-oriented language.

queue—An abstract data type that manages information in a first-in, first-out manner.

RAM—See random access memory.

random access device—A memory device whose information can be directly accessed. See also: random access memory, sequential access device.

random access memory—A term basically interchangeable with main memory. Should probably be called read-write memory, to distinguish it from read-only memory. Abbreviated RAM.

random number generator—Software which produces a pseudo–random number, generated by calculations based on a seed value.

read-only memory—Any memory device whose stored information is stored permanently when the device is created. It can be read from, but not written to. Abbreviated ROM.

recursion—The process of a method invoking itself, either directly or indirectly.

reference—A variable that holds the address of an object. In Java, a reference can be used to interact with an object, but its address cannot be accessed, set, or operated on directly.

refinement—One iteration of a cyclic development cycle in which a particular aspect of the system, such as the user interface or a particular algorithm, is addressed.

relational operator—One of several operators that determine the ordering relationship between two values: less than (<), less than or equal to (<=), greater than (>), and greater than or equal to (>=). See also: equality operator.

release—A version of a software product that is made available to the customer.

register—A small area of storage in the central processing unit (CPU) of the computer.

repetition statement—A programming construct that allows a set of statements to be executed repetitively as long as a particular condition is true. The body of the repetition statement should eventually make the condition false. Also called an iteration statement or loop. See also: while, do, for.

requirements—(1) The specification of what a program must and must not do. (2) An early phase of the software development process in which the program requirements are established.

reserved word—A word that has special meaning in a programming language, and cannot be used for any other purpose.

rest—A Java reserved word that is not currently used.

retirement—The phase of a program's life cycle in which the program is taken out of active use.

return—A Java reserved word that causes the flow of program execution to return from a method to the point of invocation.

return type—The type of value returned from a method, specified before the method name in the method declaration. Could be void, which indicates that no value is returned.

reuse—Using existing software components to create new ones.

review—The process of critically examining a design or program to discover errors. There are many types of reviews. See also: desk check, walkthrough.

RGB value—A collection of three values that define a color. Each value represents the contribution of the primary colors red, green, and blue.

ROM—See read-only memory.

run-time error—A problem that occurs during program execution that causes the program to terminate abnormally. See also: compile-time error, syntax error, logical error.

scope—See access.

searching—The process of determining the location of a target value within a list of values. See also: linear search, binary search.

secondary memory—Hardware storage devices, such as magnetic disks or tapes, which store information in a relatively permanent manner. See also: main memory.

seed value—A value used by a random number generator as a base for the calculations that produce a pseudo-random number.

selection sort—A sorting algorithm in which each value, one at a time, is placed in its final, sorted position. See also: insertion sort.

selection statement—A programming construct that allows a set of statements to be executed if a particular condition is true. See also: if, switch.

semantics—The interpretation of a program or programming construct.

sentinel value—A specific value used to indicate a special condition, such as the end of input.

service methods—Methods in an object that are declared with public visibility and define a service that the object's client can invoke.

shadowing variables—The process of defining a variable in a subclass that supersedes an inherited version.

short—A Java reserved word that represents a primitive integer type, stored using 16 bits in two's complement format.

sibling—Two items in a tree or hierarchy, such as a class inheritance hierarchy, that have the same parent.

sign bit—A bit in a numeric value that represents the sign (positive or negative) of that value.

signed numeric value—A value that stores a sign (positive or negative). All Java numeric values are signed. A Java character is stored as an unsigned value.

signature—The number, types, and order of the parameters of a method. Overloaded methods must each have a unique signature.

software—Programs and data. The intangible components of a computer system.

software component—See component.

software engineering—The discipline within computer science that addresses the process of developing high-quality software within practical constraints.

sorting—The process of putting a list of values into a well-defined order. See also: selection sort, insertion sort.

stack—A abstract data type that manages data in a last-in, first-out manner.

start angle—When defining an arc, the angle at which the arc begins. See also: arc angle.

state—The state of being of an object, defined by the values of its data. See also: behavior, identity.

statement—See programming language statement.

statement coverage—A strategy used in white-box testing in which all statements in a program are executed. See also: condition coverage.

static—A Java reserved word that serves as a modifier for methods and variables. A static method is also called a class method, and can be referenced without an instance of the class. A static variable is also called a class variable and is common to all instances of the class.

static data structure—A data structure that has a fixed size and cannot grow and shrink as needed. See also: dynamic data structure.

storage capacity—The total number of bytes that can be stored in a particular memory device.

stream—A source of input or a destination for output.

string—See character string.

string concatenation—The process of attaching the beginning of one character string to the end of another, resulting in one longer string.

strongly typed language—A programming language in which each variable is associated with a particular data type for the duration of its existence. Variables are not allowed to take on values or be used in operations that are inconsistent with their type.

structured programming—An approach to program development in which each software component has one entry and exit point and in which the flow of control does not cross unnecessarily.

stub—A method that simulates the functionality of a particular software component. Often used during unit testing.

subclass—A class derived from another class via inheritance. Also called a derived class or child class. See also: superclass.

subscript—See index.

super—A Java reserved word that is a reference to the parent class of the object making the reference. Often used to invoke a parent's constructor.

superclass—The class from which another class is derived via inheritance. Also called a base class or parent class. See also: subclass.

super reference—See super.

support methods—Methods in an object that are not intended for use outside the class. They provide support functionality for service methods. As such, they are usually not declared with public visibility.

swapping—The process of exchanging the values of two variables.

switch—A Java reserved word that specifies a compound conditional construct.

synchronization—The process of ensuring that data shared among multiple threads cannot be accessed by more than one thread at a time. See also: synchronized.

synchronized—A Java reserved word that serves as a modifier for methods. Separate threads of a process can execute concurrently in a method, unless the method is synchronized, making it a mutually exclusive resource. Methods that access shared data should be synchronized.

syntax rules—The set of specifications that govern how the elements of a programming language can be put together to form valid statements.

syntax error—An error produced by the compiler because a program did not conform to the syntax of the programming language. Syntax errors are a subset of compile-time errors. See also: syntax

rules, compile-time error, logical error, run-time error.

target value—The value that is sought when performing a search on a collection of data.

TCP/IP—The Transmission Control Protocol / Internet Protocol. Software that controls the movement of messages across the Internet.

terabyte—A unit of binary storage, equal to 2^{40} (approximately 1 trillion) bytes. Abbreviated TB.

termination—The point at which a program stops executing.

ternary operator—An operator that uses three operands.

test case—A set of input values and user actions, along with a specification of the expected output, used to find errors in a system.

testing—(1) The process of running a program with various test cases in order to discover problems. (2) The process of critically evaluating a design or program.

this—A Java reserved word that is a reference to the object executing the code making the reference. A reference to the current object is implicitly passed to all methods.

thread—An independent process executing within a program. A Java program can have multiple threads running in a program at one time.

throw—A Java reserved word that is used to start an exception propagation.

throws—A Java reserved word that specifies that a method may throw a particular type of exception.

token—A portion of a string defined by a set of delimiters.

transient—A Java reserved word that is not currently used. May be used in the future as a modifier of variables to indicate that they do not contribute to the object's persistent state, and therefore do not need to be saved.

true—A Java reserved word that serves as one of the two boolean literals (`true` and `false`).

truth table—A complete enumeration of all permutations of values involved in a boolean expression, and the computed result.

try—A Java reserved word that is used to define the context in which certain exceptions will be handled if they are thrown.

two's complement—A technique for representing numeric binary data. Used by all Java integer primitive types (`byte`, `short`, `int`, `long`).

type—See data type.

unary operator—An operator that uses only one operand.

unchecked exception—A Java exception that does not need to be caught or dealt with if the programmer so chooses.

underflow—A problem that occurs when a floating point value becomes too small for its storage size, which can result in inaccurate arithmetic processing. See also: overflow.

Unicode—The international character set used to define valid Java characters. Each character is represented using a 16-bit unsigned numeric value.

Uniform Resource Locator—A designation for a resource that can be located through a World-Wide Web browser. Abbreviated URL.

unit test—The process of testing an individual software component. May require the creation of stub modules to simulate other system components.

URL—See Uniform Resource Locator.

unsigned numeric value—A value that does not store a sign (positive or negative). The bit usually reserved to represent the sign is included in the value, doubling the magnitude of the number that can be stored. Java characters are stored as unsigned numeric values, but there are no primitive numeric types that are unsigned.

use relationship—A relationship between two classes, often shown in a class diagram, that establishes that one class uses another in some way, such as relying on its services.

user interface—The manner in which the user interacts with a software system, which is often graphical. See also: graphical user interface.

var—A Java reserved word that is not currently used.

variable—An identifier in a program that represents a memory location in which a data value is stored.

visibility modifier—A Java modifier that defines the scope in which a construct can be accessed. The Java visibility modifiers are public, protected, private, and default (no modifier used).

void—A Java reserved word that can be used as a return value for a method, indicating that no value is returned.

volatile—(1) A Java reserved word that serves as a modifier for variables. A volatile variable might be changed asynchronously and therefore indicates that the compiler should not attempt optimizations on it. (2) The characteristic of a memory device that loses stored information when the power supply is interrupted. Main memory is a volatile storage device. See also: nonvolatile.

von Neumann architecture—The computer architecture named after John von Neumann, in which programs and data are stored together in the same memory devices.

walkthrough—A form of review in which a group of developers, managers, and quality assurance personnel examine a design or program in order to find errors. Sometimes referred to as an inspection. See also: desk check.

WAN—See wide-area network.

waterfall model—One of the earliest software development process models. It defines a basically linear interaction between the requirements, design, implementation, and testing stages.

Web—See World-Wide Web.

while—A Java reserved word that represents a repetition construct. A while statement is executed zero or more times. See also: do, for.

white-box testing—Producing and evaluating test cases based on the interior logic of a software component. The test cases focus on stressing decision points and ensuring coverage. See also: condition coverage, statement coverage, black-box testing.

white space—Spaces, tabs, and blank lines that are used to set off sections of source code to make programs more readable.

wide-area network—A computer network that connects two or more LANs, usually across long geographic distances.

Abbreviated WAN. See also: local-area network.

widening conversion—A conversion between two values of different but compatible data types. Widening conversions usually maintain the data value intact because the converted type has an internal representation equal to or larger than the original storage space. See also: narrowing conversion.

word—A unit of binary storage. The size of a word varies by computer, usually two, four, or eight bytes. The word size indicates the amount of information that can be moved through the machine at one time.

World-Wide Web—Software that makes the exchange of information across a network easier by providing a common user interface for multiple types of information. Web browsers are used to retrieve and format HTML documents. Abbreviated WWW or Web.

wrapper class—A class designed to store a primitive type in an object. Usually used when an object reference is needed and a primitive type would not suffice.

WWW—See World-Wide Web.

XOR mode—A Java graphics mode that defines a reversible operation between colors. It can be used to make overlapping shapes distinct and to erase shapes by redrawing them in the same position.

Number Systems

This appendix contains a detailed introduction to number systems and their underlying characteristics. The particular focus is on the binary number system, its use with computers, and its similarities to other number systems. This introduction also covers conversions between bases.

In our everyday lives, we use the *decimal number system* to represent values, count, and perform arithmetic. The decimal system is also referred to as the *base-10* number system. We use 10 digits (0 through 9) to represent values in the decimal system.

Computers use the *binary number system* to store and manage information. The binary system, also called the *base-2* number system, only has two digits (0 and 1). Each 0 and 1 is called a *bit*, short for binary digit. A series of bits is called a *binary string*.

There is nothing particularly special about either the binary or decimal systems. Long ago, humans adopted the decimal number system probably because we have 10 fingers on our hands. If humans had 12 fingers, we would probably be using a base-12 number system regularly and find it as easy to deal with as we do the decimal system now. It all depends on what you get used to. As you explore the binary system, it will become more familiar and natural.

Binary is used for computer processing because the devices used to manage and store information are less expensive and more reliable if they only have to represent two possible values. Computers have been made that use the decimal system; they just are not as convenient.

There are an infinite number of number systems, and they all follow the same basic rules. You already know how the binary number system works, but you just might not be aware that you do. It all goes back to the basic rules of arithmetic.

Place Value

In decimal, we represent the values of 0 through 9 using only one digit. To represent any value higher than 9, we must use more than one digit. The position of each digit has a *place value* that indicates the amount it contributes to the overall value. In decimal, we refer to the one's column, the ten's column, the hundred's column, and so on forever.

Each place value is determined by the *base* of the number system, raised to increasing powers as we move from right to left. In the decimal number system, the place value of the digit furthest to the right is 10^0, or 1. The place value of the next digit is 10^1, or 10. The place value of the third digit from the right is 10^2, or 100. And so on. Figure B.1 shows how each digit in a decimal number contributes to the value.

The binary system works the same way, except that we exhaust the available digits much sooner. We can represent 0 and 1 with a single bit, but to represent any value higher than one, we must use multiple bits.

The place values in binary are determined by increasing powers of the base as we move right to left, just as they are in the decimal system. But in binary, the base value is 2. Therefore the place value of the bit furthest to the right is 2^0, or 1. The place value of the next bit is 2^1, or 2. The place value of the third bit from the right is 2^2, or 4, and so on. Figure B.2 shows a binary number and its place values.

The number 1101 is a valid binary number, but it is also a valid decimal number as well. Sometimes to make it clear which number system is being used, the base value is appended as a subscript to the end of a number. Therefore you can distinguish between 1101_2, which is equivalent to 13 in decimal, and 1101_{10} (one thousand, one hundred and one), which in binary is represented as 10001001101_2.

A number system with base N has N digits (0 through $N - 1$). As we have seen, the decimal system has 10 digits (0 through 9), and the binary system has two digits (0 and 1). They all work the same way. For instance, the base-5 number system has five digits (0 to 4).

Note that, in any number system, the place value of the digit furthest to the right is 1, since any base raised to the zero power is 1. Also notice that the value 10, which we refer to as "ten" in the decimal system, always represents the base value in

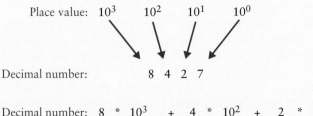

Figure B.1 Place values in the decimal system

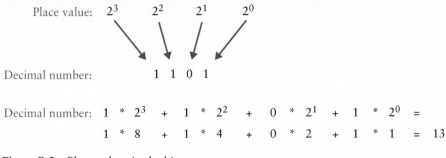

$$1 * 2^3 + 1 * 2^2 + 0 * 2^1 + 1 * 2^0 =$$
$$1 * 8 + 1 * 4 + 0 * 2 + 1 * 1 = 13$$

Figure B.2 Place values in the binary system

any number system. In base 10, 10 is one ten and zero ones. In base 2, 10 is one two and zero ones. In base 5, 10 is one five and zero ones.

Bases Higher than 10

Since all number systems with base N have N digits, then base 16 has 16 digits. But what are they? We are used to the digits 0 through 9, but in bases higher than 10, we need a single digit, a single symbol, that represents the decimal value 10. In fact, in *base 16,* which is also called *hexadecimal,* we need digits that represent the decimal values 10 through 15.

For number systems higher than 10, we use alphabetic characters as single digits for values greater than 9. The hexadecimal digits are 0 through F, where 0 through 9 represent the first 10 digits, and A represents the decimal value 10, B represents 11, C represents 12, D represents 13, E represents 14, and F represents 15.

Therefore the number 2A8E is a valid hexadecimal number. The place values are determined as they are for decimal and binary, using increasing powers of the base. So in hexadecimal, the place values are powers of 16. Figure B.3 shows how the place values of the hexadecimal number 2A8E contribute to the overall value.

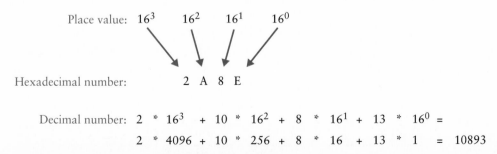

$$2 * 16^3 + 10 * 16^2 + 8 * 16^1 + 13 * 16^0 =$$
$$2 * 4096 + 10 * 256 + 8 * 16 + 13 * 1 = 10893$$

Figure B.3 Place values in the hexadecimal system

All number systems with bases greater than 10 use letters as digits. For example, base 12 has the digits 0 through B and base 19 has the digits 0 through I. But beyond having a different set of digits and a different base, the rules governing each number system are the same.

Keep in mind that when we change number systems, we are simply changing the way we represent values, not the values themselves. If you have 18_{10} pencils, it may be written as 10010 in binary or as 12 in hexadecimal, but it is still the same number of pencils.

Figure B.4 shows the representations of the decimal values 0 through 20 in several bases, including *base 8*, which is also called *octal*. Note that the larger the base, the higher the value that can be represented in a single digit.

Binary (base 2)	Octal (base 8)	Decimal (base 10)	Hexadecimal (base 16)
0	0	0	0
1	1	1	1
10	2	2	2
11	3	3	3
100	4	4	4
101	5	5	5
110	6	6	6
111	7	7	7
1000	10	8	8
1001	11	9	9
1010	12	10	A
1011	13	11	B
1100	14	12	C
1101	15	13	D
1110	16	14	E
1111	17	15	F
10000	20	16	10
10001	21	17	11
10010	22	18	12
10011	23	19	13
10100	24	20	14

Figure B.4   Counting in various number systems

Conversions

We've already seen how a number in another base is converted to decimal by determining the place value of each digit and computing the result. This process can be used to convert any number in any base to its equivalent value in base 10.

Now let's reverse the process, converting a base-10 value to another base. First, find the highest place value in the new number system that is less than or equal to the original value. Then divide the original number by that place value to determine the digit that belongs in that position. The remainder is the value that must be represented in the remaining digit positions. Continue this process, position by position, until the entire value is represented.

For example, the process of converting the decimal value 180 into binary is shown in Fig. B.5. The highest place value in binary that is less than or equal to 180 is 128 (or 2^7), which is the eighth bit position from the right. Dividing 180 by 128 yields 1 with 52 remaining. Therefore, the first bit is 1, and the decimal value 52 must be represented in the remaining seven bits. Dividing 52 by 64, which is the next place value (2^6), yields 0 with 52 remaining. So the second bit is 0. Dividing 52 by 32 yields 1 with 20 remaining. So the third bit is 1 and the remaining five bits must represent the value 20. Dividing 20 by 16 yields 1 with 4 remaining. Dividing 4 by 8 yields 0 with 4 remaining. Dividing 4 by 4 yields 0 with 0 remaining.

Since the number has been completely represented, the rest of the bits are zero. Therefore, 180_{10} is equivalent to 10110100 in binary. This can be confirmed by converting the new binary number back to decimal to make sure we get the original value.

This process works to convert any decimal value to any target base. For each target base, the place values and possible digits change. If you start with the correct place value, each division operation will yield a valid digit in the new base.

Place value	Number	Digit
128	180	1
64	52	0
32	52	1
16	20	1
8	4	0
4	4	1
2	0	0
1	0	0

$$180_{10} = 10110100_2$$

Figure B.5   Converting a decimal value into binary

Place value	Number	Digit	
256	1967	7	
16	175	A	$1967_{10} = 7AF_{16}$
1	15	F	

Figure B.6   Converting a decimal value into hexadecimal

In the example in Fig. B.5, the only digits that could have resulted from each division operation would have been 1 or 0, since we were converting to binary. However, when we are converting to other bases, any valid digit in the new base could result. For example, Fig. B.6 shows the process of converting the decimal value 1967 into hexadecimal.

The place value of 256, which is 16^2, is the highest place value less than or equal to the original number, since the next highest place value is 16^3 or 4096. Dividing 1976 by 256 yields 7 with 175 remaining. Dividing 175 by 16 yields 10 with 15 remaining. Remember that 10 in decimal can be represented as the single digit A in hexadecimal. The 15 remaining can be represented as the digit F. Therefore 1967_{10} is equivalent to 7AF in hexadecimal.

Shortcut Conversions

We have established techniques for converting any value in any base to its equivalent representation in base 10, and from base 10 to any other base. Therefore, you can now convert a number in any base to any other base by going through base 10. However, an interesting relationship exists between the bases that are powers of 2, such as binary, octal, and hexadecimal, that allows very quick conversions between them.

To convert from binary to hexadecimal, for instance, you can simply group the bits of the original value into groups of four, starting from the right, then convert each group of four into a single hexadecimal digit. The example in Fig. B.7 demonstrates this process.

To go from hexadecimal to binary, we reverse this process, and expand each hexadecimal digit into four binary digits. Note that you may have to add leading zeros to the binary version of each expanded hexadecimal digit if necessary to make four binary digits. Figure B.8 shows the conversion of the hexadecimal value 40C6 to binary.

Why do we section the bits into groups of four when converting from binary to hexadecimal? The shortcut conversions work between binary and any base that is a power of 2. We section the bits into groups of that power. Since $2^4 = 16$, we section the bits in groups of four.

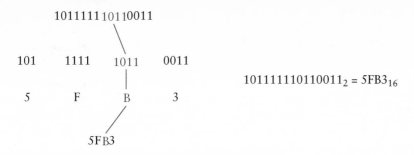

$$101111110110011_2 = 5FB3_{16}$$

Figure B.7 Shortcut conversion from binary to hexadecimal

Converting from binary to octal is the same process, except that the bits are sectioned into groups of three, since $2^3 = 8$. Likewise, when converting from octal to binary we expand each octal digit into three bits.

To convert between, say, hexadecimal and octal is now a process of doing two shortcut conversions. First convert from hexadecimal to binary, then take that result and perform a shortcut conversion from binary to octal.

By the way, these types of shortcut conversions can be performed between any base B and any base that is a power of B. For example, conversions between base 3 and base 9 can be accomplished using the shortcut grouping technique, sectioning or expanding digits into groups of two, since $3^2 = 9$.

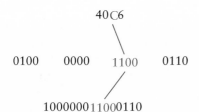

$$40C6_{16} = 100000011000110_2$$

Figure B.8 Shortcut conversion from hexadecimal to binary

Appendix C

The Unicode Character Set

The Java programming language uses the Unicode character set for managing text. A character set is simply an ordered list of characters, each corresponding to a particular numeric value. Unicode is an international character set that contains letters, symbols, and ideograms for languages all over the world. Each character is represented as a 16-bit unsigned numeric value. Unicode, therefore, can support over 65 thousand unique characters. Only about half of those values have characters assigned to them at this point. The Unicode character set continues to be refined as characters from various languages are included.

Many programming languages still use the ASCII character set. ASCII stands for the American Standard Code for Information Interchange. The 8-bit ASCII set is quite small, so the developers of Java opted to use Unicode in order to support international users. However, ASCII is essentially a subset of Unicode, including corresponding numeric values, so programmers used to ASCII should have no problems with Unicode.

Figure C.1 shows a list of commonly used characters and their Unicode numeric values. These characters also happen to be ASCII characters.

All of the characters in Fig. C.1 are called *printable characters,* since they have a symbolic representation that can be displayed on a monitor or printed by a printer. Other characters are called *nonprintable characters* because they have no such symbolic representation. Note that the space character (numeric value 32) is considered to be a printable character, even though no symbol is printed when it is displayed. Nonprintable characters are sometimes called *control characters,* since many of them can be generated by holding down the control key on a keyboard and pressing another key.

The Unicode characters with numeric values 0 through 31 are nonprintable characters. Also, the delete character, with numeric value 127, is a nonprintable

Value	Char	Value	Char	Value	Char	Value	Char	Value	Char
32	*space*	51	3	70	F	89	Y	108	l
33	!	52	4	71	G	90	Z	109	m
34	"	53	5	72	H	91	[	110	n
35	#	54	6	73	I	92	\	111	o
36	$	55	7	74	J	93	]	112	p
37	%	56	8	75	K	94	^	113	q
38	&	57	9	76	L	95	–	114	r
39	'	58	:	77	M	96	`	115	s
40	(	59	;	78	N	97	a	116	t
41	)	60	<	79	O	98	b	117	u
42	*	61	+	80	P	99	c	118	v
43	+	62	>	81	Q	100	d	119	w
44	'	63	?	82	R	101	e	120	x
45	–	64	@	83	S	102	f	121	y
46	.	65	A	84	T	103	g	122	z
47	/	66	B	85	U	104	h	123	{
48	0	67	C	86	V	105	i	124	|
49	1	68	D	87	W	106	j	125	]
50	2	69	E	88	X	107	k	126	~

Figure C.1   A small portion of the Unicode character set

character. All of these characters are also ASCII characters as well. Many of them have fairly common and well-defined uses, while others are more general. The table in Fig. C.2 lists a small sample of the nonprintable characters.

Nonprintable characters are used in many situations to represent special conditions. For example, certain nonprintable characters can be stored in a text document to indicate, among other things, the beginning of a new line. An editor will process these characters by starting the text which follows it on a new line, instead of printing a symbol to the screen. Various types of computer systems use different nonprintable characters to represent particular conditions.

Except for having no visible representation, nonprintable characters are essentially equivalent to printable characters. They can be stored in a Java character variable and be part of a character string. They are stored using 16 bits, can be converted to their numeric value, and can be compared using relational operators.

Value	Character
0	*null*
7	*bell*
8	*backspace*
9	*tab*
10	*line feed*
12	*form feed*
13	*carriage return*
27	*escape*
127	*delete*

Figure C.2   Some nonprintable characters in the Unicode character set

The first 128 characters of the Unicode character set correspond to the common ASCII character set. The second 128 characters correspond to the ISO-Latin-1 extended ASCII character set. Many operating systems and Web browsers will handle these characters, but may not be able to print the other Unicode characters.

Java Operators

Java operators are evaluated according to the precedence hierarchy shown in Fig. D.1. Operators at low precedence levels are evaluated before operators at higher levels. Operators within the same precedence level are evaluated according to the specified association, either right to left (R to L) or left to right (L to R). Operators in the same precedence level are not listed in any particular order.

The order of operator evaluation can always be forced by the use of parentheses. It is often a good idea to use parentheses even when they are not required to make it explicitly clear how an expression is evaluated.

Precedence Level	Operator	Operation	Associates
1	[ ] . (parameters) ++ −−	array indexing object member reference parameter evaluation and method invocation postfix increment postfix decrement	L to R
2	++ −− + − ~ !	prefix increment prefix decrement unary plus unary minus bitwise NOT logical NOT	R to L
3	new (type)	object instantiation cast	R to L

Figure D.1   Java operator precedence

Precedence Level	Operator	Operation	Associates
4	* / %	multiplication division remainder	L to R
5	+ + −	addition string concatenation subtraction	L to R
6	<< >> >>>	left shift right shift with sign right shift with zero	
7	< <= > >= instanceof	less than less than or equal greater than greater than or equal type comparison	L to R
8	== !=	equal not equal	L to R
9	& &	bitwise AND boolean AND	L to R
10	^ ^	bitwise XOR boolean XOR	L to R
11	| |	bitwise OR boolean OR	L to R
12	&&	logical AND	L to R
13	||	logical OR	L to R
14	?:	conditional operator	R to L
15	= += += −= *= /= %= <<= >>= >>>= &= &= ^= ^= |= |=	assignment addition, then assignment string concatenation, then assignment subtraction, then assignment multiplication, then assignment division, then assignment remainder, then assignment left shift, then assignment right shift (sign), then assignment right shift (zero), then assignment bitwise AND, then assignment boolean AND, then assignment bitwise XOR, then assignment boolean XOR, then assignment bitwise OR, then assignment boolean OR, then assignment	R to L

Figure D.1 *(continued)*

For some operators, the operand types determine which operation is carried out. For instance, if the + operator is used on two strings, string concatenation is performed, but if it is applied to two numeric types, they are added in the arithmetic sense. If only one of the operands is a string, the other is converted to a string, and string concatenation is performed. Similarly, the operators &, ^, and | perform bitwise operations on numeric operands, but boolean operations on boolean operands. Appendix E describes the bitwise and boolean operators in more detail.

The boolean operators & and | differ from the logical operators && and || in a subtle way. The logical operators are "short-circuited" in that if the result of an expression can be determined by evaluating only the left operand, then the right operand is not evaluated. The boolean versions always evaluate both sides of the expression. There is no logical operator that performs an exclusive OR (XOR) operation.

Appendix E

Java Bitwise Operators

This appendix contains a discussion of the Java *bitwise operators,* which operate on individual bits within a primitive value. They are only defined for integers and characters. They are unique among all Java operators because they let us work at the lowest level of binary storage. Figure E.1 lists the Java bitwise operators.

Three of the bitwise operators are similar to the logical operators !, &&, and ||. The bitwise NOT, AND, and OR operations work basically the same way as their logical counterparts, except they work on individual bits of a value. The rules are essentially the same. Figure E.2 shows the results of bitwise operators on all combinations of two bits. Compare this chart to the truth tables for the logical operators in Chapter 5 to see the similarities.

Operator	Description
~	bitwise NOT
&	bitwise AND
|	bitwise OR
^	bitwise XOR
<<	left shift
>>	right shift with sign
>>>	right shift with zero fill

Figure E.1 Java bitwise operators

a	b	~ a	a & b	a | b	a ^ b
0	0	1	0	0	0
0	1	1	0	1	1
1	0	0	0	1	1
1	1	0	1	1	0

Figure E.2 Bitwise operators on individual bits

The bitwise operators include the XOR operator, which stands for *exclusive OR*. The logical || operator is an *inclusive OR* operation, which means it returns true if both operands are true. The | bitwise operator is also inclusive, and yields a 1 if both corresponding bits are 1. However, the exclusive OR operator (^)yields a 0 if both operands are 1. There is no logical exclusive OR operator in Java.

When the bitwise operators are applied to integer values, the operation is performed individually on each bit in the value. For example, suppose the integer variable number is declared to be of type byte and currently holds the value 45. Stored as an 8-bit byte, it is represented in binary as 00101101. When the bitwise complement operator (~) is applied to number, each bit in the value is inverted, yielding 11010010. Since integers are stored using two's complement representation, the value represented is now negative, specifically −46.

Similarly, for all bitwise operators, the operations are applied bit-by-bit, which is where the term bitwise comes from. For binary operators (with two operands), the operations are applied to corresponding bits in each operand. For example, assume num1 and num2 are byte integers, and num1 holds the value 45, and num2 holds the value 14. Figure E.3 shows the results of several bitwise operations.

The operators &, |, and ^ can also be applied to boolean values, and they have basically the same meaning as their logical counterparts. When used with boolean values, they are called *boolean operators*. However, unlike the operators && and ||, which are "short-circuited," the boolean operators are not. Both sides of the expression are evaluated every time.

num1 & num2	num1 | num2	num1 ^ num2
00101101	00101101	00101101
& 00001110	| 00001110	^ 00001110
= 00001100	= 00001100	= 00001100

Figure E.3 Examples of bitwise operations

Like the other bitwise operators, the three bitwise shift operators manipulate the individual bits of an integer value. They all take two operands. The left operand is the value whose bits are shifted, and the right operand specifies how many positions they should move. Prior to performing a shift, `byte` and `short` values are promoted to `int` for all shift operators. Furthermore, if either of the operands is `long`, then the other operand is promoted to `long`. For readability, we only use 16 bits in the examples in this section, but the concepts are the same when carried out to 32- or 64-bit strings.

When bits are shifted, some bits are lost off one end, and others need to be filled in on the other. The *left shift* operator (<<) shifts bits to the left, filling the right bits with zeros. For example, if the integer variable `number` currently has the value 13, then the statement

```
number = number << 2;
```

stores the value 52 into `number`. Initially, `number` contains the bit string 0000000000001101. When shifted to the left, the value becomes 0000000000110100, or 52. Notice that for each position shifted to the left, the original value is multiplied by 2.

The sign bit of a number is shifted along with all of the others. Therefore, the sign of the value could change if enough bits are shifted to change the sign bit. For example, the value −8 is stored in binary two's complement form as 1111111111111000. When shifted left two positions, it becomes 1111111111100000, which is −32. However, if enough positions are shifted, a negative number can become positive, and vice versa.

There are two forms of the right shift operator: one that preserves the sign of the original value (>>) and one that fills the leftmost bits with zeros (>>>).

Let's examine two examples of the *right-shift-with-sign-fill* operator. If the `int` variable `number` currently has the value 39, then the expression (`number >> 2`) results in the value 9. The original bit string stored in `number` is 0000000000100111, and the result of a right shift two positions is 0000000000001001. The leftmost sign bit, which in this case is a zero, is used to fill from the left.

If `number` has an original value of −16, or 1111111111110000, then the right shift (with sign fill) expression (`number >> 3`) results in the binary string 1111111111111110, or −2. The leftmost sign bit is a 1 in this case, and is used to fill in the new left bits, maintaining the sign.

If maintaining the sign is not desirable, the *right-shift-with-zero-fill* operator (>>>) can be used. It operates similarly to the >> operator, but fills with zero no matter what the sign of the original value is.

Appendix F

Java Modifiers

This appendix summarizes the modifiers that give particular characteristics to Java classes, interfaces, methods, and variables. For discussion purposes, the set of all Java modifiers are divided into two groups: visibility modifiers and all others.

Java Visibility Modifiers

The table in Fig. F.1 describes the effect of Java visibility modifiers on various constructs. Some relationships are not applicable (N/A). For instance, a class cannot be declared with protected visibility. Note that each visibility modifier operates in the same way on classes and interfaces and in the same way on methods and variables.

Default visibility means that no visibility modifier was explicitly used. Default visibility is sometimes called *package visibility*, but you cannot use the reserved

Modifier	Classes and interfaces	Methods and variables
default (no modifier)	Visible in its package.	Inherited by any subclass in the same package as its class. Accessible by any class in the same package as its class.
`public`	Visible anywhere.	Inherited by all subclasses of its class. Accessible anywhere.
`protected`	N/A	Inherited by all subclasses of its class. Accessible by any class in the same package as its class.
`private`	N/A	Not inherited by any subclass. Not accessible by any other class.

Figure F.1   Java visibility modifiers

word `package` as a modifier. Classes and interfaces can only have default or public visibility; this visibility determines whether a class or interface can be referenced outside of its package.

When applied to methods and variables, the visibility modifiers dictate two specific characteristics:

- *Inheritance,* which determines whether a method or variable can be referenced in a subclass as if it were declared locally.
- *Access,* or the degree of encapsulation, which determines the scope in which a method or variable can be directly referenced. All methods and variables are accessible in the class in which they are declared.

Public methods and variables are inherited by all subclasses and can be accessed by anyone. *Private* methods and variables are not inherited by any subclasses and can only be accessed inside the class in which they are declared.

Protected visibility and default visibility (no modifier) vary in subtle ways. Note that a subclass of a parent may or may not be in the same package as the parent, and that not all classes in a package are related by inheritance.

Protected methods and variables are inherited by all subclasses, whether or not they are in the same package as the parent. Access to protected methods and variables is given to any class in the same package as the class in which they are declared. Therefore, a subclass in a different package will inherit them, but it cannot directly reference them in an instance of the parent. Furthermore, a class can directly access a protected method or variable that is declared in another class in the same package, whether or not the two classes are related by inheritance.

A method or variable with *default visibility* is inherited only by subclasses that are in the same package as the class in which the method or variable is declared. A method or variable with default visibility can be accessed by any class in the same package, whether they are related by inheritance or not.

All methods and variables declared in a parent class exist for all subclasses, but are not necessarily inherited by them. For example, when a child class is instantiated, memory space is reserved for a private variable of the parent class. However, that child class cannot refer to that variable by name since the variable was not inherited. The child class can, however, call an inherited method that references that variable. Similarly, an inherited method can invoke a method that the child class cannot call explicitly. For this reason, inheritance is carefully defined using the words "as if it were declared locally." Noninherited methods and variables can still be referenced indirectly.

A Visibility Example

Consider the situation depicted in the Fig. F.2. Class `P` is the parent class that is used to derive child classes `C1` and `C2`. Class `C1` is in the same package as `P`, but `C2` is not. Class `P` contains four methods, each with different visibility modifiers. One object has been instantiated from each of these classes.

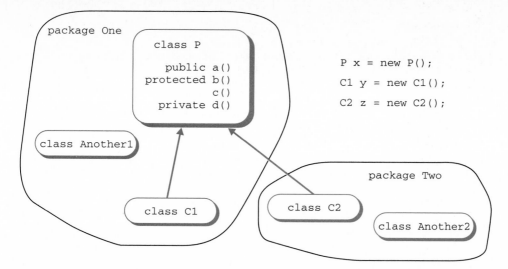

Figure F.2 A situation demonstrating Java visibility modifiers

The public method a() has been inherited by C1 and C2, and any code with access to object x can invoke x.a(). The private method d() is not inherited by C1 or C2, so objects y and z have no such method available to them. Furthermore, d() is fully encapsulated and can only be invoked from within object x.

Protected method b() is inherited by both C1 and C2. A method in y could invoke x.b(), but a method in z could not. Furthermore, an object of any class in package One could invoke x.b(), even those that are not related to class P by inheritance, such as an object created from class Another1.

Method c() has default visibility, since no visibility modifier was used to declare it. Class C1 inherits c(), but C2 does not. Therefore object y can refer to the method c() as if it were declared locally, but object z cannot. Object y can invoke x.c(), as can an object instantiated from any class in package One, such as Another1. Object z cannot invoke x.c().

These rules generalize in the same way for variables. The visibility rules may appear complicated initially, but they can be mastered with a little effort.

Other Java Modifiers

Figure F.3 summarizes the rest of the Java modifiers, which address a variety of issues. Furthermore, any given modifier has a different effect on classes, interfaces, methods, and variables. Some modifiers cannot be used with certain constructs, and therefore are listed as not applicable (N/A).

Modifier	Class	Interface	Method	Variable
abstract	The class may contain abstract methods. It cannot be instantiated.	All interfaces are inherently abstract. The modifier is optional.	No method body is defined. The method requires implementation when inherited.	N/A
final	The class cannot be used to drive new classes.	N/A	The method cannot be overridden.	The variable is a constant, whose value cannot be changed once initially set.
native	N/A	N/A	No method body is necessary since implementation is in another language.	N/A
static	N/A	N/A	Defines a class method. It does not require an instantiated object to be invoked. It cannot reference non-static methods or variables. It is implicitly final.	Defines a class variable. It does not require an instantiated object to be referenced. It is shared (common memory space) among all instances of the class.
synchronized	N/A	N/A	The execution of the method is mutually exclusive among all threads.	N/A
transient	N/A	N/A	N/A	Reserved but not currently used.
volatile	N/A	N/A	N/A	The variable is changed asynchronously. The compiler should not perform optimizations on it.

Figure F.3   The rest of the Java modifiers

The transient modifier is a reserved word in Java, but currently has no meaning. A future revision of the language may support the ability of an object to exist independently of the process which creates it. This concept is called object *persistence*. The transient modifier will probably be used to identify the variables that are not considered to be part of the object's persistent state, and therefore need not be saved.

Appendix G

Java Coding Guidelines

This appendix contains a series of guidelines that describe how to organize and format Java source code. They are designed to make programs easier to read and maintain. Some guidelines can be attributed to personal preferences, and could be modified. But it is important to have some standard set of practices that make sense and to follow them carefully.

Consistency is half of the battle. If you follow the same rules throughout a program, and follow them from one program to another, you make the effort of reading and understanding your code easier for yourself and others. It is not unusual for a programmer to develop some software that at the time seems straightforward, only to revisit it months later and have difficulty remembering how it works. If you follow consistent development guidelines, you reduce this problem considerably.

When an organization adopts a coding standard, it is easier for people to work together. A software product is often created by a team of cooperating developers, each responsible for a piece of the system. If they all follow the same development guidelines, they facilitate the process of integrating the separate pieces into one cohesive entity.

You may have to make tradeoffs between some guidelines. For example, you may be asked to make all of your identifiers easy to read, yet keep them to a reasonably short length. Use common sense on a case-by-case basis to embrace the spirit of all guidelines as much as possible.

These guidelines are followed in the example code throughout the text, with one notable exception: to save space, the header documentation guidelines presented here are not followed completely in the text.

You may opt, or be asked, to follow this set of guidelines as presented. If changes or additions are made, make sure they are clear and that they represent a conscious effort to instill good programming practices. Most of these issues are discussed further in appropriate areas of the text, but are presented succinctly here, without elaboration.

I Design Guidelines

A. Design Preparation
1. The ultimate guideline is to develop a clean design. Think before you start coding. A working program is not necessarily a good program.
2. Express and document your design with a consistent, clear notation.

B. Structured Programming
1. Do not use the `continue` statement.
2. Only use the `break` statement to terminate cases of a `switch` statement.
3. Have only one `return` statement in a method, as the last line, unless it unnecessarily complicates the method.

C. Classes and Packages
1. Do not have additional methods in the class that contains the `main` method.
2. Define the class that contains the `main` method at the top of the file it is in, followed by other classes if appropriate.
3. If only one class is used from an imported package, import that class by name. If two or more are imported, use the * symbol.

D. Modifiers
1. Do not declare variables with `public` visibility.
2. Do not use modifiers inside an interface.
3. Always use the most appropriate modifiers for each situation. For example, if a variable is used as a constant, explicitly declare it as a constant using the `final` modifier.

E. Exceptions
1. Use exception handling only for truly exceptional conditions such as terminating errors, or for significantly unusual or important situations.
2. Do not use exceptions to disguise or hide inappropriate processing.
3. Handle each exception at the appropriate level of design.

F. Miscellaneous
1. Use constants instead of literals in almost all situations.
2. Design methods so that they perform one logical function. As such, the length of a method will tend to be no longer than 50 lines of code, and usually much shorter.
3. Keep the physical lines of a source code file less than 80 characters in length.
4. Extend a logical line of code over two or more physical lines only when necessary. Divide the line at a logical place.

II Style Guidelines

A. Identifier Naming

1. Give identifiers semantic meaning. Example: Do not use single letter names such as `a` or `i`.
2. Make identifiers easy to read. Example: Use `current_value` instead of `curval`.
3. Keep identifiers to a reasonably short length.
4. Use the underscore character to separate words of an identifier.

B. Identifier Case

1. Use UPPERCASE for constants.
2. Use Title Case for class, package, and interface names.
3. Use lowercase for variable and method names. Note that all reserved words must be lowercase.

C. Indentation

1. Indent the code in any block three spaces.
2. If the body of a loop, `if` statement, or `else` clause is a single statement (not a block), indent the statement three spaces on its own line.
3. Put the left brace (`{`) starting each new block on the same line as the construct that it defines, such as a class, method, loop, `if` statement, or `else` clause. The terminating right brace (`}`) should line up with the beginning of the construct. Example:

```
while (total < 25) {
   total += 5;
   System.out.println ("The total is " + total);
}
```

4. Put the `else` clause of an `if` statement on the same line as the terminating right brace (`}`) of the block defining the body of the `if` clause. If the `if` clause contains a single statement, begin the `else` clause on a new line. Examples:

```
if (expr) {                     if (expr)
   statement1;                     statement1;
   statement2;                  else
} else                             statement2;
   statement3;
```

5. If a single `if` statement serves as the body of an `else` clause, the `if` statement should follow the `else` on the same line, and the body of the `if` should be indented only three spaces. This is an exception to guide-

line C.2. above, and keeps nested `if` statements from cascading too quickly to the right. Example:

```
if (expr1) {
    statement1;
    statement2;
} else if (expr2)
    statement3;
else if (expr3) {
    statement4;
    statement5;
} else {
    statement6;
    statement7;
}
```

   6. In a `switch` statement, indent each `case` label three spaces. Indent all code associated with a `case` three additional spaces.

D. Spacing

   1. Carefully use white space to draw attention to appropriate features of a program.
   2. Put one space after each comma in a parameter list.
   3. Put one space on either side of a binary operator.
   4. Do not put spaces immediately after a left paren or before a right paren.
   5. Do not put spaces before a semicolon.
   6. Put one space before a left paren, except before an empty parameter list.
   7. When declaring arrays, associate the brackets with the element type, as opposed to the array name, so that it applies to all variables on that line. Example:

```
int[30] list1, list2;
```

   8. When referring to the type of an array, do not put any spaces between the element type and the square brackets, such as `int[]`.

E. Messages and Prompts

   1. Do not condescend.
   2. Do not attempt to be humorous.
   3. Be informative, but succinct.
   4. Define specific input options in prompts when appropriate.
   5. Specify default selections in prompts when appropriate.

F. Output

   1. Label all output clearly.
   2. Present information to the user in a consistent manner.

III Documentation Guidelines

A. The Reader

1. Write all documentation as if the reader is computer literate and basically familiar with the Java language.
2. Assume the reader knows almost nothing about what the program is supposed to do.
3. Remember that a section of code that seems intuitive to you when you write it might not to another reader or to yourself later. Document accordingly.

B. Content

1. Make sure comments are accurate.
2. Keep comments updated as changes are made to the code.
3. Be concise but thorough.

C. Header Blocks

1. Every source code file should contain a header block of documentation providing basic information about the contents and the author.
2. Each class and interface, and each method in a class, should have a small header block that describes its role.
3. Each header block of documentation should have a distinct delimiter on the top and bottom so that the reader can visually scan from one construct to the next easily. Example:

```
//=======================================
//            header block
//=======================================
```

D. In-Line Comments

1. Use in-line documentation as appropriate to clearly describe interesting processing.
2. Put a comment on the same line with code only if the comment applies to one line of code, and can fit conveniently on that line. Otherwise, put the comment on a separate line above the line or section of code to which it applies.
3. Put a comment on the line with the terminating brace of each class, interface, method, and constructor that identifies the name of the construct.

E. Miscellaneous

1. Avoid the use of the `/*  */` style of comment, except to conform to the javadoc (`/** */`) commenting convention.
2. Don't wait until a program is finished to insert documentation. As pieces of your system are completed, comment appropriately.

Appendix H

Review Checklist

This appendix contains a checklist of issues that should be addressed during a design or code review. A *review* is a careful critique of the design or code after it has been completed. A review can take many forms. In a *desk check* a programmer reviews his or her own work. In a *walkthrough* or *inspection* a group of people meet to examine and discuss the product. No matter what form a review takes, using a checklist ensures that particular issues important to creating high-quality software are not overlooked.

Reviews involve reading through a program or design to check that objects and classes are well designed, that algorithms are implemented correctly, that code is commented properly, and that other quality attributes of the software are ensured. When a review is conducted as a walkthrough, the participants usually include the author of the code, the designer (if a separate person), one or more additional software engineers, and a person that understands the system requirements. Other people that might attend a walkthrough include managers and quality control personnel.

During a walkthrough many problems usually come to light. Errors in implementation and misunderstandings about requirements are discovered. Careful notes must be taken so that these issues can be addressed. The goal is not necessarily to solve the problems in the meeting, but at least to note them for later consideration. Many walkthroughs have been sidetracked by participants following tangents concerning one particular problem.

Walkthroughs on large software projects are an absolute necessity. Unfortunately, on small software projects walkthroughs are often overlooked or dismissed as nonessential. The same benefits that occur in reviews of a large software project also occur on smaller projects. They should never be considered unnecessary.

There is considerable evidence that as much as 70 percent of the errors in a program can be identified during a careful walkthrough.

Before a walkthrough can begin, the people involved must be prepared. The software or design must be complete and ready for review. The relevant documentation, such as design documents and requirements, must be gathered. The appropriate people to attend the walkthrough must be identified and given the documentation. By the time the meeting takes place, the participants should have reviewed all of the provided materials and prepared constructive comments and suggestions. An unsuccessful walkthrough is usually the result of a lack of preparation.

During the walkthrough, the author often initially presents a brief overview of the software or design. The author may ask the others in the meeting to concentrate on particular areas of concern. A specific person is usually designated as a recorder to capture the major questions or problems that come up. The author and reviewers then step through the code or design in detail, bringing up concerns and identifying problems at the appropriate time. After a walkthrough, the problems and corrective actions noted during the meeting should be summarized and presented to the author of the code or design so that they can be addressed.

The following checklist contains specific issues that should be covered in a review, whether conducted by yourself or in a meeting. A checklist makes the review process systematic and prevents important issues from being overlooked. Depending on your knowledge of software development and Java constructs, some of the checklist issues may not be clear. Initially, focus on those issues that you understand and incorporate others as they become familiar.

This checklist is quite small and can be augmented with other issues. Don't hesitate to add particular topics that address your own common programming and design challenges.

Review Checklist

General Issues

- ❏ Is the design or code complete?
- ❏ Can any algorithms be simplified?
- ❏ Does the program work for all valid input?
- ❏ Does the program handle invalid input appropriately?
- ❏ Does the program do everything it is supposed to?
- ❏ Does the program operate under all constraints that were established?
- ❏ Is the API being used to its fullest extent?
- ❏ Have resources (such as books and the Web) been checked for published sources of required algorithms?

Design Issues

❏ Are classes designed to encapsulate specific implementation decisions?

❏ Are classes designed to maximize reuse?

❏ Is the design modular to facilitate the inclusion of new algorithms or components?

❏ Does each inheritance derivation represent an appropriate *"is-a"* relationship?

❏ Is the class hierarchy appropriate for the problem being solved?

❏ Are abstract classes used to enhance the design of the class hierarchy?

❏ Are interfaces used properly in the design to maximize consistency among classes?

❏ Are classes grouped appropriately into packages?

❏ Are exceptions only used for handling erroneous conditions or truly unusual processing?

❏ Are threads used appropriately to minimize user response time?

Implementation Issues

❏ Are all coding standards followed?

❏ Are all comments complete and accurate?

❏ Are all variables initialized before they are used?

❏ Are constants used to make the code more readable and facilitate modifications?

❏ Are all identifiers named so that their role is clear?

❏ Do all loops terminate?

❏ Do all array indexes stay within bounds?

❏ Do all method arguments match their parameters appropriately?

❏ Are modifications to parameters in methods consistent with how those parameters are passed?

❏ Do all overriding methods have the same signature as the parent's method?

❏ Are all appropriate "clean-up" activities performed, such as files being closed?

❏ Is the implementation consistent with the design?

Comparing Java
to C++

The designers of Java based much of its syntax on the programming languages C and C++ so that developers who know those languages would feel comfortable using Java. However, Java should not be thought of as a revision of C++. There are many critical differences between them.

In fact, Java has integrated the best characteristics of several programming languages. At the heart of Java are important tenents of program design and implementation that are fundamentally distinct from the approach of C++. However, because of the similar syntax, and the popularity of C++, comparisons between these two languages are inevitable.

This appendix compares and contrasts Java and C++. It is a focussed summary of the primary similarities and differences, intended for developers with experience using C++.

Primitive Types

There are several important differences between Java and C++ concerning primitive data types and their use. These differences are summarized in Fig. I.1.

Each variable in a Java program is either associated with a primitive type (boolean, char, byte, short, int, long, float, or double) or it is a reference to an object. C++ has various primitive types, plus structs, unions, enums, arrays, and pointers. C++ pointers might or might not refer to objects.

C++ structs are subsumed by Java objects. Java does not currently have an enumerated type. The concept of unions to save memory space was considered unnecessary by Java designers. All Java primitives are signed and have a consistent size no matter what platform is used, enhancing portability.

Java	C++
Two type categories.	Various type categories.
All nonprimitive types are objects.	Separate types for structs, unions, enums, and arrays.
All numeric types are signed.	Signed and unsigned numeric types.
All primitive types are a fixed size for all platforms.	Primitive type size varies by platform.
16-bit Unicode characters.	8-bit ASCII characters.
Boolean data type primitive.	No explicit boolean data type.
Conditions must be boolean expressions.	Integer results are interpreted as boolean conditions.
Variables are automatically initialized.	No automatic initialization of variables.

Figure I.1 Java versus C++: Primitive types

All Java implementations are based on the international Unicode character set, while most C++ implementations use ASCII (American Standard Code for Information Interchange). However, since ASCII is essentially a subset of Unicode, this distinction is transparent for programmers used to using ASCII. Unicode characters can be used in identifiers and literals in a Java program.

The `boolean` type in Java cannot be cast to any other type, and vice versa. Java integers cannot be used as logical conditions. In C++ there is no boolean type and integers must be used for decision making.

No Java variables can contain garbage, since they are set to a default value if not initialized when created. However, Java compilers may warn against the use of variables before their value has been explicitly set, whether intentional or not.

Pointers and Data Structures

The absence of pointers in Java is a key difference between the two languages. The differences concerning the use of pointers, references, and basic data structures are summarized in Fig. I.2.

Java uses references that provide the functionality and versatility of pointers without their involved syntax and dangerous characteristics. Linked data structures are accomplished with references as you would with pointers in C++, but in Java it is impossible to get a segmentation fault since a reference can only refer to an object, not an arbitrary memory location.

Arrays and character strings are objects in Java, with appropriate support methods. String concatenation is a built-in operation in the Java language, and array bounds checking is automatic.

Multidimensional arrays in Java are actually arrays of arrays, in which each array is a distinct object. Therefore, for example, each row in a two-dimensional

Java	C++
References, with no explicit pointer manipulation and no pointer arithmetic.	Pointers, with dereferencing (* or ->) and address (&) operators.
Array references are not translated to pointer arithmetic.	Array references translate to pointer arithmetic.
Arrays automatically check index limits.	No automatic array bounds checking.
Array lengths in multidimensional arrays can vary from one element to the next within one dimension.	Array lengths in multidimensional arrays are all the same size in a given dimension, fixed by the declaration.
Strings are objects.	Strings are null-terminated character arrays.
Built-in string concatenation operator (+).	String concatenation through a library function.
Use string concatenation operator for long string literals.	Use line continuation (\) for long string literals.
No typedef.	typedef to define types.

Figure I.2 Java versus C++: Pointers and data structures

array can have a different number of elements. The length of each array is determined when each array object is instantiated, not when the initial declaration is made.

Defining explicit type names is not necessary in either Java or C++ since the declaration of larger structures, such as classes, implicitly defines a type name. C++ includes the typedef operation for compatibility with C.

Object-Oriented Programming

Both languages are object-oriented, but have significantly different philosophies and techniques, as summarized in Fig. I.3.

C++ supports the object-oriented approach, but it doesn't enforce it. Since C++ is essentially a superset of C, which is a procedural language, a program written in C++ could be a *hybrid* mix of procedural and object-oriented techniques. Java is a

Java	C++
Pure object-oriented language.	Hybrid between procedural and object-oriented.
All functions (methods) are part of a class.	Can have stand-alone functions.
No multiple inheritance.	Multiple inheritance.
Formal interface specifications.	No formal interface specifications.
No parameterized type.	Templates as a parameterized type.
No operator overloading.	Operator overloading.
All methods (except final methods) are dynamically bound.	Virtual functions are dynamically bound.

Figure I.3 Java versus C++: Object-oriented programming

pure object-oriented language since it enforces the object-oriented approach. As such, all functions in Java are methods, defined inside a class.

Several constructs and techniques that are a part of C++ are not included in Java, mainly to keep the complexity of the language down. These include multiple inheritance, parameterized types, and operator overloading. However, Java has the ability to define a formal interface specification, which gives the most important characteristics of multiple inheritance to Java programs. Both languages support method overloading.

In C++, a method must be explicitly declared as virtual in order to allow run-time dynamic binding of a method invocation to the appropriate definition. In Java, all methods are handled consistently and are dynamically bound, except for methods that are defined with the `final` modifier.

Special Characteristics

Some of the most highly promoted aspects of Java concern its relationship to the Web and other special characteristics that distinguish it from C++. These differences are summarized in Fig. I.4.

Links to Java applets can be embedded in HTML documents, then retrieved and executed using Web browsers. The Java API has specific support for network communication.

A C++ programmer must perform explicit dynamic memory management, releasing objects and other dynamically allocated data space when it is no longer needed. In Java, garbage collection is automatic. An object in a Java program is marked as a candidate for garbage collection after the last reference to it is removed. Therefore, Java does not support destructors, though there is the ability to define a `finalize` method for other cleanup activity.

Java source code is compiled into bytecode, a low-level representation that is not tied to any particular processor. The bytecode can then be executed on any

Java	C++
Specifically attuned to network and Web processing.	No relationship to networks or the Web.
Automatic garbage collection.	No automatic garbage collection.
Combination of compiled and interpreted.	Compiled.
Slower execution when interpreted.	Fast execution.
Architecture neutral.	Architecture specific.
Supports multithreading.	No multithreading.
Automatic generation of documentation in HTML format.	No automatic documentation generation.

Figure I.4 Java versus C++: Special characteristics

platform that has a Java interpreter. Java is therefore considered to be architecture-neutral.

When interpreted, Java programs have a slower execution speed, but because they are already compiled to a low-level representation, the interpretation overhead is not problematic for many applications. C++ compilers are specific to each type of processor.

The Java language supports multiple threads of execution, with synchronization mechanisms. It also has a special comment syntax, which can be used to generate external documentation in HTML format about the contents and structure of a Java system.

General Programming Issues

There are several specific differences between Java and C++ that affect basic programming practices. They are summarized in Fig. I.5.

Java does not support variable-length parameter lists for methods. It also does not allow parameters to be given a default value which essentially makes them optional during invocation.

Java	C++
Method bodies must be defined inside the class to which they belong.	Method bodies must be defined inside the class to which they belong.
No forward referencing required.	Explicit forward referencing required.
No preprocessor.	Heavy reliance on preprocessor.
No comma operator.	Comma operator.
No variable-length parameter lists.	Variable-length parameter lists.
No optional method parameters.	Optional function parameters.
No `const` reference parameters.	`const` reference parameters.
No `goto` statement.	`goto` statement.
Labels on `break` and `continue`.	No labels on `break` and `continue`.
Command-line arguments do not include the program name.	Command-line arguments do not include the program name.
Main method cannot return a value.	Main function can return a value.
No global variables.	Global variables.
Character escape sequences can appear in a program.	Character escape sequences must appear in a string or character literal.
Cannot mask identifiers through scope.	Can mask identifiers through scope.

Figure I.5 Java versus C++: General programming issues

Java has no comma operator, though its `for` loop syntactically allows multiple initializations and increments using the comma symbol. Java does not allow variables to be declared with global scope. In C++, you must use an explicit forward reference (function prototype) to inform the compiler that a function will be used prior to its definition, but in Java no such forward referencing is needed.

Java does not rely on a preprocessor. Most of the functionality that is provided by the C++ preprocessor is defined in the Java language itself.

There is no `goto` statement in Java, though `goto` is included in the Java reserved words. Java allows statements to be labeled, and the `break` and `continue` statements can jump to specific, labeled points in the code.

Finally, in Java, an identifier name cannot be masked by another declaration and scope, as it can in C++. For example, the following code segment is valid in C++, but causes a compile-time error in Java:

```
{
int x = 12;
   {
       int x = 25;    // same variable name with
                      // distinct memory space
   }
}
```

Appendix J

Integrating Java with Other Languages

This appendix discusses *native* methods, which allow Java programs to use software written in languages other than Java. For example, to execute a Unix operating system service that is written in the C programming language, a Java programmer can declare a `native` method that calls the underlying C function to perform the service. The `native` modifier can be used to incorporate software written in many languages. This appendix provides an overview of this process, integrating Java with C, and it assumes the reader is familiar with the C language.

There are three basic steps required to integrate a C function with a Java program:

- A `native` method needs to be declared in Java.
- A C function needs to be written or reused that implements the `native` method.
- The `native` method declaration and the C function need to be explicitly associated, so that the Java interpreter can execute the implementation of the `native` method.

The following sections provide a brief overview of how a `native` method is created, implemented, and associated with each other.

Declaring Native Methods

The following example is similar to the `Lincoln` program in Chapter 2, in that it simply prints a quote by Abraham Lincoln. However, in this version called `President`, the function that prints the quote is written in C, and the program that calls that function is written in Java. In the Java class definition below, the `speak` method is declared using the `native` modifier, and no body is given for the method.

```
// Defines a native method
class President {
   public native void speak();
   static {
      // load the c_lincoln library that contains the native
      // code implementation
      System.loadLibrary ("c_president");
   }
} // class President
```

The `static` block dynamically loads a library of code that implements the `native` method. This `static` block is executed by the Java interpreter when the class is loaded into main memory. A *shared library* is a collection of software routines that is easily accessed and can be shared among many programs. In this example, the shared library `c_president` contains the C code that implements the `speak` method.

Once the C code is associated with this program, the `President` class encapsulates the fact that the code is written in another language. Therefore calling a native method is exactly the same as calling any other method. For example, the following program contains a `main` method that invokes the `speak` method.

```
// Calls a native method
class Lincoln_Says {
   public static void main (String[] args) {
      President abe = new President();
      abe.speak();
   } // method main
} // class Lincoln_Says
```

The `javah` Program

The `javah` program is used to help create some of the software necessary to implement `native` methods. This program, which is provided with the Java Development Kit (JDK), is used to generate a header file for each class containing `native` methods. This header file is required when implementing native methods in C, because it provides a standard set of types and parameters that the Java interpreter can use. This standard set of types for parameters is known as the *Java Native Interface* (JNI).

When the `javah` program is executed it reads the specified class file and identifies the native methods. From the declaration of these methods the program generates a C header file. The header file contains a function definition that matches the class containing the native method. To generate the header file, the `javah` program is executed with the class name as its argument:

```
> javah -jni President
```

After executing these commands, a header is created in the current directory using the name of the class. In our example, the above commands create a file: `President.h`. The header file is required in the rest of the implementation of the native method. Note that we have not yet implemented the function that prints the quote. The header file contains the following declaration:

```
/*
 * Class:     President
 * Method:    speak
 * Signature: ()V
 */
JNIEXPORT void JNICALL Java_President_speak
  (JNIEnv *, jobject);
```

Native Method Implementation

Having defined the signature for the C function that matches the native method, we can proceed with its implementation. The implementation of the `native speak` method is done in several steps. First the function that prints the quote is written in C:

```
#include <stdio.h>
void speak() {
    printf ("Whatever you are, be a good one.");
}
```

Next, we create another C function that ties the header file generated by `javah` to the speak C function:

```
#include <jni.h>
#include "President.h"
JNIEXPORT void JNICALL
Java_President_speak (JNIEnv * env, jobject obj) {
    speak();
}
```

The Java interpreter executes the native method using a predefined function name created by concatenating the word Java, the class name, and the `native` method's name. In our example, the class containing the native method is `President` and the method name is `speak`, so the C function that associates the two must be called `Java_President_speak`.

Notice also that the connector function takes two parameters, even though the `native` method and the C implementation of the native method does not require any parameters. These parameters provide access to the JNI C library. These functions allow the C function to access information found in the Java execution environment. In general, the type and number of the parameters to these routines vary with the parameters of the `native` method declaration in Java.

This routine must also include the `jni.h` file and the header file generated by `javah`. After the appropriate files are generated and written, they should be compiled and linked into a shared library. This is the library that will be loaded using the `loadLibrary` method call in the static block of the class containing the native methods. In our example, this library is called `c_president`. The creation of this library is dependent on the operating system used. A programmer should consult the C compiler documentation for information on how to create shared libraries.

Issues

There are many issues to address when combining programs of different languages. Since each language contains its own interpretation of data and its own run-time execution, care must be taken when dealing with the differences between the languages. When interfacing Java with C there are four areas to understand before a native implementation can be considered correct. These issues are discussed briefly, but not exhaustively, in this section. The JNI C library provides a rich set of C functions and data types to address these issues.

The first issue relates to parameter passing and the returning of primitive data types or references. C and Java represent data types differently. Java has classes and C has structures. Java has a String class and C has a null-terminated array of characters. Each data structure used needs to be mapped correctly to its counterpart in the other language. The second issue relates to how C code can call Java methods or constructors. C code has no inherent means for executing Java code. Therefore, to accomplish this execution, the JDK provides functions associated with the JNI C library. The third issue relates to exceptions. When exceptional conditions or errors are detected in the C code, a Java exception should be thrown. However, C does not support Java exceptions. A C function named `ExceptionOccurred` of the JNI must be called to correctly construct and throw the exception. The fourth issue relates to threads. Java programs using threads must take care to be synchronized when accessing data available to multiple threads. If a variable or method is `synchronized`, the C code must implement a synchronized solution. C routines that implement Java-compatible monitors are provided by the JDK to enable the C code to respect the threaded access of data or methods.

An HTML Tutorial

This appendix contains a brief tutorial covering the HyperText Markup Language (HTML) and the creation of basic Web pages. HTML files contain instructions that describe how text, images, and multimedia are displayed by Web browsing software. Two of the more popular Web browsers are Internet Explorer by Microsoft and Navigator by Netscape.

HTML files can be created using a simple text editor. They contain the text to be displayed and *tags* that describe the layout, style, and other features of a document. Tags suggest how the browser program should display the document, but each browser interprets the meaning of a tag in its own way. Furthermore, although all browsers recognize a common set of tags, a particular browser may also recognize additional tags that others do not. Therefore what you see when you view a particular HTML document with one browser might be different than what you see when viewed with another.

In this appendix, we describe the most popular HTML tags. However, if you plan to create advanced Web pages, you may want to use additional sources covering all aspects of HTML. Many Web sites contain detailed information on specific HTML constructs. In fact, one of the best ways to learn HTML is to find interesting Web pages, and use your Web browser to view the HTML source for that document.

Basic HTML Documents

There are two basic sections to every HTML file. The first section is the head of the document, which contains a description of the document including its title. The second section is the body of the document, which contains the information to be displayed, such as text, images, and links to other documents. The following is an example of a basic HTML document for a local student activities group:

```
<HTML>
    <HEAD>
        <TITLE>Students in Action</TITLE>
    </HEAD>
    <BODY>


        Students in Action is dedicated to help our local
        community by using the volunteer effort of college
        students.  This semester our planned actions are:
        to help a local food drive for flood victims in
        the Midwest, to visit local adult care centers, and
        teach Java to grade school students.


        Our group is active, energetic, and always in need of
        donations of equipment, effort, or money.  We are
        always willing to help staff and plan community
        events.


        As always, our president (at x222) is eager and
        willing to answer questions and hear suggestions on
        how we can be more active in our community.


    </BODY>
</HTML>
```

The words such as HEAD, TITLE, and BODY are called elements. Tags are specified using an element enclosed in angle brackets (< >). Tags are often used in pairs, called a start tag and an end tag. These tags delimit, or mark, a particular region of text. Generally, the start tag uses the element name, such as <HEAD>, and the end tag uses a slash (/) followed by the element name, such as </HEAD>.

Everything between <HEAD> and </HEAD> is considered to be the introduction of the document. In this case it contains one line that defines the title of the document. The text between <TITLE> and </TITLE> appears in the title bar of the Web browser when the document is displayed.

Everything between <BODY> and </BODY> is considered to be the body of the document. In this case the body contains several paragraphs of text that will be displayed in the browser window. The text in an HTML document can be in any form convenient for its author. Browsers only pay attention to tags. Therefore, it does not matter how white space is used to separate words or lines between tags. Browsers will reformat the text to be displayed appropriately for the width and height of the browser window, independent of how the document is written. Figure K.1 shows

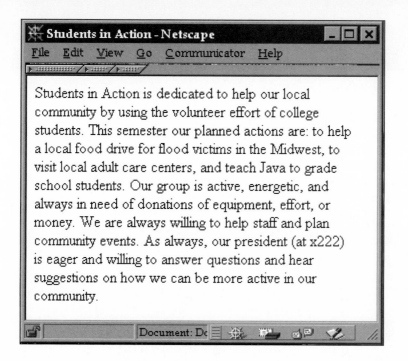

Figure K.1 Initial Web page for Students in Action

this Web page as displayed in a browser. Figure K.2 shows the same Web page, but in a differently shaped browser window. Notice how the text is reformed because of the browser's width and height.

Formatting Text

There are many tags that can be used to aid browsers with formatting text. Notice in Figs. K.1 and K.2 that the blank spaces in the paragraphs were ignored when the text was displayed. For browsers to understand how to format text, each part of the text must be marked up with tags. To indicate to the browser what paragraphs are in the text, the P element should be used. The following is a marked up version of the Students in Action Web page, so that the original paragraphs are reflected in what a browser presents, as shown in Fig. K.3.

```
<HTML>
   <HEAD>
      <TITLE>Students in Action</TITLE>
   </HEAD>
   <BODY>
```

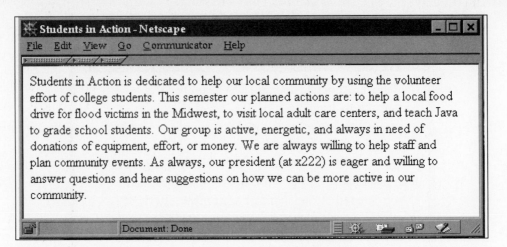

Figure K.2 Initial Web page for Students in Action reformatted

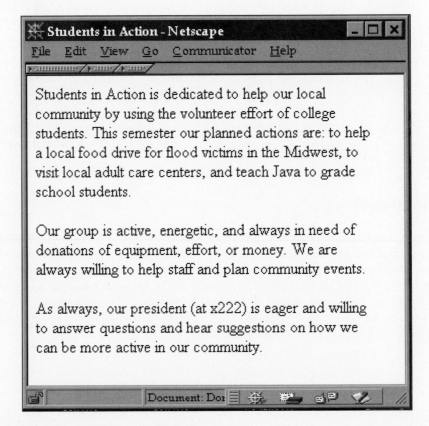

Figure K.3 Paragraph-formatted Web page

```
<P>Students in Action is dedicated to help our
local community by using the volunteer effort of
college students.  This semester our planned actions
are: to help a local food drive for flood victims
in the Midwest, to visit local adult care centers,
and teach Java to grade school students.</P>

<P>Our group is active, energetic, and always in
need of donations of equipment, effort, or money.
We are always willing to help staff and plan
community events.</P>

<P>As always, our president (at x222) is eager and
willing to answer questions and hear suggestions on
how we can be more active in our community.</P>

    </BODY>
</HTML>
```

Figure K.3 is a snapshot showing the effects of the `<P>` tag used in the text. Notice the `<P>` is not displayed by the browser, but instead a single blank line has been inserted.

Besides the P element there are many other elements that can be used to change the format of the text. The table in Fig. K.4 shows some elements and their effect on the text associated with a tag.

B, I, and U are popular elements that control the style of the font presented. They work similarly to how a word processor allows text to be bold, italic, or underlined. For example, the following HTML lines:

```
<P><B>I'd buy that for a dollar</B></P>
<P><I>May the force be with you</I></P>
<P><I><B>I'll be back</B></I></P>
```

Should be displayed by a browser as:

> **I'd buy that for a dollar**
> *May the force be with you*
> ***I'll be back***

Many elements can be nested to produce a combination of effects. Notice the use of I and B on the last line of the previous example. Usually, it is considered good practice to unnest tags in the same order as they were nested. This practice makes it

Element	Effect or Purpose
U	Underline
B	Boldface
I	Italics
STRONG	Strong type, often rendered using boldface
EM	Emphasis, often rendered using italics
STRIKE	A line drawn through the text
TT	Typewriter typeface
CODE	Code listings
KBD	Keyboard input
VAR	Variables or arguments to commands
BIG	A larger point size than the current font
SMALL	A smaller point size than the current font
SUB	Subscript
SUP	Superscript
CITE	Citation of reference documents
BLINK	Blinks on and off

Figure K.4   Some HTML text elements

easier to modify the HTML later. The rest of the elements described in Fig. K.4 also change characteristics of the font displayed by the browser.

There are several other elements similar to the P element that can be used to change the layout of the text. The <CENTER> and </CENTER> tags indicate that the browser should center the text associated with the tag. The <BR> tag forces a line break in the text. The <HR> tag tells the browser to include a horizontal rule in the document. The horizontal rule is often used to separate sections of a document visually. Note that the HR and BR elements do not have associated ending tags, because they do not affect text directly. The <NOBR> and </NOBR> tags indicate that the browser should not insert line breaks anywhere when displaying the text associated with the tags. The <Q> tag is used within a line of text to quote a few words. Text associated with the Q element is displayed within single quotes. The <BQ> tag can be used to quote a block of text, such as a paragraph.

In addition to marking up portions of the document to be displayed in a particular way, HTML header tags can provide an overall hierarchical structure to the document. Headers are used to indicate different sections of a document. HTML provides six heading levels: <H1>, <H2>, <H3>, <H4>, <H5>, and <H6>. The <H1> heading tag is the highest heading level and <H6> is the lowest. An H1 element can be thought of as marking a chapter of a book. An H2 element can be thought of as marking a section of a chapter. An H3 element is associated with a subsection, and the other headers follow suit. Generally, headings are displayed by most browsers as bolded text, and usually are larger in size (compared to the rest of the "normal" text in the document). For example, consider the following HTML document:

```
<HTML>
    <HEAD>
        <TITLE>Header Example</TITLE>
    </HEAD>
    <BODY>
        <H1> 1. Heading One
        <H2> 2. Heading Two
        <H3> 3. Heading Three
        <H4> 4. Heading Four
        <H5> 5. Heading Five
        <H6> 6. Heading Six
    </BODY>
</HTML>
```

The display of this page is shown in Fig. K.5.

There are several reasons to use headers in your web pages. The first is that headers make a document easier to read. They provide a visual cue to a reader of the

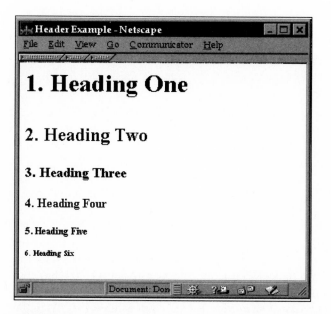

Figure K.5 Header example

different sections of your text. These cues enable a reader to easily identify and skip to the appropriate section of a web page. The second reason is that Web search engines often catalog the text associated with headers in a document. Therefore, using a good heading for a section of a document may help others find your page on the Internet. Generally, documents should contain no more than three levels of headings.

The following HTML is the Students in Action Web page marked up with a header and some font styles.

```
<HTML>
   <HEAD>
      <TITLE>Students in Action</TITLE>
   </HEAD>
   <BODY>

      <CENTER><H1>Students in Action</H1></CENTER>

      <CENTER><I>Dedicated to help our local community
      by using the volunteer effort of college
      students.</I></CENTER>

      <P>This semester our planned actions are: to help a
      local food drive for flood victims in the Midwest,
      to visit local adult care centers, and teach Java
      to grade school students.</P>

      <P>Our group is active, energetic, and always in
      need of donations of equipment, effort, or money.
      We are always willing to help staff and plan
      community events.</P>

      <P>As always, our president (at x222) is eager and
      willing to answer questions and hear suggestions on
      how we can be more active in our community.</P>

   </BODY>
</HTML>
```

The display of this page can be seen in Fig. K.6.

Besides headers, there are several other ways to structure a Web document including frames, tables, and lists. Frames and tables are more complicated than the tags we have seen so far, and are beyond the scope of this tutorial. HTML has two types of lists: an ordered list and an unordered list. Creating a list requires two parts to be identified using tags. The first is the entire list. For an ordered list, place the <OL> tag at the start of the list, and </OL> at the end of the list, and then surround

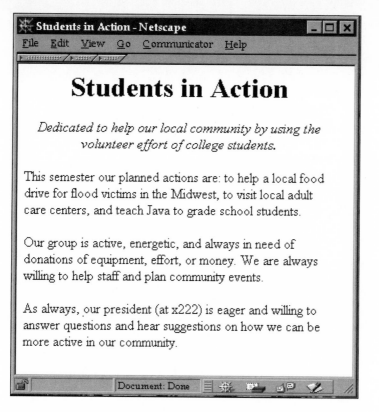

Figure K.6   Header, centering, and font changes for Web page

each item in the list with `<LI>` and `</LI>`. For example, the following HTML defines one list with three items:

```
<OL>
   <LI>First Item in the list</LI>
   <LI>Second Item in the list</LI>
   <LI>Third Item in the list</LI>
</OL>
```

This text will be formatted in browsers as:

```
1.   First Item in the list
2.   Second Item in the list
3.   Third Item in the list
```

Notice that the browser will automatically count and sequence the list items for you. Lists can also be nested within lists. Consider the following HTML code:

```
<OL>
    <LI>First Item in first list</LI>
    <OL>
        <LI>First Item in first sublist</LI>
        <LI>Second Item in first sublist</LI>
    </OL>
    <LI>Second Item in first list</LI>
    <OL>
        <LI>First Item in second sublist</LI>
        <LI>Second Item in second sublist</LI>
    <OL>
</OL>
```

This text will be formatted similar to the following:

```
1. First Item in first list
   1. First Item in first sublist
   2. Second Item in first sublist
2. Second Item in first list
   1. First Item in second sublist
   2. Second Item in second sublist
```

An unordered list is very similar to an ordered list. Unordered lists use the UL element instead of the OL element that ordered lists use. Unordered lists are usually displayed with a bullet symbol to the left of the list item. Some browsers may use a different symbol, and there are tag attributes that you can specify that will let you use images as the list item symbol.

The following uses an unordered list to represent the various activities that the Students in Action have planned for this semester. In addition, we added horizontal rules to offset the H1 element in the document.

```
<HTML>
    <HEAD>
        <TITLE>Students in Action</TITLE>
    </HEAD>
    <BODY>
        <HR>
```

```
<CENTER><H1>Students in Action</H1></CENTER>

<HR>

<CENTER><I>Dedicated to help our local community
by using the volunteer effort of college
students.</I></CENTER>

<HR>

<P>This semester our planned actions are:</P>

<UL>
    <LI> to help a local food drive for flood
    victims in the Midwest
    <LI> to visit local adult care centers
    <LI> to teach Java to grade school students
</UL>

<P>Our group is active, energetic, and always in
need of donations of equipment, effort, or money.
We are always willing to help staff and plan
community events.</P>

<P>As always, our president (at x222) is eager and
willing to answer questions and hear suggestions on
how we can be more active in our community.</P>

    </BODY>
</HTML>
```

The display of this document can be seen in Fig. K.7.

As you can see from Fig. K.7, although the content of the Web page has not changed since Fig. K.1, the presentation has changed dramatically.

Links

The World-Wide Web would not be a Web without links between documents. A link connects one document to another. The destination of the link can be a local file or a remote file hosted on another computer. Links are displayed in a number of different ways, but the most popular and recognizable is blue text that is underlined. In most browsers, when you move your pointing device (mouse, or other device) over a link in a graphical browser, the destination of the link is displayed somewhere on the

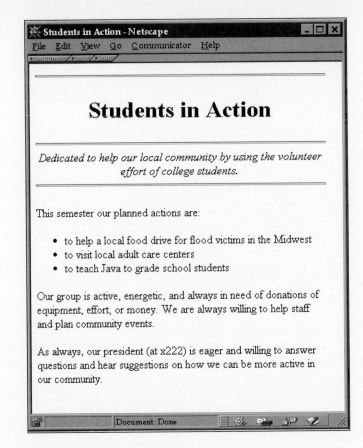

Figure K.7   Lists and lines added to Web page

screen. The most popular browsers display the destination link on the bottom of the display window.

The link tag, <A>, takes one attribute that defines its destination. Inside the link tags (also known as anchor tags) the URL of a new document is specified. For example, the following HTML creates two links

```
<A HREF="http://www.csc.vill.edu/~lewis">Dr. Lewis' Home Page Link</A>
<A HREF="http://www.yahoo.com">Yahoo Internet Search Link</A>
```

The text associated with the <A> and </A> tags is what the browser will usually display as underlined blue text. No checking is done on the validity of the destination until the user selects (or clicks on) the link. Therefore, when one writes a Web page, all links should be tested (i.e., clicked on or exercised). Following the selection of a link by a user, the browser will attempt to load the contents of the destination. When a successful connection is made to the destination link (either as a remote computer, or another file on your own computer), the browser will display the contents of the destination page.

Links are very useful for breaking up a document based on content. Links have been the driving force of the popularity of HTML and the World-Wide Web because they allow users to read documents located on computers throughout the world. The following HTML has five example links in it. The first three represent links to local documents that describe more detail about the Students in Action projects and are located on the same server. The fourth link represents an absolute URL, which can refer to any document in the World-Wide Web. The fifth link is a mailto link. This is a special type of link that allows users to send mail by clicking on the link. In the following case, the mail would be sent to `president@wpllabs.com`.

```
<HTML>
    <HEAD>
        <TITLE>Students in Action</TITLE>
    </HEAD>
    <BODY>
        <HR>

        <CENTER><H1>Students in Action</H1></CENTER>

        <HR>

        <CENTER><I>Dedicated to help our local community
        by using the volunteer effort of college
        students.</I></CENTER>

        <HR>

        <P>This semester our planned actions are:</P>

        <UL>
            <LI> to <A HREF="food.html">help a local food drive</A>
                for flood victims in the Midwest
            <LI> to <A HREF="adult.html">visit local adult care
                centers</A>
            <LI> to <A HREF="grade.html">teach Java to grade
                school students</A>
        </UL>

        <P>Our group is active, energetic, and always in
        need of donations of equipment, effort, or money.
        We are always willing to help staff and plan
        community events.</P>
```

```
<P>As always, our <A HREF="mailto:president@wpllabs.com">
president</A> (at x222) is eager and willing to answer
questions and hear suggestions on how we can be more
active in our community.</P>


<P>Visit our <A HREF="http://www.vill.edu">University Home
Page</A>.</P>

    </BODY>
</HTML>
```

Figure K.8 show how this page will be displayed by a browser.

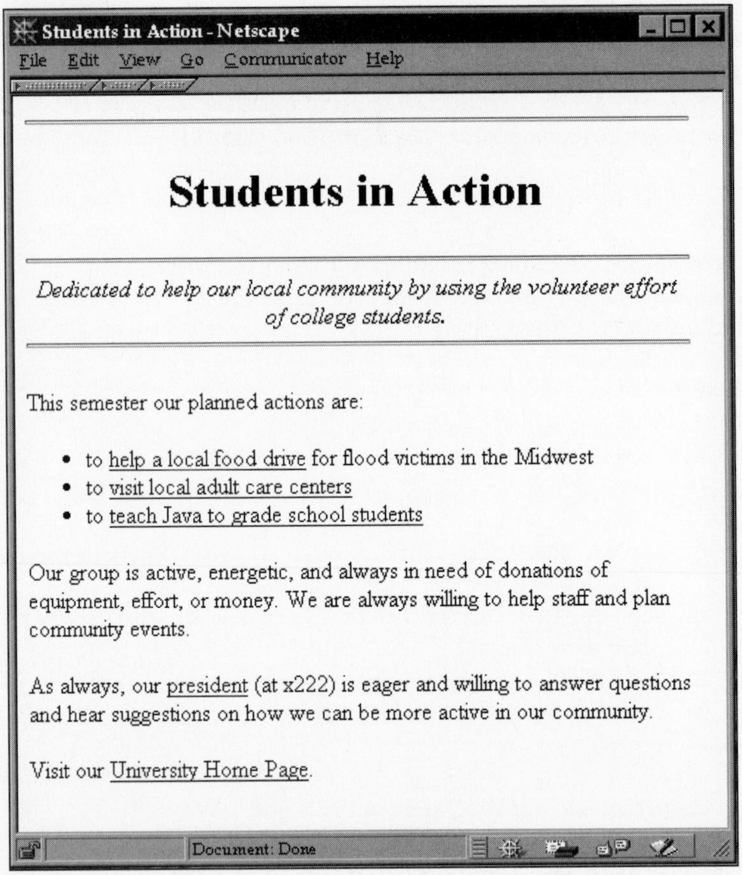

Figure K.8 Links added to Web page

Color and Images

Some of the most popular browsers (Netscape Navigator and Microsoft Internet Explorer) have introduced common extension attributes to the <BODY> tag to allow a background color or images for the document to be specified. Background images or color can dramatically improve the aesthetic appearance on a color capable display.

The first attribute is the BGCOLOR attribute. This attribute is used to set the background color of the entire document. For example, the following text will set the background color to red in a HTML document:

```
<BODY BGCOLOR=RED>
```

There are two basic methods for defining a color in HTML. The first, as seen in the previous example, uses a standard color name. Note that the display of HTML code is solely under the control of a browser; therefore these names are not truly standard, but are common color names that most browsers support. Be sure to check all browsers your users may have, to see what specific color names are accepted before choosing an appropriate color. A few de facto standard names for colors that are accepted by both Netscape and Microsoft's browsers are black, blue, gray, green, navy, purple, red, yellow, and white. The second method of choosing a color is to change the color name to an RGB value. An RGB value is a sequence of three numbers that represents the amount of red, green, and blue that will be used to create the color. The numbers represent the various strength of the colors involved (0=off, 255=full on). The combination of three values produce a specific color. The RGB values are represented as three pairs of hex characters preceded by a number sign (#) and surrounded by double quotes. For example, to represent the color in which red is 50, green is 150, and blue is 255, the <BODY> tag would look like the following:

```
<BODY BGCOLOR="#3296FF">
```

There are many good shareware programs available on the Internet that will help you determine the RGB values for a particular color.

In addition to setting the background to a single color, it is also possible to tile the background with a particular image. Most graphical browsers have implemented an extension to the <BODY> tag that will take a GIF or JPEG image and repeat it both horizontally and vertically (i.e., tiling) to create a background pattern. Some images can be fairly simple, like a single color image. Others can be more complex, representing a repeating pattern (e.g., bathroom tiles, or a stone mosaic). To use an image as a background use the BACKGROUND attribute in the

<BODY> tag and follow it with the name of the image file in quotes. For example, the piece of HTML code below uses the STONE.GIF image as a tiling background image.

```
<BODY BACKGROUND="STONE.GIF">
```

Care should be given to the type of image, and strength of its colors. Many times, using an interesting image can make the document's text difficult to read. There are many pages on the World-Wide Web that have free images that you can copy and use as backgrounds.

Graphic images can be included in an HTML document in other ways as well. Most of the popular browsers can show both GIF and JPEG image formats. To include an image use the <IMG> tag. The SRC attribute of the <IMG> tag can be used to describe the URL of the graphic image file. For example, the following HTML fragment will include an image called new.gif:

```
<IMG SRC="new.gif">
```

The following HTML code is the Students in Action Web page modified to use an image as a banner that introduces the organization, and a new image to draw attention to a portion of the page that may have changed recently.

```
<HTML>
    <HEAD>
        <TITLE>Students in Action</TITLE>
    </HEAD>
    <BODY>
        <HR>

        <CENTER><IMG SRC="SIA.gif"></CENTER>

        <HR>

        <CENTER><I>Dedicated to help our local community
        by using the volunteer effort of college
        students.</I></CENTER>

        <HR>

        <P>This semester our planned actions are:</P>

        <UL>
            <LI> to <A HREF="food.html">help a local food drive</A>
                for flood victims in the Midwest
            <LI> to <A HREF="adult.html">visit local adult care
```

```
        centers</A>
    <LI> to <A HREF="grade.html">teach Java to grade
         school students</A> <IMG SRC="new.gif">
  </UL>

  <P>Our group is active, energetic, and always in
  need of donations of equipment, effort, or money.
  We are always willing to help staff and plan
  community events.</P>

  <P>As always, our <A HREF="mailto:president@wpllabs.com">
  president</A> (at x222) is eager and willing to answer
  questions and hear suggestions on how we can be more
  active in our community.</P>

  <P>Visit our <A HREF="http://www.vill.edu">University Home
  Page</A>.</P>

  </BODY>
</HTML>
```

Figure K.9 shows how this page is displayed by a browser.

Applets

The `<APPLET>` tag is used to execute an applet in a document. The `<APPLET>` tag has many possible attributes. Its only required attribute is the `CODE` attribute. The `CODE` attribute names the class file of the applet that should execute in the document. The browser will load that applet's class file from the same URL as the document that contains the `<APPLET>` tag. For example, to execute the `Marquee` applet, the following HTML fragment is used:

```
<APPLET code=Marquee>
</APPLET>
```

A browser displaying this HTML code will load the `Marquee.class` file into the browser and execute it. Other attributes for the `<APPLET>` tag include:

- `HEIGHT`—used to define the space in pixels reserved for the display height of the applet
- `WIDTH`—used to define the space in pixels reserved for the display width of the applet
- `CODEBASE`—used to define an alternate URL for the location of the class file

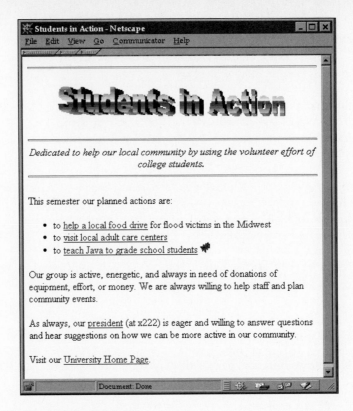

Figure K.9   Images added to Web page

In this example, we will reserve 50 pixels for the height, and 100 pixels for the width. In the code fragment below, we also reset the location of the class code to another site.

```
<APPLET CODE=Marquee WIDTH=100 HEIGHT=50
   CODEBASE="http://www.javasite.com/applets2use">
</APPLET>
```

When inserted between the `<APPLET>` and `</APPLET>` tags, the `<PARAM>` tag allows you to pass parameters to the Java applet at run time. The `<PARAM>` tag has two required attributes that allow it to pass information to the applet program. The attributes are `NAME` and `VALUE`. By defining a `NAME` and `VALUE` pair, the applet can use and decipher the information it is passed at run time. The following example sends two parameters, a state and city, to the `Map` applet:

```
<APPLET CODE=Map WIDTH=100 HEIGHT=5
   CODEBASE="http://www.javasite.com/applets2use">
```

```
<PARAM NAME="state" VALUE="pennsylvania">
<PARAM NAME="city" VALUE="philadelphia">

</APPLET>
```

The following HTML code is the Students in Action Web page, with an applet added that scrolls a message across the document as the page is browsed.

```
<HTML>
    <HEAD>
        <TITLE>Students in Action</TITLE>
    </HEAD>
    <BODY BGCOLOR="WHITE" TEXT="BLACK">
        <HR>

        <CENTER><IMG SRC="SIA.gif"></CENTER>

        <HR>

        <CENTER><I>Dedicated to help our local community
        by using the volunteer effort of college
        students.</I></CENTER>

        <HR>

        <P>This semester our planned actions are:</P>

        <UL>
            <LI> to <A HREF="food.html">help a local food drive</A>
                 for flood victims in the Midwest
            <LI> to <A HREF="adult.html">visit local adult care
                 centers</A>
            <LI> to <A HREF="grade.html">teach Java to grade
                 school students</A> <IMG SRC="new.gif">
        </UL>

        <P>Our group is active, energetic, and always in
        need of donations of equipment, effort, or money.
        We are always willing to help staff and plan
        community events.</P>

        <P>As always, our <A HREF="mailto:loftus@wpllabs.com">
        president</A> (at x222) is eager and willing to answer
        questions and hear suggestions on how we can be more
        active in our community.</P>
```

```
<APPLET CODE="Marquee.class" WIDTH=500 HEIGHT=50>
   <PARAM NAME=text
      VALUE="Join us for our Spring picnic in April!">
   <PARAM NAME=delay        VALUE="100">
   <PARAM NAME=bgcolor      VALUE="255255255">
   <PARAM NAME=fgcolor      VALUE="000000128">
</APPLET>

<P>Visit our <A HREF="http://www.vill.edu">University Home
Page</A>.</P>

   </BODY>
</HTML>
```

Figure K.10 shows how this page is displayed in a browser.

Figure K.10   Applets added to Web page

Appendix L

The Java Development Kit

This appendix contains a description of the basic command-line tools in the Java Development Kit (JDK), version 1.1. They are available free from Sun Microsystems, the creators of the Java programming language.

All of the tools make use of the CLASSPATH environment variable, which specifies the locations of the class files used by Java programs. The path is an ordered list of directories and zip files. Many of the JDK tools allow an option to override the CLASSPATH for a particular invocation of that tool.

At your site, you might have an integrated development environment (IDE) to support the creation of Java programs. If so, you will not use the tools as described below. However, some version of these tools are used by the IDE to develop and execute Java programs.

`javac`—The Java Compiler

The Java compiler translates Java source code into equivalent Java bytecode. Java source code is stored in files with a `.java` extension and the compiler creates bytecode files with `.class` extensions. A separate bytecode file is created for each class in the Java source code. The Java compiler is invoked using the following syntax:

```
javac options files
```

Multiple *files* can be submitted to the Java compiler at one time. Each file may contain only one public class. The name of the public class, not including its package name, must be the same as the name of the source code file, not including its extension. The *options* available with the Java compiler are explained in Fig. L.1.

Option	Explanation
-classpath *path*	Overrides the CLASSPATH with *path* for this invocation of the compiler.
-d *directory*	Specifies the *directory* into which the created class files will be stored. It will create the directories if they do not exist.
-depend	Requests recompilation of all dependent files.
-deprecation	Lists the specific methods used by the program that are now obsolete (deprecated).
-g	Includes debugger information in the class files.
-J *option*	Specifies an *option* to adjust the execution environment or memory usage.
-nowarn	Suppresses warnings.
-O	Optimizes the class files for faster execution.
-verbose	Produces verbose messages about the compiler's activities.

Figure L.1   Options for the java compiler (`javac`)

java—The Java Interpreter

The Java interpreter translates and executes Java bytecode stored in `.class` files. Only one class name is specified when invoking the interpreter. All additional classes required by the program are loaded automatically. The Java interpreter is invoked with the following syntax:

```
java options classname arguments
```

The interpreter is run against the class specified by *classname*, which must be fully qualified with its package name, if appropriate. The class name should not include the `.class` extension.

The class submitted to the interpreter must contain a `main` method with the appropriate signature. The optional *arguments* following the class name on the command line are passed along to the program in the string array parameter to the `main` method. The *options* available with the Java interpreter are explained in Fig. L.2.

appletviewer—The Java Applet Viewer

The Java applet viewer loads one or more HTML documents and searches them for applet tags. It then loads each applet into a separate window and executes it using the interpreter. All HTML tags other than applet tags are ignored. When it starts up, the applet viewer reads several values from a file called properties that define spe-

Option	Explanation
-classpath *path*	Overrides the CLASSPATH with *path* for this invocation of the interpreter.
-cs -checksource	Automatically recompiles the bytecode if the specified class file was created after the last modification of the source.
-debug	Generates a password to allow the Java debugger (jdb) to attach itself to the interpreter session.
-D *propertyname=value*	Sets *propertyname* to *value* in the system properties list. The Java program can look up the value by its property name.
-help	Prints the list of options that can be included.
-ms *initmem*[k|m]	Specifies that *initmem* bytes should be allocated for the heap initially. Uses kilobytes (*k*) or megabytes (*m*) if specified.
-mx *maxmem*[k|m]	Specifies that *maxmem* bytes should be used as the maximum size of the heap for dynamically allocated objects. Uses kilobytes (*k*) or megabytes (*m*) if specified.
-noasyncgc	Restricts asynchronous garbage collection. It will only occur when the interpreter runs out of memory or when it is called explicitly.
-noclassgc	Restricts class garbage collection.
-noverify	Suppresses the bytecode verifier.
-oss *stacksize*[k|m]	Sets the size of each thread's Java code stack to *stacksize* bytes. Uses kilobytes (*k*) or megabytes (*m*) if specified.
-profile: *filename*	Produces profile information to java.prof or optional *filename*.
-ss *stacksize*[k|m]	Sets the size of each thread's native code stack to *stacksize* bytes. Uses kilobytes (*k*) or megabytes (*m*) if specified.
-v -verbose	Produces a message each time the interpreter loads a class.
-verbosegc	Produces a message whenever the garbage collector frees memory.
-verify	Uses the bytecode verifier for each class that is loaded.
-verifyremote	Uses the bytecode verifier for each class loaded through a class loader (usually an untrusted location). This is the default behavior for the interpreter.
-version	Prints the version number.

Figure L.2   Options for the Java interpreter (java)

cific security restrictions on untrusted applets. The Java applet viewer is invoked with the following syntax:

```
appletviewer options urls
```

The appletviewer is run against the specified *urls*. The *options* available with the applet viewer are explained in Fig. L.3.

Option	Explanation
-debug	Starts the appletviewer within the Java debugger (jdb)
-J *option*	Specifies an *option* to adjust the execution environment or memory usage.

Figure L.3 Options for the Java applet viewer (`appletviewer`)

`jdb`—The Java Debugger

The Java debugger is a command-line tool that works in concert with the Java interpreter. Its purpose is to help the user find defects in software by allowing the user to analyze the executing program. The Java debugger can be executed on its own, which starts a new copy of the interpreter, or it can be attached to an interpreter session that is already running by specifying the appropriate password. The Java debugger is invoked with the following syntax:

```
jdb intoptions classname
```

or

```
jdb options
```

When used to start a new session, the interpreter is run against `classname`, using the Java interpreter options specified by `intoptions`. When used to connect to an existing interpreter session, the `options` of the Java debugger are used as explained in Fig. L.4.

`javadoc`—The Java Documentation Generator

The Java documentation generator creates HTML files that describe the specified package or source code files. The documentation describes each public class or inter-

Option	Explanation
-host *hostname*	Specifies that *hostname* is the host upon which the interpreter session is running.
-password *password*	Confirms the *password* that was generated by the Java interpreter using its debug option. It is a required option when attaching to a running interpreter.

Figure L.4 Options for the Java debugger (jdb)

face, its inheritance hierarchy, and each nonprivate variable and method in the class. The documentation also includes any comments from the source code that begin with /** and end with */. The Java documentation generator is invoked with the following syntax:

```
javadoc options packagename
```

or

```
javadoc options files
```

When the documentation generator is run against a package specified by package-name, the directory corresponding to the package is searched for java source code *files*. Documentation is generated for each class in those files. The documentation generator also creates an HTML index of the classes in the package. When run against a set of Java source code *files*, documentation is generated for each public class defined in those files. The *options* available with the Java documentation generator are explained in Fig. L.5.

Option	Explanation
-author	Includes @author tags, which are omitted by default.
-classpath *path*	Overrides the CLASSPATH with *path* for this invocation of the documentation generator.
-d *directory*	Specifies the *directory* into which the created HTML files will be stored. It will create the directories if they do not exist.
-J *option*	Specifies an *option* to adjust the execution environment or memory usage.
-noindex	Suppresses the package index, which is produced by default.
-nodeprecated	Suppresses paragraphs with the @deprecated tag.
-notree	Suppresses the class hierarchy, which is produced by default.
-public	Shows only public classes, variables, and methods.
-protected	Shows protected and public classes, variables, and methods. This option is the default if no visibility option is explicitly specified.
-package	Shows package, protected, and public classes, variables, and methods.
-private	Shows all classes, variables, and methods.
-sourcepath *path*	Specifies the search *path* for source files.
-verbose	Produces verbose messages about the documentation generator's activities.
-version	Includes @version tags, which are omitted by default.

Figure L.5 Options for the Java documentation generator (javadoc)

`javah`—The Java Native Method C File Generator

The Java native method C file generator creates C header (.h) files and C source code (.c) files used to form the relationship between a Java native method and its implementation in C. Appendix J describes this process in more detail. The Java native method C file generator is invoked with the following syntax:

```
javah options classnames
```

The native method C file generator runs against the specified *classnames* (.class files). The *options* available with the Java native method C file generator are explained in Fig. L.6.

Option	Explanation
-classpath *path*	Overrides the CLASSPATH with *path* for this invocation of the native method C file generator.
-d *directory*	Specifies the *directory* into which the created files will be stored. It will create the directories if they do not exist.
-help	Prints the list of options that can be included.
-jni	Creates an output file with JNI native method function prototypes.
-o *outputfile*	Combines all header (.h) and source (.c) file output into *outputfile*.
-stubs	Generates the source (.c) stub files, and not the header (.h) files. Without this option, header files are created.
-td *directory*	Specifies the *directory* where temporary files will be stored. The default is /tmp.
-trace	Includes tracing information in the stubs file.
-private	Shows all classes, variables, and methods.
-v	Produces verbose messages about the native method C file generator's activities.
-version	Prints the build version.

Figure L.6   Options for the Java native method C file generator (`javah`)

javap—The Java Class Disassembler

The Java class disassembler creates and prints a human-readable version of the specified Java bytecode classes. By default, the disassembler prints declarations of all methods, constructors, and static initializers with public or default visibility for each of the specified classes. The Java class disassembler is invoked with the following syntax:

```
javap options classnames
```

The class disassembler runs against the specified `classnames` (`.class` files). The `options` available with the Java class disassembler are explained in Fig. L.7.

Option	Explanation
-b	Ensures backward compatibility with earlier versions of `javap`.
-c	Prints the Java Virtual Machine instructions for each method.
-classpath *path*	Overrides the CLASSPATH with *path* for this invocation of the class disassembler.
-h	Generates code appropriate for a C language header file.
-J *option*	Specifies an *option* to adjust the execution environment or memory usage.
-l	Prints line numbers and local variable information.
-p	Prints private and protected methods and variables.
-public	Shows only public classes, variables, and methods.
-protected	Shows protected and public classes, variables, and methods. This option is the default if no visibility option is explicitly specified.
-package	Shows package, protected, and public classes, variables, and methods.
-private	Shows all classes, variables, and methods.
-s	Prints internal type signatures.
-verbose	Prints additional information for each method.
-verify	Runs the verifier.
-version	Prints the version of `javap`.

Figure L.7 Options for the Java class disassembler (`javap`)

Appendix M

Java Exceptions and Errors

This appendix contains a list of run-time *exceptions* and *errors* produced by the Java language and the Java Application Programmer Interface (API). It is not an exhaustive list, but does contain most of the exceptions and errors that arise in programs within the scope of this text.

Both exceptions and errors indicate that a problem has occurred while a program was executing. Exceptions can be caught and handled under programmer control using the Java `try` block and `catch` statements. Errors represent more serious problems and generally should not be caught. Some exceptions and errors indicate the same type of problem, such as `NoSuchMethodException` and `NoSuchMethodError`. In these cases the particular situation in which the problem arises determines whether an exception or an error is thrown.

Exceptions

- `AWTException (java.awt)`
  A general exception indicating that some problem has occurred in a class of the `java.awt` package.
- `ArithmeticException (java.lang)`
  An illegal arithmetic operation was attempted, such as dividing by zero.
- `ArrayIndexOutOfBoundsException (java.lang)`
  An index into an array object is out of range.
- `ArrayStoreException (java.lang)`
  An attempt was made to assign a value to an array element of an incompatible type.

- `BindException` (`java.net`)

  A socket could not be bound to a local address and port.
- `ClassCastException` (`java.lang`)

  An attempt was made to cast an object reference to an incompatible type.
- `ClassNotFoundException` (`java.lang`)

  A specific class or interface could not be found.
- `CloneNotSupportedException` (`java.lang`)

  An attempt was made to clone an object instantiated from a class that does not implement the `Cloneable` interface.
- `EOFException` (`java.io`)

  The end of file has been encountered before normal completion of an input operation.
- `EmptyStackException` (`java.util`)

  An attempt was made to reference an element from an empty stack.
- `Exception` (`java.lang`)

  The root of the exception hierarchy.
- `FileNotFoundException` (`java.io`)

  A specified file name could not be found.
- `IOException` (`java.io`)

  A requested I/O operation could not be completed normally.
- `IllegalAccessException` (`java.lang`)

  The currently executing method does not have access to the definition of a class that it is attempting to load.
- `IllegalArgumentException` (`java.lang`)

  An invalid or inappropriate argument was passed to a method.
- `IllegalMonitorStateException` (`java.lang`)

  A thread attempted to notify or wait on another thread that is waiting on an object that it has not locked.
- `IllegalStateException` (`java.lang`)

  A method was invoked from an improper state.
- `IllegalComponentStateException` (`java.awt`)

  A component method was invoked from an improper state.
- `IllegalThreadStateException` (`java.lang`)

  An operation was attempted on a thread that was not in an appropriate state for that operation to succeed.
- `IndexOutOfBoundsException` (`java.lang`)

  An index into an object such as an array, string, or vector was out of range. The invalid index could be part of a subrange, specified by a start and end point or a start point and a length.
- `InstantiationException` (`java.lang`)

  A class could not be instantiated using the `newInstance` method of class `Class` because it is abstract, or an array, or an interface.

- InterruptedException (java.lang)

  While one thread was waiting, another thread interrupted it using the interrupt method of the Thread class.
- InterruptedIOException (java.io)

  While one thread was waiting for the completion of an I/O operation, another thread interrupted it using the interrupt method of the Thread class.
- MalformedURLException (java.net)

  A specified URL does not have an appropriate format or used an unknown protocol.
- NegativeArraySizeException (java.lang)

  An attempt was made to instantiate an array that has a negative length.
- NoRouteToHostException (java.net)

  A path could not be found when attempting to connect a socket to a remote address and port.
- NoSuchElementException (java.util)

  An attempt was made to access an element of an empty vector.
- NoSuchFieldException (java.lang)

  An attempt was made to access a nonexistent field.
- NoSuchMethodException (java.lang)

  A specified method could not be found.
- NullPointerException (java.lang)

  A null reference was used where an object reference was needed.
- NumberFormatException (java.lang)

  An operation was attempted using a number in an illegal format.
- ParseException (java.text)

  A string could not be parsed according to the specified format.
- ProtocolException (java.net)

  Some aspect of a network communication protocol was not executed correctly.
- RuntimeException (java.lang)

  The superclass of all unchecked runtime exceptions.
- SecurityException (java.lang)

  An operation was attempted which violates some kind of security measure.
- SocketException (java.net)

  An operation using a socket could not be completed normally.
- StringIndexOutOfBoundsException (java.lang)

  An index into a String or StringBuffer object is out of range.
- TooManyListenersException (java.util)

  An event source has registered too many listeners.
- UTFDataFormatException (java.io)

  An attempt was made to convert a string to or from UTF-8 format, but the string was too long or the data were not in valid UTF-8 format.

- UnknownHostException (`java.net`)

  A specified network host name could not be resolved into a network address.
- UnknownServiceException (`java.net`)

  An attempt was made to request a service that the current network connection does not support.

Errors

- AWTError (`java.awt`)

  A general error indicating that a serious problem has occurred in a class of the `java.awt` package.
- AbstractMethodError (`java.lang`)

  An attempt was made to invoke an `abstract` method.
- ClassCircularityError (`java.lang`)

  A circular dependency was found while performing class initialization.
- ClassFormatError (`java.lang`)

  The format of the bytecode in a class file is invalid.
- Error (`java.lang`)

  The root of the error hierarchy.
- ExceptionInInitializerError (`java.lang`)

  An exception has occurred in a static initializer.
- IllegalAccessError (`java.lang`)

  An attempt was made to reference a class, method, or variable that was not accessible.
- IncompatibleClassChangeError (`java.lang`)

  An illegal operation was attempted on a class.
- InstantiationError (`java.lang`)

  An attempt was made to instantiate an abstract class or an interface.
- InternalError (`java.lang`)

  An error occurred in the Java interpreter.
- LinkageError (`java.lang`)

  An error occurred while attempting to link classes or resolve dependencies between classes.
- NoClassDefFoundError (`java.lang`)

  The definition of a specified class could not be found.
- NoSuchFieldError (`java.lang`)

  A specified field could not be found.
- NoSuchMethodError (`java.lang`)

  A specified method could not be found.
- OutOfMemoryError (`java.lang`)

  The interpreter has run out of memory and cannot reclaim more through garbage collection.

- StackOverflowError (java.lang)

  A stack overflow has occurred in the Java interpreter.
- ThreadDeath (java.lang)

  The stop method of a thread has caused a thread (but not the interpreter) to terminate. No error message is printed.
- UnknownError (java.lang)

  An error has occurred in the Java Virtual Machine (JVM).
- UnsatisfiedLinkError (java.lang)

  All of the links in a loaded class could not be resolved.
- VerifyError (java.lang)

  A class failed the bytecode verification procedures.
- VirtualMachineError (java.lang)

  The superclass of several errors relating to the Java Virtual Machine (JVM).

Java Syntax

This appendix contains a complete description of the syntax of the Java language, expressed as a formal grammar. Such a description is often used to learn the detailed syntax of the language or to explain a particular syntax error. The grammar is represented in *Backus-Naur Form* (BNF), a common notation for describing language syntax.

This particular grammar is based on one produced by Sriram Sankar of Sun Microsystems and is easily modified for use in various compiler construction tools.

```
// Program structuring syntax follows.

CompilationUnit :

    [ PackageDeclaration ]
    ( ImportDeclaration )*
    ( TypeDeclaration )*
    <EOF>

PackageDeclaration :
    "package" Name ";"

ImportDeclaration :
    "import" Name [ "." "*" ] ";"

TypeDeclaration :
    ClassDeclaration |
    InterfaceDeclaration |
    ";"
```

```
                ration syntax follows.
             laration :
                abstract" | "final" | "public" )*
             odifiedClassDeclaration


          fiedClassDeclaration :
          lass" <IDENTIFIER> [ "extends" Name ] [ "implements" NameList ]
          lassBody

ClassBody :
    "{" ( ClassBodyDeclaration )* "}"

NestedClassDeclaration :
    ( "static"  "abstract"  "final"  "public"
        "protected"  "private" )*
    UnmodifiedClassDeclaration

ClassBodyDeclaration :
    Initializer
    NestedClassDeclaration
    NestedInterfaceDeclaration
    ConstructorDeclaration
    MethodDeclaration
    FieldDeclaration

InterfaceDeclaration :
    ( "abstract"  "public" )*
    UnmodifiedInterfaceDeclaration

NestedInterfaceDeclaration :
    ( "static" | "abstract" | "final" | "public"
        "protected" | "private" )*
    UnmodifiedInterfaceDeclaration

UnmodifiedInterfaceDeclaration :
    "interface" <IDENTIFIER> [ "extends" NameList ]
    "{" ( InterfaceMemberDeclaration )* "}"

InterfaceMemberDeclaration :
    NestedClassDeclaration
    NestedInterfaceDeclaration
    MethodDeclaration
    FieldDeclaration
```

```
FieldDeclaration :
    ( "public" | "protected" | "private" | "static" |
        "final" | "transient" | "volatile" )*
    Type VariableDeclarator ( "," VariableDeclarator )* ";"

VariableDeclarator :
    VariableDeclaratorId [ "=" VariableInitializer ]

VariableDeclaratorId :
    <IDENTIFIER> ( "[" "]" )*

VariableInitializer :
    ArrayInitializer
    Expression

ArrayInitializer :
    "{" [ VariableInitializer ( "," VariableInitializer )* ]
        [ "," ] "}"

MethodDeclaration :
    ( "public" | "protected" | "private" | "static" |
        "abstract" | "final" | "native" | "synchronized" )*
    ResultType MethodDeclarator [ "throws" NameList ]
    ( Block   ";" )

MethodDeclarator :
    <IDENTIFIER> FormalParameters ( "[" "]" )*

FormalParameters :
    "(" [ FormalParameter ( "," FormalParameter )* ] ")"

FormalParameter :
    [ "final" ] Type VariableDeclaratorId

ConstructorDeclaration :
    [ "public" | "protected" | "private" ]
    <IDENTIFIER> FormalParameters [ "throws" NameList ]
    "{"
      [ ExplicitConstructorInvocation ]
      ( BlockStatement )*
    "}"

ExplicitConstructorInvocation :
    "this" Arguments ";"
```

```
        ion :
        ssion ( "&&" InclusiveOrExpression )*


        n :
        ssion ( "" ExclusiveOrExpression )*


        on :
        ( "^" AndExpression )*

AndExpression :
    EqualityExpression ( "&" EqualityExpression )*

EqualityExpression :
    InstanceOfExpression ( ( "=="  "!=" ) InstanceOfExpression )*

InstanceOfExpression :
    RelationalExpression [ "instanceof" Type ]

RelationalExpression :
    ShiftExpression ( ( "<"  ">"  "<="  ">=" ) ShiftExpression )*

ShiftExpression :
    AdditiveExpression ( ( "<<"  ">>"  ">>>" ) AdditiveExpression )*

AdditiveExpression :
    MultiplicativeExpression ( ( "+"  "-" ) MultiplicativeExpression )*

MultiplicativeExpression :
    UnaryExpression ( ( "*"  "/"  "%" ) UnaryExpression )*

UnaryExpression :
    ( "+"  "-" ) UnaryExpression |
    PreIncrementExpression |
    PreDecrementExpression |
    UnaryExpressionNotPlusMinus

PreIncrementExpression :
    "++" PrimaryExpression

PreDecrementExpression :
    "--" PrimaryExpression

UnaryExpressionNotPlusMinus :
    ( "~"  "!" ) UnaryExpression
```

```
             [ PrimaryExpression "." ] "super" Arguments ";"

    Initializer :
         [ "static" ] Block

    // Type, name and expression syntax follows.

    Type :
         ( PrimitiveType  Name ) ( "[" "]" )*

    PrimitiveType :
         "boolean" | "char" | "byte" | "short" | "int" |
         "long" | "float" | "double"

    ResultType :
         "void"  Type

    Name :
         <IDENTIFIER>
         ( "." <IDENTIFIER> )*

    NameList :
         Name ( "," Name )*

    // Expression syntax follows.

    Expression :
         Assignment
         ConditionalExpression

    Assignment :
         PrimaryExpression AssignmentOperator Expression

    AssignmentOperator :
         "=" | "*=" | "/=" | "%=" | "+=" | "-=" |
           "<<=" | ">>=" | ">>>=" | "&=" | "^=" | "=" 

    ConditionalExpression :
         ConditionalOrExpression
         [ "?" Expression ":" ConditionalExpression ]

    ConditionalOrExpression :
         ConditionalAndExpression ( " " ConditionalAndExpression )*
```

```
        CastExpression
        PostfixExpression

PostfixExpression :
        PrimaryExpression [ "++"  "--" ]

CastExpression :
        "(" Type ")" UnaryExpression
        "(" Type ")" UnaryExpressionNotPlusMinus

PrimaryExpression :
        PrimaryPrefix ( PrimarySuffix )*

PrimaryPrefix :
        Literal
        Name
        "this"
        "super" "." <IDENTIFIER>
        "(" Expression ")"
        AllocationExpression

PrimarySuffix :
        "." "this"
        "." "class"
        "." AllocationExpression
        "[" Expression "]"
        "." <IDENTIFIER>
        Arguments

Literal :
        <INTEGER_LITERAL>
        <FLOATING_POINT_LITERAL>
        <CHARACTER_LITERAL>
        <STRING_LITERAL>
        BooleanLiteral
        NullLiteral

BooleanLiteral :
        "true"  "false"

NullLiteral :
        "null"

Arguments :
        "(" [ ArgumentList ] ")"
```

```
ArgumentList :
    Expression ( "," Expression )*

AllocationExpression :
    "new" PrimitiveType ArrayDimensions [ ArrayInitializer ] |
    "new" Name
      (
        ArrayDimensions [ ArrayInitializer ]
        Arguments [ ClassBody ]
      )

ArrayDimensions :
    ( "[" Expression "]" )+ ( "[" "]" )*

// Statement syntax follows.

Statement :
    LabeledStatement |
    Block |
    EmptyStatement |
    StatementExpression ";" |
    SwitchStatement |
    IfStatement |
    WhileStatement |
    DoStatement |
    ForStatement |
    BreakStatement |
    ContinueStatement |
    ReturnStatement |
    ThrowStatement |
    SynchronizedStatement |
    TryStatement

LabeledStatement :
    <IDENTIFIER> ":" Statement

Block :
    "{" ( BlockStatement )* "}"

BlockStatement :
    LocalVariableDeclaration ";"
    Statement
    UnmodifiedClassDeclaration
```

```
LocalVariableDeclaration :
    [ "final" ] Type VariableDeclarator ( "," VariableDeclarator )*


EmptyStatement :
    ";"


StatementExpression :
    PreIncrementExpression |
    PreDecrementExpression |
    Assignment |
    PostfixExpression


SwitchStatement :
    "switch" "(" Expression ")" "{"
        ( SwitchLabel ( BlockStatement )* )*
    "}"


SwitchLabel :
    "case" Expression ":"
    "default" ":"


IfStatement :
    "if" "(" Expression ")" Statement [ "else" Statement ]


WhileStatement :
    "while" "(" Expression ")" Statement


DoStatement :
    "do" Statement "while" "(" Expression ")" ";"


ForStatement :
    "for" "(" [ ForInit ] ";" [ Expression ] ";"
                [ ForUpdate ] ")" Statement


ForInit :
    LocalVariableDeclaration
    StatementExpressionList


StatementExpressionList :
    StatementExpression ( "," StatementExpression )*


ForUpdate :
    StatementExpressionList
```

```
BreakStatement :
    "break" [ <IDENTIFIER> ] ";"

ContinueStatement :
    "continue" [ <IDENTIFIER> ] ";"

ReturnStatement :
    "return" [ Expression ] ";"

ThrowStatement :
    "throw" Expression ";"

SynchronizedStatement :
    "synchronized" "(" Expression ")" Block

TryStatement :
    "try" Block
    ( "catch" "(" FormalParameter ")" Block )*
    [ "finally" Block ]
```

Appendix 0

The Java API

This appendix contains a succinct summary of the Java Application Programming Interface (API), version 1.1. The first part of the appendix contains diagrams of several of the Java API packages, showing the inheritance relationships between classes. The classes in blue are explored further in the second part of this appendix, which lists the variables, constants, constructors, and methods of each class. It is intended to serve as a quick reference for the support provided by Java's class libraries. The classes are listed in alphabetical order and the package each class is contained in is given in parentheses after the class name.

java.applet

java.awt (part 1 of 3)

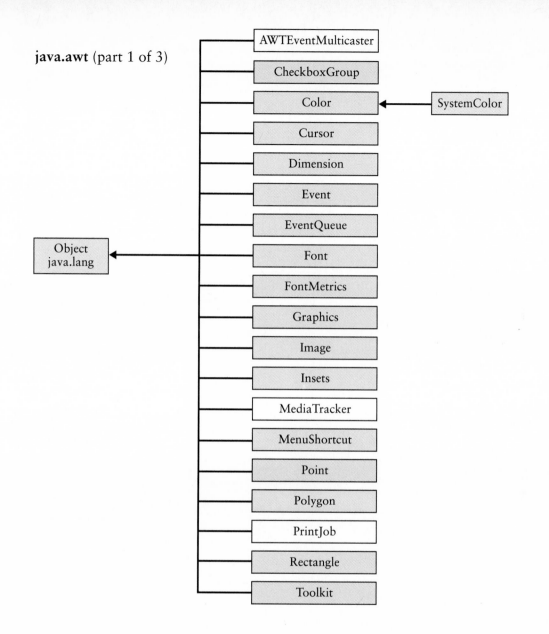

java.awt (part 2 of 3)

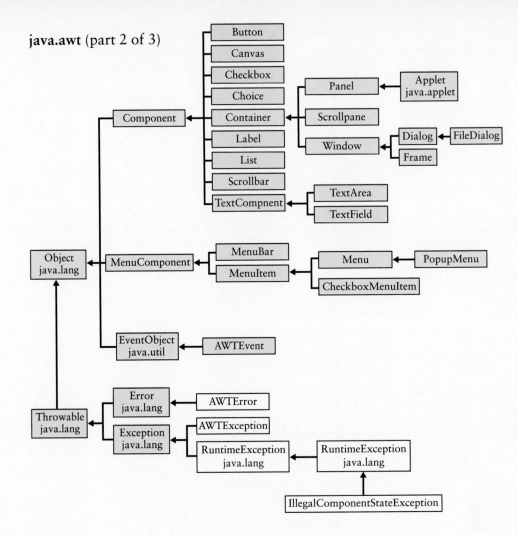

java.awt (part 3 of 3)

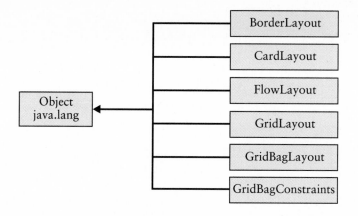

java.awt.event

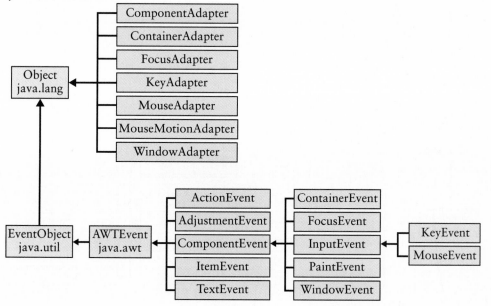

java.io (part 1 of 2)

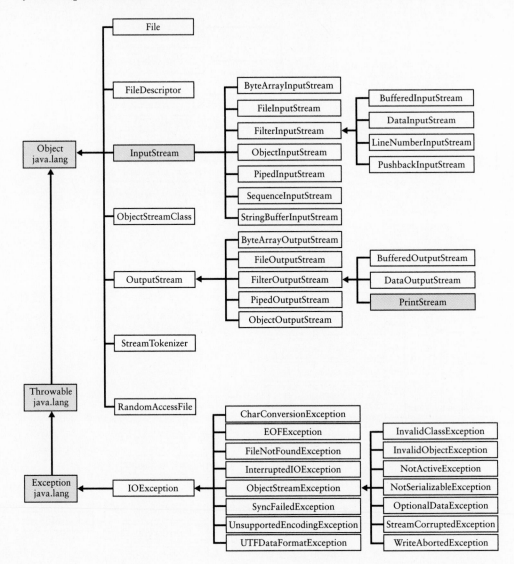

java.io (part 2 of 2)

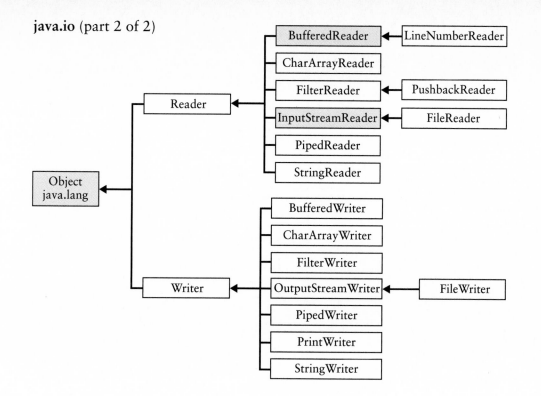

java.lang (part 1 of 3)

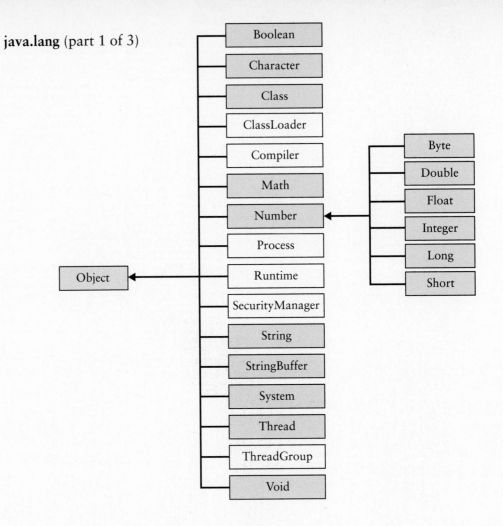

java.lang (part 2 of 3)

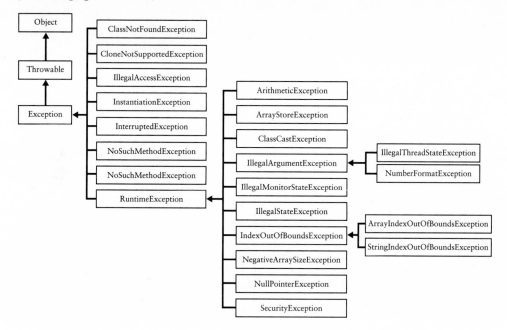

java.lang (part 3 of 3)

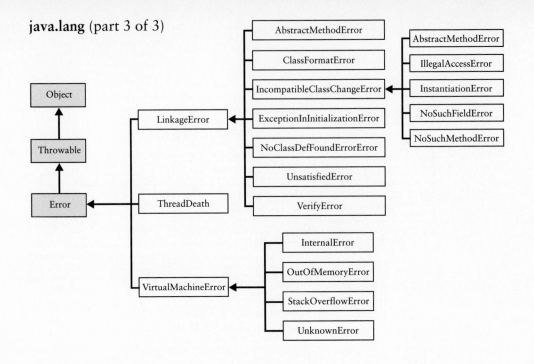

java.math

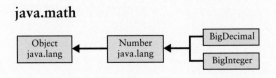

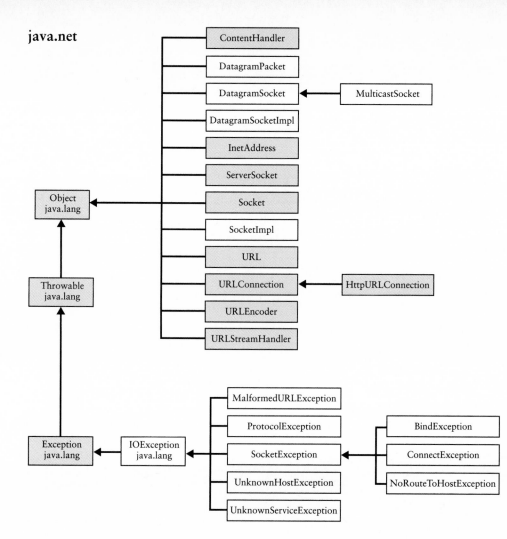

java.text

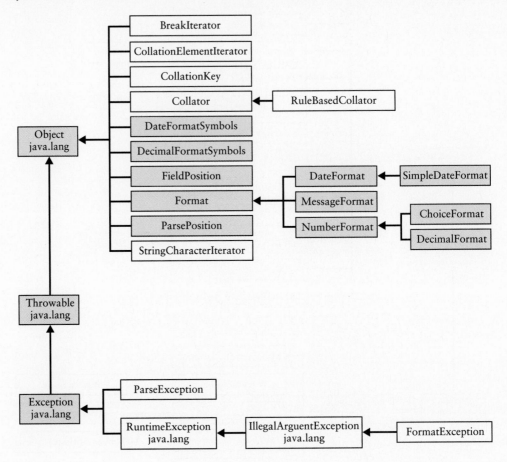

java.util

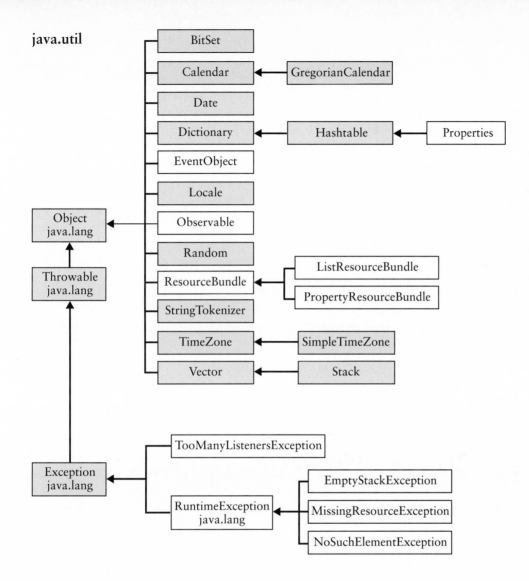

ActionEvent (`java.awt.event`)

A public class, derived from `AWTEvent`, that represents an AWT action event (from a component such as a `Button`, `List`, `MenuItem` or `TextField`).

Variables and Constants

- `public static final int ALT_MASK`
- `public static final int CTRL_MASK`
- `public static final int META_MASK`
- `public static final int SHIFT_MASK`
    Constant values which represent masks for the Alt, Control, Meta, and Shift keys being pressed during an action event.
- `public static final int ACTION_FIRST`
- `public static final int ACTION_LAST`
    Constant values that represent the index of the first and last action event ids.
- `public static final int ACTION_PERFORMED`
    A constant value that represents an action performed AWT event type.

Constructors

- `public ActionEvent(Object src, int type, String cmd)`
- `public ActionEvent(Object src, int type, String cmd, int keys)`
    Creates a new instance of an `ActionEvent` from the specified source object, event type, and command string. Additionally, a mask value can be set that defines the types of keys depressed during the event.

Methods

- `public String getActionCommand()`
    Returns the command string associated with this action.
- `public int getModifiers()`
    Returns the mask of the modifiers (special keys) depressed during this event.
- `public String paramString()`
    Returns a string containing the parameters of this `ActionEvent`.

AdjustmentEvent (`java.awt.event`)

A public class, derived from `AWTEvent`, that represents an AWT adjustment event (from a component such as a `Scrollbar` or `ScrollPane`).

- `public static final int ADJUSTMENT_FIRST`

- `public static final int ADJUSTMENT_LAST`
  Constant values that represent the index of the first and last adjustment event ids.
- `public static final int ADJUSTMENT_VALUE_CHANGED`
  A constant value that represents an adjustment value change event.
- `public static final int BLOCK_DECREMENT`
- `public static final int BLOCK_INCREMENT`
  Constant values that represent block decrement and increment events.
- `public static final int TRACK`
  A constant value which represents an absolute tracking adjustment event.
- `public static final int UNIT_DECREMENT`
- `public static final int UNIT_INCREMENT`
  Constant values which represent unit decrement and increment events.

Constructors

- `public AdjustmentEvent(Adjustable source, int id, int type, int val)`
  Creates a new instance of an `AdjustmentEvent` from a specified source and having a specified `id`, `type`, and `value`.

Methods

- `public Adjustable getAdjustable()`
  Returns the adjustable object that originated this AWT `AdjustmentEvent`.
- `public int getAdjustmentType()`
  Returns the type of adjustment for this event.
- `public int getValue()`
  Returns the current value of this `AdjustmentEvent`.
- `public String paramString()`
  Returns a string containing the parameters of this event.

Applet (`java.applet`)

A public class, derived from `Panel`, that is intended to be used as a program running inside a Web page.

Constructors

- `public Applet()`
  Creates a new instance of an applet for inclusion on a Web page.

Methods

- `public void destroy()`

  Destroys the applet and all of its resources. This method contains no functionality and should be overridden by subclasses.

- `public AppletContext getAppletContext()`

  Returns this applet's context (the environment in which it is running).

- `public String getAppletInfo()`

  Returns a string representation of information regarding this applet. This method contains no functionality and should be overridden by subclasses.

- `public AudioClip getAudioClip(URL audio)`

- `public AudioClip getAudioClip(URL base, String filename)`

  Returns the `AudioClip` requested. The location of the audio clip can be given by the `base` URL and the `filename` relative to that `base`.

- `public URL getCodeBase()`

- `public URL getDocumentBase()`

- `public Locale getLocale()`

  Returns the URL of this applet, the document that contains this applet, or the locale of this applet.

- `public Image getImage(URL image)`

- `public Image getImage(URL base, String filename)`

  Returns the image requested. The location of the image can be given by the `base` URL and the `filename` relative to that `base`.

- `public String getParameter(String param)`

- `public String[][] getParameterInfo()`

  Returns the value of the specified parameter for this applet. An array of string elements containing information about each parameter for this applet can also be obtained. Each element of the returned array should be comprised of three strings (parameter name, type, and description). This method contains no functionality and should be overridden by subclasses.

- `public void init()`

  This method provides initialization functionality to the applet prior to the first time that the applet is started. It is automatically called by the browser or the `appletviewer` program. This method contains no functionality and should be overridden by subclasses.

- `public boolean isActive()`

  Returns a true value if this applet is currently active. An applet is considered active just prior to execution of its `start` method and is no longer active just after execution of its `stop` method.

- `public void play(URL source)`

- `public void play(URL base, String filename)`

  Plays the audio clip located at `source`. The location of the audio clip can be given as a `base` URL and the `filename` relative to that `base`.

- `public void resize(Dimension dim)`

- `public void resize(int w, int h)`
  Resizes this applet according to the specified dimension.
- `public final void setStub(AppletStub stub)`
  Sets the interface between this applet and the browser or appletviewer program.
- `public void showStatus(String message)`
  Prints the specified `message` in the browser's status window.
- `public void start()`
  This method generally contains functionality relevant to the starting of this applet. It is called after the applet has been initialized (with the `init` method) and every time the applet is reloaded in the browser or `appletviewer` program. This method contains no functionality and should be overridden by subclasses.
- `public void stop()`
  This method generally contains functionality relevant to the stopping of this applet. It is called by the browser (when the containing Web page is replaced) or appletviewer program. This method contains no functionality and should be overridden by subclasses.

AWTEvent (`java.awt`)

A public class, derived from `EventObject`, that is the root class for all of the AWT event classes.

Variables and Constants

- `public final static long ACTION_EVENT_MASK`
- `public final static long ADJUSTMENT_EVENT_MASK`
- `public final static long COMPONENT_EVENT_MASK`
- `public final static long CONTAINER_EVENT_MASK`
- `public final static long FOCUS_EVENT_MASK`
- `public final static long ITEM_EVENT_MASK`
- `public final static long KEY_EVENT_MASK`
- `public final static long MOUSE_EVENT_MASK`
- `public final static long MOUSE_MOTION_EVENT_MASK`
- `public final static long TEXT_EVENT_MASK`
- `public final static long WINDOW_EVENT_MASK`
  Constant values representing the AWT event masks for various events.
- `protected boolean consumed`
  A variable representing the state of the event. A true value means that it has not been sent to the appropriate peer, false indicates that it has.
- `protected int id`
  The numeric identification for this event.

Constructors

- `public AWTEvent(Event evt)`
  Creates a new `AWTEvent` from the specified event.
- `public AWTEvent(Object src, int type)`
  Creates a new `AWTEvent` from a specified source, and having a defined type.

Methods

- `protected void consume()`
  Targets this `AWTEvent` to be sent to the appropriate peer.
- `public int getID()`
  Returns this event's type.
- `protected boolean isConsumed()`
  Returns a true value if this `AWTEvent` has been sent to the appropriate peer.
- `public String paramString()`
  Returns the parameter string for this `AWTEvent`.
- `public String toString()`
  Returns a string representation of this AWTEvent.

BigDecimal (`java.math`)

A public class, derived from `Number`, which can be used to represent a decimal number with a definable precision.

Variables and Constants

- `ROUND_CEILING`
  A constant that represents a rounding mode in which the value of the `BigDecimal` is rounded up (away from zero) if the number is positive, and down (closer to zero) if the number is negative.
- `ROUND_DOWN`
  A constant that represents a rounding mode in which the value of the `BigDecimal` is rounded closer to zero (decreasing a positive number and increasing a negative number).
- `ROUND_FLOOR`
  A constant that represents a rounding mode in which the value of the `BigDecimal` is rounded down (closer to zero) if the number is positive, and up (away from zero) if the number is negative.
- `ROUND_HALF_DOWN`
  A constant that represents a rounding mode in which the value of the `BigDecimal` is rounded as in `ROUND_UP` if the fraction of the number is greater than 0.5 and as `ROUND_DOWN` in all other cases.

- ROUND_HALF_EVEN

  A constant that represents a rounding mode in which the value of the BigDecimal is rounded as in ROUND_HALF_UP if the number to the left of the decimal is odd and as ROUND_HALF_DOWN when the number is even.

- ROUND_HALF_UP

  A constant that represents a rounding mode in which the value of the BigDecimal is rounded as in ROUND_UP if the fraction of the number is greater than or equal to 0.5 and as in ROUND_DOWN in all other cases.

- ROUND_UNNECESSARY

  A constant that represents a rounding mode in which the value of the BigDecimal is not rounded (if possible) and an exact result be returned.

- ROUND_UP

  A constant that represents a rounding mode in which the value of the BigDecimal is rounded away from zero (increasing a positive number, and decreasing a negative number).

Constructors

- `public BigDecimal(BigInteger arg)`
- `public BigDecimal(BigInteger arg, int scale) throws NumberFormatException`
- `public BigDecimal(double arg) throws NumberFormatException`
- `public BigDecimal(String arg) throws NumberFormatException`

  Creates an instance of a BigDecimal from arg. The string argument may contain a preceding minus sign indicating a negative number. The resulting BigDecimal's scale will be the number of integers to the right of the decimal point in the string, a specified value, or 0 (zero) if none are present.

Methods

- `public double doubleValue()`
- `public float floatValue()`
- `public int intValue()`
- `public long longValue()`
- `public BigInteger toBigInteger()`
- `public String toString()`

  Converts this BigDecimal to either a Java primitive type or a BigInteger.

- `public BigDecimal abs()`

  Returns the absolute value of this BigDecimal with the same scale as this BigDecimal.

- `public BigDecimal add(BigDecimal arg)`

- `public BigDecimal subtract(BigDecimal arg)`
  Returns the result of `arg` added to or subtracted from this `BigDecimal`, with the resulting scale equal to the larger of the two `BigDecimal`'s scales.
- `public int compareTo(BigDecimal arg)`
  This method compares this `BigDecimal` to `arg` and will return a −1 if this `BigDecimal` is less than `arg`, 0 if equal to `arg` or a 1 if greater than `arg`. If the values of the two `BigDecimals` are identical and the scales are different, they are considered equal.
- `public BigDecimal divide(BigDecimal arg, int mode)`
  `throws ArithmeticException, IllegalArgumentException`
- `public BigDecimal divide(BigDecimal arg, int scale, int mode) throws ArithmeticException, IllegalArgumentException`
  Returns the result of this `BigDecimal` divided by `arg`. If required the rounding `mode` is used. The resulting `BigDecimal`'s scale is identical to this `BigDecimal`'s scale or a specified value.
- `public boolean equals(Object arg)`
  Returns a true value if this `BigDecimal`'s value and scale are equal to `arg`'s value and scale.
- `public int hashCode()`
  Returns the hash code of this `BigDecimal`.
- `public BigDecimal max(BigDecimal arg)`
- `public BigDecimal min(BigDecimal arg)`
  Returns the greater or lesser of this `BigDecimal` and `arg`.
- `public BigDecimal movePointLeft(int num)`
- `public BigDecimal movePointRight(int num)`
  Returns this `BigDecimal` with the decimal point moved num positions.
- `public BigDecimal multiply(BigDecimal arg)`
  Returns the result of this `BigDecimal` multiplied with the value of `arg`. The scale of the resulting `BigDecimal` is the result of the addition of the two `BigDecimal`'s scales.
- `public BigDecimal negate()`
  Returns the negation of this `BigDecimal`'s value with the same scale.
- `public int scale()`
  Returns the scale of this `BigDecimal`.
- `public BigDecimal setScale(int val) throws ArithmeticException, IllegalArgumentException`
- `public BigDecimal setScale(int val, int mode) throws ArithmeticException, IllegalArgumentException`
  Returns a `BigDecimal` whose value is the same as this `BigDecimal`'s and has a new scale specified by `val`. If rounding is necessary, a rounding `mode` can be specified.
- `public int signum()`
  Returns a −1 if this `BigDecimal` is negative, 0 if zero, and 1 if positive.
- `public static BigDecimal valueOf(long value)`

- `public static BigDecimal valueOf(long value, int scale) throws NumberFormatException`

   Returns a `BigDecimal` with a defined `value`. The scale of the returned number is specified or it defaults to 0 (zero).

BigInteger (`java.math`)

A public class, derived from `Number`, that can be used to represent an integer in a two's complement format of any precision.

Constructors

- `public BigInteger(byte[] arg) throws NumberFormatException`
- `public BigInteger(int signum, byte[] magnitude) throws NumberFormatException`

   Creates an instance of a `BigInteger` from the specified byte array. The sign of the number can be placed in `signum` (where −1 is negative, 0 is zero, and 1 is positive).

- `public BigInteger(String arg) throws NumberFormatException`
- `public BigInteger(String arg, int radix) throws NumberFormatException`

   Creates an instance of a `BigInteger` from the string `arg`, which can contain decimal numbers preceded by an optional minus sign. The argument `radix` specifies the base of the `arg` value.

- `public BigInteger(int size, Random rand) throws IllegalArgumentException`
- `public BigInteger(int size, int prob, Random rand)`

   Creates a (generally) prime instance of a `BigInteger` from a random integer, `rand`, of a specified length, `size`. The certainty parameter (`prob`) represents the amount of probability that the generated number is a prime. The probability is generated as $1 - (.5 ** prob)$.

Methods

- `public double doubleValue()`
- `public float floatValue()`
- `public int intValue()`
- `public long longValue()`
- `public String toString()`
- `public String toString(int base)`

   Converts this `BigDecimal` to either a Java primitive type or a `BigInteger`. The base can specify the radix of the number value returned.

- `public BigInteger abs()`
  Returns the absolute value of this `BigInteger`.
- `public BigInteger add(BigInteger arg) throws ArithmeticException`
- `public BigInteger subtract(BigInteger arg)`
  Adds the argument to, or subtracts `arg` from this `BigInteger` and returns the result.
- `public BigInteger and(BigInteger arg)`
- `public BigInteger andNot(BigInteger arg)`
- `public BigInteger not()`
- `public BigInteger or(BigInteger arg)`
- `public BigInteger xor(BigInteger arg)`
  Returns the result of a logical operation of this `BigInteger` and the value of `arg`. The `not` method returns the logical not of this `BigInteger`.
- `public int bitCount()`
  Returns the number of bits from this `BigInteger` that are different from the sign bit.
- `public int bitLength()`
  Returns the number of bits from this `BigInteger`, excluding the sign bit.
- `public BigInteger clearBit(int index) throws ArithmeticException`
  Returns the modified representation of this `BigInteger` with the bit at position `index` cleared.
- `public int compareTo(BigInteger arg)`
  Compares this `BigInteger` to the parameter `arg`. If this `BigInteger` is less than `arg`, a -1 is returned, if equal to `arg` a 0 (zero) is returned, and if greater than `arg`, a 1 is returned.
- `public BigInteger divide(BigInteger arg) throws ArithmeticException`
- `public BigInteger[] divideAndRemainder(BigInteger arg) throws ArithmeticException`
  Returns the result of this `BigInteger` divided by `arg`. The `divideAndRemainder` method returns as the first element ([0]) the quotient, and the second element ([1]) the remainder.
- `public boolean equals(Object arg)`
  Returns a true value if this `BigInteger` is equal to the parameter `arg`.
- `public BigInteger flipBit(int index) throws ArithmeticException`
  Returns the modified representation of this `BigInteger` with the bit at position `index` flipped.
- `public BigInteger gcd(BigInteger arg)`
  Returns the greatest common denominator of the absolute value of this `BigInteger` and the absolute value of the parameter `arg`.
- `public int getLowestSetBit()`

Returns the index of the rightmost bit that is equal to one from this `BigInteger`.

- `public int hashCode()`

  Returns the hash code of this `BigInteger`.

- `public boolean isProbablePrime(int prob)`

  Returns a true value if this `BigInteger` is probably a prime number. The parameter `prob` represents the certainty of the decision, calculated as $1 - (.5**prob)$.

- `public BigInteger max(BigInteger arg)`
- `public BigInteger min(BigInteger arg)`

  Returns the larger or smaller of this `BigInteger` or `arg`.

- `public BigInteger mod(BigInteger arg)`
- `public BigInteger modInverse(BigInteger arg) throws ArithmeticException`
- `public BigInteger modPow(BigInteger exp, BigInteger arg)`

  Returns the result of this `BigInteger` mod `arg`. The `modInverse` returns the modular multiplicative inverse. `modPow` returns the result of this (`BigInteger` ** `exp`) mod `arg`.

- `public BigInteger multiply(BigInteger arg)`

  Returns the result of this `BigInteger` multiplied by `arg`.

- `public BigInteger negate()`

  Returns this `BigInteger` negated (this `BigInteger` * -1).

- `public BigInteger pow(int exp) throws ArithmeticException`

  Returns the result of this `BigInteger` ** `exp`.

- `public BigInteger remainder(BigInteger arg) throws ArithmeticException`

  Returns the result of this `BigInteger` mod `arg`.

- `public BigInteger setBit(int index) throws ArithmeticException`

  Returns the result of this `BigInteger` with the bit at the specified index set.

- `public BigInteger shiftLeft(int num)`
- `public BigInteger shiftRight(int num)`

  Returns the result of this `BigInteger` shifted num bits.

- `public int signum()`

  Returns a -1 if the value of this `BigInteger` is negative, 0 if zero, and 1 if positive.

- `public boolean testBit(int index) throws ArithmeticException`

  Returns a true value if the bit at the specified index is set.

- `public byte[] toByteArray()`

  Returns the two's complement of this `BigInteger` in an array of bytes.

- public static BigInteger valueOf(long arg)

  Returns a `BigInteger` from the value of `arg`.

BitSet (`java.util`)

A public final class, derived from `Object` and implementing `Cloneable` and `Serializable`, that allows for the manipulation of a vectored array of bits.

Constructors

- public BitSet()
- public BitSet(int size)

  Creates a new instance of a bit sequence of `size` bits (the default is 64). Each of the initial bits are set to false.

Methods

- public void and(BitSet arg)
- public void or(BitSet arg)
- public void xor(BitSet arg)

  Places all of the bits from both this BitSet AND/OR/XORed with the bits of `arg` into this `BitSet`.
- public void clear(int index)
- public void set(int index)

  Clears or sets the bit (sets it to false) at location `index`.
- public Object clone()

  Returns a clone of this `BitSet`.
- public boolean equals(Object arg)

  Returns a true if `arg` is not null and all bits are equal to this `BitSet`.
- public boolean get(int index)

  Returns the boolean value of the bit at location `index`.
- public int hashCode()

  Returns the hash code of this `BitSet`.
- public int size()

  Returns the size of this `BitSet`.
- public String toString()

  Returns a string representation of this `BitSet` in set notation (i.e., {1, 2, 5})

Boolean (`java.lang`)

A public final class, derived from `Object` and implementing `Serializable`, that contains boolean logic operations, constants, and methods as a wrapper around the Java primitive type `boolean`.

Variables and Constants

- `public final static Boolean TRUE`
- `public final static Boolean FALSE`
    Boolean constant values of true or false.
- `public final static Class TYPE`
    The `Boolean` constant value of the boolean type class.

Constructors

- `public Boolean(boolean arg)`
- `public Boolean(String arg)`
    Creates an instance of the `Boolean` class from the parameter `arg`.

Methods

- `public boolean booleanValue()`
    The boolean value of the current object.
- `public boolean equals(Object arg)`
    Returns the result of an equality comparison against `arg`. Here `arg` must be a boolean object with the same value as this `Boolean` for a resulting true value.
- `public static boolean getBoolean(String str)`
    Returns a `Boolean` representation of the system property named in `str`.
- `public int hashCode()`
    Returns the hash code for this object.
- `public String toString()`
    Returns the string representation of the state of the current object (i.e., "true" or "false").
- `public static Boolean valueOf(String str)`
    Returns a new Boolean initialized to the value of `str`.

BorderLayout (`java.awt`)

A public class, derived from `Object` and implementing `LayoutManager2` and `Serializable`, that lays out a container using five distinct areas (North, South, East, West, and Center).

Variables and Constants

- `public final static String CENTER`
- `public final static String EAST`
- `public final static String NORTH`

- public final static String SOUTH
- public final static String WEST
  Constant values indicating areas of the border layout manager.

Constructors

- public BorderLayout()
- public BorderLayout(int hgap, int vgap)
  Creates a new instance of a BorderLayout. If no initial horizontal and vertical gaps are specified, they default to zero.

Methods

- public void addLayoutComponent(Component item, Object constraints)
- public void removeLayoutComponent(Component item)
  Adds or removes a component to this layout manager. When adding a component, it is possible to restrict the component to the specified constraints.
- public int getHgap()
- public int getVgap()
  Returns the horizontal or vertical gap of components laid out by this layout manager.
- public float getLayoutAlignmentX(Container parent)
- public float getLayoutAlignmentY(Container parent)
  Returns the horizontal or vertical alignment value of the specified container.
- public void invalidateLayout(Container cont)
  Forces this layout manager to discard any cached layout information about the specified container.
- public void layoutContainer(Container cont)
  Lays out the specified container with this layout manager.
- public Dimension maximumLayoutSize(Container cont)
- public Dimension minimumLayoutSize(Container cont)
- public Dimension preferredLayoutSize(Container cont)
  Returns the maximum, minimum or preferred size of the specified container when laid out by this layout manager.
- public void setHgap(int hgap)
- public void setVgap(int vgap)
  Sets the horizontal or vertical gap in pixels of components laid out by this layout manager.
- public String toString()
  Returns a string representation of this layout manager.

BufferedReader (`java.io`)

A public class, derived from `Reader`, that provides a buffered stream of character-based input.

Constructors

- `public BufferedReader(Reader rdr)`
- `public BufferedReader(Reader rdr, int size)`

  Creates a `BufferedReader` from the specified `Reader`, by using a specified size (in characters). The default size is 8192 characters.

Methods

- `public void close() throws IOException`

  Closes this `BufferedReader`.
- `public void mark(int readAheadLimit) throws IOException`

  Sets a mark in the stream where attempts to reset this `BufferedReader` will return to. The `readAheadLimit` determines how far ahead the stream can be read before the mark expires.
- `public boolean markSupported()`

  An overridden method from `Reader` that determines if this stream supports the setting of a mark.
- `public int read() throws IOException`
- `public String readLine() throws IOException`

  Reads a single character or an entire line from this `BufferedReader` stream. The character is returned as an `int`, the line as a string. A line of text is considered to be a series of characters ending in a carriage return (\r), a line feed (\n), or a carriage return followed by a line (\r\n).
- `public int read(char[] dest, int offset, int size) throws IOException`

  Reads `size` characters from this `BufferedReader` stream. Reading will skip `offset` characters into the current location in the stream, and place them in the destination array. This method will return the number of characters read from the stream or a −1 if the end of the stream was reached.
- `public boolean ready() throws IOException`

  Returns a true value if this `BufferedReader` is capable of being read from. This state can only be true if the buffer is not empty.
- `public void reset() throws IOException`

  Resets this `BufferedReader` to the last mark.
- `public long skip(long num) throws IOException`

Skips forward num characters in the stream and returns the actual number of characters skipped.

Button (`java.awt`)

A public class, derived from `Component`, that creates a graphical button that a user can push to initiate an action.

Constructors

- `public Button()`
- `public Button(String str)`
  Creates a new instance of a button with a label of `str` (or none, in the case of the first constructor).

Methods

- `public void addActionListener(ActionListener listener)`
- `public void removeActionListener(ActionListener listener)`
  Adds or removes the specified action `listener` to this button.
- `public void addNotify()`
  Creates this button's peer.
- `public String getActionCommand()`
- `public void setActionCommand(String str)`
  Returns or sets the name of the command initiated by this button.
- `public String getLabel()`
- `public void setLabel(String str)`
  Returns or sets the label of this button.
- `protected String paramString()`
  Returns a string containing the parameters of this button.
- `protected void processActionEvent(ActionEvent event)`
  Handles an AWT event for this button, sending it to a registered listener.
- `protected void processEvent(AWTEvent event)`
  Processes an AWT event for this button, sending it to the `processAWTEvent` method if it is an AWT event, otherwise forwarding it to the superclass' `processAWTEvent` method.

Byte (`java.lang`)

A public final class, derived from `Number`, that contains byte logic operations, constants, and methods as a wrapper around the Java primitive type `byte`.

Variables and Constants

- `public final static byte MAX_VALUE`
- `public final static byte MIN_VALUE`
  A constant value that holds the maximum (127) and minimum (−128) values a byte can contain.
- `public final static Class TYPE`
  The `Byte` constant value of the byte type class.

Constructors

- `public Byte(byte arg)`
- `public Byte(String arg) throws NumberFormatException`
  Creates a new instance of a `Byte` from `arg`.

Methods

- `public byte byteValue()`
- `public double doubleValue()`
- `public float floatValue()`
- `public int intValue()`
- `public long longValue()`
- `public short shortValue()`
  Returns the value of this `Byte` as a Java primitive type.
- `public static Byte decode(String str) throws NumberFormatException`
  Returns the given string (`str`) as a `Byte`. The parameter string may be encoded as an octal, hexadecimal, or binary number.
- `public boolean equals(Object arg)`
  Returns a true value if this `Byte` is equal to the parameter object `arg`.
- `public int hashCode()`
  Returns the hash code of this `Byte`.
- `public static byte parseByte(String str) throws NumberFormatException`
- `public static byte parseByte(String str, int base) throws NumberFormatException`
  Returns the value of the parsed string (`str`) as a byte. The radix of the string can be specified in `base`.
- `public String toString()`
- `public static String toString(byte prim)`
  Returns a string representation of this `Byte` or the specified primitive byte (`prim`), whose radix is assumed to be 10.
- `public static Byte valueOf(String str) throws NumberFormatException`

- public static Byte valueOf(String str, int base)
  throws NumberFormatException
    Returns a Byte object whose initial value is the result of the parsed para-
    meter (str). The parameter is assumed to be the text representation of a
    byte and its radix 10 (unless specified in base).

Calendar (`java.util`)

A public abstract class, derived from `Object` and implementing `Cloneable` and
`Serializable`, that allows for the manipulation of a `Date` object.

Variables and Constants

- public static final int AM
- public static final int PM
    Constant values that represent ante and post meridiem.
- public static final int ERA
- public static final int YEAR
- public static final int MONTH
- public static final int WEEK_OF_YEAR
- public static final int WEEK_OF_MONTH
- public static final int DATE
- public static final int DAY_OF_MONTH
- public static final int DAY_OF_YEAR
- public static final int DAY_OF_WEEK
- public static final int DAY_OF_WEEK_IN_MONTH
- public static final int AM_PM
- public static final int HOUR
- public static final int HOUR_OF_DAY
- public static final int MINUTE
- public static final int SECOND
- public static final int MILLISECOND
- public static final int ZONE_OFFSET
- public static final int DST_OFFSET
    Constant values that represent the index to the field where particular data
    is stored representing an instance of time (to millisecond precision). The
    combination of all of these fields yields a full representation of a moment
    of time with respect to a particular calendar (i.e., `GregorianCalendar`).
- public static final int JANUARY
- public static final int FEBRUARY
- public static final int MARCH
- public static final int APRIL
- public static final int MAY
- public static final int JUNE

- public static final int JULY
- public static final int AUGUST
- public static final int SEPTEMBER
- public static final int OCTOBER
- public static final int NOVEMBER
- public static final int DECEMBER
- public static final int UNDECIMBER

  Constant values representing various calendar months. UNDECIMBER represents the 13th month of a Gregorian calendar (lunar month).
- public static final int SUNDAY
- public static final int MONDAY
- public static final int TUESDAY
- public static final int WEDNESDAY
- public static final int THURSDAY
- public static final int FRIDAY
- public static final int SATURDAY

  Constant values representing the days of a week.
- protected boolean areFieldsSet

  A boolean flag that indicates if the time fields have been set for this Calendar.
- public static final int FIELD_COUNT

  A constant value that represents the number of date/time fields stored by a Calendar.
- protected int fields[]

  The integer array that contains the values that make up the information about this Calendar.
- protected boolean isSet[]

  The boolean array that contains status values used to indicate if a corresponding time field has been set.
- protected boolean isTimeSet

  A boolean flag field that is used to indicate if the time is set for this Calendar.
- protected long time

  A long int field that contains the time set for this Calendar.

Methods

- public abstract void add(int field, int val)

  Adds (or subtracts in the case of a negative val) an amount of days or time from the specified field.
- public abstract boolean after(Object arg)
- public abstract boolean before(Object arg)

  Returns a true value if this Calendar date is after or before the date specified by arg.
- public final void clear()

- `public final void clear(int field)`

  Clears the value from the specified time `field` from this `Calendar`. The `clear` method will clear all of the values from this `Calendar`.

- `public Object clone()`

  Returns a clone of this `Calendar`.

- `protected void complete()`

  Attempts to complete any empty date/time fields by calling the `completeTime()` and `completeFields()` methods of this `Calendar`.

- `protected abstract void computeFields()`

- `protected abstract void computeTime()`

  Computes the values of the time fields based on the currently set time (`computeFields()`) or computes the time based on the currently set time fields (`computeTime()`) for this `Calendar`.

- `public abstract boolean equals(Object arg)`

  Returns a true value if this `Calendar` is equal to the value of `arg`.

- `public final int get(int fld)`

  Returns the value of the specified time field from this `Calendar`.

- `public static synchronized Locale[] getAvailableLocales()`

  Returns the list of locales that are available.

- `public int getFirstDayOfWeek()`

- `public void setFirstDayOfWeek(int val)`

  Returns or sets the first day of the week to `val` for this `Calendar`.

- `public abstract int getGreatestMinimum(int fld)`

  Returns the largest allowable minimum value for the specified field.

- `public static synchronized Calendar getInstance()`

- `public static synchronized Calendar getInstance(Locale locale)`

- `public static synchronized Calendar getInstance(TimeZone tz)`

- `public static synchronized Calendar getInstance(TimeZone tz, Locale locale)`

  Returns an instance of a `Calendar` based on the default time zone and locale, or from a specified time zone and/or locale.

- `public abstract int getLeastMaximum(int fld)`

  Returns the smallest allowable maximum value for the specified field.

- `public abstract int getMaximum(int fld)`

- `public abstract int getMinimum(int fld)`

  Returns the largest or smallest allowable value for the specified field.

- `public int getMinimalDaysInFirstWeek()`

- `public void setMinimalDaysInFirstWeek(int val)`

  Returns or sets the smallest allowable number of days in the first week of the year, based on the locale.

- `public final Date getTime()`

- `public final void setTime(Date dt)`

Returns or sets the time for this `Calendar`.
- `protected long getTimeInMillis()`
- `protected void setTimeInMillis(long ms)`
  Returns or sets the time in milliseconds for this `Calendar`.
- `public TimeZone getTimeZone()`
- `public void setTimeZone(TimeZone val)`
  Returns or sets the time zone for this `Calendar`.
- `protected final int internalGet(int fld)`
  An internal method used to obtain field values to be used by subclasses of `Calendar`.
- `public boolean isLenient()`
- `public void setLenient(boolean flag)`
  Returns or sets the flag indicating leniency for date/time input.
- `public final boolean isSet(int fld)`
  Returns a true value if a value is set for the specified field.
- `public abstract void roll(int fld, boolean direction)`
  Adds one single unit of time to the specified date/time field. A true value specified for `direction` increases the field's value, false decreases it.
- `public final void set(int fld, int val)`
  Sets a single specified field to a value.
- `public final void set(int year, int month, int date)`
- `public final void set(int year, int month, int date, int hour, int min)`
- `public final void set(int year, int month, int date, int hour, int min, int sec)`
  Sets the year, month, date, hour, minute, and seconds of the time fields for this `Calendar`.

Canvas (`java.awt`)

A public class, derived from `Component`, that creates a graphical drawing canvas.

Constructors

- `public Canvas()`
  Creates a new instance of a canvas.

Methods

- `public void addNotify()`
  Creates this canvas' peer.
- `public void paint(Graphics gc)`
  Repaints this canvas with the graphics context `gc`.

CardLayout (`java.awt`)

A public class, derived from `Object` and implementing `LayoutManager2` and `Serializable`, that lays out components in a series of separate cards, only one of which is visible at any time. The visibility of the cards can be changed, essentially providing the ability to sequence through the cards.

Constructors

- `public CardLayout()`
- `public CardLayout(int hg, int vg)`
  Creates a new instance of a card layout with a specified horizontal and vertical gap (or no gap in the case of the first constructor).

Methods

- `public void addLayoutComponent(Component item, Object constr)`
- `public void removeLayoutComponent(Component item)`
  Adds or removes a component to this layout manager. While adding, it is possible to restrict the component to the specified constraints (`constr`).
- `public void first(Container cont)`
- `public void last(Container cont)`
  Moves to the first or last card in the layout. `cont` is the container that is laid out by this layout manager.
- `public int getHgap()`
- `public int getVgap()`
  Returns the horizontal or vertical gap between the components laid out by this layout manager.
- `public float getLayoutAlignmentX(Container parent)`
- `public float getLayoutAlignmentY(Container parent)`
  Returns the horizontal or vertical alignment value of the specified container.
- `public void invalidateLayout(Container cont)`
  Forces this layout manager to discard any cached layout information about the specified container.
- `public void layoutContainer(Container cont)`
  Lays out the specified container with this layout manager.
- `public Dimension maximumLayoutSize(Container cont)`
- `public Dimension minimumLayoutSize(Container cont)`
- `public Dimension preferredLayoutSize(Container cont)`
  Returns the maximum, minimum or preferred size of the specified container when laid out by this layout manager.
- `public void next(Container cont)`

- `public void previous(Container cont)`
  Cycles to the next or previous card. `cont` is container that is laid out by this layout manager.
- `public void setHgap(int hg)`
- `public void setVgap(int vg)`
  Sets the horizontal or vertical gap in pixels of components laid out by this layout manager.
- `public void show(Container cont, String str)`
  Cycles to the card the contains the component with the name `str`. When found, the specified container is laid out with this layout manager.
- `public String toString()`
  Returns a string representation of this layout manager.

Character (`java.lang`)

A public class, derived from `Object` and implementing `Serializable`, that contains character constants and methods to convert and identify characters.

Variables and Constants

- `public final static byte COMBINING_SPACING_MARK`
- `public final static byte CONNECTOR_PUNCTUATION`
- `public final static byte CONTROL`
- `public final static byte CURRENCY_SYMBOL`
- `public final static byte DASH_PUNCTUATION`
- `public final static byte DECIMAL_DIGIT_NUMBER`
- `public final static byte ENCLOSING_MARK`
- `public final static byte END_PUNCTUATION`
- `public final static byte FORMAT`
- `public final static byte LETTER_NUMBER`
- `public final static byte LINE_SEPARATOR`
- `public final static byte LOWERCASE_LETTER`
- `public final static byte MATH_SYMBOL`
- `public final static byte MODIFIER_LETTER`
- `public final static byte MODIFIER_SYMBOL`
- `public final static byte NON_SPACING_MARK`
- `public final static byte OTHER_LETTER`
- `public final static byte OTHER_NUMBER`
- `public final static byte OTHER_PUNCTUATION`
- `public final static byte OTHER_SYMBOL`
- `public final static byte PARAGRAPH_SEPARATOR`
- `public final static byte PRIVATE_USE`
- `public final static byte SPACE_SEPARATOR`

- `public final static byte START_PUNCTUATION`
- `public final static byte SURROGATE`
- `public final static byte TITLECASE_LETTER`
- `public final static byte UNASSIGNED`
- `public final static byte UPPERCASE_LETTER`

    Constant values representing various character symbols and types.

- `public final static int MAX_RADIX`

    A constant value that represents the largest possible value of a radix (base).

- `public final static char MAX_VALUE`

    A constant value that represents the largest possible value of a character in Java = `\uffff`'.

- `public final static int MIN_RADIX`

    A constant value that represents that smallest possible value of a radix (base).

- `public final static char MIN_VALUE`

    A constant value that represents the smallest possible value of a character in Java = `\u0000`'.

- `public final static Class TYPE`

    The `Character` constant value of the character type class.

Constructors

- `public Character(char prim)`

    Creates an instance of the `Character` class from the primitive parameter `prim`.

Methods

- `public char charValue()`

    Returns the value of this `Character` as a primitive character.

- `public static int digit(char c, int base)`
- `public static char forDigit(int c, int base)`

    Returns the numeric value or the character depiction of the parameter `c` in radix base.

- `public boolean equals(Object arg)`

    Returns a true value if this `Character` is equal to the parameter `arg`.

- `public static int getNumericValue(char c)`

    Returns the Unicode representation of the character parameter (`c`) as a nonnegative integer. If the character has no numeric representation, a -1 is returned. If the character cannot be represented as a nonnegative number, -2 will be returned.

- `public static int getType(char c)`

Returns an integer value that represents the type of character the parameter c is.
- `public int hashCode()`
  Returns a hash code for this `Character`.
- `public static boolean isDefined(char c)`
- `public static boolean isISOControl(char c)`
  Returns a true value if the parameter c has a defined meaning in Unicode or is an ISO control character.
- `public static boolean isIdentifierIgnorable(char c)`
  Returns a true value if the parameter c is a character that can be ignored in a Java identifier (such as control characters).
- `public static boolean isJavaIdentifierPart(char c)`
- `public static boolean isJavaIdentifierStart(char c)`
  Returns a true value if the parameter c can be used in a valid Java identifier in any but the leading character. `isJavaIdentifierStart` returns a true value if the parameter c can be used as the leading character in a valid Java identifier.
- `public static boolean isDigit(char c)`
- `public static boolean isLetter(char c)`
- `public static boolean isLetterOrDigit(char c)`
- `public static boolean isLowerCase(char c)`
- `public static boolean isSpaceChar(char c)`
- `public static boolean isTitleCase(char c)`
- `public static boolean isUnicodeIdentifierPart(char c)`
- `public static boolean isWhitespace(char c)`
- `public static boolean isUnicodeIdentifierStart(char c)`
- `public static boolean isUpperCase(char c)`
  Returns a true value if the parameter c is a digit; letter; letter or a digit; lowercase character; space character; titlecase character; can be used in a valid Unicode identifier in any but the leading character; a white space character; can be used as the leading character in a valid Unicode identifier or an uppercase character (respectively).
- `public static char toLowerCase(char c)`
- `public String toString()`
- `public static char toTitleCase(char c)`
- `public static char toUpperCase(char c)`
  Returns a lowercase character, string representation, titlecase, or uppercase character of the parameter c.

Checkbox (`java.awt`)

A public class, derived from `Component` and implementing `ItemSelectable`, that creates a graphical box with an "on" and "off" state that the user can toggle with a mouse click.

Constructors

- `public Checkbox()`
- `public Checkbox(String str)`
- `public Checkbox(String str, boolean toggle)`

  Creates a new instance of a checkbox (possibly with a label of `str`), to the value of `toggle` (or false by default), and not a member of a checkbox group.

- `public Checkbox(String str, CheckboxGroup grp, boolean toggle)`
- `public Checkbox(String str, boolean toggle, CheckboxGroup grp)`

  Creates a new instance of a checkbox with a label (`str`), belonging to a checkbox group and having an initial state of `toggle`.

Methods

- `public void addItemListener(ItemListener listener)`
- `public void removeItemListener(ItemListener listener)`

  Adds or removes the specified `listener` to this checkbox.

- `public void addNotify()`

  Creates this checkbox's peer.

- `public CheckboxGroup getCheckboxGroup()`
- `public void setCheckboxGroup(CheckboxGroup cg)`

  Returns or sets the group of this checkbox.

- `public String getLabel()`
- `public void setLabel(String str)`

  Returns or sets the label of this checkbox.

- `public Object[] getSelectedObjects()`

  Returns an array of size 1 containing the label of the checkbox if it is selected, otherwise a null is returned.

- `public boolean getState()`
- `public void setState(boolean toggle)`

  Returns or sets the state of this checkbox.

- `protected String paramString()`

  Returns a string containing this checkbox's parameters.

- `protected void processEvent(AWTEvent event)`

  Processes an `AWTEvent` for this checkbox, sending it to the `processItemEvent` method if it is an `ItemEvent`; otherwise, it forwards the event to the superclass' `processEvent` method.

- `protected void processItemEvent(ItemEvent event)`

  Handles an `ItemEvent` for this checkbox, sending it to a registered `ItemListener`.

CheckboxGroup (`java.awt`)

A public class, derived from `Object` and implementing `Serializable`, that manages a list of checkboxes, allowing only one to be "on" at any time.

Constructors

- `public CheckboxGroup()`
  Creates a new checkbox group.

Methods

- `public Checkbox getSelectedCheckbox()`
  Returns the currently selected checkbox.
- `public synchronized void setSelectedCheckbox(Checkbox checkbox)`
  Selects the specified `checkbox` in this checkbox group.
- `public String toString()`
  Returns a string representation of this checkbox group.

CheckboxMenuItem (`java.awt`)

A public class, derived from `MenuItem` and implementing `Serializable`, that creates a menu item that has a part of its label as a checkbox. The user can change the start of the checkbox by clicking on the box.

Constructors

- `public CheckboxMenuItem()`
- `public CheckboxMenuItem(String str)`
- `public CheckboxMenuItem(String str, boolean toggle)`
  Creates a new instance of a checkbox menu item with a label of `str` (or none by default), and initially set to `toggle` (or false by default).

Methods

- `public void addItemListener(ItemListener listener)`
- `public void removeItemListener(ItemListener listener)`
  Adds or removes the specified `listener` to this checkbox menu item.
- `public void addNotify()`
  Creates this checkbox menu item's peer.

- `public synchronized Object[] getSelectedObjects()`

    Returns an array of size 1 containing the checkbox item if it is checked to a true value; otherwise, a null is returned.
- `public boolean getState()`
- `public void setState(boolean toggle)`

    Returns or sets the current state of this checkbox menu item.
- `public String paramString()`

    Returns a string containing the parameters for this checkbox menu item.
- `protected void processEvent(AWTEvent event)`

    Processes an AWT event for this checkbox menu item, sending it to the `processItemEvent` method if it is an `ItemEvent`; otherwise, it forwards the event to the superclass' `processEvent` method.
- `protected void processItemEvent(ItemEvent event)`

    Handles an `ItemEvent` for this checkbox menu item, sending it to a registered `ItemListener`.

Choice (`java.awt`)

A public class, derived from `Component` and implementing `ItemSelectable`, that creates and manages a graphical list of items from which the user can choose.

Constructors

- `public Choice()`

    Creates a new instance of a choice menu with no items in it.

Methods

- `public synchronized void add(String str) throws NullPointerException`
- `public void addItem(String str) throws NullPointerException`

    Adds the specified item to this choice menu.
- `public void addItemListener(ItemListener listener)`
- `public void removeItemListener(ItemListener listener)`

    Adds or removes the specified `listener` to this choice menu.
- `public void addNotify()`

    Creates this choice menu's peer.
- `public String getItem(int index)`

    Returns the label of the item at position `index`.
- `public int getItemCount()`

Returns the number of items in this choice menu.

- `public int getSelectedIndex()`
- `public String getSelectedItem()`

  Returns the index or the label of the currently selected item in this choice menu.

- `public synchronized Object[] getSelectedObjects()`

  Returns an array of size 1 containing the currently selected item from this choice menu.

- `public synchronized void insert(String str, int idx) throws IllegalArgumentException`
- `public synchronized void remove(int idx)`
- `public synchronized void remove(String str)`

  Inserts or removes the item `str` in this choice menu at the specified index (`idx`).

- `protected String paramString()`

  Returns a string containing the parameters for this choice menu.

- `protected void processEvent(AWTEvent event)`

  Processes an `AWTEvent` for this choice menu, sending it to the `processItemEvent` method (if the event is an `ItemEvent`); otherwise, the event is sent to the superclass' `processEvent` method.

- `protected void processItemEvent(ItemEvent event)`

  Handles an `ItemEvent` for this choice menu, sending it to a registered listener.

- `public void select(int pos) throws IllegalArgumentException`

  Selects the item at position `pos` in this choice menu.

- `public synchronized void removeAll()`

  Removes all of the items from the choice menu.

- `public synchronized void select(int idx)`
- `public void select(String str)`

  Selects this item with the specified label or at a specific index in this choice menu.

ChoiceFormat (`java.text`)

A public class, derived from `NumberFormat`, that facilitates the formatting of values based on a range of numbers.

Constructors

- `public ChoiceFormat(String str)`

  Creates a new instance of a `ChoiceFormat` from the specified string pattern.

- public ChoiceFormat(double[] lims, String[] formats)

  Creates a new instance of a `ChoiceFormat` from the specified range of double limits, and a set of string formats that correspond to a limit.

Methods

- public void applyPattern(String str)

  Sets the pattern for this `ChoiceFormat`.
- public Object clone()

  Returns a copy of this `ChoiceFormat`.
- public boolean equals(Object arg)

  Returns a true value if this `ChoiceFormat` is equal to arg.
- public StringBuffer format(double num, StringBuffer dest, FieldPosition pos)
- public StringBuffer format(long num, StringBuffer dest, FieldPosition pos)

  Formats the specified long or double number, starting at position pos, placing the result in the destination buffer. This method returns the value of the buffer.
- public Object[] getFormats()
- public double[] getLimits()

  Returns the set of formats and limits for this `ChoiceFormat`.
- public int hashCode()

  Returns the hash code for this `ChoiceFormat`.
- public static final double nextDouble(double num)

  Returns the smallest double value greater than the specified number.
- public static double nextDouble(double num, boolean toggle)

  Returns the smallest double value larger than the specified number.
- public Number parse(String str, ParsePosition pos)

  Parses the source string, starting at position pos, and returns a long (if possible) or double value corresponding to the string.
- public static final double previousDouble(double num)

  Returns the largest double value less than the specified number.
- public void setChoices(double[] lims, String[] formats)

  Sets the limits and formats for this `ChoiceFormat`.
- public String toPattern()

  Returns the pattern of this `ChoiceFormat`.

Class (`java.lang`)

A public final class, derived from `Object` and implementing `Serializable`, that describes both interfaces and classes in the currently running Java program.

Methods

- `public static Class forName(String class) throws ClassNotFoundException`

  Returns a `Class` object that corresponds with the named `class`. The name of the specified class must be a fully qualified class name (as in `java.io.Reader`).

- `public Class[] getClasses()`
- `public Class[] getDeclaredClasses() throws SecurityException`

  Returns an array of `Classes` that contains all of the interfaces and classes that are members of this `Class` (excluding superclasses). `getClasses` returns only the list of public interfaces and classes.

- `public ClassLoader getClassLoader()`

  Returns the `ClassLoader` for this `Class`.

- `public Class getComponentType()`

  Returns the `Component` type of the array that is represented by this `Class`.

- `public Constructor getConstructor(Class[] types) throws NoSuchMethodException, SecurityException`
- `public Constructor[] getConstructors() throws SecurityException`

  Returns the `Constructor` object or an array containing the public constructors for this class. The signature of the public constructor that is returned must match exactly the types and sequence of the parameters specified by the `types` array.

- `public Constructor getDeclaredConstructor(Class[] types) throws NoSuchMethodException, SecurityException`
- `public Constructor[] getDeclaredConstructors() throws SecurityException`

  Returns the `Constructor` object or an array containing the constructors for this class. The signature of the public constructor that is returned must match exactly the types and sequence of the parameters specified by the `types` array parameter.

- `public Field getDeclaredField(String field) throws NoSuchFieldException, SecurityException`
- `public Field[] getDeclaredFields() throws SecurityException`

  Returns the `Field` object or an array containing all of the fields for the specified matching `field` name for this `Class`.

- `public Method getDeclaredMethod(String method, Class[] types) throws NoSuchMethodException, SecurityException`
- `public Method[] getDeclaredMethods() throws SecurityException`

  Returns a `Method` object or an array containing all of the methods for the specified `method` of this `Class`. The requested method's parameter list must match identically the types and sequence of the elements of the `types` array.

- `public Class getDeclaringClass()`
  Returns the declaring class of this `Class`, provided that this `Class` is a member of another class.
- `public Field getField(String field) throws NoSuchFieldException, SecurityException`
- `public Field[] getFields() throws SecurityException`
  Returns a `Field` object or an array containing all of the fields of a specified matching `field` name for this `Class`.
- `public Class[] getInterfaces()`
  Returns an array containing all of the interfaces of this `Class`.
- `public Method getMethod(String method, Class[] types) throws NoSuchMethodException, SecurityException`
- `public Method[] getMethods() throws SecurityException`
  Returns a `Method` object or an array containing all of the public methods for the specified public `method` of this `Class`. The requested method's parameter list must match identically the types and sequence of the elements of the `types` array.
- `public int getModifiers()`
  Returns the encoded integer visibility modifiers for this `Class`. The values can be decoded using the `Modifier` class.
- `public String getName()`
  Returns the string representation of the name of the type that this `Class` represents.
- `public URL getResource(String arg)`
  Returns a URL representing the system resource for the class loader of this `Class`.
- `public InputStream getResourceAsStream(String arg)`
  Returns an input stream representing the `named` system resource from the class loader of this `Class`.
- `public Object[] getSigners()`
  Returns an array of `Object`s that contains the signers of this `Class`.
- `public Class getSuperclass()`
  Returns the superclass of this `Class`, or null if this `Class` is an interface or of type `Object`.
- `public boolean isArray()`
  Returns a true value if this `Class` represents an array type.
- `public boolean isAssignableFrom(Class other)`
  Returns a true value if this `Class` is the same as a superclass or superinterface of the `other` class.
- `public boolean isInstance(Object target)`
  Returns a true value if the specified `target` object is an instance of this `Class`.

- `public boolean isInterface()`
- `public boolean isPrimitive()`

  Returns a true value if this `Class` represents an interface class or a primitive type in Java.
- `public Object newInstance() throws`
  `InstantiationException, IllegalAccessException`

  Creates a new instance of this `Class`.
- `public String toString()`

  Returns a string representation of this `Class` in the form of the word class or interface, followed by the fully qualified name of this `Class`.

Color (`java.awt`)

A public final class, derived from `Object` and implementing `Serializable`, that is used to represent colors. A color is defined by three components, red, blue, and green, that each have a value ranging from 0 to 255.

Variables and Constants

- `public final static Color black`
- `public final static Color blue`
- `public final static Color cyan`
- `public final static Color darkGray`
- `public final static Color gray`
- `public final static Color green`
- `public final static Color lightGray`
- `public final static Color magenta`
- `public final static Color orange`
- `public final static Color pink`
- `public final static Color red`
- `public final static Color white`
- `public final static Color yellow`

  A constant value that describes the colors black (0, 0, 0), blue (0, 0, 255), cyan (0, 255, 255), darkGray (64, 64, 64), gray (128, 128, 128), green (0, 255, 0), lightGray (192, 192, 192), magenta (255, 0, 255), orange (255, 200, 0), pink (255, 175, 175), red (255, 0, 0), white (255, 255, 255) and yellow (255, 255, 0) as a set of RGB values.

Constructors

- `public Color(float r, float g, float b)`
- `public Color(int rgb)`
- `public Color(int r, int g, int b)`

Creates a new instance of the color described by the `rgb` value. When passed as a single integer value, the red component is represented in bits 16 to 23, green in 15 to 8, and blue in 0 to 7.

Methods

- `public Color brighter()`
- `public Color darker()`
  Returns a brighter or darker version of this color.
- `public static Color decode(String str) throws NumberFormatException`
  Returns the color specified by `str`.
- `public boolean equals(Object arg)`
  Returns a true value if this color is equal to `arg`.
- `public int getBlue()`
- `public int getGreen()`
- `public int getRed()`
  Returns the blue, green, or red component value for this color.
- `public static Color getColor(String str)`
- `public static Color getColor(String str, Color default)`
- `public static Color getColor(String str, int default)`
  Returns the color represented in the string `str` (where its value is an integer). If the value is not determined, the color `default` is returned.
- `public static Color getHSBColor(float h, float s, float b)`
  Returns a color specified by the Hue-Saturation-Brightness model for colors, where `h` is the hue, `s` is the saturation, and `b` is the brightness of the desired color.
- `public int getRGB()`
  Returns an integer representation of the RGB value for this color.
- `public int hashCode()`
  Returns the hash code for this color.
- `public static int HSBtoRGB(float hue, float saturation, float brightness)`
  Converts a `hue`, `saturation`, and `brightness` representation of a color to a RGB value.
- `public static float[] RGBtoHSB(int r, int g, int b, float[] hsbvals)`
  Converts a RGB representation of a color to a HSB value, placing the converted values into the `hsbvals` array. The RGB value is represented via a red (`r`), green (`g`), and blue (`b`) value.
- `public String toString()`
  Returns a string representation of this color.

Component (`java.awt`)

A public abstract class, derived from `Object` and implementing `ImageObserver`, `MenuContainer`, and `Serializable`, that is the superclass to every AWT item that is represented on screen with a specific size and position.

Variables and Constants

- `public final static float BOTTOM_ALIGNMENT`
- `public final static float LEFT_ALIGNMENT`
- `public final static float RIGHT_ALIGNMENT`
- `public final static float TOP_ALIGNMENT`
  Constant values that represent specified alignments within the component.
- `protected Locale locale`
  Holds the locale for this component.

Constructors

- `protected Component()`
  Creates a new instance of a component.

Methods

- `public synchronized void add(PopupMenu popmenu)`
- `public synchronized void remove(MenuComponent popmenu)`
  Adds or removes the specified popup menu to this component.
- `public synchronized void addComponentListener
  (ComponentListener listener)`
- `public synchronized void addFocusListener
  (FocusListener listener)`
- `public synchronized void addKeyListener(KeyListener
  listener)`
- `public synchronized void addMouseListener
  (MouseListener listener)`
- `public synchronized void addMouseMotionListener
  (MouseMotionListener listener)`
- `public synchronized void removeComponentListener
  (ComponentListener listener)`
- `public synchronized void removeFocusListener
  (FocusListener listener)`
- `public synchronized void removeKeyListener(KeyListener
  listener)`
- `public synchronized void removeMouseListener
  (MouseListener listener)`

- `public synchronized void`
  `removeMouseMotionListener(MouseMotionListener listener)`
    Adds or removes the specified `listener` to this component.
- `public void addNotify()`
- `public void removeNotify()`
    Notifies the component that a peer must be created or destroyed.
- `public int checkImage(Image img, ImageObserver obs)`
- `public int checkImage(Image img, int width, int`
  `height, ImageObserver obs)`
    Returns the status of the construction of a scaled image `img`. The image created can be scaled to a `width` and `height`. The image `obs` will be informed of the status of the image.
- `public boolean contains(int x, int y)`
- `public boolean contains(Point pt)`
    Returns a true value if this component contains the specified position.
- `public Image createImage(ImageProducer prod)`
- `public Image createImage(int width, int height)`
    Returns a new image created from `prod`. The second method creates another Image which is generally offscreen (having `width` and `height`), used for double-buffering drawings.
- `protected final void disableEvents(long mask)`
- `protected final void enableEvents(long mask)`
    Disables or enables all events specified by the `mask` for this component.
- `public final void dispatchEvent(AWTEvent event)`
    Dispatches an `AWTEvent` to this component or one of its subcomponents.
- `public void doLayout()`
    Lays out this component.
- `public float getAlignmentX()`
- `public float getAlignmentY()`
    Returns the horizontal or vertical alignment for this component.
- `public Color getBackground()`
- `public Color getForeground()`
- `public void setBackground(Color clr)`
- `public void setForeground(Color clr)`
    Returns or sets the background or foreground color for this component.
- `public Rectangle getBounds()`
- `public void setBounds(int x, int y, int width, int`
  `height)`
    Returns or sets the bounds of this component. Setting the bounds resizes and reshapes this component to the bounding box of <x, y> to <x+width, y+height>.
- `public ColorModel getColorModel()`
    Returns the color model of this component.
- `public Component getComponentAt(int x, int y)`
- `public Component getComponentAt(Point pt)`

Returns the component located at the specified point.
- `public Cursor getCursor()`
- `public synchronized void setCursor(Cursor csr)`
  Returns or sets the cursor set for this component.
- `public Font getFont()`
- `public void setFont(Font ft)`
  Returns or sets the font of this component.
- `public FontMetrics getFontMetrics(Font ft)`
  Returns the font metrics of the specified font.
- `public Graphics getGraphics()`
  Returns the graphics context for this component.
- `public Locale getLocale()`
- `public void setLocale(Locale locale)`
  Returns or sets the locale for this component.
- `public Point getLocation()`
- `public Point getLocationOnScreen()`
  Returns the location of this component relative to the containing or screen space.
- `public Dimension getMaximumSize()`
- `public Dimension getMinimumSize()`
- `public Dimension getPreferredSize()`
  Returns the maximum, minimum or preferred size of this component.
- `public String getName()`
- `public void setName(String str)`
  Returns or sets the name of this component.
- `public Container getParent()`
  Returns the parent container of this component.
- `public Dimension getSize()`
- `public void setSize(Dimension dim)`
- `public void setSize(int width, int height)`
  Returns the size of or resizes this component to the specified dimension(s).
- `public Toolkit getToolkit()`
  Returns the toolkit of this component.
- `public final Object getTreeLock()`
  Returns the AWT object that is used as the base of the component tree and layout operations for this component.
- `public boolean imageUpdate(Image src, int flags, int x, int y, int width, int height)`
  Draws more of an image (`src`) as its information becomes available. The exact value of the `x`, `y`, `width`, and `height` variables is dependent on the value of the `flags` variable.
- `public void invalidate()`
  Forces this component to be laid out again by making it "invalid."
- `public boolean isEnabled()`

- `public void setEnabled(boolean toggle)`
  Returns or sets the enabled state of this component.
- `public boolean isFocusTraversable()`
  Returns a true value if this component can be traversed using Tab or Shift-Tab sequences.
- `public boolean isShowing()`
- `public boolean isValid()`
  Returns a true value if this component is visible on screen or does not need to be laid out (valid).
- `public boolean isVisible()`
- `public void setVisible(boolean toggle)`
  Returns or sets the state of this component's visibility.
- `public void list()`
- `public void list(PrintStream outstrm)`
- `public void list(PrintStream outstrm, int spc)`
- `public void list(PrintWriter outstrm)`
- `public void list(PrintWriter outstrm, int spc)`
  Prints a listing of this component's parameters to the print writer stream `outstrm` (default of `System.out`), indenting `spc` spaces (default of 0).
- `public void paint(Graphics gc)`
- `public void print(Graphics gc)`
  Paints or prints this component with the graphics context `gc`.
- `public void paintAll(Graphics gc)`
- `public void printAll(Graphics gc)`
  Paints or prints this component and all of its subcomponents with the graphics context `gc`.
- `protected String paramString()`
  Returns a string describing the parameters of this component.
- `public boolean prepareImage(Image src, ImageObserver obs)`
- `public prepareImage(Image src, int width, int height, ImageObserver obs)`
  Downloads the `src` for display. The image can be scaled to a `width` and `height`. The `obs` is informed of the status of the image.
- `protected void processComponentEvent(ComponentEvent event)`
- `protected void processFocusEvent(FocusEvent event)`
- `protected void processKeyEvent(KeyEvent event)`
- `protected void processMouseEvent(MouseEvent event)`
- `protected void processMouseMotionEvent(MouseEvent event)`
  Processes the specified event for this component, sending the event to a registered event listener.
- `protected void processEvent(AWTEvent event)`

Processes an AWT event for this component, sending it to the appropriate processing routine (i.e., `processComponentEvent` method) for further handling.

- `public void repaint()`
- `public void repaint(int x, int y, int width, int height)`
  Repaints a rectangular portion of this component from <x, y> to <x+width, y+height>.
- `public void repaint(long msec)`
- `public void repaint(long msec, int x, int y, int width, int height)`
  Repaints a rectangular portion of this component from <x, y> to <x+width, y+height> after a delay of `msec` milliseconds.
- `public void requestFocus()`
  Requests that this component get the input focus.
- `public void setLocation(int x, int y)`
- `public void setLocation(Point pt)`
  Moves this component to the specified point in the containing space.
- `public String toString()`
  Returns a string representation of this component.
- `public void transferFocus()`
  Transfers focus from this component to the next component.
- `public void update(Graphics gc)`
  Updates this component using graphics context `gc`.
- `public void validate()`
  Validates this component if needed.

ComponentAdapter (`java.awt.event`)

A public abstract class, derived from `Object` and implementing `ComponentListener`, that permits a derived class to override the predefined no-op component events.

Constructors

- `public ComponentAdapter()`
  Creates a new instance of a `ComponentAdapter`.

Methods

- `public void componentHidden(ComponentEvent event)`
- `public void componentMoved(ComponentEvent event)`
- `public void componentResized(ComponentEvent event)`
- `public void componentShown(ComponentEvent event)`

Empty methods that should be overridden in order to implement event handling for AWT components.

ComponentEvent (`java.awt.event`)

A public class, derived from `AWTEvent`, that represents an AWT component event.

Variables and Constants

- `public static final int COMPONENT_FIRST`
- `public static final int COMPONENT_LAST`
  Constant values that represent the index of the first and last component event ids.
- `public static final int COMPONENT_MOVED`
- `public static final int COMPONENT_RESIZED`
- `public static final int COMPONENT_SHOWN`
- `public static final int COMPONENT_HIDDEN`
  Constant values that represent AWT component event ids.

Constructors

- `public ComponentEvent(Component src, int type)`
  Creates a new instance of a `ComponentEvent` from the specified source and of a specific type.

Methods

- `public Component getComponent()`
  Returns the AWT component that triggered this event.
- `public String paramString()`
  Returns a string containing the parameters of this event.

Container (`java.awt`)

A public abstract class, derived from `Component`, that is the superclass to any AWT component that can contain one or more AWT components.

Constructors

- `protected Container()`
  Creates a new instance of a container.

Methods

- `public Component add(Component item)`
- `public Component add(Component item, int idx)`
- `public void add(Component item, Object constr)`
- `public void add(Component item, Object constr, int idx)`
- `public Component add(String str, Component item)`

  Adds component `item` to this container at index `idx` (or to the end by default). The new item can have constraints (`constr`) applied to it. A string name can be associated with the added component in the case of the last constructor.

- `public void addContainerListener(ContainerListener listener)`
- `public void removeContainerListener(ContainerListener listener)`

  Adds or removes the specified `listener` to this container.

- `protected void addImpl(Component item, Object constr, int idx)`

  Adds component `item` to this container at index `idx`, and passes the constraints for the new item (`constr`) to the layout manager for this container.

- `public void addNotify()`
- `public void removeNotify()`

  Creates or destroys this container's peer.

- `public void doLayout()`

  Lays out the components of this container.

- `public float getAlignmentX()`
- `public float getAlignmentY()`

  Returns the horizontal or vertical alignment value of this container.

- `public Component getComponent(int idx) throws ArrayIndexOutOfBoundsException`
- `public Component getComponentAt(int x, int y)`
- `public Component getComponentAt(Point pt)`

  Returns the component that is located at the specified point or index.

- `public int getComponentCount()`

  Returns the number of components in this container.

- `public Component[] getComponents()`

  Returns an array of all of the components in this container.

- `public Insets getInsets()`

  Returns the insets of this container.

- `public LayoutManager getLayout()`
- `public void setLayout(LayoutManager layout)`

  Returns or sets the layout manager of this container.

- `public Dimension getMaximumSize()`
- `public Dimension getMinimumSize()`
- `public Dimension getPreferredSize()`

Returns the maximum, minimum, or preferred size of this container.

- `public void invalidate()`
  Marks the layout of this container as invalid, forcing the need to lay out the components again.
- `public boolean isAncestorOf(Component comp)`
  Returns a true value if the specified component (`comp`) is contained in the component hierarchy of this container.
- `public void list(PrintStream outstream, int spaces)`
- `public void list(PrintWriter outstream, int spaces)`
  Prints a listing of all of the components of this container to print stream `outstream`, indented a specified number of `spaces` (default of 0).
- `public void paint(Graphics gwin)`
- `public void print(Graphics gwin)`
  Paints or prints this container with graphics context `gwin`.
- `public void paintComponents(Graphics gwin)`
- `public void printComponents(Graphics gwin)`
  Repaints or prints all of the components in this container with graphics context `gwin`.
- `protected String paramString()`
  Returns a string representation of this container's parameters.
- `protected void processContainerEvent(ContainerEvent event)`
  Processes any container `event`, passing the event to a registered container listener.
- `protected void processEvent(AWTEvent event)`
  Handles any `AWTEvent`, invoking `processContainerEvent` for container events, and passing the event to the superclass' `processEvent` otherwise.
- `public void remove(Component comp)`
- `public void remove(int idx)`
  Removes the specified component (or the component at the specified index) from this container.
- `public void removeAll()`
  Removes all components from this container.
- `public void validate()`
  Validates this container and all of the subcomponents in it.
- `protected void validateTree()`
  Validates this container and all subcontainers in it.

ContainerAdapter (`java.awt.event`)

A public abstract class, derived from `Object` and implementing `ContainerListener`, that permits a derived class to override the predefined no-op container events.

Constructors

- `public ContainerAdapter()`
  Creates a new instance of a `ContainerAdapter`.

Methods

- `public void componentAdded(ContainerEvent event)`
- `public void componentRemoved(ContainerEvent event)`
  Empty methods that should be overridden in order to implement event handling for AWT containers.

ContainerEvent (`java.awt.event`)

A public class, derived from `ComponentEvent`, that describes a particular AWT container event.

Variables and Constants

- `public static final int COMPONENT_ADDED`
- `public static final int COMPONENT_REMOVED`
  Constant values that represent various container events (a component being added or removed to this container).
- `public static final int CONTAINER_FIRST`
- `public static final int CONTAINER_LAST`
  Constant values that represent the index of the first and last component event ids.

Constructors

- `public ContainerEvent(Component src, int type, Component comp)`
  Creates a new instance of a `ContainerEvent` with a specified source component, event type and a defined component (which is being added or removed).

Methods

- `public Component getChild()`
  Returns the child component that was added or removed, triggering this event.
- `public Container getContainer()`
  Returns the container in which this event was triggered.

- public String paramString()
  Returns a string containing the parameters of this ComponentEvent.

ContentHandler (`java.net`)

A public abstract class, derived from Object, that is the superclass to URL-handling classes. Its purpose is to return an object as the target of a URL.

Constructors

- public ContentHandler()
  Creates a new instance of a ContentHandler.

Methods

- public abstract Object getContent(URLConnection src)
  throws IOException
  Retrieves the content at src and returns it as an Object. This abstract method is overridden by subclasses.

Cursor (`java.awt`)

A public class, derived from Object and implementing Serializable, that represents the different states and images of the mouse cursor in a graphical application or applet.

Variables and Constants

- public final static int CROSSHAIR_CURSOR
- public final static int DEFAULT_CURSOR
- public final static int E_RESIZE_CURSOR
- public final static int HAND_CURSOR
- public final static int MOVE_CURSOR
- public final static int N_RESIZE_CURSOR
- public final static int NE_RESIZE_CURSOR
- public final static int NW_RESIZE_CURSOR
- public final static int S_RESIZE_CURSOR
- public final static int SE_RESIZE_CURSOR
- public final static int SW_RESIZE_CURSOR
- public final static int TEXT_CURSOR
- public final static int W_RESIZE_CURSOR
- public final static int WAIT_CURSOR

Constant values that represent various cursors.
- `protected static Cursor predefined[]`
  An array used to hold the cursors as they are defined and implemented.

Constructors

- `public Cursor(int cursortype)`
  Creates a new instance of a cursor of the specified type (`cursortype`).

Methods

- `public static Cursor getDefaultCursor()`
  Returns the default cursor.
- `public static Cursor getPredefinedCursor(int cursortype)`
  Returns the cursor of the specified type (`cursortype`).
- `public int getType()`
  Returns the type of this cursor.

Date (`java.util`)

A public class, derived from `Object` and implementing `Serializable` and `Cloneable`, that creates and manipulates a single moment of time.

Constructors

- `public Date()`
- `public Date(long date)`
  Creates a new instance of a `Date` from a specified `date` (time in milliseconds since midnight, January 1, 1970 GMT) or by using the current time.

Methods

- `public boolean after(Date arg)`
- `public boolean before(Date arg)`
  Returns a true value if this `Date` is after/before the date specified in `arg`.
- `public boolean equals(Object arg)`
  Returns a true value if this `Date` is equal to `arg`.
- `public long getTime()`
- `public void setTime(long tm)`
  Returns or sets the time specified by this `Date`. The time is represented as a long integer equal to the number of seconds since midnight, January 1, 1970 UTC.

- `public int hashCode()`
  Returns the hash code for this `Date`.
- `public String toString()`
  Returns a string representation of this `Date`.

DateFormat (`java.text`)

A public abstract class, derived from `Cloneable`, that is used to convert date/time objects to locale-specific strings, and vice versa.

Variables and Constants

- `public static final int DEFAULT`
- `public static final int FULL`
- `public static final int LONG`
- `public static final int MEDIUM`
- `public static final int SHORT`
  Constant values that represent formatting styles.
- `public static final int AM_PM_FIELD`
- `public static final int DATE_FIELD`
- `public static final int DAY_OF_WEEK_FIELD`
- `public static final int DAY_OF_WEEK_IN_MONTH_FIELD`
- `public static final int DAY_OF_YEAR_FIELD`
- `public static final int ERA_FIELD`
- `public static final int HOUR0_FIELD`
- `public static final int HOUR1_FIELD`
- `public static final int HOUR_OF_DAY0_FIELD`
- `public static final int HOUR_OF_DAY1_FIELD`
- `public static final int MILLISECOND_FIELD`
- `public static final int MINUTE_FIELD`
- `public static final int MONTH_FIELD`
- `public static final int SECOND_FIELD`
- `public static final int TIMEZONE_FIELD`
- `public static final int WEEK_OF_MONTH_FIELD`
- `public static final int WEEK_OF_YEAR_FIELD`
- `public static final int YEAR_FIELD`
  Constant values that represent various fields for date/time formatting.
- `protected Calendar calendar`
  Holds the calendar that this `DateFormat` uses to produce its date/time formatting.
- `protected NumberFormat numberFormat`
  Holds the number format that this `DateFormat` uses to produce its number formatting.

Constructors

- `protected DateFormat()`
  Creates a new instance of a `DateFormat`.

Methods

- `public Object clone()`
  Returns a copy of this `DateFormat`.
- `public boolean equals(Object arg)`
  Returns a true value is this `DateFormat` is equal to `arg`.
- `public final String format(Date src)`
  Formats the specified `Date` object into a string.
- `public abstract StringBuffer format(Date src, StringBuffer dest, FieldPosition pos)`
- `public final StringBuffer format(Object src, StringBuffer dest, FieldPosition pos)`
  Formats the source object into the specified destination, starting at field `pos`. This method returns the same value as the destination buffer.
- `public static Locale[] getAvailableLocales()`
  Returns the set of available locales for this `DateFormat`.
- `public Calendar getCalendar()`
- `public void setCalendar(Calendar cal)`
  Returns or sets the calendar associated with this `DateFormat`.
- `public static final DateFormat getDateInstance()`
- `public static final DateFormat getDateInstance(int style)`
- `public static final DateFormat getDateInstance(int style, Locale locale)`
  Returns the `DateFormat` for the specified or default locale (using the default or specified date formatting style).
- `public static final DateFormat getDateTimeInstance()`
- `public static final DateFormat getDateTimeInstance(int dstyle, int tstyle)`
- `public static final DateFormat getDateTimeInstance(int dstyle, int tstyle, Locale locale)`
  Returns the `DateFormat` for the specified or default locale (using the default or specified date and time formatting styles).
- `public static final DateFormat getInstance()`
  Returns the `DateFormat` for the default locale using the short formatting style.
- `public NumberFormat getNumberFormat()`
- `public void setNumberFormat(NumberFormat format)`
  Returns or sets the `NumberFormat` for this `DateFormat`.

- public static final DateFormat getTimeInstance()
- public static final DateFormat getTimeInstance(int style)
- public static final DateFormat getTimeInstance(int style, Locale locale)

  Returns the DateFormat for the specified or default locale (using the default or specified time formatting style).
- public TimeZone getTimeZone()
- public void setTimeZone(TimeZone tz)

  Returns or sets the time zone for this DateFormat.
- public int hashCode()

  Returns the hash code for this DateFormat.
- public boolean isLenient()
- public void setLenient(boolean lenient)

  Returns or sets the state of the leniency for this DateFormat.
- public Date parse(String src) throws ParseException

  Parses the specified source to a Date object.
- public abstract Date parse(String src, ParsePosition pos)
- public Object parseObject(String src, ParsePosition pos)

  Parses the specified source string to a Date or Object, starting at the specified position.

DateFormatSymbols (`java.text`)

A public class, derived from Object and implementing Serializable and Cloneable, that contains functionality for formatting both date and time values. This class is usually utilized as part of a DateFormat class (or subclass).

Constructors

- public DateFormatSymbols()
- public DateFormatSymbols(Locale locale)

  Creates a new instance of DateFormatSymbols using the specified or default locale.

Methods

- public Object clone()

  Returns a clone of this DateFormatSymbols.
- public boolean equals(Object arg)

Returns a true value if this `DateFormatSymbols` is equal to `arg`.

- `public String[] getAmPmStrings()`
- `public void setAmPmStrings(String[] newstr)`
  Returns or sets the AM/PM strings for this set of symbols.
- `public String[] getEras()`
- `public void setEras(String[] newstr)`
  Returns or sets the eras for this set of symbols.
- `public String getLocalPatternChars()`
- `public void setLocalPatternChars(String newchars)`
  Returns or sets the local pattern characters for date and time for this set of symbols.
- `public String[] getMonths()`
- `public void setMonths(String[] newmon)`
  Returns or sets the full names of months for this set of symbols.
- `public String[] getShortMonths()`
- `public void setShortMonths(String[] newmon)`
  Returns or sets the short names of months for this set of symbols.
- `public String[] getShortWeekdays()`
- `public void setShortWeekdays(String[] newdays)`
  Returns or sets the short names of weekdays for this set of symbols.
- `public String[] getWeekdays()`
- `public void setWeekdays(String[] newdays)`
  Returns or sets the full names of weekdays for this set of symbols.
- `public String[][] getZoneStrings()`
- `public void setZoneStrings(String[][] newzone)`
  Returns or sets the time zone strings for this set of symbols.
- `public int hashCode()`
  Returns the hash code for this set of symbols.

DecimalFormat (`java.text`)

A public class, derived from `NumberFormat`, that is used to format decimal numbers to locale-based strings, and vice versa.

Constructors

- `public DecimalFormat()`
- `public DecimalFormat(String str)`
- `public DecimalFormat(String str, DecimalFormatSymbols sym)`
  Creates a new instance of a `DecimalFormat` from the specified or default pattern, specified or default symbols and using the default locale.

Methods

- `public void applyLocalizedPattern(String str)`
- `public String toLocalizedPattern()`

  Sets or returns the pattern of this `DecimalFormat`. The specified pattern is in a locale-specific format.

- `public void applyPattern(String str)`
- `public String toPattern()`

  Sets or returns the pattern of this `DecimalFormat`.

- `public Object clone()`

  Returns a copy of this `DecimalFormat`.

- `public boolean equals(Object arg)`

  Returns a true value if this `DecimalFormat` is equal to arg.

- `public StringBuffer format(double num, StringBuffer dest, FieldPosition pos)`
- `public StringBuffer format(long num, StringBuffer dest, FieldPosition pos)`

  Formats the specified Java primitive type starting at pos, according to this `DecimalFormat`, placing the resulting string in the specified destination buffer. This method returns the value of the string buffer.

- `public DecimalFormatSymbols getDecimalFormatSymbols()`
- `public void setDecimalFormatSymbols (DecimalFormatSymbols symbols)`

  Returns or sets the decimal number format symbols for this `DecimalFormat`.

- `public int getGroupingSize()`
- `public void setGroupingSize(int val)`

  Returns or sets the size of groupings for this `DecimalFormat`.

- `public int getMultiplier()`
- `public void setMultiplier(int val)`

  Returns or sets the value of the multiplier for use in percent calculations.

- `public String getNegativePrefix()`
- `public void setNegativePrefix(String val)`

  Returns or sets the prefix for negative numbers for this `DecimalFormat`.

- `public String getNegativeSuffix()`
- `public void setNegativeSuffix(String val)`

  Returns or sets the suffix for negative numbers for this `DecimalFormat`.

- `public String getPositivePrefix()`
- `public void setPositivePrefix(String val)`

  Returns or sets the prefix for positive numbers for this `DecimalFormat`.

- `public String getPositiveSuffix()`
- `public void setPositiveSuffix(String val)`

  Returns or sets the suffix for positive numbers for this `DecimalFormat`.

- `public int hashCode()`

Returns the hash code for this `DecimalFormat`.
- `public boolean isDecimalSeparatorAlwaysShown()`
- `public void setDecimalSeparatorAlwaysShown(boolean toggle)`
  Returns or sets the state value that allows/prevents the display of the decimal point when formatting integers.
- `public Number parse(String src, ParsePosition pos)`
  Parses the specified string as a long (if possible) or double, starting a position pos, and returns a `Number`.

DecimalFormatSymbols (`java.text`)

A public class, derived from `Object` and implementing `Serializable` and `Cloneable`, that contains functionality for formatting decimal values. This class is usually utilized as part of a `DecimalFormat` class (or subclass).

Constructors

- `public DecimalFormatSymbols()`
- `public DecimalFormatSymbols(Locale locale)`
  Creates a new instance of `DecimalFormatSymbols` using the specified or default locale.

Methods

- `public Object clone()`
  Returns a clone of this `DecimalFormatSymbols`.
- `public boolean equals(Object arg)`
  Returns a true value if this `DecimalFormatSymbols` is equal to arg.
- `public char getDecimalSeparator()`
- `public void setDecimalSeparator(char separator)`
  Returns or sets the character used to separate decimal numbers in this set of symbols.
- `public char getDigit()`
- `public void setDigit(char num)`
  Returns or sets the character used as a digit placeholder in a pattern for this set of symbols.
- `public char getGroupingSeparator()`
- `public void setGroupingSeparator(char separator)`
  Returns or sets the character used to separate groups of thousands for this set of symbols.
- `public String getInfinity()`

- public void setInfinity(String str)

  Returns or sets the string used to represent the value of infinity for this set of symbols.
- public char getMinusSign()
- public void setMinusSign(char minus)

  Returns or sets the character used to represent the minus sign for this set of symbols.
- public String getNaN()
- public void setNaN(String str)

  Returns or sets the character used to represent a NAN value for this set of symbols.
- public char getPatternSeparator()
- public void setPatternSeparator(char separator)

  Returns or sets the character used to separate positive and negative numbers in a pattern from this set of symbols.
- public char getPercent()
- public void setPercent(char percent)

  Returns or sets the character used as a percent sign for this set of symbols.
- public char getPerMill()
- public void setPerMill(char perMill)

  Returns or sets the character used as a mille percent sign for this set of symbols.
- public char getZeroDigit()
- public void setZeroDigit(char zero)

  Returns or sets the character used to represent zero for this set of symbols.
- public int hashCode()

  Returns the hash code for this set of symbols.

Dialog (`java.awt`)

A public class, derived from `Window`, that creates a graphical window that requests input from the user.

Constructors

- public Dialog(Frame pframe)
- public Dialog(Frame pframe, boolean toggle)
- public Dialog(Frame pframe, String str)
- public Dialog(Frame pframe, String str, boolean toggle)

Creates a new instance of a dialog window with a parent frame (`pframe`) and an initial title (`str`). The resulting dialog window can be made modal by setting `toggle` (default is false, not modal).

Methods

- `public void addNotify()`
  Creates this dialog's peer.
- `public String getTitle()`
- `public void setTitle(String str)`
  Returns or sets the title of this dialog.
- `public boolean isModal()`
- `public void setModal(boolean toggle)`
  Returns or sets the modal state for this dialog.
- `public boolean isResizable()`
- `public void setResizable(boolean toggle)`
  Returns or sets the resizable state for this dialog.
- `protected String paramString()`
  Returns a string containing the parameters of this dialog.
- `public void show()`
  Makes this dialog window visible and places it on top of any other window currently displayed.

Dictionary (`java.util`)

A public abstract class, derived from `Object`, that associates keys with elements.

Constructors

- `public Dictionary()`
  Creates a new instance of a `Dictionary`.

Methods

- `public abstract Enumeration elements()`
  Returns an enumerated list of the elements of this `Dictionary`.
- `public abstract Object get(Object idx)`
- `public abstract Object put(Object idx, Object val)`
  `throws NullPointerException`
- `public abstract Object remove(Object idx)`
  Returns, inserts or removes an element, `val`, into the `Dictionary` with a key value of `idx`.

- `public abstract boolean isEmpty()`
    Returns a true value if this `Dictionary` contains no elements or keys.
- `public abstract Enumeration keys()`
    Returns an enumerated list of keys of this `Dictionary`.
- `public abstract int size()`
    Returns the number of elements in the `Dictionary`.

Dimension (`java.awt`)

A public class, derived from `Object` and implementing `Serializable`, that is used to encapsulate an object's dimensions (height and width).

Variables and Constants

- `public int height`
- `public int width`
    Variables which contain the height and width of an object.

Constructors

- `public Dimension()`
- `public Dimension(Dimension dim)`
- `public Dimension(int width, int height)`
    Creates a new instance of a dimension from specified dimensions (or 0 width and 0 height by default).

Methods

- `public boolean equals(Object arg)`
    Returns a true value if this dimension is equal to `arg`.
- `public Dimension getSize()`
- `public void setSize(Dimension dim)`
- `public void setSize(int width, int height)`
    Returns or sets the size of this dimension.
- `public String toString()`
    Returns the string representation of this dimension.

Double (`java.lang`)

A public final class, derived from `Number`, that contains floating point math operations, constants, methods to compute minimum and maximum numbers, and string manipulation routines related to the `double` primitive type.

Variables and Constants

- `public final static double MAX_VALUE`
- `public final static double MIN_VALUE`
  Constant values that contain the maximum (1.79769313486231570e+308d) and minimum (4.94065645841246544e−324d) possible values of an integer in Java.
- `public final static double NaN`
  A constant value that contains the representation of the Not-A-Number double (0.0d).
- `public final static double NEGATIVE_INFINITY`
- `public final static double POSITIVE_INFINITY`
  Constant values that contain the negative (−1.0d / 0.0d) and positive (1.0d / 0.0d) infinity double.
- `public final static Class TYPE`
  A constant value of the `Double` type class.

Constructors

- `public Double(double arg)`
- `public Double(String arg) throws NumberFormatException`
  Creates an instance of the `Double` class from the parameter `arg`.

Methods

- `public byte byteValue()`
- `public double doubleValue()`
- `public float floatValue()`
- `public int intValue()`
- `public long longValue()`
- `public short shortValue()`
  Returns the value of the current object as a Java primitive type.
- `public static long doubleToLongBits(double num)`
- `public static double longBitsToDouble(long num)`
  Returns a long bit stream or a double representation of parameter `num`. Bit 63 of the returned `long` is the sign bit, bits 52 to 62 are the exponent, and bits 0 to 51 are the mantissa.
- `public boolean equals(Object param)`
  Returns a true value if this `Double` is equal to the specified parameter (`param`).
- `public int hashCode()`
  Returns a hash code for this `Double`.
- `public boolean isInfinite()`
- `public static boolean isInfinite(double num)`

Returns true if the current object or num is positive or negative infinity, false in all other cases.

- `public boolean isNaN()`
- `public static boolean isNaN(double num)`
  Returns true if the current object or num is Not-A-Number, false in all other cases.
- `public String toString()`
- `public static String toString(double num)`
  Returns the string representation of the current object or num in base 10 (decimal).
- `public static Double valueOf(String str) throws NumberFormatException`
  Returns a `Double` initialized to the value of `str`.

Error (`java.lang`)

A public class, derived from `Throwable`, that is used to signify program-terminating errors that should not be caught.

Constructors

- `public Error()`
- `public Error(String str)`
  Creates a new instance of an error. A message can be provided via `str`.

Event (`java.awt`)

A public class, derived from `Object`, that represents event obtained from a graphical user interface.

Variables and Constants

- `public final static int ACTION_EVENT`
  A constant that represents the user desires an action.
- `public final static int ALT_MASK`
- `public final static int CTRL_MASK`
- `public final static int META_MASK`
- `public final static int SHIFT_MASK`
  Constant values which represent the mask for Alt, Control, Meta, and Shift keys modifying events.
- `public Object arg`

An optional argument used by some events.

- `public final static int BACK_SPACE`
- `public final static int CAPS_LOCK`
- `public final static int DELETE`
- `public final static int DOWN`
- `public final static int END`
- `public final static int ENTER`
- `public final static int ESCAPE`
- `public final static int F1`
- `public final static int F2`
- `public final static int F3`
- `public final static int F4`
- `public final static int F5`
- `public final static int F6`
- `public final static int F7`
- `public final static int F8`
- `public final static int F9`
- `public final static int F10`
- `public final static int F11`
- `public final static int F12`
- `public final static int HOME`
- `public final static int INSERT`
- `public final static int LEFT`
- `public final static int NUM_LOCK`
- `public final static int PAUSE`
- `public final static int PGDN`
- `public final static int PGUP`
- `public final static int PRINT_SCREEN`
- `public final static int RIGHT`
- `public final static int SCROLL_LOCK`
- `public final static int TAB`
- `public final static int UP`

  Constant values that represent keyboard keys.

- `public int clickCount`

  The number of consecutive clicks during a MOUSE_DOWN event.

- `public Event evt`

  The next event to take place, as in a linked list.

- `public final static int GOT_FOCUS`

  An id field constant that represents when an AWT component gets the focus.

- `public int id`

  The numeric identification for this event.

- `public int key`

The keyboard key that was pressed during this event.

- `public final static int KEY_ACTION`
- `public final static int KEY_ACTION_RELEASE`

  Constant values that represent when the user presses or releases a function key.
- `public final static int KEY_PRESS`
- `public final static int KEY_RELEASE`

  Constant values that represent when the user presses or releases a keyboard key.
- `public final static int LIST_DESELECT`
- `public final static int LIST_SELECT`

  Constant values that represent when the user deselects or selects a list item.
- `public final static int LOAD_FILE`
- `public final static int SAVE_FILE`

  Constant values that represent when a file load or save event occurs.
- `public final static int LOST_FOCUS`

  An id field constant that represents when an AWT component loses the focus.
- `public int modifiers`

  Value of any key modifiers for this event.
- `public final static int MOUSE_DOWN`
- `public final static int MOUSE_DRAG`
- `public final static int MOUSE_ENTER`
- `public final static int MOUSE_EXIT`
- `public final static int MOUSE_MOVE`
- `public final static int MOUSE_UP`

  Constant values that represent mouse events.
- `public final static int SCROLL_ABSOLUTE`

  An id field constant that represents when the user has moved the bubble in a scrollbar.
- `public final static int SCROLL_BEGIN`
- `public final static int SCROLL_END`

  Constant values that represent the scroll begin or ending event.
- `public final static int SCROLL_LINE_DOWN`
- `public final static int SCROLL_LINE_UP`

  Constant values that represent when the user has clicked in the line down or up area of the scrollbar.
- `public final static int SCROLL_PAGE_DOWN`
- `public final static int SCROLL_PAGE_UP`

  Constant values that represent when the user has clicked in the page down or up area of the scrollbar.
- `public Object target`

  The object that this event was created from or took place over.

- `public long when`

  The time stamp of this event. Represented as the number of milliseconds since midnight, January 1, 1970 UTC.
- `public final static int WINDOW_DEICONIFY`
- `public final static int WINDOW_DESTROY`
- `public final static int WINDOW_EXPOSE`
- `public final static int WINDOW_ICONIFY`
- `public final static int WINDOW_MOVED`

  Constant values that represent various window events.
- `public int x`
- `public int y`

  The horizontal or vertical coordinate location of this event.

Constructors

- `public Event(Object obj, int id, Object arg)`
- `public Event(Object obj, long ts, int id, int x, int y, int key, int state)`
- `public Event(Object obj, long ts, int id, int x, int y, int key, int state, Object arg)`

  Creates a new instance of an event with an initial target Object (`obj`), `id`, `x` location, `y` location, `key`, modifier `state`, time stamp (`ts`), and argument (`arg`).

Methods

- `public boolean controlDown()`
- `public boolean metaDown()`
- `public boolean shiftDown()`

  Returns a true value if the Control, Meta, or Shift key is down for this event.
- `protected String paramString()`

  Returns the parameter string for this event.
- `public String toString()`

  Returns a string representation of this event.
- `public void translate(int xval, int yval)`

  Translates this event, modifying the `x` and `y` coordinates for this event by adjusting the `x` location by `xval` and the `y` location by `yval`.

EventQueue (`java.awt`)

A public class, derived from `Object`, that represents an event queue.

Constructors

- `public EventQueue()`
  Creates a new instance of an `EventQueue`.

Methods

- `public synchronized AWTEvent getNextEvent() throws`
  `InterruptedException`
  Removes the next event from the queue and returns it to the calling method. If the queue is currently empty, this method will block until an event arrives.
- `public synchronized AWTEvent peekEvent()`
- `public synchronized AWTEvent peekEvent(int type)`
  Returns the next event if any, of the specified `type` from this queue but does not remove it.
- `public synchronized void postEvent(AWTEvent event)`
  Places a Java 1.0 AWT event at the end of this queue.

Exception (`java.lang`)

A public class, derived from `Throwable`, that catches conditions that are thrown by methods.

Constructors

- `public Exception()`
- `public Exception(String str)`
  Creates a new instance of an exception. A message can be provided via `str`.

FieldPosition (`java.text`)

A public class, derived from `Object`, that is used to identify specific fields in formatted output. This class is generally used by the `Format` class (and subclasses).

Constructors

- `public FieldPosition(int field)`
  Creates a new instance of a `FieldPosition` from the specified field.

Methods

- `public int getBeginIndex()`
- `public int getEndIndex()`
  Returns the beginning or ending character index for this field.
- `public int getField()`
  Returns the identifier value for this field.

FileDialog (`java.awt`)

A public class, derived from `Dialog`, that creates a graphical window from which the user can select a file.

Variables and Constants

- `public final static int LOAD`
- `public final static int SAVE`
  Constant values that specify that this file dialog is intended for loading or saving a file.

Constructors

- `public FileDialog(Frame prt)`
- `public FileDialog(Frame prt, String str)`
- `public FileDialog(Frame prt, String str, int lsmode)`
  Creates a new instance of a file dialog with a specified parent frame, an initial title (`str`) and an initial mode (LOAD (default) or SAVE).

Methods

- `public void addNotify()`
  Creates this file dialog's peer.
- `public String getDirectory()`
- `public void setDirectory(String str)`
  Returns or sets the directory currently displayed by this file dialog.
- `public String getFile()`
- `public void setFile(String str)`
  Returns or sets the name of the file currently selected in this file dialog.
- `public FilenameFilter getFilenameFilter()`
- `public void setFilenameFilter(FilenameFilter fltr)`
  Returns or sets the current value of this file dialog's file filter.
- `public int getMode()`
- `public void setMode(int md)`

Returns or sets the current mode of this file dialog.
- `protected String paramString()`
  Returns a string containing the parameters of this file dialog.

Float (`java.lang`)

A public final class, derived from `Number`, that contains floating point math operations, constants, methods to compute minimum and maximum numbers, and string manipulation routines related to the primitive `float` type.

Variables and Constants

- `public final static float MAX_VALUE`
- `public final static float MIN_VALUE`
  Constant values that contain the maximum possible value (3.40282346638528860e+38f) or the minimum possible value (1.40129846432481707e−45f) of a float in Java.
- `public final static float NaN`
  A constant value that contains the representation of the Not-A-Number float (0.0f).
- `public final static float NEGATIVE_INFINITY`
- `public final static float POSITIVE_INFINITY`
  Constant values that contain the representation of the negative (−1.0f / 0.0f) or positive (1.0f / 0.0f) infinity float.
- `public final static Class TYPE`
  The `Float` constant value of the float type class.

Constructors

- `public Float(double arg)`
- `public Float(float arg) throws NumberFormatException`
- `public Float(String arg)`
  Creates an instance of the Float class from the parameter `arg`.

Methods

- `public byte byteValue()`
- `public float floatValue()`
- `public double doubleValue()`
- `public int intValue()`
- `public long longValue()`
- `public short shortValue()`
  Returns the value of the current object as a Java primitive type.

- public boolean equals(Object arg)
  Returns the result of an equality comparison against arg.
- public static int floatToIntBits(float num)
- public static float intBitsToFloat(int num)
  Returns the bit stream or float equivalent of the parameter num as an int. Bit 31 of the int returned value is the sign bit, bits 23 to 30 are the exponent, while bits 0 to 22 are the mantissa.
- public int hashCode()
  Returns a hash code for this object.
- public boolean isInfinite()
- public static boolean isInfinite(float num)
  Returns true if the current object or num is positive or negative infinity, false in all other cases.
- public boolean isNaN()
- public static boolean isNaN(float num)
  Returns true if the current object or num is Not-A-Number, false in all other cases.
- public String toString()
- public static String toString(float num)
  Returns the string representation of the current object or num.
- public static Float valueOf(String str) throws NumberFormatException
  Returns a Float initialized to the value of str.

FlowLayout (java.awt)

A public class, derived from Object implementing LayoutManager and Serializable, that lays out components in a sequential horizontal order using their preferred size.

Variables and Constants

- public final static int CENTER
- public final static int LEFT
- public final static int RIGHT
  Constant values indicating areas of the flow layout manager.

Constructors

- public FlowLayout()
- public FlowLayout(int al)
- public FlowLayout(int al, int hg, int vg)

Creates a new instance of a flow layout and gives it `al` alignment (default of centered) with a `vg` vertical and `hg` horizontal gap (default of 0).

Methods

- `public void addLayoutComponent(String str, Component cpnt)`
- `public void removeLayoutComponent(Component cpnt)`
  Adds or removes a component to/from this layout manager. When adding a component, a name may be specified.
- `public int getAlignment()`
- `public void setAlignment(int alg)`
  Returns or sets the alignment value for this layout manager.
- `public int getHgap()`
- `public int getVgap()`
  Returns the value of the horizontal or vertical gap between components laid out by this layout manager.
- `public void layoutContainer(Container cont)`
  Lays out the specified container with this layout manager.
- `public Dimension minimumLayoutSize(Container cont)`
- `public Dimension preferredLayoutSize(Container cont)`
  Returns the minimum or preferred size of the specified container when laid out by this layout manager.
- `public void setHgap(int hg)`
- `public void setVgap(int vg)`
  Sets the horizontal or vertical gap for this layout manager.
- `public String toString()`
  Returns a string representation of this layout manager.

FocusAdapter (`java.awt.event`)

A public abstract class, derived from `Object` and implementing `FocusListener`, that permits derived classes to override the predefined no-op focus events.

Constructors

- `public FocusAdapter()`
  Creates a new instance of a `FocusAdapter`.

Methods

- `public void focusGained(FocusEvent event)`
- `public void focusLost(FocusEvent event)`
  Empty methods that should be overridden in order to implement event handling for AWT focus-based events.

FocusEvent (`java.awt.event`)

A public class, derived from `ComponentEvent`, that describes a particular AWT focus event.

Variables and Constants

- `public static final int FOCUS_FIRST`
- `public static final int FOCUS_LAST`
  Constant values that represent the index of the first and last focus event ids.
- `public static final int FOCUS_GAINED`
- `public static final int FOCUS_LOST`
  Constant values that represent the gain and loss of focus events.

Constructors

- `public FocusEvent(Component src, int type)`
- `public FocusEvent(Component src, int type, boolean toggle)`
  Creates a new instance of a `FocusEvent` from the specified source, having a defined event type and toggling this event as a temporary change of focus (false by default).

Methods

- `public boolean isTemporary()`
  Returns the status value of the temporary focus toggle.
- `public String paramString()`
  Returns a string containing the parameters of this `FocusEvent`.

Font (`java.awt`)

A public class, derived from `Object` and implementing `Serializable`, that represents a GUI font.

Variables and Constants

- `public final static int BOLD`
- `public final static int ITALIC`
- `public final static int PLAIN`
  Constant values that indicate the style of the font.
- `protected String name`
  The name of the font.

- `protected int size`
  The size of the font in pixels.
- `protected int style`
  The style of the font.

Constructors

- `public Font(String str, int st, int sz)`
  Creates a new font with an initial name (`str`), style (`st`), and size (`sz`).

Methods

- `public static Font decode(String arg)`
  Returns the requested font from a specified string.
- `public boolean equals(Object obj)`
  Returns a true value if this font is equal to `obj`.
- `public String getFamily()`
  Returns the name of the family this font belongs to.
- `public static Font getFont(String str)`
- `public static Font getFont(String str, Font ft)`
  Returns the font named `str`. If the font cannot be located, the second method returns `ft` as the default.
- `public String getName()`
  Returns the name of this font.
- `public FontPeer getPeer()`
  Returns the peer of this font.
- `public int getSize()`
- `public int getStyle()`
  Returns the size or style of this font.
- `public int hashCode()`
  Returns the hash code for this font.
- `public boolean isBold()`
- `public boolean isItalic()`
- `public boolean isPlain()`
  Returns a true value if this font is bolded, italicized, or plain.
- `public String toString()`
  Returns a string representation of this font.

FontMetrics (`java.awt`)

A public class, derived from `Object` and implementing `Serializable`, that provides detailed information about a particular font.

Variables and Constants

- `protected Font font`
  The font upon which the metrics are generated.

Constructors

- `protected FontMetrics(Font f)`
  Creates a new instance of metrics from a given font `f`.

Methods

- `public int bytesWidth(byte[] src, int offset, int size)`
- `public int charsWidth(char[] src, int offset, int size)`
  Returns the advance width for displaying the subarray of `src`, starting at index `offset`, and having a length of `size`.
- `public int charWidth(char c)`
- `public int charWidth(int c)`
  Returns the advance width of the character `c` for the font in this font metric.
- `public int getAscent()`
- `public int getDescent()`
  Returns the amount of ascent or descent for the font in this font metric.
- `public Font getFont()`
  Returns the font in this font metric.
- `public int getHeight()`
  Returns the standard height of the font in this font metric.
- `public int getLeading()`
  Returns the standard leading of the font in this font metric.
- `public int getMaxAdvance()`
  Returns the maximum amount of advance for the font in this font metric.
- `public int getMaxAscent()`
- `public int getMaxDescent()`
  Returns the maximum amount of ascent or descent for the font in this font metric.
- `public int[] getWidths()`
  Returns an `int` array containing the advance widths of the first 256 characters of the font.
- `public int stringWidth(String str)`
  Returns the advance width of the string `str` as represented by the font in this font metric.
- `public String toString()`
  Returns a string representation of the font metrics.

Format (`java.text`)

A public abstract class, derived from `Object` and implementing `Cloneable` and `Serializable`, which is used to format locale-based values into Strings, and vice versa.

Constructors

- `public Format()`
  Creates a new instance of a `Format`.

Methods

- `public Object clone()`
  Returns a copy of this `Format`.
- `public final String format(Object arg)`
  Returns a formatted string from `arg`.
- `public abstract StringBuffer format(Object arg, StringBuffer dest, FieldPosition pos)`
  Formats the specified argument (starting at field `pos`) into a string, and appends it to the specified `StringBuffer`. This method returns the same value as the destination buffer.
- `public Object parseObject(String src) throws ParseException`
  Parses the specified source string into a formatted object.
- `public abstract Object parseObject(String src, ParsePosition pos)`
  Parses the specified source string into a formatted object starting at the specified `ParsePosition`.

Frame (`java.awt`)

A public class, derived from `Window` and implementing `MenuContainer`, that creates a graphical window with a border and a title bar. A frame may also contain a menu bar.

Variables and Constants

- `public final static int CROSSHAIR_CURSOR`
- `public final static int DEFAULT_CURSOR`
- `public final static int E_RESIZE_CURSOR`
- `public final static int HAND_CURSOR`
- `public final static int MOVE_CURSOR`
- `public final static int N_RESIZE_CURSOR`

- `public final static int NE_RESIZE_CURSOR`
- `public final static int NW_RESIZE_CURSOR`
- `public final static int S_RESIZE_CURSOR`
- `public final static int SE_RESIZE_CURSOR`
- `public final static int SW_RESIZE_CURSOR`
- `public final static int TEXT_CURSOR`
- `public final static int W_RESIZE_CURSOR`
- `public final static int WAIT_CURSOR`
    Constant values that define a frame cursor.

Constructors

- `public Frame()`
- `public Frame(String str)`
    Creates a new instance of a frame with a title of `str` (or no title present).

Methods

- `public void addNotify()`
    Creates this frame's peer.
- `public void dispose()`
    Removes this frame and all resources associated with it.
- `public Image getIconImage()`
- `public void setIconImage(Image img)`
    Returns or sets the icon image for this frame.
- `public MenuBar getMenuBar()`
- `public void setMenuBar(MenuBar bar)`
    Returns or sets the menu bar for this frame.
- `public String getTitle()`
- `public void setTitle(String str)`
    Returns or sets the title for this frame.
- `public boolean isResizable()`
- `public void setResizable(boolean toggle)`
    Returns or sets the state of the resizability of this frame.
- `protected String paramString()`
    Returns a string containing the parameters for this frame.
- `public void remove(MenuComponent mc)`
    Removes the specified menu component from this frame.

Graphics (`java.awt`)

A public abstract class, derived from `Object`, that provides many useful drawing methods and tools for the manipulation of graphics. A `Graphics` object defines a context in which the user draws.

Constructors

- `protected Graphics()`
  Creates a new `Graphics` instance. This constructor cannot be called directly.

Methods

- `public abstract void clearRect(int x, int y, int width, int height)`
  Draws a rectangle (with no fill pattern) in the current background color at position <x, y>, and having a `width` and `height`.
- `public abstract void clipRect(int x, int y, int width, int height)`
  Sets a clipping rectangle at position <x, y> and having a `width` and `height`.
- `public abstract void copyArea(int x, int y, int width, int height, int newx, int newy)`
  Copies a graphic rectangular area at position <x, y> and having a `width` and `height`, to position `newx` and `newy`.
- `public abstract Graphics create()`
- `public Graphics create(int x, int y, int width, int height)`
  Returns a copy of this graphics context from position <x, y>, and having a `width` and `height`. In the case of the first method, the entire area is copied.
- `public abstract void dispose()`
  Disposes this graphics context.
- `public void draw3DRect(int x, int y, int width, int height, boolean toggle)`
  Draws a 3D rectangle at position <x, y> and having a `width` and `height`. If `toggle` is true, the rectangle will appear raised; otherwise, it will appear indented.
- `public abstract void drawArc(int x, int y, int width, int height, int sAngle, int aAngle)`
  Draws an arc with a starting position <x, y> and having a `width` and `height`. The start angle (`sAngle`) and arc angle (`aAngle`) are both measured in degrees and describe the starting and ending angle of the arc.
- `public void drawBytes(byte[] src, int index, int ln, int x, int y)`
- `public void drawChars(char[] src, int index, int ln, int x, int y)`
  Draw `ln` bytes or characters of array `src` (starting at the offset `index`) at position <x, y>.

- public abstract boolean drawImage(Image src, int x,
  int y, Color bgc, ImageObserver obsv)
- public abstract boolean drawImage(Image src, int x,
  int y, ImageObserver obsv)

  Draws a graphic image (src) at position <x, y>. Any transparent color pixels are drawn as bgc, and the obsv monitors the progress of the image.
- public abstract boolean drawImage(Image src, int x, int
  y, int width, int height, Color bgc, ImageObserver
  obsv)
- public abstract boolean drawImage(Image src, int x,
  int y, int width, int height, ImageObserver obsv)

  Draws a graphic image (src) at position <x, y> and having a width and height. Any transparent color pixels are drawn as bgc, and the obsv monitors the progress of the image.
- public abstract boolean drawImage(Image src, int xsrc1,
  int ysrc1, int xsrc1, int ysrc2, int xdest1, int ydest1,
  int xdest1, int ydest2, Color bgc, ImageObserver obsv)
- public abstract boolean drawImage(Image src, int
  xsrc1, int ysrc1, int xsrc1, int ysrc2, int xdest1,
  int ydest1, int xdest1, int ydest2, ImageObserver
  obsv)

  Draws a graphic image (src) from the area defined by the bounding rectangle <xsrc1, ysrc1> to <xsrc2, ysrc2> in the area defined by the bounding rectangle <xdest1, ydest1> to <xdest2, ydest2>. Any transparent color pixels are drawn as bgc, and the obsv monitors the progress of the image.
- public abstract void drawLine(int xsrc, int ysrc, int
  xdest, int ydest)

  Draws a line from position <xsrc, ysrc> to <xdest, ydest>.
- public abstract void drawOval(int xsrc, int ysrc, int
  width, int height)

  Draws an oval starting at position <xsrc, ysrc> and having a width and height.
- public abstract void drawPolygon(int[] x, int[] y,
  int num)
- public void drawPolygon(Polygon poly)

  Draws a polygon constructed from poly or an array of x points, y points and a number of points in the polygon (num).
- public void drawRect(int xsrc, int ysrc, int width,
  int height)
- public abstract void drawRoundRect(int xsrc, int ysrc,
  int width, int height, int awd, int aht)

  Draws a rectangle with or without rounded corners at position <xsrc, ysrc> and having a width and height. The shape of the rounded corners are determined by the width of the arc (awd) and the height of the arc (aht).

- `public abstract void drawString(String str, int x, int y)`

  Draws the string `str` at position `<x, y>` in this `Graphic`'s current font and color.

- `public void fill3DRect(int x, int y, int width, int height, boolean toggle)`

  Draws a filled 3D rectangle at position `<x, y>` and having a `width` and `height`. The rectangle is filled with this `Graphic`'s current color, and if `toggle` is true, the rectangle is drawn raised. (Otherwise it is drawn indented.)

- `public abstract void fillArc(int x, int y, int width, int height, int sAngle, int aAngle)`

  Draws a filled arc at position `<x, y>` and having a `width` and `height`. The arc has a starting angle of `sAngle` and an ending angle of `aAngle`.

- `public abstract void fillOval(int x, int y, int width, int height)`

  Draws a filled oval at position `<x, y>` and having a `width` and `height`.

- `public abstract void fillPolygon(int[] x, int[] y, int num)`

- `public void fillPolygon(Polygon poly)`

  Draws a filled polygon defined by `poly` or the arrays `x`, `y` and the number of points in the polygon, `num`.

- `public abstract void fillRect(int x, int y, int width, int height)`

- `public abstract void fillRoundRect(int x, int y, int width, int height, int aWidth, int aHeight)`

  Draws a filled rectangle with or without rounded corners at position `<x, y>` and having a `width` and `height`. The shape of the rounded corners are determined by the width of the arc (`aWidth`) and the height of the arc (`aHeight`).

- `public void finalize()`

  Disposes of the current graphics context.

- `public abstract Shape getClip()`

  Returns a shape object of the current clipping area for this graphics context.

- `public abstract Rectangle getClipBounds()`

  Returns a rectangle describing the bounds of the current clipping area for this graphics context.

- `public abstract Color getColor()`

- `public abstract void setColor(Color clr)`

  Returns or sets the current color for this graphics context.

- `public abstract Font getFont()`

- `public abstract void setFont(Font ft)`

  Returns or sets the current font of this graphics context.

- `public FontMetrics getFontMetrics()`

- `public abstract FontMetrics getFontMetrics(Font fn)`

Returns the font metrics associated with this graphics context or font `fn`.

- `public abstract void setClip(int x, int y, int width, int height)`
- `public abstract void setClip(Shape shp)`
  Sets the clipping area for this graphics context to be at position `<x, y>` and having a `width` and `height` or to be of a specified shape (`shp`).
- `public abstract void setPaintMode()`
  Sets the current graphics context's paint mode to overwrite any subsequent destinations with the current color.
- `public abstract void setXORMode(Color clr)`
  Sets the current graphics context's paint mode to overwrite any subsequent destinations with the alternating current color and `clr` color.
- `public String toString()`
  Returns a string representation of this graphics context.
- `public abstract void translate(int x, int y)`
  Modifies the origin of this graphics context to be relocated to `<x, y>`.

GregorianCalendar (`java.util`)

A public class, derived from `Calendar`, that represents the standard world Gregorian calendar.

Variables and Constants

- AD
- BC
  Constant values representing periods of an era.

Constructors

- `public GregorianCalendar()`
- `public GregorianCalendar(Locale locale)`
- `public GregorianCalendar(TimeZone zone)`
- `public GregorianCalendar(TimeZone zone, Locale locale)`
  Creates a new `GregorianCalendar` from the current time in the specified time zone (or the default) and the specified locale (or the default).
- `public GregorianCalendar(int year, int month, int date)`
- `public GregorianCalendar(int year, int month, int date, int hour, int min)`
- `public GregorianCalendar(int year, int month, int date, int hour, int min, int sec)`
  Creates a new `GregorianCalendar`, setting the year, month, date, hour, minute, and seconds of the time fields.

Methods

- `public void add(int field, int val)`
  Adds (or subtracts in the case of a negative `val`) an amount of days or time from the specified `field`.
- `public boolean after(Object arg)`
- `public boolean before(Object arg)`
  Returns a true value if this `GregorianCalendar` date is after or before the date specified by `arg`.
- `public Object clone()`
  Returns a clone of this `GregorianCalendar`.
- `protected void computeFields()`
- `protected void computeTime()`
  Computes the values of the time fields based on the currently set time (`computeFields()`) or computes the time based on the currently set time fields (`computeTime()`) for this `GregorianCalendar`.
- `public boolean equals(Object arg)`
  Returns a true value if this `GregorianCalendar` is equal to the value of arg.
- `public int getGreatestMinimum(int fld)`
- `public int getLeastMaximum(int fld)`
  Returns the largest allowable minimum or smallest allowable maximum value for the specified field.
- `public final Date getGregorianChange()`
- `public void setGregorianChange(Date dt)`
  Returns or sets the date of the change from Julian to Gregorian calendars for this calendar. The default value is October 15, 1582 (midnight local time).
- `public int getMaximum(int fld)`
- `public int getMinimum(int fld)`
  Returns the largest or smallest allowable value for the specified field.
- `public synchronized int hashCode()`
  Returns the hash code for this `GregorianCalendar`.
- `public boolean isLeapYear(int year)`
  Returns a true value if the specified year is a leap year.
- `public void roll(int fld, boolean direction)`
  Adds one single unit of time to the specified date/time field. A true value specified for `direction` increases the field's value, false decreases it.

GridBagConstraints (`java.awt`)

A public class, derived from `Object` and implementing `Cloneable`, that specifies the layout constraints for each component laid out with a `GridBagLayout`.

Variables and Constants

- `public int anchor`
  Determines where to place a component that is smaller in size than its display area in the gridbag.
- `public final static int BOTH`
- `public final static int HORIZONTAL`
- `public final static int NONE`
- `public final static int VERTICAL`
  Constant values that indicate the direction(s) that the component should grow.
- `public final static int CENTER`
- `public final static int EAST`
- `public final static int NORTH`
- `public final static int NORTHEAST`
- `public final static int NORTHWEST`
- `public final static int SOUTH`
- `public final static int SOUTHEAST`
- `public final static int SOUTHWEST`
- `public final static int WEST`
  Constant values that indicate where the component should be placed in its display area.
- `public int fill`
  Determines how to resize a component that is smaller than its display area in the gridbag.
- `public int gridheight`
- `public int gridwidth`
  Specifies the number of vertical and horizontal cells the component shall occupy.
- `public int gridx`
- `public int gridy`
  Describes horizontal and vertical cell locations (indices) in the gridbag, where `gridx=0` is the leftmost cell and `gridy=0` is the topmost cell.
- `public Insets insets`
  Defines the amount of space (in pixels) around the component in its display area.
- `public int ipadx`
- `public int ipady`
  Defines the amount of space (in pixels) to add to the minimum horizontal and vertical size of the component.
- `public final static int RELATIVE`
  A constant that specifies that this component is the next to last item in its gridbag row or that it should be placed next to the last item added to the gridbag.
- `public final static int REMAINDER`

A constant that specifies that this component is the last item in its grid-bag row.

- `public double weightx`
- `public double weighty`
  Specifies the weight of horizontal and vertical growth of this component relative to other components during a resizing event. A larger value indicates a higher percentage of growth for this component.

Constructors

- `public GridBagConstraints()`
  Creates a new instance of `GridBagConstraints`.

Methods

- `public Object clone()`
  Creates a copy of these gridbag constraints.

GridBagLayout (`java.awt`)

A public class, derived from `Object` and implementing `Serializable` and `LayoutManager`, that creates a gridlike area for component layout. Unlike `GridLayout`, `GridBagLayout` does not force the components to be the same size or to be constrained to one cell.

Variables and Constants

- `public double columnWeights[]`
- `public int columnWidths[]`
  Holds the weights and widths of each column of this `GridBagLayout`.
- `protected Hashtable comptable`
  A hashtable of the components managed by this layout manager.
- `protected GridBagConstraints defaultConstraints`
  Holds the default constraints for any component laid out by this layout manager.
- `protected GridBagLayoutInfo layoutInfo`
  Holds specific layout information (such as the list of components or the constraints of this manager) for this `GridBagLayout`.
- `protected final static int MAXGRIDSIZE`
  A constant value that contains the maximum (512) number of grid cells that can be laid out by this `GridBagLayout`.
- `protected final static int MINSIZE`
  A constant value that contains the minimum (1) number of cells contained within this `GridBagLayout`.

- `protected final static int PREFERREDSIZE`
  A constant value that contains the preferred (2) number of cells contained within this `GridBagLayout`.
- `public int rowHeights[]`
- `public double rowWeights[]`
  Holds the heights and weights of each row of this `GridBagLayout`.

Constructors

- `public GridBagLayout()`
  Creates a new instance of a `GridBagLayout`.

Methods

- `public void addLayoutComponent(Component item, Object constraints)`
  Adds the component `item` to this layout manager using the specified constraints on the item.
- `public void addLayoutComponent(String str, Component item)`
  Adds the component `item` to this layout manager and names it `str`.
- `protected void AdjustForGravity(GridBagConstraints constraints, Rectangle rect)`
  Sets the characteristics of `rect` based on the specified constraints.
- `protected void ArrangeGrid(Container parent)`
  Arranges the entire grid on the parent.
- `public GridBagConstraints getConstraints(Component item)`
  Returns a copy of the constraints for the `item` component.
- `public float getLayoutAlignmentX(Container parent)`
- `public float getLayoutAlignmentY(Container parent)`
  Returns the horizontal and vertical alignment values for the specified container.
- `public int[][] getLayoutDimensions()`
  Returns a two-dimensional array in which the zero index of the first dimension holds the minimum width of each column and the one index of the first dimension holds the minimum height of each column.
- `protected GridBagLayoutInfo GetLayoutInfo(Container parent, int sizeflag)`
  Computes and returns a `GridBagLayoutInfo` object for components associated with the specified parent container.
- `public Point getLayoutOrigin()`
  Returns this layout's point of origin.
- `public double[][] getLayoutWeights()`

Returns a two-dimensional array in which the zero index of the first dimension holds the weight in the *x* direction of each column and the one index of the first dimension holds the weight in the *y* direction of each column.

- `protected Dimension GetMinSize(Container parent, GridBagLayoutInfo info)`
  Returns the minimum size for the specified parent container based on laying out the container using the specified `GridBagLayoutInfo`.
- `public void invalidateLayout(Container cont)`
  Forces this layout manager to discard any cached layout information about the specified container.
- `public void layoutContainer(Container cont)`
  Lays out the specified container with this layout manager.
- `public Point location(int x, int y)`
  Returns the upper right corner of the cell in this `GridBagLayout` with dimensions greater than the specified `<x, y>` coordinate.
- `protected GridBagConstraints lookupConstraints(Component item)`
  Returns the actual constraints for the specified component.
- `public Dimension maximumLayoutSize(Container cont)`
- `public Dimension minimumLayoutSize(Container cont)`
- `public Dimension preferredLayoutSize(Container cont)`
  Returns the maximum, minimum, or preferred size of the specified container when laid out by this layout manager.
- `public void removeLayoutComponent(Component comp)`
  Removes the specified component from this layout manager.
- `public void setConstraints(Component item, GridBagConstraints constraints)`
  Sets the `constraints` for the `item` component in this layout manager.
- `public String toString()`
  Returns a string representation of this layout manager.

GridLayout (`java.awt`)

A public class, derived from `Object` and implementing `Serializable` and `LayoutManager`, that creates a grid area of equal sized rectangles to lay out components in.

Constructors

- `public GridLayout()`
- `public GridLayout(int r, int c)`
  Creates a new instance of a `GridLayout` with a dimension of `r` rows and `c` columns (default of 1 by any).
- `public GridLayout(int r, int c, int hg, int vg)`

Creates a new instance of a `GridLayout` with a dimension of r rows and c columns. The grid cells have a hg pixel horizontal gap and a vg pixel vertical gap.

Methods

- `public void addLayoutComponent(String str, Component comp)`
- `public void removeLayoutComponent(Component comp)`
  Adds or removes the specified component. When adding, the component can be given a name (`str`).
- `public int getColumns()`
- `public void setColumns(int val)`
  Returns or sets the number of columns of this layout manager.
- `public int getHgap()`
- `public int getVgap()`
  Returns the value of the horizontal or vertical gap for this layout manager.
- `public int getRows()`
- `public void setRows(int val)`
  Returns or sets the number of rows of this layout manager.
- `public void layoutContainer(Container cont)`
  Lays out the specified container with this layout manager.
- `public Dimension minimumLayoutSize(Container cont)`
- `public Dimension preferredLayoutSize(Container cont)`
  Returns the minimum or preferred size of the specified container when laid out with this layout manager.
- `public void setHgap(int val)`
- `public void setVgap(int val)`
  Sets the horizontal or vertical gap for this layout manager to `val`.
- `public String toString()`
  Returns a string representation of this layout manager.

Hashtable (`java.util`)

A public class, derived from `Dictionary` and implementing `Serializable` and `Cloneable`, that allows for the storing of objects that have a relationship with a key. You can then use this key to access the object stored.

Constructors

- `public Hashtable()`
- `public Hashtable(int size)`
- `public Hashtable(int size, float load) throws IllegalArgumentException`

Creates a new instance of a hashtable, setting the initial capacity (or using the default size of 101) and a load factor (default of 0.75). The initial capacity sets the number of objects the table can store, and the load factor value is the percentage filled the table may become before being resized.

Methods

- `public void clear()`
  Removes all keys and elements from this `Hashtable`.
- `public Object clone()`
  Returns a clone of this `Hashtable` (the keys and values are not cloned).
- `public boolean contains(Object arg) throws NullPointerException`
  Returns a true value if this `Hashtable` contains a key that is related to the element `arg`.
- `public boolean containsKey(Object index)`
  Returns a true value if this `Hashtable` contains an entry for the key at `index`.
- `public Enumeration elements()`
- `public Enumeration keys()`
  Returns an enumerated list of all of the elements or keys of this `Hashtable`.
- `public Object get(Object index)`
- `public Object put(Object index, Object arg) throws NullPointerException`
- `public Object remove(Object index)`
  Returns, inserts or removes the element `arg` corresponds to the key at `index`.
- `public boolean isEmpty()`
  Returns a true value if the `Hashtable` is empty.
- `protected void rehash()`
  Resizes this `Hashtable`. The method is invoked automatically when the number of keys exceeds the capacity and load factor.
- `public int size()`
  Returns the number of elements in this `Hashtable`.
- `public String toString()`
  Returns a string representation of this `Hashtable`'s key-element pairings.

HttpURLConnection (`java.net`)

A public class, derived from `URLConnection`, that supports HTTP–protocol-based exchanges.

Variables and Constants

- `public final static int HTTP_ACCEPTED`
- `public final static int HTTP_BAD_GATEWAY`
- `public final static int HTTP_BAD_METHOD`
- `public final static int HTTP_BAD_REQUEST`
- `public final static int HTTP_CLIENT_TIMEOUT`
- `public final static int HTTP_CONFLICT`
- `public final static int HTTP_CREATED`
- `public final static int HTTP_ENTITY_TOO_LARGE`
- `public final static int HTTP_FORBIDDEN`
- `public final static int HTTP_GATEWAY_TIMEOUT`
- `public final static int HTTP_GONE`
- `public final static int HTTP_INTERNAL_ERROR`
- `public final static int HTTP_INTERNAL_ERROR`
- `public final static int HTTP_MOVED_PERM`
- `public final static int HTTP_MOVED_TEMP`
- `public final static int HTTP_MULT_CHOICE`
- `public final static int HTTP_NO_CONTENT`
- `public final static int HTTP_NOT_ACCEPTABLE`
- `public final static int HTTP_NOT_AUTHORITATIVE`
- `public final static int HTTP_NOT_FOUND`
- `public final static int HTTP_NOT_MODIFIED`
- `public final static int HTTP_OK`
- `public final static int HTTP_PARTIAL`
- `public final static int HTTP_PAYMENT_REQUIRED`
- `public final static int HTTP_PRECON_FAILED`
- `public final static int HTTP_PROXY_AUTH`
- `public final static int HTTP_REQ_TOO_LONG`
- `public final static int HTTP_RESET`
- `public final static int HTTP_SEE_OTHER`
- `public final static int HTTP_SERVER_ERROR`
- `public final static int HTTP_UNAUTHORIZED`
- `public final static int HTTP_UNAVAILABLE`
- `public final static int HTTP_UNSUPPORTED_TYPE`
- `public final static int HTTP_USE_PROXY`
- `public final static int HTTP_VERSION`
  A constant that represents an HTTP v1.1 response code (for example: `HTTP_NOT_FOUND=404`).
- `protected String method`
  Contains the method of the URL request for this HttpURLConnection.
- `responseCode`
  Contains the HTTP response code for last exchange.
- `responseMessage`
  Contains the HTTP response message for last exchange.

Constructors

- `protected HttpURLConnection(URL src)`
  Creates an instance of an `HttpURLConnection` to the specified URL (`src`).

Methods

- `public abstract void disconnect()`
  Disconnects the connection to the URL.
- `public static boolean getFollowRedirects()`
- `public static void setFollowRedirects(boolean follow)`
  Returns or sets the state if this `HttpURLConnection` will follow HTTP redirects.
- `public String getRequestMethod()`
- `public void setRequestMethod(String method) throws ProtocolException`
  Returns or sets the current request method for this `HttpURLConnection`.
- `public int getResponseCode() throws IOException`
- `public String getResponseMessage() throws IOException`
  Returns the last HTTP response code or message for this `HttpURLConnection`.
- `public abstract boolean usingProxy()`
  Returns a true value if this `HttpURLConnection` is passing through a proxy.

Image (`java.awt`)

A public abstract class, derived from `Object`, that is used to manage graphic images.

Variables and Constants

- `public final static int SCALE_AREA_AVERAGING`
- `public final static int SCALE_DEFAULT`
- `public final static int SCALE_FAST`
- `public final static int SCALE_REPLICATE`
- `public final static int SCALE_SMOOTH`
  Constant values used to indicate specific scaling algorithms.
- `public final static Object UndefinedProperty`
  A constant value that is returned whenever an undefined property for an image is attempted to be obtained.

- `public boolean isConsumed()`
    Returns a true value if this event is consumed.
- `public boolean isAltDown()`
- `public boolean isControlDown()`
- `public boolean isMetaDown()`
- `public boolean isShiftDown()`
    Returns a true value if the Alt, Control, Meta, or Shift key is depressed during this event.

InputStream (`java.io`)

A public abstract class, derived from `Object`, that is the parent class of any type of input stream that reads bytes.

Constructors

- `public InputStream()`
    Generally called only by subclasses, this constructor creates a new instance of an `InputStream`.

Methods

- `public int available() throws IOException`
    Returns the number of available bytes that can be read. This method returns a 0 (zero) value and should be overridden by a subclass implementation.
- `public void close() throws IOException`
    Closes the input stream. This method has no functionality and should be overridden by a subclass implementation.
- `public void mark(int size)`
    Sets a mark in the input stream, allowing a rereading of the stream data to occur if the reset method is invoked. The `size` parameter indicates how many bytes may be read following the mark being set, before the mark is considered invalid.
- `public boolean markSupported()`
    Returns a true value if this `InputStream` object supports the mark and reset methods. This method always returns a false value and should be overridden by a subclass implementation.
- `public abstract int read() throws IOException`
    Reads the next byte of data from this `InputStream` and returns it as an `int`. This method has no functionality and should be implemented in a subclass. Execution of this method will block until data is available to be read, the end of the input stream occurs, or an exception is thrown.

- `public int read(byte[] dest) throws IOException`
- `public int read(byte[] dest, int offset, int size) throws IOException`

  Reads from this InputStream into the array `dest`, and returns the number of bytes read. `size` specifies the maximum number of bytes read from this InputStream into the array `dest[]` starting at index `offset`. This method returns the actual number of bytes read or −1, indicating that the end of the stream was reached. To read `size` bytes and throw them away, call this method with `dest[]` set to null.
- `public synchronized void reset() throws IOException`

  Resets the read point of this `InputStream` to the location of the last mark set.
- `public long skip(long offset) throws IOException`

  Skips over `offset` bytes from this `InputStream`. Returns the actual number of bytes skipped, as it is possible to skip over less than `offset` bytes.

InputStreamReader (`java.io`)

A public class, derived from `Reader`, that is an input stream of characters.

Constructors

- `public InputStreamReader(InputStream input)`
- `public InputStreamReader(InputStream input, String encoding) throws UnsupportedEncodingException`

  Creates an instance of `InputStreamReader` from the `InputStream` `input` with a specified `encoding`.

Methods

- `public void close() throws IOException`

  Closes this `InputStreamReader`.
- `public String getEncoding()`

  Returns the string representation of this `InputStreamReader`'s encoding.
- `public int read() throws IOException`

  Reads a single character from this `InputStreamReader`. The character read is returned as an `int`, or a −1 is returned if the end of this `InputStreamReader` was encountered.
- `public int read(char[] dest, int offset, int size) throws IOException`

Reads no more than `size` bytes from this `InputStreamReader` into the array `dest[]` starting at index `offset`. This method returns the actual number of bytes read or −1, indicating that the end of the stream was reached. To read `size` bytes and throw them away, call this method with `dest[]` set to null.

- `public boolean ready() throws IOException`
  Returns a true value if this `InputStreamReader` is capable of being read from. This state can only be true if the buffer is not empty.

Insets (`java.awt`)

A public class, derived from `Object` and implementing `Serializable` and `Cloneable`, that specify the margins of a container.

Variables and Constants

- `public int bottom`
- `public int left`
- `public int right`
- `public int top`
  Contains the value of the inset for a particular margin.

Constructors

- `public Insets(int t, int l, int b, int r)`
  Creates an instance of insets with initial top (`t`), bottom (`b`), left (`l`) and right (`r`) inset values.

Methods

- `public Object clone()`
  Creates a copy of this group of inset values.
- `public boolean equals(Object arg)`
  Returns a true value if this inset is equal to the object `arg`.
- `public String toString()`
  Returns a string representation of this group of inset values.

Integer (`java.lang`)

A public final class, derived from `Number`, that contains integer math operations, constants, methods to compute minimum and maximum numbers, and string manipulation routines related to the primitive `int` type.

Variables and Constants

- `public final static int MAX_VALUE`
- `public final static int MIN_VALUE`

  Constant values that contain the maximum possible value (2147483647) or minimum possible value (−2174783648) of an integer in Java.

- `public final static Class TYPE`

  The `Integer` constant value of the integer type class.

Constructors

- `public Integer(int num)`
- `public Integer(String num) throws NumberFormatException`

  Creates an instance of the `Integer` class from the parameter `num`.

Methods

- `public byte byteValue()`
- `public double doubleValue()`
- `public float floatValue()`
- `public int intValue()`
- `public long longValue()`
- `public short shortValue()`

  Returns the value of this integer as a Java primitive type.

- `public static Integer decode(String str) throws NumberFormatException`

  Decodes the given string (`str`) and returns it as an `Integer`. The decode method can handle octal, hexadecimal, and decimal input values.

- `public boolean equals(Object num)`

  Returns the result of an equality comparison against `num`.

- `public static Integer getInteger(String str)`
- `public static Integer getInteger(String str, int num)`
- `public static Integer getInteger(String str, Integer num)`

  Returns an `Integer` representation of the system property named in `str`. If there is no property corresponding to `num`, or the format of its value is incorrect, then the default `num` is returned as an `Integer` object.

- `public int hashCode()`

  Returns a hash code for this object.

- `public static int parseInt(String str) throws NumberFormatException`
- `public static int parseInt(String str, int base) throws NumberFormatException`

  Evaluates the string `str` and returns the `int` equivalent in radix `base`.

- `public static String toBinaryString(int num)`

- `public static String toHexString(int num)`
- `public static String toOctalString(int num)`
  Returns the string representation of parameter num in base 2 (binary), 8 (octal), or 16 (hexadecimal).
- `public String toString()`
- `public static String toString(int num)`
- `public static String toString(int num, int base)`
  Returns the string representation of this integer or num. The radix of num can be specified in base.
- `public static Integer valueOf(String str) throws NumberFormatException`
- `public static Integer valueOf(String str, int base) throws NumberFormatException`
  Returns an Integer initialized to the value of str in radix base.

ItemEvent (`java.awt.event`)

A public class, derived from AWTEvent, that represents an AWT item event (from a component such as a Checkbox, CheckboxMenuItem, Choice, or List).

Variables and Constants

- `public static final int DESELECTED`
- `public static final int SELECTED`
  Constant values representing the deselection or selection of an AWT item component.
- `public static final int ITEM_FIRST`
- `public static final int ITEM_LAST`
  Constant values that represent the index of the first and last item event ids.
- `public static final int ITEM_STATE_CHANGED`
  A constant value that represents the event of the change of state for an AWT item.

Constructors

- `public ItemEvent(ItemSelectable src, int type, Object obj, int change)`
  Creates a new instance of an ItemEvent from the specified source, having a specific type, item object, and state change.

Methods

- `public Object getItem()`
  Returns the specific item that triggered this event.
- `public ItemSelectable getItemSelectable()`

Returns the `ItemSelectable` object that triggered this event.
- `public int getStateChange()`
  Returns the state change type (deselection or selection) that triggered this event.
- `public String paramString()`
  Returns a parameter string containing the values of the parameters for this event.

KeyAdapter (`java.awt.event`)

A public abstract class, derived from `Object` and implementing `KeyListener`, that permits derived classes to override the predefined no-op keyboard events.

Constructors

- `public KeyAdapter()`
  Creates a new instance of a `KeyAdapter`.

Methods

- `public void keyPressed(KeyEvent event)`
- `public void keyReleased(KeyEvent event)`
- `public void keyTyped(KeyEvent event)`
  Empty methods that should be overridden in order to implement event handling for keyboard events.

KeyEvent (`java.awt.event`)

A public class, derived from `InputEvent`, that represents an AWT keyboard event.

Variables and Constants

- `public static final int VK_0`
- `public static final int VK_1`
- `public static final int VK_2`
- `public static final int VK_3`
- `public static final int VK_4`
- `public static final int VK_5`
- `public static final int VK_6`
- `public static final int VK_7`
- `public static final int VK_8`
- `public static final int VK_9`

Constant values that represent the keyboard keys 0–9.

- `public static final int KEY_FIRST`
- `public static final int KEY_LAST`

Constant values that represent the index of the first and last key event ids.

- `public static final int KEY_PRESSED`
- `public static final int KEY_RELEASED`
- `public static final int KEY_TYPED`

Constant values that represent the ids of a key being pressed, released, or typed.

- `public static final char CHAR_UNDEFINED`

A constant value that represents an event of a key press or release that does not correspond to a Unicode character.

- `public static final int VK_LEFT`
- `public static final int VK_RIGHT`
- `public static final int VK_UP`
- `public static final int VK_DOWN`
- `public static final int VK_HOME`
- `public static final int VK_END`
- `public static final int VK_PAGE_UP`
- `public static final int VK_PAGE_DOWN`

Constant values that represent various keyboard directional keys.

- `public static final int VK_INSERT`
- `public static final int VK_DELETE`

Constant values that represent various keyboard editing control keys.

- `public static final int VK_NUMPAD0`
- `public static final int VK_NUMPAD1`
- `public static final int VK_NUMPAD2`
- `public static final int VK_NUMPAD3`
- `public static final int VK_NUMPAD4`
- `public static final int VK_NUMPAD5`
- `public static final int VK_NUMPAD6`
- `public static final int VK_NUMPAD7`
- `public static final int VK_NUMPAD8`
- `public static final int VK_NUMPAD9`
- `public static final int VK_ADD`
- `public static final int VK_SUBTRACT`
- `public static final int VK_MULTIPLY`
- `public static final int VK_DIVIDE`
- `public static final int VK_ENTER`
- `public static final int VK_DECIMAL`

Constant values that represent various keyboard number pad keys.

- `public static final int VK_PERIOD`
- `public static final int VK_EQUALS`
- `public static final int VK_OPEN_BRACKET`
- `public static final int VK_CLOSE_BRACKET`

- `public static final int VK_BACK_SLASH`
- `public static final int VK_SLASH`
- `public static final int VK_COMMA`
- `public static final int VK_SEMICOLON`
- `public static final int VK_SPACE`
- `public static final int VK_BACK_SPACE`
- `public static final int VK_QUOTE`
- `public static final int VK_BACK_QUOTE`
- `public static final int VK_TAB`
- `public static final int VK_SLASH`

  Constant values that represent various keyboard character keys.
- `public static final int VK_PAUSE`
- `public static final int VK_PRINTSCREEN`
- `public static final int VK_SHIFT`
- `public static final int VK_HELP`
- `public static final int VK_CONTROL`
- `public static final int VK_ALT`
- `public static final int VK_ESCAPE`
- `public static final int VK_META`
- `public static final int VK_ACCEPT`
- `public static final int VK_CANCEL`
- `public static final int VK_CLEAR`
- `public static final int VK_CONVERT`
- `public static final int VK_NONCONVERT`
- `public static final int VK_MODECHANGE`
- `public static final int VK_SEPARATER`
- `public static final int VK_KANA`
- `public static final int VK_KANJI`
- `public static final int VK_FINAL`

  Constant values that represent various keyboard command and control keys.
- `public static final int VK_UNDEFINED`

  A constant value for KEY_TYPED events for which there is no defined key value.
- `public static final int VK_F1`
- `public static final int VK_F2`
- `public static final int VK_F3`
- `public static final int VK_F4`
- `public static final int VK_F5`
- `public static final int VK_F6`
- `public static final int VK_F7`
- `public static final int VK_F8`
- `public static final int VK_F9`
- `public static final int VK_F10`
- `public static final int VK_F11`

- `public static final int VK_F12`
  Constant values that represent the keyboard keys F1–F12.
- `public static final int VK_CAPS_LOCK`
- `public static final int VK_NUM_LOCK`
- `public static final int VK_SCROLL_LOCK`
  Constant values that represent various keyboard control keys.
- `public static final int VK_A`
- `public static final int VK_B`
- `public static final int VK_C`
- `public static final int VK_D`
- `public static final int VK_E`
- `public static final int VK_F`
- `public static final int VK_G`
- `public static final int VK_H`
- `public static final int VK_I`
- `public static final int VK_J`
- `public static final int VK_K`
- `public static final int VK_L`
- `public static final int VK_M`
- `public static final int VK_N`
- `public static final int VK_O`
- `public static final int VK_P`
- `public static final int VK_Q`
- `public static final int VK_R`
- `public static final int VK_S`
- `public static final int VK_T`
- `public static final int VK_U`
- `public static final int VK_V`
- `public static final int VK_W`
- `public static final int VK_X`
- `public static final int VK_Y`
- `public static final int VK_Z`
  Constant values that represent the keyboard keys A–Z.

Constructors

- `public KeyEvent(Component src, int id, long when, int modifiers, int keyCode)`
- `public KeyEvent(Component src, int id, long when, int modifiers, int keyCode, char keyChar)`
  Creates a new instance of a `KeyEvent` from the specified source, having a specific type (`id`), time stamp, modifiers, key code, and/or key character.

Methods

- `public char getKeyChar()`
- `public void setKeyChar(char character)`
  Returns or sets the character associated with this `KeyEvent`. For events that have no corresponding character, a `CHAR_UNDEFINED` is returned.
- `public int getKeyCode()`
- `public void setKeyCode(int code)`
  Returns or sets the code associated with this `KeyEvent`. For events that have no corresponding code, a `VK_UNDEFINED` is returned.
- `public static String getKeyModifiersText(int mods)`
- `public static String getKeyText(int keyCode)`
  Returns a string representation of the `KeyEvent` modifiers key code (i.e., "Meta+Shift" or "F1").
- `public boolean isActionKey()`
  Returns a true value if this event is from an action key.
- `public String paramString()`
  Returns a string representation of the parameters of this event.
- `public void setModifiers(int mods)`
  Sets the key event modifiers for this event.

Label (`java.awt`)

A public class, derived from `Component`, that places a text string in a container.

Variables and Constants

- `public final static int CENTER`
- `public final static int LEFT`
- `public final static int RIGHT`
  Constant values that indicate the alignment of the label's text.

Constructors

- `public Label()`
- `public Label(String str)`
- `public Label(String str, int align)`
  Creates a new label with the text string `str`, with `align` justification (default is `LEFT`).

Methods

- `public void addNotify()`
  Creates this label's peer.
- `public int getAlignment()`

- public void setAlignment(int align) throws
  IllegalArgumentException
    Returns or sets the alignment of this label.
- public String getText()
- public void setText(String str)
    Returns or sets the text string of this label.
- protected String paramString()
    Returns a string containing this label's parameters.

List (java.awt)

A public class, derived from Component, that graphically shows a group of items from which the user can select one or more.

Constructors

- public List()
- public List(int num)
- public List(int num, boolean toggle)
    Creates a new list with an initial number of visible rows of data (default is 0). If toggle is true, then more than one item from the list can be selected at a time.

Methods

- public void addItem(String str)
- public void addItem(String str, int idx)
    Adds an item with the label str to the list in position idx (or the bottom as the default).
- public void addActionListener(ActionListener listener)
- public void removeActionListener(ActionListener listener)
    Adds or removes the specified action listener from this list.
- public void addItemListener(ItemListener listener)
- public void removeItemListener(ItemListener listener)
    Adds or removes the specified item listener to this list.
- public void addItem(String str)
- public synchronized void addItem(String str, int idx)
    Adds an item with the label str to the list in position idx (or the bottom as the default).
- public void addNotify()
- public void removeNotify()
    Creates or removes this list's peer.
- public void delItem(int idx)

Removes an item from index idx.

- `public void deselect(int idx)`
- `public void select(int idx)`
  Deselects or selects the item at idx.
- `public String getItem(int idx)`
  Returns the label for the item at idx
- `public int getItemCount()`
  Returns the number of items in this list.
- `public synchronized String[] getItems()`
  Returns an array of the items in this list.
- `public Dimension getMinimumSize()`
- `public Dimension getMinimumSize(int num)`
- `public Dimension getPreferredSize()`
- `public Dimension getPreferredSize(int num)`
  Returns the minimum or preferred size of this list. If a new number of rows is specified, the minimum/preferred size for the change is returned.
- `public int getRows()`
  Returns the current number of visible rows in this list.
- `public int getSelectedIndex()`
- `public int[] getSelectedIndexes()`
  Returns the index(s) of the currently selected item.
- `public String getSelectedItem()`
- `public String[] getSelectedItems()`
  Returns the string label of the currently selected item(s) from this list.
- `public Object[] getSelectedObjects()`
  Returns an array of objects of the currently selected items from this list.
- `public int getVisibleIndex()`
  Returns the index of the last item made visible by the `makeVisible` method.
- `public boolean isIndexSelected(int idx)`
  Returns a true value if the item at position idx is currently selected.
- `public boolean isMultipleMode()`
  Returns a true value if this list is allowed to have more than one item selected at a time.
- `public void makeVisible(int idx)`
  Scrolls the list so the item at position idx is visible.
- `protected String paramString()`
  Returns a string value of the parameters of this list.
- `protected void processActionEvent(ActionEvent event)`
  Handles any action event for this list by passing it to a registered action listener.
- `protected void processEvent(AWTEvent event)`
  Processes an incoming event for this list, passing it to `processActionEvent` if it is an action event, or to `processItemEvent` if it is

an item event; otherwise, the specified event is passed to the superclass' `processEvent` method.

- `protected void processItemEvent(ItemEvent event)`
  Handles any item `event` for this list by passing them to a registered item listener.
- `public synchronized void remove(int idx)`
- `public synchronized void remove(String str)`
  Removes the item at a specified index or the first occurrence of item `str` from this list.
- `public synchronized void removeAll()`
  Removes all items from this list.
- `public void replaceItem(String str, int idx)`
  Changes the value of the label for the item at position `idx` to `str`.
- `public synchronized void setMultipleMode(boolean toggle)`
  If `toggle` is set to true, this list will allow for multiple selections at one time.

Locale (`java.util`)

A public class, derived from `Object` and implementing `Serializable` and `Cloneable`, that represents geographic-specific or political-specific information.

Variables and Constants

- `public static final Locale CANADA`
- `public static final Locale CANADA_FRENCH`
- `public static final Locale CHINA`
- `public static final Locale FRANCE`
- `public static final Locale GERMANY`
- `public static final Locale ITALY`
- `public static final Locale JAPAN`
- `public static final Locale KOREA`
- `public static final Locale PRC`
- `public static final Locale TAIWAN`
- `public static final Locale UK`
- `public static final Locale US`
  Constant values that represent locales based on countries.
- `public static final Locale CHINESE`
- `public static final Locale ENGLISH`
- `public static final Locale FRENCH`
- `public static final Locale GERMAN`
- `public static final Locale ITALIAN`
- `public static final Locale JAPANESE`

- public static final Locale KOREAN
- public static final Locale SIMPLIFIED_CHINESE
- public static final Locale TRADITIONAL_CHINESE
  Constant values that represent locales based on languages.

Constructors

- public Locale(String lang, String country)
- public Locale(String lang, String country, String var)
  Creates a new locale from the specified two character ISO codes for a language and country. A computer and browser variant of a locale can also be included. These usually take the form of WIN for Windows or MAC for Macintosh.

Methods

- public Object clone()
  Returns a copy of this locale.
- public boolean equals(Object arg)
  Returns a true value if this locale is equal to arg.
- public String getCountry()
- public String getLanguage()
- public String getVariant()
  Returns the character code for the name of this locale's country, language or variant.
- public static synchronized Locale getDefault()
- public static synchronized void setDefault(Locale locale)
  Returns or sets the default locale.
- public final String getDisplayCountry()
- public String getDisplayCountry(Locale displaylocale)
  Returns the display version of the country name for this locale in either the specified or default locales.
- public final String getDisplayLanguage()
- public String getDisplayLanguage(Locale displaylocale)
  Returns the display version of the language name for this locale in either the specified or default locales.
- public final String getDisplayName()
- public String getDisplayName(Locale displaylocale)
  Returns the display version of the name for this locale in either the specified or default locales.
- public final String getDisplayVariant()
- public String getDisplayVariant(Locale displaylocale)
  Returns the display version of the variant for this locale in either the specified or default locales.

- `public String getISO3Country() throws MissingResourceException`
- `public String getISO3Language() throws MissingResourceException`

  Returns the three-character ISO abbreviation for the country or language for this locale.
- `hashCode()`

  Returns the hash code for this locale.
- `toString()`

  Returns a string representation of this locale.

Long (`java.lang`)

A public final class, derived from `Number`, that contains long integer math operations, constants, methods to compute minimum and maximum numbers, and string manipulation routines related to the primitive `long` type.

Variables and Constants

- `public final static long MAX_VALUE`
- `public final static long MIN_VALUE`

  Constant values that contain the maximum possible value (9223372036854775807L) or minimum possible value (−9223372036854775808L) of a `long` in Java.
- `public final static Class TYPE`

  The `Integer` constant value of the integer type class.

Constructors

- `public Long(long num)`
- `public Long(String num) throws NumberFormatException`

  Creates an instance of the `Long` class from the parameter `num`.

Methods

- `public byte byteValue()`
- `public double doubleValue()`
- `public float floatValue()`
- `public int intValue()`
- `public long longValue()`
- `public short shortValue()`

  Returns the value of this `Long` as a Java primitive type.
- `public boolean equals(Object arg)`

Returns the result of the equality comparison between this `Long` and the parameter `arg`.

- `public static Long getLong(String prop)`
- `public static Long getLong(String prop, long num)`
- `public static Long getLong(String prop, long num)`
  Returns a `Long` representation of the system property named in `prop`. If there is no property corresponding to `prop`, or the format of its value is incorrect, then the default `num` is returned.
- `public int hashCode()`
  Returns a hash code for this `Long`.
- `public static Long parseLong(String str) throws NumberFormatException`
- `public static Long parseLong(String str, int base) throws NumberFormatException`
  Evaluates the string `str` and returns the long equivalent in radix `base`.
- `public static String toBinaryString(long num)`
- `public static String toHexString(long num)`
- `public static String toOctalString(long num)`
  Returns the string representation of parameter `num` in base 2 (binary), 8 (octal), or 16 (hexadecimal).
- `public String toString()`
- `public static String toString(long num)`
- `public static String toString(long num, int base)`
  Returns the string representation of this `long` or `num` in base 10 (decimal). The radix of the returned number can also be specified in `base`.
- `public static Long valueOf(String str) throws NumberFormatException`
- `public static Long valueOf(String str, int base) throws NumberFormatException`
  Returns a `Long` initialized to the value of `str` in radix `base`.

Math (`java.lang`)

A public final class, derived from `Object`, that contains integer and floating point constants, and methods to perform various math operations, compute minimum and maximum numbers, and generate random numbers.

Variables and Constants

- `public final static double E`
- `public final static double PI`
  Constant values that contain the natural base of logarithms (2.7182818284590452354) and the ratio of the circumference of a circle to its diameter (3.14159265358979323846).

Methods

- `public static double abs(double num)`
- `public static float abs(float num)`
- `public static int abs(int num)`
- `public static long abs(long num)`
  Returns the absolute value of the specified parameter.
- `public static double acos(double num)`
- `public static double asin(double num)`
- `public static double atan(double num)`
  Returns the arc cosine, arc sine, or arc tangent of parameter `num` as a double.
- `public static double atan2(double x, double y)`
  Returns the component θ of the polar coordinate $\{r,\theta\}$ that corresponds to the cartesian coordinate <x, y>.
- `public static double ceil(double num)`
  Returns the smallest integer value that is not less than the argument `num`.
- `public static double cos(double num)`
- `public static double sin(double num)`
- `public static double tan(double num)`
  Returns the cosine, sine, or tangent of parameter `num`.
- `public static double exp(double num)`
  Returns e to the `num`, where e is the base of natural logarithms.
- `public static double floor(double num)`
  Returns a double that is the largest integer value that is not greater than the parameter `num`.
- `public static double IEEEremainder(double arg1, double arg2)`
  Returns the mathematical remainder between `arg1` and `arg2` as defined by IEEE 754.
- `public static double log(double num) throws ArithmeticException`
  Returns the natural logarithm of parameter `num`.
- `public static double max(double num1, double num2)`
- `public static float max(float num1, float num2)`
- `public static int max(int num1, int num2)`
- `public static long max(long num1, long num2)`
  Returns the larger of parameters `num1` and `num2`.
- `public static double min(double num1, double num2)`
- `public static float min(float num1, float num2)`
- `public static int min(int num1, int num2)`
- `public static long min(long num1, long num2)`
  Returns the minimum value of parameters `num1` and `num2`.
- `public static double pow(double num1, double num2) throws ArithmeticException`

Returns the result of num1 to num2.

- `public static double random()`
  Returns a random number between 0.0 and 1.0.
- `public static double rint(double num)`
  Returns the closest integer to parameter num.
- `public static long round(double num)`
- `public static int round(float num)`
  Returns the closest `long` or `int` to parameter num.
- `public static double sqrt(double num) throws`
  `ArithmeticException`
  Returns the square root of parameter num.

Menu (`java.awt`)

A public class, derived from `MenuItem` and implementing `MenuContainer`, that contains a selection of items that "pop-down," from which the user can choose one.

Constructors

- `public Menu()`
- `public Menu(String lbl)`
- `public Menu(String lbl, boolean toggle)`
  Creates a new instance of a menu with a label (or none if not specified). If `toggle` is true, then the menu can be "torn" from the menu bar, staying on the screen after the menu is no longer selected.

Methods

- `public MenuItem add(MenuItem item)`
- `public void add(String lbl)`
  Adds an item with a label (`lbl`) to this menu. If the item is a `MenuItem`, the added menu item is returned.
- `public void addNotify()`
- `public void removeNotify()`
  Creates or removes the menu's peer.
- `public void addSeparator()`
- `public void insertSeparator(int idx)`
  Adds a separator line to the end, or inserts it at the specified index, of this menu.
- `public MenuItem getItem(int num)`
  Returns the menu item at position num from this menu.
- `public int getItemCount()`
  Returns the number of items in this menu.

- public synchronized void insert(MenuItem item, int idx)
- public void insert(String lbl, int idx)
  Inserts an item into this list at the specified index. The inserted item can have a string label of lbl.
- public boolean isTearOff()
  Returns true if this menu can be torn off.
- public String paramString()
  Returns the parameter string for this menu.
- public void remove(int idx)
- public void remove(MenuComponent item)
  Removes the specified menu item from this menu.
- public synchronized void removeAll()
  Removes all of the menu items from this menu.

MenuBar (`java.awt`)

A public class, derived from `MenuComponent` and implementing `MenuContainer`, that creates graphical menu regions that are bound to frames and allow graphical menus to be attached.

Constructors

- public MenuBar()
  Creates a new instance of a menu bar.

Methods

- public Menu add(Menu arg)
  Adds menu arg to this menu bar.
- public void addNotify()
- public void removeNotify()
  Creates or destroys this menu bar's peer.
- public void deleteShortcut(MenuShortcut shortcut)
  Removes the specified menu shortcut from this menu bar.
- public Menu getHelpMenu()
- public void setHelpMenu(Menu helpmenu)
  Returns or sets the menu designated as the help menu for this menu bar.
- public Menu getMenu(int idx)
  Returns the menu indexed at position idx on this menu bar.
- public int getMenuCount()
  Returns the number of menus attached to this menu bar.

- public MenuItem getShortcutMenuItem(MenuShortcut shortcut)

  Returns the menu item that is associated with the specified menu shortcut, or null if none exists.
- public void remove(int idx)
- public void remove(MenuComponent comp)

  Removes the specified menu component or item at index idx from this menu.
- public synchronized Enumeration shortcuts()

  Returns an enumerated list of all of the menu shortcuts from this menu bar.

MenuComponent (`java.awt`)

A public abstract class, derived from `Object` and implementing `Serializable`, that is the superclass to all menu component classes.

Constructors

- public MenuComponent()

  Creates a new instance of a menu component.

Methods

- public final void dispatchEvent(AWTEvent evt)

  Sends the specified event (evt) to this menu component or one of its sub-menu component objects.
- public Font getFont()
- public void setFont(Font fnt)

  Returns or sets the font for this menu component.
- public String getName()
- public void setName(String str)

  Returns or sets the name of this menu component.
- public MenuContainer getParent()

  Returns this menu component's parent container.
- protected String paramString()

  Overridden by subclasses, this method returns a string containing the parameters for this menu component.
- public boolean postEvent(Event arg)

  Posts event arg to this menu component.
- protected void processEvent(AWTEvent evt)

An abstract method used to process incoming events (evt) from this menu component.

- public void removeNotify()
  Removes this menu component's peer.
- public String toString()
  Returns a string representation of this menu component.

MenuItem (`java.awt`)

A public class, derived from `MenuComponent`, that represents a single choice in a menu.

Constructors

- public MenuItem()
- public MenuItem(String str)
- public MenuItem(String str, MenuShortcut shortcut)
  Creates a new instance of a menu item. Item can have both a label and a shortcut associated with it.

Methods

- public void addActionListener(ActionListener listener)
- public void removeActionListener(ActionListener listener)
  Adds or removes the specified `listener` to this menu item.
- public void addNotify()
  Creates this menu item's peer.
- public void deleteShortcut()
  Removes the shortcut associated with this menu item.
- protected final void disableEvents(long mask)
- protected final void enableEvents(long mask)
  Disables or enables events from the specified `mask` from being handled by this menu item.
- public String getActionCommand()
- public void setActionCommand(String command)
  Returns or sets the name of the command that results from selection of this menu item.
- public String getLabel()
- public synchronized void setLabel(String str)
  Returns or sets the label of this menu item.

- `public MenuShortcut getShortcut()`
- `public void setShortcut(MenuShortcut shortcut)`
  Returns or sets the menu shortcut associated with this menu item.
- `public boolean isEnabled()`
- `public synchronized void setEnabled(boolean toggle)`
  Returns or sets the current enabled state for this menu item.
- `public String paramString()`
  Returns the string parameter of this menu item.
- `protected void processActionEvent(ActionEvent evt)`
  Handles any action events (`evt`) for this menu item, sending them to a registered listener.
- `protected void processEvent(AWTEvent evt)`
  Handles any events (`evt`) on this menu item, sending all action events to this menu item's `processActionEvent` method.

MenuShortcut (`java.awt`)

A public class, derived from `Object` and implementing `Serializable`, that is a combination of keyboard actions that yield a menu item selection.

Constructors

- `public MenuShortcut(int value)`
- `public MenuShortcut(int value, boolean toggle)`
  Creates an instance of a menu shortcut using the specified key code value. If `toggle` is true, then the Shift key must be depressed in order for this shortcut to function.

Methods

- `public boolean equals(MenuShortcut arg)`
  Returns a true value if this menu shortcut is equal to the specified shortcut (`arg`).
- `public int getKey()`
  Returns the key code value for this menu shortcut.
- `protected String paramString()`
  Returns the parameter string for this menu shortcut.
- `public String toString()`
  Returns a string representation of this menu shortcut.
- `public boolean usesShiftModifier()`
  Returns a true value if this menu shortcut requires the use of a shift key.

MessageFormat (`java.text`)

A public class, derived from `Format`, that is used to build formatted message strings.

Constructors

- `public MessageFormat(String str)`
  Creates a new instance of a `MessageFormat` from the specified string pattern.

Methods

- `public void applyPattern(String str)`
- `public String toPattern()`
  Sets and returns the pattern for this `MessageFormat`.
- `public Object clone()`
  Returns a copy of this `MessageFormat`.
- `public boolean equals(Object arg)`
  Returns a true value if this `MessageFormat` is equal to `arg`.
- `public final StringBuffer format(Object src, StringBuffer dest, FieldPosition ignore)`
- `public final StringBuffer format(Object[] src, StringBuffer dest, FieldPosition ignore)`
  Formats the specified source object with this `MessageFormat`, placing the result in `dest`. This method returns the value of the destination buffer.
- `public static String format(String str, Object[] args)`
  Formats the given string applying specified arguments. This method allows for message formatting with the creation of a `MessageFormat`.
- `public Format[] getFormats()`
- `public void setFormats(Format[] newFormats)`
  Returns and sets the formats for this `MessageFormat`.
- `public Locale getLocale()`
- `public void setLocale(Locale locale)`
  Returns and sets the locale for this `MessageFormat`.
- `public int hashCode()`
  Returns the hash code for this `MessageFormat`.
- `public Object[] parse(String src) throws ParseException`
- `public Object[] parse(String src, ParsePosition pos)`
  Parses the string source (starting at position `pos`, or 0 by default), returning its objects.

- public Object parseObject(String src, ParsePosition pos)

    Parses the string source (starting at position pos, or 0 by default), returning one object.
- public void setFormat(int var, Format fmt)

    Sets an individual format at index var.

MouseAdapter (`java.awt.event`)

A public abstract class, derived from `Object` and implementing `MouseListener`, that permits derived classes to override the predefined no-op mouse events.

Constructors

- public MouseAdapter()

    Creates a new instance of a `MouseAdapter`.

Methods

- public void mouseClicked(MouseEvent event)
- public void mouseEntered(MouseEvent event)
- public void mouseExited(MouseEvent event)
- public void mousePressed(MouseEvent event)
- public void mouseReleased(MouseEvent event)

    Empty methods which should be overridden in order to implement event handling for mouse events.

MouseEvent (`java.awt.event`)

A public class, derived from `InputEvent`, that represents events triggered by the mouse.

Variables and Constants

- public static final int MOUSE_CLICKED
- public static final int MOUSE_DRAGGED
- public static final int MOUSE_ENTERED
- public static final int MOUSE_EXITED
- public static final int MOUSE_MOVED

- public static final int MOUSE_PRESSED
- public static final int MOUSE_RELEASED
    Constant variables that represent a variety of mouse events.
- public static final int MOUSE_FIRST
- public static final int MOUSE_LAST
    Constant values that represent the index of the first and last mouse event ids.

Constructors

- public MouseEvent(Component src, int type, long time-stamp, int mods, int x, int y, int clickCount, boolean popupTrigger)
    Creates a new instance of a MouseEvent from a given source, with a specified type, timestamp, keyboard modifiers, x and y locations, number of clicks and a state value, if this event triggers a popup menu.

Methods

- public int getClickCount()
    Returns the number of mouse clicks in this event.
- public Point getPoint()
    Returns the point location of this event, relative to the source component's space.
- public int getX()
- public int getY()
    Returns the x or y location of this event, relative to the source component's space.
- public boolean isPopupTrigger()
    Returns a true value if this event is a trigger for popup-menus.
- public String paramString()
    Returns a string representation of the parameters of this MouseEvent.
- public synchronized void translatePoint(int xoffset, int yoffset)
    Offsets the x and y locations of this event by the specified amounts.

MouseMotionAdapter (`java.awt.event`)

A public abstract class, derived from Object and implementing MouseMotionListener, that permits a derived class to override the predefined no-op mouse motion events.

Constructors

- `public MouseMotionAdapter()`
  Creates a new instance of a `MouseMotionAdapter`.

Methods

- `public void mouseDragged(MouseEvent event)`
- `public void mouseMoved(MouseEvent event)`
  Empty methods that should be overridden in order to implement event handling for mouse motion events.

Number (`java.lang`)

A public abstract class, derived from `Object` and implementing `Serializable`, that is the parent class to the wrapper classes `Byte`, `Double`, `Integer`, `Float`, `Long` and `Short`.

Constructors

- `public Number()`
  Creates a new instance of a `Number`.

Methods

- `public byte byteValue()`
- `public abstract double doubleValue()`
- `public abstract float floatValue()`
- `public abstract int intValue()`
- `public abstract long longValue()`
- `public short shortValue()`
  Returns the value of this `Number` as a Java primitive type.

NumberFormat (`java.text`)

A public abstract class, derived from `Format` and implementing `Cloneable`, that is used to convert number objects to locale-specific strings, and vice versa.

Variables and Constants

- `public static final int FRACTION_FIELD`
- `public static final int INTEGER_FIELD`
  Constant values that indicate field locations in a `NumberFormat`.

Constructors

- `public NumberFormat()`
  Creates a new instance of a `NumberFormat`.

Methods

- `public Object clone()`
  Returns a copy of this `NumberFormat`.
- `public boolean equals(Object arg)`
  Returns a true value if this `NumberFormat` is equal to `arg`.
- `public final String format(double num)`
- `public final String format(long num)`
  Formats the specified Java primitive type according to this `NumberFormat`, returning a string.
- `public abstract StringBuffer format(double num, StringBuffer dest,FieldPosition pos)`
- `public abstract StringBuffer format(long num, StringBuffer dest, FieldPosition pos)`
- `public final StringBuffer format(Object num, StringBuffer dest, FieldPosition pos)`
  Formats the specified Java primitive type (or object) starting at `pos`, according to this `NumberFormat`, placing the resulting string in the specified destination buffer. This method returns the value of the string buffer.
- `public static Locale[] getAvailableLocales()`
  Returns the available locales.
- `public static final NumberFormat getCurrencyInstance()`
- `public static NumberFormat getCurrencyInstance(Locale locale)`
  Returns the `NumberFormat` for currency for the default or specified locale.
- `public static final NumberFormat getInstance()`
- `public static NumberFormat getInstance(Locale locale)`
  Returns the default number format for the default or specified locale.
- `public int getMaximumFractionDigits()`
- `public void setMaximumFractionDigits(int val)`
  Returns or sets the maximum number of fractional digits allowed in this `NumberFormat`.
- `public int getMaximumIntegerDigits()`
- `public void setMaximumIntegerDigits(int val)`
  Returns or sets the maximum number of integer digits allowed in this `NumberFormat`.
- `public int getMinimumFractionDigits()`

- public void setMinimumFractionDigits(int val)
  Returns or sets the minimum number of fractional digits allowed in this NumberFormat.
- public int getMinimumIntegerDigits()
- public void setMinimumIntegerDigits(int val)
  Returns or sets the minimum number of integer digits allowed in this NumberFormat.
- public static final NumberFormat getNumberInstance()
- public static NumberFormat getNumberInstance(Locale locale)
  Returns the NumberFormat for numbers for the default or specified locale.
- public static final NumberFormat getPercentInstance()
- public static NumberFormat getPercentInstance(Locale locale)
  Returns the NumberFormat for percentages for the default or specified locale.
- public int hashCode()
  Returns the hash code for this NumberFormat.
- public boolean isGroupingUsed()
- public void setGroupingUsed(boolean toggle)
  Returns or sets the toggle flag for the use of the grouping indicator by this NumberFormat.
- public boolean isParseIntegerOnly()
- public void setParseIntegerOnly(boolean toggle)
  Returns or sets the toggle flag for the use of parsing numbers as integers only by this NumberFormat.
- public Number parse(String str) throws ParseException
  Parses the specified string as a number.
- public abstract Number parse(String str, ParsePosition pos)
- public final Object parseObject(String str, ParsePosition pos)
  Parses the specified string as a long (if possible) or double, starting a position pos. Returns a number or an object.

Object (java.lang)

A public class that is the root of the hierarchy tree for all classes in Java.

Constructors

- public Object()
  Creates a new instance of the object class.

Methods

- `protected Object clone() throws OutOfMemoryError, CloneNotSupportedException`
  Returns an exact copy of the current object.
- `public boolean equals(Object arg)`
  Returns a true value if the current object is equal to `arg`.
- `protected void finalize() throws Throwable`
  The finalize method contains code that is called as the object is being destroyed.
- `public final Class getClass()`
  Returns the class of the current object.
- `public int hashCode()`
  Returns a hash code for the current object.
- `public final void notify() throws IllegalMonitorStateException`
- `public final void notifyAll() throws IllegalMonitorStateException`
  Informs a paused thread that it may resume execution. `notifyAll` informs all paused threads.
- `public String toString()`
  Returns a string representation of the current object.
- `public final void wait() throws IllegalMonitorStateException, InterruptedException`
- `public final void wait(long msec) throws IllegalMonitorStateException, InterruptedException`
- `public final void wait(long msec, int nsec) throws IllegalMonitorStateException, InterruptedException, IllegalArgumentException`
  Causes a thread to suspend execution for `msec` milliseconds and `nsec` nanoseconds. The `wait()` method (without parameters) causes a thread to suspend execution until further notice.

PaintEvent (`java.awt.event`)

A public class, derived from `ComponentEvent`, that describes a particular AWT paint event.

Variables and Constants

- `public static final int PAINT`
- `public static final int UPDATE`
  Constant values representing the paint and update event types.
- `public static final int PAINT_FIRST`

- public static final int PAINT_LAST

  Constant values that represent the index of the first and last paint event ids.

Constructors

- public PaintEvent(Component src, int type, Rectangle rect)

  Creates a new instance of a `PaintEvent` from a specified source component, having an event type and a defined rectangular region to update.

Methods

- public Rectangle getUpdateRect()
- public void setUpdateRect(Rectangle rect)

  Returns or sets the rectangular region that is updated as a result of this `PaintEvent`.

- public String paramString()

  Returns a string containing the parameters of this `PaintEvent`.

Panel (`java.awt`)

A public class, derived from `Container`, that allocates space in which you can place other components and containers.

Constructors

- public Panel()
- public Panel(LayoutManager mgr)

  Creates a new instance of a panel with the specified layout manager or uses `FlowLayout` as the default.

Methods

- public void addNotify()

  Creates this panel's peer.

ParsePosition (`java.text`)

A public class, derived from `Object`, that is used to track the position of the index during parsing. This class is generally used by the `Format` class (and its subclasses).

Constructors

- `public ParsePosition(int index)`
  Creates a new instance of a `ParsePosition` from the specified index.

Methods

- `public int getIndex()`
- `public void setIndex(int num)`
  Returns or sets the parse position.

Point (`java.awt`)

A public class, derived from `Object` and implementing `Serializable`, that defines and manipulates a location on a two-dimensional coordinate system.

Variables and Constants

- `public int x`
- `public int y`
  The x and y locations of this point.

Constructors

- `public Point()`
- `public Point(Point pt)`
- `public Point(int x, int y)`
  Creates a new instance of a `Point` from the specified coordinates, the specified point, or using <0, 0> by default.

Methods

- `public boolean equals(Object arg)`
  Returns a true value if this point is identical to `arg`.
- `public Point getLocation()`
- `public void move(int x, int y)`
- `public void setLocation(Point pt)`
- `public void setLocation(int x, int y)`
  Returns or relocates the position of this point.
- `public int hashCode()`
  Returns the hash code of this point.
- `public String toString()`
  Returns a string representation of this point.

- public void translate(int xoffset, int yoffset)
  Relocates this point to <x+xoffset, y+yoffset>.

Polygon (`java.awt`)

A public class, derived from `Object` and implementing `Shape` and `Serializable`, that maintains a list of points that define a polygon shape.

Variables and Constants

- protected Rectangle bounds
  The bounds of this polygon.
- public int npoints
  The total number of points of this polygon.
- public int xpoints[]
- public int ypoints[]
  The arrays of x and y locations for the points of this polygon.

Constructors

- public Polygon()
- public Polygon(int[] x, int[] y, int np)
  Creates a new instance of a polygon, initially defined by the arrays of x and y locations <x, y> and comprised of np points. The default constructor creates a new polygon that contains no points.

Methods

- public void addPoint(int newx, int newy)
  Adds the point located at <newx, newy> to this polygon.
- public boolean contains(int x, int y)
- public boolean contains(Point pt)
  Returns a true value if this polygon contains the specified point.
- public Rectangle getBounds()
  Returns the bonds of this polygon.
- public void translate(int xoffset, int yoffset)
  Relocates all of the x and y points of this polygon by xoffset and yoffset.

PopupMenu (`java.awt`)

A public class, derived from `Menu`, that can produce a menu inside a component.

Constructors

- `public PopupMenu()`
- `public PopupMenu(String lbl)`
  Creates a new instance of a popup menu with the specified label (or having no label in the case of the first constructor).

Methods

- `public synchronized void addNotify()`
  Creates this popup menu's peer.
- `public void show(Component source, int x, int y)`
  Displays the popup menu at the position `<x, y>` relative to the specified component.

PrintStream (`java.io`)

A public class, derived from `FilterOutputStream`, that provides methods to print data types in a format other than byte-based.

Constructors

- `public PrintStream(OutputStream out)`
- `public PrintStream(OutputStream out, boolean autoflush)`
  Creates a new instance of a `PrintStream` on `out`. If the `autoflush` value is set to true, then the output buffer is flushed at every occurrence of a newline.

Methods

- `public boolean checkError()`
  Flushes this print stream's buffer and returns a true value if an error occurred.
- `public void close()`
  Closes this print stream.
- `public void flush()`
  Flushes this print stream's buffer.
- `public void print(boolean b)`
- `public void print(char c)`
- `public void print(char[] s)`
- `public void print(double d)`
- `public void print(float f)`

- `public void print(int i)`
- `public void print(long l)`
- `public void print(Object obj)`
- `public void print(String s)`
- `public void println()`
- `public void println(boolean b)`
- `public void println(char c)`
- `public void println(char[] s)`
- `public void println(double d)`
- `public void println(float f)`
- `public void println(int i)`
- `public void println(long l)`
- `public void println(Object obj)`
- `public void println(String s)`

    Prints the specified Java primitive type, Object, or blank line to this print stream. When using a character, only the lower byte is printed.

- `public void write(int b)`
- `public void write(byte[] b, int off, int len)`

    Writes a byte or `len` bytes from the array `b`, starting at index `off` to this print stream.

Random (`java.util`)

A public class, derived from `Object` and implementing `Serializable`, that produces sequences of pseudo-random numbers.

Constructors

- `public Random()`
- `public Random(long rnd)`

    Creates a new instance of a random class using the value of `rnd` as the random number seed. When the default constructor is used, the current time in milliseconds is the seed.

Methods

- `protected int next(int b)`

    Returns the next random number (from the specified number of bits).
- `public void nextBytes(byte[] b)`

    Generates an array of random bytes as defined by `b[]`.
- `public double nextDouble()`
- `public float nextFloat()`

- `public int nextInt()`
- `public long nextLong()`

  Returns the next random number between 0.0 and 1.0 in a selected Java primitive type.

- `public double nextGaussian()`

  Returns a Gaussian double random number with a mean value of 0.0 and a standard deviation of 1.0.

- `public void setSeed(long rnd)`

  Sets the seeds for this random number generator to `rnd`.

Rectangle (`java.awt`)

A public class, derived from `Object` and implementing `Shape` and `Serializable`, that represents a rectangular shape that is described by an `x` and `y` location, and a width and height.

Variables and Constants

- `public int height`
- `public int width`

  The height and width of this rectangle.

- `public int x`
- `public int y`

  The `x` and `y` locations of the upper-left corner of this rectangle.

Constructors

- `public Rectangle()`
- `public Rectangle(Dimension dim)`
- `public Rectangle(Point pt)`

  Creates a new instance of a `Rectangle` with an initial location of the corresponding values of `pt` or `dim`, with a height of 0 and width of 0. If neither `pt` or `dim` are specified, then the initial location is <0, 0> and the height and width are set to 0.

- `public Rectangle(Rectangle rect)`
- `public Rectangle(Point pt, Dimension dim)`

  Creates a new instance of a `Rectangle` with initial location and size values the same as corresponding values in `rect`, or with an initial location of the corresponding values of `pt`, and with a width and height corresponding to the values of `dim`.

- `public Rectangle(int width, int height)`
- `public Rectangle(int x, int y, int width, int height)`

Creates a new instance of a `Rectangle` with an initial location of <x, y> (or <0, 0> by default), and with a `height` and `width`.

Methods

- `public void add(int x, int y)`
- `public void add(Point point)`
- `public void add(Rectangle rect)`

  Adds the specified point in space, defined by coordinates, a point, or the initial location of the specified `Rectangle`, to this `Rectangle`. This method may expand the `Rectangle` (if the point lies outside) or reduce the `Rectangle` (if the point lies inside).

- `public boolean contains(int x, int y)`
- `public boolean contains(Point pt)`

  Returns a true value if this `Rectangle` contains the specified point.

- `public boolean equals(Object rect2)`

  Returns a true value if this `Rectangle` and the rectangle `rect2` are identical.

- `public Rectangle getBounds()`

  Returns the bounds of this `Rectangle`.

- `public Point getLocation()`
- `public Dimension getSize()`

  Returns the location or size of this `Rectangle`.

- `public void grow(int width, int height)`

  Increases this `Rectangle` by `height` and `width` pixels.

- `public int hashCode()`

  Returns the hash code for this `Rectangle`.

- `public Rectangle intersection(Rectangle rect2)`

  Returns the intersection of this `Rectangle` and the specified rectangle (`rect2`).

- `public boolean intersects(Rectangle rect2)`

  Returns a true value if this `Rectangle` intersects `rect2`.

- `public boolean isEmpty()`

  Returns a true value if this `Rectangle` is empty (height and width <= 0).

- `public void setBounds(int x, int y, int width, int height)`
- `public void setBounds(Rectangle rect)`

  Resets the x and y locations, width and height of this `rectangle` to the respective values of `rect` or the specified values of x, y, width, and height.

- `public void setLocation(int x, int y)`
- `public void setLocation(Point pt)`

  Resets the location of this `Rectangle` to the specified point.

- `public void setSize(Dimension dim)`
- `public void setSize(int width, int height)`
  Resets the size to `width` and `height`, or the corresponding values of `dim`.
- `public String toString()`
  Returns a string representation of this `Rectangle`.
- `public void translate(int width, int height)`
  Adds the specified `width` and `height` to this `Rectangle`'s width and height values.
- `public Rectangle union(Rectangle rect2)`
  Returns the union of this `Rectangle` and `rect2`.

Scrollbar (`java.awt`)

A public class, derived from `Component` and implementing `Adjustable`, that creates a graphical representation of a range of values which the user can set.

Variables and Constants

- `public final static int HORIZONTAL`
- `public final static int VERTICAL`
  Constant values representing the orientation of a horizontal or vertical scrollbar.

Constructors

- `public Scrollbar()`
- `public Scrollbar(int direction) throws IllegalArgumentException`
- `public Scrollbar(int direction, int val, int size, int min, int max)`
  Creates a new scrollbar in the specified `direction` that ranges from `min` to `max`. The initial value is set to `val`, and the size of the bubble is set to `size`. If the default constructor is used, a vertical scrollbar is created. The first and second constructors use initial values of 0, 10, 0, 100 for the initial value, size of the bubble, min, and max values, respectively.

Methods

- `public void addAdjustmentListener(AdjustmentListener listener)`
- `public void removeAdjustmentListener(AdjustmentListener listener)`
  Adds or removes the specified `listener` to this scrollbar.
- `public void addNotify()`

Creates this scrollbar's peer.

- `public int getBlockIncrement()`
- `public synchronized void setBlockIncrement(int val)`
  Returns or sets the amount of the increment when the user pushes the increment/decrement device of this scrollbar.
- `public int getMaximum()`
- `public int getMinimum()`
  Returns the maximum or minimum value of this scrollbar.
- `public int getOrientation()`
- `public synchronized void setOrientation(int direction)`
  Returns or sets the orientation of this scrollbar.
- `public int getUnitIncrement()`
- `public synchronized void setUnitIncrement(int num)`
  Returns or sets the unit increment for this scrollbar.
- `public int getValue()`
  Returns the current value of this scrollbar.
- `public int getVisibleAmount()`
- `public synchronized void setVisibleAmount(int bubble)`
  Returns or sets the visible amount of this scrollbar.
- `protected String paramString()`
  Returns a string representation of this scrollbar's parameters.
- `protected void processAdjustmentEvent(AdjustmentEvent event)`
  Handles the adjustment event for this scrollbar, sending it to the appropriate registered listener.
- `protected void processEvent(AWTEvent event)`
  Processes all events for this scrollbar, passing them to the `processAdjustmentEvent` if they apply, otherwise the event is passed to the superclass' `processEvent` method.
- `public synchronized void setMaximum(int num)`
- `public synchronized void setMinimum(int num)`
  Sets the maximum or minimum value for this scrollbar to num.
- `public void setValue(int num)`
  Sets this scrollbar's value to num.
- `public void setValues(int num, int size, int min, int max)`
  Sets the value (num), bubble `size`, min, and max values of this scrollbar.

ScrollPane (`java.awt`)

A public class, derived from `Container`, that creates a graphical pane area which can contain a single GUI component. The pane of the area can contain scrollbars for easier viewing of the component.

Variables and Constants

- `public final static int SCROLLBARS_ALWAYS`
- `public final static int SCROLLBARS_AS_NEEDED`
- `public final static int SCROLLBARS_NEVER`

    Constant values indicating the policy for the creation of scrollbars at instantiation of this scroll pane.

Constructors

- `public ScrollPane()`
- `public ScrollPane(int policy)`

    Creates a new instance of a scroll pane, using the specified `policy` (or the default of `SCROLLBARS_AS_NEEDED`, in the case of the default constructor) for the creation of scrollbars.

Methods

- `protected final void addImpl(Component obj, Object constraints, int index)`

    Adds the specified component object to this scroll pane at `index`. The `constraints` parameter is not presently used.
- `public void addNotify()`

    Creates the peer for this scroll pane.
- `public void doLayout()`

    Lays out this scroll pane by resizing the component to the preferred size.
- `public Adjustable getHAdjustable()`
- `public Adjustable getVAdjustable()`

    Returns the state of the horizontal or vertical scrollbar if it exists; otherwise, it returns a null.
- `public int getHScrollbarHeight()`
- `public int getVScrollbarWidth()`

    Returns the height in pixels of the horizontal scrollbar or the width in pixels of the vertical scrollbar (even if they are not created).
- `public int getScrollbarDisplayPolicy()`

    Returns the creation and display policy for the scrollbars of this scroll pane.
- `public Point getScrollPosition()`

    Returns the `x` and `y` coordinate of the embedded component that is aligned with the upper right corner of the scroll pane's view window.
- `public Dimension getViewportSize()`

    Returns the current size in pixels of this scroll pane's view window.
- `public String paramString()`

    Returns a string representation of the parameters of this scroll pane.
- `public void printComponents(Graphics dest)`

Prints the component of this scroll pane on the specified graphics destination (dest).
- public final void setLayout(LayoutManager manager)
  Sets the layout manager for this scroll pane to manager.
- public void setScrollPosition(int xpos, int ypos)
- public void setScrollPosition(Point dest)
  Scrolls the embedded component to the specified position.

ServerSocket (java.net)

A public final class, derived from Object, that represents a socket which listens for connection requests, receives data, and potentially returns a result to the requestor.

Constructors

- public ServerSocket(int num) throws IOException
- public ServerSocket(int num, int queue) throws IOException
- public ServerSocket(int num, int queue, InetAddress addr) throws IOException
  Creates a new instance of a ServerSocket on local port num (a value of 0 means connect to any free port), setting an incoming queue length for the socket (default is 50 connections), bound to the local machine addr.

Methods

- public Socket accept() throws IOException
  Accept an incoming request on this socket.
- public void close() throws IOException
  Closes this server socket.
- public InetAddress getInetAddress()
  Returns the Internet address for the machine this socket has connected to. If no connection yet exists, a null value is returned.
- public int getLocalPort()
  Returns the number of the local port this socket is bound to.
- public synchronized int getSoTimeout() throws IOException
- public synchronized void setSoTimeout(int num) throws SocketException
  Returns or sets the timeout value for this socket in milliseconds.
- protected final void implAccept(Socket arg) throws IOException

This method is provided so that subclasses of `ServerSocket` can override the accept method.

- `public static void setSocketFactory(SocketImplFactory sif) throws IOException, SocketException`
  Sets the `ServerSocket` implementation factory for this `ServerSocket` to the specified value.
- `public String toString()`
  Returns a string representation for this socket.

Short (`java.lang`)

A public class, derived from `Number`, that contains integer math operations, constants, methods to compute minimum and maximum numbers, and string manipulation routines related to the primitive `short` type.

Variables and Constants

- `public final static short MAX_VALUE`
- `public final static short MIN_VALUE`
  A constant value that contains the maximum possible value (32767) or minimum possible value (-32768) of an integer in Java.
- `public final static Class TYPE`
  The `Short` constant value of the short type class.

Constructors

- `public Short(short num)`
- `public Short(String num) throws NumberFormatException`
  Creates a new instance of a `Short` from the specified num.

Methods

- `public byte byteValue()`
- `public double doubleValue()`
- `public float floatValue()`
- `public int intValue()`
- `public long longValue()`
- `public short shortValue()`
  Returns the value of this `Short` as a Java primitive type.
- `public static Short decode(String str) throws NumberFormatException`
  Returns the short representation of the coded argument (`str`). The argument can be coded in decimal, hexadecimal or octal formats.

- public boolean equals(Object arg)

  Returns a true value if this `Short` is equal to the parameter `arg`.
- public int hashCode()

  Returns the hash code for this `Short`.
- public static short parseShort(String str) throws NumberFormatException
- public static short parseShort(String str, int base) throws NumberFormatException

  Returns the string argument (`str`) as a short in base 10. The radix of the returned number can be specified in `base`.
- public static String toString(short num)
- public String toString()

  Returns a string representation of this `Short` or num.
- public static Short valueOf(String str) throws NumberFormatException
- public static Short valueOf(String str, int base) throws NumberFormatException

  Returns an instance of a new `Short` object initialized to the value specified in `str`. The radix of the returned number can be specified in `base`.

SimpleDateFormat (`java.text`)

A public class, derived from `DateFormat`, that allows for the parsing of dates to locale-based strings, and vice versa.

Constructors

- public SimpleDateFormat()
- public SimpleDateFormat(String str)
- public SimpleDateFormat(String str, Locale locale)

  Creates a new instance of a `SimpleDateFormat` using the specified or default pattern and the specified or default locale.
- public SimpleDateFormat(String str, DateFormatSymbols format)

  Creates a new instance of a `SimpleDateFormat` using the specified pattern and format data.

Methods

- public void applyLocalizedPattern(String str)
- public String toLocalizedPattern()

  Sets or returns the locale-based string that describes this `SimpleDateFormat`.

- public void applyPattern(String str)
- public String toPattern()

  Sets or returns the non-locale-based string that describes this SimpleDateFormat.
- public Object clone()

  Returns a copy of this SimpleDateFormat.
- public boolean equals(Object arg)

  Returns a true value if this SimpleDateFormat is equal to arg.
- public StringBuffer format(Date date, StringBuffer dest, FieldPosition pos)

  Formats the specified string, starting at field pos, placing the result in the specified destination buffer. This method returns the value of the buffer.
- public DateFormatSymbols getDateFormatSymbols()
- public void setDateFormatSymbols(DateFormatSymbols symbols)

  Returns or sets the date/time formatting symbols for this SimpleDateFormat.
- public int hashCode()

  Returns the hash code for this SimpleDateFormat.
- public Date parse(String str, ParsePosition pos)

  Parses the specified string, starting at position pos, and returns a Date object.

SimpleTimeZone (`java.util`)

A public class, derived from TimeZone, that represents a time zone in a Gregorian calendar.

Constructors

- public SimpleTimeZone(int offset, String id)
- public SimpleTimeZone(int offset, String id, int stMonth, int stNthDayWeekInMonth, int stDayOfWeek, int stTime, int endMonth, int endNthDayWeekInMonth, int endDayOfWeek, int endTime)

  Creates a new SimpleTimeZone from an offset from GMT and a time zone id. ID should be obtained from the TimeZone.getAvailableIDs method. You can also define the starting and ending times for daylight savings time. Each period has a starting and ending month (stMonth, endMonth), day of the week in a month (stNthDayWeekInMonth, endNthDayWeekInMonth), day of the week (stDayOfWeek, endDayOfWeek), and time (stTime, endTime).

Methods

- `public Object clone()`
  Returns a copy of this `SimpleTimeZone`.
- `public boolean equals(Object arg)`
  Returns a true value if this `SimpleTimeZone` is equal to arg.
- `public int getOffset(int era, int year, int month, int day, int dayOfWeek, int millisec)`
  Returns the offset from the Greenwich Mean Time (GMT), taking into account daylight savings time.
- `public int getRawOffset()`
- `public void setRawOffset(int millisec)`
  Returns or sets the offset from Greenwich Mean Time (GMT) for this `SimpleTimeZone`. These methods do not take daylight savings time into account.
- `public synchronized int hashCode()`
  Returns the hash code for this `SimpleTimeZone`.
- `public boolean inDaylightTime(Date dt)`
  Returns a true value if the specified date falls within Daylight Savings Time.
- `public void setEndRule(int month, int dyWkInMo, int dyWk, int tm)`
- `public void setStartRule(int month, int dyWkInMo, int dyWk, int tm)`
  Sets the starting and ending times for Daylight Savings Time for this `SimpleTimeZone` to a specified month, day of a week in a month, day of a week, and time (in milliseconds).
- `public void setStartYear(int year)`
  Sets the Daylight Savings starting year for this `SimpleTimeZone`.
- `public boolean useDaylightTime()`
  Returns a true value if this `SimpleTimeZone` uses Daylight Savings Time.

Socket (`java.net`)

A public final class, derived from `Object`, that defines a client-side socket.

Constructors

- `protected Socket()`
- `protected Socket(SocketImpl implementation) throws SocketException`
  Creates a new instance of a socket, (not connected to any machine). A socket implementation can be specified or a default one is utilized.

- `public Socket(InetAddress dest, int num) throws IOException`
- `public Socket(InetAddress dest, int num, InetAddress local, int lnum) throws IOException`
- `public Socket(String dest, int num) throws IOException`
- `public Socket(String dest, int num, InetAddress local, int lnum) throws IOException`

  Creates a new instance of a socket to a destination at port `num`. The socket can be connected to the local machine (`local`) on a local port (`lnum`).

Methods

- `public void close() throws IOException`
  Closes this socket.
- `public InetAddress getInetAddress()`
  Returns the Internet address this socket is connected to.
- `public InputStream getInputStream() throws IOException`
  Returns the input stream this socket utilizes for reading.
- `public InetAddress getLocalAddress()`
  Returns the local host this socket is bound to.
- `public int getLocalPort()`
  Returns the local port this socket is using for its connection.
- `public OutputStream getOutputStream() throws IOException`
  Returns the output stream this socket uses for writing.
- `public int getPort()`
  Returns the port number the socket is connected to on the destination machine.
- `public int getSoLinger() throws SocketException`
- `public void setSoLinger(boolean toggle, int num) throws SocketException`
  Returns or sets the socket linger time in milliseconds.
- `public synchronized int getSoTimeout() throws SocketException`
- `public synchronized void setSoTimeout(int num) throws SocketException`
  Returns or sets the socket timeout value in milliseconds.
- `public boolean getTcpNoDelay() throws SocketException`
- `public void setTcpNoDelay(boolean toggle) throws SocketException`
  Returns or sets a true value if the TCP_NODELAY is set for this socket.
- `public static void setSocketImplFactory(SocketImplFactory arg) throws IOException, SocketException`

Sets the socket implementation factory for this socket to arg.
- `public String toString()`
  Returns a string representation of this socket.

Stack (`java.util`)

A public class, derived from `Vector`, that represents a last-in-first-out stack.

Constructors

- `public Stack()`
  Creates a new instance of an empty stack.

Methods

- `public boolean empty()`
  Returns a true value if this stack contains no elements.
- `public Object peek() throws EmptyStackException`
  Returns the item on the top of the stack, but does not remove it.
- `public Object pop() throws EmptyStackException`
- `public Object push(Object obj)`
  Returns and removes the item on the top of the stack (pop) or pushes a new item onto the stack (push).
- `public int search(Object obj)`
  Returns the relative position of item `obj` from the top of the stack, or −1 if the item is not in this stack.

String (`java.lang`)

A public final class, derived from `Object` and implementing `Serializable`, that contains methods for creating and parsing strings. Because the contents of a string cannot be modified, many of the methods return a new string.

Constructors

- `public String()`
- `public String(byte[] arg)`
- `public String(byte[] arg, int index, int count)`
- `public String(byte[] arg, String code) throws UnsupportedEncodingException`
- `public String(byte[] arg, int index, int count, String code) throws UnsupportedEncodingException`
  Creates a new instance of the `String` class from the array `arg`. The parameter `index` indicates which element of `arg` is the first character of

the resulting string, and the parameter `count` is the number of characters to add to the new string. The `String()` method creates a new string of no characters. The characters are converted using `code` encoding format.

- `public String(char[] chars)`
- `public String(char[] chars, int index, int count)`
  `throws StringIndexOutOfBoundsException`
  Creates an instance of the `String` class from the array `chars`. The parameter `index` indicates which element of `chars` is the first character of the resulting string, and the parameter `count` is the number of characters to add to the new string.
- `public String(String str)`
- `public String(StringBuffer str)`
  Creates an instance of the `String` class from the parameter `str`.

Methods

- `public char charAt(int idx) throws`
  `StringIndexOutOfBoundsException`
  Returns the character at index `idx` in the current object. The first character of the source string is at index 0.
- `public int compareTo(String str)`
  Compares the current object to `str`. If both strings are equal, 0 (zero) is returned. If the current string is lexicographically less than the argument, an `int` less than zero is returned. If the current string is lexicographically greater than the argument, an `int` greater than zero is returned.
- `public String concat(String source)`
  Returns the product of the concatenation of argument `source` to the end of the current object.
- `public static String copyValueOf(char[] arg)`
- `public static String copyValueOf(char[] arg, int index, int count)`
  Returns a new `String` that contains the characters of `arg`, beginning at index `index`, and of length `count`.
- `public boolean endsWith(String suff)`
  Returns true if the current object ends with the specified suffix.
- `public boolean equals(Object arg)`
- `public boolean equalsIgnoreCase(String arg)`
  Returns true if the current object is equal to `arg`. `arg` must not be null, and must be of exact length and content as the current object. `equalsIgnoreCase` disregards the case of the characters.
- `public byte[] getBytes()`
- `public byte[] getBytes(String enc) throws`
  `UnsupportedEncodingException`

Returns the contents of the current object in an array of bytes decoded with enc. When a decoding format is not present, the platform default it used.

- `public void getChars(int start, int end, char[] dest, int destStart)`

  Copies the contents of the current object starting at index `start` and ending at `end` into the character array `dest` starting at index `destStart`.

- `public int hashCode()`

  Returns the hash code of the current object.

- `public int indexOf(int c)`
- `public int indexOf(int c, int index)`

  Returns the index of the first occurrence of the character `c` in the current object, no less than `index` (default of 0). Returns a -1 if there is no such occurrence.

- `public int indexOf(String str)`
- `public int indexOf(String str, int index)`

  Returns the index of the first occurrence of the string `str` in the current object, no less than `index` (default of 0). Returns a -1 if there is no such occurrence.

- `public String intern()`

  Creates a new canonical string with identical content to this string.

- `public int lastIndexOf(int c)`
- `public int lastIndexOf(int c, int index)`

  Returns the index of the last occurrence of the character `c` in the current object, no less than `index` (default of 0). Returns a -1 if there is no such occurrence.

- `public int lastIndexOf(String str)`
- `public int lastIndexOf(String str, int index)`

  Returns the index of the last occurrence of the string `str` in the current object, no less than `index` (default of 0). Returns a -1 if there is no such occurrence.

- `public int length()`

  Returns the integer length of the current object.

- `public boolean regionMatches(boolean case, int cindex, String str, int strindex, int size)`
- `public boolean regionMatches(int cindex, String str, int strindex, int size)`

  Returns a true result if the subregion of parameter `str` starting at index `strindex` and having length `size`, is identical to a substring of the current object starting at index `cindex` and having the same length. If `case` is true, then character case is ignored during the comparisons.

- `public String replace(char oldC, char newC)`

  Returns a new string with all occurrences of the `oldC` replaced with the `newC`.

- `public boolean startsWith(String str)`
- `public boolean startsWith(String str, int index)`

    Returns a true if the current object starts with the string `str` at location `index` (default of 0).

- `public String substring(int startindex) throws StringIndexOutOfBoundsException`
- `public String substring(int startindex, int lastindex) throws StringIndexOutOfBoundsException`

    Returns the substring of the current object starting with `startindex` and ending with `lastindex-1` (or the last index of the string in the case of the first method).

- `public char[] toCharArray()`
- `public String toString()`

    Returns the current object as an array of characters or a string. Is present due to the automatic use of the `toString` method in output routines.

- `public String toLowerCase()`
- `public String toLowerCase(Locale loc)`

    Returns the current object with each character in lower case, taking into account variations of the specified locale (`loc`).

- `public String toUpperCase()`
- `public String toUpperCase(Locale loc)`

    Returns the current object with each character in uppercase, taking into account variations of the specified locale (`loc`).

- `public String trim()`

    Returns the current object with leading and trailing white space removed.

- `public static String valueOf(boolean arg)`
- `public static String valueOf(char arg)`
- `public static String valueOf(char[] arg)`
- `public static String valueOf(char[] arg, int index, int size)`
- `public static String valueOf(double arg)`
- `public static String valueOf(float arg)`
- `public static String valueOf(int arg)`
- `public static String valueOf(long arg)`
- `public static String valueOf(Object arg)`

    Returns a string representation of the parameter `arg`. A starting `index` and specified `size` are permitted.

StringBuffer (`java.lang`)

A public class, derived from `Object` and implementing `Serializable`, that contains methods for creating, parsing and modifying string buffers. Unlike a `String`, the content and length of a `StringBuffer` can be changed dynamically.

Constructors

- `public StringBuffer()`
- `public StringBuffer(int size) throws NegativeArraySizeException`

  Creates an instance of the `StringBuffer` class that is empty but has an initial capacity of `size` characters (16 by default).

- `public StringBuffer(String arg)`

  Creates an instance of the `StringBuffer` class from the string `arg`.

Methods

- `public StringBuffer append(boolean arg)`
- `public StringBuffer append(char arg)`
- `public StringBuffer append(char[] arg)`
- `public StringBuffer append(char[] arg, int index, int size)`
- `public StringBuffer append(double arg)`
- `public StringBuffer append(float arg)`
- `public StringBuffer append(int arg)`
- `public StringBuffer append(long arg)`
- `public StringBuffer append(Object arg)`
- `public StringBuffer append(String arg)`

  Returns the current object with the `String` parameter `arg` appended to the end. A substring of a character array can be appended by specifying an `index` and `size`.

- `public int capacity()`

  Returns the capacity of this `StringBuffer`.

- `public char charAt(int idx) throws StringIndexOutOfBoundsException`

  Returns the character at the specified index of this `StringBuffer`.

- `public void ensureCapacity(int min)`

  Sets the minimum capacity of this `StringBuffer` to be no less than `min`. The new capacity set by this method may actually be greater than `min`.

- `public void getChars(int start, int end, char[] dest, int destindex) throws StringIndexOutOfBoundsException`

  Copies the characters at index `start` to `end` from this `StringBuffer` to `dest`, starting at index `destindex`.

- `public StringBuffer insert(int index, boolean arg) throws StringIndexOutOfBoundsException`
- `public StringBuffer insert(int index, char arg) throws StringIndexOutOfBoundsException`
- `public StringBuffer insert(int index, char[] arg) throws StringIndexOutOfBoundsException`

- `public StringBuffer insert(int index, double arg)`
  `throws StringIndexOutOfBoundsException`
- `public StringBuffer insert(int index, float arg)`
  `throws StringIndexOutOfBoundsException`
- `public StringBuffer insert(int index, int arg) throws`
  `StringIndexOutOfBoundsException`
- `public StringBuffer insert(int index, long arg) throws`
  `StringIndexOutOfBoundsException`
- `public StringBuffer insert(int index, Object arg)`
  `throws StringIndexOutOfBoundsException`
- `public StringBuffer insert(int index, String arg)`
  `throws StringIndexOutOfBoundsException`

  Inserts the string representation of parameter `arg` into this `StringBuffer` at index `index`. Characters to the right of the specified index of this `StringBuffer` are shifted to the right.
- `public int length()`

  Returns the length of this `StringBuffer`.
- `public StringBuffer reverse()`

  Returns the value of this `StringBuffer` with the order of the characters reversed.
- `public void setCharAt(int idx, char c)`

  Sets the character at the specified index to c.
- `public void setLength(int size) throws`
  `StringIndexOutOfBoundsException`

  Truncates this `StringBuffer`, if needed, to the new length of `size`.
- `public String toString()`

  Returns the `String` representation of this `StringBuffer`.

StringTokenizer (`java.util`)

A public class, derived from `Object` and implementing `Enumeration`, that manipulates string values into tokens separated by delimiter characters.

Constructors

- `public StringTokenizer(String arg)`
- `public StringTokenizer(String arg, String delims)`
- `public StringTokenizer(String arg, String delims,`
  `boolean tokens)`

  Creates a new instance of a `StringTokenizer` with the string initialized to `arg`, and utilizing the specified delimiters or the defaults (`" \t\n\r"`: a space, tab, newline, and carriage return). If `tokens` is true, the delimiters are treated as words within the string and are subject to being returned as tokens.

Methods

- `public int countTokens()`
  Returns the number of tokens present in this string tokenizer.
- `public boolean hasMoreElements()`
- `public boolean hasMoreTokens()`
  Returns a true value if there are more tokens to be returned by this string tokenizer. `hasMoreElements()` is identical to `nextToken()` and is implemented to complete the implementation of the `Enumerated` interface.
- `public Object nextElement() throws NoSuchElementException`
- `public String nextToken() throws NoSuchElementException`
- `public String nextToken(String delims) throws NoSuchElementException`
  Returns the next token in the string. `nextElement()` is identical to `nextToken()` and is implemented to complete the implementation of the `Enumerated` interface. New delimiters can be specified in the last method.

System (`java.lang`)

A public final class, derived from `Object`, that contains the standard input, output, and error streams, as well as various system related methods.

Variables and Constants

- `public static PrintStream err`
- `public static InputStream in`
- `public static PrintStream out`
  Constant values that are the standard error output stream (stderr), standard input stream (stdin), and the standard output stream (stdout).

Methods

- `public static void arraycopy(Object source, int srcindex, Object dest, int destindex, int size) throws ArrayIndexOutOfBoundsException, ArrayStoreException`
  Copies a subarray of `size` objects from `source`, starting at index `srcindex`, to `dest` starting at `destindex`.
- `public static long currentTimeMillis()`

Returns the current system in milliseconds from midnight, January 1st, 1970 UTC.

- `public static void exit(int num) throws SecurityException`
  Exits the program with the status code of num.
- `public static void gc()`
  Executes the `gc` method of the `Runtime` class, which attempts to garbage collect any unused objects, freeing system memory.
- `public static Properties getProperties() throws SecurityException`
- `public static void setProperties(Properties newprops) throws SecurityException`
  Returns or sets the current system properties.
- `public static String getProperty(String name) throws SecurityException`
- `public static String getProperty(String name, String default) throws SecurityException`
  Returns the system property for name, or returns the value `default` as a default result if no such name exists.
- `public static SecurityManager getSecurityManager()`
- `public static void setSecurityManager(SecurityManager mgr) throws SecurityException`
  Returns or sets the security manager for the current application. If no security manager has been initialized, then a null value is returned by the `get` method.
- `public static int identityHashCode(Object arg)`
  Returns the hash code for the specified object. This will return the default hash code, in the event that the object's `hashCode` method has been overridden.
- `public static void load(String name) throws UnsatisfiedLinkError, SecurityException`
  Loads name as a dynamic library.
- `public static void loadLibrary(String name) throws UnsatisfiedLinkError, SecurityException`
  Loads name as a system library.
- `public static void runFinalization()`
  Requests that the Java Virtual Machine execute the finalize method on any outstanding objects.
- `public static void runFinalizersOnExit(boolean toggle)`
  Allows the execution of the finalizer methods for all objects, when toggle is true.
- `public static void setErr(PrintStream strm)`
- `public static void setIn(InputStream strm)`

- public static void setOut(PrintStream strm)
  Reassigns the error stream, input stream, or output stream to strm.

SystemColor (`java.awt`)

A public final class, derived from `Color` and implementing `Serializable`, that represents the current window system color for the current system. If the user changes the window system colors for this system and the window system can update the new color selection, these color values will change as well.

Variables and Constants

- public final static int ACTIVE_CAPTION
  Constant index to the active caption color in the system color array.
- public final static int ACTIVE_CAPTION_BORDER
- public final static int ACTIVE_CAPTION_TEXT
  Constant indices to the active caption border and text colors in the system color array.
- public final static int CONTROL
  Constant index to the control color in the system color array.
- public final static int CONTROL_DK_SHADOW
- public final static int CONTROL_SHADOW
  Constant indices to the control shadow and control dark shadow colors in the system color array.
- public final static int CONTROL_HIGHLIGHT
- public final static int CONTROL_LT_HIGHLIGHT
  Constant indices to the control highlight and light highlight colors in the system color array.
- public final static int CONTROL_TEXT
  Constant index to the control text color in the system color array.
- public final static int DESKTOP
  Constant index to the desktop color in the system color array.
- public final static int INACTIVE_CAPTION
  Constant index to the inactive caption color in the system color array.
- public final static int INACTIVE_CAPTION_BORDER
- public final static int INACTIVE_CAPTION_TEXT
  Constant indices to the inactive caption border and text colors in the system color array.
- public final static int INFO
  Constant index to the information (help) text background color in the system color array.
- public final static int INFO_TEXT
- public final static int MENU_TEXT

Constant indices to the information (help) and menu text colors in the system color array.

- `public final static int NUM_COLORS`
  Constant value that holds the number of colors in the system color array.
- `public final static int SCROLLBAR`
  Constant index to the scrollbar background color in the system color array.
- `public final static int TEXT`
  Constant index to the background color of text components in the system color array.
- `public final static int TEXT_HIGHLIGHT`
- `public final static int TEXT_HIGHLIGHT_TEXT`
  Constant indices to the background and text colors for highlighted text in the system color array.
- `public final static int TEXT_INACTIVE_TEXT`
  Constant index to the inactive text color in the system color array.
- `public final static int TEXT_TEXT`
  Constant index to the color of text components in the system color array.
- `public final static int WINDOW`
  Constant index to the background color of windows in the system color array.
- `public final static int WINDOW_BORDER`
- `public final static int WINDOW_TEXT`
  Constant indices to the border and text colors of windows in the system color array.
- `public final static SystemColor activeCaption`
  The system's background color for window border captions.
- `public final static SystemColor activeCaptionBorder`
- `public final static SystemColor activeCaptionText`
  The system's border and text colors for window border captions.
- `public final static SystemColor control`
  The system's color for window control objects.
- `public final static SystemColor controlDkShadow`
- `public final static SystemColor controlShadow`
  The system's dark shadow and regular shadow colors for control objects.
- `public final static SystemColor controlHighlight`
- `public final static SystemColor controlLtHighlight`
  The system's highlight and light highlight colors for control objects.
- `public final static SystemColor controlText`
  The system's text color for control objects.
- `public final static SystemColor desktop`
  The system's color of the desktop background.

- public final static SystemColor inactiveCaption
  The system's background color for inactive caption areas of window borders.
- public final static SystemColor inactiveCaptionBorder
- public final static SystemColor inactiveCaptionText
  The system's border and text colors for inactive caption areas of window borders.
- public final static SystemColor info
  The system's background color for information (help) text.
- public final static SystemColor infoText
  The system's text color for information (help) text.
- public final static SystemColor menu
  The system's background color for menus.
- public final static SystemColor menuText
  The system's text color for menus.
- public final static SystemColor scrollbar
  The system's background color for scrollbars.
- public final static SystemColor text
  The system's color for text components.
- public final static SystemColor textHighlight
  The system's background color for highlighted text.
- public final static SystemColor textHighlightText
- public final static SystemColor textInactiveText
  The system's text color for highlighted and inactive text.
- public final static SystemColor textText
  The system's text color for text components.
- public final static SystemColor window
  The system's background color for windows.
- public final static SystemColor windowBorder
- public final static SystemColor windowText
  The system's border and text colors for windows.

Methods

- public int getRGB()
  Returns the RGB values of this SystemColor's symbolic color.
- public String toString()
  Returns a string representation of this SystemColor's values.

TextArea (java.awt)

A public class, derived from TextComponent, that provides a graphical multiline area for displaying text.

Variables and Constants

- `public final static int SCROLLBARS_BOTH`
- `public final static int SCROLLBARS_HORIZONTAL_ONLY`
- `public final static int SCROLLBARS_NONE`
- `public final static int SCROLLBARS_VERTICAL_ONLY`
  Constant values indicating the creation policy of scrollbars for this text area during instantiation.

Constructors

- `public TextArea()`
- `public TextArea(int r, int c)`
- `public TextArea(String str)`
- `public TextArea(String str, int r, int c)`
- `public TextArea(String str, int r, int c, int sb)`
  Creates a new instance of a text area from the string `str`, of the size `r` rows by `c` columns and creating scrollbars according to the direction of the value of `sb` (scrollbar visibility constant). Default values for these constructors include 0 rows and columns, and `SCROLLBARS_BOTH` for the scrollbar creation policy.

Methods

- `public void addNotify()`
  Creates this text area's peer.
- `public void append(String str)`
  Appends the specified string to the text area.
- `public int getColumns()`
- `public void setColumns(int num)`
  Returns or sets the number of columns in this text area.
- `public Dimension getMinimumSize()`
- `public Dimension getPreferredSize()`
  Returns the minimum and preferred size of this text area.
- `public Dimension getMinimumSize(int r, int c)`
- `public Dimension getPreferredSize(int r, int c)`
  Returns the minimum and preferred size of this text area, sized to `r` rows and `c` columns.
- `public void getRows()`
- `public void setRows(int num)`
  Sets the number of rows for this text area to `num`.
- `public int getScrollbarVisibility()`
  Returns the scrollbar visibility status, corresponding to this scrollbar's constant values.

- `public void insert(String src, int index)`
  Inserts the string `src` into this text area at position `index`.
- `protected String paramString()`
  Return a string containing the parameters of this text area.
- `public synchronized void replaceRange(String newtxt, int begin, int end)`
  Replaces the current text from position `begin` to end with `newtxt`.

TextComponent (`java.awt`)

A public class, derived from `Component`, that allows for the editing of text in a window toolkit component.

Variables and Constants

- `protected transient TextListener textListener`
  The current text listener for this text component.

Methods

- `public void addTextListener(TextListener listener)`
- `public void removeTextListener(TextListener listener)`
  Adds or removes the specified `listener` to this text component.
- `public int getCaretPosition()`
- `public void setCaretPosition(int pos)`
  Returns or sets the position of the insertion caret for this text component.
- `public synchronized String getSelectedText()`
  Returns a string containing the entire text in this text component.
- `public synchronized String getText()`
- `public synchronized void setText(String str)`
  Returns or sets the text contained in this text component.
- `public synchronized int getSelectionEnd()`
- `public synchronized int getSelectionStart()`
  Returns the index of the starting or ending of the current selection from this text component.
- `public boolean isEditable()`
- `public synchronized void setEditable(boolean toggle)`
  Returns or sets the status variable that indicates if this text component can be edited by the user.
- `protected String paramString()`
  Returns the string representation of the parameters for this text component.

- protected void processEvent(AWTEvent event)

  Handles the specified event, passing it to the processTextEvent method if event is a TextEvent; otherwise, this method passes the event to the parent's processEvent method.
- protected void processTextEvent(TextEvent event)

  Processes this text event, sending it to the appropriate registered listener.
- public void removeNotify()

  Removes the peer for this text component.
- public synchronized void select(int start, int end)

  Selects the text in this text component, starting at index position start, and ending at index position end.
- public synchronized void selectAll()

  Selects all of the text from this text component.
- public synchronized void setSelectionEnd(int pos)
- public synchronized void setSelectionStart(int pos)

  Sets the starting or ending position of the selection area in this text component to index position pos.

TextEvent (`java.awt.event`)

A public class, derived from AWTEvent, that describes a particular AWT text-based event.

Variables and Constants

- public static final int TEXT_FIRST
- public static final int TEXT_LAST

  Constant values that represent the index of the first and last text event ids.
- public static final int TEXT_VALUE_CHANGED

  A constant value that represents the event of a text component's text value changing.

Constructors

- public TextEvent(Object src, int type)

  Creates a new instance of a TextEvent from a specified source object and having a defined event type.

Methods

- public String paramString()

  Returns a string containing the parameters of this TextEvent.

TextField (`java.awt`)

A public class, derived from `TextComponent`, that provides a graphical single line of text that can be edited by the user.

Constructors

- `public TextField()`
- `public TextField(int num)`
- `public TextField(String str)`
- `public TextField(String str, int num)`
  Creates a new instance of a text field from the specified string, `num` columns wide. The first constructor creates a text field with no string present, and 0 columns wide. The third constructor sizes the field based on the number of characters in the string.

Methods

- `public void addActionListener(ActionListener listener)`
- `public void removeActionListener(ActionListener listener)`
  Adds or removes the specified `listener` to this text field.
- `public void addNotify()`
  Creates this text field's peer.
- `public boolean echoCharIsSet()`
  Returns a true value if the echo character for this text field is set.
- `public int getColumns()`
- `public void setColumns(int num)`
  Returns or sets the number of columns for this text field.
- `public char getEchoChar()`
- `public void setEchoChar(char c)`
  Returns or sets the current echo character for this text field.
- `public Dimension getMinimumSize()`
- `public Dimension getPreferredSize()`
  Returns the minimum or preferred size needed to display this text field.
- `public Dimension getMinimumSize(int num)`
- `public Dimension getPreferredSize(int num)`
  Returns the minimum or preferred size needed to display this text field of `num` columns.
- `protected String paramString()`
  Returns a string containing this text field's parameters.
- `protected void processActionEvent(ActionEvent event)`
  Handles the specified `event` for this text field, sending it to any registered listener.

- **protected void processEvent(AWTEvent event)**
  Handles any event on this text field, passing to the processActionEvent method if it is an action event. Otherwise, the event is passed to the parent's processEvent method.

Thread (`java.lang`)

A public class, derived from `Object` and implementing `Runnable`, that handles the implementation and management of Java execution threads.

Variables and Constants

- **public final static int MAX_PRIORITY**
- **public final static int MIN_PRIORITY**
- **public final static int NORM_PRIORITY**
  Constant values that contain the maximum (10), minimum (1), and normal (6) priority values a thread can have.

Constructors

- **public Thread()**
  Creates a new instance of a thread.
- **public Thread(Runnable arg)**
  Creates a new instance of a thread. `arg` specifies which object's run method is invoked to start the thread.
- **public Thread(String str)**
- **public Thread(Runnable arg, String str)**
  Creates a new instance of a thread, named `str`. `arg` specifies which object's run method is invoked to start the thread.
- **public Thread(ThreadGroup tgrp, String str) throws SecurityException**
- **public Thread(ThreadGroup tgrp, Runnable arg) throws SecurityException**
- **public Thread(ThreadGroup tgrp, Runnable arg, String str) throws SecurityException**
  Creates a new instance of a thread, named `str` and belonging to thread group `tgrp`. The `arg` parameter specifies which object's run method is invoked to start the thread.

Methods

- **public static int activeCount()**
  Returns the number of active threads in this thread's group.
- **public void checkAccess() throws SecurityException**

Validates that the current executing thread has permission to modify this thread.

- `public int countStackFrames() throws IllegalThreadStateException`
  Returns the number of stack frames in this thread. The thread must be in a suspended state.
- `public static Thread currentThread()`
  Returns the currently executing thread.
- `public void destroy()`
  Destroys this thread.
- `public static void dumpStack()`
  Dumps a trace of the stack for the current thread.
- `public static int enumerate(Thread[] dest)`
  Copies each of the members of this thread's group into the thread array dest.
- `public final String getName()`
- `public final int getPriority()`
- `public final ThreadGroup getThreadGroup()`
  Returns the name, priority, or thread group of this thread.
- `public void interrupt()`
  Interrupts this thread's execution.
- `public static boolean interrupted()`
  Returns a true value if the current thread's execution has been interrupted.
- `public final boolean isAlive()`
- `public boolean isInterrupted()`
  Returns a true value if this thread's execution is alive or has been interrupted.
- `public final boolean isDaemon()`
  Returns a true value if this thread is a daemon thread.
- `public final void join() throws InterruptedException`
- `public final void join(long msec) throws InterruptedException`
- `public final void join(long msec, int nsec) throws InterruptedException`
  Waits up to msec milliseconds and nsec nanoseconds for this thread to die. The `join()` method waits forever for this thread to die.
- `public final void resume() throws SecurityException`
  Resumes this thread's execution.
- `public void run()`
  Method containing the main body of the executing thread code. Run methods can run concurrently with other thread run methods.
- `public final void setDaemon(boolean flag) throws IllegalThreadStateException`

Sets this thread as a daemon thread, if `flag` is true.

- `public final void setName(String str) throws SecurityException`
- `public final void setPriority(int val) throws SecurityException`

  Sets the name of this thread to `str` or the priority to `val`.
- `public static void sleep(long msec) throws InterruptedException`
- `public static void sleep(long msec, int nsec) throws InterruptedException`

  Causes the current thread to sleep for `msec` milliseconds and `nsec` nanoseconds.
- `public void start() throws IllegalThreadStateException`

  Start this thread's execution, calling this thread's run method.
- `public final void stop() throws SecurityException`
- `public final void stop(Throwable arg) throws SecurityException`

  Stop this thread's execution and throw `arg` as an exception.
- `public final void suspend() throws SecurityException`

  Suspends this thread's execution.
- `public String toString()`

  Returns a string representation of this thread.
- `public static void yield()`

  Causes the currently executing thread to pause in execution, allowing other threads to run.

Throwable (`java.lang`)

A public class, derived from `Object` and implementing `Serializable`, that is the superclass of all of the errors and exceptions thrown.

Constructors

- `public Throwable()`
- `public Throwable(String str)`

  Creates a new instance of a throwable object with the specified message (`str`) or none present.

Methods

- `public Throwable fillInStackTrace()`

  Fills in the executable stack trace for this throwable object.
- `public String getLocalizedMessage()`

Returns a locale specific description of this object. Locale specific messages should override this method; otherwise, the same message that the getMessage method produces will be returned.

- public String getMessage()
  Returns the detail message for this throwable.
- public void printStackTrace()
- public void printStackTrace(PrintStream stream)
- public void printStackTrace(PrintWriter stream)
  Prints the stack trace for this throwable to the standard error stream or to the specified stream.
- public String toString()
  Returns a string representation of this throwable object.

TimeZone (`java.util`)

A public abstract class, derived from Object and implementing Serializable and Cloneable, that represents an amount of time offset from GMT that results in local time. Functionality is provided to allow for Daylight Savings Time within a time zone.

Methods

- clone()
  Returns a copy of this TimeZone.
- public static synchronized String[] getAvailableIDs()
- public static synchronized String[] getAvailableIDs(int offset)
  Returns a list of all of the supported time zone ids, or only those for a specified time zone offset.
- public static synchronized TimeZone getDefault()
- public static synchronized void setDefault(TimeZone tz)
  Returns or sets the default time zone.
- public String getID()
  Returns the id of this time zone.
- public abstract int getOffset(int era, int year, int month, int day, int dayOfWeek, int milliseconds)
  Returns the offset from the Greenwich Mean Time (GMT), taking into account daylight savings time.
- public abstract int getRawOffset()
- public abstract void setRawOffset(int millisec)
  Returns or sets the offset from Greenwich Mean Time (GMT) for this SimpleTimeZone. These methods do not take daylight savings time into account.
- public static synchronized TimeZone getTimeZone(String id)

Returns the time zone corresponding to the specified id value.
- `public abstract boolean inDaylightTime(Date dt)`
  Returns a true result if the specified date falls within the Daylight Savings Time for this `TimeZone`.
- `public void setID(String id)`
  Sets the id value of this `TimeZone`.
- `public abstract boolean useDaylightTime()`
  Returns a true value if this `TimeZone` uses Daylight Savings Time.

Toolkit (`java.awt`)

A public class, derived from `Object`, that is used to tie abstract window classes provided in the AWT to their native implementation on a destination system.

Constructors

- `public Toolkit()`
  Creates an instance of a toolkit.

Methods

- `public abstract void beep()`
  Plays a beep, created by the audio device.
- `public abstract int checkImage(Image img, int width, int height, ImageObserver obs)`
  Returns the status of an image (`img`) that is being loaded by the specified observer (`obs`) at a `width` and `height` on the screen.
- `protected abstract ButtonPeer createButton(Button arg)`
- `protected abstract CanvasPeer createCanvas(Canvas arg)`
- `protected abstract CheckboxPeer createCheckbox(Checkbox arg)`
- `protected abstract CheckboxMenuItemPeer createCheckboxMenuItem(CheckboxMenuItem arg)`
- `protected abstract ChoicePeer createChoice(Choice arg)`
- `protected LightweightPeer createComponent(Component arg)`
- `protected abstract DialogPeer createDialog(Dialog arg)`
- `protected abstract FileDialogPeer createFileDialog(FileDialog arg)`
- `protected abstract FramePeer createFrame(Frame arg)`
- `protected abstract LabelPeer createLabel(Label arg)`
- `protected abstract ListPeer createList(List arg)`
- `protected abstract MenuPeer createMenu(Menu arg)`

- protected abstract MenuBarPeer createMenuBar(MenuBar arg)
- protected abstract MenuItemPeer createMenuItem(MenuItem arg)
- protected abstract PanelPeer createPanel(Panel arg)
- protected abstract PopupMenuPeer createPopupMenu(PopupMenu arg)
- protected abstract ScrollbarPeer createScrollbar(Scrollbar arg)
- protected abstract ScrollPanePeer createScrollPane(ScrollPane arg)
- protected abstract TextAreaPeer createTextArea(TextArea arg)
- protected abstract TextFieldPeer createTextField(TextField arg)
- protected abstract WindowPeer createWindow(Window arg)

  Creates a new AWT component and returns its peer.
- public Image createImage(byte[] image)
- public abstract Image createImage(byte[] image, int index, int size)
- public abstract Image createImage(ImageProducer prod)

  Creates a new image from the specified array of bytes or image producer. The second method allows for an offset from the start of the array as well as the number of bytes to use from the array.
- public abstract ColorModel getColorModel()

  Returns the color model provided from this toolkit.
- public static synchronized Toolkit getDefaultToolkit() throws AWTError

  Returns the default toolkit.
- public abstract String[] getFontList()

  Returns the list of available fonts provided from this toolkit.

URL (java.net)

A public final class, derived from Object and implementing Serializable, that represents a Web Uniform Resource Locator (URL).

Constructors

- public URL(String arg) throws MalformedURLException
- public URL(URL url, String type) throws MalformedURLException

  Creates a URL instance from a string argument, or by parsing a type (http, gopher, ftp) and the remaining base.

- public URL(String proto, String source, int num, String doc) throws MalformedURLException
- public URL(String proto, String source, String doc) throws MalformedURLException

  Creates a URL instance using a defined protocol (proto), source system, destination port num, and document (doc).

Methods

- public boolean equals(Object obj)

  Returns a true value if this URL is equal in all respects (protocol, source, port, and document) to obj.
- public final Object getContent() throws IOException

  Returns the retrieved contents as an Object.
- public String getFile()
- public String getRef()

  Returns the name of the file (document) or its anchor this URL will attempt to retrieve.
- public String getHost()
- public int getPort()

  Returns the name of the host (source) or the port this URL will attempt to connect to.
- public String getProtocol()

  Returns the protocol this URL will use in retrieving the data.
- public int hashCode()

  Returns the hash code for this URL.
- public URLConnection openConnection() throws IOException
- public final InputStream openStream() throws IOException

  Returns a connection to this URL and returns the connection or a stream.
- public boolean sameFile(URL arg)

  Returns a true value if this URL retrieves the same file as the arg URL.
- protected void set(String proto, String source, int num, String doc, String anchor)

  Sets the protocol (proto), source, port num, file (doc) and reference (anchor) for this URL.
- public static void setURLStreamHandlerFactory(URLStreamHandlerFactory fac) throws Error

  Sets the URL StreamHandlerFactory for this application to fac.
- public String toExternalForm()
- public String toString()

  Returns a string representation of this URL.

URLConnection (`java.net`)

A public abstract class, derived from `Object`, that is the superclass to any class that establishes a connection between a specified URL and an application.

Variables and Constants

- `protected boolean allowUserInteraction`
  When true, allows for user interaction with some types of URLs (such as password dialogs).
- `protected boolean connected`
  Holds the status of the current connection.
- `protected boolean doInput`
- `protected boolean doOutput`
  When true, signifies that this URL is used for reading and writing.
- `protected long ifModifiedSince`
  Holds a time value used in determining if a URL's object should be fetched if it has been modified more recently than this time.
- `public static FileNameMap fileNameMap`
  Holds the file name mapping of a file name to a MIME type for this URLConnection.
- `protected URL url`
  The remote file or object this connection will communicate with.
- `protected boolean useCaches`
  When true, allows the protocol to use cached information, if possible.

Constructors

- `protected URLConnection(URL arg)`
  Creates a new `URLConnection` to arg.

Methods

- `public abstract void connect() throws IOException`
  Opens a connection to this URL.
- `public boolean getAllowUserInteraction()`
- `public void setAllowUserInteraction(boolean flag)`
  Returns or sets the state of the `allowUserInteraction` field.
- `public Object getContent() throws IOException, UnknownServiceException`
- `public String getContentEncoding()`
- `public int getContentLength()`
- `public String getContentType()`
- `public URL getURL()`

Returns the document encoding value, content, length, type, or URL for this `URLConnection`.

- `public long getDate()`
- `public long getExpiration()`
- `public long getLastModified()`

Returns the date field or expiration time from the header of this `URLConnection`. `getLastModified` returns the number of seconds since midnight, January 1, 1970 UTC that the URL content for this URLConnection was last modified.

- `public static boolean getDefaultAllowUserInteraction()`
- `public static void setDefaultAllowUserInteraction(boolean flag)`

Returns or sets the default value of the `allowUserInteraction` field.

- `public static String getDefaultRequestProperty(String prop)`
- `public static void setDefaultRequestProperty(String prop, String val)`

Returns or sets the default request property, named `prop`, for this URLConnection.

- `public boolean getDefaultUseCaches()`
- `public void setDefaultUseCaches(boolean flag)`

Returns or sets the default value of the `useCaches` field.

- `public boolean getDoInput()`
- `public boolean getDoOutput()`
- `public void setDoInput(boolean flag)`
- `public void setDoOutput(boolean flag)`

Returns or sets a true value if this connection is used for reading input or writing output.

- `public String getHeaderField(int num)`
- `public String getHeaderField(String key)`

Returns the `num`th header field or the value that corresponds to `key` of the URL.

- `public long getHeaderFieldDate(String key, long default)`
- `public int getHeaderFieldInt(String key, int default)`
- `public String getHeaderFieldKey(int num)`

Returns the value of the header field named `key`, or the `default` if there is no such field. The key can also be specified as an index number.

- `public long getIfModifiedSince()`
- `public void setIfModifiedSince(long since)`

Returns or sets the value of the `ifModifiedSince` field.

- `public InputStream getInputStream() throws UnknownServiceException`

- public OutputStream getOutputStream() throws
  IOException, UnknownServiceException
    Returns the input or output stream for this URLConnection.
- public String getRequestProperty(String prop)
- public void setRequestProperty(String prop, String
  val)
    Returns or sets the value of the request property, prop, for this
    URLConnection.
- public boolean getUseCaches()
- public void setUseCaches(boolean flag)
    Returns or sets the value of the useCaches field of this
    URLConnection.
- protected static String
  guessContentTypeFromName(String name)
- protected static String
  guessContentTypeFromStream(InputStream strm) throws
  IOException
    Returns a guess of the type of content from a data stream or a name.
- public static void
  setContentHandlerFactory(ContentHandlerFactory arg)
  throws Error
    Sets the ContentHandlerFactory for this application to arg.
- public String toString()
    Returns a string representation of this URLConnection.

URLEncoder (`java.net`)

A public class, derived from Object, that converts a string to a MIME format.

Methods

- public static String encode(String str)
    Encodes the string str into MIME "x-www-form-urlencoded" format.

URLStreamHandler (`java.net`)

A public abstract class, derived from Object, that is the superclass for all stream-based protocol handling classes.

Constructors

- public URLStreamHandler()
    Creates a new instance of a URLStreamHandler.

Methods

- protected abstract URLConnection openConnection(URL dest) throws IOException
  Opens a connection to the specified URL.
- protected void parseURL(URL url, String src, int init, int end)
  Parses the string representation of a URL (url), starting at index position init and ending at index end, into dest.
- protected void setURL(URL url, String prot, String src, int num, String doc, String anchor)
  Sets the URL (url) fields to prot (name of the protocol), src (name of the remote machine), num (port number of connection on remote machine), doc (object to retrieve), and anchor (anchor reference).
- protected String toExternalForm(URL url)
  Returns a string representation of the specified URL.

Vector (java.util)

A public class, derived from Object and implementing Serializable and Cloneable, that manages an array of objects. Elements can be added or removed from this list and the size of the list can change dynamically.

Variables and Constants

- protected int capacityIncrement
  The amount of element spaces to be added to the vector each time that an increase must occur. A capacityIncrement of 0 indicates that the list will double in size at every resizing.
- protected int elementCount
- protected Object elementData[]
  The number of elements and the array containing the elements currently in this Vector.

Constructors

- public Vector()
- public Vector(int size)
- public Vector(int size, int incr)
  Creates a new instance of a vector with an initial size of size (or using the default of 10). An initial capacityIncrement can also be specified.

Methods

- `public final void addElement(Object arg)`
- `public final void insertElementAt(Object arg, int index) throws ArrayIndexOutOfBoundsException`
    Adds element `arg` to the end of this `Vector` or at a specific `index`. The capacity of the vector is adjusted if needed.
- `public final int capacity()`
- `public final void ensureCapacity(int size)`
    Returns the current capacity of this `Vector`, or ensures that it can contain at least `size` elements
- `public Object clone()`
    Returns the clone of this `Vector`.
- `public final boolean contains(Object arg)`
    Returns a true value if this `Vector` contains object `arg`.
- `public final void copyInto(Object[] dest)`
    Copies each of the elements of this `Vector` into the array `dest`.
- `public final Object elementAt(int index) throws ArrayIndexOutOfBoundsException`
    Returns the element at location `index` from this `Vector`.
- `public final Enumeration elements()`
    Returns an `Enumeration` of the elements in this `Vector`.
- `public final Object firstElement() throws NoSuchElementException`
- `public final Object lastElement() throws NoSuchElementException`
    Returns the first or last element in this `Vector`.
- `public final int indexOf(Object arg)`
- `public final int indexOf(Object arg, int index)`
    Returns the index of the first occurrence of element `arg`, starting at `index`. A −1 value is returned if the element is not found.
- `public final boolean isEmpty()`
    Returns a true value if this `Vector` contains no elements.
- `public final int lastIndexOf(Object arg)`
- `public final int lastIndexOf(Object arg, int index)`
    Returns the first index that object `arg` occurs at in this `Vector`, starting a backwards search at the specified index. If the object is not located, a −1 is returned.
- `public final void removeAllElements()`
- `public final boolean removeElement(Object arg)`
- `public final void removeElementAt(int index) throws ArrayIndexOutOfBoundsException`
    Removes element `arg` and returns a true value. If the object requested is not located, a false value is returned. An element can also be removed at a specific `index` value, or all elements can be removed.

- `public final void setElementAt(Object arg, int index)`
  `throws ArrayIndexOutOfBoundsException`
    Sets the element at the specified `index` equal to object `arg`.
- `public final void setSize(int size)`
    Sets the size of this `Vector` to `size`.
- `public final int size()`
    Returns the number of elements in this `Vector`.
- `public final String toString()`
    Returns a string representation of this `Vector`.
- `public final void trimToSize()`
    Reduces the size of this `Vector` to contain all of the elements present.

Void (`java.lang`)

An uninstantiable class that acts as a placeholder for the primitive `void` type in the `Class` object.

Variables and Constants

- `public final static Class TYPE`
    The `Void` constant value of the void type class.

Window (`java.awt`)

A public class, derived from `Container`, that creates a graphical area that has no borders or menus and can be used to contain AWT components.

Constructors

- `public Window(Frame frm)`
    Creates a new instance of a window that has a parent frame (`frm`). The window is initially not visible.

Methods

- `public void addNotify()`
    Creates this window's peer.
- `public synchronized void`
  `addWindowListener(WindowListener listener)`
- `public synchronized void`
  `removeWindowListener(WindowListener listener)`

Removes or adds the specified window listener (`listener`) for this window.

- `public void dispose()`
  Removes this window and deletes any resources used by this window.
- `public Component getFocusOwner()`
  Returns the component from this active window that currently has the focus.
- `public Locale getLocale()`
  Returns the locale for this window.
- `public Toolkit getToolkit()`
  Returns the toolkit for this window.
- `public final String getWarningString()`
  Returns the warning string for this window.
- `public boolean isShowing()`
  Returns a true value if this window is currently visible on the screen.
- `public void pack()`
  Causes all of the components of this window to be laid out according to their preferred size.
- `protected void processEvent(AWTEvent event)`
  Processes the specified event for this window. If the event is a `WindowEvent`, then this method calls the process `WindowEvent` method of this window, otherwise it will call the parent class' `processEvent` method.
- `protected void processWindowEvent(WindowEvent event)`
  Handles any `WindowEvent` (event) generated on this window, and passes them to a registered listener for that event.
- `public void show()`
  Makes this window visible to the user and brings it to the front (on top of other windows).
- `public void toBack()`
- `void toFront()`
  Sends this window to the back or front of other windows currently displayed on the screen.

WindowAdapter (`java.awt.event`)

A public abstract class, derived from `Object` and implementing `WindowListener`, that permits a derived class to override the predefined no-op AWT window events.

Constructors

- `public WindowAdapter()`
  Creates a new instance of a `WindowAdapter`.

Methods

- `public void windowActivated(WindowEvent event)`
- `public void windowClosed(WindowEvent event)`
- `public void windowClosing(WindowEvent event)`
- `public void windowDeactivated(WindowEvent event)`
- `public void windowDeiconified(WindowEvent event)`
- `public void windowIconified(WindowEvent event)`
- `public void windowOpened(WindowEvent event)`

    Empty methods that should be overridden in order to implement event handling for window events.

WindowEvent (`java.awt.event`)

A public class, derived from `ComponentEvent`, that describes a particular AWT window-based event.

Variables and Constants

- `public static final int WINDOW_ACTIVATED`
- `public static final int WINDOW_CLOSED`
- `public static final int WINDOW_CLOSING`
- `public static final int WINDOW_DEACTIVATED`
- `public static final int WINDOW_DEICONIFIED`
- `public static final int WINDOW_FIRST`
- `public static final int WINDOW_ICONIFIED`
- `public static final int WINDOW_LAST`
- `public static final int WINDOW_OPENED`

    Constant values which represent a variety of window event types.

Constructors

- `public WindowEvent(Window src, int type)`

    Creates a new instance of a `WindowEvent` from a specified source window and having a specific event type.

Methods

- `public Window getWindow()`

    Returns the source window that this event was triggered in.
- `public String paramString()`

    Returns a string containing the parameters for this `WindowEvent`.

Index

command line-argument
  arrays used to store, 221
  use of, 53–54
comments, 34, 37–39, 69. *See also* documentation
  implementation issues for, 608
common features
  and reuse potential, 306
communication lines
  sharing of, 21, 28
communication sockets, 18
compact discs, 6
compatible references
  and polymorphism, 317
compiler, 46–48, 82. *See also* javac (Java compiler)
  in class library, 61
compile-time error, 50, 51, 53
  message for, 52
ComponentAdapter class, 709–710
Component class, 705–709
  to construct GUIs, 358
  in java.awt package, 368
ComponentEvent class, 710
component hierarchy, 370
components and containers, 368–372, 403. *See also* GUI components
  component hierarchies, 370–372
  containers, 369–370, 403
computer architecture, 11–13
computer languages
  historical development of, 44
computer networks, 1, 11–21
computer processing
  basic, 2–3
  impact of Internet on, 28
computer resources
  and operating system, 4
computers
  binary number system used by, 581
  hardware specifications of, 11
  networks of, 1, 20–21
computer systems, 10, 31
  analog vs. digital signals, 7–8
  basic computer processing, 2–3
  binary numbers, 9–11
  digital computers, 6–9
  hardware components, 11–19
  network components, 11–19
  software categories, 3–5
concurrent processing, 498, 499
condition, 103
  at end of loop, 194
  evaluation of, 196–197
conditional coverage, 417

conditional operators, 188
conditional statements, 93
Confucius applet, 65–66, 67, 68, 69
consistency
  between design and implementation, 608
  in Java coding guidelines, 601
constant declarations, 341
constants, 82–83, 116
  in interfaces, 340–341, 352
constraints
  in GridBagLayout class, 391
constructors, 124, 140
  using Super with, 290–292
ContainerAdapter class, 712–713
Container class, 369, 370, 710–712
ContainerEvent class, 713–714
containers, 369. *See also* components and containers
  class hierarchy for, 369
  and layout managers, 382
content
  documentation guidelines for, 605
ContentHandler class, 714
continue statement, 199–202, 602, 614
control characters, 588
  in ASCII set, 77, 78
controllers, 12, 18
control unit
  of central processing unit, 17
conversion categories, 177–181
  in number systems, 585–586
coordinate system
  for graphics, 252–254
  within Java applets, 66
Countdown program, 41–42
Counter program, 103
countTokens method, 378
  of StringTokenizer class, 238, 239
coupling, 542. *See also* cohesion
C programming language, 44, 45, 49, 609, 615
  Java language interfaced with, 615–618
CPU. *See* central processing unit
current fonts, 276
Cursor class, 714–715

D

DARPA, 427
data. *See also* Objects for organizing data
  comparing, 99–100
  and hardware components, 1
  kinds of, 76
  and memory location, 14, 15, 28

hexadecimal number system, 581
  converting from binary to, 586, 587
high-density floppy disks, 15
high-level languages, 44, 45, 46, 70
HORIZONTAL constant
  for Scrollbar, 380
Horse class, 287
HTML. *See* HyperText Markup Language
HttpURL Connection class, 750–752
hybrid techniques, 611
hypermedia, 25
hypertext, 25
Hypertext Markup Language (HTML), 25,
    29. *See also* World-Wide Web applets,
    253, 635–638
  applet transmitted over Web via, 68
  basic HTML documents, 619–621, 629
  color and images, 633–635
  formatting text in, 621–629
  Java applets embedded in documents, 612
  links, 629–632
  tutorial, 619–638
HyperText Transfer Protocol, 27

I

IBM PC, 44
icons, 4
IDE. *See* integrated development environment
identifiers (and identifier naming), 39, 40
  and coding guidelines, 601
  consistent case conventions for, 70
  implementation issues for, 608
  Java versus C++, 614
  length of, 39, 40
  style guidelines for, 603
identity
  of object, 122
IEEE. *See* International Electronic and
    Electrical Engineering Organization
I element (in HTML), 623
if-else statement, 116, 188, 189
  semantics of, 102
  switch statements implemented as, 202
if statements, 14, 102, 189, 417, 603
  else portion of, 112
  nested, 101–102
  syntax of, 93
Image class, 752–753
Image_File class, 336, 337, 344
Image_Prototype class, 426
immutable string object, 125
implementation, 108, 111, 112, 114–115,
    116, 523, 532
  cohesion within abstract data type, 542

errors in, 606
evolution of, 415
of native methods, 616–618
of programs, 108
recursive, 463
review checklist on, 608
implements, 339
import statement, 63–64, 350–352
inclusive OR operator, 595
increment and decrement operators, 181–183,
    202
increments
  for scrollbar, 380
indentation
  crucial need for consistent, 102
  style guidelines for, 603
in-depth focus
  analog vs. digital signals, 7
  command-lines arguments, 53–54
  comparing data, 99–100
  coupling and cohesion, 542
  defining custom layout manager, 396
  direct vs. indirect recursion, 450
  expressions and for statement, 200
  garbage collection, 133
  scaling fonts, 278
  search analysis, 478
  shadowing variables, 299
  stub methods, 524
  synchronized statement, 505
  throw-away and evolutionary prototypes,
    427
  vector efficiency, 236
index (or subscript), 208
  in string, 126
index operator, 211
indirect recursion, 450
inequality operator, 95
InetAddress class, 753–754
infinite loop, 106
  avoiding, 116, 196
infinite recursion, 443, 445
information hiding
  and encapsulation, 346–347
inheritance, 60, 61, 65, 70, 285–325, 326,
    520, 522. *See also* object-oriented pro-
    gramming
  class hierarchies, 305–315
  of methods, 288
  overriding methods, 296–305
  polymorphism, 315–325
  and software reuse, 287
  subclass creation and, 286–296
  of variables, 288
  and visibility modifiers, 598
inherited methods, 288

N

NAME attribute, 636
name parameter
    in `Font` class, 276
NaN value, 176
narrowing conversions, 179, 202
    and information loss, 178
native methods
    declaring of, 615–616
native modifier, 615
nativespeak method, 617, 618
natural language, 49
`Nature` applet
    `setColor` method used in, 256
n comparisons, 470, 478
negative infinity, 176
negative start angle, 270, 271
negative values, 76
negative zero, 176
nested `if` statements, 101–102, 116
    style guidelines for, 604
Netscape Communications Corporation, 25
Netscape Navigator browser, 25, 26 (fig.
    1.19), 619, 633
    colors accepted by, 633
network address, 20
network resources, 28
networks, 19–27, 28
    Internet, 22–24
    local-area and wide-area, 21–22
    network connections, 20–21
    Uniform Resource Locator, 26–27
    World-Wide Web, 24–25
newline character, 36, 38
new operator, 167
    instantiating array with use of, 209, 210
nextInt method
    of `Random` class, 131
next method
    of `CardLayout` class, 390
next reference, 539, 541
nextToken method
    of `StringTokenizer` class, 238, 241
N factorial, 446
`Node` class, 546, 547
nonabstract class, 352
nonprintable (or invisible) characters, 77, 588,
    589, 590
nonvolatile secondary memory devices, 16, 28
`No_Parking` applet, 67
North location, 386, 387, 388
`NoSuchMethodException`, 646
not a number (NaN value), 176
NOT bitwise operator, 594
null

array initialized to, 219
null-terminated array of characters
    in C language, 618
null value, 539, 540
`Number` class, 780
`NumberFormat` class, 780–782
`NumberFormatException` class, 491–492
number systems, 581–586
    bases higher than 10, 583–584
    conversions between, 585–586
    counting in, 584
    and place value in, 582–583
    shortcut conversions between, 586–587
number variable, 595
numeric values, 76, 77, 115
    linear search with, 474–475
number systems,10
numeric input, 87–89

O

`Object` class, 233, 548, 551, 782–783
    within class hierarchies, 313–315
    Java classes derived from, 326
object-oriented concepts
    and abstraction, 146, 167
object-oriented design
    and class relationship organizations, 331
object-oriented development process, 515, 517
    (fig. 15.2)
    class and object identification, 519–520
    detailed design, 522–523
    evolutionary development, 516–518
    implementation, 523
    refinement scope establishment, 518–519,
        532
    relationship identification, 520–522
    unit and integration testing, 523–525
object-oriented programming, 33, 56, 65, 70,
    121, 516–517, 518, 532
    and inheritance, 286
    Java versus C++ languages, 611–612
    objects and classes, 58–61
    and refinement process, 532
    software engineering, 54–58
object persistence, 600
object reference. *See* references
objects and classes, 58, 59, 61, 70, 122–125.
objects
    aliases, 131–133
    arrays of, 220–224
    behaviors of, 167
    CD collection: example, 148–149
    classes, 123–124, 140–143
    creation and use of, 85

quotations
 use of, 85
Quote_GUI, 395
Quotes applet, 395, 397

R

Raindrop class, 163
RAM. *See* random-access memory
random-access device, 16
random-access memory (RAM), 17, 55
Random class, 130–131, 788–789
random number generator, 130
Random_Robot class, 432, 434
 code for implementing of, 435–436
readability
 of code, 37, 39
Readable_Files class, 345
readers
 documentation guidelines for, 605
readLine method, 85, 112
 instantiation by, 221
read-only memory (ROM), 17
read/write heads, 16
read-write memory, 17
real numbers
 standard IEEE 754 floating point format to
  represent, 176, 202
real-world objects, 58, 60
Rectangle class, 789–791
 Java definition of, 142–143
 visibility modifiers with, 147
rectangles
 applet, 265
 bounding, 281
 class, 264–265
 drawing of, 263–268
 and Graphics class, 252
 methods for drawing, 263–264
 ovals and rounded, 266
recursion, 443–461
 definitions, 444
 infinite, 444, 445
 in math, 446
 recursive programming, 446–451
 recursive thinking, 444–446, 459
 using, 451–458
recursive binary search, 478–480, 482
recursive paths
 termination of, 458
recursive programming, 446–451
 recursion vs. iteration, 448–450
redundancy
 elimination of, 113, 114
references, 121
 as aliases of each other, 132

and class hierarchies, 315–319
and instantiation, 124–125
to an object, 124
reference types, 179
refinements, 516
 for slide puzzle, 527
 and stubs, 524
refinement scope, 532
 establishment of, 518–519
registers
 of central processing unit, 17
relational operators, 95
release
 of program, 408
remainder operator, 89, 91
removeElement method
 of Vector class, 233
removeLayoutComponent method, 396
Repeating_Pictures applet, 451–453
repetition, 75, 102–106
 infinite loops, 106
 while statement, 102–105
repetition statement, 102, 194–202
 and break statement used in loops, 199
 continue statement, 199–201
 do statement, 194–196
 for statement, 196–199
 labels, 201–202
 and logical operators, 184
requirements
 and design, 607
 misunderstandings about, 606
 for robot search simulator, 417–420
 for slide puzzle, 525–526
 for Storm applet, 160
 and verb *shall*, 439
requirements analysis
 in software development process, 515
reserved words, 40, 50
resources, 240
retirement, 409
return statement, 135–136, 602
return type, 135
reusable codes, 56
reverse method
 of StringBuffer class, 242
Reverse_Numbers program, 212–213
reversibility
 of XOR mode effect, 259
review checklist, 606–608
reviewers, 607
RGB value, 255, 257, 633
 color defined by, 281
right boundary, 477
RIGHT integer constant, 373, 384
right-shift-with-sign-fill operator, 596

right-shift-with-zero-fill operator, 596
Rings_Display applet, 370, 371
   component hierarchy of, 372
Rings from Canvas class, 370
Robot class, 422, 425
   code for implementing of, 431–432
robotic engineers, 418, 419
robot search applet, 438
robot search simulator requirements, 417–420
   revising, 418–420
   robot search problem, 418
Robot_Sim class, 422, 423
robust programs, 50, 112, 113
Roll_Call program, 222–224
ROM. See read-only memory
ROM chips, 18
Rotating_Disk applet, 264
Rounded rectangles
   applet, 266
rows
   for Grid_Bag applet, 334
run method, 500, 501, 511
Runnable interface, 499, 511
run-time error, 50, 51

S

Sales_Analysis class, 217
sampling rate, 6
Sankar, Sriram, 651
Savings_Account class, 302–305, 307–312
scanners, 13
scenario diagrams, 407, 522, 532
   for slide puzzle, 530
screen layouts, 107
Scrollbar class, 791–792
scrollbars, 379–382, 403
ScrollPane class, 792–794
search analysis, 478
Search_Engines class, 473
searching, 463, 473–482
   binary search, 475–478, 482
   hashing, 480–482
   linear search, 473–475, 482
   recursive binary search, 478–480
secondary memory, 3, 14–17, 19. See also
    main memory
   devices, 2, 13
   nonvolatility of, 16, 28
seed value, 130
selection sort algorithm, 463, 464–466, 482
selection statements, 93, 98, 189–194
   and logical operators, 184
   switch statement, 189–194
semantic meanings

for identifiers, 603
semantics. See also syntax
   in programming languages, 33, 48–49
semicolons, 52
sentinel values, 110, 113
sequential-access device, 16
sequential processing, 499
ServerSocket class, 794–795
service methods, 144
services
   encapsulated objects with, 143, 144
setAlignment method, 373
setBackground method
   in Nature applet, 256
setCharAt method
   of StringBuffer class, 242
setColor method
   in Graphics class, 255
setFont method, 276
setLayout method, 383
setLength method
   of StringBuffer class, 242
setMultipleMode method, 378
setSize method
   parameters to, 253
setText method, 373, 375
setXORMode method
   of Graphics class, 258
shadowing variables, 299
shapes
   arcs, 268–271
   drawing of, 260–275
   ovals, 260–263
   polygons, 271–273
   polylines, 273–274
   rectangles, 263–268
shared libraries, 615, 618
short-circuited operators, 185
Short class, 795–796
shortcut conversions
   in number systems, 586–587
short data type, 76, 77, 115, 609
siblings, 306
signature
   of method, 152
   of overloaded method, 167
signed integer
   converted to integral type, 178
signed numeric types, 76
signs, 175, 176
simple animation
   and graphics, 251
SimpleDateFormat class, 796–797
Simple_IO package
   Reader class as part of, 349, 350, 351
   Writer class of, 350, 351, 352

SimpleTimeZone class, 797–798
Simultaneous program, 501
single inheritance, 346
16–bit machines, 15
64–bit machines, 15
size
  and initializer list, 216
  of Java arrays, 212
  of refinement, 518, 519, 532
size method
  of Vector class, 233
slashes
  in comments, 38
sleep method, 506, 511
slide puzzle: example
  architectural design, 526
  refinements, 527, 532
  requirements, 525–526
  user interface refinement, 527–532
Slider applet, 533
Slogan class, 332, 333, 334
Smalltalk language, 44, 45
Socket class, 798–800
Soda class, 500, 501
Soda_Survey class, 230, 231
Soda_Survey program, 231
software, 2, 27. *See also* hardware and hard-
    ware components; software development
    process
  activities for development of, 106–107
  categories of, 3–5
  components, 56–58, 59, 70
  crisis in, 55
  design, 107–108, 116, 420–426
  and Internet, 23, 24, 28
  life cycle, 408–411
  maintenance, 408, 438
  object-oriented, 12, 515
  objects, 122
  procedural approach to developing of, 54
  programming languages for writing of,
    44–45
  and random numbers, 130
  requirements, 107, 116
  reuse of, 285, 287, 326
  review checklist for high-quality,
    606–608
  TCP/IP, 23, 28
  tools, 46
  Web, 24–25, 408
software development models
  development process models, 411–413
  and iterative process, 413–415
  software life cycle, 408–411
software development process, 407–442,
    515–536

and computer networks, 1
cornerstones of high quality, 75
design, 407, 420–426
implementation, 407, 426–438
object-oriented development process,
    516–525
robot search simulator requirements,
    417–420
slide puzzle: example, 525–532
software development models, 408–417
software engineering, 54–58
software engineers, 606
software objects, 58, 60
software reuse, 287
Sortable interface, 470, 471
sort comparison, 469–470, 482
sorting and searching, 463–485
  comparing sorts, 469–470, 482
  insertion sort, 467–469, 482
  of objects, 470–473, 482
  searching, 473–482
  selection sort, 464–466, 482
  sorting, 464–473, 482
sound, 25, 68
source code, 47, 70, 612
  and implementation, 108
South location, 386, 387
spacing
  style guidelines for, 604
Sparc processor, 44
speakers, 2, 13
Sqrt method
  of Math class, 151
square, drawing, 260
stack abstract data type
  operations for, 551
Stack class, 551, 552, 800
Stack operations, 551
Stack trace, 490, 495
stacks, 538, 550–553
  message decoding: example, 552–553
  Stack class, 551–552
Staff_Member class, 319–325
standard input
  abbreviation for, 85
start angle, 268
start method, 162, 436, 500, 501, 511
state
  of objects, 122
statement list, 491, 497
statements, 505
  coverage, 417
  execution of, 93, 116
  threads and order of executing, 498
static block, 516
static constants, 276

white space, 36–37, 70
  style guidelines for, 604
wide-area networks (WANs), 22. *See also*
    local-area networks
widening conversions, 178. *See also* narrowing
    conversions
WIDTH constant, 436
WindowAdapter class, 828–829
Window class, 827–828
WindowEvent class, 829
windows, 4
Windows 95, 4, 349
word, 15
word processors, 4
Words program, 290–291
Words2 program, 291
World-Wide Web (WWW), 24–26, 27, 607
  free images on, 634
  impact and significance of, 1, 29
  and Java applet, 64, 68, 69, 70
  Java programming language relationship
    with, 25, 27, 33, 56, 62, 612
  links between documents within, 629–632
  and prototyping efforts, 427
  Uniform Resource Locators used with, 240
  Web page creation, 619

WPL Laboratories, Inc., 24
wrapper classes, 78
WWW. *See* World-Wide Web

X

x-axis coordinates
  in graphics coordinate system, 252, 253
x-coordinate
  of oval, 263
  of Raindrop object, 165
XOR mode, 258–260, 277, 281
  and oval drawing, 263
XOR operator, 595

Y

y-axis coordinates
  in graphics coordinate system, 252, 253
y-coordinate
  of Raindrop object, 165

Z

ZZ_Top program, 234–235